Applied Probability and Statistics (*Continued*)

CHAKRAVARTI, LAHA and ROY · Handbook of Methods of Applied Statistics, Vol. II

CHERNOFF and MOSES · Elementary Decision Theory

CHEW · Experimental Designs in Industry

CHIANG · Introduction to Stochastic Processes in Biostatistics

CLELLAND, deCANI, BROWN, BURSK, and MURRAY · Basic Statistics with Business Applications

COCHRAN · Sampling Techniques, *Second Edition*

COCHRAN and COX · Experimental Designs, *Second Edition*

COX · Planning of Experiments

COX and MILLER · The Theory of Stochastic Processes

DEMING · Sample Design in Business Research

DODGE and ROMIG · Sampling Inspection Tables, *Second Edition*

DRAPER and SMITH · Applied Regression Analysis

· GOLDBERGER · Econometric Theory

GUTTMAN and WILKS · Introductory Engineering Statistics

HALD · Statistical Tables and Formulas

HALD · Statistical Theory with Engineering Applications

HANSEN, HURWITZ, and MADOW · Sample Survey Methods and Theory, Volume I

HOEL · Elementary Statistics, *Second Edition*

JOHNSON and LEONE · Statistics and Experimental Design: In Engineering and the Physical Sciences, Volumes I and II

KEMPTHORNE · An Introduction to Genetic Statistics

MEYER · Symposium on Monte Carlo Methods

PRABHU · Queues and Inventories: A Study of Their Basic Stochastic Processes

SARHAN and GREENBERG · Contributions to Order Statistics

TIPPETT · Technological Applications of Statistics

WILLIAMS · Regression Analysis

WOLD and JUREEN · Demand Analysis

YOUDEN · Statistical Methods for Chemists

Tracts on Probability and Statistics

BILLINGSLEY · Ergodic Theory and Information

CRAMÉR and LEADBETTER · Stationary and Related Stochastic Processes

RIORDAN · Combinatorial Identities

TAKÁCS · Combinatorial Methods in the Theory of Stochastic Processes

Theory of Games and
Statistical Decisions

Theory of Games and Statistical Decisions

DAVID BLACKWELL

Professor of Mathematics
Howard University

M. A. GIRSHICK

Professor of Statistics
Stanford University

New York · London · Sydney · John Wiley & Sons, Inc.

Dedicated
To the Memory of
ABRAHAM WALD

Preface

DECISION THEORY APPLIES TO STATISTICAL PROBLEMS THE PRIN-
ciple that a statistical procedure should be evaluated by its consequences
in various circumstances, a principle first clearly emphasized by Neyman
and Pearson in their theory of testing hypotheses. The extension of this
principle to all statistical problems was proposed by A. Wald in 1939,
and developed by him in a series of papers culminating in his book,
Statistical Decision Functions, Wiley, 1950. The importance of Wald's
approach has been widely recognized, and the decision-theory viewpoint
has been adopted in much recent research in statistics. This book is
intended primarily as a textbook in decision theory for first-year grad-
uate students in statistics.

Wald's mathematical model for decision theory is a special case of
that for game theory, as introduced by E. Borel in 1921 and more gener-
ally by J. von Neumann in 1928, and expanded in the definitive book
by von Neumann and O. Morgenstern, *Theory of Games and Economic
Behavior*, Princeton, 1944. Many of the results in von Neumann and
Morgenstern's book, e.g., the reduction of games to normal form, the
minimax theorem, and the utility theorem, and much of the research
stimulated by that book are of basic importance for decision theory, so
that our book begins with a treatment of the relevant parts of game
theory. Occasionally we have permitted ourselves the luxury of discuss-
ing topics in game theory not strictly relevant to statistics: perfect-
information games, for example. For an excellent treatment of numer-
ous aspects of game theory not treated here, the reader is referred to
J. C. C. McKinsey's *Introduction to the Theory of Games*, McGraw-Hill,
1952.

Many have contributed to the development of game theory and deci-
sion theory, and in most cases the reader will find in the references indi-
cated at the end of the book a more complete treatment of the topics
presented here.

The mathematical prerequisite for reading this book is a course in
elementary analysis, covering such topics as limits of sequences, uniform
convergence, the Riemann integral, and the Heine-Borel theorem. For
a few sections, some knowledge of matrices, determinants, and linear

dependence is required. The statistical concepts used are defined in the book, but the reader who has no previous knowledge of statistics may find some parts difficult. Only discrete distributions appear in the formal development, but continuous distributions, e.g., the normal, are used for illustrative purposes. For a fuller treatment of the probability and statistical concepts used here, the reader is referred to two excellent books: W. Feller, *An Introduction to Probability Theory and Its Applications*, Wiley, 1950; and A. M. Mood, *Introduction to the Theory of Statistics*, McGraw-Hill, 1950.

We are indebted to the Office of Naval Research, for its continuing support which made it possible for us to write this book. We are also indebted to our former colleagues at the Rand Corporation, countless discussions with whom helped to clarify our ideas, to Herman Rubin and Patrick Suppes, whose participation amounts practically to co-authorship, to J. C. C. McKinsey for numerous improvements, particularly in Chapters 1 and 2, to Oscar Wesler for introducing a great deal of clarity and rigor in the final revision of this book, to Rosedith Sitgreaves and Russell N. Bradt for substantial contributions, to Gladys Garabedian for preparing the figures for the draftsman, and to many other people for assistance and criticisms. We are grateful to Phyllis Winkler, who typed two versions of this book, performing 1–1 transformations of notation and deciphering cryptic instructions from the authors, without ever losing her sunny disposition.

DAVID BLACKWELL

M. A. GIRSHICK

February 1954

Contents

ix

CHAPTER 1

Games in Normal Form

1.1. Introduction

A game is characterized by a set of rules having a certain formal struc-
ture, governing the behavior of certain individuals or groups, the players.
Chess and bridge are examples of games in the sense considered here,
and will be used for illustrative purposes.

Broadly speaking, the rules provide that the game shall consist of a
finite sequence of moves in a specified order, and the nature of each
move is prescribed. Moves are of two kinds, *personal moves* and *chance
moves*. A personal move is a choice by one of the players of one of a
specified, possibly infinite, set of alternatives; for instance, each move
in chess is a personal move; the first move is a choice by White of 1 of
20 specified alternatives. The actual decision made in a particular
play of a game at a given personal move we shall call *the choice* at that
move. A chance move also results in the choice of one of a specified
set of alternatives; here the alternative is selected not by one of the
players, but by a chance mechanism, with the probabilities with which
the mechanism selects the various alternatives specified by the rules of
the game. For instance, the first move in bridge consists of dealing
the first card to a specified player. This is a chance move with 52 al-
ternatives; the rules require that each alternative shall have proba-
bility $\frac{1}{52}$ of being selected. The actual selection made in a particular
play of a game at a given chance move we shall call *the outcome* at that
move.

In terms of moves, the rules of a game have the following structure.
For the first move, the rules specify whether it is to be a personal move
or a chance move. If it is a personal move, the rules list the available
alternatives and specify which player is to make the choice; if it is a
chance move, the rules list the available alternatives and specify the
probabilities with which they are to be selected. For moves after the
first, say the kth move with $k > 1$, the rules specify, *as a function of
the choices and outcomes at the first $k - 1$ moves* (*a*) whether the kth
move is to be a personal move or a chance move, (*b*) if a chance move,

1

the alternatives and their probabilities of selection, and (c) if a personal
move, the alternatives, the player who is to make the choice, and the
information concerning the choices and outcomes at the first $k - 1$
moves that is given to him before he makes his choice. Finally, the
rules specify, as a function of the choices and outcomes at the succes-
sive moves, when the game shall terminate and the score, not neces-
sarily numerical, that is to be assigned to each player.

Various points should be noted in connection with the above descrip-
tion. (1) For $k > 1$, the characteristics of the kth move depend on the

<p style="text-align:center">Figure 1</p>

results of previous moves. In bridge, for instance, when the first three
bids are "pass," the move after the fourth bid will be a chance move,
i.e., a new deal, if the fourth bid is "pass," and a personal move, i.e.,
a bid by the next player, if the fourth bid is anything other than "pass."
(2) The information given to a player when he is to make a certain move
does not necessarily include the information that was given to him at
an earlier move. In bridge, for instance, two partners are best consid-
ered as a single player; each partner has complete knowledge of his own
hand throughout the play, but not of his partner's hand. (3) The num-
ber of moves occurring in an actual play is not fixed in advance but de-
pends on the successive outcomes and choices. The rules must guaran-
tee, however, that the game will terminate eventually. (4) The con-
cept of move is to some extent indeterminate. For instance, the deal
in bridge may be considered either as a single chance move or as a suc-
cession of 52 chance moves.

An interesting graphical representation of a game can be given in
terms of a *tree* as is illustrated in Figure 1. In this figure the *vertices*
represent various positions for the players as the result of the outcomes

of a sequence of moves. No vertex is occupied by more than one player. Play begins at a specified vertex O, and each move is a change in position from a vertex to one of the adjoining higher vertices. When any vertex without branches is reached, the play of the game is over. Each non-terminal vertex has a label (in Figure 1, the labels I and II are for players I and II, respectively), specifying who is to move if that vertex is reached, and the number of alternatives is simply the number of branches at the vertex. The information available to the players is specified by a partition S of the vertices into sets V, called *information sets*, such that, when a vertex $v \, \varepsilon \, V$ is reached, the player who is to move is told only the set V, and not, unless V contains only a single element, the exact position v. Certain obvious requirements are imposed on the information partition S: (1) all $v \, \varepsilon \, V$ must have the same mover and the same number of alternatives, and (2) if $v_1 \, \varepsilon \, V$ and v_2 is attainable from v_1, then $v_2 \notin V$. In the game given by Figure 1, the information partition S contains five information sets as members, and three of these, V_1, V_3, V_4, are sets containing only one element. When *every* information set V of a game contains only one element, the game is said to be a *game of perfect information*. This special class of games is discussed in Section 1.7.

A formal mathematical description of the structure of a game in terms of the concepts of moves and information will not be attempted here. One of the most important results in the theory of games is the fact that all games, no matter what their detailed formal structure, may be reduced to an exceedingly simple form, the so-called normal form. In the next two sections we give an informal description of how this reduction is effected.

1.2. The Concept of a Strategy

Imagine that you are to play the White pieces in a single game of chess, and that you discover you are unable to be present for the occasion. There is available a deputy, who will represent you on the occasion, and who will carry out your instructions exactly, but who is absolutely unable to make any decisions of his own volition. Thus, in order to guarantee that your deputy will be able to conduct the White pieces throughout the game, your instructions to him must envisage every possible circumstance in which he may be required to move, and must specify, for each such circumstance, what his choice is to be. Any such complete set of instructions constitutes what we shall call a *strategy*. Thus, a strategy for White must specify a first move and, for each possible reply by Black, a corresponding next move and, in

general, for each possible sequence of choices $m_1, \cdots, m_{2k}, k \geq 0$, a choice $c(m_1, \cdots, m_{2k})$ for his $(k + 1)$st move (the $[2k + 1]$st move of the game) among the alternatives available to him as a result of the situation m_1, \cdots, m_{2k}. Of course, the specification of a strategy that has a reasonable chance of winning against an opponent who will actually be present would be a formidable job, mainly because you would have to make a tremendous number of decisions, most of which would turn out to be irrelevant in any particular play of the game, since most of the situations for which decisions had to be made will simply not turn up. For instance, a White player who is actually present must make two decisions in order to make his first two moves, whereas one who is operating by deputy must make 21 decisions to guarantee that his deputy will be able to make two moves. Thus the use of strategies would make the actual play of a single chess game a major undertaking; nevertheless, we shall see that the concept of strategy leads to great simplification for theoretical purposes.

In general, a strategy for a given player in a given game consists of a specification, for each situation that could arise in which he would be required to make a personal move, of his choice in that situation. It is to be emphasized that the choice of a strategy imposes no theoretical handicap on a player; specifically he is not required to make any decision on the basis of less information than he would have in the actual play at the stage where this decision was required, since the decisions whose totality constitutes a strategy are conditional ones of the form "If a situation should arise in which I am informed that it is my move and I am given information z about the results of previous moves (chance and personal) and I am told that the set of alternatives open to me is S, my choice will be s (a point of S)." Properly speaking, the information z about the results of previous moves includes the information that it is his turn to move and the specification of the alternatives open to him, since these latter facts in general constitute information about the results of previous moves. With the understanding that information z includes specification of S and of the fact that it is his turn to move, we may describe a player's strategy as a listing of all possible z's and an assignment to each z of an s in the set S of available alternatives specified by z, i.e., if Z is the space of possible z's (in terms of the tree, the space of all information sets V with the player's label) and $S(z)$ is the set of alternatives specified by z (the set of branches leading out of a vertex of the particular information set), the player's strategy is a function f such that $f(z) \varepsilon S(z)$ for all $z \varepsilon Z$ (i.e., f is a rule that specifies, for each information set, which branch is to be selected). The space of all possible strategies f for a given player will be designated by

F. (The number of elements in F is clearly given by $\prod\limits_{i=1}^{n} r_i$, where n is the number of information sets with the player's label and r_i is the number of alternatives for the ith information set.)

Let Z_1, Z_2 be the Z spaces for White and Black in chess, and let f_1, f_2 be any strategies for White and Black respectively. A referee, given f_1 and f_2, could conduct the entire game without further instructions from either player and announce the result. For the information z_1 that no previous moves have been made, that it is now White's turn, and that $S(z_1)$ consists of the 20 legal opening moves for White is a point in Z_1, so that $m_1 = f_1(z_1)\ \varepsilon\ S(z_1)$ is White's opening move. The information z_2 that White's opening move was m_1, that no other moves have been made by either player, that it is now Black's turn to move, and that $S(z_2)$ consists of the 20 legal moves for Black at this stage will be an element of Z_2, so that $f_2(z_2) = m_2$ will be Black's reply, etc. Thus the outcome of the game is determined uniquely by the strategies f_1, f_2 chosen by the players.

The fact noted above for chess, that the outcome of the game is determined once each player has selected a strategy, will clearly continue to hold for any game in which each move is a personal move by some player, but will fail for bridge, for instance, where chance moves occur and influence the outcome. In discussing chance moves, we make the conceptual simplification corresponding to that of strategy for personal moves of a given player. Let W be the set of all possible circumstances w in which a chance move would be required. Each w includes specification of the nature of the chance move to be performed, i.e., of the set $S(w)$ of alternatives among which one is to be selected, and for each w of the probability distribution p over $S(w)$ according to which the selection of $s\ \varepsilon\ S(w)$ is to be made. Suppose that a referee performs in advance each chance experiment that may be required in the course of the game, i.e., for each w he selects an element $s\ \varepsilon\ S(w)$ according to the distribution p, the selections for different w's being independent. Now a particular selection of an s from $S(w)$ for each w constitutes a function h defined on W with $h(w)\ \varepsilon\ S(w)$. (In terms of the tree, h is a rule which specifies, for each information set labeled "chance move," which branch is selected.) Also, the distributions p, together with the requirement of independent selection, determine an over-all distribution P on these functions h. Consequently, the totality of experiments performed by the referee may be viewed as a single experiment, namely, selecting a function $h\ \varepsilon\ \mathfrak{K}$ according to the probability function P. Thus, just as the totality of all decisions to be made by a given player can be described by a single decision—the choice of a strategy—so can

the totality of chance experiments to be performed be replaced by a single over-all chance move.

We can now describe quite simply the structure of a game. Suppose there are k players, and let F_i be the space of possible strategies f_i for player i, \mathcal{X} the space of possible outcomes h of the over-all chance experiment, and G the space of $(k+1)$-tuples $g = (f_1, \cdots, f_k, h)$, where $f_i \, \varepsilon \, F_i$, $h \, \varepsilon \, \mathcal{X}$. Any $(k+1)$-tuple $g \, \varepsilon \, G$ determines uniquely the course of the play. For each play the rules of the game determine a unique *outcome r* belonging to the space of outcomes R, and consequently for each game there is a function q defined over the space G mapping G onto R; i.e., the range of q is the entire space R. For fixed $f = (f_1, \cdots, f_k)$, the probability distribution P, according to which h is selected, determines a probability distribution Q over G, and thus a probability distribution π_f over R. Hence, every game can be described by k spaces F_1, \cdots, F_k, a space R, and the association with each k-tuple (f_1, \cdots, f_k), $f_i \, \varepsilon \, F_i$, of a probability distribution π_f over R. The game is played as follows: Player i chooses a point $f_i \, \varepsilon \, F_i$, the k choices being made simultaneously and independently; a point $r \, \varepsilon \, R$ is then selected according to the probability distribution π_f associated with the k choices (f_1, \cdots, f_k).

An analysis of the following simple game will provide an illustration of the concepts introduced in this section. Player I moves first and selects one of the two integers 1, 2. The referee then tosses a coin, and, if the outcome is "head," he informs player II of player I's choice, and not otherwise. Player II then moves and selects one of the two integers 3, 4. The fourth move is again a chance move by the referee and consists of selecting one of the three integers 1, 2, 3 with respective probabilities 0.4, 0.2, 0.4. The numbers selected in the first, third, and fourth moves are then added, and that amount in dollars is paid by II to I if the sum is even, and by I to II if the sum is odd.

The tree of this game is shown in Figure 2. The numbers at the terminal vertices represent the possible winnings in dollars of the two players. The symbol 0 is used to designate chance moves.

In terms of the two spaces F_1 and F_2, the strategies of the two players can be described as follows: The space F_1 consists simply of the two single element sets (1) and (2). That is,

$$F_1 = \{(1), (2)\}$$

The space F_2 consists of eight ordered triples (i, j, k) with $i, j, k = 3, 4$; i.e.,

$$F_2 = \{(3, 3, 3), (3, 3, 4), (3, 4, 3), (3, 4, 4), (4, 3, 3), (4, 3, 4),$$

$$(4, 4, 3), (4, 4, 4)\}$$

where the first position in the triple is conditioned upon the coin falling head and player I choosing 1, the second position in the triple is conditioned upon the coin falling head and player I choosing 2, and the third position in the triple is conditioned upon the coin falling tail. The

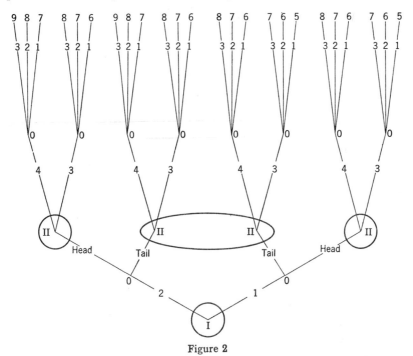

Figure 2

space \mathcal{H} and the values of the probability distribution P for each $h \; \varepsilon \; \mathcal{H}$ are given by

$$\mathcal{H}: \quad \{(H, 1), \quad (H, 2), \quad (H, 3), \quad (T, 1), \quad (T, 2), \quad (T, 3)\}$$

$$P: \quad \{ \quad 0.2 \qquad 0.1 \qquad 0.2 \qquad 0.2 \qquad 0.1 \qquad 0.2 \; \}$$

where the letter H stands for head and T for tail. The space G of all triples $g = (f_1, f_2, h)$ clearly contains 96 elements. The space of outcomes R consists of the 5 elements \$5.00, \$6.00, \$7.00, \$8.00, \$9.00. Typical values of the function q which maps G onto the space of outcomes is

$$q(g) = \$5.00 \quad \text{for} \quad g = ((1), (3, 3, 4), (H, 1))$$

$$q(g) = \$8.00 \quad \text{for} \quad g = ((1), (4, 4, 3), (H, 3))$$

$$q(g) = \$7.00 \quad \text{for} \quad g = ((2), (3, 4, 4), (T, 1))$$

$$q(g) = \$9.00 \quad \text{for} \quad g = ((2), (4, 3, 4), (T, 3))$$

These values are most easily computed by referring to Figure 2. The tree representation of the game also facilitates the computation of the probability distribution π_f on R for each $f = (f_1, f_2)$. Thus, for example, if $f = ((1), (3, 3, 4))$,

$$\pi_f(\$5.00) = \pi_f(\$8.00) = 0.2; \qquad \pi_f(\$6.00) = \pi_f(\$7.00) = 0.3;$$
$$\pi_f(\$9.00) = 0$$

and, if $f = ((2), (3, 4, 4))$,

$$\pi_f(\$5.00) = \pi_f(\$6.00) = 0; \qquad \pi_f(\$7.00) = \pi_f(\$9.00) = 0.4;$$
$$\pi_f(\$8.00) = 0.2$$

PROBLEMS

1.2.1. In the above illustrative example compute $\pi_f(r)$ for each f and r, and present the results in tabular form.

1.2.2. From the results of Problem 1.2.1, compute the expected gain for player I for each f, and present the results in a 2-by-8 matrix with the rows representing the strategies of player I and the columns the strategies of player II.

1.2.3. Reduce the following game to the matrix form as in the previous problem, and sketch its tree:

Move 1. Player I chooses $i = 0$ or 1.
Move 2. A chance move, selecting $j = 0$ or 1 with equal probabilities.
Move 3. Player II chooses $k = 0$ or 1.
Outcome: If $i + j + k = 1$, I pays II one unit; otherwise II pays I one unit.
Information of II at move 3: II is told the value of j but not the value of i.

1.2.4. Reduce to matrix form and sketch the tree for the variations of Problem 1.2.3, with the same moves and outcomes, but with the following information for II at move 3.

(1) II is told neither the value of i nor the value of j.
(2) II is told the values of both i and j.
(3) II is told the value of $i + j$ (but not the separate values of i and j).
(4) II is told the value of the product of i and j (but not the separate values of i and j).

1.3. The Normal Form

So far we have not mentioned the motivations of the players—an essential element of any game. The description of a game at the end of Section 1.2 was simply a listing of the strategies of the players and the outcome of any set of choices of strategies, without regard to the attitudes of the players toward various outcomes. We now indicate briefly how the final simplification of a game—the normal form—is obtained, by taking into account the preferences of the players.

We have seen in Section 1.2 that the result of any set of strategies f_1, \cdots, f_k is a probability distribution π_f over the set R of possible outcomes. It would be particularly convenient if a given player could ex-

press his preference pattern in R by a bounded numerical function u defined on R, such that he prefers r_1 to r_2 if and only if $u(r_1) > u(r_2)$ (so that $u(r_1) = u(r_2)$ denotes indifference between r_1 and r_2) and such that, if for any probability distribution ξ over R, we define $U(\xi)$ as the expected value of $u(r)$ computed with respect to ξ, i.e.,

$$U(\xi) = \sum_{r \,\varepsilon\, R} \xi(r)u(r)$$

he prefers ξ_1 to ξ_2 if and only if $U(\xi_1) > U(\xi_2)$. It is a remarkable fact that, under extremely plausible hypotheses concerning the preference pattern, such a function u exists. The function U defined for all probability distributions ξ over R, is called the player's *utility function*. It is unique, for a given preference pattern, up to a linear transformation. We shall discuss this question in some detail in Chapter 4; for the present we shall simply suppose that each player has such a utility function.

Thus the aim of each player in the game is to maximize his expected utility. If U_i is the utility function of player i, his aim is to make $M_i(f_1, \cdots, f_k) = U_i(\pi_f)$ as large as possible, where π_f is the probability distribution (for fixed f_1, \cdots, f_k) over R determined by the over-all chance move. We are now in a position to give a description of the normal form of a game: A game consists of k spaces F_1, \cdots, F_k and k bounded numerical functions $M_i(f_1, \cdots, f_k)$ defined on the space of all k-tuples (f_1, \cdots, f_k), $f_i \,\varepsilon\, F_i$, $i = 1, \cdots, k$. The game is played as follows: Player i chooses an element f_i of F_i, the k choices being made simultaneously and independently; player i then receives the amount $M_i(f_1, \cdots, f_k)$, $i = 1, \cdots, k$. The aim of player i is to make M_i as large as possible. The statement "Player i then receives the amount $M_i(f_1, \cdots, f_k)$" is a shorthand way of saying "a situation results whose utility for player i is $M_i(f_1, \cdots, f_k)$." We shall often speak as though the changes in utility are effected simply by money receipts or payments. This terminology is used because of its convenience and suggestiveness.

In the theory of games it is usual to treat first a special class of games, the two-person zero-sum games. The theory of these games is particularly simple and complete, and only these games will be treated in this book. A *two-person* game is of course a game with $k = 2$; a *zero-sum* game is one in which $\sum_{i=1}^{k} M_i(f_1, \cdots, f_k) = 0$ for all f_1, \cdots, f_k; more precisely, since each M_i is unique only up to linear transformations, a game is zero-sum if there is a determination of M_1, \cdots, M_k for which $\sum_{i=1}^{k} M_i(f_1, \cdots, f_k) = 0$ for all f_1, \cdots, f_k. Thus a two-person

zero-sum game is a game between two players in which their interests are diametrically opposed: One player gains only at the expense of the other. Consequently, there is no motive for collusion between the players; it is precisely the fact that collusion is unprofitable that simplifies the theory.

Notice that a constant-sum game, i.e., one in which $\sum_{i=1}^{k} M_i(f_1, \cdots, f_k)$ $= c$ for all f_1, \cdots, f_k is zero-sum in the sense defined above, since an alternative choice of utility functions is $M^*_1 = M_1 - c$, $M^*_i = M_i$ for $i \neq 1$, and $\sum_{1}^{k} M^*_i \equiv 0$. Thus the theory developed below for zero-sum two-person games applies equally to constant-sum two-person games. A slightly different kind of game falling within our definition of zero-sum games is illustrated by the following example. Player I has two strategies, 1 and 2, and player II has a single strategy 1*. If I chooses 1, nothing happens; if he chooses 2, he loses $1 and II wins $10. If we suppose that I prefers the result of 1 to that of 2 and that II has the opposite preference, an appropriate choice of utility functions yields

$$M_1(1, 1^*) = M_2(1, 1^*) = 0, \qquad M_1(2, 1^*) = -1, \qquad M_2(2, 1^*) = 10$$

and the game is zero-sum. According to the theory developed below, rational play for I in this situation is to choose strategy 1, so that nothing happens.

What often does happen in situations of this kind is that II approaches I, offering him a fee of, say, $5 if I will choose strategy 2. If I accepts this offer, the result is that I nets $4, II nets $5, and both have improved their positions. This means simply that our original description of the game was incomplete, as we failed to list certain strategies, involving offering and acceptance of fees, which were in fact available to the players. A more complete description, taking these possibilities into account, would yield a non-zero-sum game. Thus it is important, in applying game theory to an actual situation, to be sure to list all available strategies for the players.

Since for a two-person zero-sum game we have

$$M_2(f_1, f_2) = -M_1(f_1, f_2)$$

we need specify only M_1. The term "game" will hereafter always mean "zero-sum two-person game." Thus we have

Definition 1.3.1. A game G in the normal form is a triple (X, Y, M), where X, Y are arbitrary spaces and M is a bounded numerical function

defined on the product space $X \times Y$ of pairs (x, y), $x \, \varepsilon \, X$, $y \, \varepsilon \, Y$. The points x (y) are called strategies for player I (II), and the function M is called the payoff.

The game G is played as follows: I chooses $x \, \varepsilon \, X$, II chooses $y \, \varepsilon \, Y$, the choices being made independently and simultaneously. II then pays I the amount $M(x, y)$.

Note that, although it was useful, for the understanding of the argument leading to the simplification of a game to the normal form, to restrict the spaces X and Y to be finite, this restriction is removed in Definition 1.3.1 and will not be assumed, unless specified otherwise, in the remainder of this book.

1.4. Equivalent Games

If in a given game one relabels the strategies of either player, the new game is not essentially different from the old: Every statement about either game can be translated into a corresponding statement about the other, and we wish to consider the two games as equivalent. Another simple transformation which does not alter the essential character of a game is the deletion of duplicated strategies; in other words, if player I has two strategies x_1, x_2, such that $M(x_1, y) = M(x_2, y)$ for all y, the deletion of x_2 from X is an inessential change in the game, even though it might, for example, destroy such properties as symmetry.

Definition 1.4.1. Let $G_1 = (X_1, Y_1, M_1)$ and $G_2 = (X_2, Y_2, M_2)$ be two games. Then G_2 is a reduction of G_1, written: $G_2 \, r \, G_1$, if either
(a) $X_2 = X_1$, and there is a function f from Y_1 onto Y_2, such that $M_1(x, y) = M_2(x, f(y))$ for all $x \, \varepsilon \, X_1$, $y \, \varepsilon \, Y_1$, or
(b) $Y_2 = Y_1$, and there is a function g from X_1 onto X_2, such that $M_1(x, y) = M_2(g(x), y)$ for all $x \, \varepsilon \, X_1$, $y \, \varepsilon \, Y_1$.

If f is a $1-1$ transformation, G_2 is obtained from G_1 by a relabeling of strategies; if f is not $1-1$, G_2 is obtained from G_1 by deletions of certain duplicated strategies and relabeling.

Definition 1.4.2. Two games G and G' are called equivalent, written $G \sim G'$, if there is a finite sequence of games G_0, G_1, \cdots, G_n with $G_0 = G$, $G_n = G'$, and, for each $i = 1, \cdots, n$, either $G_{i-1} \, r \, G_i$ or $G_i \, r \, G_{i-1}$.

An example of two equivalent games is the following. Let $G = (X, Y, M)$ be a game, where $X = (x_1, \cdots, x_N)$, a set of N real numbers;

$Y = (y_1, \cdots, y_R)$, also a set of R real numbers; and, for $x \varepsilon X$, $y \varepsilon Y$,

$$M(x, y) = \frac{xy}{|x||y|}$$

Then $G' = (X', Y', M')$, where $x' = ax$ and $y' = by$ with a and b positive constants, and

$$M'(x', y') = \frac{x'y'}{|x'||y'|}$$

is equivalent to G.

Definition 1.4.3. A game $G = (X, Y, M)$ is called finite if both X and Y contain only a finite number of elements.

A finite game $G = (X, Y, M)$ with $X = (x_1, \cdots, x_m)$, $Y = (y_1, \cdots, y_n)$ is clearly equivalent to the game $G' = (I_m, I_n, M')$, where I_k denotes the set of positive integers $1, \cdots, k$, and $M'(i, j) = M(x_i, y_j)$. This equivalence leads to the following useful definition.

Definition 1.4.4. If $G = (X, Y, M)$ is a finite game with $X = (x_1, \cdots, x_m)$ and $Y = (y_1, \cdots, y_n)$, then the $m \times n$ matrix $A = \|a_{ij}\|$ with $a_{ij} = M(x_i, y_j)$ is called the matrix of the game G.

We remark that most properties of games in which we shall be interested are invariant under equivalence. By means of the transformation function f used in defining the concept of reduction, any statement about a game G can be translated into a statement about an equivalent game G'. Thus, although from a logical point of view a game G could be defined as a class of equivalent triples (X, Y, M), we shall not make this abstraction but shall consider each triple as constituting a game and, when convenient, replace any game by an equivalent one. A few theorems on invariance under equivalence are proved in later sections of this chapter.

PROBLEMS

1.4.1. Two games with matrices A and B are equivalent if B is obtained from A by a permutation of rows or columns.

1.4.2. If $X_1 \subset X$, a sufficient condition that the game $G_1 = (X_1, Y, M_1)$ with $M_1(x, y) = M(x, y)$ for $x \varepsilon X_1$, $y \varepsilon Y$ be equivalent to $G = (X, Y, M)$ is that for every $x \varepsilon X$ there is an $x_1 \varepsilon X_1$ with $M(x_1, y) = M(x, y)$.

1.4.3. Call $G = (X, Y, M)$ *completely reduced* if $x_1 \neq x_2$ implies $M(x_1, y) \neq M(x_2, y)$ and $y_1 \neq y_2$ implies $M(x, y_1) \neq M(x, y_2)$. Every game is equivalent to a completely reduced game. (First reduce the game by deleting all duplicated strategies in X; then delete all duplicated strategies in Y. The resulting game is completely reduced.)

1.4.4. Two games G_1 and G_2 are called *isomorphic* if there exist 1-1 mappings f and g of X_1 onto X_2 and Y_1 onto Y_2 respectively, such that $M_1(x_1, y_1) = M_2(f(x_1), g(y_1))$ for all $x_1 \varepsilon X_1$, $y_1 \varepsilon Y_1$. Two games are equivalent if and only if their completely reduced forms are isomorphic.

1.4.5. If $G' \sim G$ and G' is reduced, there is a game G_1 such that G_1 r G and G' r G_1.

1.4.6. Problems 1.4.3 and 1.4.5 imply that the n of Definition 1.4.2 need never exceed 4. Give an example where n must be at least 4.

1.4.7. Show that the condition of Problem 1.4.2 is also necessary if either X or Y, when duplicated strategies are deleted, is finite.

1.5. Illustrative Examples

To illustrate the concepts of normal form and equivalence we give several examples.

Game G_1. Matching Pennies. Players I and II simultaneously place coins on a table. If the coins agree, i.e., both show heads or both tails, II pays I one unit. If not, I pays II one unit.

Clearly each player has two strategies—heads and tails. The game is equivalent to one with matrix $\overset{\mathcal{I}}{\begin{pmatrix} 1 & -1 \\ -1 & 1 \end{pmatrix}}$. ⟿ I's payoff matrix

Game G_2. Matching Pennies with Spying. This game is like matching pennies, except that I is required to place his coin first, and II is permitted to see the result before placing his own coin.

I still has two strategies—heads and tails. A strategy for II now specifies his choice when he sees heads and his choice when he sees tails, so that II has four strategies. Denoting heads by 1, tails by 2, and by (i, j) the strategy that chooses i when I chooses 1, and j when I chooses 2, we obtain the matrix

$$
\begin{array}{cccc}
\overset{H\ H}{(1,\,1)} & \overset{H\ T}{(1,\,2)} & \overset{T\ H}{(2,\,1)} & \overset{T\ T}{(2,\,2)} \\
\end{array}
$$

$$
\begin{array}{c}
\overset{H}{1} \\
\overset{T}{2}
\end{array}
\begin{pmatrix}
1 & 1 & -1 & -1 \\
-1 & 1 & -1 & 1
\end{pmatrix}
$$

Game $G_3(p)$. Matching Pennies with Imperfect Spying. After I makes his choice, a coin is tossed that has probability p of showing I's choice and $1 - p$ of showing the opposite. The result of the toss is revealed to II, who then makes his choice.

Again I has two strategies and II has four. The matrix is

$$
\begin{array}{cccc}
\overset{H\ H}{(1,\,1)} & \overset{H\ T}{(1,\,2)} & \overset{T\ H}{(2,\,1)} & \overset{T\ T}{(2,\,2)} \\
\end{array}
$$

$$
\begin{array}{c}
\overset{H}{1} \\
\overset{T}{2}
\end{array}
\begin{pmatrix}
1 & 2p - 1 & 1 - 2p & -1 \\
-1 & 2p - 1 & 1 - 2p & 1
\end{pmatrix}
$$

where (i, j) now denotes the strategy: II chooses i when 1 is announced, j when 2 is announced.

Game $G_4(k, N)$. Addition. I and II alternately choose integers, each choice being one of the integers $1, \cdots, k$, and each choice being made with knowledge of all preceding choices. As soon as the sum of the chosen integers exceeds N, the last player to choose pays his opponent one unit.

The situation in which player I finds himself at his rth move is described by a sequence $s_r = (i_1, i_2, \cdots, i_{2r-2})$, with each i_j being one of the integers $1, \cdots, k$ and

$$\sum_{j=1}^{2r-2} i_j \leq N$$

Denote by S_r the set of possible sequences s_r, where $r = 1, \cdots, [N/2] + 1$ and $[z]$ denotes the largest integer not exceeding z. A strategy x for I consists of a set of $[N/2] + 1$ functions $f_1, \cdots, f_{[N/2]+1}$, where f_r is a function defined on S_r assuming only the values $1, 2, \cdots, k$: f_r specifies I's rth move when the previous history of the play is s_r. Similarly, a strategy y for II is a set of $[(N + 1)/2]$ functions $g_1, \cdots, g_{[(N+1)/2]}$, where g_r is defined for the set T_r of all sequences $t_r = (i_1, \cdots, i_{2r-1})$ with each i_j being one of the integers $1, 2, \cdots, k$ and

$$\sum_{j=1}^{2r-1} i_j \leq N$$

Define $i_1(x, y) = f_1$ and, inductively for $j > 0$,

$$i_{2j}(x, y) = g_j(i_1(x, y), \cdots, i_{2j-1}(x, y))$$

$$i_{2j+1}(x, y) = f_{j+1}(i_1(x, y), \cdots, i_{2j}(x, y))$$

(this induction describes the manner in which a referee would carry out the instructions of the players) and let $j^*(x, y)$ be the largest j for which $i_j(x, y)$ is defined. Then

$$M(x, y) = \quad 1 \quad \text{if} \quad j^*(x, y) \quad \text{is even}$$

$$-1 \quad \text{if} \quad j^*(x, y) \quad \text{is odd}$$

This game is again discussed in Section 1.7.

PROBLEMS

1.5.1. Is $G_3(1)$ equivalent to G_2? Is $G_3(1/2)$ equivalent to G_1?

1.5.2. Let $G_4(k, N)$ be modified so that each choice is made with knowledge only of the sum of all previous choices. Is the modified game equivalent to the original game?

1.5.3. Let $G = (X, Y, M)$ be any game. We modify G by introducing an irrelevant move as follows. Player I chooses an integer $z = 1$ or 2; his choice is announced to II. After this preliminary, the original G is played: x and y are chosen independently, and II pays I the amount $M(x, y)$. What is the normal form of the modified game? Is it equivalent to the original game?

1.6. Lower and Upper Pure Value

In a game $G = (X, Y, M)$, the consequences of a strategy x_0 are described by the function $M(x_0, y)$. Using x_0, player I is certain to receive at least

$$\Lambda_G(x_0) = \inf_{y \,\varepsilon\, Y} M(x_0, y)$$

and cannot be certain of any definite larger amount (where for any set S of real numbers, $\inf S$ and $\sup S$ denote the largest number s_0 with $s_0 \leq s$ for all $s \,\varepsilon\, S$ and the smallest number s_1 with $s_1 \geq s$ for all $s \,\varepsilon\, S$ respectively). Thus the number

$$\lambda^*{}_G = \sup_{x \,\varepsilon\, X} \Lambda_G(x)$$

is the upper limit to the amount I can guarantee getting: for every $\epsilon > 0$, he can, simply by choosing a suitable x, be certain of at least $\lambda^*{}_G - \epsilon$, and for no $\epsilon > 0$ is there an x which makes him certain to receive at least $\lambda^*{}_G + \epsilon$ against all y. Similarly, we define

$$\Upsilon_G(y_0) = \sup_{x \,\varepsilon\, X} M(x, y_0), \quad v^*{}_G = \inf_{y \,\varepsilon\, Y} \Upsilon_G(y)$$

by selecting a y suitably, player II can with certainty restrict his loss to $v^*{}_G + \epsilon$ but not to $v^*{}_G - \epsilon$ for any $\epsilon > 0$. For subsequent reference these definitions are stated formally.

Definition 1.6.1. If $G = (X, Y, M)$ is a game, then, for $x_0 \,\varepsilon\, X$, $\Lambda_G(x_0) = \inf\limits_{y \,\varepsilon\, Y} M(x_0, y)$.

Definition 1.6.2. If $G = (X, Y, M)$ is a game, then, for $y_0 \,\varepsilon\, Y$, $\Upsilon_G(y_0) = \sup\limits_{x \,\varepsilon\, X} M(x, y_0)$.

Definition 1.6.3. If $G = (X, Y, M)$ is a game, then the lower pure value of G is the number

$$\lambda^*{}_G = \sup_{x \,\varepsilon\, X} \Lambda_G(x) = \sup_{x \,\varepsilon\, X} \inf_{y \,\varepsilon\, Y} M(x, y)$$

max gain with certainty

Definition 1.6.4. If $G = (X, Y, M)$ is a game, then the upper pure value of G is the number

$$v^*{}_G = \inf_{y \,\varepsilon\, Y} \Upsilon_G(y) = \inf_{y \,\varepsilon\, Y} \sup_{x \,\varepsilon\, X} M(x, y)$$

min loss with certainty

Theorem 1.6.1. If $G = (X, Y, M)$ is a game, then, for every $x_0 \in X$ and $y_0 \in Y$,

$$\Lambda_G(x_0) \leq \Upsilon_G(y_0) \quad \text{and} \quad \lambda^*_G \leq v^*_G$$

Proof. $\Lambda_G(x_0) \leq M(x_0, y_0) \leq \Upsilon(y_0)$. Thus $\lambda^*_G \leq \Upsilon_G(y_0)$, for all $y_0 \in Y$, and $\lambda^*_G \leq v^*_G$.

Consider now any game G. No method of play for I can guarantee him more than v^*_G, since II can restrict his loss to v^*_G, and no method of play for II can with certainty reduce his loss below λ^*_G, since I can guarantee this amount. Thus, if $\lambda^*_G = v^*_G = v$, say, no method of play can guarantee either player any improvement over v, and we have seen that each player can attain v (more precisely, approximate v as closely as he wishes). Thus, for such games, choosing an x_0 with $\Lambda_G(x_0) = v$ is an unimprovable method of play for I in the sense that no method of play can guarantee more, and similarly for II. This situation leads to the following definitions.

Definition 1.6.5. If $G = (X, Y, M)$ is a game, and if $\lambda^*_G = v^*_G = v_G$, then the number v_G is called the pure value of G.

Definition 1.6.6. If $G = (X, Y, M)$ is a game, and if v_G is the pure value of G, then a good strategy for player I in G is any $x_0 \in X$, with $\Lambda_G(x_0) = v_G$, and a good strategy for player II in G is any $y_0 \in Y$, with $\Upsilon_G(y_0) = v_G$.

Theorem 1.6.2. If two games $G_1 = (X_1, Y_1, M_1)$ and $G_2 = (X_2, Y_2, M_2)$ are equivalent, then $\lambda^*_{G_1} = \lambda^*_{G_2}$ and $v^*_{G_1} = v^*_{G_2}$.

Proof. It is sufficient to prove the theorem in the special case where one of the games is a reduction of the other. Suppose for definiteness that G_2 is a reduction of G_1 and that f is a function mapping X_1 onto X_2. Since, for all $x \in X_1$ and all $y \in Y_1 (= Y_2)$,

$$M_1(x, y) = M_2(f(x), y)$$

we have

$$\inf_{y \in Y_1} M_1(x, y) = \inf_{y \in Y_2} M_2(f(x), y)$$

Hence, for all $x \in X_1$,

$$\Lambda_{G_1}(x) = \Lambda_{G_2}(f(x))$$

so that

$$\lambda^*_{G_1} = \sup_{x \in X_1} \Lambda_{G_1}(x) = \sup_{x \in X_1} \Lambda_{G_2}(f(x)) = \lambda^*_{G_2}$$

The proof that $v^*_{G_1} = v^*_{G_2}$ is similar.

PROBLEMS

1.6.1. If there are strategies x_0, y_0 such that $M(x_0, y) = c_1$ for all $y \in Y$, $M(x, y_0)$ $= c_2$ for all $x \in X$, then $c_1 = c_2 = \lambda^*_G = v^*_G$.

1.6.2. If there are strategies x_0, y_0 and a number v such that $M(x_0, y) \geq v \geq M(x, y_0)$ for all x, y, then $\lambda^*_G = v^*_G = v$, and x_0, y_0 are good strategies for I, II.

1.6.3. For any $G = (X, Y, M)$ in which X, Y are closed bounded subsets of m- and n-dimensional Cartesian spaces and M is continuous on $X \times Y$ (i.e., M is uniformly continuous on $X \times Y$), $\Lambda_G(x)$ and $\Upsilon_G(y)$ are continuous in x, y respectively.

1.6.4. In any game $G = (X, Y, M)$ in which Y is a closed bounded subset of n space and M is for each x continuous in y, there exists a $y' \in Y$ such that $\Upsilon_G(y') = v^*_G$.

1.6.5. Show that, if G_1 and G_2 are equivalent, and if a player has a good strategy in G_1, he also has a good strategy in G_2.

1.6.6. Find λ^*_G and v^*_G for matching pennies, matching pennies with spying, and matching pennies with imperfect spying.

1.6.7. I chooses a number x, $0 \leq x \leq 1$. II consists of two partners II_1 and II_2. II_1 observes x, then chooses a number z, $0 \leq z \leq 1$, and z, but not x, is communicated to II_2. II_2 then chooses a number y, $0 \leq y \leq 1$, and II pays I the amount $z + |x - y|$. Describe this game in normal form and evaluate λ^*_G, v^*_G. Does either player I or II have good strategies?

1.6.8. For any game $G = (X, Y, M)$ let $T(G)$ be the game played as follows: I chooses $x \in X$ and this x is announced to II. II then chooses $y \in Y$ and pays I the amount $M(x, y)$. Describe $T(G)$ in normal form. Show that $\lambda^*_{T(G)} = v^*_{T(G)} = \lambda^*_G$.

1.6.9. Let $T(G)$ be defined as in Problem 1.6.8, and let $U(G)$ be the corresponding game in which II moves first. Is $T(G)$ equivalent (a) to $T(T(G))$, (b) to $U(T(G))$?

1.7. Perfect-Information Games

We have seen that some very simple games, e.g., matching pennies, do not have a pure value. Among the games that do have a pure value are the so-called perfect-information games of which chess, checkers, and tic-tac-toe are examples. In this section we shall consider such games in some detail. We remark, however, that the theorems and concepts discussed here, though interesting, are not needed for the understanding of the remainder of the book, and may be skipped by the reader.

Essentially, a game of perfect information is one that can be described in terms of successive moves in such a way that, at each personal move, the mover knows the choices and outcomes of all preceding personal and chance moves. In terms of the description of games in extensive form in Section 1.2, perfect-information games may be characterized as games in which every information set is a unit set. It is intuitively clear that this condition is equivalent to the requirement that every branch of the tree of the game also be a tree of some game. This latter condition leads to an inductive definition for games

in normal form. In this definition, the *order* of a perfect-information game intuitively corresponds to the maximum number of moves in that game.

Definition 1.7.1. A game $G = (X, Y, M)$ is a perfect-information game of order 0, if and only if $M(x, y)$ is constant; and a game $G = (X, Y, M)$ is a perfect-information game of order $n + 1$, if and only if there is a set A and a class \mathcal{G}_A of games $G_a = (X_a, Y_a, M_a)$ for $a \,\varepsilon\, A$, such that each G_a is a perfect-information game of order n, and such that either

Case 1. X consists of all pairs $x = (a, z)$ with $a \,\varepsilon\, A$, $z \,\varepsilon\, X_a$, Y consists of all functions y defined on A with $y(a) \,\varepsilon\, Y_a$ for all a, and

$$M((a, z), y) = M_a(z, y(a)) \quad \text{or}$$

Case 2. Y consists of all pairs $y = (a, z)$ with $a \,\varepsilon\, A$, $z \,\varepsilon\, Y_a$, X consists of all functions x defined on A with $x(a) \,\varepsilon\, X_a$ for all a, and

$$M(x, (a, z)) = M_a(x(a), z) \quad \text{or}$$

Case 3. X, Y consist of all functions x, y defined on A with $x(a) \,\varepsilon\, X_a$, $y(a) \,\varepsilon\, Y_a$ for all a, and

$$M(x, y) = \sum_{a \,\varepsilon\, A} p(a) M_a(x(a), y(a))$$

where $p(a) \geq 0$, $\sum_{a \,\varepsilon\, A} p(a) = 1$. A game G is called a perfect-information game if G is a perfect-information game of order n for some n.

Our inductive description corresponds to the fact that the result of the first move in a perfect-information game with n moves is a perfect-information game with $n - 1$ moves, so that the first move can be considered as a choice of one of a given collection of perfect-information games with $n - 1$ moves, with the three possible cases corresponding to the cases in which the first move—the choice of a—is a personal move of I, a personal move of II, or a chance move. For any perfect-information game G of order n, the first k moves of G may be considered as a game of perfect information, whose outcome is however not a number, but a game of perfect information of order $n - k$, so that the first k moves of G may be regarded as a struggle to determine which game with $n - k$ moves shall be played. Our inductive definition is the case $k = 1$. Reference to the tree and matrix of the game in Problem 1.7.1 will make the previous discussion clearer and help in an understanding of what follows.

Theorem 1.7.1. Every perfect-information game has a pure value. Moreover, if $G = (X, Y, M)$ is a perfect-information game of order $n + 1$, and \mathcal{G}_A is the class of perfect-information games $G_a = (X_a, Y_a, M_a)$, $a \, \varepsilon \, A$, of order n, as required by Definition 1.7.1, then, corresponding to the three cases for \mathcal{G}_A in Definition 1.7.1, the pure value v_G of G is given by either

Case 1. $$v_G = \sup_{a \, \varepsilon \, A} v_G(a) \qquad \text{or}$$

Case 2. $$v_G = \inf_{a \, \varepsilon \, A} v_G(a) \qquad \text{or}$$

Case 3. $$v_G = \sum_{a \, \varepsilon \, A} p(a) v_G(a)$$

where $v_G(a)$ is the pure value of G_a. In addition, if there is a $b \, \varepsilon \, A$, such that $v_G(b) = v_G$, and, for every $a \, \varepsilon \, A$, there are good strategies $x^*_a \, \varepsilon \, X_a$, $y^*_a \, \varepsilon \, Y_a$ in G_a, then good strategies $x^* \, \varepsilon \, X$, $y^* \, \varepsilon \, Y$ exist in G and, corresponding to the three cases in Definition 1.7.1, are given by either

Case 1. $x^* = (b, x^*_b)$, $y^*(a) = y^*_a$ for all $a \, \varepsilon \, A$

Case 2. $y^* = (b, y^*_b)$, $x^*(a) = x^*_a$ for all $a \, \varepsilon \, A$

Case 3. $x^*(a) = x^*_a$, $y^*(a) = y^*_a$ for all $a \, \varepsilon \, A$

Proof. The theorem is obvious for $n = 0$, and we may suppose the theorem true for all perfect-information games of order less than $n + 1$.

Case 1. Let $v = \sup_{a \, \varepsilon \, A} v_G(a)$. For any $\epsilon > 0$, choose $x^* = (b, z)$ and y^* such that

$$v_G\,(b) \qquad > v - \epsilon$$

$$\Lambda_{G_b}(z) \qquad > v_G(b) - \epsilon$$

$$\Upsilon_{G_a}(y^*(a)) < v_G(a) + \epsilon$$

Then, for all $y \, \varepsilon \, Y$,

(1) $\qquad M(x^*, y) = M_b(z, y(a)) \geq \Lambda_{G_b}(z) > v - 2\epsilon$

and, for all $x \, \varepsilon \, X$,

(2) $M(x, y^*) = M_a(x_a, y^*(a)) \leq \Upsilon_{G_a}(y^*(a)) < v_G(a) + \epsilon \leq v + \epsilon$

Thus G has pure value $v_G = v$. Furthermore, if the supremum of $v_G(a)$ is attained by some $b \, \varepsilon \, A$ and there are good strategies $x^*_a \, \varepsilon \, X_a$, $y^*_a \, \varepsilon \, Y_a$ for every G_a, then, since equations 1 and 2 are valid for all $\epsilon > 0$, the choices $x^* \, \varepsilon \, X$, $y^* \, \varepsilon \, Y$ are good strategies in G. The proofs in cases 2 and 3 are similar.

The inductive description of the value and good strategies in perfect-information games can be used to solve such games. We illustrate the method by solving the game addition, denoted by $G(k, N)$ and described in Section 1.5. If we denote by $G'(k, N)$ the game addition in which player II moves first, we notice that the initial choice of $a = 1$, \cdots, k by I produces a situation equivalent to the game $G'(k, N - a)$, and similarly for initial choices by II in $G'(k, N)$, where $G(k, N)$ and $G'(k, N)$ are of order 0 for $N \leq 0$. Thus $G(k, N)$ and $G'(k, N)$ are perfect-information games of order N for $N \geq 0$. Denoting by $v(k, N)$ the pure value of $G(k, N)$, we have

$$v(k, 0) = -1$$
$$v(k, N) = \quad 1 \quad \text{for} \quad N = 1, \cdots, k$$

Since at each stage the set A contains the k integers $1, \cdots, k$, we obtain, for $N \geq 0$,

$$v(k, N) = \max (v'(k, N - 1), \cdots, v'(k, N - k))$$

and, since the value $v'(k, N) = -v(k, N)$ for every integer N, we obtain inductively

$$v(k, 1) = \max (1, -1, -1, \cdots, -1) = 1$$
$$v(k, 2) = \max (-1, 1, -1, \cdots, -1) = 1$$

$$\cdot \ \cdot$$

$$v(k, k) = \max (-1, -1, -1, \cdots, -1, 1) = 1$$
$$v(k, k + 1) = \max (-1, -1, -1, \cdots, -1, -1) = -1$$
$$v(k, k + 2) = \max (1, -1, -1, \cdots, -1) = 1$$

$$\text{etc.}$$

Thus, for $N \geq 0$, $v(k, N) = -1$ if N is a multiple of $k + 1$ and $v(k, N) = 1$ otherwise. If N is not a multiple of $k + 1$, the initial move in a good strategy for I is to choose a so that $N - a$ is a multiple of $k + 1$, since this a maximizes $-v(k, N - a)$; if N is a multiple of $k + 1$, all initial moves are equally worthless.

If a finite game $G = (X, Y, M)$ with matrix A has a pure value v_G, both players will have good strategies, say, $x_{i*} \, \varepsilon \, X$, $y_{j*} \, \varepsilon \, Y$. Thus, in accordance with Definition 1.4.4, $v_G = a_{i*j*}$, and

$$a_{ij*} \leq a_{i*j*} \leq a_{i*j}, \quad \text{for all } i, j$$

We may restate this inequality as follows: a_{i*j*} is the minimum element in its row and the maximum element in its column. Such an element is called a *saddle point* of the matrix. Conversely, if a matrix A has a

saddle point a_{i*j*}, then the game $G = (X, Y, M)$ with matrix A has pure value $v_G = a_{i*j*}$, and $x_{i*} \varepsilon X$ and $y_{j*} \varepsilon Y$ are good strategies for players I and II respectively. Using Theorem 1.7.1, we obtain the following result for perfect-information games.

Theorem 1.7.2. The matrix of a finite game of perfect information has a saddle point.

We remark, however, that by no means all matrices with saddle points correspond to perfect-information games; the matrices of perfect-information games have a further property which we shall describe below.

We begin with an example. Suppose that, as in $G(2, 2)$, players I and II alternately choose integers, each choice being 1 or 2 and each made with knowledge of all preceding choices, until the sum of the integers chosen exceeds 2. (The reader is advised to draw the tree for this game.) Strategies for both players may be described by listing those situations in which the player chooses the number 1; there are clearly four strategies for each player. For player I they are [1]: never choose 1; [2]: choose 1 only at first move; [3]: choose 1 only at second move; [4]: always choose 1. For player II they are [1]: never choose 1; [2]: choose 1 only if I chose 1 on first move; [3]: choose 1 only if I chose 2 on first move; [4]: always choose 1. The possible plays are (2, 2), (2, 1), (1, 2), (1, 1, 2), (1, 1, 1), and if the payoff to I for these plays is A, B, C, D, E, we have the matrix

I \ II	[1]	[2]	[3]	[4]
[1]	A	A	B	B
[2]	C	D	C	D
[3]	A	A	B	B
[4]	C	E	C	E

Theorem 1.7.2 asserts that, no matter what values are assigned to A, B, C, D, E, the resulting matrix will have a saddle point. For instance, the values $A = 2$, $B = 4$, $C = 1$, $D = 0$, $E = 3$, yield, after deleting row [3] as a duplication of row [1], the matrix

I \ II	[1]	[2]	[3]	[4]
[1]	2	2	4	4
[2]	1	0	1	0
[4]	1	3	1	3

which has the upper left element as a saddle point. Now instead of looking for saddle points, one could proceed as follows. A comparison of rows [2] and [4] shows that, no matter what II chooses, strategy [4] is at least as good as strategy [2], so that I may delete row [2] from consideration, yielding

I \ II	[1]	[2]	[3]	[4]
[1]	2	2	4	4
[4]	1	3	1	3

A comparison of the columns of this matrix shows that, against either of I's *remaining* strategies, strategy [1] for II is at least as good as [2], [3], or [4], so that II may delete [2], [3], and [4] from consideration, leaving

I \ II	[1]
[1]	2
[4]	1

Finally, against II's strategy [1], I should play [1], yielding

I \ II	[1]
[1]	2

Thus, not only is there a saddle point, but also we can discover it by successive deletion of "inferior" strategies. This is the property that all matrices of games of perfect information possess, as we shall show. On the other hand, the matrix

$$\begin{Vmatrix} 2 & 3 & 4 \\ 1 & 4 & 0 \\ 1 & 0 & 6 \end{Vmatrix}$$

has a saddle point in the upper left corner, but no deletions of inferior strategies are possible, so that it cannot be the matrix of a perfect-information game.

Theorem 1.7.3. If $G = (X, Y, M)$ is a finite game of perfect information, the matrix of G may be reduced to a single element by successive deletion of inferior (including duplicated) strategies.

Proof. If G is of order 0, the theorem is clear. Suppose the theorem true for all finite perfect-information games of order $k < n$, and let G be of order n. We consider the three cases of Definition 1.7.1.

Case 1. (Player I makes the first move.) Let $A = (1, \cdots, r)$, and let B_1, \cdots, B_r be the matrices of G_1, \cdots, G_r, where matrix B_a has elements $b(a, i, j)$, $1 \le i \le m_a$, $1 \le j \le n_a$. With the set $S = (B_1, \cdots, B_r)$ we associate a matrix $T(S)$ whose rows are in $1-1$ correspondence with the set of all couples (a, i), where $a \, \varepsilon \, A$ and $1 \le i \le m_a$; whose columns are in $1-1$ correspondence with the set of all r-tuples (j_1, \cdots, j_r), where $1 \le j_a \le n_a$ for $1 \le a \le r$; and which is such that, if I corresponds to (a, i) and J to (j_1, \cdots, j_r), then the element t_{IJ} in the Ith row and Jth column of T is given by the formula

$$t_{IJ} = b(a, i, j_a)$$

Then $T(S)$ is the matrix of G, and the following assertions are easily verified:

1. If i^* is an inferior row in $B_a{}^*$, then $I^* = (a^*, i^*)$ is an inferior row in $T(S)$, and, if S' is obtained from S by deleting row i^* from B_{a*}, then $T(S')$ is obtained from $T(S)$ by deleting row I^*.

2. If j^* is an inferior column in B_{a*}, then all columns J with $j_{a*} = j^*$ are inferior columns in $T(S)$, and, if S' is obtained from S by deleting column j^* from B_{a*}, then $T(S')$ is obtained from $T(S)$ by deleting all columns with $j_{a*} = j^*$.

Thus assertion 1 associates with each permissible row deletion in any B a corresponding permissible row deletion in T, and assertion 2 associates with each permissible column deletion in any B a corresponding set of permissible column deletions in T. The induction hypothesis asserts that there is a series of permissible deletions reducing S to a collection S^* of r one-element matrices. The corresponding permissible deletions reduce $T(S)$ to $T(S^*)$, which has only a single column. Clearly $T(S^*)$ can be further reduced to a single element—the maximum element of $T(S^*)$.

Case 2. The proof in case 2 (player II makes the first move) is similar.

Case 3. (The first move is a chance move.) Let $A = (1, \cdots, r)$, and, with the same notation as in case 1, let B_1, \cdots, B_r be the corresponding matrices. Let $p(a)$ be the probability with which a is selected; we associate with S the matrix $U(S)$ whose rows are specified by r-tuples $I = (i_1, \cdots, i_r)$, $1 \le i_a \le m_a$, whose columns are specified by r-tuples $J = (j_1, \cdots, j_r)$, $1 \le j_a \le n_a$, with

$$U_{IJ} = \sum_a p(a)b(a, i_a, j_a)$$

The following assertion is easily verified: If i^* is an inferior row in B_{a*}, then all rows in U for which $i_{a*} = i^*$ are inferior rows in U, and, if S' is obtained from S by deleting i^* from B_{a*}, $U(S')$ is obtained from $U(S)$ by deleting from $U(S)$ all rows with $i_{a*} = i^*$; similar facts hold for columns.

Thus, as in case 1, each permissible deletion in any B is associated with a corresponding set of permissible deletions in U; the induction hypothesis yields a series of deletions reducing S to a collection S^* of one-element matrices, and the corresponding series reduces $T(S)$ to $T(S^*)$, which is itself a one-element matrix. This completes the proof.

Corollary. Let $G = (X, Y, M)$ be a finite game of perfect information, and let $M(x_0, y_0)$ be the single element to which the matrix of G reduces; then G has pure value $v_G = M(x_0, y_0)$ and x_0, y_0 are good strategies for players I, II.

Proof. The corollary follows from the fact that, if a matrix A_1 is obtained from A by deletion of an inferior strategy, any saddle point in A_1 is also a saddle point in A. Since the final single-element matrix $M(x_0, y_0)$ has a saddle point at (x_0, y_0), (x_0, y_0) is also a saddle point of the original $M(x, y)$.

We remark that the proof and corollary of Theorem 1.7.3 yield, for finite games, a second proof of Theorem 1.7.2.

PROBLEMS

1.7.1. Draw the tree for the following game: An unbiased coin is tossed, and, if the outcome is "head," player I chooses one of the two integers 1, 6. If the outcome is "tail," he chooses one of the two integers 2, 7. Player II then chooses one of the two integers 3, 9. The choices of the two players are added to yield the sum s. A coin is then tossed which has 0.8 probability of falling head and 0.2 probability of falling tail. If the outcome of the toss is head, II pays I s dollars; if the outcome is tail, I pays II s dollars. The outcome and choices at each move are known to both players.

1.7.2. Compute the payoff matrix of the above game, and indicate which strategies for the players result in a saddle point. Show that the matrix may be reduced to a single element by successive deletion of inferior strategies.

1.8. Mixed Strategies

In matching pennies, we have $v^*_G = 1$; either of II's strategies has a counter by I which wins for I every time. In matching pennies with the extremely imperfect spying represented by $p = 1/2$ on the other hand, the matrix is

$$
\begin{array}{cc}
& (1,\,1) \quad (1,\,2) \quad (2,\,1) \quad (2,\,2) \\
\begin{matrix} 1 \\ 2 \end{matrix} & \left(\begin{matrix} 1 & 0 & 0 & -1 \\ -1 & 0 & 0 & 1 \end{matrix} \right)
\end{array}
$$

and $v^*_G = 0$: II can reduce his expected loss to zero simply by believing that the face shown does represent I's choice, i.e., choosing strategy $(2, 1)$, or by disbelieving, i.e., choosing $(1, 2)$. Notice that, since $p = 1/2$, the coin that II observes could as well have been tossed in ignorance of I's choice: II can achieve the same effect in the original matching-pennies game simply by tossing a fair coin and believing (or acting as if he believed) that the result represents I's choice.

Suppose, then, that, in matching pennies, II tosses a coin and bases his choice on the result of the toss. We may regard the coin toss either as a device employed by II for choosing a strategy in the original game or as a new chance move introduced into the game by II, whose result is observed only by him, and which has no influence on the payoff, except in so far as II bases his play on its result. We shall adopt the second point of view and extend every game by introducing four new moves at the beginning of the game: a personal move by player I— the selection of a chance device—and a chance move performed by the device selected by I, whose result is announced to him, and the similar moves for II.

A strategy for player I consists of (1) choosing a chance device and (2) specifying for every outcome of the chance device selected in (1), a strategy x in the original game. We have not yet specified the class of chance devices available to I; we shall restrict attention to chance devices with a countable (which we take to include finite) number of possible outcomes and shall suppose that, for any sequence

$$
\xi = (\xi(1),\ \xi(2),\ \cdots,), \qquad \xi(i) \geq 0, \quad \Sigma\xi(i) = 1
$$

player I has available a chance device with different possible outcomes $r_1,\ r_2,\ \cdots$, with the probabilities $\xi(1),\ \xi(2),\ \cdots$. Part 2 of I's strategy then assigns to each r_i a corresponding $x_i \,\varepsilon\, X$. Now the exact nature of $r_1,\ r_2,\ \cdots$, is irrelevant except that they must be distinguishable, and I's choice of $\xi = (\xi(1),\ \xi(2),\ \cdots,)$ and $(x_1,\ x_2,\ \cdots,)$ is in effect a decision to choose $x_1,\ x_2,\ \cdots$, with probabilities $\xi(1),\ \xi(2),\ \cdots$. Thus a permutation of $(\xi(1),\ \xi(2),\ \cdots,)$ associated with the same permutation of $(x_1,\ x_2,\ \cdots)$ is in effect the same strategy as the original. Finally, we may suppose that $x_1,\ x_2,\ \cdots$, are distinct, since, for instance, $(1/2, 1/4, 1/4)$, $(x',\ x',\ x'')$ has the same result as $(3/4, 1/4)$, $(x',\ x'')$. A strategy for I becomes, then, simply a probability distribution ξ over X, where by a probability distribution ξ over X we mean the following.

Definition 1.8.1. A (discrete) probability distribution ξ over a space X is a non-negative, numerical function ξ defined over X such that $\xi(x) = 0$ except for a countable number of x's in X and $\sum_{x \, \varepsilon \, X} \xi(x) = 1$. Similarly, a strategy for II is a probability distribution η over Y.

Definition 1.8.2. Let $G = (X, Y, M)$ be a game. Then the game $\Gamma = (\Xi, \mathrm{H}, \mathrm{M})$, where Ξ, H consist of all probability distributions ξ, η over X, Y, and

$$M(\xi, \eta) = \sum_{x, \, y} M(x, y)\xi(x)\eta(y)$$

is called the mixed extension of G.

We shall often use the same symbol M for the payoff in G and Γ. This is to emphasize the fact that Γ is an extension of G. The strategy ξ with $\xi(x_0) = 1$, $\xi(x) = 0$ for $x \neq x_0$ we shall denote simply by x_0. Thus the symbol $M(x, y)$ denotes either the value of the original M at the point (x, y) of $X \times Y$ or the value of M at the point (ξ, η) of $\Xi \times \mathrm{H}$, where $\xi(x) = 1$ and $\eta(y) = 1$. Of course, the value is the same with either interpretation since we are describing the same thing: the payoff to I when he chooses $x \, \varepsilon \, X$ and II chooses $y \, \varepsilon \, Y$.

Definition 1.8.3. Let $\Gamma = (\Xi, \mathrm{H}, \mathrm{M})$ be the mixed extension of the game $G = (X, Y, M)$. Then the points $x \, \varepsilon \, X$, $y \, \varepsilon \, Y$ are called *pure strategies* in G and the points $\xi \, \varepsilon \, \Xi$, $\eta \, \varepsilon \, \mathrm{H}$ *mixed strategies* in G.

Theorem 1.8.1. If $G = (X, Y, M)$ is a game and $\Gamma = (\Xi, \mathrm{H}, \mathrm{M})$ is the mixed extension of G, then

(a) $\qquad\qquad \Lambda_\Gamma(\xi) = \inf_{y \, \varepsilon \, Y} M(\xi, y)$ and $\lambda^*_G \leq \lambda^*_\Gamma$

(b) $\qquad\qquad \Upsilon_\Gamma(\eta) = \sup_{x \, \varepsilon \, X} M(x, \eta)$ and $v^*_G \geq v^*_\Gamma$

Proof. (a) For any $\eta \, \varepsilon \, \mathrm{H}$,

$$M(\xi, \eta) = \sum_{y} M(\xi, y)\eta(y) \geq \inf_{y \, \varepsilon \, Y} M(\xi, y)$$

Thus

$$\Lambda_\Gamma(\xi) \geq \inf_{y \, \varepsilon \, Y} M(\xi, y)$$

Also, since H contains every $y \, \varepsilon \, Y$,

$$\inf_{y \, \varepsilon \, Y} M(\xi, y) \geq \inf_{\eta \, \varepsilon \, \mathrm{H}} M(\xi, \eta) = \Lambda_\Gamma(\xi)$$

and the first part of the theorem follows. Furthermore, for every $x \, \varepsilon \, X$

$$\Lambda_G(x) = \Lambda_\Gamma(x) \leq \lambda^*_\Gamma$$

so that $\lambda^*_G \leq \lambda^*_\Gamma$. The proof of (b) is similar.

Since $\lambda^*_G \leq \lambda^*_\Gamma \leq v^*_\Gamma \leq v^*_G$ whenever G has a pure value, Γ will have the same pure value, and, since $\Lambda_G(x) = \Lambda_\Gamma(x)$, any good strategy in G is a good strategy in Γ. The purpose of introducing Γ, however, was to analyze those games for which $\lambda^*_G < v^*_G$. We hope that for a large class of games it will turn out that $\lambda^*_\Gamma = v^*_\Gamma$, as we would then have a reasonable theory for Γ and hence for G.

Definition 1.8.4. Let $G = (X, Y, M)$ be a game and let $\Gamma = (\Xi, H, M)$ be the mixed extension of G. Then, if Γ has a pure value v_Γ, we shall say that G has value $v = v_\Gamma$, and we shall call any good strategy in Γ a good strategy in G.

Definition 1.8.5. Let $G = (X, Y, M)$ be a game, and let $\Gamma = (\Xi, H, M)$ be the mixed extension of G. If there exists a $\xi_0 \, \varepsilon \, \Xi$ such that $\Lambda_\Gamma(\xi_0) = \lambda^*_\Gamma$, then ξ_0 is called a maximin strategy for player I. If there exists an $\eta_0 \, \varepsilon \, H$ such that $\Upsilon_\Gamma(\eta_0) = v^*_\Gamma$, then η_0 is called a minimax strategy for player II.

Note that, if Γ has a value, then ξ_0, η_0 are good strategies for the two players.

It is the basic theorem of the theory of games that every finite game has a value and both players have good strategies, so that, for finite games, the introduction of Γ provides a satisfactory theory. This theorem and some extensions will be proved in Section 2.3.

Example. Matching Pennies. The matrix A of G is $A = \begin{pmatrix} 1 & -1 \\ -1 & 1 \end{pmatrix}$, $\Gamma = (\Xi, H, M)$ where Ξ consists of elements $\xi = (\alpha, 1 - \alpha)$, H consists of elements $\eta = (\beta, 1 - \beta)$, $0 \leq \alpha, \beta \leq 1$, and

$$M(\xi, \eta) = \alpha\beta + (1 - \alpha)(1 - \beta) - \alpha(1 - \beta) - \beta(1 - \alpha)$$

$$= 1 - 2\alpha - 2\beta + 4\alpha\beta$$

Thus

$$\Lambda_\Gamma(\xi) = \min[M(\xi, 1), M(\xi, 2)] = \min[2\alpha - 1, 1 - 2\alpha]$$

and

$$\lambda^*_\Gamma = \Lambda_\Gamma(1/2) = 0$$

Similarly

$$\Upsilon_\Gamma(\eta) = \max[2\beta - 1, 1 - 2\beta]$$

and

$$v^*_\Gamma = \Upsilon_\Gamma(1/2) = 0$$

We see that matching pennies has value 0, and that each player has a good strategy—choosing heads and tails each with probability $1/2$.

We conclude this section with the following theorem.

Theorem 1.8.2. If two games are equivalent, so are their mixed extensions.

Proof. It is sufficient to prove the theorem in the special case where one of the two equivalent games $G_1 = (X, Y, M_1)$ and $G_2 = (X', Y, M_2)$ is a reduction of the other. Suppose for definiteness that G_2 is a reduction of G_1 and that f maps X onto X'. For every $x' \varepsilon X'$ we define $S_{x'}$ as the set of all $x \varepsilon X$ such that $f(x) = x'$. Consider now the mixed extensions $\Gamma_1 = (\Xi_1, H, M_1)$ and $\Gamma_2 = (\Xi_2, H, M_2)$. For every $x' \varepsilon X'$ and every $\xi_1 \varepsilon \Xi_1$ we define the function ξ^*_2 by

$$\xi^*_2(x') = \sum_{x \varepsilon S_{x'}} \xi_1(x)$$

Then $\xi^*_2 \varepsilon \Xi_2$, and we define the mapping F from Ξ_1 to Ξ_2 by setting $F(\xi_1) = \xi^*_2$. Let g be a function defined over X' such that, for every $x' \varepsilon X'$, $g(x') \varepsilon S_{x'}$. Then, for every $x \varepsilon X$ and every $\xi_2 \varepsilon \Xi_2$, we define the function ξ^*_1 by

$$\xi^*_1(x) = \xi_2(x') \quad \text{if there is an } x' \varepsilon X' \text{ with } g(x') = x$$

$$0 \quad \text{if there is no } x' \varepsilon X' \text{ with } g(x') = x$$

Then $\xi^*_1 \varepsilon \Xi_1$ and $F(\xi^*_1) = \xi_2$. Thus, for every element $\xi_2 \varepsilon \Xi_2$, there is an element $\xi^*_1 \varepsilon \Xi_1$ such that $F(\xi^*_1) = \xi_2$. In addition, for every $\xi_1 \varepsilon \Xi_1$ and every $\eta \varepsilon H$,·

$$M_1(\xi_1, \eta) = \sum_{x \varepsilon X} \sum_{y \varepsilon Y} M_1(x, y)\xi_1(x)\eta(y)$$

$$= \sum_{x \varepsilon X} \sum_{y \varepsilon Y} M_2(f(x), y)\xi_1(x)\eta(y)$$

$$= \sum_{x' \varepsilon X'} \sum_{y \varepsilon Y} \sum_{x \varepsilon S_{x'}} M_2(x', y)\xi_1(x)\eta(y)$$

$$= \sum_{x' \varepsilon X'} \sum_{y \varepsilon Y} M_2(x', y)\xi^*_2(x')\eta(y)$$

$$= M_2(F(\xi_1), \eta)$$

which completes the proof.

PROBLEMS

1.8.1. Let G be a game, and let Γ be its mixed extension. Show that the mixed extension of Γ is equivalent to Γ.

◦ **1.8.2.** Let G be a game whose payoff matrix is

$$A = \begin{pmatrix} 1 & 12 & 7 & 0 \\ 3 & 0 & 1 & 9 \end{pmatrix}$$

Determine the value of G and the good mixed strategies for the players. [For any $2 \times n$ matrix (a_{ij}), $i = 1, 2; j = 1, 2, \cdots, n$, a good strategy for player I can most easily be obtained graphically by drawing the n lines $z_j = \alpha a_{1j} + (1 - \alpha)a_{2j}$, delineating for each α, min z_j (i.e., $\Lambda(\xi)$) which is a concave curve made up of line segments, and then selecting a value of α for which this curve attains its maximum.]

◦ **1.8.3.** Solve the game of matching pennies with imperfect spying, i.e., find the value and good strategies.

1.8.4. Let $G = (X, Y, M)$ where $X = (0 \leq x \leq 1)$, $Y = (0 \leq y \leq 1)$ and $M(x, y) = x - 2xy + \frac{1}{2}y$. Draw the graphs of $\Lambda(x)$ and $\Upsilon(y)$, and locate on these graphs λ^* and v^* respectively.

CHAPTER 2

Values and Optimal
Strategies in Games

2.1. Introduction

We have proved in Chapter I that finite games with perfect informa-
tion always have a value and each player has a good pure strategy.
In this chapter we shall consider some general conditions under which
games have values and the players have good (mixed) strategies. We
shall here prove the basic theorem of the theory of games—that, for
finite games, $\lambda^*_\Gamma = v^*_\Gamma$, and that good mixed strategies exist for both
players. This theorem can be considered as an assertion about convex
sets in Cartesian n-dimensional space, and certain useful extensions of
this theorem, which will also be given in this chapter, involve the asso-
ciated concept of convex functions. To facilitate the understanding of
these game-theoretic results, it will be necessary to introduce a sum-
mary of the relevant facts about convex sets and convex functions.
Games in which one of the players has a finite number of pure strategies
are of particular interest in statistics and will be studied in some detail.
Methods for solving games will also be considered.

2.2. Convex Sets and Convex Functions

We shall denote by S_n the Cartesian n-dimensional space of all vec-
tors $\mathbf{s} = (s_1, \cdots, s_n)$, where each s_i is a real number; S_n is also referred
to as n space. (Henceforth, if we wish to emphasize that an element is
or can be represented as a point in n space with $n > 1$, we shall desig-
nate it by a letter in boldface type.) For any $\mathbf{s} = (s_1, \cdots, s_n) \, \varepsilon \, S_n$
and any number λ, $\lambda\mathbf{s}$ denotes the vector $(\lambda s_1, \cdots, \lambda s_n)$, and, for any
$\mathbf{t} = (t_1, \cdots, t_n) \, \varepsilon \, S_n$, $\mathbf{s} + \mathbf{t}$ denotes the vector $(s_1 + t_1, \cdots, s_n + t_n)$,
and $\mathbf{s} - \mathbf{t}$ denotes $\mathbf{s} + (-1)\mathbf{t}$. The vector $(0, 0, \cdots, 0)$ will be denoted
by \mathbf{e}. For any \mathbf{s}, \mathbf{t} with $\mathbf{s} \neq \mathbf{t}$, the set of all points representable as
$\lambda\mathbf{s} + (1 - \lambda)\mathbf{t}$ is called the *line* containing \mathbf{s} and \mathbf{t}, and the subset of

this line with $0 \leq \lambda \leq 1$ is the *line segment* joining \mathbf{s} and \mathbf{t}. For any \mathbf{s} and \mathbf{t}, the number $\sum_1^n s_i t_i$ is called the *inner product* of \mathbf{s} and \mathbf{t} and will be denoted by $\mathbf{s} \cdot \mathbf{t}$. For any $\mathbf{u} \neq \mathbf{e}$ and any constant c, the set of all vectors \mathbf{x} with $\mathbf{u} \cdot \mathbf{x} = c$ is called a *hyperplane*. For any line l and any point \mathbf{x}_0 the hyperplane $(\mathbf{s}_1 - \mathbf{s}_2) \cdot \mathbf{x} = (\mathbf{s}_1 - \mathbf{s}_2) \cdot \mathbf{x}_0$, where $\mathbf{s}_1 \, \varepsilon \, l$, $\mathbf{s}_2 \, \varepsilon \, l$, $\mathbf{s}_1 \neq \mathbf{s}_2$, is independent of \mathbf{s}_1, \mathbf{s}_2 and is called *the hyperplane through* \mathbf{x}_0 *perpendicular to* l. If S and T are sets and $\mathbf{u} \cdot \mathbf{x} = c$ is a hyperplane in S_n such that, for $\mathbf{x} \, \varepsilon \, S$, $\mathbf{u} \cdot \mathbf{x} \geq c$ and, for $\mathbf{x} \, \varepsilon \, T$, $\mathbf{u} \cdot \mathbf{x} \leq c$, then the hyperplane $\mathbf{u} \cdot \mathbf{x} = c$ is said to *separate* S and T. For any $\mathbf{u} \neq \mathbf{e}$ and any constant c, the set of all vectors \mathbf{x} with $\mathbf{u} \cdot \mathbf{x} \geq c$ is called a *half-space*. The number $\left(\sum_1^n x^2_i \right)^{1/2}$ is called the *length* of \mathbf{x}, written $|\mathbf{x}|$, and, for any \mathbf{x}_0 and any $r > 0$, the set of all \mathbf{x} with $|\mathbf{x} - \mathbf{x}_0| < r$ (we denote this set by the symbol $\{\mathbf{x} : |\mathbf{x} - \mathbf{x}_0| < r\}$) is called the *sphere* about \mathbf{x}_0 of radius r. A point $\mathbf{u} \, \varepsilon \, U$ is called an *inner point* of U if there is a sphere with center \mathbf{u} which is a subset of U. A set U all of whose points are inner points is called *open*, and a set V for which the *complementary set* U of all points $\mathbf{u} \notin V$ is open is called *closed*. For every set U, there is a smallest closed set containing U, called the *closure* of U and denoted by \bar{U}. A point \mathbf{s} is called a *boundary point* of a set U if every sphere about \mathbf{s} contains points $\mathbf{u} \, \varepsilon \, U$ and points $\mathbf{v} \notin U$. The closure of a set is obtained by adjoining to it all its boundary points not already in it. Since half-spaces are closed, any hyperplane separating S and T also separates their closures \bar{S} and \bar{T}. The *diameter* of a set $R \subset S_n$ is the least upper bound of $|\mathbf{x}_1 - \mathbf{x}_2|$, where \mathbf{x}_1 and \mathbf{x}_2 are in R. If δ is the diameter of R, then, for all \mathbf{x}_1, $\mathbf{x}_2 \, \varepsilon \, R$, $|\mathbf{x}_1 - \mathbf{x}_2| \leq \delta$. A set of finite diameter is called *bounded*.

A set that has no points in it is called the *null set* and will be designated by the symbol \varnothing. If S and T are any two sets then by the *intersection* of S and T is meant the set of points common to both S and T, which will be designated by the symbol $S \cap T$. Thus, if S and T have no points in common, $S \cap T = \varnothing$. By the *union* of S and T is meant the set of all points in at least one of S and T, which will be designated by $S \cup T$. If S_1, S_2, \cdots are a sequence of sets then we shall sometimes write $\bigcap_i S_i$ for $S_1 \cap S_2 \cap \cdots$ and $\bigcup_i S_i$ for $S_1 \cup S_2 \cup \cdots$.

A subset S of S_n is called *convex* if for any two points \mathbf{s}_1 and \mathbf{s}_2 of S, the entire line segment joining \mathbf{s}_1 and \mathbf{s}_2 is contained in S; i.e., $\lambda \mathbf{s}_1 + (1 - \lambda) \mathbf{s}_2 \, \varepsilon \, S$ for $0 \leq \lambda \leq 1$. Examples of convex sets are points, lines, line segments, spheres, hyperplanes, and half-spaces. For any set R, the set R^* of all points \mathbf{r}^* which are centers of gravity of a finite set of

points in R with appropriate weights, i.e., which are all representable as

$$\mathbf{r}^* = \lambda_1 \mathbf{r}_1 + \cdots + \lambda_k \mathbf{r}_k$$

where

$$\lambda_i \geq 0, \quad \sum_1^k \lambda_i = 1, \quad \mathbf{r}_i \, \varepsilon \, R, \quad i = 1, \cdots, k; \quad k = 1, 2, \cdots,$$

is clearly a convex set containing R. Moreover, since

$$\sum_{i=1}^{k+1} \lambda_i \mathbf{r}_i = \sum_{i=1}^{k} \lambda_i \left[\frac{\displaystyle\sum_{i=1}^{k} \lambda_i \mathbf{r}_i}{\displaystyle\sum_{i=1}^{k} \lambda_i} \right] + \lambda_{k+1} \mathbf{r}_{k+1}$$

when

$$\sum_{i=1}^{k} \lambda_i \neq 0$$

it is seen by induction on k that any convex set containing R also contains R^*. Thus R^* is the smallest convex set containing R. R^* is called the *convex hull* of R. For example, the convex hull of two points is the line segment joining them; the convex hull of a circle is the circle and its interior.

The following elementary properties of convex sets are easy to prove and are left as exercises at the end of the section: The intersection of any number of convex sets is convex. The closure of a convex set is convex. The set of inner points of a convex set is convex. (Note that a line segment, considered as a subset of 2-space, does not have any inner points, but does have inner points when considered as a subset of the infinite line, the 1-space containing it. Thus, a point \mathbf{x} belonging to a set S will be called a *relative* inner point of S if it is an inner point of S considered as a subset of the lowest dimensional space, that is, hyperplane, containing it. Similarly, for a *relative* boundary point.) A convex set always has (relative) inner points.

Lemma 2.2.1. (*a*) Let S be a convex set, \mathbf{x} an inner point of S, \mathbf{y} a boundary point of S (belonging to S or not). Then the points $(1 - \lambda)\mathbf{x} + \lambda \mathbf{y}$ are inner points of S for $0 \leq \lambda < 1$, and exterior points of S for $\lambda > 1$. (*b*) A convex set S and its closure \bar{S} have the same boundary points, inner points, and exterior points.

Proof. (*a*) Choose $\mathbf{y}_n \, \varepsilon \, S$ such that $\mathbf{y}_n \to \mathbf{y}$. If $\mathbf{z} = (1 - \lambda)\mathbf{x} + \lambda \mathbf{y}$, $0 < \lambda < 1$, is not an inner point of S, there is a sequence $\mathbf{z}_n \notin S$ with $\mathbf{z}_n \to \mathbf{z}$. Define \mathbf{x}_n by $\mathbf{z}_n = (1 - \lambda)\mathbf{x}_n + \lambda \mathbf{y}_n$; i.e., $\mathbf{x}_n = (\mathbf{z}_n - \lambda \mathbf{y}_n)/(1 - \lambda)$. Then $\mathbf{x}_n \notin S$; otherwise, since $\mathbf{y}_n \, \varepsilon \, S$, we would have $\mathbf{z}_n \, \varepsilon \, S$.

As $n \to \infty$, $\mathbf{x}_n \to (\mathbf{z} - \lambda\mathbf{y})/(1 - \lambda) = \mathbf{x}$, contradicting the hypothesis that \mathbf{x} is an inner point of S. For $\lambda > 1$, if there were an inner or boundary point of S on the line from \mathbf{x} through \mathbf{y} and beyond \mathbf{y}, then the preceding argument would make \mathbf{y} an inner point of S, contradicting the assumption. (b) Since $S \subset \bar{S}$, an inner point of S is obviously an inner point of \bar{S}, an exterior point of \bar{S} is an exterior point of S. For an exterior point \mathbf{x} of S there is by definition a sphere about \mathbf{x} containing no points of S, hence no limit point of S, consequently no points of \bar{S}, so that \mathbf{x} is exterior to \bar{S} as well; that is to say, in general, *any* set and its closure have the same exterior points. Let \mathbf{y} be an inner point of \bar{S}, let T be a sphere with center \mathbf{y} contained in \bar{S}, and let \mathbf{s} be an inner point of $S \cap T$; such an \mathbf{s} exists; otherwise $S \cap T$ would be contained in a hyperplane, and $\overline{S \cap T} = \bar{S} \cap T = T$ would be contained in the same hyperplane. From (a), every point within a line segment joining \mathbf{s} to a boundary point of $S \cap T$ is an inner point of $S \cap T$. Since all points of the boundary of T are boundary points of $S \cap T$, every point of T is within such a line segment, every point of T is an inner point of $S \cap T$, and therefore in S. Thus the inner points of S and \bar{S} coincide. By exclusion, the boundary points of S and \bar{S} coincide.

Theorem 2.2.1. (i) If S and T are closed convex sets without common points and at least one of S and T is bounded, there is a hyperplane $\mathbf{u} \cdot \mathbf{x} = c$ with $\mathbf{u} \cdot \mathbf{x} > c$ for $\mathbf{x} \, \varepsilon \, S$ and $\mathbf{u} \cdot \mathbf{x} < c$ for $\mathbf{x} \, \varepsilon \, T$.

(ii) If S and T are convex sets and if there exists a sequence of convex sets S_N such that (a) S_N and T have a separating hyperplane for each N and (b) every sphere about any point of S contains points in all but a finite number of S_N, then S and T have a separating hyperplane.

Proof. We first prove (i); say S is bounded. Figure 3 illustrates the construction used in the proof.

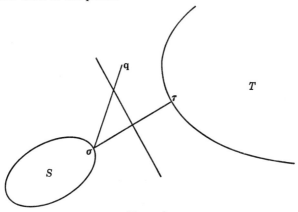

Figure 3

Since T is closed and S is bounded and closed, there exist sequences $\{\sigma_n\}$, $\{\tau_n\}$, with $\sigma_n \varepsilon S$ and $\tau_n \varepsilon T$ such that

$$\left| \sigma_n - \tau_n \right| \to \inf_{s \varepsilon S, t \varepsilon T} \left| s - t \right|$$

and such that $\{\tau_n\}$ is bounded, as can be seen from the inequality

$$\left| \left| \sigma_n \right| - \left| \tau_n \right| \right| \leq \left| \sigma_n - \tau_n \right|$$

and the fact that $\{\sigma_n\}$ is bounded. Hence there are points $\sigma \varepsilon S$, $\tau \varepsilon T$ with

$$\left| \sigma - \tau \right| = \min_{s \varepsilon S, t \varepsilon T} \left| s - t \right|$$

Then the hyperplane which passes through the midpoint of the line segment joining σ and τ and is perpendicular to this line segment, i.e.,

$$(\sigma - \tau) \cdot \mathbf{x} = (\sigma - \tau) \cdot \left(\frac{\sigma + \tau}{2} \right) = c$$

has the required property. For, let \mathbf{q} be any point with

$$(1) \qquad (\sigma - \tau) \cdot \mathbf{q} \leq c$$

Then the square of the distance from τ to any point on the line joining σ and \mathbf{q} is

$$(2) \qquad f(\lambda) = \left| \lambda \mathbf{q} + (1 - \lambda)\sigma - \tau \right|^2$$

and from (2) by expansion, we get

$$(3) \qquad f(\lambda) = \left| \mathbf{q} - \sigma \right|^2 \lambda^2 + 2(\mathbf{q} - \sigma) \cdot (\sigma - \tau)\lambda + \left| \sigma - \tau \right|^2$$

The result of taking the derivative of (3) with respect to λ and setting $\lambda = 0$ is

$$(4) \qquad f'(0) = 2(\mathbf{q} - \sigma) \cdot (\sigma - \tau) = 2\mathbf{q} \cdot (\sigma - \tau) - 2\sigma \cdot (\sigma - \tau)$$
$$\leq 2c - 2\sigma \cdot (\sigma - \tau)$$

Now, from the definition of c,

$$(5) \qquad \sigma \cdot (\sigma - \tau) - c = (\sigma - \tau) \cdot \left(\sigma - \frac{\sigma + \tau}{2} \right)$$
$$= \tfrac{1}{2} \left| \sigma - \tau \right|^2 > 0$$

From (4) and (5) we conclude that

$$f'(0) < 0$$

Hence there are points \mathbf{w} on the line segment joining σ and \mathbf{q} with

$|\mathbf{w} - \tau| < |\sigma - \tau|$, so that $q \notin S$, and, since q is any point satisfying (1), we conclude that, for all $\mathbf{x} \, \varepsilon \, S$,

$$(\sigma - \tau) \cdot \mathbf{x} > c$$

Similarly, $(\sigma - \tau) \cdot \mathbf{x} < c$, for all $\mathbf{x} \, \varepsilon \, T$.

To prove (ii), suppose the hyperplane

$$\mathbf{u}_N \cdot \mathbf{x} = c_N$$

separates S_N from T, i.e., $\mathbf{u}_N \cdot \mathbf{x} \geq c_N$ for $\mathbf{x} \, \varepsilon \, S_N$, $\mathbf{u}_N \cdot \mathbf{x} \leq c_N$ for $\mathbf{x} \, \varepsilon \, T$. We may suppose, replacing \mathbf{u}_N, c_N by $\mathbf{u}_N / |\mathbf{u}_N|$, $c_N / |\mathbf{u}_N|$, that $|\mathbf{u}_N| = 1$ for all N. Let $\mathbf{t} \, \varepsilon \, T$ and let the points \mathbf{s}_N be a bounded sequence with $\mathbf{s}_N \, \varepsilon \, S_N$. Using Schwarz inequality, we then obtain

$$-|\mathbf{t}| \leq \mathbf{u}_N \cdot \mathbf{t} \leq c_N \leq \mathbf{u}_N \cdot \mathbf{s}_N \leq |\mathbf{s}_N|$$

so that c_N is bounded, and we may choose a subsequence of \mathbf{u}_N, c_N with $\mathbf{u}_N \to \mathbf{u}$, $c_N \to c$ as $N \to \infty$ through the chosen subsequence. Moreover, $|\mathbf{u}| = 1$, so that $\mathbf{u} \neq \mathbf{e}$. Since $\mathbf{u}_N \cdot \mathbf{t} \leq c_N$ for all $\mathbf{t} \, \varepsilon \, T$ and all N, we have $\mathbf{u} \cdot \mathbf{t} \leq c$ for all $\mathbf{t} \, \varepsilon \, T$. For $\mathbf{s} \, \varepsilon \, S$, there is a sequence $\mathbf{s}_N \, \varepsilon \, S_N$ with $\mathbf{s}_N \to \mathbf{s}$ as $N \to \infty$. Since $\mathbf{u}_N \cdot \mathbf{s}_N \geq c_N$ for all N, letting $N \to \infty$ through the chosen subsequence yields $\mathbf{u} \cdot \mathbf{s} \geq c$. This completes the proof. Note that, in view of part (ii), we can, at the expense of replacing the strict inequalities of part (i) by weak inequalities, remove the requirement in part (i) that S be bounded, for, by taking S_N to be the intersection of S with the sphere K_N with center at the origin and radius N, the hypotheses of (ii) are satisfied by (i).

Corollary 1. If \mathbf{s} is a boundary point of a convex set T, there is a hyperplane $\mathbf{u} \cdot \mathbf{x} = c$ containing \mathbf{s} such that $\mathbf{u} \cdot \mathbf{x} \leq c$ for $\mathbf{x} \, \varepsilon \, T$.

Proof. Choose a sequence $\mathbf{s}_N \to \mathbf{s}$ with $\mathbf{s}_N \notin \overline{T}$. [See Problem 2.2.2 and Lemma 2.2.1(*b*).] Then \overline{T} and the sets S_N each consisting of the single element \mathbf{s}_N satisfy the hypotheses of part (ii) of the theorem, so that \mathbf{s} and \overline{T} have a separating hyperplane $\mathbf{u} \cdot \mathbf{x} = c$. Since $\mathbf{u} \cdot \mathbf{s} \geq c$ and $\mathbf{u} \cdot \mathbf{s} \leq c$, we have $\mathbf{u} \cdot \mathbf{s} = c$.

The plane $\mathbf{u} \cdot \mathbf{x} = c$ of the above corollary is called a *supporting hyperplane* to the convex set T at the point \mathbf{s}.

Corollary 2. If S and T are convex sets without common points, they have a separating hyperplane.

Proof. Let $\{\mathbf{s}_N\}$, $\{\mathbf{t}_N\}$ be sequences of points with $\mathbf{s}_N \, \varepsilon \, S$, $\mathbf{t}_N \, \varepsilon \, T$ such that every sphere about any point of S, T contains at least one \mathbf{s}_N, \mathbf{t}_N respectively. If S_N, T_M are the convex hulls of $(\mathbf{s}_1, \cdots, \mathbf{s}_N)$, $(\mathbf{t}_1, \cdots, \mathbf{t}_M)$ respectively, S_N, T_M are closed bounded convex sets without common points and have a separating hyperplane from part (i) of the theorem. Then for fixed M the sets S, T_M satisfy the hypotheses of

part (ii) of the theorem and consequently have a separating hyperplane. Then S and T also satisfy the hypotheses of (ii), using the sequence T_M, so that they have a separating hyperplane.

Theorem 2.2.2. For any subset R of n space, every point \mathbf{r}^* in the convex hull R^* of R is representable in the form

$$\mathbf{r}^* = \sum_0^n \lambda_i \mathbf{r}_i, \quad \lambda_i \geq 0, \quad \sum_0^n \lambda_i = 1, \quad \mathbf{r}_i \, \varepsilon \, R$$

If \mathbf{r}^* is a boundary point of R^*, λ_0 can be chosen to be zero.

Proof. Suppose first that \mathbf{r}^* is a boundary point of R^*, and let $\mathbf{u} \cdot \mathbf{x} = c$ be a hyperplane through \mathbf{r}^* with $\mathbf{u} \cdot \mathbf{x} \leq c$ for all $\mathbf{x} \, \varepsilon \, R^*$. Say $\mathbf{r}^* = \sum_1^k \lambda_i \mathbf{r}_i$, $\lambda_i > 0$. Then $\mathbf{u} \cdot \mathbf{r}_i = c$ for $i = 1, \cdots, k$. We show that, if $k > N$, we can choose constants a_1, \cdots, a_k not all zero such that $\sum_1^k a_i = 0$, $\sum_1^k a_i \mathbf{r}_i = \mathbf{e}$. We use the fact that any set of more than n vectors in n space is linearly dependent. If $c \neq 0$, choose a_i not all zero so that $\sum_1^k a_i \mathbf{r}_i = \mathbf{e}$. Then

$$\sum_{i=1}^k a_i(\mathbf{u} \cdot \mathbf{r}_i) = \mathbf{e} \cdot \mathbf{u} = 0$$

and hence

$$c \sum_1^k a_i = 0 = \sum_1^k a_i$$

If $c = 0$, choose a_i not all zero so that $\sum_1^k a_i(\mathbf{r}_i + \mathbf{u}) = \mathbf{e}$. Then

$$\sum_{i=1}^k a_i(\mathbf{u} + \mathbf{r}_i) \cdot \mathbf{u} = \mathbf{e} \cdot \mathbf{u} = 0$$

and hence

$$|\mathbf{u}|^2 \sum_1^k a_i = 0 = \sum_1^k a_i$$

and since $\sum_{i=1}^k a_i(\mathbf{r}_i + \mathbf{u}) = \mathbf{e}$,

$$\sum_1^k a_i \mathbf{r}_i = \mathbf{e}$$

Consequently, for any real number t

$$\sum_1^k (\lambda_i + ta_i) = 1$$

and

$$\sum_1^k (\lambda_i + ta_i)\mathbf{r}_i = \mathbf{s}$$

Choosing

$$t = -\min_{a_i>0} \frac{\lambda_i}{a_i}$$

makes $\lambda_i + ta_i$ zero for some i and non-negative for all i, so that, if $k > n$, a representation of \mathbf{r}^* with less than k points of \mathbf{r} is possible.

For non-boundary points of R^*, consider the sets Q, Q^* of all points in $(n + 1)$-space of the form $(\mathbf{r}, 0)$, $(\mathbf{r}^*, 0)$, where $\mathbf{r} \, \varepsilon \, R$, $\mathbf{r}^* \, \varepsilon \, R^*$. Then Q^* is the convex hull of Q and all points of Q^* are boundary points. Thus, for any $\mathbf{r}^* \, \varepsilon \, R^*$, there is a representation

$$(\mathbf{r}^*, 0) = \sum_0^n \lambda_i(\mathbf{r}_i, 0)$$

where

$$\mathbf{r}_i \, \varepsilon \, R, \qquad \lambda_i \geq 0, \qquad \sum_0^n \lambda_i = 1$$

so that

$$\mathbf{r}^* = \sum_0^n \lambda_i \mathbf{r}_i.$$

This completes the proof.

A point \mathbf{s} in a convex set S is called an *extreme point* of S if it is not interior to any line segment of S, i.e., if there do not exist two points $\mathbf{s}_1 \, \varepsilon \, S$, $\mathbf{s}_2 \, \varepsilon \, S$ with $\mathbf{s}_1 \neq \mathbf{s}_2$ and $\mathbf{s} = \lambda\mathbf{s}_1 + (1 - \lambda)\mathbf{s}_2$, $0 < \lambda < 1$.

Theorem 2.2.3. A closed bounded convex set has extreme points in every supporting hyperplane.

Proof. Say $\mathbf{u} \cdot \mathbf{x} = c$ is a supporting hyperplane of the closed, bounded convex set S, and let T be the intersection of S with $\mathbf{u} \cdot \mathbf{x} = c$, so that T is a closed, bounded non-empty convex subset of S. Any extreme point of T is also an extreme point of S, since $\mathbf{t} = \lambda\mathbf{s}_1 + (1 - \lambda)\mathbf{s}_2$, $\mathbf{t} \, \varepsilon \, T$, $\mathbf{s}_1 \, \varepsilon \, S$, $\mathbf{s}_2 \, \varepsilon \, S$, $0 < \lambda < 1$ imply $\mathbf{s}_1 \, \varepsilon \, T$, $\mathbf{s}_2 \, \varepsilon \, T$. Thus it suffices to show that T has extreme points. Now, for any closed bounded convex set T, the point $\mathbf{t}^* \, \varepsilon \, T$ farthest from the origin is an extreme point, since, if

$\mathbf{t}^* = \lambda_0\mathbf{t}_1 + (1 - \lambda_0)\mathbf{t}_2$, $\mathbf{t}_1 \neq \mathbf{t}_2$, $0 < \lambda_0 < 1$, the quadratic function

$$f(\lambda) = \big|\, \lambda\mathbf{t}_1 + (1 - \lambda)\mathbf{t}_2 \,\big|^2 = \lambda^2\big|\, \mathbf{t}_1 - \mathbf{t}_2 \,\big|^2 + 2\lambda[(\mathbf{t}_1 - \mathbf{t}_2)\cdot\mathbf{t}_2] + \big|\, \mathbf{t}_2 \,\big|^2$$

has a positive coefficient for λ^2, so that at least one of $f(0) = \big|\, \mathbf{t}_2 \,\big|^2$ and $f(1) = \big|\, \mathbf{t}_1 \,\big|^2$ must exceed $f(\lambda_0) = \big|\, \mathbf{t}^* \,\big|^2$. This completes the proof.

Theorem 2.2.4. If a closed bounded convex set has only a finite number of extreme points, it is the convex hull of its extreme points.

Proof. Say $\mathbf{x}_1, \cdots, \mathbf{x}_k$ are the extreme points of the closed bounded convex set S, and let S^* be the convex hull of $\mathbf{x}_1, \cdots, \mathbf{x}_k$. If there is a point $\mathbf{s}_0 \,\varepsilon\, S$, $\mathbf{s}_0 \notin S^*$, there is a hyperplane $\mathbf{u}\cdot\mathbf{x} = c$ with $\mathbf{u}\cdot\mathbf{s}_0 > c$, $\mathbf{u}\cdot\mathbf{s}^* < c$, for $\mathbf{s}^* \,\varepsilon\, S^*$. If $c_1 = \max_{\mathbf{x}\,\varepsilon\, S} (\mathbf{u}\cdot\mathbf{x})$, $\mathbf{u}\cdot\mathbf{x} = c_1$ is a supporting hyperplane of S not containing any of the extreme points $\mathbf{x}_1, \cdots, \mathbf{x}_k$ and therefore contradicting Theorem 2.2.3.

If S is a convex set of S_n, a numerical function f defined on S is said to be *convex* if for all $\mathbf{x}_1, \mathbf{x}_2 \,\varepsilon\, S$ and all λ, $0 \leq \lambda \leq 1$ we have

$$f[\lambda\mathbf{x}_1 + (1 - \lambda)\mathbf{x}_2] \leq \lambda f(\mathbf{x}_1) + (1 - \lambda)f(\mathbf{x}_2)$$

and it is said to be *concave* if

$$f[\lambda\mathbf{x}_1 + (1 - \lambda)\mathbf{x}_2] \geq \lambda f(\mathbf{x}_1) + (1 - \lambda)f(\mathbf{x}_2)$$

If the above inequalities are strict for $\mathbf{x}_1 \neq \mathbf{x}_2$, $0 < \lambda < 1$, f is called *strictly convex* or *strictly concave*, respectively. Geometrically, a function is convex if every line segment joining two points on its graph lies entirely on or above the graph, and it is concave if the line segment lies entirely on or below the graph. By induction on k we obtain that, for any k points $\mathbf{x}_1, \cdots, \mathbf{x}_k$ in S and any non-negative numbers $\lambda_1, \cdots, \lambda_k$ with $\sum_1^k \lambda_i = 1$, we have

$$f\left(\sum_1^k \lambda_i\mathbf{x}_i\right) \leq \sum_1^k \lambda_i f(\mathbf{x}_i)$$

if f is convex, and

$$f\left(\sum_1^k \lambda_i\mathbf{x}_i\right) \geq \sum_1^k \lambda_i f(\mathbf{x}_i)$$

if f is concave. A function f is convex (concave) if and only if the function φ with

$$\varphi(\lambda, \mathbf{x}_1, \mathbf{x}_2) = f[\lambda\mathbf{x}_1 + (1 - \lambda)\mathbf{x}_2]$$

is a convex (concave) function of λ on $0 \leq \lambda \leq 1$ for all $\mathbf{x}_1, \mathbf{x}_2 \,\varepsilon\, S$ [see Problem 2.2.6]. Thus the verification that a certain function of n vari-

ables is convex (concave) reduces to verifying that certain functions of one variable are convex (concave).

Theorem 2.2.5. Let a function φ be defined and possess the first two derivatives throughout the closed interval (a, b). Then φ is convex on (a, b) if $\varphi'' \geq 0$ on (a, b).

Proof. Since for any two points c and d in (a, b) with $c < d$, the mean-value theorem states that

$$(1) \qquad \varphi(d) - \varphi(c) = \varphi'(\varsigma)(d - c), \quad c < \varsigma < d$$

we have, for $a \leq y_1 < y_2 \leq b$ and $0 < \alpha < 1$,

$$(2) \qquad \varphi[\alpha y_1 + (1 - \alpha)y_2] - \varphi(y_1) = (1 - \alpha)(y_2 - y_1)\varphi'(\varsigma_1)$$

where $y_1 < \varsigma_1 < \alpha y_1 + (1 - \alpha)y_2$, and

$$(3) \qquad \varphi(y_2) - \varphi[\alpha y_1 + (1 - \alpha)y_2] = \alpha(y_2 - y_1)\varphi'(\varsigma_2)$$

where $\alpha y_1 + (1 - \alpha)y_2 < \varsigma_2 < y_2$. Solving (2) and (3) for $\varphi'(\varsigma_1)$ and $\varphi'(\varsigma_2)$ and noting that $\varphi'(\varsigma_1) \leq \varphi'(\varsigma_2)$, since $\varphi''(y) \geq 0$, we obtain

$$(4) \qquad \varphi[\alpha y_1 + (1 - \alpha)y_2] \leq \alpha\varphi(y_1) + (1 - \alpha)\varphi(y_2)$$

which proves the theorem.

Examples of convex functions are:

$$\sum_{i=1}^{n} a_i x_i; \quad |x_i|^\alpha, \quad \alpha \geq 1; \quad \text{and} \quad e^{\sum_{i=1}^{n} a_i x_i}$$

The following relation exists between convex functions and convex sets [see Problem 2.2.7]: For any convex function f defined on a closed convex subset S of S_n, the set T of all points $(\mathbf{x}, y) \varepsilon S_{n+1}$ with $\mathbf{x} \varepsilon S$, $y \geq f(\mathbf{x})$ is convex; if in addition f is continuous, T is closed.

Theorem 2.2.6. If f is a continuous convex function defined on a closed convex set S of S_n, for any $\epsilon > 0$ and any $\mathbf{x}_0 \varepsilon S$ there is a linear function l such that $l(\mathbf{x}) \leq f(\mathbf{x})$ for $\mathbf{x} \varepsilon S$ and $l(\mathbf{x}_0) > f(\mathbf{x}_0) - \epsilon$. If \mathbf{x}_0 is an interior point of S, there is a linear function l_1 with $l_1(\mathbf{x}) \leq f(\mathbf{x})$ for $\mathbf{x} \varepsilon S$ and $l_1(\mathbf{x}_0) = f(\mathbf{x}_0)$.

Proof. Since the set T of points (\mathbf{x}, y) with $\mathbf{x} \varepsilon S$, $y \geq f(\mathbf{x})$ is a closed convex subset of S_{n+1} not containing the point $(\mathbf{x}_0, f(\mathbf{x}_0) - \epsilon)$, there is a strictly separating hyperplane, i.e., a $\mathbf{u} \varepsilon S_n$ and numbers a, c with

$$\mathbf{u} \cdot \mathbf{x} + af(\mathbf{x}) > c \qquad \text{for} \quad \mathbf{x} \varepsilon S$$

$$\mathbf{u} \cdot \mathbf{x}_0 + a[f(\mathbf{x}_0) - \epsilon] < c$$

Then $a > 0$ and the linear function l with

$$l(x) = \frac{c - \mathbf{u} \cdot \mathbf{x}}{a}$$

has the required property.

Let \mathbf{x}_0 be an interior point of S. The set T has a supporting hyperplane at $(\mathbf{x}_0, f(\mathbf{x}_0))$, i.e., there is a $\mathbf{u}_1 \, \varepsilon \, S_n$ and a number a with

(1) $$\mathbf{u}_1 \cdot \mathbf{x} + ay \geq \mathbf{u}_1 \cdot x_0 + af(\mathbf{x}_0)$$

for all $\mathbf{x} \, \varepsilon \, S$ and $y \geq f(\mathbf{x})$. We shall show that $a > 0$ in (1). We consider two cases; $\mathbf{u}_1 = \mathbf{e}$ and $\mathbf{u}_1 \neq \mathbf{e}$. If $\mathbf{u}_1 = \mathbf{e}$ then (1) becomes $ay \geq af(\mathbf{x}_0)$ and, by definition of a hyperplane, $a \neq 0$. Since y can be taken arbitrarily large, it follows that $a > 0$. If $\mathbf{u}_1 \neq \mathbf{e}$, then for a sufficiently small $\epsilon > 0$, $\mathbf{x}' = \mathbf{x}_0 - \epsilon\mathbf{u}_1$ is an interior point of S. Moreover,

(2) $$\mathbf{u}_1 \cdot \mathbf{x}' < \mathbf{u}_1 \cdot \mathbf{x}_0$$

so that substituting \mathbf{x}' for \mathbf{x} in (1) and employing (2) yields $ay > af(\mathbf{x}_0)$ for all y. Thus in both cases $a > 0$, and consequently the linear function l_1 defined by

(3) $$l_1(\mathbf{x}) = \frac{\mathbf{u}_1 \cdot (\mathbf{x}_0 - \mathbf{x})}{a} + f(\mathbf{x}_0)$$

has the required property.

It follows from Theorem 2.2.6 that a continuous convex function f on a closed set S is the upper bound of all linear functions l which never exceed it. If f is not continuous, this need not occur, as shown by $f(x) = 0$, $x > 0$, $f(0) = 1$, where $S = \{x : x \geq 0\}$. A partial converse to Theorem 2.2.6, which will be used later, is

Theorem 2.2.7. *If A is a bounded subset of n space, the function φ defined by $\varphi(\mathbf{x}) = \sup_{\mathbf{a} \, \varepsilon \, A} (\mathbf{a} \cdot \mathbf{x})$ is continuous and convex on n space.*

Proof. For every $\epsilon > 0$ there is a finite set $A_N = \{\mathbf{a}_1, \cdots, \mathbf{a}_N\}$ in A which is ϵ-*dense* in A, i.e., for every $\mathbf{a} \, \varepsilon \, A$ there is an $\mathbf{a}_i \, \varepsilon \, A_N$ with $|\mathbf{a}_i - \mathbf{a}| < \epsilon$. Now $|\mathbf{a}_i - \mathbf{a}| < \epsilon$ implies

(1) $$|\mathbf{a}_i \cdot \mathbf{x} - \mathbf{a} \cdot \mathbf{x}| < \epsilon |\mathbf{x}|$$

so that, writing $f(\mathbf{x}) = \sup_i (\mathbf{a}_i \cdot \mathbf{x})$, we have $f(\mathbf{x}) \geq \mathbf{a} \cdot \mathbf{x} - \epsilon|\mathbf{x}|$ for all $\mathbf{a} \, \varepsilon \, A$ and hence $f(\mathbf{x}) \geq \varphi(\mathbf{x}) - \epsilon|\mathbf{x}|$. But $\varphi(\mathbf{x}) \geq f(\mathbf{x})$. Hence

(2) $$\varphi(\mathbf{x}) \geq f(\mathbf{x}) \geq \varphi(\mathbf{x}) - \epsilon|\mathbf{x}|$$

for all \mathbf{x}. Choosing $\epsilon = 1/M$ yields a sequence f_M which converges uni-

formly to φ on every bounded set. Since each f_M is convex [see Problem 2.2.8] and continuous, φ is convex [see Problem 2.2.9] and continuous (since the convergence to φ is uniform).

Theorem 2.2.8. Let f be any continuous convex function defined on S_n, let $\{\mathbf{x}_m\}$ be a sequence of points in S_n, and let $\{\lambda_m\}$ be a sequence of non-negative numbers with $\sum_1^\infty \lambda_m = 1$. If $\sum_1^\infty \lambda_m |\mathbf{x}_m| < \infty$, then

$$f\left(\sum_1^\infty \lambda_m \mathbf{x}_m\right) \leq \sum_1^\infty \lambda_m f(\mathbf{x}_m)$$

with actual inequality if f is strictly convex, unless $(\mathbf{x}_i - \mathbf{x}_j)\lambda_i\lambda_j = 0$ for all i, j. If $f(\mathbf{x}) \to +\infty$ as $|\mathbf{x}| \to \infty$ and $\Sigma\lambda_m f(\mathbf{x}_m)$ converges, then $\Sigma\lambda_m |\mathbf{x}_m|$ converges.

Proof. Say $\mathbf{x}_0 = \sum_1^\infty \lambda_m \mathbf{x}_m$. According to Theorem 2.2.6 there is a linear function l such that $l(\mathbf{x}) = \mathbf{u}\cdot\mathbf{x} + c$ with $l(\mathbf{x}) \leq f(\mathbf{x})$ for all \mathbf{x} and $l(\mathbf{x}_0) = f(\mathbf{x}_0)$. Moreover, if f is strictly convex, $l(\mathbf{x}) < f(\mathbf{x})$ for $\mathbf{x} \neq \mathbf{x}_0$, since $l(\mathbf{x}_1) = f(\mathbf{x}_1)$ will yield

$$f\left(\frac{\mathbf{x}_0 + \mathbf{x}_1}{2}\right) < \frac{f(\mathbf{x}_0) + f(\mathbf{x}_1)}{2} = \frac{l(\mathbf{x}_0) + l(\mathbf{x}_1)}{2} = l\left(\frac{\mathbf{x}_0 + \mathbf{x}_1}{2}\right)$$

unless $\mathbf{x}_1 = \mathbf{x}_0$. Then

$$\sum_1^\infty \lambda_m f(\mathbf{x}_m) \geq \sum_1^\infty \lambda_m l(\mathbf{x}_m) = l(\mathbf{x}_0) = f(\mathbf{x}_0)$$

with, for strictly convex f, actual inequality unless $\mathbf{x}_m = \mathbf{x}_0$ whenever $\lambda_m > 0$.

The last part of the theorem will follow if we show that there exist constants $a > 0$, b with $f(\mathbf{x}) > a|\mathbf{x}| + b$ for all \mathbf{x}. We may suppose, adding a constant to $f(\mathbf{x})$ if necessary, that $f(\mathbf{x}) \geq 1$ for all \mathbf{x}. Unless there is an $a > 0$ with $f(\mathbf{x}) > a|\mathbf{x}|$ for all \mathbf{x}, there is a sequence $\{\mathbf{x}'_m\}$ with

(1) $$f(\mathbf{x}'_m) < |\mathbf{x}'_m|/m$$

Since $f(\mathbf{x}'_m) \geq 1$ for all m, it follows from (1) that $|\mathbf{x}'_m| > mf(\mathbf{x}'_m) > m$. Thus $|\mathbf{x}'_m| \to \infty$, and by hypothesis $f(\mathbf{x}'_m) \to \infty$, so that, by (1) again, $|\mathbf{x}'_m|/m \to \infty$. Write $\mathbf{y}_m = c_m\mathbf{x}'_m$, where $c_m = m/|\mathbf{x}'_m|$; then $c_m \to 0$, and $|\mathbf{y}_m| \to \infty$ as $m \to \infty$ since $|\mathbf{y}_m| = m$. Then, for m large enough,

$0 < c_m < 1$, and, since f is convex,

$$f(\mathbf{y}_m) \leq (1 - c_m)f(0) + c_m f(\mathbf{x}'_m) \leq f(0) + 1$$

This contradicts the hypothesis that $f(\mathbf{y}_m) \to +\infty$ as $|\mathbf{y}_m| \to \infty$ and completes the proof.

PROBLEMS

2.2.1. The intersection of any number of convex sets is convex.

2.2.2. The closure of a convex set is convex.

2.2.3. (a) A convex set always has (relative) inner points. (b) The set of inner points of a convex set is convex.

2.2.4. For any set R, the convex hull of the closure of R is contained in the closure of the convex hull of R, with equality if R is bounded.

2.2.5. Give an example to show that the following is not in general true: If S and T are closed convex sets without common points there is a hyperplane $\mathbf{u} \cdot \mathbf{x} = c$ with $\mathbf{u} \cdot \mathbf{x} > c$ for $\mathbf{x} \,\varepsilon\, S$ and $\mathbf{u} \cdot \mathbf{x} < c$ for $\mathbf{x} \,\varepsilon\, T$.

2.2.6. A function f defined on a convex subset S of S_n is convex if and only if the function φ with $\varphi(\lambda, \mathbf{x}_1, \mathbf{x}_2) = f[\lambda \mathbf{x}_1 + (1 - \lambda)\mathbf{x}_2]$ is a convex function of λ on $0 \leq \lambda \leq 1$ for all $\mathbf{x}_1, \mathbf{x}_2 \,\varepsilon\, S$.

2.2.7. For any convex function f defined on a closed convex subset S of S_n, the set T of all points $(\mathbf{x}, y) \,\varepsilon\, S_{n+1}$ with $\mathbf{x} \,\varepsilon\, S$, $y \geq f(\mathbf{x})$ is convex; if in addition f is continuous, T is closed.

2.2.8. If f_t is for each t convex in \mathbf{x} on a convex set S and if $f(\mathbf{x}) = \sup_t f_t(\mathbf{x})$ is finite for each $\mathbf{x} \,\varepsilon\, S$, then f is convex on S.

2.2.9. If f_1, f_2, \cdots, is a sequence of convex functions all defined on a convex set S, which converges pointwise to a function f, then f is convex on S.

2.2.10. Give an example to show that in the last sentence of Theorem 2.2.6 the hypothesis that \mathbf{x}_0 is an interior point is necessary.

2.3. Games with a Value

The basic result of the theory of finite games is

Theorem 2.3.1. Every finite game has a value, and each player has at least one good (mixed) strategy.

Proof. Let G be any finite game, and let $A = ||a_{ij}||$, $i = 1, \cdots, m$; $j = 1, \cdots, n$ be the matrix of G. We must show that the mixed extension $\Gamma = (\Xi, H, M)$ of G has a pure value and each player has a good pure strategy in Γ, where Ξ, H consist of all points $\boldsymbol{\xi} = (\xi(1), \cdots, \xi(m))$, $\boldsymbol{\eta} = (\eta(1), \cdots, \eta(n))$ in S_m, S_n with $\xi(i) \geq 0$, $\sum_1^m \xi(i) = 1$, $\eta(j) \geq 0$, $\sum_1^n \eta(j) = 1$ respectively, and

$$M(\boldsymbol{\xi}, \boldsymbol{\eta}) = \sum_{i, j} a_{ij}\xi(i)\eta(j)$$

Let S^* be the convex hull of the n points $\mathbf{c}_1, \cdots, \mathbf{c}_n$ of S_m whose coordinates are the columns of A, i.e., $\mathbf{c}_j = (a_{1j}, \cdots, a_{mj})$. Then

$$(1) \qquad M(\xi, \eta) = \sum_i \xi(i) \left(\sum_j \eta(j) a_{ij} \right) = \xi \cdot \mathbf{s}$$

where $\mathbf{s} = \sum_1^n \eta(j) \mathbf{c}_j \, \varepsilon \, S^*$, and, since every $\mathbf{s} \, \varepsilon \, S^*$ has a representation

$\mathbf{s} = \sum_1^n \eta(j) \mathbf{c}_j$, $\eta \, \varepsilon \, H$, Γ is equivalent to the game $\Gamma_1 = (\Xi, S^*, M_1)$ with $M_1(\xi, \mathbf{s}) = \xi \cdot \mathbf{s}$. To show that Γ_1 has a pure value, it is sufficient, from Theorem 1.6.1, to show that

$$(2) \qquad v^*_{\Gamma_1} \le \lambda^*_{\Gamma_1}$$

We have

$$(3) \qquad \Upsilon_{\Gamma_1}(\mathbf{s}) = \max_{\xi \, \varepsilon \, \Xi} (\xi \cdot \mathbf{s}) = \max (s_1, \cdots, s_m)$$

and

$$(4) \qquad v^*_{\Gamma_1} = \min_{\mathbf{s} \, \varepsilon \, S^*} \Upsilon_{\Gamma_1}(\mathbf{s}) = \Upsilon_{\Gamma_1}(\mathbf{s}_0)$$

where $\mathbf{s}_0 \, \varepsilon \, S^*$. To establish (2), it is sufficient to find a $\xi_0 \, \varepsilon \, \Xi$ such that, for all $\mathbf{s} \, \varepsilon \, S^*$,

$$(5) \qquad v^*_{\Gamma_1} \le \xi_0 \cdot \mathbf{s}$$

since it would follow from this fact that

$$v^*_{\Gamma_1} \le \inf_{\mathbf{s}} \xi_0 \cdot \mathbf{s} = \Lambda_{\Gamma_1}(\xi_0) \le \lambda^*_{\Gamma_1}$$

Let T consist of all points $\mathbf{t} = (t_1, \cdots, t_m) \, \varepsilon \, S_m$ with $t_i < v^*_{\Gamma_1}$ for $i = 1, \cdots, m$. Then T is a convex set not intersecting S^*, since it follows from (3) and (4) that any point $\mathbf{s} \, \varepsilon \, S^*$ has at least one coordinate $\ge v^*_{\Gamma_1}$. Hence, by corollary 2 of Theorem 2.2.1 there is a hyperplane $\mathbf{a} \cdot \mathbf{x} = c$ with $\mathbf{a} \cdot \mathbf{x} \ge c$ for $\mathbf{x} \, \varepsilon \, S^*$ and $\mathbf{a} \cdot \mathbf{x} \le c$ for $\mathbf{x} \, \varepsilon \, \overline{T}$. Let δ_i be the point in S_m whose ith coordinate is 1 and whose remaining coordinates are zero. Then the point $\mathbf{s}_0 - \delta_i \, \varepsilon \, \overline{T}$, and

$$\mathbf{a} \cdot \mathbf{s}_0 = c \ge \mathbf{a} \cdot (\mathbf{s}_0 - \delta_i)$$

so that

$$\mathbf{a} \cdot \delta_i \ge 0$$

and thus

$$a_i \ge 0 \quad \text{for} \quad i = 1, \cdots, m$$

Let $\xi_0 = \mathbf{a} \Big/ \sum_{i=1}^m a_i$ and $v = c \Big/ \sum_{i=1}^m a_i$. Then $\xi_0 \varepsilon \, \Xi$ and

(6)
$$\boldsymbol{\xi}_0 \cdot \mathbf{s} \geq v \quad \text{for} \quad \mathbf{s} \, \varepsilon \, S$$
$$\boldsymbol{\xi}_0 \cdot \mathbf{t} \leq v \quad \text{for} \quad \mathbf{t} \, \varepsilon \, \overline{T}$$

In particular, the point $\mathbf{t}^* = (v^*_{\Gamma_1}, \cdots, v^*_{\Gamma_1}) \, \varepsilon \, \overline{T}$, so that

(7)
$$\boldsymbol{\xi}_0 \cdot \mathbf{t}^* = v^*_{\Gamma_1} \leq v$$

and consequently we conclude from (6) and (7) that, for all $\mathbf{s} \, \varepsilon \, S$,

$$\boldsymbol{\xi}_0 \cdot \mathbf{s} \geq v \geq v^*_{\Gamma_1}$$

which establishes (5). Thus v is the value of G and $\boldsymbol{\xi}_0$ and \mathbf{s}_0 are good (mixed) strategies for I and II respectively, which completes the proof.

Notice that the good strategy \mathbf{s}_0 for player II is a boundary point of S^*, since $\mathbf{s}_0 - \epsilon(1, \cdots, 1) \notin S^*$ for any $\epsilon > 0$. According to Theorem 2.2.2, \mathbf{s}_0 can be represented as a convex linear combination of m of the points $(\mathbf{c}_1, \cdots, \mathbf{c}_n)$. A similar argument applies to player I. Thus we have

Theorem 2.3.2. If $G = (X, Y, M)$ is a finite game with matrix $\| a_{ij} \|$, $i = 1, \cdots, m$, $j = 1, \cdots, n$, then each player has a good strategy which is a mixture of at most $\min(m, n)$ pure strategies.

Various extensions of Theorem 2.3.1 to infinite games have been given. A simple criterion for a game to have a value is

Theorem 2.3.3. A game $G = (X, Y, M)$ has a value if the following condition is satisfied: For every $\epsilon > 0$ there exists a finite set x_1, \cdots, x_m of elements of X such that, for every x in X, there exists a mixture ξ of x_1, \cdots, x_m, such that, for all y in Y,

$$M(\xi, y) \geq M(x, y) - \epsilon$$

Proof. In view of Definition 1.8.4 and Theorem 1.6.1, it is sufficient to show that

$$v^*_\Gamma = \lambda^*_\Gamma$$

which will be proved if we can show that, for every $\epsilon > 0$,

(1)
$$v^*_\Gamma - \lambda^*_\Gamma \leq 2\epsilon$$

Let ϵ be any positive number, and let x_1, \cdots, x_m be elements of X such that, for every element x of X, there exists a mixture $\xi^{(x)}$ of x_1, \cdots, x_m such that

(2)
$$M(\xi^{(x)}, y) \geq M(x, y) - \epsilon \quad \text{for all } y \text{ in } Y$$

The set S of all vectors $\mathbf{v}(y) = (M(x_1, y), \cdots, M(x_m, y))$ for $y \, \varepsilon \, Y$ is a bounded subset of S_m, since M is a bounded function. Hence S contains

a finite subset $\mathbf{v}(y_1), \cdots, \mathbf{v}(y_n)$ such that, for every y there is a j such that

(3) $$\left| \mathbf{v}(y) - \mathbf{v}(y_j) \right| < \epsilon$$

Since for any vector $\mathbf{z} = (z_1, z_2, \cdots, z_m)$, $\left| z_i \right| \leq (\Sigma z^2{}_i)^{1/2} = \left| \mathbf{z} \right|$ for all i, inequality (3) implies that for every y there is a j such that

(4) $$\left| M(x_i, y) - M(x_i, y_j) \right| < \epsilon \quad \text{for} \quad i = 1, \cdots, m$$

Now we set $X_0 = (x_1, \cdots, x_m)$ and $Y_0 = (y_1, \cdots, y_n)$. Then the game $G_0 = (X_0, Y_0, M)$ is finite and by Theorem 2.3.1 has a value v and good strategies $\boldsymbol{\xi}^* = (\xi^*(1), \cdots, \xi^*(m))$ and $\boldsymbol{\eta}^* = (\eta^*(1), \cdots, \eta^*(n))$ for the two players. Thus, for all mixtures ξ and η of X_0 and Y_0 respectively, we have

(5) $$M(\xi, \boldsymbol{\eta}^*) \leq v_0 \leq M(\boldsymbol{\xi}^*, \eta)$$

From (2), we obtain, for $j = 1, \cdots, n$,

(6) $$M(x, y_j) \leq M(\xi^{(x)}, y_j) + \epsilon$$

and hence, multiplying (6) by $\eta^*(j)$ and summing, we obtain

(7) $$M(x, \boldsymbol{\eta}^*) = \sum_{j=1}^{n} M(x, y_j)\eta^*(j) \leq \sum_{j=1}^{n} M(\xi^{(x)}, y_j)\eta^*(j) + \epsilon$$
$$= M(\xi^{(x)}, \boldsymbol{\eta}^*) + \epsilon$$

From (5) and (7) we have for all $x \; \varepsilon \; X$

(8) $$M(x, \boldsymbol{\eta}^*) \leq M(\xi^{(x)}, \boldsymbol{\eta}^*) + \epsilon \leq v_0 + \epsilon$$

and thus taking the supremum of (8) with respect to x yields

(9) $$v^*{}_{\Gamma} \leq \Upsilon_{\Gamma}(\boldsymbol{\eta}^*) \leq v_0 + \epsilon$$

Also, from (4) we infer that for every y there is a j such that

$$M(x_i, y) \geq M(x_i, y_j) - \epsilon \quad \text{for} \quad i = 1, \cdots, m$$

and thus

$$M(\boldsymbol{\xi}^*, y) \geq M(\boldsymbol{\xi}^*, y_j) - \epsilon$$

and hence from (5)

$$M(\boldsymbol{\xi}^*, y) \geq v_0 - \epsilon$$

and thus

(10) $$\lambda^*{}_{\Gamma} \geq \Lambda_{\Gamma}(\boldsymbol{\xi}^*) \geq v_0 - \epsilon$$

From (9) and (10) we infer (1) which completes the proof.

Corollary 1. Any game $G = (X, Y, M)$ where X is finite has a value, and player I has a good strategy.

Proof. Since the condition of the theorem is satisfied, G has a value v. Let $X = (x_1, \cdots, x_m)$, and let $\Gamma = (\Xi, \text{H}, M)$ be the mixed extension of G. Then

$$\lambda^*{}_\Gamma = v = \sup_{\xi \, \varepsilon \, \Xi} \Lambda_\Gamma(\xi)$$

and there exists a sequence $\xi^{(1)}, \xi^{(2)}, \cdots,$ in Ξ such that $\Lambda_\Gamma(\xi^{(k)}) \rightarrow \lambda^*{}_\Gamma$ as $k \rightarrow \infty$, where

$$\xi^{(k)} = (\xi^{(k)}(1), \xi^{(k)}(2), \cdots, \xi^{(k)}(m))$$

Since all the vectors $\xi^{(k)}$ lie in the m-dimensional cube with side 1 (more exactly, in the fundamental probability simplex in m space), there is a convergent subsequence which approaches a vector $\xi^* = (\xi^*(1), \cdots, \xi^*(m))$, with $\xi^*(i) \geq 0$, $\sum_{i=1}^{m} \xi^*(i) = 1$. Since the function M is continuous and linear in the components of $\xi^{(k)}$, $M(\xi^{(k)}, y) \rightarrow M(\xi^*, y)$ for all y as $k \rightarrow \infty$. Also, since

$$M(\xi^{(k)}, y) \geq \Lambda_\Gamma(\xi^{(k)}) \quad \text{for all } y$$

we obtain

$$M(\xi^*, y) = \lim_{k \to \infty} M(\xi^{(k)}, y) \geq \lim_{k \to \infty} \Lambda_\Gamma(\xi^{(k)}) = \lambda^*{}_\Gamma \quad \text{for all } y$$

and ξ^* is a good strategy for player I.

Corollary 2. Any game $G = (X, Y, M)$ where X, Y are closed bounded subsets of S_m, S_n and M is continuous has a value.

Proof. Since $M(x, y)$ is defined for \mathbf{x} in S_m and \mathbf{y} in S_n, we can consider M as a function of one variable $\mathbf{z} \, \varepsilon \, Z = X \times Y$ in S_{m+n}. Since M is continuous on Z, it is uniformly continuous: For every $\epsilon > 0$ there is a $\delta > 0$ such that $\left| M(\mathbf{z}_1) - M(\mathbf{z}_2) \right| < \epsilon$ whenever $\left| \mathbf{z}_1 - \mathbf{z}_2 \right| < \delta$. Let $\mathbf{x}_1, \cdots, \mathbf{x}_r$ be a finite subset of X such that for every $\mathbf{x} \, \varepsilon \, X$ there is an i with $\left| \mathbf{x}_i - \mathbf{x} \right| < \delta$. Then $\left| (\mathbf{x}_i, \mathbf{y}) - (\mathbf{x}, \mathbf{y}) \right| = \left| \mathbf{x}_i - \mathbf{x} \right| < \delta$ for all \mathbf{y}, and $\left| M(\mathbf{x}, \mathbf{y}) - M(\mathbf{x}_i, \mathbf{y}) \right| < \epsilon$ for all \mathbf{y}. Thus Theorem 2.3.3 applies.

If a game has a value, then either player can, by a suitable choice of strategies, approximate this value to within ϵ for any $\epsilon > 0$ no matter how small. Such strategies are called *ϵ-good strategies* for each player and are defined as follows:

Definition 2.3.1. Let $\Gamma = (\Xi, \text{H}, M)$ be the mixed extension of the game $G = (X, Y, M)$, let $\epsilon > 0$ be given, let Γ have value v_Γ, and let ξ

be an element of Ξ and η be an element of H such that

$$\Lambda_\Gamma(\xi) \geq v_\Gamma - \epsilon$$

$$\Upsilon_\Gamma(\eta) \leq v_\Gamma + \epsilon$$

Then ξ and η are called ϵ-good (mixed) strategies for players I and II respectively.

PROBLEMS

*, **2.3.1.** In a finite game the set of good strategies for either player is bounded, closed, and convex.

*, **2.3.2.** Carry out the steps of the proof of Theorem 2.3.1 for the finite game with matrix

$$A = \begin{pmatrix} 4 & 5 & 8 & 2 & 6 \\ 1 & 8 & 5 & 6 & 6 \end{pmatrix}$$

and find the value and good strategies for both players.

2.4. *S* Games

The games in which player I has a finite number of pure strategies have an interesting and useful geometrical interpretation, even when the number of pure strategies for player II is infinite. Let $G = (X, Y, M)$ be a game in which $X = (x_1, \cdots, x_m)$. We associate with each $y \, \epsilon \, Y$ the point $\mathbf{s}(y)$ in m space with coordinates $M(x_1, y), \cdots, M(x_m, y)$, and let S be the set of all points $\mathbf{s}(y)$ as y varies over Y. Then G is equivalent to a game which is played in the following manner: Player II selects a point $\mathbf{s} = (s_1, s_2, \cdots, s_m)$ from the set S. Independently of his choice, player I selects a coordinate. The payoff to player I is the value of this coordinate. Such games will be called S games and are formally defined as follows:

Definition 2.4.1. Let I_m consist of the integers $i = 1, \cdots, m$, let S be a bounded subset of m space, and, for $i \, \epsilon \, I_m$, $\mathbf{s} \, \epsilon \, S$, let

$$M(i, \mathbf{s}) = s_i$$

where s_i is the ith coordinate of s. Then the game $G_1 = (I_m, S, M)$ is called an S game.

A mixed strategy for player I in the original game G, as well as in the S game, is a vector $\boldsymbol{\xi} = (\xi(1), \xi(2), \cdots, \xi(m))$ with $\xi(i) \geq 0$ and $\sum_{i=1}^{m} \xi(i) = 1$. A mixed strategy for player II in the original game is a choice of a probability distribution η over Y, which in the S game is equivalent to selecting a point in S_m which is attainable as a countable

convex linear combination of points in S. Thus the mixed extension of an S game is equivalent to the game $\Gamma_1 = (\Xi, R, M)$ where Ξ consists of all the vectors $\boldsymbol{\xi}$ defined above, R is the set of all points \mathbf{r} of m space which are countable convex linear combinations of points of S and

$$M(\boldsymbol{\xi}, \mathbf{r}) = \boldsymbol{\xi} \cdot \mathbf{r}$$

It is clear from the definition of the convex hull of a set that R contains the convex hull S^* of S. We shall now prove that R is in fact identical with S^*.

Theorem 2.4.1. Let S be any set in S_m, S^* the convex hull of S. Then any convergent convex mixture of a countable number of points of S belongs to S^*.

Proof. We first show that any such point \mathbf{s}, given by $\mathbf{s} = \sum_1^\infty \lambda_i \mathbf{s}_i$, where without loss of generality we take $\lambda_i > 0$, and $\Sigma \lambda_i = 1$, $\mathbf{s}_i \, \varepsilon \, S$ for all i, belongs to the closure $\overline{S^*}$ of S^*. We write

$$\mathbf{s} = \lim_{n \to \infty} \sum_{i=1}^n \lambda_i \mathbf{s}_i = \lim_{n \to \infty} \left(\sum_{i=1}^n \lambda_i \right) \left(\sum_{i=1}^n \zeta_i \mathbf{s}_i \right)$$

where $\zeta_i = \lambda_i \Big/ \sum_{i=1}^n \lambda_i > 0$, $\sum_{i=1}^n \zeta_i = 1$. Since $\sum_1^n \lambda_i \to 1$ as $n \to \infty$, we have

$$\mathbf{s} = \lim_{n \to \infty} \sum_{i=1}^n \zeta_i \mathbf{s}_i = \lim_{n \to \infty} \mathbf{z}_n$$

where $\mathbf{z}_n \, \varepsilon \, S^*$. Hence $\mathbf{s} \, \varepsilon \, \overline{S^*}$.

Now let Q_k, of dimension $k \le m$, be the lowest dimensional hyperplane containing the points \mathbf{s}_1, \mathbf{s}_2, \cdots, let P^* be the convex hull of \mathbf{s}_1, \mathbf{s}_2, \cdots, and let N be an integer so large that the convex hull P^*_N of \mathbf{s}_1, \mathbf{s}_2, \cdots, \mathbf{s}_N is a k-dimensional convex set (simplex) in Q_k, i.e., has inner points in Q_k. By definition of Q_k, such an N clearly exists. Also $P^* \subset S^*$, and $P^*_N \subset P^* \subset Q_k$. As above, we write

$$\mathbf{s} = \sum_1^\infty \lambda_i \mathbf{s}_i = \sum_1^N \lambda_i \mathbf{s}_i + \sum_{N+1}^\infty \lambda_i \mathbf{s}_i$$

$$= \left(\sum_1^N \lambda_i \right) \left(\sum_1^N \zeta_i \mathbf{s}_i \right) + \left(\sum_{N+1}^\infty \lambda_i \right) \left(\sum_{N+1}^\infty \gamma_i \mathbf{s}_i \right)$$

$$= \mu \mathbf{t}_1 + (1 - \mu) \mathbf{t}_2$$

where $0 < \mu = \sum_1^N \lambda_i < 1$, $\sum_1^N \zeta_i = 1$, $\sum_{N+1}^\infty \gamma_i = 1$, ζ_i, $\gamma_i > 0$, so that $\mathbf{t}_1 = \sum_1^N \zeta_i \mathbf{s}_i$ is an inner point of P^*_N, consequently an inner point of P^*, and $\mathbf{t}_2 = \sum_{N+1}^\infty \gamma_i \mathbf{s}_i$ belongs to $\overline{P^*}$ by the first part of the proof. Hence, by Lemma 2.2.1, $\mathbf{s} \, \varepsilon \, P^* \subset S^*$, and the theorem is proved.

Corollary 1 of Theorem 2.3.3 asserts that every S game has a value v and that I has a good strategy $\boldsymbol{\xi}$, so that $\boldsymbol{\xi} \cdot \mathbf{s} \geq v$ for all $\mathbf{s} \, \varepsilon \, S^*$. Player II will generally not have a good strategy, but there will exist a sequence $\mathbf{s}_n = (s_{n1}, \cdots, s_{nm}) \, \varepsilon \, S^*$ with $\max_i (s_{ni}) \to v$ as $n \to \infty$. If S^* is closed, a subsequence of \mathbf{s}_n converges to an $\mathbf{s}^* = (s^*_1, \cdots, s^*_m) \, \varepsilon \, S^*$, and $\max_i (s^*_i) = v$, so that \mathbf{s}^* is a good strategy for II. The main facts are summarized in

Theorem 2.4.2. Every S game has a value and player I has a good strategy. Moreover, if (I_m, S, M) is an S game and if S is closed (or more generally, if the convex hull S^* of S is closed), then player II has a good strategy which is a mixture of at most m pure strategies. If S is closed and convex, player II has a good pure strategy.

Proof. If II has a good strategy \mathbf{s}, it is a boundary point of S^*, and thus, by Theorem 2.2.2, \mathbf{s} is a convex linear combination of at most m points of S. If S is closed and convex, $S^* = S$, so that II has a good strategy in S. The remaining facts have already been proved.

We observe that the proof of the fundamental theorem of the theory of games [Theorem 2.3.1] was accomplished by first converting it into an S game, with S consisting of the points $\mathbf{c}_1, \cdots, \mathbf{c}_n$ in S_m. The finiteness of the set S was not essential to the proof. What was required there was the closure of S^*, to insure that the minimum of $\Upsilon(\mathbf{s})$, for $\mathbf{s} \, \varepsilon \, S^*$, would be assumed by a point $\mathbf{s}_0 \, \varepsilon \, S^*$. Thus the same proof can be employed to give the more general result contained in Theorem 2.4.2. It could also be used to establish the truth of corollary 1 to Theorem 2.3.3.

The proof of the fundamental theorem also suggests the following geometric method for locating the value and good strategies in an S game. For any real number a, let $T_a = \{ \mathbf{t} = (t_1, t_2, \cdots, t_m) \, \varepsilon \, S_m : t_i < a$, $i = 1, 2, \cdots, m \}$, i.e., T_a is the "negative orthant" in m space shifted so that the vertex $(0, 0, \cdots, 0)$ is at the point (a, a, \cdots, a). T_a is obviously convex. Let $a^* = \sup_a \{ a : T_a \cap S^* = \varnothing \}$. (In the proof of Theorem 2.3.1, a^* is in fact equal to $v^*_{\Gamma_1}$, the value of the game.) $T_{a^*} \cap S^*$

$= \varnothing$; hence by corollary 2 to Theorem 2.2.1 there exists a hyperplane $\xi_0 \cdot \mathbf{x} = c$ separating T_{a*} and S^*, where without loss of generality we can assume $\xi_0 \, \varepsilon \, \Xi$. Then ξ_0 will be a good strategy for player I, and $a^* = c$ is the value of the game. Further, $\overline{T_{a*}} \cap \overline{S^*} \neq \varnothing$. Let \mathbf{s}^* be any point in $\overline{T_{a*}} \cap \overline{S^*}$. If S^* is closed, then $\mathbf{s}^* \, \varepsilon \, S^*$ and is a good strategy for player II, which is a mixture of at most m pure strategies in S. If S^* is not closed, then there exists a sequence of points \mathbf{s}^*_1, \mathbf{s}^*_2, \cdots in S^* such that $\mathbf{s}^*_n \to \mathbf{s}^*$, \mathbf{s}^*_n a mixture of at most $m + 1$ pure strategies in S, and such that $\max_i (s^*_{ni}) \to a^*$.

The above discussion also shows that the assumption of boundedness for the payoff function M of the original game G is not required. What is required is the weaker condition that M be *bounded from below*, i.e., there exists a positive constant K such that $M(x, y) > -K$ for all x and y.

The notion of S games and their mixed extensions are capable of a further useful generalization. Consider the game $G = (S, T, M)$ where S and T are bounded convex subsets in m space; player I chooses a point \mathbf{s} in S, player II independently chooses a point \mathbf{t} in T, and the payoff $M(\mathbf{s}, \mathbf{t})$ to player I is $\mathbf{s} \cdot \mathbf{t}$ units. From Theorem 2.4.1 and the convexity of S and T, it follows that any mixing of strategies on the part of the players by means of a chance device can add nothing new to the game—that G is identical with its mixed extension. If, in addition, S and T are assumed to be closed, it follows from corollary 2 to Theorem 2.3.3, since M is continuous, that the game G has a value v, hence a pure value. By Problem 1.6.3 it follows at once that there exist points \mathbf{s}^* in S, \mathbf{t}^* in T (i.e., good strategies for the two players), such that

$$\min_{\mathbf{t} \, \varepsilon \, T} (\mathbf{s}^* \cdot \mathbf{t}) = \max_{\mathbf{s} \, \varepsilon \, S} (\mathbf{s} \cdot \mathbf{t}^*) = v = \mathbf{s}^* \cdot \mathbf{t}^*$$

As we shall have occasion to use these results in later portions of the book, we summarize them in

Theorem 2.4.3. Let $G = (S, T, M)$ be a game, S and T bounded, closed, convex subsets of S_m, $M(\mathbf{s}, \mathbf{t}) = \mathbf{s} \cdot \mathbf{t}$ for $\mathbf{s} \, \varepsilon \, S$, $\mathbf{t} \, \varepsilon \, T$. Then G has a value, and each player has a good pure strategy. Equivalently, for any closed bounded convex sets S, T of S_m, there are points $\mathbf{s}^* \, \varepsilon \, S$, $\mathbf{t}^* \, \varepsilon \, T$ with

$$\mathbf{s} \cdot \mathbf{t}^* \leq \mathbf{s}^* \cdot \mathbf{t}^* \leq \mathbf{s}^* \cdot \mathbf{t}$$

for all $\mathbf{s} \, \varepsilon \, S$, $\mathbf{t} \, \varepsilon \, T$.

PROBLEMS

2.4.1. Find the value and good strategies for the following S games in 2-space, with points $\mathbf{x} = (x_1, x_2)$:

(a) $S = \{\mathbf{x}: (x_1 - 8)^2 + (x_2 - 3)^2 \leq 9\}$

(b) $S = \{\mathbf{x}: (x_1 - 10)^2 + (x_2 - 10)^2 \leq 50\}$

(c) $S = \left\{\mathbf{x}: x_1 > 0, x_2 \geq \dfrac{1}{2x_1}\right\}$

2.4.2. Find the value and good strategies for the game $G = (S^*, T^*, M)$, where S^* is the convex hull in 2-space of the three points $(2, 8)$, $(4, 3)$, $(7, 2)$ and T^* is the convex hull of two points $(1, 0)$ and $(0, 1)$.

2.5. Games with Convex Payoff

We have seen that any game in which X and Y are closed and bounded subsets of S_m, S_n and in which the payoff M is continuous has a value. A further restriction on the payoff, convexity in y for fixed x, enables us to obtain a more precise result—that player II has a good pure strategy and that player I has a good strategy which is a mixture of at most $n + 1$ pure strategies. This fact is the main result of the present section and is incorporated in the following theorem and corollaries.

Theorem 2.5.1. If $G = (X, Y, M)$ is a game such that Y is a closed bounded convex subset of S_n and $M(x, \mathbf{y})$ is for each x a continuous convex function of \mathbf{y}, then G has a value, player II has a good pure strategy, and, for every $\epsilon > 0$, player I has an ϵ-good strategy which is a mixture of at most $n + 1$ pure strategies.

Proof. Since

(1) $\Upsilon(\mathbf{y}) = \sup_{x} M(x, \mathbf{y});\qquad v^* = \inf_{y} \Upsilon(\mathbf{y})$

we can select a sequence $\{\mathbf{y}_m\}$ such that $\lim\limits_{m \to \infty} \Upsilon(\mathbf{y}_m) = v^*$. Since Y is closed and bounded, we can choose the sequence $\{\mathbf{y}_m\}$ so that $\lim\limits_{m \to \infty} \mathbf{y}_m = \mathbf{y}'$ and $\mathbf{y}' \, \varepsilon \, Y$. Also, for each x, $M(x, \mathbf{y}_m) \leq \Upsilon(\mathbf{y}_m)$, and hence by Problem 1.6.4,

(2) $M(x, \mathbf{y}') \leq \Upsilon(\mathbf{y}') = v^*$

Consider the collection \mathcal{L} of linear functions l, defined on Y, for which there is an $x \, \varepsilon \, X$ with $l(\mathbf{y}) \leq M(x, \mathbf{y})$ for all $\mathbf{y} \, \varepsilon \, Y$; and, for l in \mathcal{L} and any $\epsilon > 0$, let H_l be the set of all \mathbf{y} such that $l(\mathbf{y}) > v^* - \epsilon$. Since l is continuous, H_l is open in Y. We shall show that the sets H_l cover Y; i.e., every $\mathbf{y} \, \varepsilon \, Y$ belongs to some H_l. Select $\mathbf{y}_0 \, \varepsilon \, Y$. Then, there exists an x_0 in X such that $M(x_0, \mathbf{y}_0) > v^* - \epsilon/2$, since

(3) $\sup_{x} M(x, \mathbf{y}_0) = \Upsilon(\mathbf{y}_0) \geq v^*$

Now by Theorem 2.2.6 there exists a linear function l_0 such that $l_0(\mathbf{y}) \leq M(x_0, \mathbf{y})$ for all \mathbf{y} and $l_0(\mathbf{y}_0) > M(x_0, \mathbf{y}_0) - \epsilon/2$. But, since $M(x_0, \mathbf{y}_0) > v^* - \epsilon/2$, $l_0(\mathbf{y}_0) > v^* - \epsilon$, and hence, $\mathbf{y}_0 \, \varepsilon \, H_{l_0}$. Thus the open sets H_l cover Y so that, by the Heine-Borel theorem, we can find a finite sub-collection of these sets which cover Y. There is then a finite set of linear functions l_1, \cdots, l_N each in the collection \mathcal{L}, with $\max_i l_i(\mathbf{y}) > v^* - \epsilon$ for each $y \, \varepsilon \, Y$. Since l_i is in \mathcal{L}, there is an $x_i \, \varepsilon \, X$ with $l_i(\mathbf{y}) \leq M(x_i, \mathbf{y})$ for all \mathbf{y}.

Let $\boldsymbol{\xi} = (\xi(1), \xi(2), \cdots, \xi(n))$ be a mixed strategy for player I in which he selects x_i $(i = 1, 2, \cdots, N)$ with probability $\xi(i)$. Then

$$(4) \qquad M(\boldsymbol{\xi}, \mathbf{y}) = \sum_{i=1}^{N} \xi(i) M(x_i, \mathbf{y}) \geq \sum_{i=1}^{N} \xi(i) l_i(\mathbf{y})$$

for all $\mathbf{y} \, \varepsilon \, Y$. We need now to show that we can find a $\boldsymbol{\xi}^*$ with at most $n + 1$ of its components different from zero such that $\sum_{i=1}^{N} \xi^*(i) l_i(\mathbf{y}) \geq v^* - \epsilon$. Suppose

$$(5) \qquad l_i(\mathbf{y}) = \sum_{j=1}^{n} a_{ij} y_j + a_{i,n+1}$$

Let U be the convex hull in S_{n+1} of the set of points $\mathbf{u}_i = (a_{i1}, a_{i2}, \cdots, a_{i,n+1})$, and let V be the set of all points of the form $(\mathbf{y}, 1)$, where $\mathbf{y} \, \varepsilon \, Y$. Then V is closed and convex. We apply Theorem 2.4.3 to the sets U, V, obtaining points $\mathbf{u}^* \, \varepsilon \, U$, $\mathbf{v}^* = (\mathbf{y}^*, 1) \, \varepsilon \, V$ such that

$$(6) \qquad \mathbf{u} \cdot \mathbf{v}^* \leq \mathbf{u}^* \cdot \mathbf{v}^* \leq \mathbf{u}^* \cdot \mathbf{v}$$

for all $\mathbf{u} \, \varepsilon \, U$, $\mathbf{v} \, \varepsilon \, V$. There is an i for which $l_i(\mathbf{y}^*) > v^* - \epsilon$; i.e., $\mathbf{u} \cdot \mathbf{v}^* > v^* - \epsilon$, so that $\mathbf{u}^* \cdot \mathbf{v}^* > v^* - \epsilon$ and $\mathbf{u}^* \cdot \mathbf{v} > v^* - \epsilon$ for all $\mathbf{v} \, \varepsilon \, V$. Moreover, \mathbf{u}^* is a boundary point of U; otherwise there would be a $\delta > 0$ such that the point \mathbf{u}_δ obtained by adding δ to the $(n + 1)$st co-ordinate of \mathbf{u}^* would be in U, and $\mathbf{u}_\delta \cdot \mathbf{v}^* = \mathbf{u}^* \cdot \mathbf{v}^* + \delta$, contradicting the inequality $\mathbf{u}_\delta \cdot \mathbf{v}^* \leq \mathbf{u}^* \cdot \mathbf{v}^*$. Theorem 2.2.2 then implies that $\mathbf{u}^* = \sum_{i=1}^{N} \xi^*(i) \mathbf{u}_i$ with $\xi^*(i) \geq 0$, $\sum_{i=1}^{N} \xi^*(i) = 1$, and at most $(n + 1)$ of the $\xi^*(i)$'s are different from zero. Then, for all $\mathbf{y} \, \varepsilon \, Y$,

$$(7) \qquad \sum_{i=1}^{N} \xi^*(i) l_i(\mathbf{y}) = \mathbf{u}^* \cdot (\mathbf{y}, 1) > v^* - \epsilon$$

From (2), (4), and (7) we see that v^* is the value of the game; from (2), therefore, that \mathbf{y}' is a good strategy for player II; and, from (7), that $\boldsymbol{\xi}^*$ is an ϵ-good strategy for player I.

Corollary 1. If in addition X is a closed bounded subset of S_m and M is for each \mathbf{y} continuous in \mathbf{x}, then I has a good strategy which is a mixture of at most $n + 1$ pure strategies.

Proof. Let $\boldsymbol{\xi}^{(k)}$, mixing $\mathbf{x}^{(k)}{}_1,\ \cdots,\ \mathbf{x}^{(k)}{}_{n+1}$ in proportion $\xi^{(k)}(1),\ \cdots,$ $\xi^{(k)}(n + 1)$ be a mixed strategy for player I such that $M(\boldsymbol{\xi}^{(k)}, \mathbf{y}) > v^*$ $- 1/k$ for all \mathbf{y}. Choose a subsequence of k for which $\mathbf{x}^{(k)}{}_i \to \mathbf{x}^*{}_i$, $\xi^{(k)}(i) \to \xi^*(i)$ for $i = 1, 2, \cdots, n + 1$, as $k \to \infty$ through this subsequence. Then

$$M(\boldsymbol{\xi}^{(k)}, \mathbf{y}) = \sum_{i=1}^{n+1} \xi^{(k)}(i) M(\mathbf{x}^{(k)}{}_i, \mathbf{y}) \to M(\boldsymbol{\xi}^*, \mathbf{y})$$

as $k \to \infty$ through the subsequence, where $\boldsymbol{\xi}^*$ mixes $\mathbf{x}^*{}_1, \cdots, \mathbf{x}^*{}_{n+1}$ in the proportions $\xi^*(1), \cdots, \xi^*(n + 1)$, so that $M(\boldsymbol{\xi}^*, \mathbf{y}) \geq v^*$ for all \mathbf{y} and $\boldsymbol{\xi}^*$ is a good strategy for player I.

Corollary 2. If $G = (X, Y, M)$ is a game in which X, Y are closed bounded convex subsets of S_n and $M(\mathbf{x}, \mathbf{y})$ is for each \mathbf{y} a continuous concave function in \mathbf{x} and for each \mathbf{x} a continuous convex function in \mathbf{y}, then G has a value and each player has a good pure strategy.

Corollary 3. If $G = (X, Y, M)$ is a game in which X, Y are closed bounded subsets of S_n and for each $\mathbf{x} = (x_1, \cdots, x_n) \in X$ and $\mathbf{y} =$ $(y_1, \cdots, y_n) \in Y$, $M(\mathbf{x}, \mathbf{y}) = \sum_{i=1}^{n} x_i y_i$, then G has a value and each player has a good strategy which is a mixture of at most $n + 1$ pure strategies.

Proof. Let Γ be the mixed extension of G. Then Γ is equivalent to the game $\Gamma_1 = (X^*, Y^*, M)$ where X^* is the convex hull of X, Y^* is the convex hull of Y, and $M(\mathbf{x}, \mathbf{y}) = \sum_{i=1}^{n} x_i y_i$, $\mathbf{x} \in X^*$, $\mathbf{y} \in Y^*$. Hence, by corollary 2 above, Γ_1 has a value and each player has a good pure strategy in Γ_1. By Theorem 2.2.2, each pure strategy of Γ_1 can be represented as a mixture of at most $n + 1$ pure strategies in G. This completes the proof.

Note that this corollary also follows from Theorem 2.4.3.

PROBLEMS

2.5.1. If in corollary 1 to Theorem 2.5.1, $M(\mathbf{x}, \mathbf{y})$ is for each \mathbf{x} a continuous and strictly convex function of \mathbf{y}, then player II's good pure strategy is unique.

2.5.2. Let $G = (X, Y, M)$ be a game in which X, Y are closed bounded subsets of S_n and $M(\mathbf{x}, \mathbf{y}) = \sum_{i,j} a_{ij} x_i y_j$. Then G has a value, and each player has a good strategy which is a mixture of at most $n + 1$ pure strategies.

2.5.3. If, in Theorem 2.5.1, X is finite, player I has a good strategy which is a mixture of at most $n + 1$ pure strategies.

2.5.4. Find the value and good strategies for the following games $G = (X, Y, M)$ where $X = (0 \leq x \leq 1)$ and $Y = (0 \leq y \leq 1)$ and

(a) $$M(x, y) = (y - x)^2$$

(b) $$M(x, y) = x^2 - x + y - y^2$$

(c) $$M(x, y) = y - 2xy + 1$$

2.6. Extended Mixed Strategies

Any game $G = (X, Y, M)$ where X, Y are closed bounded subsets of S_m, S_n and M is continuous on $X \times Y$ has a value according to corollary 2 of Theorem 2.3.3. Thus this corollary guarantees ϵ-good strategies to the two players. However, if the concept of mixed strategies is suitably extended, good strategies for both players can be shown to exist for all games of this type. That this does not hold with our restriction to discrete distributions is illustrated in the following example.

Example. $X = (0 \leq x \leq 1)$, $Y = (0 \leq y \leq 1)$, $M(x, y) = f(x - y)$, where $f(t) = t(1 - t)$ for $0 \leq t \leq 1$ and $f(t) = f(t + 1)$ for $-1 \leq t \leq 0$. Notice that, for every fixed y_0,

$$\int_0^1 M(x, y_0)\, dx = \int_0^{y_0} f(x + 1 - y_0)\, dx + \int_{y_0}^1 f(x - y_0)\, dx$$

$$= \int_{1-y_0}^1 f(u)\, du + \int_0^{1-y_0} f(u)\, du = \int_0^1 f(u)\, du = \frac{1}{6}$$

Thus, for every mixed strategy η, $\int_0^1 M(x, \eta)\, dx = 1/6$. Now $M(x, \eta) = \sum_1^\infty \eta(i)f(x - y_i)$ cannot be identically $1/6$, since at $x = y_i$ the derivative of $\eta(i)f(x - y_i)$ with respect to x fails to exist, while the derivatives of the other terms do exist at this point, so that $\dfrac{dM(x, \eta)}{dx}$ fails to exist at $x = y_i$. Since $\int_0^1 M(x, \eta)\, dx = 1/6$ and $M(x, \eta) \not\equiv 1/6$, there is an x_0 with $M(x_0, \eta) > 1/6$, i.e., $\Upsilon(\eta) > 1/6$ for every η. Similarly $\int_0^1 M(\xi, y)\, dy = 1/6$ for all ξ and $M(\xi, y) \not\equiv 1/6$, so that there is a y_0 with $M(\xi, y_0) < 1/6$ and $\Lambda(\xi) < 1/6$ for all ξ. From corollary 2

above, $\lambda^* = v^*$, so that their common value is 1/6. Thus neither player has a good strategy.

It is clear that in this example, the players fail to have good strategies only because our concept of mixed strategy is too restricted. If we permit player I to choose a number at random on the unit interval, so that the probability that the number chosen falls in an interval (a, b) is $b - a$ $(0 \leq a \leq b \leq 1)$, then his expected gain against any y is $\int_0^1 M(x, y)\,dx$ $= 1/6$, and similarly for player II. Even if the choice of a number at random is not permitted as a mixed strategy, it still serves a useful purpose in the above example: it permitted us to find the value of the game. Moreover, using the fact that a Riemann integral can be approximated by a sum, we can for any $\epsilon > 0$, find ϵ-good mixed strategies for each player in the following way: Since the function $M(x, y)$ is uniformly continuous, for every $\epsilon > 0$ we can find a $\delta > 0$ such that

$$\big| M(x_1, y) - M(x_2, y) \big| < \epsilon$$

for all y whenever $\big| x_1 - x_2 \big| < \delta$. Choose n so large that $1/n < \delta$, and let ξ be the mixed strategy assigning probability $1/n$ to each of the points $x_i = i/n$, $1 \leq i \leq n$. Then

$$M(\xi, y) = \frac{1}{n} \sum_1^n M(x_i, y) \geq \sum_1^n \int_{x_{i-1}}^{x_i} M(x, y)\,dx - \epsilon = \frac{1}{6} - \epsilon$$

where $x_0 = 0$. Thus ξ is an ϵ-good strategy for I. In a similar manner, we get ϵ-good strategies for player II.

Pursuing the idea suggested by the above example, we define extended mixed strategies.

Definition 2.6.1. Let $\Gamma = (\Xi, \mathrm{H}, M)$ be the mixed extension of the game $G = (X, Y, M)$, and let T be any function which associates with $M(x, y)$ a real valued function φ defined on Y. Then, if for every $\epsilon > 0$ there is a mixed strategy $\xi \,\varepsilon\, \Xi$ such that for all $y \,\varepsilon\, Y$,

$$\big| \varphi(y) - M(\xi, y) \big| \leq \epsilon$$

we call T an extended mixed strategy.

We may consider T purely as a convenient mathematical device for finding the value of a game and ϵ-good strategies. In games in which X is an n space, the T's which are particularly useful, and which are the only ones considered in this book, are the *density functions* on X.

Definition 2.6.2. Let X be an n space, and let f be a non-negative function defined on X. Then if the integral

$$\int_X f(\mathbf{x})\, d\mathbf{x}$$

exists and is equal to 1, we call f a density on X.

In a game (X, Y, M), a density f on X associates with $M(x, y)$ the function

$$\varphi(y) = M(f, y) = \int_X M(\mathbf{x}, y)f(\mathbf{x})\, d\mathbf{x}$$

In order for f to be an extended mixed strategy, we must verify that $M(f, y)$ is uniformly (in y) approximable by $M(\xi, y)$, and this will not always be the case. A convenient criterion is given by the next theorem, for which we need some preliminary definitions.

Definition 2.6.3. Let E be a set of real-valued functions Ψ, each of which is defined over a bounded subset $A \subset S_n$. If, for every $\epsilon > 0$, there is a $\delta > 0$, such that, for every subdivision $R = (R_1, \cdots, R_k)$ of A into sets R_i, where $\int_{R_i} d\mathbf{x}$ exists and the diameter of each R_i is less than δ, we have, for each ψ

$$\sum_{i=1}^{k} [\sup_{\mathbf{x} \in R_i} \Psi(\mathbf{x}) - \inf_{\mathbf{x} \in R_i} \Psi(\mathbf{x})]\int_{R_i} d\mathbf{x} < \epsilon$$

then the set E of functions is said to be uniformly Riemann-integrable over A.

Definition 2.6.4. Let M be a real-valued function of two variables $\mathbf{x} \in X$, $y \in Y$, $X \subset S_n$, and let E be the set of real-valued functions ψ defined on X such that $\psi \in E$ if and only if, for some y in Y,

$$\psi(\mathbf{x}) = M(\mathbf{x}, y) \quad \text{for all } \mathbf{x} \text{ in } X$$

Then, if E is uniformly Riemann-integrable over a bounded subset $A \subset S_n$, we say that $M(\mathbf{x}, y)$ is uniformly (in y) Riemann-integrable over A.

Theorem 2.6.1. Let $G = (X, Y, M)$ be a game, let X be a subset of S_n; and suppose that $M(\mathbf{x}, y)$ is uniformly (in y) Riemann-integrable over every bounded subset X_1 of X. Then every density function over X is an extended mixed strategy for player I.

Proof. From the definition of a density on X, it is apparent that, for any such function f and any $\epsilon > 0$, there is a bounded subset X_1 of X such that f is bounded on X_1, and

$$(1) \qquad \int_{X_1} f(\mathbf{x})\, d\mathbf{x} = 1 - \epsilon$$

Let A be the upper bound of $|M(\mathbf{x}, y)|$, and let $X{-}X_1$ be those points of X that are not in X_1. Then, from (1) we obtain

$$A \int_{X-X_1} f(\mathbf{x})\, d\mathbf{x} = A\left(1 - \int_{X_1} f(\mathbf{x})\, d\mathbf{x}\right) = A\epsilon$$

and, from this,

$$\left| \int_{X-X_1} M(\mathbf{x}, y) f(\mathbf{x})\, d\mathbf{x} \right| \le A\epsilon$$

and then, from the definition of $M(f, y)$,

$$(2) \qquad \left| M(f, y) - \int_{X_1} M(\mathbf{x}, y) f(\mathbf{x})\, d\mathbf{x} \right| \le A\epsilon$$

Define

$$g(\mathbf{x}) = \frac{1}{1 - \epsilon} f(\mathbf{x}) \quad \text{for} \quad \mathbf{x} \in X_1$$

$$0 \qquad\qquad \text{for} \quad \mathbf{x} \notin X_1$$

Thus $\int_{X_1} g(\mathbf{x})\, d\mathbf{x} = 1$, and $g(\mathbf{x})$ is a density on X_1. From this definition and (1) we obtain

$$(3) \quad \left| \int_{X_1} M(\mathbf{x}, y) f(\mathbf{x})\, d\mathbf{x} - M(g, y) \right|$$

$$= \left| (1 - \epsilon) \int_{X_1} M(\mathbf{x}, y) g(\mathbf{x})\, d\mathbf{x} - M(g, y) \right|$$

$$= \epsilon |M(g, y)| \le \epsilon A \int_{X_1} g(\mathbf{x})\, d\mathbf{x} = \epsilon A$$

From (2) and (3), by the triangle inequality, we get

$$(4) \qquad |M(f, y) - M(g, y)| \le 2A\epsilon$$

Our aim is to find a mixed strategy ξ such that, for all y,

$$(5) \qquad |M(f, y) - M(\xi, y)| \le \epsilon$$

Because of (4), it will be sufficient to find a ξ such that, for all y,

$$(6) \qquad |M(g, y) - M(\xi, y)| \leq \epsilon$$

Let K be the upper bound of g. From the definition of a density function and the hypothesis of the theorem, we see that one may choose a subdivision R_1, \cdots, R_n of X_1 such that, for all y,

$$(7) \qquad \sum_{1}^{n} [\sup_{\mathbf{x} \in R_i} M(\mathbf{x}, y) - \inf_{\mathbf{x} \in R_i} M(\mathbf{x}, y)] \int_{R_i} d\mathbf{x} < \frac{\epsilon}{K}$$

Define $\xi(i) = \int_{R_i} g(\mathbf{x}) \, d\mathbf{x}$. Let $\mathbf{x}_1, \cdots, \mathbf{x}_n$ be any points in R_1, \cdots, R_n, respectively, and let $\boldsymbol{\xi}$ be the mixed-strategy assigning probability $\xi(i)$ to \mathbf{x}_i, for $i = 1, \cdots, n$.

Then, for all y,

$$(8) \qquad M(\boldsymbol{\xi}, y) \leq \sum_{i=1}^{n} \xi(i) \sup_{\mathbf{x} \in R_i} M(\mathbf{x}, y)$$

and

$$(9) \qquad M(\boldsymbol{\xi}, y) \geq \sum_{i=1}^{n} \xi(i) \inf_{\mathbf{x} \in R_i} M(\mathbf{x}, y)$$

and $M(g, y)$ satisfies the same inequalities.

Define

$$M_i(y) = \sup_{\mathbf{x} \in R_i} M(\mathbf{x}, y), \qquad m_i(y) = \inf_{\mathbf{x} \in R_i} M(\mathbf{x}, y)$$

From (8) and (9) and the fact that $M(g, y)$ also satisfies these inequalities, we infer

$$(10) \qquad |M(g, y) - M(\xi, y)| \leq \sum_{1}^{n} \xi(i)[M_i(y) - m_i(y)]$$

Now

$$(11) \qquad \xi(i) = \int_{R_i} g(\mathbf{x}) \, d\mathbf{x} \leq K \int_{R_i} d\mathbf{x}$$

From (10), (11), and (7), we obtain

$$|M(g, y) - M(\xi, y)| \leq \sum_{1}^{n} [M_i(y) - m_i(y)] \int_{R_i} d\mathbf{x} < \epsilon$$

which completes the proof.

Corollary. Let $G = (X, Y, M)$ be a game. If X, Y are closed, bounded subsets of S_m, S_n and M is continuous, then every density for either player is an extended mixed strategy.

Proof. The function M is uniformly continuous on $X \times Y$ and therefore is uniformly (in **y**) integrable over X and uniformly (in **x**) integrable over Y.

An example in which densities are not approximable by discrete mixed strategies is the following. Player I chooses a number x with $0 \leq x \leq 1$, and player II chooses a finite set y of numbers (y_1, \cdots, y_n), $0 \leq y_i \leq 1$. If the number chosen by I is in the set chosen by II, the payoff is zero; if not, I wins 1 unit. Thus X is the unit interval, Y consists of all finite subsets of the unit interval, and $M(x, y) = 0$ if $x \,\varepsilon\, y$, $M(x, y) = 1$ if $x \notin y$. For any mixed strategy ξ for I, $M(\xi, y_n) \to 0$ as $n \to \infty$, where y_n is the set of the first n x's in an ordering x_1, x_2, \cdots, of the countable x set for which $\xi(x) > 0$. Thus $\Lambda(\xi) = 0$ for all ξ, and $\lambda^* = 0$. Also, for any η, $M(x, \eta) = 1$ for x, outside the countable set which is the union of those y's for which $\eta(y) > 0$, so that $\Upsilon(\eta) = 1$ for all η, $v^* = 1$. The game has lower value 0, upper value 1.

However, if f is the density function $f(x) \equiv 1$ for $0 \leq x \leq 1$, corresponding to choosing a number at random in the unit interval, $M(f, y)$
$$= \int_0^1 M(x, y)\, dx = 1 \text{ for all } y,$$
since, for a fixed y_0, $M(x, y_0) = 1$ except on a finite set. Thus, if we insist that player I can really choose a number at random on the unit interval, the game has a value; if we restrict his choice to discrete mixtures over finite sets, the game does not have a value. Now the difficulty here is not mathematical; we simply have two mathematical models, and the question is which describes more accurately a certain situation. In fact, in the general theory of games, even the requirement that a function T be ϵ-approximable by a discrete mixed strategy, in order for T to be an extended mixed strategy, is usually relaxed.

We turn now to an example of a different kind, a game that simply fails to have a value, even if we permit arbitrary probability distributions as mixed strategies. The game is this: Players I and II choose positive integers, and whoever chooses the larger integer wins. Thus $X = Y =$ the set of positive integers,

$$M(x, y) = \quad 1 \quad \text{if} \quad x > y$$

$$= \quad 0 \quad \text{if} \quad x = y$$

$$= -1 \quad \text{if} \quad x < y$$

Now the most general probability distribution over X is a sequence $\xi = (\xi(1), \xi(2), \cdots)$ with $\xi(i) \geq 0$, $\Sigma\xi(i) = 1$, where $\xi(i)$ is the prob-

ability that $x = i$, and similarly for Y. For such a ξ, we have

$$M(\xi, y) = \sum_{i>y} \xi(i) - \sum_{i<y} \xi(i)$$

As $y \to \infty$, $M(\xi, y) \to -1$, so that $\Lambda(\xi) = -1$, $\lambda^* = -1$. Similarly $\Upsilon(\eta) = 1$ for all η and $v^* = 1$.

2.7. Solving Games

There are various methods for solving a game, i.e., finding the value and the good strategies for both players. In principle, any finite game can be solved by solving a finite number of systems of linear equations, as will be noted below, but no universally valid method is known for solving infinite games. However, if a pair of strategies ξ^*, η^* is obtained in any way whatever, it is usually easy to evaluate $\Lambda(\xi^*)$ and $\Upsilon(\eta^*)$; if $\Lambda(\xi^*) = \Upsilon(\eta^*)$, their common value is the value of the game, and ξ^* and η^* are good strategies; even if $\Lambda(\xi^*) < \Upsilon(\eta^*)$, the value is somewhere in the interval $(\Lambda(\xi^*), \Upsilon(\eta^*))$, so that we have an upper bound, $\Upsilon(\eta^*) - \Lambda(\xi^*)$, on the loss that either player suffers by using ξ^* or η^*. Thus, in considering methods for solving games, we need not be unduly troubled by the fact that a method cannot be guaranteed in advance to yield the solution; if a method often yields strategies (ξ^*, η^*) that can be verified directly to be solutions, it is worth knowing. There is such a method, suggested by the following

Theorem 2.7.1. If the game $G = (X, Y, M)$ has a value v, and if ξ^* is a good strategy for player I and η^* is a good strategy for player II, then

(a)
$$\sum_{\{x:\, M(x,\, \eta^*)\, <v\}} \xi^*(x) = 0$$

and

(b)
$$\sum_{\{y:\, M(\xi^*,\, y)\, >v\}} \eta^*(y) = 0$$

Proof. (We shall prove assertion a only; the proof of assertion b is similar.) We have $M(\xi^*, y) \geq v$ for all y, so that $M(\xi^*, \eta^*) \geq v$. However $M(x, \eta^*) \leq v$ for all x, so that $M(\xi^*, \eta^*) = v$. Let

$$U = \{x: M(x, \eta^*) < v\}; \qquad U_n = \{x: M(x, \eta^*) < v - 1/n\}$$

Then

(1)
$$v = \sum_{x\,\varepsilon\,X} \xi^*(x) M(x, \eta^*)$$

$$= \sum_{x\,\varepsilon\,U_n} \xi^*(x) M(x, \eta^*) + \sum_{x\,\varepsilon\,C(U_n)} \xi^*(x) M(x, \eta^*)$$

$$\leq \left(v - \frac{1}{n}\right) \sum_{x \,\varepsilon\, U_n} \xi^*(x) + v \sum_{x \,\varepsilon\, C(U_n)} \xi^*(x)$$

for all n. But

(2)
$$\sum_{x \,\varepsilon\, U_n} \xi^*(x) + \sum_{x \,\varepsilon\, C(U_n)} \xi^*(x) = 1$$

so that

(3)
$$v \leq v - \frac{1}{n} \sum_{x \,\varepsilon\, U_n} \xi^*(x)$$

and hence $\sum_{x \,\varepsilon\, U_n} \xi^*(x) = 0$. Since this holds for all n, we have $\sum_{x \,\varepsilon\, U} \xi^*(x)$ = 0, as was to be shown.

We remark that, if X is an m space and Y an n space, and if ξ^* is a density which is an extended good strategy for player I and η^* is a density which is an extended good strategy for player II, then

(c)
$$\int_{\{\mathbf{x}:\, M(\mathbf{x},\, \eta^*) \,<\, v\}} \xi^*(\mathbf{x}) \, d\mathbf{x} = 0$$

and

(d)
$$\int_{\{\mathbf{y}:\, M(\xi^*,\, \mathbf{y}) \,>\, v\}} \eta^*(\mathbf{y}) \, d\mathbf{y} = 0$$

The proof of the theorem has been stated in a way that easily transfers to the case of densities.

The above theorem implies, for example, that, if Y is finite and II has a good strategy η^* with $\eta^*(y) > 0$ for all y, then any good strategy ξ^* for I will have $M(\xi^*, y) = v$ for all y. Also, if $Y = S_n$, and $\eta^*(y)$ is a density such that $\eta^*(y) > 0$ in some interval I_n, then $M(\xi^*, y) = v$ for all $y \,\varepsilon\, I_n$. Now in solving a game we will usually not know v, but we can often find those strategies ξ for which $M(\xi, y)$ is constant and can check to see whether ξ is in fact a good strategy. This procedure is best explained by working out a few examples.

Example 1. I is to look for II in one of the locations A, B, C. II is now at A but, at a cost of 1 unit, may move to B or C or, at a cost of 2 units, may move to D. The cost of moving, if any, is paid to I after the search is over, and he receives an additional 3 units if he locates II.

Solution. The matrix is

	A	B	C	D
A	3	1	1	2
B	0	4	1	2
C	0	1	4	2

We look for strategies η with $M(x, \eta) = $ constant; i.e., we solve the system

$$3\eta(1) + \eta(2) + \eta(3) + 2\eta(4) = k$$
$$4\eta(2) + \eta(3) + 2\eta(4) = k$$
$$\eta(2) + 4\eta(3) + 2\eta(4) = k$$
$$\eta(1) + \eta(2) + \eta(3) + \eta(4) = 1$$

There are two linearly independent solutions $\eta_1 = (1/3, 1/3, 1/3, 0)$ and $\eta_2 = (0, 0, 0, 1)$, with $M(x, \eta_1) = 5/3$, $M(x, \eta_2) = 2$. Thus η_2 is not the solution; if η_1 is, we must have $M(\xi^*, y) = 5/3$ for any good strategy ξ^* for I and $y = A, B,$ or C. This leads to the system

$$3\xi(1) = 5/3$$
$$\xi(1) + 4\xi(2) + \xi(3) = 5/3$$
$$\xi(1) + \xi(2) + 4\xi(3) = 5/3$$
$$\xi(1) + \xi(2) + \xi(3) = 1$$

which has the solution $\xi^* = (5/9, 2/9, 2/9)$. Thus $v = 5/3$ and ξ^*, η_1 are the unique good strategies.

Example 2. A is to arrive at a station at a time t selected at random in $(0, 1)$ and waits there until time 1 or until I or II arrives. Each of I, II chooses a time in $(0, 1)$ to appear at the station; he looks for A and departs immediately, with A if A is present. If either I or II succeeds in meeting A, he receives one unit from the other.

Solution. If x, y are the times chosen by I, II, the payoff is

$$M(x, y) = x - (y - x) = 2x - y \quad \text{for} \quad x < y$$
$$= 0 \quad \text{for} \quad x = y$$
$$(x - y) - y = x - 2y \quad \text{for} \quad x > y$$

The payoff is discontinuous, but we shall assume that the game has a value and that any density is an extended mixed strategy. We shall therefore look for a density ξ for which $M(\xi, y) = $ constant.

$$M(\xi, y) = \int_0^1 M(x, y)\xi(x)\, dx = \int_0^y (2x - y)\xi(x)\, dx + \int_y^1 (x - 2y)\xi(x)\, dx$$
$$= \int_0^y (x + y)\xi(x)\, dx + \int_0^1 (x - 2y)\xi(x)\, dx$$

If $M(\xi, y)$ is constant, $\dfrac{\partial^2 M}{\partial y^2} = 0$. This yields

$$2 \frac{\partial}{\partial y} [y\xi(y)] + \xi(y) = 0; \qquad 2y \frac{\xi'}{\xi} + 3 = 0; \qquad \xi(y) = ky^{-\frac{3}{2}}$$

Since $\displaystyle\int_0^1 x^{-\frac{3}{2}} dx$ is infinite, we cannot use a density $kx^{-\frac{3}{2}}$ throughout $(0, 1)$. Since arriving very early is unlikely to succeed anyway, we try

$$\xi_a(x) = 0 \qquad \text{for} \quad x < a$$

$$k_a x^{-\frac{3}{2}} \quad \text{for} \quad a \leq x \leq 1$$

where $0 < a < 1$, and

$$k^{-1}{}_a = \int_a^1 x^{-\frac{3}{2}} dx = 2 \frac{1 - a^{\frac{1}{2}}}{a^{\frac{1}{2}}}$$

For $a \leq y \leq 1$,

$$M(\xi_a, y) = 2k_a[(2 - a^{-\frac{1}{2}})y - 2a^{\frac{1}{2}} + 1]$$

Thus $M(\xi_a, y)$ can be made constant for $a \leq y \leq 1$ by setting the coefficient of y equal to zero and solving for a. This yields $a = 1/4$, and hence

$$\xi^*(x) = 0 \qquad \text{for} \quad x < \tfrac{1}{4}$$

$$\tfrac{1}{2} x^{-\frac{3}{2}} \quad \text{for} \quad \tfrac{1}{4} \leq x \leq 1$$

We also have

$$M(\xi^*, y) = 0 \qquad \text{for} \quad \tfrac{1}{4} \leq y \leq 1$$

$$M(\xi^*, y) = \tfrac{1}{2} - 2y \quad \text{for} \quad y \leq \tfrac{1}{4}$$

The same density η^* for II yields

$$M(x, \eta^*) = 0 \qquad \text{for} \quad \tfrac{1}{4} \leq x \leq 1$$

$$M(x, \eta^*) = 2x - \tfrac{1}{2} \quad \text{for} \quad x \leq \tfrac{1}{4}$$

Thus ξ^*, η^* are good strategies for I, II; the value of the game is, of course, zero.

For games in which one player has only two or three pure strategies, direct geometric methods are useful. For instance, if player I has only two pure strategies, 1, 2, each strategy y of II may be represented by the point $\mathbf{s}(y) = [M(1, y), M(2, y)]$ in the plane. Let S denote the convex set determined by the points $\mathbf{s}(y)$. The point \mathbf{s}^* in S whose maximum coordinate is minimized can be spotted directly; the maximum coordinate of \mathbf{s}^* is the value of the game, and any mixture of y's for

which the same convex linear combination of $\mathbf{s}(y)$'s yields \mathbf{s}^* is a good strategy for II.

Example 3. I chooses a number $i = 1$ or 2. A number t is chosen at random in $(0, 1)$, and the number $z = t^i$ is announced to II. II then guesses which integer I chose; he pays I the amount 0 or 1, according as his guess is correct or not.

Solution. A strategy for II is specified by a subset T of $(0, 1)$ such that he guesses 1 when $z \,\varepsilon\, T$. The payoff is

$$M(1, T) = 1 - \int_T dt$$

$$M(2, T) = \int_{\{t:\, t^2 \,\varepsilon\, T\}} dt = \frac{1}{2} \int_{t \,\varepsilon\, T} t^{-\frac{1}{2}} dt$$

(Note that, for a fixed $i = 1, 2$, M is a function whose arguments are those subsets of $(0, 1)$ for which the integral exists.) We need not plot the set of all points $\mathbf{s}(T) = (M(1, T), M(2, T))$, since only the lower left boundary is of interest. For fixed $M(1, T) = a$, the minimum value of $M(2, T)$ over T clearly occurs when T is the interval $(a, 1)$ and is $(1 - a^{\frac{1}{2}})$. The lower boundary of the set of points $\mathbf{s}(T)$ is thus the curve $y = 1 - x^{\frac{1}{2}}$, $0 \le x \le 1$. This curve is convex and is the lower boundary of the convex set S. The point whose maximum coordinate is minimum is the intersection of this curve with the line $y = x$ and is (v, v), where $v = \dfrac{3 - 5^{\frac{1}{2}}}{2} = 0.382$ approximately. The value of the game is v, and II has the good pure strategy $T = (v, 1)$. The good strategy for I mixes 1, 2 in proportion to the coefficients of x and y in the equations of the tangent line to $y = 1 - x^{\frac{1}{2}}$ at (v, v). This equation is $\zeta x + (1 - \zeta)y = v$, where we write. $\boldsymbol{\xi} = (\zeta, 1 - \zeta)$ and

$$\zeta = \frac{v^{-\frac{1}{2}}}{2 + v^{-\frac{1}{2}}} = 5^{-\frac{1}{2}} = 0.447$$

approximately, so that I mixes 1, 2 in the proportions $(0.447, 0.553)$.

In games in which $M(x, y)$ is convex in y for fixed x, the simplest procedure is often a direct evaluation of $\Upsilon(y)$.

Example 4. $X = Y =$ unit interval; $M(x, y) = |x - y|$. $\Upsilon(y) = \max(y, 1 - y)$, $v^* = \min_y \Upsilon(y) = \Upsilon(1/2) = 1/2$. Thus $v = 1/2$, and $y = 1/2$ is a good strategy for II. Since 0 and 1 are the only pure strategies x for I with $M(x, 1/2) = 1/2$, any good strategy ξ for I is a mixture of 0 and 1. If $\xi(0) = \zeta$,

$$M(\xi, y) = \zeta y + (1 - \zeta)(1 - y), \qquad \Lambda(\xi) = \min(\zeta, 1 - \zeta)$$

Thus $\Lambda(\xi) = 1/2$ only if $\zeta = 1/2$; the only good strategy for I mixes 0 and 1 equally.

In finite games there is a constructive method for obtaining the extreme points of the set Ξ^* (H*) of good strategies for player I (II) which is given below. It turns out that the set Ξ^* (H*) is the convex hull of a finite set of extreme points, so that, from Theorem 2.2.4, this method yields an explicit parametric representation of Ξ^* (H*).

First we define simple solutions of arbitrary games.

Definition 2.7.1. Let $G = (X, Y, M)$ be a game, and let ξ^* and η^* be mixed strategies such that

$$M(\xi^*, y) = M(x, \eta^*) = \text{constant}$$

for all x in X and y in Y. Then we call the couple (ξ^*, η^*) if it exists, a simple solution of G. If G is a finite game with matrix A, we call (ξ^*, η^*) a simple solution of A. It is obvious that the constant is the value of the game and that ξ^* and η^* are good strategies.

Theorem 2.7.2. Let $A = (a_{ij})$, $i, j = 1, \cdots, n$ be a nonsingular matrix and let $\bar{A} = (A_{ij})$ be the adjoint of A. Then a necessary and sufficient condition that A have a simple solution is that the quantities

$$R_i = \sum_{j=1}^{n} A_{ij} \quad \text{for} \quad i = 1, \cdots, n$$

$$C_j = \sum_{i=1}^{n} A_{ij} \quad \text{for} \quad j = 1, \cdots, n$$

all be of the same sign.

Proof. (Sufficiency.) Assume that R_i and C_j are of the same sign, and consider the linear equation

(1) $$A(\xi, j) = \sum_{i=1}^{n} a_{ij}\xi(i) = v, \qquad (j = 1, \cdots, n)$$

where v is a nonzero constant of value not yet specified. Using Cramer's rule, the solution of these equations is

(2) $$\xi(i) = \frac{vR_i}{a}, \qquad (i = 1, 2, \cdots, n)$$

where $a = |A|$, the determinant of the matrix A. Now v can be chosen so that

(3)
$$\sum_{i=1}^{n} \xi(i) = v\frac{\sum_{i=1}^{n} R_i}{a} = 1$$

that is

(4)
$$v = \frac{a}{\sum_{i=1}^{n} R_i} = \frac{a}{\Sigma\Sigma A_{ij}} ; \qquad \xi(i) = \frac{R_i}{\Sigma\Sigma A_{ij}}$$

Since we assume that all R_i are of the same sign, then, by (4), $\xi(i) \geq 0$ for all i and, in view of (3), $\boldsymbol{\xi} = (\xi(1), \cdots, \xi(n)) \in \Xi$.

In a similar way we conclude that $\boldsymbol{\eta} = (\eta(1), \cdots, \eta(n)) \in H$, where $\eta(j) = C_j/\Sigma\Sigma A_{ij}$ is a solution of the equations

(5)
$$A(i, \boldsymbol{\eta}) = \sum_{j=1}^{n} a_{ij}\eta(j) = v', \qquad (i = 1, \cdots, n)$$

But, as above,

(6)
$$v' = \frac{a}{\sum_{j=1}^{n} C_j} = \frac{a}{\Sigma\Sigma A_{ij}} = v$$

so that $A(\boldsymbol{\xi}, j) = A(i, \boldsymbol{\eta}) = v$ for all i and j.

(Necessity.) To prove the necessity, we are given

(7)
$$\sum_{i=1}^{n} a_{ij}\xi(i) - v, \qquad (j = 1, \cdots, n); \qquad \xi(i) \geq 0, \qquad \sum_{1}^{n} \xi(i) = 1$$

$$\sum_{j=1}^{n} a_{ij}\eta(j) = v, \qquad (i = 1, \cdots, n); \qquad \eta(j) \geq 0, \qquad \sum_{j=1}^{n}\eta(j) = 1$$

and, consequently,

(8)
$$\xi(i) = \frac{R_i}{\Sigma\Sigma A_{ij}}, \qquad \eta(j) = \frac{C_j}{\Sigma\Sigma A_{ij}}, \qquad v = \frac{a}{\Sigma\Sigma A_{ij}}$$

and, since $\xi(i) \geq 0$ and $\eta(j) \geq 0$, we must have all R_i and all C_j of the same sign as $\sum_{i=1}^{n}\sum_{j=1}^{n} A_{ij}$.

Note that, if A is nonsingular and admits a simple solution, the good strategies for the two players and the value of the game are given by (8).

Corollary. If a nonsingular square matrix admits a simple solution, then the solution is unique.

Proof. The proof follows from the fact that, since matrix A is nonsingular, the sets of equations

$$\sum_{i=1}^{n} a_{ij}\xi(i) = v; \qquad \sum_{j=1}^{n} a_{ij}\eta(j) = v$$

have a unique solution.

Theorem 2.7.3. Let A be an $m \times n$ matrix, such that the value v of the game with matrix A is not zero. Let Ξ^* (H*) be the set of all good strategies for Player I (II) in the finite game whose matrix is A. Then a necessary and sufficient condition that a ξ^* in Ξ^* and an η^* in H* be extreme points of Ξ^* and H*, respectively, is that A contain a nonsingular submatrix B such that (ξ^*_B, η^*_B) is a simple solution of B— where ξ^*_B is the vector obtained from ξ^* by deleting the components corresponding to the rows deleted to obtain B from A, and η^*_B is the vector obtained from η^* by deleting the components corresponding to the columns deleted to obtain B from A.

Proof. (Sufficiency.) We assume that there is an $r \times r$ nonsingular matrix B in A, such that (ξ^*_B, η^*_B) is a simple solution of B, and show that this implies that ξ^* and η^* are extreme points of Ξ^* and H*, respectively. Assume the contrary; then there exist ξ', $\xi'' \varepsilon \Xi^*$ with $\xi' \neq \xi''$ such that

(1) $$\xi^* = \lambda\xi' + (1 - \lambda)\xi''$$

$0 < \lambda < 1$. Let I_B represent the row subscripts and J_B the column subscripts of B. Then, by hypothesis,

(2) $$v = B(\xi^*_B, j) = \lambda B(\xi'_B, j) + (1 - \lambda)B(\xi''_B, j)$$

for all $j \varepsilon J_B$. But $v \geq B(\xi'_B, j)$ and $v \geq B(\xi''_B, j)$ for $j \varepsilon J_B$, and hence it must follow that

(3) $$v = B(\xi'_B, j) = B(\xi''_B, j) \quad \text{for} \quad j \varepsilon J_B$$

and (ξ'_B, η^*_B), (ξ''_B, η^*_B) are simple solutions of B, so that by corollary to Theorem 2.7.2

(4) $$\xi'_B = \xi''_B$$

Since by hypothesis (ξ^*_B, η^*_B) is a simple solution of B, the components of ξ^* corresponding to rows of A not in B are all zero. Hence we con-

clude from (1) and (4) that

$$(5) \qquad\qquad \boldsymbol{\xi}' = \boldsymbol{\xi}''$$

which contradicts the assumption that $\boldsymbol{\xi}' \neq \boldsymbol{\xi}''$. The proof that $\boldsymbol{\eta}^*$ is an extreme point of H* is similar.

(Necessity.) Let I_1 and I_2 be the sets of row subscripts of A such that $\xi^*(i) > 0$ for $i \,\varepsilon\, I_1$ and $A(i, \boldsymbol{\eta}^*) = v$ for $i \,\varepsilon\, I_2$ where v is the value of the game. Similarly let J_1 and J_2 be sets of column subscripts of A such that $\eta^*(j) > 0$ for $j \,\varepsilon\, J_1$ and $A(\boldsymbol{\xi}^*, j) = v$ for $j \,\varepsilon\, J_2$. Then $I_2 \supset I_1$, $J_2 \supset J_1$. Now in the submatrix A_2 of A with $i \,\varepsilon\, I_2$, $j \,\varepsilon\, J_2$, the row vectors \mathbf{r}_i for $i \,\varepsilon\, I_1$, are linearly independent; for suppose there exists a non-zero vector \mathbf{t} with $\mathbf{t} \cdot \mathbf{c}_j = 0$ for all $j \,\varepsilon\, J_2$, where $t_i = 0$ for $i \notin I_1$, and where \mathbf{c}_j is the jth column vector of A_2. Then, since

$$(6) \qquad\qquad \sum_{j \,\varepsilon\, J_2} \eta^*(j)\mathbf{c}_j = v\boldsymbol{\delta}, \qquad \boldsymbol{\delta} = \begin{bmatrix} 1 \\ 1 \\ \cdot \\ \cdot \\ \cdot \\ 1 \end{bmatrix}$$

we have

$$(7) \qquad\qquad 0 = \mathbf{t} \cdot \sum_{j \,\varepsilon\, J_2} (\eta^*(j)\mathbf{c}_j)' = v(\mathbf{t} \cdot \boldsymbol{\delta}')$$

where for any column vector \mathbf{w}, \mathbf{w}' represents the corresponding raw vector.

Since $v \neq 0$, $\mathbf{t} \cdot \boldsymbol{\delta}' = 0$. Thus

$$(8) \qquad\qquad \boldsymbol{\xi}^{(\epsilon)} = \boldsymbol{\xi}^* + \epsilon \mathbf{t}$$

is a mixed strategy for $|\,\epsilon\,|$ sufficiently small. Moreover, for all $j \,\varepsilon\, J_2$,

$$(9) \qquad A(\boldsymbol{\xi}^{(\epsilon)}, j) = \sum_{i \,\varepsilon\, I_1} a_{ij}(\xi^*(i) + \epsilon t_i) = v + \epsilon \sum_{i \,\varepsilon\, I_1} a_{ij}t_i = v$$

and, since $A(\boldsymbol{\xi}^*, j) > v$ for $j \notin J_2$, $A(\boldsymbol{\xi}^{(\epsilon)}, j) > v$ for $j \notin J_2$ and $|\,\epsilon\,|$ sufficiently small. Thus there is an $\epsilon_0 > 0$ for which $\boldsymbol{\xi}^{(\epsilon_0)}$ and $\boldsymbol{\xi}^{(-\epsilon_0)}$ are good strategies for player I, with $\boldsymbol{\xi}^* = \frac{1}{2}(\boldsymbol{\xi}^{(\epsilon_0)} + \boldsymbol{\xi}^{(-\epsilon_0)})$ contradicting the hypothesis that $\boldsymbol{\xi}^*$ is an extreme point in Ξ^*. Similarly, the column vectors \mathbf{c}_j of A_2 are linearly independent for $j \,\varepsilon\, J_1$. Let r be the rank of A_2. Then

$$(10) \qquad\qquad r \geq \max\,[N(I_1), N(J_1)]$$

where for any finite set S the symbol $N(S)$ stands for the number of elements in S. Thus there exists an $r \times r$ nonsingular submatrix B in A_2 with $I_B \supset I_1, J_B \supset J_1$, where I_B and J_B are the sets of i, j determining the matrix B. We also have

$$(11) \qquad B(\xi^*_B, j) = B(i, \eta^*_B) = v$$

for $i \, \varepsilon \, I_B, j \, \varepsilon \, J_B$, which completes the proof of the theorem.

The restriction in Theorem 2.7.3 that $v \neq 0$ is unimportant, since by adding the same constant to all elements of A we obtain a new matrix all of whose elements are positive, and its associated game has exactly the same sets of good strategies as that of A. Thus Theorems 2.7.2 and 2.7.3 give us a fairly complete theory for the solutions of finite games. We examine all square submatrices of A for simple solutions; that is, we test them to see whether all R_i and C_j are of the same sign. For each submatrix where this is true, we compute the simple solutions according to the method of Theorem 2.7.2. We then try these solutions to see if they determine good strategies for both players, i.e., whether $A(\xi^*, j) \leq v$ for all j and $A(i, \eta^*) \geq v$ for all i. If the answer is in the affirmative, we obtain two extreme points, one in Ξ^* and one in H^*. Once all the extreme points have been thus obtained, we can then give a complete characterization of Ξ^* and H^*.

We have seen in Chapter 1 that in games of perfect information the good strategies and value may often be obtained by an inductive process. The same method may sometimes be applied with success to games that cannot be strictly classified as games of perfect information. An interesting instance of this is given in the following example:

Example 5. In an archery contest, two contestants of equal skill (i.e., equal accuracy) approach their respective targets from the same distance and with the same speed. Contestant I has m arrows, contestant II n arrows; also, each knows how many arrows the other has and when his opponent shoots. We assume that at the start the probability of hitting the bull's eye is a, where $a \leq 1/(m + n)$, and increases to 1 monotonically as the two contestants approach their targets. We can describe the location of a contestant by the probability of a hit. If I scores before II, then II pays I one unit, and the game is over. If II scores before I, then I pays II one unit, and the game is over. If both contestants exhaust their arrows without scoring, or if both score simultaneously, then the payoff is 0. We denote this game by $G(a, m, n)$. The problem is: At what points x should contestant I shoot his arrows, and at what points y should contestant II shoot his arrows, provided neither has yet scored?

Solution. Let us first consider the case $m = n = 1$, i.e., the game $G(a, 1, 1)$. The payoff function M is

(1)
$$M(x, y) = x - (1 - x)y \quad \text{if} \quad x < y$$
$$0 \qquad\qquad\qquad \text{if} \quad x = y$$
$$(1 - y)x - y \quad \text{if} \quad y > x$$

It is clear that I gains by waiting, so long as II does not shoot. However, if I waits past $x = 1/2$, II may shoot before I and make the expected payoff negative. This suggests that the best I can do (if II has not shot) is to shoot at $x = 1/2$, which yields an expected payoff of 0, and II can prevent him from gaining more by also shooting at that distance. We easily verify in fact that $x = y = 1/2$ is a saddle point; i.e.,

(2)
$$M(x, 1/2) \leq M(1/2, 1/2) \leq M(1/2, y)$$

for all x and y, and thus $x = 1/2$ is a good strategy for I, $y = 1/2$ is a good strategy for II, and the value of the game is of course 0.

For arbitrary m and n, neither player has a good strategy in $G(a, m, n)$ but both have ϵ-good strategies [see Definition 2.3.1]. In order to understand how to "guess" a correct solution for the general case, we suggest that the reader work out the case for $m = 1$, $n = 2$ and then generalize on these results. We begin the study of the general case by describing a certain strategy for each player in $G(a, m, n)$.

For any $\epsilon > 0$ and for m and n positive integers, we describe inductively the ϵ-*designated strategy* $S_1(\epsilon, m, n)$ for player I in $G(a, m, n)$. For I to use $S_1(\epsilon, 1, 1)$ in $G(a, 1, 1)$ is to play as follows: If II does not shoot before $y = 1/2$, then I shoots at $x = 1/2$; if II shoots before $y = 1/2$, then I shoots at $x = 1$. To use $S_1(\epsilon, m, n)$ in $G(a, m, n)$ is for I to play as follows:

Case 1. $m \geq n$. (a) If II shoots at $y < 1/(m + n)$, then I uses $S_1(\epsilon, m, n - 1)$ in the game $G(y, m, n - 1)$.

(b) If II does not shoot before $\dfrac{1}{m + n}$, player I shoots at $\dfrac{1}{m + n}$ and then uses strategy $S_1(\epsilon, m - 1, n)$ in the game $G\left(\dfrac{1}{m + n}, m - 1, n\right)$ or $S_1(\epsilon, m - 1, n - 1)$ in $G\left(\dfrac{1}{m + n}, m - 1, n - 1\right)$ according as II does not or does shoot at $\dfrac{1}{m + n}$.

Case 2. $m < n$. I chooses δ such that

(3) $$\delta = \min\left[\dfrac{(2m + n)(m + n - 1)\epsilon}{2m^2}, \qquad \dfrac{1}{(m + n)(m + n - 1)}\right]$$

and uses the rectangular distribution over the closed interval $\left(\dfrac{1}{m+n},\right.$

$\left.\dfrac{1}{m+n} + \delta\right)$ to pick a point x_0 in this interval before each play of the game.

(a) If II shoots at $y < x_0$, then I uses $S_1(\epsilon/2, m, n-1)$ in the game $G(y, m, n-1)$.

(b) If II does not shoot before x_0, I shoots at x_0 and then uses $S(\epsilon/2, m-1, n)$ in the game $G(x_0, m-1, n)$. (Of course, if II shoots at x_0, I uses $S(\epsilon/2, m-1, n-1)$ in $G(x_0, m-1, n-1)$, but the probability of this happening is zero.)

An ϵ-designated strategy for player II is described in a similar way with m and n interchanged.

We now prove that for every $\epsilon > 0$, the ϵ-designated strategy for player I (player II) is an ϵ-good strategy for player I (player II) in the game $G(a, m, n)$ and that the value of $G(a, m, n)$ is $(m-n)/(m+n)$.

We introduce the notation $E(\epsilon, m, n)$ to designate the least amount that player I can expect to get if he uses the ϵ-designated strategy $S_1(\epsilon, m, n)$ in the game $G(a, m, n)$. Since the proof for player II is exactly similar to the proof for player I, it will be sufficient to prove that, against any strategy adopted by II,

$$(4) \qquad E(\epsilon, m, n) \geq \frac{m-n}{m+n} - \epsilon$$

The proof proceeds by induction on $m+n$. We see from (1) and (2) that $S_1(\epsilon, 1, 1)$ is a good strategy and, a fortiori an ϵ-good strategy in $G(a, 1, 1)$, and thus

$$E(\epsilon, 1, 1) > 0 - \epsilon$$

We assume that the theorem is proved for $m+n < k$, and prove it for $m+n = k$.

Case 1. $m \geq n$. (a) II shoots at $y < 1/(m+n)$.

$$E(\epsilon, m, n) \geq -y + (1-y)E(\epsilon, m, n-1)$$

$$= E(\epsilon, m, n-1) - y(1 + E(\epsilon, m, n))$$

$$\geq \left(\frac{m-n+1}{m+n-1} - \epsilon\right) - \left(\frac{1}{m+n}\right)\left(1 + \frac{m-n+1}{m+n-1} - \epsilon\right)$$

$$> \frac{m-n}{m+n} - \epsilon$$

(b_1) II shoots at $y = 1/(m+n)$.

$$E(\epsilon, m, n) \geq x(1 - y) - y(1 - x) + (1 - x)(1 - y)E(\epsilon, m - 1, n - 1)$$

$$\geq \left(1 - \frac{1}{m+n}\right)^2 \left(\frac{m-n}{m+n-2} - \epsilon\right)$$

$$> \left(\frac{m-n}{m+n}\right)\frac{(m+n-1)^2}{(m+n)(m+n-2)} - \epsilon > \frac{m-n}{m+n} - \epsilon$$

(b_2) II shoots at $y > 1/(m+n)$.

$$E(\epsilon, m, n) \geq x + (1 - x)E(\epsilon, m - 1, n)$$

$$\geq \frac{1}{m+n} + \left(1 - \frac{1}{m+n}\right)\left(\frac{m-n-1}{m+n-1} - \epsilon\right) > \frac{m-n}{m+n} - \epsilon$$

Case 2. $m < n$. (a) II shoots at $y \leq 1/(m+n)$.

$$E(\epsilon, m, n) \geq -y + (1 - y)E(\epsilon/2, m, n - 1)$$

$$\geq -\frac{1}{m+1} + \left(\frac{m+n-1}{m+n}\right)\left(\frac{m-n+1}{m+n-1} - \frac{\epsilon}{2}\right)$$

$$> \frac{m-n}{m+n} - \epsilon$$

(b) II shoots at $y_0 = [1/(m+n)] + \lambda\delta$, $0 \leq \lambda \leq 1$.

$$E(\epsilon, m, n) \geq \lambda\left[\frac{1}{\lambda\delta}\int_{y_0-\lambda\delta}^{y_0} x\, dx + \left(1 - \frac{1}{\lambda\delta}\int_{y_0-\lambda\delta}^{y_0} x\, dx\right)E\left(\frac{\epsilon}{2}, m - 1, n\right)\right]$$

$$+ (1 - \lambda)\left[-y + (1 - y)E\left(\frac{\epsilon}{2}, m, n - 1\right)\right]$$

$$> -\frac{\epsilon}{2} + \lambda\left[\left(\frac{1}{m+n} + \frac{\lambda\delta}{2}\right)\right.$$

$$+ \left(1 - \frac{1}{m+n} - \frac{\lambda\delta}{2}\right)\left(\frac{m-n-1}{m+n-1}\right)\right]$$

$$+ (1 - \lambda)\left[-\frac{1}{m+n} - \lambda\delta\right.$$

$$+ \left(1 - \frac{1}{m+n} - \lambda\delta\right)\left(\frac{m-n-1}{m+n-1}\right)\right]$$

$$> -\frac{\epsilon}{2} + \frac{m-n}{m+n} + \left[\frac{\lambda^2}{2}\left(1 - \frac{m-n-1}{m+n-1}\right)\right.$$

$$\left. - (\lambda - \lambda^2)\left(1 + \frac{m-n+1}{m+n-1}\right)\right]\delta$$

To complete the proof of case 2(b), we need only show that, for all λ with $0 \leq \lambda \leq 1$,

$$\left[\frac{\lambda^2}{2}\left(1 - \frac{m-n-1}{m+n-1}\right) - (\lambda - \lambda^2)\left(1 + \frac{m-n+1}{m+n-1}\right)\right]\delta \geq -\frac{\epsilon}{2}$$

It is easy to show that the coefficient of δ is minimal at

$$\lambda = m/(2m + n)$$

Consequently, it suffices to prove that

$$(5) \quad \left[\frac{m^2}{2(2m+n)^2}\left(1 - \frac{m-n-1}{m+n-1}\right)\right.$$

$$\left. - \left(\frac{m}{2m+n}\right)\left(1 - \frac{m}{2m+n}\right)\left(1 + \frac{m-n+1}{m+n-1}\right)\right]\delta \geq -\frac{\epsilon}{2}$$

Rearranging and factoring (5), we obtain

$$\left(\frac{m}{2m+n}\right)^2\left(\frac{1}{m+n-1}\right)(2m+n)\delta \geq -\frac{\epsilon}{2}$$

and, using (3), we get the desired result.

(c) II shoots at $y > 1/(m+n) + \delta = y_1$.

$$E(\epsilon, m, n) \geq \frac{1}{\delta}\int_{y_1-\delta}^{y_1} x\, dx + \left(1 - \frac{1}{\delta}\int_{y_1-\delta}^{y_1} x\, dx\right)E\left(\frac{\epsilon}{2}, m-1, n\right)$$

$$\geq \frac{1}{m+n} + \frac{\delta}{2} + \left(1 - \frac{1}{m+n} - \frac{\delta}{2}\right)\left(\frac{m-n-1}{m+n-1} - \frac{\epsilon}{2}\right)$$

$$\geq \frac{m-n}{m+n} - \frac{\epsilon}{2} + \frac{\delta}{2}\left(1 - \frac{m-n-1}{m+n-1}\right) > \frac{m-n}{m+n} - \epsilon$$

which completes the proof.

PROBLEMS

2.7.1. Solve the games with the following matrices:

(a) $\begin{Vmatrix} a & 0 & 0 \\ 0 & b & 0 \\ 0 & 0 & c \end{Vmatrix}$

(b) $\begin{Vmatrix} 1 & 2 & 3 & 4 \\ 2 & 3 & 4 & 1 \\ 3 & 4 & 1 & 2 \\ 4 & 1 & 2 & 3 \end{Vmatrix}$

(c) $\begin{Vmatrix} 5 & 3 & 2 & 1 \\ 1 & 4 & 1 & 0 \\ -3 & 2 & 3 & -1 \\ -2 & -1 & 3 & 2 \\ -1 & 0 & 1 & 2 \end{Vmatrix}$

(d) $a_{ij} = i - j \quad i, j = 1, 2, \cdots, n$

(e) $a_{ij} = 1$ if $|i - j| = 0$ or 1,

$i, j = 1, \cdots, n$

$a_{ij} = 0$ otherwise.

2.7.2. Solve the following game:

$$X = (0 < x < 1), \quad Y = (0 < y < 1), \quad M(x, y) = \varphi(x/y)$$

where $\varphi(t) = 1$ if the first non-zero digit in the decimal expansion of t is 1, $\varphi(t) = 0$ otherwise.

2.7.3. Solve the following game:

$$X = (0 \leq x \leq 1), \quad Y = (0 \leq y \leq 1), \quad M(x, y) = |x - y| - (x - y)^2$$

2.7.4. In Example 5 of this section, solve the game for $m = n = 1$ when (a) the two contestants are separated by a partition so that neither knows whether the opponent has shot his arrow, (b) contestant I has this information but not contestant II. Assume in either case that the probability of hitting a bull's eye at the start is zero. Also, assume in part b that contestant II will delay his shot until the end with positive probability.

CHAPTER 3

General Structure
of Statistical Games

3.1. Introduction

In the previous two chapters we considered general two-person, zero-sum games defined by a triple (X, Y, M) where X and Y are the spaces of pure strategies for the two players and M is a real-valued function defined on $X \times Y$ and represents the payoff to one of the players. What characterizes a particular game, or a given class of games, is the structure assigned to X and Y and the form given to M. One kind of specialization of these spaces and payoff functions leads to a class of games known as *statistical games*. The study of such games will be the concern of the remainder of this book.

In statistical games the two players will be referred to as nature and the statistician. Nature will be designated as player I and the statistician as player II. The fact that, in statistical games, nature cannot be considered as a conscious opponent who can take advantage of mistakes made by the statistician raises the important and as yet unsolved problem of what constitutes a rational way of playing games of this type. Various aspects of this problem will be considered in Chapters 4 and 5. The existence of such problems does not, however, in any way change the basic fact that statistics *can* be viewed as a game against nature, and this viewpoint has already led to important advances in statistics.

In this chapter we will not deal with any specific class of games of a statistical nature but rather will attempt to describe certain general features common to all such games. We will also introduce some basic probability concepts which are essential to the understanding of the structure of such games. The study of special classes of statistical games which arise in a variety of statistical-decision situations will be undertaken in the last six chapters of this book.

Before we embark on a discussion of statistical games, we introduce a few mathematical notions and notations which will be employed in this and subsequent chapters of this book.

75

Let φ be a function which is defined on a product space $A \times B$. Then by φ_b, for $b \,\varepsilon\, B$, we mean the function defined on A such that

$$\varphi_b(a) = \varphi(a, b)$$

for all a in A.

If φ and f are functions such that the domain of definition of φ contains the range of f and the domain of f is a space Z, then by the *composition* of φ and f, written $\varphi \bigcirc f$, we mean the function h such that for all $z \,\varepsilon\, Z$

$$h(z) = \varphi[f(z)]$$

By a *partition* of a space Z we mean a division of Z into mutually exclusive sets whose union is Z. A partition will be designated by the symbol \mathcal{S} and a set of partitions by the symbol \mathfrak{S}. A function f defined on Z *determines* a partition \mathcal{S}_f of sets S_a defined by

$$S_a = \{z : f(z) = a\}$$

where a is an element in the range of f.

Let Y be any space and y any element of it; then by the symbol $\{y\}$ we shall mean the set in Y consisting of the single element y. However, if y has a subscript or superscript, this symbol will designate a sequence of elements of Y.

3.2. The Sample Space

In the background of each statistical game there is postulated a *sample space* which describes all conceivable *outcomes* of an experiment that the statistician can perform. The possibility of "spying" on the opponent by performing experiments is a distinguishing characteristic of all statistical games. The manner in which this spying is done will form a basic part of the statistician's strategy, as will be described later.

The structure of the space Z of outcomes of an experiment can be simple or exceedingly complex. An example of a relatively simple space is one in which the elements are the 2^n possible outcomes of n tosses of a coin. Each point in this space is a sequence of n "heads" and "tails" of the form $HTH \cdots T$. An example of a complex space is one in which the elements are possible temperatures that can be recorded during a 24-hour period in a given locality. A point in this space is a function z with values $z(t)$ representing the temperature at time t.

A set S of points of the space of outcomes is called an *event*. Thus, in the coin-tossing experiment, the set of $\binom{n}{m}$ points each of which contains exactly m heads and $n - m$ tails is an event. In the temperature-

recording experiment, a possible event might be the set of all functions z with $\max_t z(t) \leq 80°$ F.

Associated with the space Z is a *parameter space* Ω with elements ω, and a function p defined on $Z \times \Omega$ such that, for a fixed ω, p_ω is a probability distribution on Z; i.e., p_ω is a non-negative function defined on Z with $p_\omega(z) = 0$ except on a countable set, and $\sum_{z \varepsilon Z} p_\omega(z) = 1$. [See Definition 1.8.1.] The set Ω can also be fruitfully considered as an *index set* for the class of probability distributions on Z. The elements of Ω need not be real numbers or vectors, although in many statistical problems Ω is, in fact, a subset of n space.

We now formally define the notion of a sample space.

Definition 3.2.1. Let Z and Ω be two non-empty sets, and let p be a function defined on $Z \times \Omega$ such that, for a fixed $\omega \varepsilon \Omega$, p_ω is a probability distribution on Z. Then the triple $\mathcal{Z} = (Z, \Omega, p)$ is called a *sample space*.

Though formally the sample space \mathcal{Z} is defined as a triple, we do not always make the distinction between it and the first element of the triple. Thus we speak of an event as a set in the sample space when in fact it is a subset of Z. This ambiguity will cause no difficulty and helps to emphasize that an event is associated with a set of probabilities, one for each $\omega \varepsilon \Omega$. For any $\omega \varepsilon \Omega$ and any event $S \subset Z$, the *probability of the event* S is given by

$$P_\omega(S) = \sum_{z \varepsilon S} p_\omega(z)$$

From the point of view of statistical games, the elements ω in Ω constitute *the pure strategies for nature*. Thus the space Ω corresponds to the space X in a general game. An element in Ω will sometimes be referred to as a *state* of nature. For any $\omega \varepsilon \Omega$, the value of the function p_ω will be denoted by $p_\omega(z)$ and also by $p(z \mid \omega)$. We define

$$\mathcal{P}_\Omega = \{p_\omega : \omega \varepsilon \Omega\}$$

It is easily verified that for every $S \subset Z$ and every $\omega \varepsilon \Omega$

(a) $$0 \leq P_\omega(S) \leq 1$$

(b) $$\text{If} \quad S \subset T, \quad \text{then} \quad P_\omega(S) \leq P_\omega(T)$$

(c) $$P_\omega(S) + P_\omega(C(S)) = 1$$

where $C(S)$ stands for the complement of the set S, and

(d) $$P_\omega(S \cup T) \leq P_\omega(S) + P_\omega(T)$$

with equality holding if S and T are disjoint. We also have the following

Theorem 3.2.1. Let $\mathcal{Z} = (Z, \Omega, p)$ be a sample space. For every ω in Ω and every sequence of disjoint events S_1, S_2, \cdots,

$$P_\omega \left(\bigcup_{i=1}^\infty S_i \right) = \sum_{i=1}^\infty P_\omega(S_i)$$

Proof.

$$P_\omega \left(\bigcup_{i=1}^\infty S_i \right) = \sum_{z \,\epsilon\, \bigcup_i S_i} p_\omega(z) = \sum_i \sum_{z \,\epsilon\, S_i} p_\omega(z) = \sum_i P_\omega(S_i)$$

3.3. The Space of Pure Strategies for the Statistician

The structure of the space of the statistician's pure strategies is somewhat more complex than that for nature. To begin with, the statistician has at his disposal a class A of possible actions which he can take (or decisions he can make) in the face of the (to him) unknown state of nature ω. If he decides to take an action without experimentation, we assume that he incurs a numerical loss $L(\omega, a)$, a known function of the state of nature ω and the action a which he selects from A. However, the possibility of performing experiments and thus reducing the loss by gaining at least partial information about ω is open to the statistician. The possibility greatly enlarges the class of strategies that he can employ. He must now decide which experiments he is to perform, in what sequence he is to perform them, when he is to terminate experimentation, and what action he is to take once experimentation is terminated.

What prevents the statistician from getting full knowledge of ω by unlimited experimentation is the cost of the experiments. This cost may depend linearly or otherwise on the number and kind of experiments he performs, or it may also depend on the outcome of the experiments. However this cost is measured, it is an essential factor which enters in his choice of a strategy.

What then is a strategy for the statistician? Before we can answer this question, we must introduce the notion of a random variable and the new sample space to which it gives rise.

3.4. The Notion of a Random Variable

Previously it was stated that in the background of each statistical game there is a sample space \mathcal{Z}. Because of cost considerations and

other reasons which will be made clear in Chapter 8, the experimenter often will not observe the elements of Z directly but rather a numerical or *vector-valued* function defined on Z where by a vector-valued function is meant a function whose values are points in n space. Thus, for example, in the coin-tossing experiment, the statistician may not observe the actual sequence of heads and tails but rather the values of the function f where $f(z)$ represents the number of heads in the sequence, or the values of the function g, where $g(z)$ represents the number of runs in the sequence, or the values of the vector function h, where $h(z) = (f(z), g(z))$. Similarly in the temperature-recording experiment he may observe not $z(t)$ but rather the values of the function f, where

$$f(z) = \frac{1}{t_2 - t_1} \int_{t_1}^{t_2} z(t)\, dt$$

is the mean temperature in the time interval (t_1, t_2); or the values of the function g, where $g(z) = \max_t z(t)$—the highest temperature in a 24-hour period; or the values of the vector function h, where

$$h(z) = (z(1), z(2), \cdots, z(24))$$

and where $z(j)$ is the temperature reading at the jth hour of the day. The functions f, g, h of these examples are *random variables*.

Random variables are usually thought of as being numerical or vector-valued. In many statistical situations, however, a more general point of view is desirable. Thus, for example, a rule that assigns to each outcome of an experiment a decision, out of a class of possible decisions, is clearly a random variable in the same sense as the above functions f, g, and h, even when the decisions are not expressed as numbers. Thus we are led to the following formal definition.

Definition 3.4.1. Let $\mathcal{Z} = (Z, \Omega, p)$ be a sample space. A function defined on Z is called a random variable.

Let f be a random variable. Then f generates a new sample space $\mathfrak{X} = (X, \Omega, q)$ where X is the range of f and q_ω is the probability distribution of f induced by p_ω. (The class of probability distributions q_ω for each ω in Ω will be denoted by \mathcal{Q}_Ω.) Thus we see that a choice of a random variable f is equivalent to a choice of a sample space \mathfrak{X} which in turn is equivalent to a choice of an experiment whose outcomes are the elements of X. The meaning of the symbol q will be made more precise by Theorem 3.4.1 and the definitions that precede it.

Definition 3.4.2. Let $\mathcal{Z} = (Z, \Omega, p)$ be a sample space, let f_1, \cdots, f_m be random variables defined on Z, let the sets B_1, \cdots, B_m be the ranges

of f_1, \cdots, f_m, respectively, and let B be the product space of B_1, \cdots, B_m. Then for any ω in Ω the function q_ω, such that for every b in B

$$q_\omega(b) = q_\omega(b_1, \cdots, b_m) = P_\omega\{z: f_1(z) = b_1, \cdots, f_m(z) = b_m\}$$

is called the joint probability distribution of f_1, \cdots, f_m, given ω.

Definition 3.4.3. Let $\mathcal{Z} = (Z, \Omega, p)$ be a sample space, and let f be a vector-valued random variable defined on Z. Then for any ω in Ω if the series

$$\sum_{z \varepsilon Z} |f(z)| p_\omega(z)$$

converges, the vector

$$\sum_{z \varepsilon Z} f(z) p_\omega(z)$$

is called the expectation (mean or expected value) of f, given ω (where as in Chapter 2, $|f(z)|$ stands for $\sqrt{f_1{}^2(z) + \cdots + f_k{}^2(z)}$ and $f_1(z)$, $\cdots, f_k(z)$ are the components of the vector $f(z)$). This vector is denoted by $E_\omega(f)$.

Theorem 3.4.1. Let $\mathcal{Z} = (Z, \Omega, p)$ be a sample space, let f be a random variable defined on Z, and let φ be a vector-valued function whose domain of definition includes the range B of f. Then, for any ω in Ω,

Note:
$\bigcirc =_{df}$ Composite.

$$E_\omega(\varphi \circ f) = \sum_{b \varepsilon B} \varphi(b) q_\omega(b)$$

where q_ω is the probability distribution of f given ω.

Proof.

$$E_\omega(\varphi \circ f) = \sum_{z \varepsilon Z} \varphi(f(z)) p_\omega(z)$$

$$= \sum_{b \varepsilon B} \varphi(b) \sum_{\{z: f(z) = b\}} p_\omega(z) = \sum_{b \varepsilon B} \varphi(b) q_\omega(b)$$

Theorem 3.4.1 asserts that it is sufficient to know the probability distribution of f to compute the expectation of any function of the values of f. In particular, if φ is the *characteristic function* of a set S in X, i.e., $\varphi[f(z)] = 1$ if $f(z) \varepsilon S$ and $\varphi[f(z)] = 0$ if $f(z) \notin S$, the probability of an event S can be computed without any reference to the space \mathcal{Z}. In subsequent discussions it will entail no loss of generality and it will sometimes be convenient to take as our sample space the triple $\mathfrak{X} = (X, \Omega, q)$. When f is vector-valued, which is often the case in statistics, its range X is a subset of n space.

As a final remark, we wish to point out that any random variable f, and hence any experiment, may be viewed as a partition \mathcal{S}_f of the space

Z into sets S_x defined by

$$S_x = \{z : f(z) = x\}$$

where $x \, \varepsilon \, X$.

3.5. Statistician's Space of Strategies for Single Experiments

We now turn to the problem of characterizing the structure of the space of strategies for the statistician. For expository reasons it will be convenient first to treat the special case where the statistician is restricted to performing a *single experiment*. Such an experiment might consist of firing N bullets at a target and observing the distance of each shot from the point of aim, planting k varieties of wheat on r plots each and measuring the mean yield per plot for each variety, counting the number of bacteria on each of N Petri dishes, measuring during a period of a year the weekly gain in weight of N animals which were fed a special diet, and so forth. A single experiment usually consists of a finite number of subexperiments, and the outcome of a subexperiment may itself be a vector with a fixed number of components. What makes an experiment a *single experiment* is the fact that a prescribed number of subexperiments are performed. A single experiment is often referred to as a *fixed sample-size* experiment, and the number of components in the resulting vector is called the *size of the sample*.

As was previously indicated, the space of pure strategies for the statistician in a statistical game with no experimentation is simply a space A whose elements are the possible actions that he can take. In a game with a single experiment, the number of strategies for the statistician becomes vastly increased, for he must now decide on a rule that will associate with each possible outcome of the experiment a point a in A. Such a rule is a *decision function*, which is defined as follows.

Definition 3.5.1. Let $Z = (Z, \Omega, p)$ be a sample space, and let A be an arbitrary space of actions or decisions. Then a function d which is defined on Z and which maps Z into A is called a decision function. The class D of decision functions is the class of pure strategies for the statistician.

We remark that a decision function d in D is a random variable, and it can be considered as a partition of the set Z into mutually exclusive subsets

$$S_a = \{z : d(z) = a\}$$

whose union is Z. If the outcome of a single experiment is an element in S_a, action a is taken. Thus, for example, if A consists of two elements

a_1 and a_2, then a strategy d is a division of Z into a set S, sometimes called a *critical region*, and its complement $C(S)$ such that, if $z \in S$, action a_1 is taken, and, if $z \in C(S)$, action a_2 is taken.

In order to define a statistical game with a single experiment, we need to introduce only two more concepts, that of a loss function and that of a payoff or risk function. These two concepts, as well as those already defined, are illustrated in the example following Definition 3.5.4. These concepts will be treated in greater detail in the next chapter, but formal definitions are given here for the sake of completeness.

Definition 3.5.2. Let $Z = (Z, \Omega, p)$ be a sample space, and let A be an arbitrary space of actions. Then a bounded numerical function L defined on the product space $\Omega \times A$ with values $L(\omega, a)$ is called a loss function.

In the definition of *risk function* we use the composition of the functions L_ω and d, where L is a loss function and d a decision function.

Definition 3.5.3. Let $Z = (Z, \Omega, p)$ be a sample space, let A be an arbitrary space of actions, let D be a class of decision functions mapping Z into A, and let L be a loss function defined on $\Omega \times A$. Then the payoff or risk function is the function ρ defined on $\Omega \times D$ such that

$$\rho(\omega, d) = \sum_{z \in Z} L(\omega, d(z))p_\omega(z)$$

We remark that, since the loss function L is bounded, the risk function ρ is bounded, and the number $\rho(\omega, d)$ always exists.

In view of the foregoing discussion, we are now in a position to give a general definition of a statistical game with a single experiment.

Definition 3.5.4. Let $Z = (Z, \Omega, p)$ be a sample space, let A be an arbitrary space of actions, let D be a class of decision functions mapping Z into A, and let ρ be a risk function defined on $\Omega \times D$. Then the game $G = (\Omega, D, \rho)$ is called a statistical game with a single experiment (or a fixed sample-size game).

The following is an illustration of a statistical game with a single experiment.

A chemist desires to estimate the average number of inert particles per cubic centimeter of a liquid produced by a chemical process. It is assumed that the number z of particles in any volume v of the liquid produced by the process has a Poisson distribution. That is to say,

(1) $$p(z \mid \omega) = \frac{(\omega v)^z e^{-\omega v}}{z!}, \qquad 0 \leq \omega < \infty$$

where ω is the expected number of particles per cubic centimeter of the liquid. The chemist decides to base his estimate on the number of particles he finds in a microscopic examination of a specified volume v of the liquid. He measures the loss by a multiple of the square of the difference between his estimated value of ω and the true value of ω which is unknown to him.

In this example, the space Z consists of all non-negative integers. Nature's space of pure strategies Ω is the non-negative half of the real line. The sample space is the triple (Z, Ω, p) where p is given by (1). The space of decisions A consists of all real numbers a with $0 \le a < \infty$. For any a and ω, the loss function L is defined by

$$(2) \qquad L(\omega, a) = k(\omega - a)^2$$

where k is a positive constant. A decision function d is a rule, which to each possible number z of particles counted in a selected volume v assigns a number a in A which the chemist is to consider as an estimate of ω. Thus a possible decision function d is

$$(3) \qquad d(z) = z/v$$

For any decision function d, the risk function ρ for this problem is given by

$$(4) \qquad \rho(\omega, d) = k \sum_{z=0}^{\infty} [\omega - d(z)]^2 \frac{(\omega v)^z e^{-\omega v}}{z!}$$

If, for example, d is defined by (3), then

$$\rho(\omega, d) = \frac{k}{v^2} \sum_{z=0}^{\infty} (\omega v - z)^2 \frac{(\omega v)^z e^{-\omega v}}{z!} = \frac{k\omega}{v}$$

which is linear in ω.

We observe that the loss function L defined by (2) is unbounded so that $\rho(\omega, d)$ may not exist for all d. In many estimation problems [see Chapter 11] the requirement that L be bounded will often be replaced by the weaker requirement that L be bounded from below, i.e., that there exist a positive constant K such that $L(\omega, a) > -K$ for all a and ω.

3.6. Mixed Strategies for Single-Experiment Games

Having defined a single-experiment game G, the definition of the mixed extension $\Gamma = (\Xi, H, \rho)$ of G presents no difficulties and is, in fact, the same as that given in Definition 1.8.2 for general games. There is, however, a difference in nomenclature between general games and

statistical games. A mixed strategy for nature is, in statistical language, often called an *a priori probability distribution* for the states on which ξ is defined, and the space Ξ of mixed strategies is called the space of a priori probability distributions. Another concept which plays an important role in statistical games is that of an *a posteriori probability distribution*. To define a posteriori probability and the related concept of the *a posteriori risk* we need to introduce the more general notion of *conditional probability* and *conditional expectation*.

Definition 3.6.1. Let S be an event in a sample space $Z = (Z, \Omega, p)$ and let f be any vector-valued random variable defined on Z. For any $\omega \, \varepsilon \, \Omega$ for which $P_\omega(S) > 0$, the vector

$$(3.6.1) \qquad\qquad \sum_{z \, \varepsilon \, S} \frac{f(z) p_\omega(z)}{P_\omega(S)}$$

is called the conditional expectation of f, given S and ω, provided $\sum_{z \, \varepsilon \, S} |f(z)| \, p_\omega(z)$ is finite, and is denoted by $E_\omega(f \mid S)$. If f is the characteristic function of a set T, the number $E_\omega(f \mid S)$ is called the conditional probability of the event T, given S and ω, and is denoted by $P_\omega(T \mid S)$.

In statistical terminology, the quantity $P_\omega(T \mid S)$ is the probability that the outcome of an experiment will be a point in a set T in Z, given that the outcome is a point in a set S in Z and given that nature is in state ω. Note that $P_\omega(T \mid S)$ exists for all ω such that $P_\omega(S) > 0$. Also $P_\omega(T \mid S) = 0$ unless $T \cap S$ is not empty. If $T \cap S$ is not empty, then

$$(3.6.2) \qquad\qquad P_\omega(T \mid S) = \frac{\sum_{z \, \varepsilon \, T \cap S} p_\omega(z)}{P_\omega(S)}$$

and, if $T = S$, $P_\omega(S \mid S) = 1$. The above remarks are summarized in the following theorem:

Theorem 3.6.1. Let S be an event in a sample space $Z = (Z, \Omega, p)$, and let Ω_S consist of all $\omega \, \varepsilon \, \Omega$ such that $P_\omega(S) > 0$. Assume Ω_S is not empty. Let $p^*_\omega(z) = p_\omega(z \mid S)$ for all $\omega \, \varepsilon \, \Omega_S$. Then $Z^* = (Z, \Omega_S, p^*)$ is a sample space. If expectations on the new sample space are denoted by E^*, then $E^*_\omega(f) = E_\omega(f \mid S)$ for all random variables f.

The above theorem asserts among other things that conditional expectations are simply expectations for a new sample space so that all theorems about expectations are valid also for conditional expectations. Thus, for instance

$$E_\omega[(f_1 + f_2) \mid S] = E_\omega(f_1 \mid S) + E_\omega(f_2 \mid S)$$

Definition 3.6.2. Let $Z = (Z, \Omega, p)$ be a sample space. For any partition S of Z, any $\omega \, \varepsilon \, \Omega$, and any random variable f, the random variable h which for each $z \, \varepsilon \, S \, \varepsilon \, S$ has the constant value

$$h(z) = E_\omega(f \mid S)$$

is called the conditional expectation of f with respect to the partition S and is denoted by $E_\omega(f \mid S)$.

Note that $E_\omega(f \mid S)$ may fail to exist for either of two reasons: (1) For some $S \, \varepsilon \, S$, $P_\omega(S) = 0$, or (2) $\sum\limits_{z \, \varepsilon \, S} |f(z)| \, p_\omega(z)$ diverges.

Definition 3.6.3. Let g be any random variable, and let v be any point in the range of g. The sets $S_v = \{z : g(z) = v\}$ form a partition S_g on the sample space determined by g. For a fixed ω, the random variable $E_\omega(f \mid S_g)$, also written $E_\omega(f \mid g)$, is called the conditional expectation of f, given g.

Let $Z = (Z, \Omega, p)$ be a sample space, and let Ξ be a class of randomized strategies for nature defined on Ω. We are interested in finding a function q such that, for each $\xi \, \varepsilon \, \Xi$, q_ξ is a probability distribution on $Z \times \Omega$ which assigns the value $\xi(\omega)$ to the event $Z \times \{\omega\}$ and the value $p(z \mid \omega)$ to the conditional event $\{z\} \times \Omega$, given that the event $Z \times \{\omega\}$ has occurred. More precisely, we are looking for a function q such that the sample space

$$Z' = (Z \times \Omega, \Xi, q)$$

has the property that for every z, ω, and ξ

(1) $$Q_\xi(Z \times \{\omega\}) = \xi(\omega)$$

and for $\xi(\omega) > 0$

(2) $$Q_\xi(\{z\} \times \Omega \mid Z \times \{\omega\}) = p(z \mid \omega)$$

where for any set S in $Z \times \Omega$

$$Q_\xi(S) = \sum\limits_{(z, \, \omega) \, \varepsilon \, S} q_\xi(z, \omega)$$

Consider any ω for which $\xi(\omega) > 0$. Then, since Q_ξ satisfies (1) and (2), we have by (3.6.2)

(3) $$q_\xi(z, \omega) = p(z \mid \omega)\xi(\omega)$$

If $\xi(\omega) = 0$, then (3) holds by (1) since, if a set has probability zero, every element in it has probability zero. Conversely, a function q satisfying (3) also satisfies (1) and (2) as can be seen by direct computation.

Let $Z' = Z \times \Omega$, and let g and h be two random variables defined on Z' such that for $z' = (z, \omega)\ \varepsilon\ Z'$

$$g(z') = z \quad \text{and} \quad h(z') = \omega$$

Then, by Definition 3.4.2, the function q_ξ is the joint probability distribution of g and h, given ξ.

It follows from (2) that if nature employs a mixed strategy ξ, the quantity $p(z \mid \omega)$ is then in fact the conditional probability of z, given ω.

Let S be any set in $Z' = Z \times \Omega$ such that $Q_\xi(S) > 0$. Then for any vector-valued random variable f defined on Z' the conditional expected value of f, given S [see Definition 3.6.1], is

$$E_\xi(f \mid S) = \frac{\displaystyle\sum_{z' \,\varepsilon\, S} f(z')q_\xi(z')}{Q_\xi(S)}$$

We consider two special cases for f and S which are of statistical importance.

Case 1. $f(z') = 1$ for $z' = (z, \omega)$; $f(z') = 0$ otherwise; $S = \{z\} \times \Omega$. Then

$$E_\xi(f \mid S) = \frac{p(z \mid \omega)\xi(\omega)}{\displaystyle\sum_{\theta\, \varepsilon\, \Omega} p(z \mid \theta)\xi(\theta)}$$

That is, $E_\xi(f \mid S)$ represents in this case the conditional probability that nature's randomized choice is ω, given that the outcome of the experiment is z. This conditional probability is known as the a posteriori probability of ω, given z, and is designated by $\xi_z(\omega)$. (The expression for $\xi_z(\omega)$ is also known as Bayes' formula.) Formally we have the following definition:

Definition 3.6.4. Let $\mathcal{Z} = (Z, \Omega, p)$ be a sample space, and let Ξ be a class of probability functions defined on Ω. Then the a posteriori probability distribution of ω, given z, is the conditional distribution of ω, given z, i.e., the function ξ_z which for a fixed $z\ \varepsilon\ Z$ is defined on $\Xi \times \Omega$ and which is such that

$$\xi_z(\omega) = \frac{p(z \mid \omega)\xi(\omega)}{\displaystyle\sum_{\theta\, \varepsilon\, \Omega} p(z \mid \theta)\xi(\theta)}$$

Case 2. $f(z') = L(\omega, d(z))$ for some $d \varepsilon D$; and $S = \{z\} \times \Omega$. Then

$$E_\xi(f \mid S) = \frac{\sum\limits_{\omega \varepsilon \Omega} L(\omega, d(z)) p(z \mid \omega) \xi(\omega)}{\sum\limits_{\omega \varepsilon \Omega} p(z \mid \omega) \xi(\omega)}$$

$$= \sum_{\omega \varepsilon \Omega} L(\omega, d(z)) \xi_z(\omega)$$

That is, $E_\xi(f \mid S)$ is the conditional risk, given z. This quantity will be designated by $\tau_z(d)$. The dependence of this function upon ξ will be suppressed, since in any given discussion ξ will be fixed. Formally we have the following definition.

Definition 3.6.5. Let $Z = (Z, \Omega, p)$ be a sample space, let A be an arbitrary space of actions, let D be a class of decision functions mapping Z into A, let L be a loss function defined on $\Omega \times A$, let Ξ be a class of probability distributions defined on Ω, and let ξ_z be the a posteriori probability distribution of ω for ξ in Ξ and z in Z. Then the function τ_z which for a fixed $z \varepsilon Z$ is defined on $\Xi \times D$ and which is such that

$$\tau_z(d) = \sum_{\omega \varepsilon \Omega} L(\omega, d(z)) \xi_z(\omega)$$

is called the conditional or a posteriori risk function given z and d. For $a \varepsilon A$, $\tau_z(a)$ denotes the number $\tau_z(d)$ for the particular function d with $d(z) \equiv a$.

It will often be found convenient to consider an equivalent class [see Theorems 7.2.1 and 8.3.1] of randomized strategies for the statistician defined not on the space of functions D but rather on the sample space.

Definition 3.6.6. Let $Z = (Z, \Omega, p)$ be a sample space, let A be a space of actions, and let Φ be a class of functions φ defined on $A \times Z$ such that, for each $z \varepsilon Z$, φ_z is a probability distribution on A. Then Φ is a space of randomized strategies for the statistician.

To select a randomized strategy φ from Φ is to select the following rule of behavior: For every outcome z of a single experiment, the statistician chooses action a with probability $\varphi_z(a) = \varphi(a \mid z)$. The risk function ρ is then defined as follows:

Definition 3.6.7. Let $Z = (Z, \Omega, p)$ be a sample space, let A be a space of actions, let Φ be a space of randomized strategies for the statistician, and let L be a loss function defined on $\Omega \times A$. Then the (ran-

domized) risk function is the function ρ defined on $\Omega \times \Phi$, such that

$$\rho(\omega, \varphi) = \sum_{a \,\epsilon\, A} L(\omega, a) E_\omega(\varphi(a \mid z)) = \sum_{a \,\epsilon\, A} \sum_{z \,\epsilon\, Z} L(\omega, a)\varphi(a \mid z)p(z \mid \omega)$$

where φ is in Φ.

3.7. Games Involving Densities

In order to enlarge the scope of the applicability of the statistical theory to be developed, it will be necessary for illustrative purposes to discard the restriction that every $\omega \,\epsilon\, \Omega$ is zero except on a countable set in Z. For these purposes a sample space is defined as a triple $\mathfrak{X} = (X, \Omega, p)$ where X is an n space and for each $\omega \,\epsilon\, \Omega$, p_ω is a *density* defined on X (see Definition 2.6.2). A vector-valued function f defined on X is a *random variable*, and, if the integral

$$\int_X f(\mathbf{x})p_\omega(\mathbf{x}) \, d\mathbf{x}$$

exists, it is called the *expectation* of f, given ω, and is denoted by $E_\omega(f)$. In particular, if f is the characteristic function of a set B in X, then $E_\omega(f)$ is called the *probability of the set B, given ω*. For $\mathbf{x} = (x_1, \cdots, x_n)$ any element of X, let $f_{\mathbf{x}}$ be the characteristic function of the set

$$B_{\mathbf{x}} = \{\mathbf{y} : \mathbf{y} = (y_1, \cdots, y_n) \,\epsilon\, X, y_1 \leq x_1, \cdots, y_n \leq x_n\}$$

Then the function F_ω such that

$$F_\omega(\mathbf{x}) = E_\omega(f_{\mathbf{x}})$$

is called the *cumulative distribution function (cdf) of the vector \mathbf{x}, given ω.*

Let \mathcal{P}_Ω consist of densities, and let d be a function mapping X into the space of actions A. The risk function ρ is defined by

(1) $$\rho(\omega, d) = \int_X L(\omega, d(\mathbf{x}))p_\omega(\mathbf{x}) \, d\mathbf{x}$$

We conclude this section by defining the a posteriori probability distribution $\xi_{\mathbf{x}}$ of ω, given \mathbf{x}, and the a posteriori risk function $\tau_{\mathbf{x}}$ for the case where Ξ is a class of densities defined on Ω. For this purpose we take Ω to be a k-dimensional Cartesian space. Each element in Ω determines a probability distribution or density on X. The function $\xi_{\mathbf{x}}$ is then defined by the equation

$$\xi_{\mathbf{x}}(\omega) = \frac{p(\mathbf{x} \mid \omega)\xi(\omega)}{\displaystyle\int_{-\infty}^{\infty} \cdots \int_{-\infty}^{\infty} p(\mathbf{x} \mid \theta)\xi(\theta) \, d\theta_1, \cdots, d\theta_k}$$

and the a posteriori risk function $\tau_{\mathbf{x}}$ is defined by the equation

$$\tau_{\mathbf{x}}(d) = \int_{-\infty}^{\infty} \cdots \int_{-\infty}^{\infty} L(\boldsymbol{\omega}, d(\mathbf{x})) \xi_{\mathbf{x}}(\boldsymbol{\omega}) \, d\omega_1, \cdots, d\omega_k$$

3.8. Preliminary Remarks Concerning Sequential Games

The single-experiment game, though often encountered in statistical-decision theory and practice, is a very special type of game. By restricting the experimenter to a fixed sample-size experiment, the class of strategies open to him deals only with the type of action he is to take once he knows the outcome of the experiment. But clearly the conduct of the experiment itself can be made into a legitimate strategy for him. Thus, for example, instead of exhausting all N observations, the experimenter might take observations in sequence and at each stage decide on the basis of the information thus far collected whether to stop experimenting and select an element from A or to take another observation. If the observations were costless, the enlargement of the class of strategies by introducing sequential-sampling procedures of the above type would not alter his behavior, since he couldn't lose and might actually gain by taking all N observations (assuming he is restricted to that many). However, in most real situations, observations are costly, and the experimenter might greatly improve his situation if at each stage of experimentation he balances the cost of taking future observations against the expected gain in information from such observations.

As an illustration of what might be gained by allowing sequential procedures as part of the decision maker's strategy, consider the following example: An inspector at an Army Proving Ground has to decide whether to accept or reject a lot of rocket-propellent powder on the basis of the performance of 5 randomly selected rockets which he is to fire. A propellent is called defective if the pressure developed in the rocket chamber is 3000 lb. or more per square inch. The acceptability of the lot depends on the proportion of defective items in the lot, and the decision is to be based on the number of defective rockets found in the sample of 5. (In practice, the actual pressures observed would presumably form the basis for a decision. The problem as stated is somewhat artificial but has been chosen as an illustration because of the simplicity of the resulting space of outcomes X.)

For each rocket fired, let x be the random variable which has value 1 if the propellent is defective and 0 otherwise. Then, if all 5 rockets are fired, the space of outcomes X consists of the 32 points x_1, \cdots, x_{32} given on the next page.

Space of Outcomes for a Binomial Variable with 5 Observations

$x_1 = (0, 0, 0, 0, 0)$	$x_9 = (0, 0, 0, 1, 0)$	$x_{17} = (0, 0, 0, 0, 1)$	$x_{25} = (0, 0, 0, 1, 1)$
$x_2 = (0, 1, 0, 0, 0)$	$x_{10} = (0, 1, 0, 1, 0)$	$x_{18} = (0, 1, 0, 0, 1)$	$x_{26} = (0, 1, 0, 1, 1)$
$x_3 = (1, 0, 0, 0, 0)$	$x_{11} = (1, 0, 0, 1, 0)$	$x_{19} = (1, 0, 0, 0, 1)$	$x_{27} = (1, 0, 0, 1, 1)$
$x_4 = (1, 1, 0, 0, 0)$	$x_{12} = (1, 1, 0, 1, 0)$	$x_{20} = (1, 1, 0, 0, 1)$	$x_{28} = (1, 1, 0, 1, 1)$
$x_5 = (0, 0, 1, 0, 0)$	$x_{13} = (0, 0, 1, 1, 0)$	$x_{21} = (0, 0, 1, 0, 1)$	$x_{29} = (0, 0, 1, 1, 1)$
$x_6 = (0, 1, 1, 0, 0)$	$x_{14} = (0, 1, 1, 1, 0)$	$x_{22} = (0, 1, 1, 0, 1)$	$x_{30} = (0, 1, 1, 1, 1)$
$x_7 = (1, 0, 1, 0, 0)$	$x_{15} = (1, 0, 1, 1, 0)$	$x_{23} = (1, 0, 1, 0, 1)$	$x_{31} = (1, 0, 1, 1, 1)$
$x_8 = (1, 1, 1, 0, 0)$	$x_{16} = (1, 1, 1, 1, 0)$	$x_{24} = (1, 1, 1, 0, 1)$	$x_{32} = (1, 1, 1, 1, 1)$

The space A of actions consists of only two points, a_1, a_2 where a_1 stands for the acceptance and a_2 the rejection of the lot.

It will be shown in Chapter 7 that, however the Government measures losses from a wrong decision, a class of "admissible" strategies [see Definition 5.4.9] if all 5 rockets are fired is given by the following: Let m stand for the number of coordinates that have value 1 in x, and let k be any integer from 0 to 4. Then accept the lot if $m \leq k$ (i.e., define $d(x) = a_1$ if $m \leq k$), and reject the lot if $m > k$ (i.e., define $d(x) = a_2$ if $m > k$).

Now it is clear that, since firing a rocket is costly, the Government might gain appreciably if the rockets were fired one at a time and the appropriate decision made as soon as the value of d became known. Thus, for example, if $k = 0$, after the first observation it becomes known that $d(x_i) = a_2$ for $i = 3$, 4, 7, 8, 11, 12, 15, 16, 19, 20, 23, 24, 27, 28, 31, and 32; after the second observation it becomes known that $d(x_i) = a_2$ for $i = 2$, 6, 10, 14, 18, 22, 26, and 30, and so forth. In fact, only if the outcome of the experiment is x_1 or x_{17} will all 5 observations be required to make a decision. Similarly, if $k = 2$, after 3 observations it becomes known that $d(x_i) = a_2$ for $i = 8$, 16, 24, 32 and $d(x_i) = a_1$ for $i = 1$, 9, 17, 25. Thus we see that, though the above class of decision procedures is admissible as a costless fixed sample-size experiment, it is definitely not admissible if the cost of the observations is taken into account. To find a class of admissible decision procedures in the latter case, we must enlarge the class of strategies by introducing sequential-sampling procedures.

3.9. Space of Statistician's Strategies in Truncated Sequential Games

To define a statistical game with sequential-sampling procedures as possible strategies for the statistician, we must envisage an experiment as consisting of a series of subexperiments, each subexperiment being a choice of a random variable defined on a fixed sample space \mathcal{Z}. To avoid technical complications we make the following two assumptions:

(1) The total number of possible subexperiments does not exceed a certain preassigned integer N.

(2) The sequence in which these experiments are to be performed is predetermined and is not part of the statistician's strategy.

Assumption 1 states that we shall be dealing only with *truncated* sequential procedures. This restriction is necessary since the notion of a joint probability distribution has been defined only for a finite number of random variables (see Definition 3.4.2). However, in Chapter 9 this restriction will be removed for a large class of statistical-decision problems. Assumption 2 is of no consequence if the random variables arising from the choice of the subexperiments are independently and identically distributed for each $\omega \, \varepsilon \, \Omega$ [see Definition 3.11.3]. In all other cases the sequence in which the subexperiments are performed does matter and complicates the characterization of a general sequential procedure.

Under assumptions 1 and 2 the sample space $\mathfrak{X} = (X, \, \Omega, \, q)$ has the following structure: For each ω in Ω the function q_ω is a probability distribution defined on X and each point $x \, \varepsilon \, X$ is an N-tuple $x = (x_1, \, x_2, \, \cdots, \, x_N)$ where each x_i, $i = 1, \, \cdots, \, N$, is the value of a random variable, but we allow the possibility of not observing all the coordinates of a point x but only the first $j = 1, \, 2, \, \cdots, \, N$ of them before a decision is made. That is, we shall now consider rules that to each point x of X assign two numbers, an integer $j = 1, \, 2, \, \cdots, \, N$ which specifies the number of coordinates of x to observe before terminating experimentation, and an element a of A which specifies what action is to be taken once experimentation is terminated. It is clear that, if a rule assigns the value $(j, \, a)$ to a point $x \, \varepsilon \, X$ and if a point $y \, \varepsilon \, X$ has the same first j coordinates as x, the rule must assign the same value $(j, \, a)$ to y also. Thus a truncated sequential procedure is a decision function δ with values $\delta(x) = (\nu(x), \, \alpha(x))$ which maps every point $x = (x_1, \, \cdots, \, x_N)$ of X into the product space $J \times A$ with elements $(j, \, a)$ where J stands for the set of integers $(0, \, 1, \, \cdots, \, N)$ and A is the set of terminal actions, and, if $\delta(x) = (j_0, \, a_0)$, then, for every $y = (y_1, \, \cdots, \, y_N) \, \varepsilon \, X$ such that $y_i = x_i$ for $0 < i \leq j_0$, $\delta(y) = (j_0, \, a_0)$ also. The reason zero is included in the set J is to permit taking an action without experimentation which may sometimes be desirable in case the cost of taking observations is high. Thus for any function δ such that $\delta(x) = (0, \, a)$ for any $x \, \varepsilon \, X$ then $\delta(x) = (0, \, a)$ for all $x \, \varepsilon \, X$.

As an illustration of sequential sampling rules, consider the rocket-firing experiment with the sample space X discussed above. A possible sequential rule is as follows: fire the rockets 1 at a time and stop as soon as 2 defectives are found; in any case stop when all 5 rockets have been

fired. Let n be the number of rockets fired by this rule. Suppose that the first problem is to decide whether to accept or reject the lot. A possible criterion is the following: accept the lot (i.e., take action a_1) if $n \geq 4$; reject the lot (i.e., take action a_2) otherwise. The function δ then has the following values:

$\delta(x_1) = (5, a_1)$	$\delta(x_9) = (5, a_1)$	$\delta(x_{17}) = (5, a_1)$	$\delta(x_{25}) = (5, a_1)$
$\delta(x_2) = (5, a_1)$	$\delta(x_{10}) = (4, a_1)$	$\delta(x_{18}) = (5, a_1)$	$\delta(x_{26}) = (4, a_1)$
$\delta(x_3) = (5, a_1)$	$\delta(x_{11}) = (4, a_1)$	$\delta(x_{19}) = (5, a_1)$	$\delta(x_{27}) = (4, a_1)$
$\delta(x_4) = (2, a_2)$	$\delta(x_{12}) = (2, a_2)$	$\delta(x_{20}) = (2, a_2)$	$\delta(x_{28}) = (2, a_2)$
$\delta(x_5) = (5, a_1)$	$\delta(x_{13}) = (4, a_1)$	$\delta(x_{21}) = (5, a_1)$	$\delta(x_{29}) = (4, a_1)$
$\delta(x_6) = (3, a_2)$	$\delta(x_{14}) = (3, a_2)$	$\delta(x_{22}) = (3, a_2)$	$\delta(x_{30}) = (3, a_2)$
$\delta(x_7) = (3, a_2)$	$\delta(x_{15}) = (3, a_2)$	$\delta(x_{23}) = (3, a_2)$	$\delta(x_{31}) = (3, a_2)$
$\delta(x_8) = (2, a_2)$	$\delta(x_{16}) = (2, a_2)$	$\delta(x_{24}) = (2, a_2)$	$\delta(x_{32}) = (2, a_2)$

Suppose now that the second problem is to estimate the proportion p of defective items in the lot. The space of actions A in this case is the closed interval $(0, 1)$. A possible sequential estimation rule is the following: Let m be the number of defectives found; if $n < 5$, take $(m - 1)/(n - 1)$ as an estimate of p, and if $n = 5$, take $m/5$ as an estimate. For this estimation procedure, the function δ has the following values:

$\delta(x_1) = (5, 0)$	$\delta(x_9) = (5, 1/5)$	$\delta(x_{17}) = (5, 1/5)$	$\delta(x_{25}) = (5, 2/5)$
$\delta(x_2) = (5, 1/5)$	$\delta(x_{10}) = (4, 1/3)$	$\delta(x_{18}) = (5, 2/5)$	$\delta(x_{26}) = (4, 1/3)$
$\delta(x_3) = (5, 1/5)$	$\delta(x_{11}) = (4, 1/3)$	$\delta(x_{19}) = (5, 2/5)$	$\delta(x_{27}) = (4, 1/3)$
$\delta(x_4) = (2, 1)$	$\delta(x_{12}) = (2, 1)$	$\delta(x_{20}) = (2, 1)$	$\delta(x_{28}) = (2, 1)$
$\delta(x_5) = (5, 1/5)$	$\delta(x_{13}) = (4, 1/3)$	$\delta(x_{21}) = (5, 2/5)$	$\delta(x_{29}) = (4, 1/3)$
$\delta(x_6) = (3, 1/2)$	$\delta(x_{14}) = (3, 1/2)$	$\delta(x_{22}) = (3, 1/2)$	$\delta(x_{30}) = (3, 1/2)$
$\delta(x_7) = (3, 1/2)$	$\delta(x_{15}) = (3, 1/2)$	$\delta(x_{23}) = (3, 1/2)$	$\delta(x_{31}) = (3, 1/2)$
$\delta(x_8) = (2, 1)$	$\delta(x_{16}) = (2, 1)$	$\delta(x_{24}) = (2, 1)$	$\delta(x_{32}) = (2, 1)$

It is clear from the above examples that every sequential-sampling plan and terminal-decision rule defines a function δ of the type considered. It is not, however, immediately obvious that a sequential-decision function δ is in fact a rule that tells the experimenter at each stage whether to take another observation or to stop experimenting and make the specified decision. To see that this is the case we give a second definition of a sequential procedure where such a rule is clearly implied and show that the two definitions are equivalent.

Let J be the set of integers $(0, 1, 2, \cdots, N)$, and let K be any subset of J. A set S in X is called *a cylinder set over K* if whenever $x_i = y_i$ for all $i \in K$, $i \neq 0$; then $x \in S$ if and only if $y \in S$. (Note that, in order to prove that a set is a cylinder set over K, it is sufficient to prove the "if"

part or the "only if" part since the definition is symmetric in x and y.)
In terms of cylinder sets we define a sequential procedure as follows:

A sequential procedure δ^* consists of a partition \mathcal{S} of X with elements S_0, S_1, \cdots, S_N such that each S_j is a cylinder set over $K = \{r \varepsilon J : 0 < r \leq j\}$, together with a sequence of functions d_0, d_1, \cdots, d_N such that, for each j, d_j is a function of the first j coordinates of x only and maps S_j into A. We shall call the partition \mathcal{S} a sequential-sampling plan and the sequence of functions $\{d_j\}$ a terminal-decision rule. We remark that S_0 is either all of X, in which case S_j is empty for $j > 0$, or S_0 is empty. Also the sequence of functions $\{d_j\}$ will generally depend on the partition \mathcal{S}. This dependence will not however be exhibited in what follows.

We now show that the two definitions are equivalent. Assume that δ^* consisting of a sequential-sampling plan \mathcal{S} and terminal-decision rule $\{d_j\}$ is given. To find a sequential function δ, we let $\nu(x)$ be that j such that $x \varepsilon S_j$ and define $\alpha(x) = d_{\nu(x)}(x)$. Clearly, the function δ which for every $x \varepsilon X$ has the value

$$\delta(x) = (\nu(x), \alpha(x))$$

is a uniquely defined sequential-decision rule. Conversely, let a sequential-decision rule δ with $\delta(x) = (\nu(x), \alpha(x))$ be given, we shall find a sampling plan \mathcal{S} and a decision rule $\{d_j\}$. If δ is such that $\delta(x) \equiv (0, a)$, we take for \mathcal{S} the set $S_0 = X$ and for $\{d_j\}$ the single function d_0 with $d_0(x) \equiv a$. Otherwise, we define

$$S_k = \{x : \nu(x) = k\}$$

and show that S_k is a cylinder set. Suppose $x \varepsilon S_k$, and let y be such that, for $0 < i \leq k$, $x_i = y_i$. Then, by the definition of δ, $\delta(x) = \delta(y)$ so that $\nu(x) = \nu(y) = k$, and hence $y \varepsilon S_k$ also. To define a terminal-decision function d_k for each S_k, we set $d_k(x) = \alpha(x)$. Then $d_k(x)$ depends only on the first k coordinates of x since, if $y_i = x_i$ for $0 < i \leq k$, then, by the definition of S_k and the condition on δ, $\delta(x) = \delta(y)$ and $\alpha(x) = \alpha(y)$, and, consequently, $d_k(x) = d_k(y)$. Thus, d_k is a mapping of the required type.

Finally, simple considerations show that, if we start with a sequential-decision function δ and apply the above construction to obtain a sequential procedure δ^* and from this δ^* in turn obtain a sequential-decision rule δ', then $\delta' = \delta$. Conversely, if we start with a δ^* and obtain a δ and from this δ a δ^{**}, then $\delta^* = \delta^{**}$.

In many statistical problems, the sequential-sampling plan \mathcal{S} is fixed. What is required is to find an optimal terminal-decision rule. For this and other reasons which will become clear in Chapter 9, it is con-

venient to remove the dependence of the terminal-decision rule $\{d_j\}$ upon the partition S. To this end we define a general class D of terminal-decision functions d, mapping the product space $J \times X$ into A such that, if $d(j, x) = a$ and y is any other point in X such that $y_i = x_i$ for $0 < i \leq j$, then $d(j, y) = a$ also. Clearly, given any sequential-sampling plan S and any $d \, \varepsilon \, D$, then d determines a sequence of terminal-decision functions d_j such that d_j maps $S_j \, \varepsilon \, S$ into A. We now give a formal definition of a class of sequential-decision functions which will be employed in this book.

Definition 3.9.1. Let $Z = (Z, \Omega, p)$ be a sample space, let f_1, \cdots, f_N be random variables defined on Z, let $\mathfrak{X} = (X, \Omega, q)$ be the sample space such that $X = X_1 \times X_2 \times \cdots \times X_N$ where X_i is the range of f_i, $i = 1, 2, \cdots, N$, \mathcal{Q}_Ω is obtained from \mathcal{P}_Ω according to Definition 3.4.2. In addition, let A be an arbitrary space of actions, let $J = \{0, 1, \cdots, N\}$, and let \mathfrak{S} be the class of partitions of X such that, if $S = (S_0, S_1, \cdots, S_N) \, \varepsilon \, \mathfrak{S}$, then each element S_j of S is a cylinder set over $K = \{r \, \varepsilon \, J : 0 < r \leq j\}$. Moreover, let D be the class of functions d which map $J \times X$ into A and are such that, if x and y are in X, $x_i = y_i$ for $0 < i \leq j$ and $d(j, x) = a$, then $d(j, y) = a$ also. Then the product space $\mathfrak{S} \times D$ is called the class of sequential-decision functions.

We remark that the elements (S, d) of $\mathfrak{S} \times D$ are the pure strategies for the statistician in a sequential game. We also remark that formally speaking the reference to the sample space Z and the random variables f_1, \cdots, f_N could be omitted. These concepts were introduced here to make clearer the underlying structure of sequential procedures. It is to be remembered, however, that the f_i's are not necessarily identically distributed random variables, and the spaces X_i may be different for each i.

As an illustration of a partition S, consider the sequential procedure for the rocket-firing experiment given in the second table. Here $S = (S_2, S_3, S_4, S_5)$ where

$$S_2 = \{x_4, x_8, x_{12}, x_{16}, x_{20}, x_{24}, x_{28}, x_{32}\}$$

$$S_3 = \{x_6, x_7, x_{14}, x_{15}, x_{22}, x_{23}, x_{30}, x_{31}\}$$

$$S_4 = \{x_{10}, x_{11}, x_{13}, x_{26}, x_{27}, x_{29}\}$$

$$S_5 = \{x_1, x_2, x_3, x_5, x_9, x_{17}, x_{18}, x_{19}, x_{21}, x_{25}\}$$

The function d maps the sets S_4 and S_5 into a_1; S_2 and S_3 into a_2.

3.10. Definition of Truncated Sequential Games

Having characterized the spaces of pure strategies for the two players, it remains only to specify the payoff or risk function in order to complete the definition of truncated sequential games. However, to define the risk function for games with sequential-sampling rules, it is necessary to take into account the cost of performing each subexperiment. This cost may depend only on the number of subexperiments performed, or, more generally, it may depend on the outcome of these experiments, such as, for example, in medical experiments on animals, where the cost of the observation depends on whether or not the animal survives.

Definition 3.10.1. Let $\mathfrak{X} = (X, \Omega, q)$ be a sample space, where $X = X_1 \times \cdots \times X_N$, let $J = \{0, 1, \cdots, N\}$, and let c be a non-negative function defined on $J \times X$ such that if x and y are in X and $x_i = y_i$, $i = 1, 2, \cdots, j$, then $c(j, x) = c(j, y)$. Then c is called a cost function.

Thus, for example, if the cost is simply proportional to the number of subexperiments performed, then $c(j, x) = kj$ for all x for which the decision rule requires terminating sampling with j observations and where k is a positive constant.

In what follows we shall write $c_j(x)$ for $c(j, x)$.

Definition 3.10.2. Let $\mathfrak{X} = (X, \Omega, q)$ be a sample space, where $X = X_1 \times \cdots \times X_N$, let A be a space of actions, let $\mathfrak{S} \times D$ be the class of sequential decision functions (for \mathfrak{X} and A), let L be a loss function defined on $\Omega \times A$, and let c be a cost function defined on $J \times X$, where $J = \{0, 1, \cdots, N\}$. Then the payoff or sequential risk function is the function ρ defined on $\Omega \times \mathfrak{S} \times D$ such that

$$\rho(\omega, \mathcal{S}, d) = \sum_{j=0}^{N} \sum_{x \, \varepsilon \, S_j} [c_j(x) + L(\omega, d(j, x))] q_\omega(x)$$

As in the case of a single experiment, $\rho(\omega, \mathcal{S}, d)$ will exist for all decision functions (\mathcal{S}, d) of the type considered. If X is an N space and the elements of \mathcal{Q}_Ω are densities, then the equivalent risk function is defined by

$$\rho(\omega, \mathcal{S}, d) = \sum_{j=0}^{N} \int_{S_j} \cdots \int [c_j(\mathbf{x}) + L(\omega, d(j, \mathbf{x}))] q_\omega(\mathbf{x}) \, dx_1, \cdots, dx_N$$

We now give a general definition of a truncated sequential game.

Definition 3.10.3. Let $\mathcal{Z} = (Z, \Omega, p)$ be a sample space, let f_1, \cdots, f_N be random variables defined on Z, let $\mathfrak{X} = (X, \Omega, q)$ be the sample space such that $X = X_1 \times \cdots \times X_N$, where X_i is the range of f_i, for $i = 1$,

\cdots, N, and \mathcal{Q}_Ω is obtained from \mathcal{P}_Ω according to Definition 3.4.2, let A be a space of actions, let $\mathfrak{S} \times D$ be the class of sequential-decision functions (for \mathfrak{X} and A), and let ρ be a sequential risk function defined on $\Omega \times \mathfrak{S} \times D$. Then the game $(\Omega, \mathfrak{S} \times D, \rho)$ is called a truncated-sequential game.

3.11. Some Further Theorems on Probability

The following definitions and theorems will be used in the subsequent chapters of this book.

Definition 3.11.1. Let $\mathcal{Z} = (Z, \Omega, p)$ be a sample space, let S_1, S_2, \cdots, S_n be subsets of Z, and let ω be an arbitrary element of Ω. The subsets (events) S_1, S_2, \cdots, S_n are said to be independent with respect to p_ω if, for every set of subscripts i_1, i_2, \cdots, i_k, no two equal,

$$P_\omega(S_{i_1} \cap S_{i_2} \cap \cdots \cap S_{i_k}) = P_\omega(S_{i_1})P_\omega(S_{i_2}) \cdots P_\omega(S_{i_k})$$

for $k = 2, 3, \cdots, n; i_j = 1, 2, \cdots, n$.

Definition 3.11.2. Let $\mathcal{Z} = (Z, \Omega, p)$ be a sample space, let \mathfrak{S}_1, \mathfrak{S}_2, \cdots, \mathfrak{S}_n be n partitions of Z, and let ω be an arbitrary element of Ω. The partitions \mathfrak{S}_1, \mathfrak{S}_2, \cdots, \mathfrak{S}_n are said to be independent with respect to p_ω if every collection of n sets S_1, S_2, \cdots, S_n that can be formed by taking one element from each of the n partitions is independent with respect to p_ω.

Definition 3.11.3. Let $\mathcal{Z} = (Z, \Omega, p)$ be a sample space, let f_1, f_2, \cdots, f_n be n random variables defined on Z, and let ω be an arbitrary element of Ω. The random variables f_1, f_2, \cdots, f_n are said to be independent with respect to p_ω if the partitions \mathfrak{S}_{f_1}, \mathfrak{S}_{f_2}, \cdots, \mathfrak{S}_{f_n} determined by f_1, f_2, \cdots, f_n, respectively, are independent with respect to p_ω.

Definition 3.11.4. The n events S_1, S_2, \cdots, S_n (or n partitions \mathfrak{S}_1, \mathfrak{S}_2, \cdots, \mathfrak{S}_n, or n random variables f_1, f_2, \cdots, f_n) are said to be independent with respect to \mathcal{P}_Ω if they are independent with respect to p_ω for every $\omega \varepsilon \Omega$.

Theorem 3.11.1. The partitions \mathfrak{S}_1, \mathfrak{S}_2, \cdots, \mathfrak{S}_n are independent with respect to p_ω if and only if for every collection of n sets S_1, S_2, \cdots, S_n with $S_i \varepsilon \mathfrak{S}_i$

(i) $$P_\omega(S_1 \cap \cdots \cap S_n) = P_\omega(S_1) \cdots P_\omega(S_n)$$

Proof. It follows from Definition 3.11.2 that if the partitions are independent then (i) holds. Conversely, suppose (i) holds, we must

show that the partitions are independent; i.e., for every arbitrary collection of n sets S_1, \cdots, S_n with $S_i \, \varepsilon \, \mathcal{S}_i$,

$$(1) \qquad P_\omega(S_{i_1} \cap \cdots \cap S_{i_k}) = P_\omega(S_{i_1}) \cdots P_\omega(S_{i_k})$$

where i_1, i_2, \cdots, i_k with $2 \le k \le n$ are any k arbitrary subscripts, no two of which are equal. We shall prove (1) by a backward induction on k. For $k = n$

$$(2) \qquad P_\omega(S_1 \cap \cdots \cap S_n) = \prod_{i=1}^{n} P_\omega(S_i)$$

by hypothesis. Assume that (1) holds for $k = n - 1, n - 2, \cdots,$ m $(m \ge 3)$. To show that it holds for $k = m - 1$, let i_1, i_2, \cdots, i_m be m distinct subscripts. Then since

$$(3) \qquad S_{i_1} \cap \cdots \cap S_{i_{m-1}} = \bigcup_{S_{i_m} \, \varepsilon \, \mathcal{S}_{i_m}} [S_{i_1} \cap \cdots \cap S_{i_{m-1}} \cap S_{i_m}]$$

we have

$$(4) \quad P_\omega(S_{i_1} \cap \cdots \cap S_{i_{m-1}}) = P_\omega \left[\bigcup_{S_{i_m} \, \varepsilon \, \mathcal{S}_{i_m}} (S_{i_1} \cap \cdots \cap S_{i_{m-1}} \cap S_{i_m}) \right]$$

so that, by the induction hypothesis,

$$(5) \qquad P_\omega(S_{i_1} \cap \cdots \cap S_{i_{m-1}}) = \sum_{S_{i_m} \, \varepsilon \, \mathcal{S}_{i_m}} \prod_{k=1}^{m-1} P_\omega(S_{i_k}) P_\omega(S_{i_m})$$

$$= \prod_{k=1}^{m-1} P_\omega(S_{i_k}) \sum_{S_{i_m} \, \varepsilon \, \mathcal{S}_{i_m}} P_\omega(S_{i_m})$$

But $\bigcup S_{i_m} = Z$ so that $\Sigma P_\omega(S_{i_m}) = 1$ and consequently

$$(6) \qquad P_\omega(S_{i_1} \cap \cdots \cap S_{i_{m-1}}) - \prod_{k=1}^{m-1} P_\omega(S_{i_k})$$

which proves the theorem.

Corollary 1. The random variables f_1, f_2, \cdots, f_n are independent with respect to p_ω if and only if

$$q_\omega(v_1, v_2, \cdots, v_n) = q_{1\omega}(v_1) q_{2\omega}(v_2) \cdots q_{n\omega}(v_n)$$

where q_ω is the joint probability distribution of f_1, \cdots, f_n and $q_{i\omega}$ is the distribution of f_i.

Definition 3.11.5. Let \mathfrak{I} be a partition of Z. A collection \mathcal{S} of sets of Z is called a subpartition of \mathfrak{I} if (a) \mathcal{S} is a partition of Z and (b) each $S \varepsilon \mathcal{S}$ is a subset of some T in \mathfrak{I}.

Theorem 3.11.2. Let \mathcal{S}_i $(i = 1, 2, \cdots, n)$ be subpartitions of the n partitions \mathfrak{I}_i of Z. Then, if the collection $(\mathcal{S}_1, \mathcal{S}_2, \cdots, \mathcal{S}_n)$ are independent with respect to some $p_\omega \varepsilon \mathcal{P}_\Omega$, so is the collection $\mathfrak{I}_1, \mathfrak{I}_2, \cdots, \mathfrak{I}_n$.

Before we prove this theorem, we require the following lemma.

Lemma 3.11.1. If \mathcal{S} is a subpartition of \mathfrak{I}, then any $T \varepsilon \mathfrak{I}$ is the union of sets in \mathcal{S}.

Proof. Let S_T be the set of elements of \mathcal{S} which are subsets of T. We shall show that T is the union of these sets. Since, for every $S \varepsilon S_T$, $S \subset T$, it follows that

$$\bigcup_{S \varepsilon S_T} S \subset T$$

Hence, it is sufficient to show that there exist no elements in T that are not in $\bigcup\limits_{S \varepsilon S_T} S$. Assume the contrary, and let $z \varepsilon T \cap C \left(\bigcup\limits_{S \varepsilon S_T} S \right)$. Then, since \mathcal{S} is a partition of Z, there exists some $S^* \varepsilon \mathcal{S}$ such that $z \varepsilon S^*$. Now let T' be that element of \mathfrak{I} such that $S^* \subset T'$. Hence, since $z \varepsilon T$ and $z \varepsilon S^*$, it follows that $z \varepsilon T \cap T'$, and, since the sets in a partition are disjoint, $T = T'$. Thus $S^* \subset T$; i.e., $S^* \varepsilon S_T$ and $z \notin C \left(\bigcup\limits_{S \varepsilon S_T} S \right)$. This contradiction proves the lemma.

We now return to the proof of the theorem.

In order to prove that $\mathfrak{I}_1, \cdots, \mathfrak{I}_n$ are independent, it is sufficient, by Theorem 3.11.1, to show that for any arbitrary sets $T_i \varepsilon \mathfrak{I}_i$ $(i = 1, 2, \cdots, n)$

$$P_\omega(T_1 \cap \cdots \cap T_n) = \prod_{i=1}^{n} P_\omega(T_i)$$

Now, by Lemma 3.11.1,

$$T_k = \bigcup_{S_k \varepsilon S_{T_k}} S_k, \qquad S_k \varepsilon \mathcal{S}_k$$

so that

$$T_1 \cap \cdots \cap T_n = \bigcup_{S_1 \varepsilon S_{T_1}} \cdots \bigcup_{S_n \varepsilon S_{T_n}} (S_1 \cap \cdots \cap S_n)$$

and since the partitions \mathcal{S}_i are independent

$$P_\omega(T_1 \cap \cdots \cap T_n) = \sum_{S_1 \,\varepsilon\, S_{T1}} \cdots \sum_{S_n \,\varepsilon\, S_{T_n}} P_\omega(S_1) \cdots P_\omega(S_n)$$

$$= \sum_{S_1 \,\varepsilon\, S_{T_1}} P_\omega(S_1) \cdots \sum_{S_n \,\varepsilon\, S_{T_n}} P_\omega(S_n)$$

$$= P_\omega\left(\bigcup_{S_1 \,\varepsilon\, S_{T_1}} S_1\right) \cdots P_\omega\left(\bigcup_{S_n \,\varepsilon\, S_{T_n}} S_n\right)$$

$$= P_\omega(T_1) \cdots P_\omega(T_n)$$

which proves the theorem.

Theorem 3.11.3. Let f_1, f_2, \cdots, f_n be n random variables which are independent with respect to some $p_\omega \,\varepsilon\, \mathcal{P}_\Omega$, and let g_1, g_2, \cdots, g_n be n vector-valued functions. Then the random variables $g_1 \bigcirc f_1, \cdots,$ $g_n \bigcirc f_n$ are independent with respect to p_ω where $g_i \bigcirc f_i$ stands for the composition of the two functions g_i and f_i.

Proof. The proof of this theorem follows from Theorem 3.11.2 since S_{f_i} is a subpartition of $S_{g_i \bigcirc f_i}$. [See Lemma 8.2.1.]

Theorem 3.11.4. For two independent numerical random variables f and g

$$E_\omega(fg) = E_\omega(f)E_\omega(g)$$

provided $E_\omega(f)$ and $E_\omega(g)$ exist.

Proof. Let r_ω be the joint probability distribution of f and g. Then

$$r_\omega(v, w) = p_\omega(v)q_\omega(w)$$

where p_ω is the probability distribution of f and q_ω is the probability distribution of g, where v is in the range of f and w is in the range of g. Now

$$E_\omega(f)E_\omega(g) = \sum_i v_i p_\omega(v_i) \sum_j w_j q_\omega(w_j) = \sum_{i,\,j} v_i w_j p_\omega(v_i) q_\omega(w_j)$$

$$= \sum_{i,\,j} v_i w_j r_\omega(v_i, w_j) = \sum_u u \sum_{v_i w_j = u} r_\omega(v_i, w_j)$$

$$= \sum_u u P_\omega\{z : f(z)g(z) = u\} = E_\omega(fg)$$

Theorem 3.11.5. Let $\mathcal{Z} = (Z, \Omega, p)$ be any sample space, and suppose that, for all $z \, \varepsilon \, Z$,

$$p_{\omega_n}(z) \to p_\omega(z) \quad \text{as} \quad n \to \infty,$$

$$f_n(z) \to f(z) \quad \text{as} \quad n \to \infty,$$

$$\left| f_n(z) \right| \le M \quad \text{for all } n$$

Then $E_{\omega_n}(f_n) \to E_\omega(f)$ as $n \to \infty$.

Proof. Fix $\epsilon > 0$, and choose z_1, \cdots, z_k, so that

$$\sum_{i=1}^{k} p_\omega(z_i) > 1 - \epsilon$$

Now choose N so large that, for $n \ge N$ and $i = 1, \cdots, k$,

$$\left| p_{\omega_n}(z_i) - p_\omega(z_i) \right| < \epsilon/k$$

Then, for $n \ge N$,

$$\sum_1^k p_{\omega_n}(z_i) > \sum_1^k p_\omega(z_i) - \epsilon > 1 - 2\epsilon$$

Thus, for $n \ge N$,

$$(1) \quad \left| E_{\omega_n}(f_n) - E_\omega(f_n) \right| \le \sum_1^k \left| p_{\omega_n}(z_i) - p_\omega(z_i) \right| \left| f_n(z_i) \right|$$

$$+ \sum_{z \ne z_1, \cdots, z_k} [p_{\omega_n}(z) + p_\omega(z)] \left| f_n(z) \right|$$

$$< \epsilon M + \epsilon M + 2\epsilon M = 4\epsilon M$$

and, for all n,

$$(2) \quad \left| E_\omega(f_n) - E_\omega(f) \right| \le \sum_{i=1}^k p_\omega(z_i) \left| f_n(z_i) - f(z_i) \right|$$

$$+ \sum_{z \ne z_1, \cdots, z_k} p_\omega(z) \left| f_n(z) - f(z) \right| < \sum_{i=1}^k p_\omega(z_i) \left| f_n(z_i) - f(z_i) \right| + 2\epsilon M$$

Taking the limit superior of both sides in (1) and (2), we obtain [see problem 3.11.7]

$$(3) \qquad \limsup_{n \to \infty} \left| E_{\omega_n}(f_n) - E_\omega(f_n) \right| \le 4\epsilon M$$

and

$$(4) \qquad \limsup_{n \to \infty} \left| E_\omega(f_n) - E_\omega(f) \right| \le 2\epsilon M$$

Since ϵ is any positive number, (3), (4), and problem 3.11.7 imply

$$E_{\omega_n}(f_n) \to E_\omega(f)$$

Corollary. $E_\omega(f_n) \to E_\omega(f)$.

Proof. Choose $\omega_n \equiv \omega$ for all n, and the hypotheses of the theorem are satisfied.

PROBLEMS

Prove the following theorems on conditional expectations defined on a sample space $Z = (Z, \Omega, p)$.

3.11.1. $E_\omega[f \mid \{z: g(z) \, \varepsilon \, B\}] = E_\omega[E_\omega(f \mid g) \mid \{z: g(z) \, \varepsilon \, B\}]$.

3.11.2. Let \mathcal{S} be a partition of Z, and let $E_\omega(f)$ exist. Then

$$E_\omega[E_\omega(f \mid \mathcal{S})] = E_\omega(f).$$

In particular, if \mathcal{S}_g is the partition determined by the random variable g, then

$$E_\omega[E_\omega(f \mid g)] = E_\omega(f)$$

3.11.3. Let \mathcal{S} be a partition of Z. Then

$$E_\omega[E_\omega(f \mid \mathcal{S}) \mid \mathcal{S}] = E_\omega(f \mid \mathcal{S})$$

3.11.4. Let \mathcal{J} be a partition of Z, and let \mathcal{S} be a subpartition of \mathcal{J}. Then

$$E_\omega(f \mid \mathcal{J}) = E_\omega[E_\omega(f \mid \mathcal{S}) \mid \mathcal{J}]$$

In particular, if $h \circ g$ stands for the composition of the two functions h and g

$$E_\omega(f \mid h \circ g) = E_\omega[E_\omega(f \mid g) \mid h \circ g]$$

3.11.5. For any convex function h

$$E_\omega[h \circ f] \geq E_\omega[h \circ g]$$

where $g = E_\omega(f \mid \mathcal{S})$ and \mathcal{S} is a partition of Z.

3.11.6. Let $h = E_\omega(f \mid \mathcal{J})$. Show that $E_\omega(f \mid h) = h$.

3.11.7. Given a sequence of real numbers $\{a_n\}$, let

$$\limsup_{n \to \infty} a_n = \inf_k \sup_{m \geq k} a_m$$

$$\liminf_{n \to \infty} a_n = \sup_k \inf_{m \geq k} a_m$$

($k, m = 1, 2, 3, \cdots$). Show that a necessary and sufficient condition that $\lim_{n \to \infty} a_n = 0$ is that $\limsup_{n \to \infty} |a_n| = 0$.

3.11.8. Let

$$I_n = \sum_x p(x) f_n(x), \qquad f_n(x) \to f(x), \qquad I = \sum_x p(x) f(x)$$

If there is a $g(x)$ such that

(1) $$|f_n(x)| \leq g(x) \quad \text{for all } n, x$$

(2) $$\sum_x p(x) g(x) \quad \text{converges}$$

then $I_n \to I$ as $n \to \infty$.

3.11.9. Show that the corollary of Theorem 3.11.5 is a special case of Problem 3.11.8.

CHAPTER 4

Utility and Principles
of Choice

4.1. Introduction

The theory of zero-sum two-person games developed in Chapters 1 and 2 is intended as a theory of rational behavior in an unknown situation, when the unknown factor is the strategy chosen by an intelligent opponent whose interests are diametrically opposed to one's own. The statistical games discussed in Chapter 3, on the other hand, aim at an analysis of situations in which the unknown factor is the state of a presumably neutral world. Games against an intelligent opponent and statistical games have the same formal structure, being characterized by a triple (X, Y, M).

However, in stating that a game is a triple (X, Y, M), where M is a bounded numerical function defined on $X \times Y$, we already assume the concept of numerical utility, since, for x in X and y in Y, $M(x, y)$ is interpreted as the negative of the utility to player II (the decision maker) of the outcome resulting from the choice of strategy x by I and strategy y by II. Our task in this chapter thus naturally falls into two parts: to develop the theory of numerical utility and then to examine various principles for choosing a strategy, once the utilities of the various possible outcomes are given. Before turning to the first part of this task, it will be useful to elaborate upon the description of the structure of a game given in Section 1.2.

Every two-person game can be described by (i) two spaces F_1 and F_2 of strategies for players I and II, respectively, (ii) an outcome space R, and (iii) the association with each pair $f = (f_1, f_2)$ in $F_1 \times F_2$ of a probability distribution π_f over R. Since the theory of utility is developed in the next section in terms of the utilities of the probability distributions on R, it is important to realize how probability distributions enter in the games under discussion here. As was pointed out in Chapters 1 and 2, in games against an intelligent opponent, probability distributions enter in the form of chance moves by the referee and also

through the use of mixed strategies by either player. In statistical games, F_1 is a parameter space, or index set for probability distributions on the sample space. Correspondingly F_2 is the space D of decision functions mapping Z into a space A of possible actions by the decision maker. Each decision function $d \, \varepsilon \, D$ is a random variable defined on Z with values in A, and thus [see Definition 3.4.2] for each $d \, \varepsilon \, D$ there is a function p_d defined on $A \times \Omega$ with values $p_d(a \mid \omega)$ such that, for each $\omega \, \varepsilon \, \Omega$, p_d is a probability distribution on A. (Alternatively, each $d \, \varepsilon \, D$ generates a sample space $(A, \, \Omega, \, p_d)$.) The decision maker may also use a mixed strategy by selecting a d in D according to a probability distribution η over D or by randomizing over the sample space [see Definition 3.6.6]. A choice of an $\eta \, \varepsilon \, H$ also induces a probability distribution on A for each ω, namely

$$q_\eta(a \mid \omega) = \sum_{d \, \varepsilon \, D} \eta(d) \sum_{\{z: \, d(z) = a\}} p(z \mid \omega)$$

which in terms of the function p_d is given by

$$q_\eta(a \mid \omega) = \sum_{d \, \varepsilon \, D} \eta(d) p_d(a \mid \omega)$$

Now a specific action a by the decision maker results in a specific outcome r in R. More precisely, in any decision problem there is a fixed function g which maps A into R. This function is a random variable, and for a fixed η and ω it induces a probability distribution on R.

We see then that in general games and statistical games what we are faced with in a decision problem is a choice of one of a set of probability distributions on R. An essential question we must answer in choosing a strategy is: What is the relative value (i.e., utility) of the various possible probability distributions over R?

For the analysis of the problems central to this chapter we make the following concise formulation of the decision problem. Let Ω be the space of strategies of the opponent. Each η in H determines a function k_η defined on Ω and taking values in P, the set of probability distributions on R. We may replace the space H by the space K of functions mapping Ω into P; the decision maker is then required to choose exactly one k from K.

These concepts are illustrated in the following example. Suppose that a coin is about to be tossed, and that a man must choose among d_1, betting a dollar on heads; d_2, betting a dollar on tails; and d_3, not betting. If ω is completely unknown, Ω consists of the unit interval $0 \leq \omega \leq 1$, and, for each $\omega \, \varepsilon \, \Omega$, $p_\omega \equiv \omega$ is the probability with which the coin falls heads. The space H consists of all randomized mixtures

of the three elements d_1, d_2, and d_3 of D, so that an η in H is specified by a triple $\eta = (\lambda_1, \lambda_2, \lambda_3)$, with $\lambda_i \geq 0$ and $\lambda_1 + \lambda_2 + \lambda_3 = 1$, where λ_i is the probability with which the man chooses d_i. The outcome set R is $(1, 0, -1)$, corresponding to winning, not betting, and losing a dollar, respectively. The class K consists of (employing the subscript i to represent the decision d_i):

(i) The function k_1 defined on Ω with $k_1(\omega) = (\omega, 0, 1 - \omega)$, where $(\omega, 0, 1 - \omega)$ is a probability distribution on $R = (1, 0, -1)$.

(ii) The function k_2 with $k_2(\omega) = (1 - \omega, 0, \omega)$.

(iii) The function k_3 with $k_3(\omega) = (0, 1, 0)$.

(iv) All convex linear combinations of these three functions.

Thus, in general, $k_\eta(\omega)$ is given by

$$q_1 = \omega\lambda_1 + (1 - \omega)\lambda_2$$

$$q_0 = \lambda_3$$

$$q_{-1} = \omega\lambda_2 + (1 - \omega)\lambda_1$$

4.2. Utility

If ω were known (or, more generally, if the mixed strategy of the opponent were known), the problem of the decision maker would be simply that of choosing one of a given set of probability distributions over R. But, whether ω is known or not, the decision maker must be able to judge the relative value to him of any two probability distributions over R. In particular, we shall suppose that the decision maker has formulated his objectives with sufficient clarity to declare which of two outcomes he prefers (or that he is indifferent between them), and, more generally, for any two probability distributions p_1 and p_2 over R, to declare which he prefers. Formally we have the following.

Definition 4.2.1. Let R be an arbitrary set, and let P be the set of all probability distributions over R. Then a preference relation (or preference pattern) \geq on P is a binary relation such that

(i) For every p_1 and p_2 in P, either $p_2 \geq p_1$ or $p_1 \geq p_2$ (both may hold), and

(ii) If $p_3 \geq p_2$ and $p_2 \geq p_1$, then $p_3 \geq p_1$.

The relation $p_2 \geq p_1$ is to be interpreted as meaning p_2 is *preferred or indifferent to* p_1. If $p_2 \geq p_1$ but not $p_1 \geq p_2$, we say that p_2 is *preferred* to p_1, written $p_2 > p_1$. If $p_2 \geq p_1$ and $p_1 \geq p_2$, we say that p_2 is *indifferent* to p_1, written $p_2 \sim p_1$. The following properties, summarized as a theorem, are easily verified.

Theorem 4.2.1. The relation \sim is an equivalence relation; i.e., it is reflexive, symmetric, and transitive. For every p_1, p_2, exactly one of $p_2 \succ p_1, p_2 \sim p_1, p_1 \succ p_2$ holds. If $p_3 \succ p_2$ and $p_2 \succeq p_1$, then $p_3 \succ p_1$.

In the development of the theory of games we were concerned with only those preference patterns that may be described by numerical *utility functions*, i.e., for which there exists a bounded function u defined on P such that

$$(1) \qquad u\left(\sum_1^\infty \lambda_n p_n\right) = \sum_1^\infty \lambda_n u(p_n)$$

for any sequence $\lambda_n \geq 0$ with $\sum_1^\infty \lambda_n = 1$, and

$$(2) \qquad u(p_2) \geq u(p_1) \quad \text{if and only if} \quad p_2 \geq p_1$$

If such a function u exists, we define $h(r) = u(q_r)$, where q_r is the particular probability distribution over R assigning probability one to the outcome r. Since for any $p \,\varepsilon\, P$ and any $w \,\varepsilon\, R$ we have $p(w) = \sum_r p(r)q_r(w)$, it follows that

$$p = \sum_r p(r)q_r$$

Thus, replacing λ_n by $p(r)$ and p_n by q_r in (1), we get

$$(3) \qquad u(p) = \sum_r p(r)u(q_r) = \sum_r p(r)h(r)$$

Equation 3 says that the utility of any p is the expectation $E_p(h)$ of the function h with respect to p. Moreover (2) implies that p is preferred or indifferent to q if and only if $E_p(h) \geq E_q(h)$: There is then a numerical function h defined on the space of outcomes, such that the aim of the decision maker is simply to maximize the expectation of h. Conditions under which a utility function exists are given in the next theorem. In what follows, we shall write $p_1 \leq p_2$ for $p_2 \geq p_1$.

Theorem 4.2.2. Let R be an arbitrary set, and let P be the set of all probability distributions on R. Then a preference pattern \geq on P has a utility function if it satisfies

H_1: If $p_{1n} \leq p_{2n}$ for all n, then

$$(a) \qquad \Sigma\lambda_n p_{1n} \leq \Sigma\lambda_n p_{2n}$$

for any sequence $\lambda_n \geq 0$ with $\Sigma\lambda_n = 1$. If in addition $p_{1n} < p_{2n}$ for some n for which $\lambda_n > 0$,

$$(b) \qquad \Sigma\lambda_n p_{1n} < \Sigma\lambda_n p_{2n}$$

(Note that, if for all n, $p_{1n} \sim p_{2n}$, then (a) implies that $\Sigma\lambda_n p_{1n} \sim \Sigma\lambda_n p_{2n}$.)

H_2: If $p_1 \prec p_2 \prec p_3$, there are numbers λ, μ with $0 < \lambda, \mu < 1$ such that

$$\lambda p_1 + (1 - \lambda)p_3 \prec p_2, \qquad \mu p_1 + (1 - \mu)p_3 \succ p_2$$

Before turning to the proof of the theorem we remark that for any sequence $\{p_n\}$ and any sequence $\{\lambda_n\}$ of non-negative numbers with $\Sigma\lambda_n = 1$, the distribution $p = \Sigma\lambda_n p_n$ which is an element of P selects r in R with probability

$$p(r) = \Sigma\lambda_n p_n(r)$$

Thus the distribution p may be achieved by selecting an integer n according to the distribution λ, then selecting r according to p_n. Hypothesis H_1 then requires that, if for each n the decision maker would be willing to have the distribution p_{2n} rather than p_{1n} used in choosing r, then, if he is required to choose between an unspecified element of the sequence $\{p_{2n}\}$ and the corresponding element of the sequence $\{p_{1n}\}$ for the selection of r, he will prefer that the choice be made from the sequence $\{p_{2n}\}$, no matter what random mechanism is used to accomplish this choice. His preference, moreover, will be definite if the random mechanism selects with positive probability at least one n for which there is a positive preference for p_{2n} against p_{1n}. Hypothesis H_2 asserts that, if $p_1 \prec p_2 \prec p_3$, then, if an experiment is to be performed to decide whether p_1 or p_3 is to be used in selecting r and p_1 has probability λ of being chosen, there is a $\lambda < 1$ so near 1 that the decision maker will be controlled by his preference of p_2 over p_1, and a $\lambda > 0$ so small that his preference for p_3 over p_2 becomes controlling. (A looser interpretation of H_2 is that there exists no $p \,\varepsilon\, P$ that is either infinitely desirable or infinitely undesirable.)

The proof of the theorem depends on certain auxiliary propositions and runs as follows:

A. For any p_1 and p_2 in P with $p_1 \prec p_2$, and any λ and μ with $0 \leq \lambda < \mu \leq 1$,

$$\mu p_1 + (1 - \mu)p_2 \prec \lambda p_1 + (1 - \lambda)p_2$$

Proof. From H_1 and the hypothesis that $p_1 \prec p_2$, we have

$$p_1 \sim \lambda p_1 + (1 - \lambda)p_1 \prec \lambda p_1 + (1 - \lambda)p_2 \prec \lambda p_2 + (1 - \lambda)p_2 \sim p_2$$

and thus

(1) $$p_1 \prec \lambda p_1 + (1 - \lambda)p_2 \prec p_2$$

For $0 \leq \lambda < \mu \leq 1$ we have the identity

$$(2) \qquad \lambda p_1 + (1 - \lambda)p_2 = \frac{\lambda}{\mu}[\mu p_1 + (1 - \mu)p_2] + \left(1 - \frac{\lambda}{\mu}\right)p_2$$

and from (1)

$$(3) \qquad \mu p_1 + (1 - \mu)p_2 \prec p_2$$

so that by H_1 and (2)

$$(4) \quad \lambda p_1 + (1 - \lambda)p_2 \succ \frac{\lambda}{\mu}[\mu p_1 + (1 - \mu)p_2]$$

$$+ \left(1 - \frac{\lambda}{\mu}\right)[\mu p_1 + (1 - \mu)p_2] \sim \mu p_1 + (1 - \mu)p$$

which completes the proof of A.

B. For any q with $p_0 \leq q \leq p_1$ there is a unique λ such that

$$q \sim \lambda p_0 + (1 - \lambda)p_1$$

Proof. If either $p_0 \sim q$ or $q \sim p_1$ then the result is immediate. Assume then that $p_0 \prec q \prec p_1$, and let

$$T = \{\lambda \text{ with } 0 \leq \lambda \leq 1 : q \prec \lambda p_0 + (1 - \lambda)p_1\}$$

Clearly $T \neq \emptyset$. Also if $\lambda \in T$ then $\lambda \neq 1$. We shall show that T is a half-open interval $0 \leq \lambda < \lambda^*$. By A we have that, if $\lambda_2 \in T$ and $\lambda_2 > \lambda_1$, then $\lambda_1 \in T$. It remains to be shown that T does not contain a largest element.

For any $\lambda \in T$, there is by H_2 an α, $0 < \alpha < 1$ such that

$$q \prec \alpha p_0 + (1 - \alpha)[\lambda p_0 + (1 - \lambda)p_1]$$

i.e.,

$$q \prec [\lambda + \alpha(1 - \lambda)]p_0 + (1 - \alpha)(1 - \lambda)p_1$$

so that $\lambda + \alpha(1 - \lambda) \in T$. Consequently, if λ^* is the least upper bound of the interval T, then $\lambda^* \notin T$. Let now

$$U = \{\lambda \text{ with } 0 \leq \lambda \leq 1 : \lambda p_0 + (1 - \lambda)p_1 \prec q\}$$

Then by a similar argument we can show that U is a half-open interval $\mu^* < \lambda \leq 1$. Thus $\lambda^* \leq \mu^*$ and

$$q \sim \lambda p_0 + (1 - \lambda)p_1$$

if and only if $\lambda^* \leq \lambda \leq \mu^*$. But by A there cannot be more than one λ satisfying the above indifference relationship, and hence $\lambda^* = \mu^*$. This completes the proof of B.

For fixed p_0 and p_1 with $p_0 \prec p_1$ we define, for all q with $p_0 \prec q \prec p_1$, the numerical function h as follows: $h(q)$ is the unique number $1 - \lambda$ such that

$$q \sim \lambda p_0 + (1 - \lambda)p_1$$

Then from H_1, A, and B, we see that for any p and r with $p_0 \prec p \prec p_1$, $p_0 \prec r \prec p_1$

(i) $h(p) \geq h(r)$ if and only if $p \geq r$

Now from H_1 and the definition of the function h we have for any sequence $\mu_n \geq 0$ with $\Sigma \mu_n = 1$ and for any sequence q_n with $p_0 \prec q_n \prec p_1$ for all n,

$$\sum_1^\infty \mu_n q_n \sim \left[1 - h\left(\sum_1^\infty \mu_n q_n\right)\right]p_0 + h\left(\sum_1^\infty \mu_n q_n\right)p_1$$

But we also have from this definition and H_1

$$\sum_1^\infty \mu_n q_n \sim \sum_1^\infty \mu_n[(1 - h(q_n))p_0 + h(q_n)p_1]$$

$$\sim \left[1 - \sum_1^\infty \mu_n h(q_n)\right]p_0 + \sum_1^\infty \mu_n h(q_n)p_1$$

Hence we conclude from the uniqueness property of h that

(ii) $$h\left(\sum_1^\infty \mu_n q_n\right) = \sum_1^\infty \mu_n h(q_n)$$

Any numerical function defined on an "interval" $p_0 \leq q \leq p_1$ with properties (i) and (ii) above will be called a *utility function on the interval* (p_0, p_1). We have proved:

C. For any p_0 and p_1 with $p_0 \prec p_1$ there exists a utility function on (p_0, p_1).

Now fix a pair q_0, q_1 with $q_0 \prec q_1$ and consider any interval $I = \{p: p_0 \leq p \leq p_1\}$ containing q_0 and q_1. It follows from C that there is a utility function g on I and it is easy to see that for any constants a and b with $a > 0$ the function g' defined as follows for every p in I

$$g'(p) = ag(p) + b$$

is also a utility function on I.

In particular, since $g(q_0) < g(q_1)$, we can choose a and b so that

$$ag(q_0) + b = 0$$

and

$$ag(q_1) + b = 1$$

Then we define the utility function $u_{I,g}$ with values $u(p \mid I, g)$ for every p in I by

$$u(p \mid I, g) = ag(p) + b$$

D. For any two intervals I_1 and I_2 (each containing q_0 and q_1), for any utility function g_1 on I_1 and any utility function g_2 on I_2, and for every p in $I_1 \cap I_2$

$$u(p \mid I_1, g_1) = u(p \mid I_2, g_2)$$

Proof. If $p \sim q_0$ or $p \sim q_1$ the result is immediate. For each of the remaining three cases: (i) $p \prec q_0$, (ii) $q_0 \prec p \prec q_1$, (iii) $q_1 \prec p$, there exists numbers λ_i, $0 < \lambda_i < 1$, $i = 1, 2, 3$ such that

(i) $$q_0 \sim (1 - \lambda_1)p + \lambda_1 q_1$$

(ii) $$p \sim (1 - \lambda_2)q_0 + \lambda_2 q_1$$

(iii) $$q_1 \sim (1 - \lambda_3)q_0 + \lambda_3 p$$

From the additive property of the utility function $u_{I,g}$ we have in the three cases

(i) $$0 = \lambda_1 + (1 - \lambda_1)u(p \mid I_i, g_i)$$

(ii) $$u(p \mid I_i, g_i) = \lambda_2$$

(iii) $$1 = \lambda_3 u(p \mid I_i, g_i)$$

Hence, $u(p \mid I_1, g_1) = u(p \mid I_2, g_2)$ for every p in $I_1 \cap I_2$.

For any p there is an interval I containing p, q_0, and q_1. Define $u(p)$ as the common value of $u(p \mid I, g)$ for every I containing p, q_0, and q_1, and every utility function g on I. Then $u(p)$ is defined for all p, and u is a utility function for every such interval I.

E. The function u is bounded.

Proof. Suppose, for instance, that u is unbounded above. Then we can find a sequence $\{p_n\}$ such that $u(p_n) > 2^n$ and $u(p_n) > u(p_{n-1})$ for all n. Let

$$q = \sum_1^{\infty} 2^{-n}p_n, \qquad q_N = \left(\sum_1^N 2^{-n}p_n\right) + 2^{-N}p_N$$

Since

$$q = \sum_1^N 2^{-n}p_n + \sum_{N+1}^{\infty} 2^{-n}p_n$$

and

$$q_N = \sum_1^N 2^{-n}p_n + \sum_{N+1}^{\infty} 2^{-n}p_N$$

then, using H_1, we have $q > q_N$ for all N, so that $u(q) > u(q_N)$ for all N. By hypothesis $u(p_n) > 2^n$ and thus $u(q) > u(q_N) > N + 1$, for all N, which is impossible.

The proof that u is bounded below is similar.

F. For any sequence p_n and any sequence $\lambda_n \geq 0$ with $\Sigma\lambda_n = 1$,

$$u\left(\sum_1^\infty \lambda_n p_n\right) = \sum_1^\infty \lambda_n u(p_n)$$

Proof. In case λ_n is zero except for a finite number of values of n, the proof is obvious, since there exists an interval I which includes the finite set of probability distributions p_n.

Suppose $\lambda_n > 0$ for an infinite number of values of n (so that $\sum_{N+1}^\infty \lambda_n \neq 0$ for all N). Since u is a utility function on any interval I we have

$$u\left(\sum_1^\infty \lambda_n p_n\right) = u\left[\sum_1^N \lambda_n p_n + \left(\sum_{N+1}^\infty \lambda_n\right) \sum_{n=N+1}^\infty \mu_{Nn} p_n\right]$$

$$= \sum_1^N \lambda_n u(p_n) + \sum_{N+1}^\infty \lambda_n u\left(\sum_{n=N+1}^\infty \mu_{Nn} p_n\right)$$

where $\mu_{Nn} = \lambda_n / \sum_{N+1}^\infty \lambda_n$. Since u is bounded, as $N \to \infty$

$$\sum_{N+1}^\infty \lambda_n u\left(\sum_{n=N+1}^\infty \mu_{Nn} p_n\right) \to 0$$

which completes the proof of F and also of the theorem.

We remark that the loss function L which was defined in the previous chapter [Definition 3.5.2] takes as values the *negative* of the utility to the statistician of probability distributions on the space of outcomes R. It is in terms of the loss function that the theory of utility enters in statistical games.

As a simple illustration of the concept of utility we consider the coin-tossing decision problem, with the three possible gains 1, 0, -1. The class P is the set of all distributions $p = (p_1, p_0, p_{-1})$ with $p_i \geq 0$, $\Sigma p_i = 1$. If we suppose that $(1, 0, 0) > (0, 1, 0) > (0, 0, 1)$, there is a one-parameter family of possible utility functions. For, fixing $u(0, 1, 0)$

$= 0$, $u(0, 0, 1) = -1$, we may choose any $b > 0$, and set $u(1, 0, 0) = b$. Then $u(p_1, p_0, p_{-1}) = bp_1 - p_{-1}$. The number b measures the willingness of the decision maker to take risks. If $b = 1$, his utility is simply his expected gain; if $b < 1$, his expected gain must be definitely positive before he will risk a dollar, whereas, if $b > 1$, he will undertake certain risks with negative expected gain (though positive utility).

It is obvious that the determination of the utility of the probability distribution on R is seldom as easy as in the above example. In many applications the utility of a given probability distribution is identified with the expected monetary gain connected with it. However, this is not always possible, as, for instance, in decisions involving scientific research or human life. Another course often followed is simply to take as the value of the loss function the probability of making a mistake. The difficulties involved in applying utility theory to statistical decisions are often appreciable, but fortunately many of the considerations about statistical games remain the same for a large number of different loss functions.

PROBLEM

4.2.1. In the coin-tossing decision problem, define $m(p) = p_1 - p_{-1}$, $\sigma^2(p) = p_1^2 + p_{-1}^2 - [m(p)]^2$. Which, if either, of H_1, H_2 is violated for the following preference patterns?

 (1) $p > q$ if and only if $m(p) > m(q)$ or $m(p) = m(q)$ and $\sigma^2(p) < \sigma^2(q)$.
 (2) $p > q$ if and only if $m(p) > \max(m(q), 1/2)$.
 (3) $p > q$ if and only if $m(p) - \epsilon\sigma(p) > m(q) - \epsilon\sigma(q)$.
 (4) $p > q$ if and only if $p_1 > q_1$.

4.3. Principles of Choice

In terms of the utility function of the decision maker, the decision problem assumes a simple form. The problem may be represented as one of choosing a strategy in a game (Ω, F, M) where Ω is the space of strategies of the opponent (in statistical games, a class of parameters determining probability distributions on a sample space), F is a uniformly bounded collection of numerical functions defined on Ω such that, if $f_i \,\epsilon\, F$, $i = 1, 2, \cdots$, then, for $\lambda_i \geq 0$, $\Sigma\lambda_i = 1$, $\Sigma\lambda_i f_i \,\epsilon\, F$, and finally $M(\omega, f) = -f(\omega)$, where $f(\omega)$ is the utility to the decision maker of f when his opponent uses strategy ω.

Our coin-tossing decision problem again furnishes us an example. If $u(p_1, p_0, p_{-1}) = bp_1 - p_{-1}$, $b > 0$, the functions available to the decision maker are all convex linear combinations of $f_1 = b\omega - (1 - \omega)$, $f_2 = -\omega + b(1 - \omega)$, and $f_3 = 0$; i.e., all functions $f = \alpha\omega + \beta(1 - \omega)$, where (α, β) is in the convex hull T of $(b, -1)$, $(-1, b)$ and $(0, 0)$.

For $b < 1$, for instance, T is shaded in Figure 4. A decision is the choice of a point $(\alpha, \beta)\ \varepsilon\ T$. For a given (α, β), player II's utility when the coin falls heads is α, and when the coin falls tails is β; the over-all utility of (α, β) is $\alpha\omega + \beta(1 - \omega)$, where ω is the (more or less unknown) probability that the coin falls heads.

An equivalent alternative statement of the decision problem is that we are given a bounded numerical function u defined on a product space $\Omega \times D$; the decision maker must choose exactly one $d\ \varepsilon\ D$; and

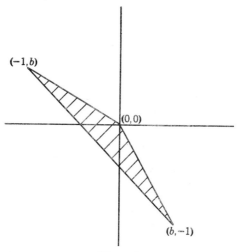

Figure 4

the utility of decision d in state ω is $u(\omega, d)$. The latter formulation exhibits most clearly the relation among games against an intelligent opponent, statistical games, and the general-decision problem. In the first case, ω is chosen by an opponent whose utility is the negative of the decision maker's; the statistical game is the case in which ω is regarded as being determined by nature. In the general-decision problem ω may for instance be partly chosen by nature and partly by various individuals whose utilities may be in any relationship to those of the decision maker.

Having completed our description of the decision problem, we turn to, but do not answer, the question of how to solve it. An answer would take the form of a *principle of choice*, i.e., a rule specifying, for each set F, which $f\ \varepsilon\ F$ should be selected. Now in the case where ω is chosen by an opponent whose utility is the negative of our own, i.e., the case of (zero-sum) games against an intelligent opponent, we have seen that the minimax principle furnishes a reasonable theory.

Minimax Principle. Choose d so as to maximize inf $u(\omega, d)$.
ω

In our coin-tossing decision problem, the minimax principle tells us to choose the point (α, β) ε T whose minimum coordinate is maximized. This point is (v, v), where $v = \max\left(0, \dfrac{b-1}{2}\right)$. Thus, for $b < 1$, $v = 0$, and $(0, 0)$ is attained only by not betting, for $b = 1$, $v = 0$, and any $\eta = (\lambda_1, \lambda_2, \lambda_3)$ with $\lambda_1 = \lambda_2$ is satisfactory, and, for $b > 1$, $v = (b-1)/2$, and only $\eta = (1/2, 1/2, 0)$ is satisfactory. [See Problem 2.4.2.]

The minimax principle is distinctly less satisfactory in statistical games and in some situations prescribes courses of action that would be regarded as unreasonable by all but the most incurable pessimists.

Suppose, for instance, that a manufacturer has a process for producing fuses, producing defective fuses with a constant but unknown probability ω, a fuse being regarded as defective if it fails to blow out at 20 amperes. He has produced a lot of 10,000 fuses and can either junk the lot (action 1) or sell the fuses at 10 cents each, with a double-your-money-back guarantee for each fuse that proves defective (action 2). His income, which we consider as his utility, if he junks the lot is zero and if he sells the lot is $1000(1 - 2\omega)$.

Thus $u(\omega, \lambda) = \lambda 1000(1 - 2\omega)$, where λ denotes the probability with which the manufacturer accepts the lot. We have min $u(\omega, \lambda) =$
ω
-1000λ, and the minimax principle requires the manufacturer to junk the lot if he regards all ω, or even $\omega > 1/2$, as remotely possible. This conclusion is simply the reflection of the fact that, if ω were chosen by a hostile opponent, ω would be chosen as large as possible. Notice that introduction of the possibility of sampling does not change the minimax conclusion at all: If the manufacturer tests N fuses, and decides on the basis of the results whether to junk or sell the remaining $10,000 - N$, a non-randomized decision function is a subset S of the integers $0, \cdots, N$, specifying those integers s for which he proposes to junk the lot if s defectives are found in the sample. We have

$$u(\omega, S) = (1 - 2\omega)(1000 - 0.1N) \sum_{s \not\in S} \binom{N}{s} \omega^s (1 - \omega)^{N-s}$$

and

$$U(\omega, \eta) = \sum_{S} \eta(S)u(\omega, S)$$

where η is any probability distribution over the class of subsets S of

$J^* = (0, 1, \cdots, N)$. Since for $1/2 < \omega < 1$, $u(\omega, S) < 0$ unless $S = J^*$, we have

$$U(\omega, \eta) < 0 \quad \text{for} \quad 1/2 < \omega < 1 \quad \text{unless} \quad \eta(J^*) = 1$$

and $u(\omega, J^*) = 0$ for all ω. Again the minimax procedure requires the manufacturer to junk the remainder of the lot, even if no defectives are found in a sample of size N if, before the inspection, he regarded any value of ω between $1/2$ and 1 as remotely possible. Thus the minimax principle involves ignoring the results of the sample entirely, and is unsatisfactory to anyone who believes that the results of a sample are relevant in the situation described.

One modification of the minimax principle is the *minimax loss* or *regret principle:*

Minimax Loss. Choose d so as to maximize

$$v(d) = \inf_{\omega} [u(\omega, d) - \sup_d u(\omega, d)]$$

The maximum attainable utility in circumstance ω is $\sup_d u(\omega, d)$, or, in other words, it is the least risk attainable, so that to maximize the function v is to minimize maximum regret or loss. Let $\gamma(\omega) = \sup_d u(\omega, d)$. In the example described above,

$$\gamma(\omega) = (1 - 2\omega)(1000 - 0.1N) \quad \text{for} \quad \omega \le 1/2$$

and $\qquad \gamma(\omega) = 0 \qquad\qquad\qquad\qquad$ for $\quad \omega \ge 1/2$

The minimax principle is applied to

$$u_1(\omega, d) - u(\omega, d) - \gamma(\omega)$$

that is, for $\omega \le 1/2$,

$$u_1(\omega, S) = (2\omega - 1)(1000 - 0.1N) \left[1 - \sum_{s \notin S} \binom{N}{s} \omega^s (1 - \omega)^{N-s} \right]$$

$$= (2\omega - 1)(1000 - 0.1N) \sum_{s \in S} \binom{N}{s} \omega^s (1 - \omega)^{N-s}$$

and, for $\omega \ge 1/2$, $u_1 = u$.

For N odd, say $N = 2k + 1$, the set $S^* = (k + 1, \cdots, 2k + 1)$, corresponding to junking the lot if and only if more than half the sample items are defective, is easily seen from the following considerations to be a minimax loss strategy, i.e., a minimax strategy for player II in the game with payoff

$$\rho_1(\omega, S) = -u_1(\omega, S)$$

We note that

$$\rho_1(\omega, S^*) = \rho_1(1 - \omega, S^*)$$

Let ω_1 be a point in $0 \le \omega \le 1/2$ with

$$\rho_1(\omega_1, S^*) = \max_{\omega} \rho_1(\omega, S^*) = v$$

If ξ is the mixed strategy for I mixing ω_1 and $1 - \omega_1$ equally

$$\rho_1(\xi, S) = \frac{1}{2}(1 - 2\omega_1)(1000 - 0.1N)\left(\sum_{s=0}^{N}\binom{N}{s} h(s, S)\right)$$

where

$$h(s, S) = \omega_1{}^s(1 - \omega_1)^{N-s} \quad \text{for} \quad s \, \varepsilon \, S$$

$$h(s, S) = (1 - \omega_1)^s \omega_1{}^{N-s} \quad \text{for} \quad s \notin S$$

We obtain $\min_{S} \rho_1(\xi, S)$ by minimizing $h(s, S)$ for each s, i.e.; $s \, \varepsilon \, S$ if and only if

$$\omega_1{}^s(1 - \omega_1)^{N-s} \le (1 - \omega_1)^s \omega_1{}^{N-s}$$

i.e.,

$$\left(\frac{\omega_1}{1 - \omega_1}\right)^{2s-N} \le 1$$

or $s \ge N/2$. Thus

$$\min_{S} \rho_1(\xi, S) = \rho_1(\xi, S^*) = v = \max_{\omega} \rho_1(\omega, S^*)$$

and S^* is the minimax loss strategy.

Some statistical games have $\gamma(\omega) = 0$ for all ω, so that, for these games, the minimax and minimax loss principles coincide. This occurs, for instance, when ω is an unknown parameter that the statistician must estimate from a sample, and all values of ω have equal intrinsic desirability, so that the risk depends only on the error in estimation. In any case, most of the statistical games for which the minimax strategies have been investigated are games with $\gamma(\omega) \equiv 0$.

An objection often raised to the minimax and minimax loss principle, as applied to statistical games, is that they do not take into account any information the decision maker may have about ω, except to the extent that this information rules out certain ω's as being absolutely impossible. If he can describe his information about ω by a probability distribution ξ over Ω, so that $\xi(\omega)$ represents the probability, based on his information, that ω is the true state of the system, then the utility of action d is simply

$$U(\xi, d) = \sum_{\omega} \xi(\omega)u(\omega, d)$$

Thus he maximizes his utility by choosing d so as to maximize $U(\xi, d)$. This principle of choice, based on ξ, is called a *Bayes principle;* and a d which maximizes $U(\xi, d)$ is called a *Bayes solution* (of the decision problem) against ξ. Bayes principles have the objection that, in most statistical games, ξ is simply an expression of the personal judgment of the decision maker, so that two decision makers, facing the same decision problem and using Bayes principles, might well reach different conclusions from the same data collected in the course of the game, if their a priori judgments ξ, before the data were collected, differed markedly. A further objection to Bayes principles is that they never require randomization; many statisticians consider that random sampling, which is a form of randomization, is useful. [See Section 8.7.]

Bayes solutions will be studied in considerable detail in later chapters. We remark here that, in the fuse-manufacturing example discussed above, every Bayes principle leads to the choice of an integer m, with $S = \{s: s > m\}$.

In general, a principle of choice associates with each decision problem (Ω, D, ρ) a preference ordering \geq on D, with decision d_1 being preferred or indifferent to d_2 if and only if $d_1 \geq d_2$. The minimax principle leads to the ordering $d_1 \geq d_2$ if and only if

$$\sup_{\omega} \rho(\omega, d_1) \leq \sup_{\omega} \rho(\omega, d_2)$$

while the Bayes principle with respect to an a priori distribution ξ leads to $d_1 \geq d_2$ if and only if

$$\Sigma\xi(\omega)\rho(\omega, d_1) \leq \Sigma\xi(\omega)\rho(\omega, d_2)$$

One way to arrive at "reasonable" principles of choice is to specify various properties which "reasonable" principles should have, and then determine the class of all principles with these properties. As an instance of this method, we present the following discussion. We shall consider Ω as fixed, and impose requirements on the class of preference orderings as D varies. We first consider

L_1: There exists a preference ordering \geq on the space of decision functions D such that if $d_1 \geq d_2$ for some subset of D containing d_1 and d_2 then $d_1 \geq d_2$ for all D.

The principle L_1 asserts that the relative desirability of d_1 and d_2 does not depend on the other alternatives available to the decision maker. Notice that Bayes and minimax principles satisfy L_1. However, minimax regret does not; as the following example illustrates.

Consider a finite game with matrix

$$W = \begin{array}{c|cccc} \Omega & d_1 & d_2 & d_3 & d_4 \\ \hline 1 & 20 & 3 & 2 & 0 \\ 2 & 0 & 3 & 5 & 20 \end{array}$$

The "regret" matrix obtained from W is W itself so that minimax regret strategy for player II is to select d_2 with probability one and the others with zero probability. If, however, we now delete column 1 and convert the resulting matrix to a regret matrix, we obtain a new game with matrix

$$W^* = \begin{array}{c|ccc} \Omega & d_2 & d_3 & d_4 \\ \hline 1 & 3 & 2 & 0 \\ 2 & 0 & 2 & 17 \end{array}$$

in which the minimax regret strategy for player II is to select d_3 with probability one and the others with probability zero. Thus, which of the two strategies d_2 or d_3 is selected depends on whether or not d_1 is present.

A principle satisfying L_1 determines a preference ordering \geq on the set F of all bounded functions f on Ω, and we shall formulate our next requirement in terms of this ordering. It is

L_2: If $f(\omega) \geq g(\omega)$ for all ω, then $f \geq g$.

The meaning and reasonableness of L_2 are obvious, and L_2, appropriately formulated, is satisfied by all principles of choice that have been proposed.

A requirement that is not satisfied by the minimax principle is

L_3: If $f_1 \geq f_2$, then $f_1 + g \geq f_2 + g$ for all g.

This principle asserts that, in deciding between f_1 and f_2, the decision maker is guided only by the change in utility, as a function of the unknown state ω, resulting from a change from f_1 to f_2.

Theorem 4.3.1. If Ω is finite and \geq satisfies L_1, L_2, and L_3, then either all f's are indifferent or there is a probability distribution ξ on Ω such that $f_1 > f_2$ whenever

$$\sum_\omega \xi(\omega) f_1(\omega) > \sum_\omega \xi(\omega) f_2(\omega)$$

Proof. If Ω consists of n points, $\omega_1, \cdots, \omega_n$, then there is a 1–1 correspondence between numerical functions f on Ω and vectors \mathbf{x} in n space with

$$\mathbf{x} = [f(\omega_1), \cdots, f(\omega_n)]$$

Thus \geq may be considered as a preference relation among vectors. Denote by P the set of all vectors $\mathbf{p} = (p_1, \cdots, p_n)$ with $p_i > 0$ for $i = 1, \cdots, n$. Then from L_2 we conclude that for all \mathbf{p} in P

$$\mathbf{p} \geq \mathbf{e} = (0, 0, \cdots, 0)$$

If there exists a \mathbf{p}_0 in P such that $\mathbf{p}_0 \sim \mathbf{e}$, then from L_3 we see that

$$2\mathbf{p}_0 \sim \mathbf{p}_0 + \mathbf{p}_0 \sim \mathbf{e} + \mathbf{p}_0 \sim \mathbf{p}_0 \sim \mathbf{e}$$

and

$$-\mathbf{p}_0 \sim \mathbf{e} - \mathbf{p}_0 \sim \mathbf{p}_0 - \mathbf{p}_0 \sim \mathbf{e}$$

and thus $N\mathbf{p}_0 \sim \mathbf{e}$ for every positive or negative integer N. Since the components of \mathbf{p}_0 are all positive, for every n-dimensional vector \mathbf{x} there is an integer N_1 with $N_1\mathbf{p}_0 - \mathbf{x}$ in P and there is an integer N_2 with $\mathbf{x} - N_2\mathbf{p}_0$ in P. And, since $N_1\mathbf{p}_0 - \mathbf{x} \geq \mathbf{e}$ and $\mathbf{x} - N_2\mathbf{p}_0 \geq \mathbf{e}$, we have

$$N_1\mathbf{p}_0 \geq \mathbf{x} \quad \text{and} \quad \mathbf{x} \geq N_2\mathbf{p}_0$$

But $N_1\mathbf{p}_0 \sim \mathbf{e} \sim N_2\mathbf{p}_0$, so that $\mathbf{x} \sim \mathbf{e}$ for all \mathbf{x}. Thus, unless all vectors are indifferent, $\mathbf{p} > \mathbf{e}$ for all \mathbf{p} in P. We restrict attention hereafter to the case $\mathbf{p} > \mathbf{e}$ for all \mathbf{p} in P. In this case, we have also $\mathbf{q} < \mathbf{e}$ for $-\mathbf{q} \,\varepsilon\, P$, since $-\mathbf{q} > \mathbf{e}$ implies $-\mathbf{q} + \mathbf{q} > \mathbf{e} + \mathbf{q}$.

Let S be the set of all vectors $\mathbf{s} \geq \mathbf{e}$, and consider the set Q of all vectors representable as $\mathbf{s} + \mathbf{p}$, where $\mathbf{s} \,\varepsilon\, S$ and $\mathbf{p} \,\varepsilon\, P$. Taking $\mathbf{s} = \mathbf{e}$, we see that $P \subset Q$. Also $\mathbf{p} > \mathbf{e}$, and therefore by L_3

$$\mathbf{s} + \mathbf{p} > \mathbf{s} + \mathbf{e} \geq \mathbf{e}$$

so that $Q \subset S$. Thus $P \subset Q \subset S$. Moreover, Q is an open set since $P + \mathbf{s}$ is open and

$$Q = \bigcup_{\mathbf{s} \,\varepsilon\, S} (P + \mathbf{s})$$

We show that Q is convex; since Q is closed under addition, it is sufficient to show that if $\mathbf{x} \,\varepsilon\, Q$ and $\lambda > 0$ then $\lambda \mathbf{x} \,\varepsilon\, Q$. Suppose that $\mathbf{x} = \mathbf{s}_0 + \mathbf{p}_0$ with \mathbf{s}_0 in S and \mathbf{p}_0 in P. Then $(M/N)\mathbf{s}_0 \,\varepsilon\, S$ for all positive in-

tegers M and N, since $(M/N)\mathbf{s}_0 \prec \mathbf{e}$ would imply $M\mathbf{s}_0 \prec \mathbf{e}$, while $\mathbf{s}_0 \succeq \mathbf{e}$ implies $M\mathbf{s}_0 \succeq \mathbf{e}$. If $\lambda > 0$ and $\mathbf{p} \,\varepsilon\, P$, then clearly $\lambda \mathbf{p} \,\varepsilon\, P$. Thus for $\lambda > 0$,

$$\lambda(\mathbf{s}_0 + \mathbf{p}_0) = k\mathbf{s}_0 + \mathbf{p}_1$$

where k is a positive rational sufficiently near λ and $\mathbf{p}_1 \,\varepsilon\, P$. Since $k\mathbf{s}_0 \,\varepsilon\, S$, we have $\lambda \mathbf{x} \,\varepsilon\, Q$. Thus Q is an open convex set, and \mathbf{e} is a boundary point of Q.

By corollary 1 to Theorem 2.2.1, there is then a supporting hyperplane to Q through \mathbf{e}; i.e., there is a vector $\boldsymbol{\xi} \neq \mathbf{e}$ with $\boldsymbol{\xi} \cdot \mathbf{x} > 0$ for $\mathbf{x} \,\varepsilon\, Q$. Each $\xi(i) \geq 0$, for, if there were a $\xi(i) < 0$, then, since $P \subset Q$, there would exist an \mathbf{x} in Q with component x_i relatively large enough to have $\boldsymbol{\xi} \cdot \mathbf{x} < 0$. Since $\xi(i) \geq 0$ and $\boldsymbol{\xi} \neq \mathbf{e}$, we may normalize to obtain $\sum_1^n \xi(i) = 1$. Furthermore, $\boldsymbol{\xi} \cdot \mathbf{x} \geq 0$ for all \mathbf{x} in S. [See problem 4.3.4.] Thus, if $\mathbf{x} \geq \mathbf{y}, \mathbf{x} - \mathbf{y} \,\varepsilon\, S$ and $\boldsymbol{\xi} \cdot (\mathbf{x} - \mathbf{y}) \geq 0$. Hence $\boldsymbol{\xi} \cdot \mathbf{x} \geq \boldsymbol{\xi} \cdot \mathbf{y}$. Consequently, whenever $\boldsymbol{\xi} \cdot \mathbf{y} > \boldsymbol{\xi} \cdot \mathbf{x}$ we have $\mathbf{y} > \mathbf{x}$.

The meaning of the theorem is this: Anyone who uses a principle of choice satisfying L_1, L_2, and L_3 is acting *as if* he regarded the states $1, \cdots, n$ as having probabilities $\xi(1), \cdots, \xi(n)$ of occurring, at least insofar as the probabilities $\xi(1), \cdots, \xi(n)$ are decisive in differentiating between two actions. Our theorem does not guarantee $\boldsymbol{\xi} \cdot \mathbf{x} = \boldsymbol{\xi} \cdot \mathbf{y}$ implies $\mathbf{x} \sim \mathbf{y}$, and a simple two-dimensional example satisfying L_1, L_2, and L_3 where this fails is as follows:

$$(x_1, y_1) > (x_2, y_2) \quad \text{if either} \quad x_1 > x_2, \quad \text{or} \quad x_1 = x_2 \quad \text{and} \quad y_1 > y_2$$

The $\boldsymbol{\xi}$ vector is $(1, 0)$, so that the decision maker regards state 2 as having probability zero. Nevertheless, between two actions yielding the same income in state 1, he prefers that yielding the larger income in state 2.

The above theorem for the special case when Ω is finite as well as the discussion of the fuse-manufacturing example indicates rather clearly that, without assuming an a priori distribution on Ω, there is in terms of the present theory no adequate principle of choice for choosing a strategy in a statistical game. This is one reason, though by no means the most important one, why Bayes principles of choice will be studied in detail in succeeding chapters. It is also the reason why we turn to the study of various *classes* of strategies in the next chapter, the development of which is useful in studying arbitrary games as well as statistical games.

PROBLEMS

4.3.1. Consider the hypotheses

L_4: $f_1 \geq f_2$ implies $\lambda f_1 + (1 - \lambda)g \geq \lambda f_2 + (1 - \lambda)g$ for all $g \, \varepsilon \, F$ and all λ in $(0, 1)$.

L_5: If $f_n \geq g$ for all n and $f_n(\omega) \to f^*(\omega)$ for all ω, then $f^* \geq g$. Assume that Ω is finite and that the preference relation \geq on all the vectors satisfy L_1 and L_2.

(1) Show that L_4 implies L_3.

(2) Show that L_3 and L_5 imply L_4.

(3) Show that L_4 and L_5 guarantee that the equality

$$\sum_{\omega} \xi(\omega)f_1(\omega) = \sum_{\omega} \xi(\omega)f_2(\omega)$$

implies $f_1 \sim f_2$.

4.3.2. For any numerical function $h(t)$ satisfying $h(t_1 + t_2) = h(t_1) + h(t_2)$, the ordering \geq defined for two-dimensional vectors by $\mathbf{x} = (x_1, x_2) \geq \mathbf{y} = (y_1, y_2)$ if (a) $x_1 + x_2 > y_1 + y_2$ or (b) $x_1 + x_2 = y_1 + y_2$ and $h(x_1) \geq h(y_1)$ satisfies L_1, L_2, and L_3.

4.3.3. It is known that there are discontinuous functions h satisfying $h(t_1 + t_2) = h(t_1) + h(t_2)$. This provides an example showing that L_3 does not imply L_4. Employ the solution $h(t) = t$ to prove that L_4 does not imply L_5.

4.3.4. A set R in n space is said to be a *cone* if whenever $\mathbf{x} \, \varepsilon \, R$, $\lambda \mathbf{x} \, \varepsilon \, R$ for $\lambda > 0$. Thus the set Q of Theorem 4.3.1 is a cone. Is the associated set S the closure of this cone? Explain.

CHAPTER 5

Classes of Optimal Strategies

5.1. Introduction

In the previous chapter we considered some general principles of choice of optimal strategies in games where one of the players is not faced with an intelligent opponent but rather with an unknown state of nature. It was pointed out that no single principle thus far advanced seems to be compelling enough to insure a universal agreement on a rule for selecting a particular course of action among many that might be available. However, while disagreement might exist on what to do in a given situation, it might be possible to get full agreement on what *not* to do. To illustrate this point, let us assume that we are considering a game $G = (\Omega, D, \rho)$ where the possible states of nature are represented by points ω in Ω, the possible decisions of player II by points d in D, and the risk to player II by $\rho(\omega, d)$. Suppose further that a strategy η for player II is proposed as a possible candidate for consideration. Two cases may arise: (*a*) No other strategy can be found that is *better* than η. Technically, this means that there exists no η^* such that $\rho(\omega, \eta^*) \leq \rho(\omega, \eta)$ for all ω with inequality holding for some ω. (*b*) There does exist a strategy η^* that is better than η. In case *a* the strategy η can rightly be designated as *admissible* but not necessarily preferred since other admissible strategies will be competing for attention. In case *b*, however, η could clearly be dropped from consideration in favor of η^*.

The above discussion suggests that in games played against nature it would be highly desirable to construct a class \mathcal{C} of strategies such that no reasonable principle of choice would lead one to select a strategy that was outside of this class. To satisfy this requirement the class \mathcal{C} should possess the property that for every strategy η for player II that is not in \mathcal{C} there can be found a strategy η^* in \mathcal{C} which is *better*, i.e., which is as good for all possible states of nature and actually better for some states. A class \mathcal{C} of strategies with this property is called a *complete* class.

121

It is easy to see that a complete class will necessarily contain all admissible strategies. It is not true, however, that a complete class can always be restricted to only such strategies. The reason is that, if a strategy η is not admissible, it does not follow that any of the $\eta^{*'}$s that are better than it will necessarily belong to the admissible class. If the class of admissible strategies is complete, it is the smallest complete class, and, if a minimal complete class exists, it is identical with the admissible class of strategies. It will be shown in this and later chapters that the admissible class is complete in many games of statistical importance. It is obvious that for any game a complete class of strategies exists, namely, the class of all strategies; on the other hand, there are games in which the class of admissible strategies is empty.

The following example will serve to illustrate some of the concepts mentioned above: A purchaser of an oil-bearing seed is engaged in crushing seed for its yield in oil. The oil yield in pounds per bushel of seed is the value x of a random variable which is assumed to be normally distributed with mean θ and a known standard deviation σ. The price of a pound of oil is r and of a bushel of seed is q. If other costs incidental to the crushing operation are ignored, the profitability of accepting and utilizing a lot of N bushels of seed depends only on the expected oil yield per bushel, i.e., expected profit $= N(r\theta - q)$. Clearly it would pay to reject the lot whenever $N(r\theta - q) < 0$ and accept the lot whenever $N(r\theta - q) > 0$, whereas acceptance and rejection are equally profitable when $N(r\theta - q) = 0$. In other words, it is profitable to accept the lot when $\theta > \theta_0 = q/r$ and to reject the lot when $\theta < \theta_0$. If lots with "quality" $\theta > \theta_0$ are rejected, then the cost of this error will be assumed to be $L_1(\theta) = N(r\theta - q)$, and, if lots with quality $\theta < \theta_0$ are accepted, then the cost of this error will be assumed to be $L_2(\theta) = N(q - r\theta)$.

Suppose the purchaser is supplied with a sample of n bushels of seed upon which to make his decision. Then a pure strategy for him would be a rule that would specify for every possible sample point $\mathbf{x} = (x_1, x_2, \cdots, x_n)$ whether to accept or reject the lot. A mixed strategy for the purchaser can quite generally be described [see Theorem 7.2.1] as a function φ with $0 \leq \varphi(\mathbf{x}) \leq 1$ such that if $\mathbf{x} = (x_1, \cdots, x_n)$ is observed he will accept the lot with probability $\varphi(\mathbf{x})$ and reject the lot with probability $1 - \varphi(\mathbf{x})$. In terms of these mixed strategies the situation may be described as a game $\Gamma = (\Theta, \Phi, \rho)$ where Θ is the real line, Φ is the class of integrable functions φ, $0 \leq \varphi(\mathbf{x}) \leq 1$ defined on n space and

$$\rho(\theta, \varphi) = \left(\frac{1}{\sqrt{2\pi}\,\sigma}\right)^n L_1(\theta) \int_{-\infty}^{\infty} \cdots \int_{-\infty}^{\infty} [1 - \varphi(\mathbf{x})] e^{-\frac{1}{2}\sum_{i=1}^{n}\left(\frac{x_i - \theta}{\sigma}\right)^2} d\mathbf{x}$$

for $\theta \geq \theta_0$, and

$$\rho(\theta, \varphi) = \left(\frac{1}{\sqrt{2\pi}\,\sigma}\right)^n L_2(\theta) \int_{-\infty}^{\infty} \cdots \int_{-\infty}^{\infty} \varphi(\mathbf{x}) e^{-\frac{1}{2}\sum_{i=1}^{n}\left(\frac{x_i - \theta}{\sigma}\right)} d\mathbf{x}$$

for $\theta \leq \theta_0$.

It would appear that, if the purchaser knew nothing more about the situation than what was described, he would have to consider every element of Φ as a possible candidate for a final choice of a rule of action. Fortunately, this is not the case. It will be shown in Section 7.4 that only a small subclass Φ^* of φ's defined by $\varphi(x) = 1$ if $\bar{x} > k$ and $\varphi(x) = 0$ otherwise, where $\bar{x} = \Sigma x_i/n$ and k any real number, are worthy of his attention, and no other strategy need be considered. The reason for this is that the subclass Φ^* is a complete class, and in fact every element of Φ^* is an admissible strategy.

In addition to the admissible class there exist other classes of strategies which may or may not be complete but which from the point of view of decision making are of interest and will be discussed in this chapter. The theory of games developed in Chapters 1 and 2 will be used as the tool for defining and characterizing all the optimal classes we shall be concerned with. *Thus the same theory that served to delineate optimal strategies in games played against an intelligent opponent will* *serve to delineate classes of optimal strategies in games played against nature.* Since the definitions of these classes of optimal strategies depend in no way on special assumptions about statistical games, the formal definitions are stated in terms of arbitrary games. That these concepts may be found useful in general games is illustrated by the following example: Consider the two-person zero-sum game $G = (X, Y, M)$ with $X = Y = (1, \cdots, 100)$, $M(x, y) = \min(x, y)$. Any strategy for I is a good strategy; II has the unique good strategy $y = 1$. However, it is clear that the only admissible choice for I is $x = 100$. Thus, even if the minimax principle is employed, the problem of optimal classes of strategies becomes important in case the minimax strategy is not unique.

PROBLEMS

5.1.1. In the illustrative example given above, let $N = 1000$, $n = 36$, $\sigma = 10$, $r = 15$ cents, $q = \$3.00$. Let φ^* be a strategy for the purchaser defined as follows: Accept the lot if $\bar{x} > 20$ lb., reject the lot if $\bar{x} \leq 20$ lb. Consider another strategy ψ defined as follows: Let m be the number of bushels of seed in the sample whose oil yield is greater than 20 lb. Then accept the lot if $m > 18$, reject the lot if

$m < 18$, and if $m = 18$ toss a coin and accept the lot if the outcome is "head," reject the lot if the outcome is "tail."

(a) Plot $\rho(\theta, \varphi^*)$ and $\rho(\theta, \psi)$ as functions of θ, and thus show that ψ is not admissible.

(b) Show that φ^* is a minimax strategy, assuming that Φ^* is an admissible complete class.

5.1.2. Give an example of a game in which the class of admissible strategies is empty.

5.1.3. Player I chooses a number θ, $0 \leq \theta \leq 1$. A coin whose probability of falling heads is θ is tossed N times, and player II bets \$1.00 on the result of each toss, each bet made with knowledge of the results of previous tosses. Show that the minimax strategy for II of betting on heads and tails with equal probability at each toss is not admissible and that a better minimax strategy is: For every n, let x_n, y_n denote the winnings on those previous tosses when II has bet on heads, tails respectively. (x_n and y_n may be negative.) At the nth toss, II bets on heads if $x_n > y_n$, tails if $x_n < y_n$, and chooses heads and tails with equal probability if $x_n = y_n$.

5.2. Complete Classes of Strategies in S Games

In many important decision problems, we are confronted with a game in which nature has only a finite number of possible states. In such cases it is possible to obtain a full description of the structure of the complete classes under quite general conditions.

It was shown in Section 2.4 that a game G in which player I has a finite number n of pure strategies is equivalent to an S game, where S is a bounded subset of the n-dimensional Cartesian space S_n. A pure strategy for player II is a choice of a point $\mathbf{s} = (s_1, s_2, \cdots, s_n)$ in S, for player I a choice of an integer $i = 1, 2, \cdots, n$, and the payoff to player I is the number s_i. Let S^* be the mixed extension of S. Then S^* is a convex subset of S_n, and each point in S^* represents a possible mixed strategy for player II. It follows from the boundedness of S that S^* is bounded. From Definition 2.4.1 we also see that the space Ξ of mixed strategies for player I is a closed, bounded convex subset of S_n; i.e., $\Xi =$ the set of all points

$$\boldsymbol{\xi} = (\xi(1), \cdots, \xi(n)), \qquad \xi(i) \geq 0, \qquad \sum_{i=1}^{n} \xi(i) = 1$$

In Section 5.4 we shall define various classes of strategies for arbitrary games, and thus, a fortiori, for S games, but for convenience we informally state for these games the definitions of the class \mathcal{C} of admissible strategies and the class \mathcal{B} of Bayes strategies along with informal definitions of several other classes. These definitions refer to an S game (I_n, S, M) and its mixed extension (Ξ, S^*, M), where, for $\boldsymbol{\xi}$ in Ξ and \mathbf{s} in S^*, $M(\boldsymbol{\xi}, \mathbf{s}) = \boldsymbol{\xi} \cdot \mathbf{s} = \sum_{i=1}^{n} \xi(i)s_i$. (Strictly speaking, (Ξ, S^*, M)

is only equivalent to the mixed extension of (I_n, S, M), but no confusion will result from this identification.)

(1) \mathfrak{A} = the set of admissible points in S^*; i.e., a point $\mathbf{a} = (a_1, \cdots, a_n)$ in S^* belongs to \mathfrak{A} if there exists no \mathbf{s} in S^* such that $s_i \leq a_i$ for all i with inequality holding for at least one i.

(2) \mathfrak{B} = the set of Bayes points in S^*; i.e., a point $\mathbf{b} = (b_1, \cdots, b_n)$ in S^* belongs to \mathfrak{B} if there is a $\boldsymbol{\xi}$ in Ξ such that

$$\boldsymbol{\xi} \cdot \mathbf{b} = \min_{\mathbf{s} \, \varepsilon \, S^*} (\boldsymbol{\xi} \cdot \mathbf{s})$$

(The point \mathbf{b} is then said to be Bayes against $\boldsymbol{\xi}$.)

(3) Ξ_ϵ = the set of all $\boldsymbol{\xi}$ in Ξ with $\xi(i) \geq \epsilon$ for all i.
(4) Ξ_+ = the set of all $\boldsymbol{\xi}$ in Ξ with $\xi(i) > 0$ for all i.
(5) \mathfrak{D}_ϵ = the set of all \mathbf{s} in S^* which are Bayes against some $\boldsymbol{\xi}$ in Ξ_ϵ.

Because of its greater importance we give a formal definition of the next class of strategies to be introduced.

Definition 5.2.1. Let (Ξ, S^*, M) be the mixed extension of an S game, and let Ξ_+ be the set of all $\boldsymbol{\xi}$ in Ξ with $\xi(i) > 0$ for all i. Then $\mathfrak{D} =$ the set of all \mathbf{s} in S^* which are Bayes against some $\boldsymbol{\xi}$ in Ξ_+. We denote the closure of \mathfrak{D} by $\overline{\mathfrak{D}}$.

We turn now to a number of theorems about the above classes of strategies in S games. It is clearly seen that the defining properties of the classes \mathfrak{A}, \mathfrak{B}, \mathfrak{D}, and $\overline{\mathfrak{D}}$ remain unchanged if to each element of S we add a constant vector \mathbf{r}, or, equivalently, if we translate the set S in S_n.

Theorem 5.2.1. Let (Ξ, S^*, M) be the mixed extension of an S game, let $\mathbf{s}^* = (s^*_1, \cdots, s^*_n)$ be a fixed point in S^*, and let $T_{\mathbf{s}*}$ be the set of points in n space defined by $\mathbf{t} \, \varepsilon \, T_{\mathbf{s}*}$ if $t_i < s^*_i$ for all i. Then a necessary and sufficient condition that $\mathbf{s}^* \, \varepsilon \, \mathfrak{B}$ is that $T_{\mathbf{s}*} \cap S^*$ is empty.

Proof. Suppose $T_{\mathbf{s}*} \cap S^* \neq \varnothing$; say $\mathbf{s}_1 \, \varepsilon \, T_{\mathbf{s}*} \cap S^*$. Then, since $\mathbf{s}_1 \, \varepsilon \, T_{\mathbf{s}*}$, we have $s_{1i} < s^*_i$ for all i, and hence, for all $\boldsymbol{\xi}$ in Ξ,

$$\boldsymbol{\xi} \cdot \mathbf{s}_1 < \boldsymbol{\xi} \cdot \mathbf{s}^*$$

which contradicts the hypothesis that \mathbf{s}^* is Bayes, i.e., that, for some $\boldsymbol{\xi}$ in Ξ,

$$\boldsymbol{\xi} \cdot \mathbf{s}^* = \min_{\mathbf{s} \, \varepsilon \, S^*} (\boldsymbol{\xi} \cdot \mathbf{s})$$

This proves the necessity of the condition. To prove the sufficiency of the condition, we assume that $T_{\mathbf{s}*} \cap S^* = \varnothing$. Since $T_{\mathbf{s}*}$ is open and

s^* is a boundary point of T_{s*}, then by corollary 2 to Theorem 2.2.1 there exists a hyperplane $\xi \cdot x = c$ such that $\xi \cdot s^* = c$, $\xi \cdot t \leq c$ for all $t \, \varepsilon \, \overline{T}$ and $\xi \cdot s \geq c$ for all $s \, \varepsilon \, S^*$. Let δ_i be the unit vector with 1 in the ith coordinate. Then $s^* - \delta_i \, \varepsilon \, \overline{T}$, and

$$\xi \cdot (s^* - \delta_i) \leq c = \xi \cdot s^*$$

so that $\xi \cdot \delta_i \geq 0$ and thus $\xi(i) \geq 0$ for all i. Hence, we can assume, without loss of generality, that $\sum_{i=1}^{n} \xi(i) = 1$ so that $\xi \, \varepsilon \, \Xi$. Clearly s^* is Bayes against this ξ, which completes the proof of the theorem.

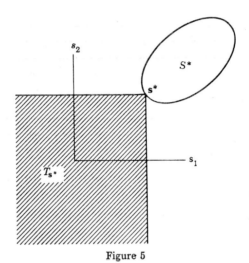

Figure 5

We observe that in any S game the class of good strategies for player II form a subset of \mathcal{B}. Thus Theorem 5.2.1 simply carries further the geometric ideas introduced in Section 2.4 following the proof of Theorem 2.4.2. Here again we point out that in a game $G = (X, Y, M)$ in which X is finite, the requirement that M is bounded can be replaced by the weaker requirement that M is bounded from below, and the geometric characterization of the class \mathcal{B} given by the above Theorem remains valid.

Theorem 5.2.2. Let (Ξ, S^*, M) be the mixed extension of an S game, where S^* is closed. Then the class \mathcal{B} of Bayes strategies in S^* is closed.

Proof. Let $\{b_m\}$ be a sequence of points in \mathcal{B} such that $b_m \to b$ as $m \to \infty$. We wish to show that $b \, \varepsilon \, \mathcal{B}$. Since $b_m \, \varepsilon \, \mathcal{B}$ then b_m is Bayes against some $\xi^{(m)} \, \varepsilon \, \Xi$; i.e., $\xi^{(m)} \cdot b_m \leq \xi^{(m)} \cdot s$ for all $s \, \varepsilon \, S^*$. Since

Ξ is closed we can choose a subsequence of $\{\xi^{(m)}\}$ which converges to $\xi^* \, \varepsilon \, \Xi$. Letting $m \to \infty$ through this subsequence yields $\xi^* \cdot \mathbf{b} \leq \xi^* \cdot \mathbf{s}$ for all $\mathbf{s} \, \varepsilon \, S^*$. Thus \mathbf{b} is Bayes against ξ^*, and hence $\mathbf{b} \, \varepsilon \, \mathfrak{B}$.

Theorem 5.2.3. Let (Ξ, S^*, M) be the mixed extension of an S game, where S^* is closed. Then,

$$\mathfrak{D} \subset \mathfrak{A} \subset \overline{\mathfrak{D}} \subset \mathfrak{B}$$

Proof. Clearly $\mathfrak{D} \subset \overline{\mathfrak{D}}$, and $\mathfrak{D} \subset \mathfrak{B}$. Since \mathfrak{B} is closed by Theorem 5.2.2, $\overline{\mathfrak{D}} \subset \mathfrak{B}$. It remains therefore to show that (a) $\mathfrak{D} \subset \mathfrak{A}$ and (b) $\mathfrak{A} \subset \overline{\mathfrak{D}}$.

Proof of a. Let $\mathbf{d} \, \varepsilon \, \mathfrak{D}$. Then there is a $\xi = (\xi(1), \cdots, \xi(n))$ with $\xi(i) > 0$ for all i such that $\xi \cdot \mathbf{d} \leq \xi \cdot \mathbf{s}$ for all $\mathbf{s} \, \varepsilon \, S^*$. Hence there cannot be an $\mathbf{s} \, \varepsilon \, S^*$ with $s_i \leq d_i$ for all i and actual inequality for some i, as this would imply that $\xi \cdot \mathbf{s} < \xi \cdot \mathbf{d}$ for that \mathbf{s}. Thus $\mathbf{d} \, \varepsilon \, \mathfrak{A}$.

Proof of b. Let $\mathbf{a} \, \varepsilon \, \mathfrak{A}$. To simplify the proof it will be assumed without loss of generality that $\mathbf{a} = \mathbf{e}$ where $\mathbf{e} = (0, \cdots, 0)$. Consider the two sets S^* and Ξ_ϵ for $\epsilon > 0$. Since both of these sets are closed, convex, and bounded, then by Theorem 2.4.3 there exists a point $\mathbf{s}^{(\epsilon)} \, \varepsilon \, S^*$ and a point $\xi^{(\epsilon)} \, \varepsilon \, \Xi_\epsilon$ such that

$$(1) \qquad \xi \cdot \mathbf{s}^{(\epsilon)} \leq \xi^{(\epsilon)} \cdot \mathbf{s}^{(\epsilon)} \leq \xi^{(\epsilon)} \cdot \mathbf{s}$$

for all $\mathbf{s} \, \varepsilon \, S^*$ and $\xi \, \varepsilon \, \Xi_\epsilon$. We shall show that we can choose a sequence $\epsilon_m \to 0$ such that the corresponding sequence $\mathbf{s}^{(\epsilon_m)} \to \mathbf{e}$.

Since by assumption $\mathbf{e} \, \varepsilon \, S^*$ we have by (1)

$$(2) \qquad \xi^{(\epsilon)} \cdot \mathbf{s}^{(\epsilon)} \leq \xi^{(\epsilon)} \cdot \mathbf{e} = 0$$

Choose a sequence $\epsilon_m \to 0$ such that $\xi^{(\epsilon_m)} \to \xi^*$ and $\mathbf{s}^{(\epsilon_m)} \to \mathbf{s}^*$. Now, by (1) and (2), $\xi \cdot \mathbf{s}^{(\epsilon_m)} \leq 0$ for all $\xi \, \varepsilon \, \Xi_\epsilon$. Therefore, since for any $\xi \, \varepsilon \, \Xi_+$, $\xi \, \varepsilon \, \Xi_{\epsilon_m}$ for sufficiently large m, it follows that, for such m, $\xi \cdot \mathbf{s}^{(\epsilon_m)} \leq 0$ for all $\xi \, \varepsilon \, \Xi_+$ and hence $\xi \cdot \mathbf{s}^* \leq 0$ for all $\xi \, \varepsilon \, \Xi_+$. Now, for any $\xi \, \varepsilon \, \Xi$, there is a sequence $\{\xi^{(m)}\}$, $\xi^{(m)} \, \varepsilon \, \Xi_+$ such that $\xi^{(m)} \to \xi$. Since $\xi^{(m)} \cdot \mathbf{s}^* \leq 0$ for all m, we have $\xi \cdot \mathbf{s}^* \leq 0$ for all $\xi \, \varepsilon \, \Xi$. In particular, $\delta_i \cdot \mathbf{s}^* = s^*_i \leq 0$ for each i where δ_i is the vector which has unity for the ith coordinate and zero for all other coordinates. But, by assumption, \mathbf{e} is admissible. Hence $s^*_i = 0$ for all i; i.e., $\mathbf{s}^* = \mathbf{e}$. Thus we have exhibited a sequence $\mathbf{s}^{(\epsilon_m)} \to \mathbf{e}$ such that, for each m, $\mathbf{s}^{(\epsilon_m)}$ is Bayes against a $\xi^{(m)} \, \varepsilon \, \Xi_+$ so that $\mathbf{e} \, \varepsilon \, \overline{\mathfrak{D}}$ and consequently $\mathfrak{A} \subset \overline{\mathfrak{D}}$.

We shall now give two examples which will show that (1) $\mathfrak{D} \neq \mathfrak{A}$ and (2) $\mathfrak{A} \neq \overline{\mathfrak{D}}$.

Example 1. Let S^* consist of all points (x, y) such that $(x - 1)^2 + (y - 1)^2 \leq 1$. Then it is easy to see that all admissible points lie on the arc of the circle $(x - 1)^2 + (y - 1)^2 = 1$ with $0 \leq x, y \leq 1$. Thus the points $(0, 1)$ and $(1, 0)$ are admissible, but they are not Bayes against any $\boldsymbol{\xi} = (\xi(1), \xi(2))$, $\xi(1) + \xi(2) = 1$ with $\xi(i) > 0$. Thus $\mathfrak{D} \neq \mathfrak{a}$.

Example 2. Let $T =$ the set of triples $(x, y, 1)$ with $0 \leq x, y \leq 1$ and $(x - 1)^2 + (y - 1)^2 = 1$, and let $a_0 = (1, 0, 0)$. Let S^* be the convex set determined by T and a_0. Consider the point $\mathbf{t}_0 = (x_0, y_0, 1)$ $\varepsilon\ T$ with $0 < x_0 < 1$. Then there are positive numbers ζ_1, ζ_2, with $\zeta_1 + \zeta_2 = 1$ such that

$$(1) \qquad\qquad x\zeta_1 + y\zeta_2 > x_0\zeta_1 + y_0\zeta_2$$

for all $t = (x, y, 1)\ \varepsilon\ T$ with $t \neq t_0$. (The ζ_i's are given by the tangent line to the circle $(x - 1)^2 + (y - 1)^2 = 1$ at the point (x_0, y_0).) In particular, setting $x = 1$, $y = 0$, we get $\zeta_1 > x_0\zeta_1 + y_0\zeta_2$. Now, pick $\epsilon > 0$ so small that

$$(2) \qquad\qquad \zeta_1 > x_0\zeta_1 + y_0\zeta_2 + \frac{\epsilon}{1 - \epsilon}$$

and consider the vector $\boldsymbol{\xi} = ((1 - \epsilon)\zeta_1, (1 - \epsilon)\zeta_2, \epsilon)\ \varepsilon\ \Xi_+$. Then, by (1) and (2), a simple calculation gives us the inequalities

$$(3) \qquad\qquad \boldsymbol{\xi} \cdot \mathbf{t} \geq \boldsymbol{\xi} \cdot \mathbf{t}_0$$

for all $\mathbf{t}\ \varepsilon\ T$, and

$$(4) \qquad\qquad \boldsymbol{\xi} \cdot \mathbf{a}_0 \geq \boldsymbol{\xi} \cdot \mathbf{t}_0$$

Taking convex linear combinations of (3) and (4) yields

$$(5) \qquad\qquad \boldsymbol{\xi} \cdot \mathbf{s} \geq \boldsymbol{\xi} \cdot \mathbf{t}_0$$

for all $\mathbf{s}\ \varepsilon\ S^*$; i.e., \mathbf{t}_0 is Bayes against $\boldsymbol{\xi}$; consequently $\mathbf{t}_0\ \varepsilon\ \mathfrak{D}$. Now let $x_0 \to 1$, $y_0 \to 0$. Then $(x_0, y_0, 1) \to (1, 0, 1)$ and $(1, 0, 1)\ \varepsilon\ \overline{\mathfrak{D}}$. But $(1, 0, 1)$ is not admissible since $(1, 0, 0)$ is better. Thus $\mathfrak{a} \neq \overline{\mathfrak{D}}$.

Theorem 5.2.4. Let (Ξ, S^*, M) be the mixed extension of an S game, where S^* is closed. Then the sets \mathfrak{a}, $\overline{\mathfrak{D}}$, and \mathfrak{B} in S^* are complete.

Proof. If a subclass of a class of strategies is complete, then the class itself is complete. Thus, in view of Theorem 5.2.3, it is sufficient to show that \mathfrak{a} is complete. That is, we have to show that for every $\mathbf{s}\ \varepsilon\ S^*$, $\mathbf{s} \notin \mathfrak{a}$ we can find an $\mathbf{a}\ \varepsilon\ \mathfrak{a}$ such that $a_i \leq s_i$ for all i with inequality holding for at least one i.

Figure 6

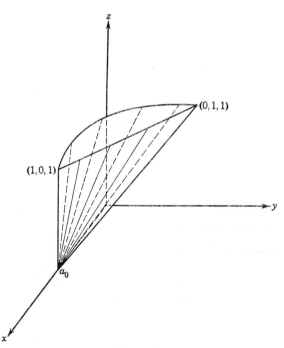

Figure 7

Let $s_0 \, \varepsilon \, S^*$, $s_0 \notin \mathcal{Q}$, and let S_1 be the set of all points $s \, \varepsilon \, S^*$ with $s_i \leq s_{0i}$ for all i. Then S_1 is closed. Let \mathbf{a}_0 be a point in S^* which minimizes $f(\mathbf{x}) = \sum_{i=1}^{n} \frac{1}{n} x_i$ on S_1. Then, since S_1 is closed, $\mathbf{a}_0 \, \varepsilon \, S_1$. Furthermore \mathbf{a}_0 is admissible since (1) by Theorem 5.2.3, \mathbf{a}_0 is admissible in S_1 as it is Bayes against a $\boldsymbol{\xi}$ with positive components: viz., $\boldsymbol{\xi} = (1/n, 1/n, \cdots, 1/n)$; (2) no point of S^* outside of S_1 can dominate \mathbf{a}_0 for, if $s_1 \notin S_1$, we have $s_{1i} > s_{0i}$ for some i while $a_{0i} \leq s_{0i}$ for all i. Finally, for at least one i, $a_{0i} < s_{0i}$ since otherwise s_0 would also be admissible which is contrary to our assumptions.

Thus far we have assumed that nature has a finite number of possible states, but no limitations were set on the possible actions (pure strategies) the statistician might have. If we assume that the statistician too can have only a finite number, say m, of pure strategies, then the game S consists of a finite number of points in S_n, and S^* is the convex hull of these points. That is, if $\mathbf{z}_1, \cdots, \mathbf{z}_m$ are the points in S then every point $s \, \varepsilon \, S^*$ is given by

$$\mathbf{s} = \left(\sum_{j=1}^{m} \eta(j) z_{j1}, \cdots, \sum_{j=1}^{m} \eta(j) z_{jn} \right) = \sum_{j=1}^{m} \eta(j) \mathbf{z}_j$$

where $\eta(j) \geq 0$ for all j and $\sum_{j=1}^{m} \eta(j) = 1$. For this special case we have the following.

Theorem 5.2.5. Let (Ξ, S^*, M) be the mixed extension of an S game, where S^* is spanned by a finite number of points, say $\mathbf{z}_1, \cdots, \mathbf{z}_m$. Then there is a finite number of $\boldsymbol{\xi}$'s in Ξ_+, say $\boldsymbol{\xi}^{(1)}, \cdots, \boldsymbol{\xi}^{(k)}$, such that $\mathfrak{D} = \mathcal{Q} = \overline{\mathfrak{D}} =$ the set of all \mathbf{s} in S^* which are Bayes against some $\boldsymbol{\xi}^{(i)}$, for $i = 1, \cdots, k$.

Proof. Before we prove this theorem, we prove the following lemma.

Lemma 5.2.1. If $s \, \varepsilon \, S^*$ is Bayes against $a \, \boldsymbol{\xi}$ and $\mathbf{s} = \sum_{j=1}^{m} \eta(j) \mathbf{z}_j$, then every \mathbf{z}_j for which $\eta(j) > 0$ is also Bayes against $\boldsymbol{\xi}$.

Proof. Let s be Bayes against $\boldsymbol{\xi}$. Then $\boldsymbol{\xi} \cdot \mathbf{z}_j \geq \boldsymbol{\xi} \cdot \mathbf{s}$ for all j, and hence $\eta(j)(\boldsymbol{\xi} \cdot \mathbf{z}_j) \geq \eta(j)(\boldsymbol{\xi} \cdot \mathbf{s})$ for all j. But the inequality sign cannot hold for any j for which $\eta(j) > 0$ since we would then have

$$\boldsymbol{\xi} \cdot \mathbf{s} = \sum_{j=1}^{m} \eta(j)(\boldsymbol{\xi} \cdot \mathbf{z}_j) > \sum_{j=1}^{m} \eta(j)(\boldsymbol{\xi} \cdot \mathbf{s}) = \boldsymbol{\xi} \cdot \mathbf{s}$$

which is impossible. Thus, for all j for which $\eta(j) > 0$, we have $\eta(j)(\boldsymbol{\xi}\cdot\mathbf{z}_j) = \eta(j)(\boldsymbol{\xi}\cdot\mathbf{s})$, and hence $\boldsymbol{\xi}\cdot\mathbf{z}_j = \boldsymbol{\xi}\cdot\mathbf{s}$, which proves the lemma. We now return to the proof of the theorem.

We shall show that $\mathfrak{D} = \bigcup_{i=1}^{k} T_i$ where T_i is closed and the elements of T_i are Bayes against a common $\boldsymbol{\xi}^{(i)} \varepsilon \,\Xi_+$. From this we will have \mathfrak{D} closed; hence $\mathfrak{D} = \overline{\mathfrak{D}}$; and, since $\mathfrak{D} \subset \mathfrak{C} \subset \overline{\mathfrak{D}}$, the conclusion will follow.

Let v_1, \cdots, v_{2^m} be the 2^m subsets of the set of integers $\{1, \cdots, m\}$. Let T_i be the convex hull of the set of those \mathbf{z}_j's for which $j \varepsilon v_i$. Let U_i be the set of all $\mathbf{s} \varepsilon \mathfrak{D}$ for which \mathbf{s} can be represented by $\mathbf{s} = \sum_{j\,\varepsilon\,v_i} \eta(j)\mathbf{z}_j$ where $\eta(j) > 0$ for $j \varepsilon v_i$, $\sum_{j\,\varepsilon\,v_i} \eta(j) = 1$. Since some U_j may be empty, let us assume for simplicity that U_i is not empty for $i \leq k$ and is empty for $i > k$ $(k \leq 2^m)$.

Now, for $i \leq k$, let $\mathbf{s}_0 \varepsilon U_i$ and \mathbf{s}_0 be Bayes against $\boldsymbol{\xi}^{(i)} \varepsilon \Xi_+$. We can write $\mathbf{s}_0 = \sum_{j\,\varepsilon\,v_i} \eta_0(j)\mathbf{z}_j$ where $\eta_0(j) > 0$ for $j \varepsilon v_i$ and $\sum_{j\,\varepsilon\,v_i} \eta_0(j) = 1$. Then, by Lemma 5.2.1, \mathbf{z}_j is Bayes against $\boldsymbol{\xi}^{(i)}$ for each $j \varepsilon v_i$. For, $\mathbf{s}_1 \varepsilon T_i$, we can write $\mathbf{s}_1 = \sum_{j\,\varepsilon\,v_i} \eta_1(j)\mathbf{z}_j$, $\eta_1(j) \geq 0$, $\sum_{j\,\varepsilon\,v_i} \eta_1(j) = 1$. Then, for each $\mathbf{s} \varepsilon S^*$,

$$\boldsymbol{\xi}^{(i)}\cdot\mathbf{s}_1 = \sum_{j\,\varepsilon\,v_i} \eta_1(j)\boldsymbol{\xi}^{(i)}\cdot\mathbf{z}_j \leq \sum_{j\,\varepsilon\,v_i} \eta_1(j)\boldsymbol{\xi}^{(i)}\cdot\mathbf{s} = \boldsymbol{\xi}^{(i)}\cdot\mathbf{s}$$

Hence, each element of T_i is Bayes against $\boldsymbol{\xi}^{(i)} \varepsilon \Xi_+$ and this for $i = 1$, $2, \cdots, k$. Clearly, from its definition T_i is closed.

The above shows $\mathfrak{D} \supset \bigcup_{i=1}^{k} T_i$. To show the opposite inclusion, suppose $\mathbf{s}_0 \varepsilon \mathfrak{D}$, $\mathbf{s}_0 = \sum_{j=1}^{m} \eta_0(j)\mathbf{z}_j$, and suppose the set of j's such that $\eta_0(j) > 0$ is v_r. Then $\mathbf{s}_0 \varepsilon U_r \subset T_r$. Hence, $\mathfrak{D} \subset \sum_{i=1}^{k} T_i$ and the proof is complete.

It might be noted that we have shown $\mathfrak{D} = \bigcup_{i=1}^{k} T_i = \bigcup_{i=1}^{k} U_i$.

The following result properly belongs to Chapter 2, but, since it is a direct consequence of the previous theorem, we state it as a corollary.

Corollary. Let (Ξ, H, M) be the mixed extension of a finite game $G = (X, Y, M)$ with matrix $\|a_{ij}\|$, $i = 1, \cdots, n$, $j = 1, \cdots, m$. Then there is a good strategy $\boldsymbol{\xi} = (\xi(1), \cdots, \xi(n))$ for player I such that $\xi(i) > 0$ for every pure strategy x_i in X which is Bayes against all good strategies of player II.

Proof. Let R be the set of all i's for which x_i is Bayes against every good strategy of player II. Then, if I is restricted to i's in R, the value of the game is unchanged, since every good strategy ξ for I will have $\xi(i) = 0$ for $i \notin R$.

If η is any good strategy in the new game, then $\sum_{j=1}^{m} a_{ij}\eta(j) = v$ for $i \varepsilon R$, for suppose $\sum_{j=1}^{m} a_{i_0 j}\eta(j) < v$ for some $i_0 \varepsilon R$. We can choose a good strategy η^* in the original game with $\sum_{j=1}^{n} a_{ij}\eta^*(j) < v$ for all $i \notin R$.

For every $\epsilon > 0$, the strategy $\eta_1 = (1 - \epsilon)\eta^* + \epsilon\eta$ satisfies $\sum_{j=1}^{m} a_{ij}\eta(j) \leq v$ for $i \varepsilon R$, and the inequality will hold for $i \notin R$ for sufficiently small ϵ. Then, for sufficiently small $\epsilon > 0$, η_1 will be a good strategy in the original game, and, since $\sum_{j=1}^{m} a_{i_0 j}\eta(j) < v$, i_0 is not in R. Thus we may suppose that every x_i, $i = 1, \cdots, n$ is Bayes against every good strategy η for II, and must prove that there is a good strategy ξ with $\xi(i) > 0$ for all i.

Let z_1, \cdots, z_m be the column vectors of $\| a_{ij} \|$, and let S^* be the convex set determined by z_1, \cdots, z_m. Then G is equivalent to the S game (I_n, S, M), where $S = \{z_1, \cdots, z_m\}$, and (Ξ, H, M) is equivalent to (Ξ, S^*, M'), where, for ξ in Ξ and s in S^*, $M'(\xi, s) = \xi \cdot s$. The point $s^* = (v, \cdots, v)$ is in S^* and is admissible, where v is the value of G. By Theorem 5.2.5, there is a $\xi \varepsilon \Xi_+$ such that s^* is Bayes against ξ; i.e., $\xi \cdot s^* \leq \xi \cdot s$ for all s in S^*. That is, $\xi \cdot s \geq v$ for all s in S^*, which completes the proof.

PROBLEMS

5.2.1. Let $x = (x_1, x_2)$ be any point in 2-space, and let $K = \{x : (x_1 - 8)^2 + (x_2 - 8)^2 \leq 100\}$; $Q = \{x : 0 \leq x_1, x_2 \leq 4\}$; $R = \{x : 2 \leq x_1 < 3, x_2 = 0\}$; $P = \{x : x_1 = 0, x_2 = 2\}$. Consider an S game with $S = K \cap Q - (P \cup R)$. (a) Draw the set S, and describe the sets \mathfrak{D}, \mathfrak{A}, and \mathfrak{B}. (b) Show how this example illustrates the fact that, if S^* is not closed, there need not exist a minimal complete class.

5.2.2. Let G be a finite game with matrix

$$A = \begin{pmatrix} 2 & 8 & 15 & 5 & 2 & 10 & 12 & 13 & 14 & 5 \\ 12 & 3 & 9 & 4 & 8 & 9 & 3 & 12 & 5 & 10 \end{pmatrix}$$

and let S^* be the mixed extension of the corresponding S game in 2-space. Draw the set S^*, and compute the strategies $\xi^{(1)}, \xi^{(2)}, \cdots, \xi^{(k)}$ guaranteed by Theorem 5.2.5.

5.2.3. Let S^* be the mixed extension of an S game in n space, and let $b \varepsilon \mathfrak{B}$. Then

(1) $\mathbf{b} = \sum_{j=1}^{r} \eta(j)\mathbf{s}^{(j)}$ where $r \leq n$; $\mathbf{s}^{(j)} = (s_1^{(j)}, \cdots, s_n^{(j)})$ and $\mathbf{s}^{(j)} \, \varepsilon \, S$ for all j; $\eta(j) > 0$ for all j, $\sum_{j=1}^{r} \eta(j) = 1$.

(2) If ξ is an element of Ξ against which \mathbf{b} is Bayes, then $\mathbf{s}^{(j)}$ is also Bayes against the same ξ for all j.

5.3. The Class of Games G_η

Definition 5.3.1. Let $G = (X, Y, M)$ be a game and (Ξ, H, M) its mixed extension, and, for every η in H, x in X, and y in Y, let

$$M_\eta(x, y) = M(x, y) - M(x, \eta)$$

Then we call the game $G_\eta = (X, Y, M_\eta)$ a game derived from G (or simply a derived game).

For simplicity of notation in dealing with derived games, we write v^*_η and λ^*_η for the upper and lower values of Γ_η, the mixed extension of G_η. Elements of H are denoted by η, μ, and ν.

Definition 5.3.2. Let $G = (X, Y, M)$ be a game, and let η, μ be any two strategies in H, and let G_η, G_μ be the corresponding derived games. The strategy μ will be said to be at least as good as η if $\Upsilon_\eta(\mu) \leq 0$; it will be said to be better than η if in addition $\Upsilon_\mu(\eta) > 0$. The two strategies μ and η will be called equivalent, written $\mu \equiv \eta$, if $\Upsilon_\eta(\mu) \leq 0$ and $\Upsilon_\mu(\eta) \leq 0$; i.e., $M(x, \mu) = M(x, \eta)$ for all x.

Note that for a strategy μ to be called *better than* η, there must exist at least one $x = x_0$ such that $M(x_0, \mu) < M(x_0, \eta)$.

Theorem 5.3.1. Let $G = (X, Y, M)$ be a game. Then in every derived game $G_\eta = (X, Y, M)$, $v^*_\eta \leq 0$.

Proof. By Definitions 5.3.1 and 1.6.2, $\Upsilon_\eta(\eta) = 0$. Hence

$$v^*_\eta = \inf_{\mu \, \varepsilon \, \mathrm{H}} \Upsilon_\eta(\mu) \leq 0$$

An immediate consequence of this theorem is that all admissible strategies in the original game G can be found only among the class of η's for which $v^*_\eta = 0$. To see this, suppose $v^*_\eta < 0$. Then there exists a strategy μ such that $\Upsilon_\eta(\mu) < -\delta < 0$; i.e., $\sup_x [M(x, \mu) - M(x, \eta)] < -\delta < 0$ or, what is equivalent, $M(x, \mu) \leq M(x, \eta) - \delta$ for all x, so that η is not admissible. This remark is made as a partial motivation for studying the class of games G_η. As will be seen below, many classes of optimal strategies will be defined in terms of the derived games G_η, and the properties of these classes will depend on the properties of these games.

Theorem 5.3.2. Let $G = (X, Y, M)$ be a game. A necessary and sufficient condition that any derived game $G_\eta = (X, Y, M_\eta)$ have a value and the value be zero is that $\lambda^*_\eta = 0$.

Proof. Assume that $\lambda^*_\eta = 0$. By Theorem 1.6.1, $\lambda^*_\eta \leq v^*_\eta$ so that, by Theorem 5.3.1, we have

(1) $$\lambda^*_\eta = v^*_\eta = 0$$

Conversely, if the value of G_η is zero, then (1) holds.

Theorem 5.3.3. Let $G_\eta = (X, Y, M_\eta)$ and $G_\mu = (X, Y, M_\mu)$ be any two games derived from $G = (X, Y, M)$. Then

$$\Upsilon_\eta(\mu) + v^*_\mu \geq v^*_\eta$$

Proof. Let η, μ, and ν be any three elements of H. Then, since for any functions f and g

$$\sup_x f(x) + \sup_x g(x) \geq \sup_x [f(x) + g(x)]$$

we have

(1) $$\sup_x [M(x, \mu) - M(x, \eta)] + \sup_x [M(x, \nu) - M(x, \mu)]$$
$$\geq \sup_x [M(x, \nu) - M(x, \eta)]$$

and (1) is equivalent to

(2) $$\Upsilon_\eta(\mu) + \Upsilon_\mu(\nu) \geq \Upsilon_\eta(\nu)$$

Taking the infimum with respect to ν on both sides of (2) yields the theorem.

Corollary. Under the conditions of the theorem

$$\Upsilon_\eta(\mu) + \Upsilon_\mu(\eta) \geq 0$$

Proof. Let $\nu = \eta$ in equation 2 above.

Theorem 5.3.4. Let (Ξ, H, M) be the mixed extension of the game $G = (X, Y, M)$, and suppose that there exists an η in H such that μ in H is a minimax strategy for player II in the derived game G_η. Then, in the derived game G_μ, $v^*_\mu = 0$.

Proof. Since μ is minimax in G_η, we have, by Definition 1.8.5,

$$\Upsilon_\eta(\mu) = v^*_\eta$$

so that, by Theorem 5.3.3, $v^*_\mu \geq 0$. But, by Theorem 5.3.1, $v^*_\mu \leq 0$. Therefore, $v^*_\mu = 0$.

PROBLEMS

5.3.1. Give a geometric interpretation of the game G_η in case G is an S game.

5.3.2. Give a geometric interpretation of all the theorems proved in this section in case G is an S game.

5.4. Definition of Classes of Optimal Strategies

In this section we formally define various classes of optimal strategies. In order to avoid repetition in the definitions, we shall omit statement of the condition that we are dealing with an arbitrary game $G = (X, Y, M)$, its mixed extension $\Gamma = (\Xi, H, M)$, and the games G_η derived from G. The same rule shall be followed in the statement of theorems and definitions in the remainder of this chapter.

Definition 5.4.1. Suppose $\epsilon > 0$. The class \mathfrak{M}_ϵ is defined as the class of all strategies μ in H for which there exists an η in H such that

$$\Upsilon_\eta(\mu) < v^*{}_\eta + \epsilon$$

The class \mathfrak{M}_ϵ consists of all strategies for player II that are within ϵ of being minimax in some game G_η.

Definition 5.4.2. The class \mathfrak{M} is defined as the class of all strategies μ in H for which there exists an η in H such that

$$\Upsilon_\eta(\mu) = v^*{}_\eta$$

The class \mathfrak{M} consists of all strategies for player II that are minimax in some game G_η.

Definition 5.4.3. The class \mathfrak{N} is defined as the class of all strategies μ in H that are minimax for player II in G.

Definition 5.4.4. Let ϵ be any positive number. The class \mathfrak{B}_ϵ of ϵ-Bayes strategies is defined as the class of all strategies η in H for which $\lambda^*{}_\eta > -\epsilon$.

An ϵ-Bayes strategy is an η which is within ϵ of being optimal against some strategy ξ_ϵ of player I in the original game G; that is, there exists a ξ_ϵ such that

$$M(\xi_\epsilon, \eta) \leq \inf_\mu M(\xi_\epsilon, \mu) + \epsilon$$

This inequality follows from the definition since

$$\lambda^*{}_\eta = \sup_\xi \inf_\mu M_\eta(\xi, \mu) > -\epsilon$$

implies that there exists a ξ_ϵ such that

$$\inf_\mu M_\eta(\xi_\epsilon, \mu) \geq -\epsilon$$

or

$$\inf_\mu M(\xi_\epsilon, \mu) - M(\xi_\epsilon, \eta) \geq -\epsilon$$

Definition 5.4.5. A strategy η in H is called extended Bayes if $\lambda^*_\eta = 0$. The class of extended Bayes strategies is designated by \mathfrak{B}_0.

A strategy η is extended Bayes if and only if it is ϵ-Bayes for every $\epsilon > 0$. In view of Theorem 5.3.2, the class \mathfrak{B}_0 can be characterized as the class of η's for which G_η has the value zero.

Definition 5.4.6. A strategy η in H is called Bayes if it is extended Bayes and there exists a ξ in Ξ with $\Lambda_\eta(\xi) = 0$. The class of Bayes strategies is designated by \mathfrak{B}.

A strategy η is Bayes if there exists a ξ against which it is optimal in the original game G; i.e.,

$$M(\xi, \eta) = \min_\mu M(\xi, \mu)$$

This follows from the definition and Theorem 5.3.2.

Definition 5.4.7. For $\epsilon > 0$ a strategy η in H is called ϵ-admissible if $v^*_\eta > -\epsilon$. The class of ϵ-admissible strategies is designated by \mathfrak{A}_ϵ.

An ϵ-admissible strategy η has the property that there exists no other strategy μ such that for all x

(1) $M(x, \mu) < M(x, \eta) - \epsilon$

This conclusion follows from the definition since

$$v^*_\eta = \inf_\mu \sup_x M_\eta(x, \mu) > -\epsilon$$

implies that

$$\sup_x [M(x, \mu) - M(x, \eta)] > -\epsilon$$

for all μ, so that for every μ there exists an x such that

$$M(x, \mu) - M(x, \eta) \geq -\epsilon$$

Hence, there can exist no μ satisfying (1) for all x.

Definition 5.4.8. A strategy η in H is called extended admissible if $v^*_\eta = 0$. The class of extended admissible strategies is designated by \mathfrak{A}_0.

A strategy η is extended admissible if and only if it is ϵ-admissible for every $\epsilon > 0$.

Definition 5.4.9. A strategy η in H is called admissible if, for all μ in H, $\Upsilon_\eta(\mu) > 0$ unless $\mu \equiv \eta$. The class of admissible strategies is designated by \mathcal{C}.

Definition 5.4.10. A class \mathcal{C} of strategies is called essentially complete if for every $\mu \, \varepsilon \, $H there exists an $\eta \, \varepsilon \, \mathcal{C}$ such that $\Upsilon_\mu(\eta) \leq 0$.

An essentially complete class of strategies has the property that for any strategy in H there is one in the class that is at least as good.

Definition 5.4.11. A class \mathcal{C} of strategies is called complete if for every $\mu \notin \mathcal{C}$ there exists an $\eta \, \varepsilon \, \mathcal{C}$ such that $\Upsilon_\mu(\eta) \leq 0$ and $\Upsilon_\eta(\mu) > 0$.

A complete class of strategies has the property that for every strategy outside the class there exists one in the class which is better.

Classes \mathcal{C}, \mathcal{B} and complete classes have been considered in the previous section in connection with S games. To illustrate the remaining classes, consider the game $G = (X, Y, M)$ where X consists of all positive integers, Y consists of all sequences $\{a_j\} = (a_1, a_2, \cdots)$ with $a_j > 0$ for all j, and, for any $x = n \, \varepsilon \, X$ and $y = \{a_j\} \, \varepsilon \, Y$, $M(x, y) = a_n$. For any $\epsilon > 0$, the class $\mathfrak{M}_\epsilon = \mathcal{C}_\epsilon = \mathcal{B}_\epsilon$ consists of the class of sequences $\{a_j\}$ such that, for at least one n, $a_n \leq \epsilon$. The class $\mathfrak{M} = \mathcal{C}_0 = \mathcal{B}_0$ consists of the class of all sequences $\{a_j\}$ which have zero as a limit point, i.e., which contain a subsequence $(a_{j_1}, a_{j_2}, \cdots)$ such that $\lim_{n \to \infty} a_{j_n} = 0$.

As a simple example of an essentially complete class, consider an S game in n space in which the set S is convex. Then the class of pure strategies (i.e., all the elements of S) form an essentially complete class in the class of all mixed strategies.

PROBLEMS

5.4.1. Prove that a strategy η is extended Bayes if and only if it is ϵ-Bayes for every $\epsilon > 0$.

5.4.2. Prove that a strategy η is extended admissible if and only if it is ϵ-admissible for every $\epsilon > 0$.

5.4.3. Prove that if $\eta \, \varepsilon \, \mathcal{B}_\epsilon$ then $v^*{}_\eta - \lambda^*{}_\eta < \epsilon$.

5.4.4. A class \mathcal{R} of strategies is said to be *closed under equivalence* if it satisfies the condition that if $\eta \, \varepsilon \, \mathcal{R}$ then all strategies μ such that $\mu \equiv \eta$ also belong to \mathcal{R}. Show that \mathcal{C} and \mathcal{C}_0 are closed under equivalence.

5.4.5. A class \mathcal{R} of strategies which is closed under equivalence is complete if and only if it is essentially complete.

5.5. Set-Theoretic Relations among the Classes of Strategies

For any arbitrary game, certain set-theoretic relations always hold among the classes of strategies defined in Section 5.4. These are summarized in

Theorem 5.5.1. In every game

$$
\begin{array}{ccc}
\mathfrak{M}_\epsilon & = \; \mathcal{A}_\epsilon \; \supset \; \mathcal{B}_\epsilon \\
\cup & \cup \quad \cup \\
\mathfrak{M} & = \; \mathcal{A}_0 \; \supset \; \mathcal{B}_0 \\
\cup & \cup \quad \cup \\
\mathfrak{N} & \mathcal{A} \quad \mathcal{B}
\end{array}
$$

Proof. (a) $\mathfrak{M}_\epsilon = \mathcal{A}_\epsilon$. Let $\mu \, \varepsilon \, \mathfrak{M}_\epsilon$. Then $\Upsilon_\eta(\mu) < v^*_\eta + \epsilon$. Using Theorem 5.3.3, we obtain $v^*_\mu > -\epsilon$, and hence $\mu \, \varepsilon \, \mathcal{A}_\epsilon$. Conversely, let $\mu \, \varepsilon \, \mathcal{A}_\epsilon$. Then $v^*_\mu > -\epsilon$ so that $0 < v^*_\mu + \epsilon$. Choosing $\eta = \mu$ yields $\Upsilon_\mu(\mu) = 0 < v^*_\mu + \epsilon$ and hence $\mu \, \varepsilon \, \mathfrak{M}_\epsilon$.

(b) $\mathcal{A}_\epsilon \supset \mathcal{B}_\epsilon$. Always $\lambda^*_\eta \leq v^*_\eta$. Hence, whenever $\lambda^*_\eta > -\epsilon$, $v^*_\eta > -\epsilon$.

(c) $\mathfrak{M} = \mathcal{A}_0$. Let $\mu \, \varepsilon \, \mathfrak{M}$. Then, by Theorem 5.3.4, $v^*_\mu = 0$, so that $\mu \, \varepsilon \, \mathcal{A}_0$. Conversely, let $\mu \, \varepsilon \, \mathcal{A}_0$. Choosing $\eta = \mu$ yields $\Upsilon_\mu(\mu) = 0 = v^*_\mu$ and hence $\mu \, \varepsilon \, \mathfrak{M}$.

(d) $\mathcal{A}_0 \supset \mathcal{B}_0$. By Theorem 5.3.1, $v^*_\eta \leq 0$. If $\eta \, \varepsilon \, \mathcal{B}_0$ then $0 = \lambda^*_\eta \leq v^*_\eta \leq 0$. Therefore $v^*_\eta = 0$ and $\eta \, \varepsilon \, \mathcal{A}_0$.

(e) $\mathfrak{M} \supset \mathfrak{N}$. Let $\eta \, \varepsilon \, \mathfrak{N}$. By Theorem 5.3.1, $v^*_\eta \leq 0$. Suppose $\eta \not\varepsilon \, \mathfrak{M}$. Then, by (c), $\eta \not\varepsilon \, \mathcal{A}_0$ and hence $v^*_\eta < 0$. Thus there exists a μ with $\Upsilon_\eta(\mu) = \delta < 0$. That is

$$
M(x, \mu) \leq M(x, \eta) + \delta
$$

for all x. Since $\delta < 0$, η cannot be minimax which contradicts the assumption that $\eta \, \varepsilon \, \mathfrak{N}$.

(f) $\mathcal{A}_0 \supset \mathcal{A}$. Let $\eta \, \varepsilon \, \mathcal{A}$. Then by definition $\Upsilon_\eta(\mu) \geq 0$ for all μ. Hence, $v^*_\eta = \inf_\mu \Upsilon_\eta(\mu) \geq 0$. But, by Theorem 5.3.1, $v^*_\eta \leq 0$ so that $v^*_\eta = 0$ and $\eta \, \varepsilon \, \mathcal{A}_0$.

The proofs of the remaining relationships follow directly from the definitions and will be omitted. Further, it can be shown by means of counter examples that each set-theoretic relation not stated in Theorem 5.5.1 is in general false.

Theorem 5.5.2. In every game G, $\mathcal{A}_\epsilon = \mathcal{B}_\epsilon$ for every $\epsilon > 0$ if and only if for every η in H the game G_η has a value.

Proof. If every game G_η has a value then for every η, $\lambda^*_\eta = v^*_\eta$ so that the two classes are identical. Conversely, if $\mathcal{C}_\epsilon = \mathcal{B}_\epsilon$ for all ϵ, we must show that G_η has a value for all η. Assume the contrary. Then there exists an η for which $\lambda^*_\eta < v^*_\eta$. Choose $\epsilon > 0$ so that $\lambda^*_\eta < -\epsilon < v^*_\eta$. Then (1) $\eta \, \epsilon \, \mathcal{C}_\epsilon$ since $v^*_\eta > -\epsilon$ and (2) $\eta \notin \mathcal{B}_\epsilon$ since $\lambda^*_\eta < -\epsilon$. Thus we have exhibited an ϵ with $\mathcal{C}_\epsilon \neq \mathcal{B}_\epsilon$ which contradicts the assumption.

Theorem 5.5.3. In every game G, $\mathcal{C}_0 = \mathcal{B}_0$ if and only if for each $\eta \, \epsilon \, \mathcal{C}_0$ the game G_η has a value (namely zero).

Proof. If each game G_η has a value for $\eta \, \epsilon \, \mathcal{C}_0$ then by Theorem 5.3.2 $\lambda^*_\eta = v^*_\eta = 0$ and hence $\mathcal{C}_0 \subset \mathcal{B}_0$. But by Theorem 5.4.1 $\mathcal{C}_0 \supset \mathcal{B}_0$ and consequently $\mathcal{C}_0 = \mathcal{B}_0$. Conversely, assume $\mathcal{C}_0 = \mathcal{B}_0$. Then G_η has a value zero for every $\eta \, \epsilon \, \mathcal{C}_0$ by Theorem 5.3.2.

Theorem 5.5.4. In every game G, $\mathcal{B}_0 = \mathcal{B}$ if and only if for each $\eta \, \epsilon \, \mathcal{B}_0$ player I has a maximin strategy in G_η.

Proof. Assume that for each $\eta \, \epsilon \, \mathcal{B}_0$ player I has a maximin strategy ξ. Then $\Lambda_\eta(\xi) = \lambda^*_\eta = 0$. Thus $\mathcal{B}_0 \subset \mathcal{B}$. But, by Theorem 5.4.1, $\mathcal{B}_0 \supset \mathcal{B}$. Therefore $\mathcal{B}_0 = \mathcal{B}$. Conversely, if $\mathcal{B}_0 = \mathcal{B}$, then, for every $\eta \, \epsilon \, \mathcal{B}_0$, player I has a maximin strategy by the definition of \mathcal{B}.

Corollary 1. In every game G, $\mathcal{C}_0 = \mathcal{B}$ if and only if for each $\eta \, \epsilon \, \mathcal{C}_0$ the game G_η has a value and player I has a good strategy.

Proof. This corollary follows from Theorems 5.5.3 and 5.5.4.

PROBLEMS

5.5.1. Prove that $\mathcal{C} \subset \mathcal{B}$ if for each $\eta \, \epsilon \, \mathcal{C}_0$ the game G_η has a value and player I has a good strategy.

5.5.2. Prove the following theorem: Let $\eta \, \epsilon \, \mathfrak{N}$. (a) If G_η has a value then $\eta \, \epsilon \, \mathcal{B}_0$. (b) If in addition player I has a good strategy in G_η then $\eta \, \epsilon \, \mathcal{B}$.

5.5.3. Let $G_f = (X, Y, M + f)$ where f is any real-valued function defined on X. Let $\mathfrak{M}_{\mathfrak{F}}$ be the class of minimax strategies in G_f for all f. Prove that $\mathfrak{M}_{\mathfrak{F}} = \mathfrak{M}$.

5.6. Conditions under Which the Classes of Strategies Are Complete

Theorem 5.6.1. In every game the class of strategies \mathcal{C}_ϵ (and hence \mathfrak{M}_ϵ) is always complete.

Proof. Let $\eta \notin \mathcal{C}_\epsilon$. We shall show that there exists a $\mu \, \epsilon \, \mathcal{C}_\epsilon$ such that $\Upsilon_\eta(\mu) < 0$. Choose a μ such that $\Upsilon_\eta(\mu) < v^*_\eta + \epsilon$. Since $v^*_\eta \leq -\epsilon$, $\Upsilon_\eta(\mu) < 0$. It remains to be shown that $\mu \, \epsilon \, \mathcal{C}_\epsilon$; i.e., $v^*_\mu > -\epsilon$. That

this is true can be seen by substituting $v^*_\eta + \epsilon$ for $\Upsilon_\eta(\mu)$ in Theorem 5.3.3.

Theorem 5.6.2. In every game G the class \mathcal{B}_ϵ is complete if each of the games G_η has a value.

Proof. If, for each η, G_η has a value, then, by Theorem 5.5.2, $\mathcal{A}_\epsilon = \mathcal{B}_\epsilon$, and, by Theorem 5.6.1, \mathcal{A}_ϵ is complete.

Theorem 5.6.3. In every game G, the class \mathcal{A}_0 (and hence \mathfrak{M}) is complete if for every η in H player II has a minimax strategy in the game G_η.

Proof. For any η let μ be a minimax strategy for player II in G_η. Since $v^*_\eta \le 0$ we have $\Upsilon_\eta(\mu) = v^*_\eta \le 0$. In view of the results in Problems 5.4.4 and 5.4.5, it remains to show that $\mu \,\varepsilon\, \mathcal{A}_0$; i.e., $v^*_\mu = 0$. But this follows from Theorem 5.3.4.

Theorem 5.6.4. In every game G, the class \mathcal{B}_0 is complete if for every η in H the game G_η has a value and player II has a good strategy.

Proof. If G_η has a value for each η, then, by Theorem 5.5.3, $\mathcal{B}_0 = \mathcal{A}_0$. The completeness of \mathcal{B}_0 now follows from Theorem 5.6.3.

Theorem 5.6.5. In every game G, the class \mathcal{B} is complete if for every η in H, the game G_η has a value and both players have good strategies.

Proof. Since player I has a good strategy in each G_η then $\mathcal{B} = \mathcal{B}_0$ by Theorem 5.5.4. The completeness of \mathcal{B} now follows from Theorem 5.6.4.

Theorem 5.6.6. In every game G, the class \mathcal{A} is a subclass of every complete class \mathcal{C}.

Proof. Let $\eta \,\varepsilon\, \mathcal{A}$. Then since \mathcal{C} is complete there exists a $\mu \,\varepsilon\, \mathcal{C}$ with $\Upsilon_\eta(\mu) \le 0$. But since η is admissible this can happen only if $\eta \equiv \mu$.

PROBLEMS

5.6.1. Prove that if \mathcal{A} is complete it is the smallest complete class, and if a smallest complete class exists it is \mathcal{A}.

5.6.2. Using the results of this section, give an alternative proof of the following theorem: Let G be an S game in which S is bounded and S^* is closed. Then the class \mathcal{B} of Bayes points in S^* is complete.

5.6.3. For each $\eta \,\varepsilon\, \mathcal{A}$, let S_η be the class of strategies $\mu \,\varepsilon\,$ H such that $\mu \equiv \eta$. Then the sets S_η form a partition S on \mathcal{A} into equivalence classes. Show that an essentially complete class necessarily contains at least one element from each equivalence class of \mathcal{A}.

5.6.4. (a) If α is complete, then every class containing one element from each of its equivalence classes is essentially complete. (b) If a smallest essentially complete class exists, it consists of one element from each of the equivalence classes of α.

5.7. Completeness of the Class of Admissible Strategies

In the previous section we were able to give conditions under which many of the classes of strategies defined in Section 5.4 were complete. However, none of the conditions considered was sufficient to make the class α of admissible strategies complete in the general case. The completeness of α appears to depend on some properties of the game G which go beyond the existence of values and optimal strategies in the class of games G_η. This is exemplified by the following

Theorem 5.7.1. The class α of admissible strategies is complete if the game $G = (X, Y, M)$ satisfies the following conditions:
(i) There exists a sequence $\{x_j\}$ in X such that for every x in X there is a subsequence $\{x_{j_n}\}$ of $\{x_j\}$ such that

$$\lim_{n \to \infty} M(x_{j_n}, \eta) = M(x, \eta)$$

for all η in H.
(ii) For every sequence η_1, η_2, \cdots for which $\Upsilon_{\eta_i}(\eta_{i+1}) \leq 0$ for all i, there exists an η^* such that $\Upsilon_{\eta_i}(\eta^*) \leq 0$ for all i.

Proof. If, for some μ, $M_\eta(x, \mu) \equiv 0$, then clearly $M_\eta(x_j, \mu) = 0$ for all j. On the other hand, if, for some x, $M_\eta(x, \mu) < 0$, then, by assumption (i), there exists a j such that $M_\eta(x_j, \mu) < 0$. Thus assumption (i) implies that $\Upsilon_\eta(\mu) \leq 0$ if and only if $M_\eta(x_j, \mu) \leq 0$ for every j. For any $\eta \varepsilon$ H we define H_η as the set consisting of all $\mu \varepsilon$ H such that $\Upsilon_\eta(\mu) \leq 0$. We also define

$$Q(\mu) = \sum_{i=1}^{\infty} \frac{M(x_i, \mu)}{2^i} \tag{1}$$

Clearly, for all $\mu \varepsilon$ H, $Q(\mu)$ exists since M is by definition a bounded function. (The quantity $Q(\mu)$ is the payoff to player I if player II employs strategy μ and player I employs the probability distribution $\xi = (1/2, 1/4, \cdots)$ over the sequence of elements x_1, x_2, \cdots.) Moreover, the function Q satisfies the condition that $Q(\mu) \leq Q(\eta)$ whenever $\Upsilon_\eta(\mu) \leq 0$, with equality holding only if $\mu \equiv \eta$.

Now a strategy η is admissible if it possesses the property that $\Upsilon_\eta(\mu) \leq 0$ implies $\Upsilon_\mu(\eta) \leq 0$ for all μ. Hence it must follow that, for all $\eta \varepsilon$ H $-$ α, there exists a μ which is *better* than η. Also it follows from the definition of the classes α and H_η that if $\mu \varepsilon \alpha \cap H_\eta$ then $\mu \not\equiv \eta$ whenever $\eta \varepsilon$ H $-$ α.

Assume that \mathfrak{C} is not complete. Then $H - \mathfrak{C} \neq \varnothing$. Moreover, there exists an $\eta_1 \,\varepsilon\, H - \mathfrak{C}$ such that $\mathfrak{C} \cap H_{\eta_1} = \varnothing$. If this were not true, then for every $\eta \,\varepsilon\, H - \mathfrak{C}$ we could find a $\mu \,\varepsilon\, \mathfrak{C}$ which is better, contradicting the assumptions that \mathfrak{C} is not complete. We now select an $\eta_2 \,\varepsilon\, H_{\eta_1}$ such that

$$Q(\eta_2) < \inf_{\mu \,\varepsilon\, H_{\eta_1}} Q(\mu) + \tfrac{1}{2}$$

and consider the set H_{η_2}. Then by an argument similar to the above we show that $H_{\eta_2} \neq \varnothing$ and $\mathfrak{C} \cap H_{\eta_2} = \varnothing$. We next select an $\eta_3 \,\varepsilon\, H_{\eta_2}$ such that

$$Q(\eta_3) < \inf_{\mu \,\varepsilon\, H_{\eta_2}} Q(\mu) + \tfrac{1}{3}$$

and so forth. In general, for $m > 1$, we select an η_m from $H_{\eta_{m-1}}$ such that

$$Q(\eta_m) < \inf_{\mu \,\varepsilon\, H_{\eta_{m-1}}} Q(\mu) + \frac{1}{m}$$

By assumption (ii) there exists an η^* such that $\Upsilon_{\eta_i}(\eta^*) \leq 0$ for all i, so that $\eta^* \,\varepsilon\, H_{\eta_i}$ for all i. We shall prove that η^* is admissible, contradicting the fact that, for all i, $\mathfrak{C} \cap H_{\eta_i} = \varnothing$. Suppose η^* is not admissible. Then there exists a $\nu \,\varepsilon\, H$ which is better; i.e.,

$$(1) \qquad \Upsilon_{\eta^*}(\nu) \leq 0 \quad \text{and} \quad \Upsilon_\nu(\eta^*) > 0$$

By substituting η_i for η, η^* for μ in expression 2 in the proof of Theorem 5.3.3 we see that $\Upsilon_{\eta_k}(\nu) \leq 0$ for all k so that $\nu \,\varepsilon\, H_{\eta_k}$ for all k. Moreover, in view of (1), $\nu \not\equiv \eta_k$ for any k, and hence for all k

$$(2) \qquad Q(\eta^*) \leq Q(\eta_k) < Q(\nu) + \frac{1}{k}$$

which implies that $Q(\eta^*) \leq Q(\nu)$. But, by (1), $Q(\nu) < Q(\eta^*)$. Thus the assumption that η^* is not admissible leads to a contradiction and the theorem is proved.

It will be shown in Chapter 7 that the conditions of Theorem 5.7.1 are satisfied for a large class of statistical games in which the statistician has a finite number of possible actions.

PROBLEMS

5.7.1. Employ Theorem 5.7.1 to give an alternative proof of the theorem that in any S game in which the set S is bounded and S^* is closed the class \mathfrak{C} is complete.

5.7.2. Prove Theorem 5.7.1 without the assumption of the boundedness of M.

Fixed Sample-Size Games
with Finite Ω

6.1. Introduction

In this chapter we shall consider fixed sample-size statistical games $G = (\Omega, D, \rho)$ in which the possible states of nature are finite in number; i.e., $\Omega = (1, 2, \cdots, h)$, where $\mathcal{Z} = (Z, \Omega, p)$ is the sample space. For a fixed $j \,\varepsilon\, \Omega$, we shall designate the probability distribution on Z either by $p_j(z)$ or by $p(z \mid j)$. Let A be the action space, and let $L(j, a)$ be the loss to the statistician if nature's state is j and he takes action $a \,\varepsilon\, A$. We define

$$(6.1.1) \quad W = \{\mathbf{w}(a) = (w_1(a), \cdots, w_h(a)): w_j(a) = L(j, a), a \,\varepsilon\, A\}$$

Then W is a subset of h space.

Consider a game G_0 in which the statistician takes an action $a \,\varepsilon\, A$ without experimentation. Then G_0 is equivalent to an S game [see Definition 2.4.1] in which the statistician chooses a point $\mathbf{w} \,\varepsilon\, W$, nature chooses a coordinate j, and the loss to the statistician (i.e., the payoff to nature) is w_j, the value of the jth coordinate of \mathbf{w}.

Suppose the statistician performs a fixed sample-size experiment and employs a decision function $d \,\varepsilon\, D$ which maps Z into A. Then, for every outcome $z \,\varepsilon\, Z$, the loss to the statistician is $u_j(z) = L(j, d(z))$ if nature is in state j. Thus, in a fixed sample-size game in which Ω is finite, a choice of a decision function $d \,\varepsilon\, D$ is equivalent to a choice of a vector-valued function u which maps Z into W and is such that for any $z \,\varepsilon\, Z$

$$\mathbf{u}(z) = (u_1(z), \cdots, u_h(z)) = (w_1, \cdots, w_h)$$

The class of decision functions D can therefore be replaced by a class U of vector-valued functions u.

Now assume that nature is in state j, the statistician performs a fixed sample-size experiment and employs a decision function $d \,\varepsilon\, D$ or,

equivalently, a vector-valued function $u \in U$. Then the risk is given by

$$(6.1.2) \qquad \rho(j, d) = \sum_{z \in Z} L(j, d(z)) p(z \mid j)$$

$$= \sum_{z \in Z} u_j(z) p(z \mid j) = E_j(u_j)$$

We now define a set S in h space by

$$(6.1.3) \quad S = \{\boldsymbol{\rho}(d) = (\rho_1(d), \cdots, \rho_h(d)): \rho_j(d) = \rho(j, d), d \in D\}$$

The original game G is then equivalent to an S game in which the statistician selects a point $\boldsymbol{\rho}(d) \in S$, nature selects a coordinate j, and the (expected) loss to the statistician is the value of the jth coordinate of the point selected.

Note that every decision function u (i.e., random variable) which maps Z into W results in a point $\boldsymbol{\rho}(u)$ in S given by

$$(6.1.4) \qquad \boldsymbol{\rho}(u) = (E_1(u_1), \cdots, E_h(u_h))$$

Thus in the game G_0 the loss to the statistician is the value of a coordinate of a point in W, whereas in the game G (i.e., when the possibility of experimentation is introduced) the loss is an average (expected value) of a coordinate of many points in W which are values of a random variable u, and this random variable is at the choice of the statistician.

In many statistical problems it is often the case that if Ω is finite so is the space A of terminal actions, though the number of states of nature does not necessarily correspond to the number of possible actions for the statistician. However, there are important situations where A is not finite. As an illustration, consider the problem of estimating the proportion of defective items in a lot of size M on the basis of a random sample of size N selected from it. Let R stand for the number of defective items in the lot and $\omega = R/M$. Then Ω consists of the $M + 1$ states $(0, 1/M, 2/M, \cdots, 1)$. On the other hand, for a given loss function it may be profitable to consider every number between 0 and 1 as a possible estimate of ω so that A may consist of all points in the closed interval $(0, 1)$.

The general case in which A is finite will be treated in the next chapter, and several theorems applicable to the present situation will be found there. However, the finiteness of Ω which is assumed here and the consequent reduction of the game G to an S game will make it possible to characterize these statistical games in greater detail, regardless of the structure of the space A.

6.2. Complete Classes of Strategies in Games with Finite Ω

In Chapter 5, Section 5.2, we have given a detailed characterization of the complete classes of strategies for player II (the statistician) in S games under the assumption that the game S^*, the mixed extension of S, is a closed, bounded, and convex subset of h space. That S^* is convex follows directly from the definition. It remains to investigate conditions under which S, and hence S^*, is closed and bounded.

Theorem 6.2.1. Let W be the subset in h space defined by (6.1.1), and let S be the corresponding subset in h space defined by (6.1.3). Then if W is closed and bounded so is S.

Proof. The boundedness of W implies the boundedness of S as can be seen from Equation 6.1.2. It remains to show that S is closed.

Since Ω is finite, there is no loss in generality in assuming that Z consists of a countable number of elements z_1, z_2, \cdots. For any $d \varepsilon D$ let

(1) $$a_{kj} = L(j, d(z_k)), \qquad k = 1, 2, \cdots$$

so that

(2) $$\rho_j(d) = \sum_k a_{kj} p_j(z_k)$$

and

(3) $$\boldsymbol{\rho}(d) = \left(\sum_k a_{k1} p_1(z_k), \cdots, \sum_k a_{kh} p_h(z_k) \right)$$

In view of the above, a decision procedure $d \varepsilon D$ and hence $u \varepsilon U$ can be thought of as a specification of a *sequence* of vectors $\{\mathbf{a}_1, \mathbf{a}_2, \cdots\}$ in W with $\mathbf{a}_k = (a_{k1}, \cdots, a_{kh})$ such that, if z_k is observed, the vector \mathbf{a}_k is chosen from the sequence.

Let $\{\boldsymbol{\rho}(d_m)\}$ be a convergent sequence of points in S. We shall show that the limit belongs to S. Let $d_m = \{\mathbf{a}^{(m)}_1, \mathbf{a}^{(m)}_2, \cdots\}$. By the Cantor diagonal method we can select a subsequence $\{d_n\}$ with $d_n = \{\mathbf{a}^{(n)}_1, \mathbf{a}^{(n)}_2, \cdots\}$ such that $\mathbf{a}^{(n)}_k \to \mathbf{a}^*_k$ as $n \to \infty$ for each k. Also $\mathbf{a}^*_k \varepsilon W$ since W is closed. It remains to show that $\boldsymbol{\rho}(d_n) \to \boldsymbol{\rho}(d^*)$ where $d^* = \{\mathbf{a}^*_1, \mathbf{a}^*_2, \cdots\}$. But this follows from Theorem 3.11.5 since each coordinate of $\boldsymbol{\rho}(d_n)$ is given by (2) with a_{kj} replaced by $a^{(n)}_{kj}$ for each j.

Theorem 6.2.1 holds not only for discrete probability distributions but also for densities. The proof, however, is beyond the scope of this book. In fact, it can be shown that, in the case of densities and under the conditions of Theorem 6.2.1, not only is S closed and bounded, but it is also convex. The implication of this result is that if \mathcal{P}_Ω consists of

a finite number of densities the statistician need never use a randomized strategy since whatever risk can be achieved with a randomized strategy can also be achieved with a pure strategy. More precisely, the pure strategies in this case form an essentially complete class. We also remark that the conditions of Theorem 6.2.1, namely, the boundedness and closure of W, are not restrictive and hold in a great many statistical problems. As was mentioned before, the boundedness of W follows from the boundedness of the loss function L. The closure of W is guaranteed, for example, in case A is finite or if A is a bounded closed subset of n space and $L(j, a)$ is a continuous function of a for each j.

We see from Theorem 5.2.1 that if Ω is finite and W is bounded (at least from below) the class \mathfrak{B} of risk vectors arising from Bayes procedures can be represented as certain boundary points of S^*—the convex hull of the set S defined by 6.1.3. If in addition W is closed, then, by Theorems 6.2.1, 5.2.3, and 5.2.4, the class \mathfrak{A} of admissible risk vectors and the class $\overline{\mathfrak{D}}$—the closure of the set of risk vectors arising from Bayes procedures against ξ's with positive components—are complete and, moreover, are subsets of \mathfrak{B}. It is of interest, therefore, to characterize those sequences of vectors in W which result in Bayes points in the set S.

Since Ω is finite, the space Ξ is an $(h - 1)$-dimensional simplex—i.e., a convex set in S_h spanned by the unit vectors $\delta_1 = (1, 0, 0, \cdots, 0)$, $\delta_2 = (0, 1, 0, \cdots, 0)$, \cdots, $\delta_h = (0, 0, 0, \cdots, 1)$ and every $\xi \, \varepsilon \, \Xi$ is given by $\xi = (\xi(1), \xi(2), \cdots, \xi(h))$, $\xi(i) \geq 0$ for all i and $\sum_{i=1}^{h} \xi(i) = 1$. Thus, for example, if $h = 3$, Ξ can be represented as an equilateral triangle of unit altitude, and, if drawn in a plane, the coordinates of a point ξ in the triangle can be taken as the perpendicular distances from the point to the 3 sides. (From elementary geometry we know that the sum of the perpendicular distances from any point in an equilateral triangle to the opposite sides is equal to the altitude, which in our case is unity.)

For any $\xi \, \varepsilon \, \Xi$, let $\xi_{z_k}(j)$ be the a posteriori probability of the state j when the outcome of the experiment is z_k. Then [see Definition 3.6.4]

$$(6.2.1) \qquad \xi_{z_k}(j) = \frac{p_j(z_k)\xi(j)}{\sum_{i=1}^{h} p_i(z_k)\xi(i)}, \qquad j = 1, 2, \cdots, h$$

We shall denote the vector $(\xi_{z_k}(1), \cdots, \xi_{z_k}(h))$ by ξ_{z_k} and the quantity $\sum_{i=1}^{h} p_i(z_k)\xi(i)$ by $P_\xi(z_k)$.

For any choice of a decision function d or, what is equivalent, for any choice of a sequence of vectors \mathbf{a}_1, \mathbf{a}_2, \cdots in W, the risk $\rho(\boldsymbol{\xi}, d)$ is given by

$$(6.2.2) \qquad \rho(\boldsymbol{\xi}, d) = \sum_{j=1}^{h} \sum_{k=1}^{\infty} a_{kj} p_j(z_k) \xi(j)$$

$$= \sum_k \left(\sum_{j=1}^{h} a_{kj} \xi_{z_k}(j) \right) P_{\boldsymbol{\xi}}(z_k)$$

$$\geq \sum_k \left(\sum_{j=1}^{h} a^*_{kj} \xi_{z_k}(j) \right) P_{\boldsymbol{\xi}}(z_k)$$

where for a fixed k

$$(6.2.3) \qquad \sum_{j=1}^{h} a^*_{kj} \xi_{z_k}(j) = \min_{\mathbf{a}_k \,\varepsilon\, W} \sum_{j=1}^{h} a_{kj} \xi_{z_k}(j)$$

Thus we have the following theorem.

Theorem 6.2.2. The sequence of vectors

$$\{\mathbf{a}^*_k\} = \{(a^*_{k1}, \cdots, a^*_{kh})\}$$

in W determined by (6.2.3) for each k is Bayes against $\boldsymbol{\xi}$, provided the minimum of $\mathbf{a}_k \cdot \boldsymbol{\xi}_{z_k}$ is assumed in W for each k.

We observe that, for any z_k and $\boldsymbol{\xi}$, the a posteriori probability $\boldsymbol{\xi}_{z_k}$ is a point in Ξ. Thus for each $\boldsymbol{\xi} \,\varepsilon\, \Xi$ the sequence of possible observations z_1, z_2, \cdots determines a sequence of vectors $\boldsymbol{\xi}_{z_1}$, $\boldsymbol{\xi}_{z_2}$, \cdots in Ξ and hence a sequence of vectors \mathbf{a}^*_1, \mathbf{a}^*_2, \cdots in W such that \mathbf{a}^*_k is Bayes against $\boldsymbol{\xi}_{z_k}$. A point in S is then a coordinate-wise weighted average of the sequence $\{\mathbf{a}^*_k\}$, the weight of the jth coordinate of the kth element of the sequence being $p(z_k \mid j)$. It is to be noted that in order to obtain the sequence $\{\mathbf{a}^*_k\}$ it is not necessary to consider all of W but only a subset of W, viz., those $\mathbf{w} \,\varepsilon\, W$ which are Bayes against some $\boldsymbol{\xi} \,\varepsilon\, \Xi$ and which form the extreme points of W^*—the convex hull of W. [See Problem 5.2.3.] If this subset contains only a finite number of distinct vectors, then the sequence $\{\mathbf{a}^*_k\}$ will also contain only a finite number of distinct vectors.

We conclude this section with the following theorem about the Bayes risk as a function of the a priori probability $\boldsymbol{\xi}$.

Theorem 6.2.3. The risk $\rho^*(\boldsymbol{\xi})$ from a Bayes decision procedure is a continuous and concave function of $\boldsymbol{\xi}$.

Proof. By definition, for any $\boldsymbol{\xi}$, and any $d \,\varepsilon\, D$,

$$\rho(\boldsymbol{\xi}, d) = \sum_{j=1}^{h} \rho_j(d)\xi(j) = \sum_{j=1}^{h} \rho(j, d)\xi(j)$$

where $\rho(j, d)$ is given by 6.1.2. Hence

$$\rho^*(\boldsymbol{\xi}) = \inf_{d} \rho(\boldsymbol{\xi}, d) \doteq \inf_{\boldsymbol{\rho}\,\varepsilon\, S} \sum_{j=1}^{h} \rho_j\xi(j) = \inf_{\boldsymbol{\rho}\,\varepsilon\, S} \boldsymbol{\rho}\cdot\boldsymbol{\xi}$$

Since $L(j, a)$ and hence S is bounded and since

$$(6.2.4) \qquad \inf_{\boldsymbol{\rho}\,\varepsilon\, S} \boldsymbol{\rho}\cdot\boldsymbol{\xi} = -\sup_{\boldsymbol{\rho}\,\varepsilon\, S} [-\boldsymbol{\rho}\cdot\boldsymbol{\xi}]$$

the theorem follows from Theorem 2.2.7.

PROBLEMS

6.2.1. Let $\mathcal{Z} = (Z, \Omega, p)$ where Z is the set of non-negative integers, Ω consists of two elements $\omega = 1$ and $\omega = 2$;

$$p(z \mid \omega) = \frac{\omega^z e^{-\omega}}{z!}$$

i.e., $p(z \mid \omega)$ is a Poisson probability.

(1) Let A consist of two elements a_1 and a_2, let $\boldsymbol{\xi} = (\xi(1), \xi(2))$, $\xi(1) = 0.6$, $\xi(2) = 0.4$, and let the loss matrix W be given by

$$W = \begin{array}{c|cc}
\Omega & a_1 & a_2 \\
\hline
1 & 0 & 100 \\
\hline
2 & 50 & 0
\end{array}$$

(a) Draw a graph of W and W^*.
(b) Compute the sequence of a posteriori probabilities $\{\boldsymbol{\xi}_z\}$, $z = 0, 1, 2, \cdots$.
(c) Compute the sequence \mathbf{a}^*_1, \mathbf{a}^*_2, \cdots resulting from the Bayes procedure.
(d) Describe the Bayes procedure in terms of a partition of Z.
(e) Determine (approximately) the corresponding Bayes point in S.
(2) Do part 1 with $A = (a_1, a_2, a_3)$ and

$$W = \begin{array}{c|ccc}
\Omega & a_1 & a_2 & a_3 \\
\hline
1 & 0 & 100 & 40 \\
\hline
2 & 50 & 0 & 50
\end{array}$$

(3) Do part 1 with $A = (a_1, a_2, a_3)$; $\xi(1) = \xi(2) = 1/2$, and

$$W = \begin{array}{c|ccc} \Omega & a_1 & a_2 & a_3 \\ \hline 1 & 0 & 20 & 10 \\ \hline 2 & 50 & 0 & 20 \end{array}$$

(4) Do part 1 with $A = \{a: 0 \le a \le 3\}$; $\xi(1) = 0.3$, $\xi(2) = 0.7$, and

$$L(\omega, a) = 100(\omega - a)^2, \qquad \omega = 1, 2, \qquad 0 \le a \le 3$$

6.2.2. Consider the sample space \mathcal{Z} in Problem 6.2.1. Let $A = (a_1, a_2)$, and let the loss matrix W be given by

$$W = \begin{array}{c|cc} \Omega & a_1 & a_2 \\ \hline 1 & 0 & 1 \\ \hline 2 & 1 & 0 \end{array}$$

(a) Characterize the Bayes points of S in terms of the probabilities of taking the two actions.

(b) Compute an *adequate number of boundary points* of S^*, and sketch the entire set S^*.

6.2.3. For any game $G = (\Omega, D, \rho)$ in which Ω is finite, say, $\Omega = (1, 2, \cdots, h)$, let the set W in h space be defined as in equation 6.1.1. In terms of the coordinates of the points in W we define

$$\underline{w_j} = \inf_{a \varepsilon A} w_j(a), \qquad \bar{w}_j = \sup_{a \varepsilon A} w_j(a), \qquad j = 1, 2, \cdots, h$$

Consider the interval $\Pi(W)$ in h space defined by

$$\Pi(W) = \{\mathbf{x} = (x_1, \cdots, x_h): \underline{w_j} \le x_j \le \bar{w}_j, \qquad j = 1, 2, \cdots, h\}$$

Clearly $W \subset \Pi(W)$. (a) Show that $S \subset \Pi(W)$ where S is defined by equation 6.1.3. (b) Explain the notion of minimax loss or regret [see Section 4.3] in terms of $\Pi(W)$.

6.2.4. Show that $W \subset S$.

6.3. Bayes Solutions for Finite Ω

We have seen that in a fixed sample-size game in which Ω is finite, the class \mathfrak{B} of Bayes solutions result in a set of risk vectors which lie on a specified portion of the boundary of a convex set S^* in an h space.

This set can be said to characterize geometrically the Bayes procedures. In this section we shall study two other types of representation of this class of strategies—one in terms of a partition of the space Ξ of a priori probabilities and the other in terms of partitions of the sample space Z by means of likelihood ratios in case A is finite also.

Theorem 6.3.1. Let W be closed and bounded. For any $\mathbf{w} \, \varepsilon \, W$ define

$$T(\mathbf{w}) = \{\boldsymbol{\xi} \, \varepsilon \, \Xi : \min_{\mathbf{u} \, \varepsilon \, W} (\boldsymbol{\xi} \cdot \mathbf{u}) = \boldsymbol{\xi} \cdot \mathbf{w}\}$$

where the symbol $\boldsymbol{\xi} \cdot \mathbf{u}$ stands for $\sum_{i=1}^{h} u_i \xi(i)$. Then the sets $T(\mathbf{w})$ are closed and convex, and, if $\mathbf{w}_1 \neq \mathbf{w}_2$, then $T(\mathbf{w}_1)$ and $T(\mathbf{w}_2)$ have no interior points in common.

Proof. That $T(\mathbf{w})$ is closed follows from the fact that it is defined in terms of equalities of continuous functions. To show that $T(\mathbf{w})$ is convex, let $\boldsymbol{\xi}_1$ and $\boldsymbol{\xi}_2$ be any two points in $T(\mathbf{w})$, and let

$$\boldsymbol{\xi}_\alpha = \alpha \boldsymbol{\xi}_1 + (1 - \alpha)\boldsymbol{\xi}_2, \qquad 0 \leq \alpha \leq 1$$

Then since $\boldsymbol{\xi} \cdot \mathbf{w}$ is linear in the components of $\boldsymbol{\xi}$, we have

$$(6.3.1) \qquad \min_{\mathbf{u} \, \varepsilon \, W} (\boldsymbol{\xi}_\alpha \cdot \mathbf{u}) \geq \alpha \min_{\mathbf{u} \, \varepsilon \, W} (\boldsymbol{\xi}_1 \cdot \mathbf{u}) + (1 - \alpha) \min_{\mathbf{u} \, \varepsilon \, W} (\boldsymbol{\xi}_2 \cdot \mathbf{u})$$

$$= \alpha(\boldsymbol{\xi}_1 \cdot \mathbf{w}) + (1 - \alpha)(\boldsymbol{\xi}_2 \cdot \mathbf{w})$$

On the other hand,

$$(6.3.2) \qquad \min_{\mathbf{u} \, \varepsilon \, W} (\boldsymbol{\xi}_\alpha \cdot \mathbf{u}) \leq \boldsymbol{\xi}_\alpha \cdot \mathbf{w} = \alpha(\boldsymbol{\xi}_1 \cdot \mathbf{w}) + (1 - \alpha)(\boldsymbol{\xi}_2 \cdot \mathbf{w})$$

so that

$$(6.3.3) \qquad \min_{\mathbf{u} \, \varepsilon \, W} (\boldsymbol{\xi}_\alpha \cdot \mathbf{u}) = \alpha(\boldsymbol{\xi}_1 \cdot \mathbf{w}) + (1 - \alpha)(\boldsymbol{\xi}_2 \cdot \mathbf{w}) = \boldsymbol{\xi}_\alpha \cdot \mathbf{w}$$

and hence $\boldsymbol{\xi}_\alpha \, \varepsilon \, T(\mathbf{w})$ which proves the convexity of $T(\mathbf{w})$. To prove the remaining part of the theorem, we observe that, for all $\boldsymbol{\xi} \, \varepsilon \, T(\mathbf{w}_1) \cap T(\mathbf{w}_2)$, we have

$$(6.3.4) \qquad \min_{\mathbf{u} \, \varepsilon \, W} (\boldsymbol{\xi} \cdot \mathbf{u}) = \sum_{j=1}^{h} w_{1j} \xi(j) = \sum_{j=1}^{h} w_{2j} \xi(j)$$

That is, the common points of $T(\mathbf{w}_1)$ and $T(\mathbf{w}_2)$ must all lie on an $(h - 2)$-dimensional hyperplane in h space and consequently cannot be interior points of the sets.

Theorem 6.3.1 gives the following characterization of Bayes solutions when Ω is finite. The space Ξ is divided into closed convex subsets $T(\mathbf{w})$ which have only boundary points in common. Let $\boldsymbol{\xi}$ be given.

Then, if the outcome of the experiment is z, compute $\boldsymbol{\xi}_z$. If $\boldsymbol{\xi}_z \,\varepsilon\, T(\mathbf{w})$, choose the vector \mathbf{w}, or, equivalently, take that action $a \,\varepsilon\, A$ which results in this vector $\mathbf{w} \,\varepsilon\, W$.

Note that this particular characterization of the Bayes solutions is independent of the functional form of $p(z \mid j)$. More precisely, all statistical situations which involve the same structure for A, the same number of states for nature, and the same loss function $L(j, a)$ will yield the same sets $T(\mathbf{w})$ and consequently the same Bayes procedures.

As an illustration, consider a statistical situation in which nature has 3 states, the statistician has 3 possible actions, and the loss matrix is of the following form.

States of Nature	Actions		
	1	2	3
1	0	50	100
2	50	0	50
3	100	100	0

Here W consists of the 3 .points $\mathbf{w}_1 = (0, 50, 100)$, $\mathbf{w}_2 = (50, 0, 100)$, $\mathbf{w}_3 = (100, 50, 0)$. Let $\boldsymbol{\xi} = (\xi(1), \xi(2), \xi(3))$ be any a priori probability of the 3 states of nature (or, alternatively, the a posteriori probability of the 3 states after the experiment has been performed). Then

$$\boldsymbol{\xi} \cdot \mathbf{w}_1 = 50\xi(2) + 100\xi(3)$$

$$\boldsymbol{\xi} \cdot \mathbf{w}_2 = 50\xi(1) + 100\xi(3)$$

$$\boldsymbol{\xi} \cdot \mathbf{w}_3 = 100\xi(1) + 50\xi(2)$$

Now action 1 will be taken if

$$\boldsymbol{\xi} \cdot \mathbf{w}_1 \leq \boldsymbol{\xi} \cdot \mathbf{w}_2 \quad \text{and} \quad \boldsymbol{\xi} \cdot \mathbf{w}_1 \leq \boldsymbol{\xi} \cdot \mathbf{w}_3$$

i.e., if $\xi(1) \geq \xi(2)$ and $\xi(1) \geq \xi(3)$. Action 2 will be taken if

$$\boldsymbol{\xi} \cdot \mathbf{w}_2 \leq \boldsymbol{\xi} \cdot \mathbf{w}_1 \quad \text{and} \quad \boldsymbol{\xi} \cdot \mathbf{w}_2 \leq \boldsymbol{\xi} \cdot \mathbf{w}_3$$

i.e., if $\xi(2) \geq \xi(1)$ and $\xi(3) \leq 1/3$. Action 3 will be taken if

$$\boldsymbol{\xi} \cdot \mathbf{w}_3 \leq \boldsymbol{\xi} \cdot \mathbf{w}_2 \quad \text{and} \quad \boldsymbol{\xi} \cdot \mathbf{w}_3 \leq \boldsymbol{\xi} \cdot \mathbf{w}_1$$

i.e., if $\xi(3) \geq 1/3$ and $\xi(3) \geq \xi(1)$.

If the space Ξ is represented as a triangle, the three regions $T(\mathbf{w}_1)$, $T(\mathbf{w}_2)$ and $T(\mathbf{w}_3)$ are shown in Figure 8. The Bayes procedure for a single experiment is to compute the vector $\boldsymbol{\xi}_z$, locate this point in the triangle, and take action i if $\boldsymbol{\xi}_z$ falls in $T(\mathbf{w}_i)$.

Suppose in addition to Ω being finite A is also finite; say $A = (1, 2, \cdots, k)$. Then in a single-experiment problem, the Bayes solutions [see

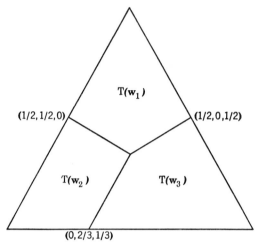

Figure 8

also Section 7.3] are as follows: We take action i if $\tau_z(i) \leq \tau_z(j)$ for all $j \neq i$ where

$$(6.3.5) \qquad \tau_z(i) = \frac{\sum\limits_{j=1}^{h} L(j, i)p(z \mid j)\xi(j)}{\sum\limits_{j=1}^{h} p(z \mid j)\xi(j)} = \sum_{j=1}^{h} L(j, i)\xi_z(j)$$

Thus, as we have seen in the previous illustration, Bayes solutions in the problem under consideration are characterized by linear inequalities in the a posteriori probabilities $\xi_z(j)$. Since only the numerator of the second term of (6.3.5) matters, the Bayes solutions can also be considered as being characterized by linear inequalities in the probabilities (or densities) $p(z \mid j)$. Moreover, we can divide each of the latter inequalities by some $p(z \mid r)$ and obtain linear inequalities in the likelihood ratios $p(z \mid j)/p(z \mid r)$. This type of characterization of a Bayes solution is especially useful in two special cases which we shall now investigate in some detail.

Case 1. $\Omega = (1, 2)$, $A = (1, 2)$. Here nature's states are represented by one of two probabilities $p_1(z)$ and $p_2(z)$, and the statistician has to decide whether the sample point z came from state 1 or state 2. This case, known as the case of a simple hypothesis against a simple alternative, has been extensively studied in statistical literature. While the assumption that nature has only two states is often artificial, the statistical procedures based on this assumption are quite general, as can be seen, for example, from Theorem 7.4.4 below.

Let $\xi = (\zeta, 1 - \zeta)$ where ζ is the a priori probability for state 1 and $1 - \zeta$ the a priori probability for state 2. The most general loss function in this case can be taken as w if nature is in state 1 and the statistician decides 2, unity if nature is in state 2 and the statistician decides 1, and zero otherwise. The Bayes procedure is to decide 1 if

$$(6.3.6) \qquad\qquad (1 - \zeta)p_2(z) \leq w\zeta p_1(z)$$

or, equivalently,

$$(6.3.7) \qquad\qquad \frac{p_2(z)}{p_1(z)} \leq \frac{w\zeta}{1 - \zeta} = c(\zeta, w)$$

and to decide 2 if the inequality is reversed.

We note that, for a fixed w, as ζ varies from 0 to 1, c varies from 0 to ∞. Similarly, for a fixed ζ, as w varies from 0 to ∞, c also varies from 0 to ∞. Thus by varying c from 0 to ∞ we generate all Bayes procedures for every possible loss and a priori probability.

In case the sample space is $\mathfrak{X} = (X, \Omega, p)$ with $x = (x_1, \cdots, x_N)$ where the x_j's are independently distributed with probability (or density) $f_i(x)$, $i = 1, 2$, then $p_i(x) = \prod_{j=1}^{N} f_i(x_j)$. Taking logarithms on both sides of (6.3.7) and setting

$$z_j = \log \frac{f_2(x_j)}{f_1(x_j)}$$

the Bayes procedure reduces to deciding 1 if $\sum_{j=1}^{N} z_j \leq k = \log c$ and deciding 2 otherwise. Since for large N approximate probability statements are often easy to obtain for sums of independent random variables, the above reduction is of great practical importance.

Let S_ζ be the set of points in the sample space satisfying inequality (6.3.7), and let $C(S_\zeta)$ be its complement. Furthermore, let $\alpha(\zeta)$ be the probability that the sample point x will fall in $C(S_\zeta)$ when nature is in state 1, $\beta(\zeta)$ be the probability that x will fall in S_ζ when nature is in

state 2, and let $\rho^*(\zeta)$ be the Bayes risk as a function of ζ. Then

(6.3.8) $\rho^*(\zeta) = \zeta w\alpha(\zeta) + (1 - \zeta)\beta(\zeta)$

By Theorem 6.2.3, the function $\rho^*(\zeta)$ is continuous and concave. Moreover, $\rho^*(0) = 0$, $\rho^*(1) = 0$ and hence $\rho^*(\zeta)$ will attain a maximum at some point $\zeta = \zeta_0$.

If $p_i(x)$ are densities, then $\rho^*(\zeta)$ when plotted against ζ will have the shape as given in Figure 9. Suppose the statistician believes that the a priori probability for state 1 is ζ' and he operates with the region

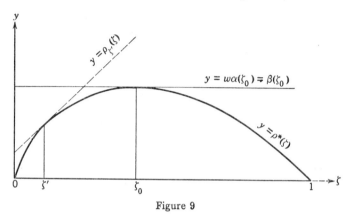

Figure 9

$S_{\zeta'}$ while in fact some other ζ is the true probability. Then his average risk $\rho_{\zeta'}(\zeta)$ is given by

(6.3.9) $\rho_{\zeta'}(\zeta) = \zeta w\alpha(\zeta') + (1 - \zeta)\beta(\zeta')$

which is linear in ζ and is tangent to the curve $y = \rho^*(\zeta)$ at the point $\zeta = \zeta'$. His loss may be great if ζ departs from ζ' by an appreciable amount as can be seen from Figure 9. On the other hand, if he is not certain of ζ and operates with the region S_{ζ_0} then his average loss will never exceed $\rho_{\zeta}(\zeta_0) = w\alpha(\zeta_0) = \beta(\zeta_0)$ since the line $y = \rho_{\zeta}(\zeta_0)$ [see Figure 9] is parallel to the ζ axis and tangent to the curve $y = \rho^*(\zeta)$ at the point $\zeta = \zeta_0$. This, of course, is the minimax procedure. We can summarize the above results by saying that, if $p_i(x)$ are densities, the minimax procedure is obtained by finding that region S for which $w\alpha(\zeta) = \beta(\zeta)$. This, of course, can be obtained by varying c in (6.3.7). Once the proper c is found, the least favorable probability ζ_0 can be obtained by solving for ζ in the equation $w\zeta/(1 - \zeta) = c$.

In case $p_i(x)$ are discrete probability distributions, the curve $y = \rho^*(\zeta)$ will generally consist of connected line segments. This follows from the fact that a whole interval of ζ's will generally yield the same

α and β. It often happens in this case that the maximum of $\rho^*(\zeta)$ occurs at a point where two line segments (one with a positive slope and one with a negative slope) meet [see Figure 10]. In this case the minimax procedure is obtained by mixing any two Bayes procedures with regions, say S_a and S_b which yield the line segment a and the line segment b respectively [see Figure 10]. More specifically, let α_a, β_a be the probabilities of errors using region S_a and α_b, β_b be the probabilities of errors using region S_b; then, if we employ region S_a with probability

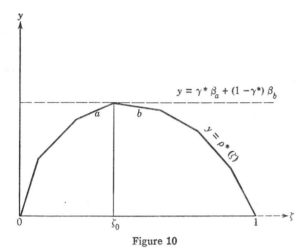

Figure 10

γ and S_b with probability $1 - \gamma$, the average risk $\rho_\gamma(\zeta)$ for any ζ is given by

$$(6.3.10) \quad \rho_\gamma(\zeta) = \gamma[\zeta w \alpha_a + (1 - \zeta)\beta_a] + (1 - \gamma)[\zeta w \alpha_b + (1 - \zeta)\beta_b]$$

and the minimax procedure is obtained by finding that $\gamma = \gamma^*$ which makes (6.3.10) independent of ζ. The minimax risk has the value $\gamma^*\beta_a + (1 - \gamma^*)\beta_b$.

Case 2. $\Omega = (1, 2, \cdots, h)$, $A = (1, 2, \cdots, h)$, and the loss is a constant, say w, if the state of nature is j and the statistician decides $i \neq j$ and the loss is zero if $i = j$. Let the associated probability distributions be designated by $p_i(z)$, $i = 1, 2, \cdots, h$, and let $\boldsymbol{\xi} = (\xi(1), \cdots, \xi(h))$ be any a priori probability distribution over the h states. Then for any decision i the a posteriori risk τ_z is given by

$$(6.3.11) \qquad \tau_z(i) = \frac{w \sum\limits_{j \neq i=1}^{h} p_j(z)\xi(j)}{\sum\limits_{j=1}^{h} p_j(z)\xi(j)}$$

Hence the Bayes procedure is to decide i $(i = 1, 2, \cdots, h)$ if

$$(6.3.12) \qquad \sum_{\neq i=1}^{h} p_j(z)\xi(j) \leq \sum_{j \neq k=1}^{h} p_j(z)\xi(j)$$

or, equivalently,

$$(6.3.13) \qquad \frac{p_k(z)}{p_i(z)} \leq \frac{\xi(i)}{\xi(k)}$$

for all $k = 1, 2, \cdots, h$. As in case 1, the Bayes procedures for this special multidecision case have a very simple representation in terms of likelihood ratios. Illustrative examples of this case will be given in the next section.

PROBLEMS

6.3.1. Let $x = (x_1, \cdots, x_{100})$ be 100 independent observations on a random variable which is normally distributed with variance $\sigma^2 = 25$ and mean μ. Let H_1 be the hypothesis that $\mu = 0$ and H_2 the hypothesis that $\mu = 2$. Let $\xi = (\zeta, 1 - \zeta)$ where ζ is the a priori probability for H_1.

(a) Plot the Bayes risk as a function of ζ if the loss matrix is given by

States of Nature	Decision	
	H_1	H_2
H_1	0	25
H_2	10	0

(b) Obtain the minimax procedure, and compute the least favorable ξ.

6.3.2. Let x be a binomial random variable with $P(x = 1) = \omega$ and $P(x = 0) = 1 - \omega$. Let H_1 be the hypothesis that $\omega = 0.4$ and H_2 the hypothesis that $\omega = 0.6$. Let ζ be the a priori probability for H_1. We wish to test H_1 against H_2 on the basis of 10 independent observations on x.

(a) Plot the Bayes risk as a function of ζ if the loss matrix is given by

States of Nature	Decision	
	H_1	H_2
H_1	0	25
H_2	25	0

(b) Obtain the minimax procedure and compute the least favorable ξ.

6.3.3. Draw the Bayes decision regions $T(w_1)$, $T(w_2)$, $T(w_3)$ in an equilateral triangle for the loss matrix

States of Nature	Actions		
	1	2	3
1	0	50	10
2	50	0	20
3	100	50	0

6.4. Illustrative Examples of Fixed Sample-Size Statistical Games in Which Ω Is Finite

Example 1. Multiple Classifications. The theory of multiple classifications or, as it is commonly known, discriminant analysis deals with the problem of assigning an individual to one of several possible groups to which he may belong on the basis of a set of measurable characteristics observed on him. For example, we may wish to classify a plant specimen into one of two species on the basis of measurements of its stem and leaves, or to assign a skull found in archeological excavations to some dynastic period on the basis of anthropometric measurements made on it, or to determine whether a candidate in a pilot training school will be a success or a failure on the basis of aptitude tests.

From a theoretical point of view, the problem of discriminant analysis is a multidecision fixed sample-size problem with finite Ω. The main distinguishing features of this problem are: (a) A decision here is usually made on the basis of a single observation on several correlated characteristics, and (b) it is not unreasonable in this problem to assume the existence of a priori probabilities since they represent the proportions in which the populations under consideration are mixed.

We shall first consider the problem of two populations which may be formulated as follows: An individual on whom we observe the characteristics x_1, \cdots, x_N is known to come from one of two populations Π_1 and Π_2, but it is not known from which. The probability distribution (or density) of these characteristics is given by $p_1(x_1, \cdots, x_N)$ if the individual belongs to Π_1, and $p_2(x_1, \cdots, x_N)$ if the individual belongs to Π_2. These functions are assumed to be known. We also assume that, if an individual comes from Π_1 and he is classified into Π_2, there is a loss of w units, and, if he belongs to Π_2 and he is classified in Π_1,

there is a loss of v units. If he is classified correctly, the loss is zero. Thus, for example, in the problem of training pilots, we might assess what it would cost us to reject a possible good pilot (w) and what it would cost us to train a "washout" (v). Without loss of generality v can be taken as unity.

We further assume that the two populations are mixed in the proportion of ζ and $1 - \zeta$, so that, if an individual is chosen at random, ζ is the a priori probability that he comes from Π_1 and $1 - \zeta$ is the a priori probability that he comes from Π_2.

On the basis of the above information we wish to set up a procedure for classifying an individual into one of the two populations. The optimal procedure here is obviously the Bayes procedure discussed under case 1, Section 6.3, above. In case ζ is unknown, the minimax procedure might be employed. The method of computing the minimax procedure can also be found under case 1, Section 6.3.

Of particular interest is the case where both $p_1(x_1, \cdots, x_N)$ and $p_2(x_1, \cdots, x_N)$ are multivariate normal with the same variance and covariance matrix (σ_{ij}) but different means $\theta_1 = (\theta_{11}, \cdots, \theta_{1N})$ and $\theta_2 = (\theta_{21}, \cdots, \theta_{2N})$ respectively. That is

$$p_k(x_1, \cdots, x_N) = \frac{|\sigma^{ij}|^{\frac{1}{2}}}{(2\pi)^{N/2}} \exp\left[-\frac{1}{2} \sum_{i=1}^{N} \sum_{j=1}^{N} \sigma^{ij}(x_i - \theta_{ki})(x_j - \theta_{kj}) \right]$$

$k = 1, 2$, where σ^{ij} are the elements of the inverse of the matrix (σ_{ij}) and $|\sigma^{ij}|$ is the determinant of the matrix (σ^{ij}). In this case, the Bayes procedure, after taking logarithms to the base e on both sides of (6.3.7), reduces to the following: Classify the individual into Π_1 if

$$(6.4.1) \qquad l(x) = \sum_{i=1}^{N} \lambda_i x_i \leq \frac{l(\theta_2) + l(\theta_1)}{2} + \log \frac{w\zeta}{1 - \zeta}$$

and into Π_2 otherwise, where

$$(6.4.2) \qquad \lambda_i = \sum_{j=1}^{N} \sigma^{ij}(\theta_{2j} - \theta_{1j})$$

Since the x's are jointly normally distributed so will $l(x)$ be in each population with mean $l(\theta_k)$, $k = 1, 2$, and common variance

$$(6.4.3) \qquad \sigma^2_l = \sum_{i=1}^{N} \sum_{j=1}^{N} \sigma^{ij}(\theta_{2i} - \theta_{1i})(\theta_{2j} - \theta_{1j}) = l(\theta_2) - l(\theta_1)$$

Let $\alpha(\zeta)$ and $\beta(\zeta)$ be the probabilities of misclassification. Then

$$(6.4.4) \qquad \alpha(\zeta) = \frac{1}{\sqrt{2\pi}} \int_u^\infty e^{-(1/2)t^2}\, dt$$

$$(6.4.5) \qquad \beta(\zeta) = \frac{1}{\sqrt{2\pi}} \int_{-\infty}^v e^{-(1/2)t^2}\, dt$$

where

$$(6.4.6) \qquad u = \frac{1}{\sigma_l}\log\frac{w\zeta}{1-\zeta} + \frac{\sigma_l}{2}, \qquad v = \frac{1}{\sigma_l}\log\frac{w\zeta}{1-\zeta} - \frac{\sigma_l}{2}$$

as can easily be verified. The minimax procedure is obtained by finding that $\zeta = \zeta_0$ which satisfies the equation $w\alpha(\zeta) = \beta(\zeta)$ and substituting the result in (6.4.1). Note that if $w = 1$ (i.e., the two losses due to misclassification are equal) then $\alpha(\zeta) = \beta(\zeta)$ for $\zeta = 1/2$, and the minimax procedure is then simply to classify the individual into Π_1 if $l(x) < \dfrac{l(\theta_1) + l(\theta_2)}{2}$ and into Π_2 if the inequality is reversed.

Before we leave the problem of two populations, the following remarks may be of some interest.

We are sometimes faced with a situation where we are dealing with n individuals who could have come from one of two populations, say Π_1 and Π_2, and we wish to choose a subset of them having the greatest probability of belonging to Π_1. For example, from a group of 100 candidates applying to a pilot training school, we might wish to choose 25 best prospects on the basis of some tests. Here we have the problem of ranking the individuals according to the likelihood that they come from Π_1.

If we know ζ, the a priori probability that an individual selected at random belongs to Π_1, we can compute for the ith individual the a posteriori probability ζ_{x_i} where $x_i = (x_{1i}, \cdots, x_{Ni})$ $(i = 1, \cdots, n)$ and then rank these ζ_{x_i}'s. It turns out, however, that we need not know ζ in order to accomplish this ranking. This follows from an easily verified theorem that a necessary and sufficient condition that $\zeta_{x_i} \geq \zeta_{x_j}$ is that

$$(6.4.7) \qquad \frac{p_1(x_{1i}, \cdots, x_{Ni})}{p_2(x_{1i}, \cdots, x_{Ni})} \geq \frac{p_1(x_{1j}, \cdots, x_{Nj})}{p_2(x_{1j}, \cdots, x_{Nj})}$$

Another situation that might be encountered is the following: We are given a pair of individuals, and it is known that one belongs to Π_1 and the other to Π_2, but it is not known which individual belongs to which population. For example, suppose two horses are racing against

each other and we wish to choose the winner on the basis of some characteristics observed on the horses. Barring a photofinish, we know that one is going to be a winner and the other necessarily a loser.

Let x'_1, x'_2, \cdots, x'_N and $x''_1, x''_2, \cdots, x''_N$ be the values of the measured characteristics on the two individuals and let $p_i(x_1, \cdots, x_N)$ be the probability (or density) of the characteristics in Π_i ($i = 1, 2$). We observe that here only one error of misclassification is possible, so that $w = v$. Moreover, the assignment of the marks "prime" and "double prime" to the two individuals might as well be made by chance see Section 8.6], thus giving an a priori probability of 1/2 that the individual marked "prime" belongs to Π_1 (and hence the one marked "double prime" belongs to Π_2). The Bayes solution is then as follows. Classify the individual marked "prime" into Π_1 if

$$(6.4.8) \qquad \frac{p_2(x'_1, \cdots, x'_N)p_1(x''_1, \cdots, x''_N)}{p_1(x'_1, \cdots, x'_N)p_2(x''_1, \cdots, x''_N)} < 1$$

and reverse the classifications otherwise. Because of the symmetry of the problem, this solution is also minimax.

The problem of multiple classifications when the number of populations involved is greater than 2 presents no theoretical difficulties insofar as the Bayes solutions are concerned and has essentially been solved in Section 6.3. The difficulties arise when we desire to compute the risk of misclassification, and this can only be done with moderate ease for some very special cases. These difficulties are, of course, not restricted to discriminant analysis but are inherent in all multidecision problems.

We shall here consider a simple illustrative example of a multiple-classification problem. We are given an individual who could have come from one of 3 populations Π_1, Π_2, Π_3, and we wish to classify him into one of the populations on the basis of N characteristics $x = (x_1, x_2, \cdots, x_N)$ observable on him. These characteristics have a known multivariate normal distribution in each of the populations with the same covariance matrix (σ_{ij}) but different means $\theta_k = (\theta_{k1}, \cdots, \theta_{kN})$, $k = 1, 2, 3$. The loss due to misclassification is assumed to be constant. The problem is to obtain a Bayes procedure for a given a priori distribution $\boldsymbol{\xi} = (\xi(1), \xi(2), \xi(3))$.

In view of the results previously obtained [see in particular, equations 6.3.13, 6.4.1, and 6.4.2], the solution is as follows: Let

$$(6.4.9) \qquad \lambda^i_{pq} = \sum_{j=1}^{N} \sigma^{ij}(\theta_{jp} - \theta_{jq}), \qquad p > q = 1, 2, 3$$

and let

(6.4.10) $$l_{pq}(x) = \sum_{i=1}^{N} \lambda^i_{pq} x_i$$

Then classify the individual into Π_1 if

$$l_{21}(x) < \frac{l_{21}(\theta_2) + l_{21}(\theta_1)}{2} + \log \frac{\xi(1)}{\xi(2)}$$

and

$$l_{31}(x) < \frac{l_{31}(\theta_3) + l_{31}(\theta_1)}{2} + \log \frac{\xi(1)}{\xi(3)}$$

Classify the individual into Π_2 if

$$l_{21}(x) > \frac{l_{21}(\theta_2) + l_{21}(\theta_1)}{2} + \log \frac{\xi(1)}{\xi(2)}$$

and

$$l_{32}(x) < \frac{l_{32}(\theta_3) + l_{32}(\theta_2)}{2} + \log \frac{\xi(2)}{\xi(3)}$$

Classify the individual into Π_3 if

$$l_{32}(x) > \frac{l_{32}(\theta_3) + l_{32}(\theta_2)}{2} + \log \frac{\xi(2)}{\xi(3)}$$

and

$$l_{31}(x) > \frac{l_{31}(\theta_3) + l_{31}(\theta_1)}{2} + \log \frac{\xi(1)}{\xi(3)}$$

We note that this Bayes procedure involves 3 linear functions of normally distributed variables and hence have themselves a trivariate normal distribution with means, variances, and covariances which can easily be computed. The probability that an individual who belongs, say, to Π_1 will be classified into Π_2 or Π_3 can be computed from a bivariate normal distribution.

Example 2. The Problem of the n-Faced Die. The following problem is very similar to the last two discussed above and admits a variety of generalizations. We are given an n-faced die in which one side has a higher probability of appearing than any of the other sides. More specifically, we assume that one side has a known probability p of appearing and each of the remaining sides has a probability $(1 - p)/(n - 1)$ of appearing with $p > (1 - p)/(n - 1)$. The problem is to decide on the basis of N tosses of the die which of the n sides is the biased one.

Suppose we label the faces of the die with, say, the integers, 1, 2, \cdots, n. Then we will be considering n alternative hypotheses, H_1, H_2, \cdots, H_n where H_i is the hypothesis that the face labeled with the integer i is the biased one. In view of the symmetry of the problem, it is entirely appropriate to label the faces randomly [see Section 8.6] thus inducing an a priori probability of $1/n$ for each of the alternative hypotheses. Moreover, it is also appropriate to consider here a constant loss due to a wrong decision. Thus this problem can be reduced to the multiple-decision problem considered in case 2, Section 6.3 with $\xi(i) = 1/n$ for all i.

Suppose the die is tossed N times and the outcome is $\mathbf{r} = (r_1, r_2, \cdots, r_n)$ with $\sum_{i=1}^{n} r_i = N$ where r_i represents the number of times the face labeled i has appeared. Then letting $p_i(\mathbf{r})$ stand for the probability of the outcome \mathbf{r} under the hypothesis H_i, we have

$$(6.4.11) \qquad p_i(\mathbf{r}) = \frac{N!}{r_1! \cdots r_n!} p^{r_i} \left(\frac{1-p}{n-1}\right)^{N-r_i}$$

Now according to (6.3.13), the Bayes procedure is to accept H_i if

$$(6.4.12) \qquad \frac{p_k(\mathbf{r})}{p_i(\mathbf{r})} = \left[\frac{(n-1)p}{1-p}\right]^{r_k-r_i} \leq 1$$

for all k. Since by assumption $p > (1-p)/(n-1)$, the above simply implies that we accept H_i if $r_i = \max(r_1, r_2, \cdots, r_n)$.

Thus far we have considered examples in which the number of possible decisions the statistician can make equaled the number of possible states for nature. We shall now consider several examples where this situation does not hold.

Example 3. A Hypothesis with a Two-Sided Alternative. We are given a normally distributed random variable with unit variance and a mean which can have the value $-\mu$, 0, or μ. The problem is to decide on the basis of N independent observations x_1, x_2, \cdots, x_N whether the mean is zero. If the mean is zero (hypothesis H_0) and we decide that it isn't zero, i.e., that it is either $-\mu$ or μ, our loss is w. On the other hand, if the mean is not zero and we decide that it is, our loss is unity. Here we are faced with a situation where Ω consists of 3 elements while A consists only of 2 elements.

Let $\boldsymbol{\xi} = (\xi(1), \xi(2), \xi(3))$ be the a priori probability for the three states $(-\mu, 0, \mu)$ respectively. The Bayes solution is to accept the

hypothesis H_0 if

(6.4.13)
$$\frac{\xi(1)p(\bar{x} \mid -\mu) + \xi(3)p(\bar{x} \mid \mu)}{\xi(2)p(\bar{x} \mid 0)} \leq w$$

and to reject it otherwise, where

(6.4.14)
$$p(\bar{x} \mid \theta) = \frac{\sqrt{N}}{\sqrt{2\pi}} e^{-(N/2)(\bar{x} - \theta)}$$

The inequality (6.4.13) simplifies to

(6.4.15) $$\xi(3)e^{N\mu\bar{x}} + \xi(1)e^{-N\mu\bar{x}} \leq \xi(2)we^{(N/2)\mu^2}$$

which in turn is equivalent to

(6.4.16) $$c_1(w, \boldsymbol{\xi}) \leq \bar{x} \leq c_2(w, \boldsymbol{\xi})$$

where c_1 and c_2 are the two roots of equation 6.4.15 with the equality sign holding.

Thus the class of Bayes procedures are characterized by intervals (c_1, c_2) on the real line such that if \bar{x} falls in this interval the hypothesis H_0 is accepted, and if it falls outside of this interval this hypothesis is rejected. The fact that the Bayes procedures are characterized by intervals follows from a general result [corollary 1, Theorem 7.4.3] to be proved later. Moreover, it will also be shown [corollary 3 of the same theorem] that this class is admissible.

Example 4. A Problem in Which $\Omega = (1, 2)$, $A = (1, 2, 3)$. A manufacturer who produces complex items sells these items in lots with a guarantee that each item will be well functioning. Before selling a lot, he tests N items from it and obtains the random variable f whose values are $x = (x_1, x_2, \cdots, x_N)$. The decision he makes on the basis of the outcome is either to sell the lot as is (action 1) or to reassemble each item in it (action 2). Each lot comes to him from a production process which is in one of two states [i.e., $\Omega = (1, 2)$] with known probabilities ζ and $1 - \zeta$. In state 1, the probability distribution of f is given by $p_1(x)$, and in state 2 by $p_2(x)$ [see Definition 3.4.2]. He will always take action 1 if he decides that the lot comes from state 1 and action 2 if he decides that the lot comes from state 2. Knowing the expected proportion of defective items in both states, the cost of having items returned to him due to the guarantee, and the cost of reassembling the items in a lot, he assesses his losses due to wrong decisions as w_{12} dollars if the lot comes from state 1 and he takes action 2 and w_{21} dollars if the lot comes from state 2 and he takes action 1.

Suppose after determining the Bayes procedure and computing the Bayes risk resulting from it (which is the best he can accomplish) he discovers that this risk is higher than he can tolerate. He then decides to introduce a third action, viz. to sell some of the lots at a cheaper price but without a guarantee. He assesses his new loss matrix as follows:

States of Nature	Actions		
	1	2	3
1	0	w_{12}	w_{13}
2	w_{21}	0	w_{23}

The problem is: What conditions must the elements of the loss matrix satisfy (other than the obvious conditions that $w_{13} < w_{12}$ and $w_{23} < w_{21}$) before it will be profitable for him to take action 3, and for what outcomes x will he take action 3? The solution is easily obtainable and is as follows: Let $\tau_x(i)$, $i = 1, 2, 3$ be the a posteriori risk if the manufacturer takes action i. Then

$$\tau_x(1) = \frac{(1 - \zeta)w_{21}p_2(x)}{\zeta p_1(x) + (1 - \zeta)p_2(x)}$$

(6.4.17) $$\tau_x(2) = \frac{\zeta w_{12}p_1(x)}{\zeta p_1(x) + (1 - \zeta)p_2(x)}$$

$$\tau_x(3) = \frac{\zeta w_{13}p_1(x) + (1 - \zeta)w_{23}p_2(x)}{\zeta p_1(x) + (1 - \zeta)p_2(x)}$$

and he will take action i if $\tau_x(i)$ is the smallest of the 3 τ_x's. More specifically, he will take action 1 if

(6.4.18) $$\frac{p_2(x)}{p_1(x)} \leq \frac{\zeta w_{12}}{(1 - \zeta)w_{21}} \quad \text{and} \quad \frac{p_2(x)}{p_1(x)} \leq \frac{\zeta w_{13}}{(1 - \zeta)(w_{21} - w_{23})},$$

he will take action 2 if

(6.4.19) $$\frac{p_2(x)}{p_1(x)} \geq \frac{\zeta w_{12}}{(1 - \zeta)w_{21}} \quad \text{and} \quad \frac{p_2(x)}{p_1(x)} \geq \frac{\zeta(w_{12} - w_{13})}{(1 - \zeta)w_{23}},$$

he will take action 3 if

$$(6.4.20) \quad \frac{p_2(x)}{p_1(x)} \geq \frac{\zeta w_{13}}{(1 - \zeta)(w_{21} - w_{23})} \quad \text{and} \quad \frac{p_2(x)}{p_1(x)} \leq \frac{\zeta(w_{12} - w_{13})}{(1 - \zeta)w_{23}}$$

We observe that action 3 will never be taken unless

$$(6.4.21) \quad \frac{\zeta w_{13}}{(1 - \zeta)(w_{21} - w_{23})} \leq \frac{\zeta(w_{12} - w_{13})}{(1 - \zeta)w_{23}}$$

or equivalently

$$(6.4.22) \quad\quad w_{12}w_{21} \geq w_{12}w_{23} + w_{21}w_{13}$$

But, if (6.4.22) is satisfied, the second inequality in both (6.4.18) and (6.4.19) implies the first, as can easily be verified. Thus we see that it will generally be profitable for the manufacturer to introduce the 3rd action, provided condition 6.4.22 is satisfied. The profitability of this action follows from the fact that the described procedure is Bayes and hence must be better than the original procedure which is a possible procedure for the new loss matrix.

Note that (6.4.22) is a condition on the risk matrix only. Hence we can state that, in any decision situation where $\Omega = (1, 2)$ and $A = (1, 2, 3)$ and where the risk matrix satisfies condition 6.4.22, the class of Bayes solutions is characterized by three intervals on the real line, $I_1 = (-\infty, c_1)$, $I_3 = (c_1, c_2)$, $I_2 = (c_2, \infty)$, where

$$(6.4.23) \quad c_1 = \frac{\zeta w_{13}}{(1 - \zeta) (w_{21} - w_{23})}, \quad c_2 = \frac{\zeta(w_{12} - w_{13})}{(1-\zeta)w_{23}}$$

and, for any ζ, the Bayes procedure is to take action j if the likelihood ratio $p_2(x)/p_1(x)$ falls in I_j.

An interesting consequence of the above discussion is that in a situation where Ω and A are both finite, the Bayes procedure may sometimes lead us to decide that nature is in state i, even if it is known that the a priori probability for that state is zero. Thus, for example, let the loss if nature is in state i and the statistician takes action j, be represented by a matrix (w_{ij}) ($i, j = 1, 2, 3$) with $w_{ii} = 0$, and let the elements of (w_{ij}) satisfy condition 6.4.22. Then the Bayes procedure will sometimes lead us to take action 3, even if the a priori probability for state 3 is zero. This situation is illustrated in Problem 6.3.3.

Example 5. Estimation of the Fraction Defective in Finite Lots When the Loss Function Is Quadratic. We are given a lot of M items where each item is classified as either defective or non-defective. The number R of defective items is unknown. It is desired to estimate the fraction

$\omega = R/M$ of defective items in the lot on the basis of a random sample [see Section 7.7] of N items selected from it. Let x_i represent the quality of the ith item selected for inspection; i.e., $x_i = 1$ if the item is defective and $x_i = 0$ if it is non-defective, and let $x = (x_1, x_2, \cdots, x_N)$. The probability distribution of $r = \sum_{i=1}^{N} x_i$ is

$$(6.4.24) \qquad q(r \mid R) = \frac{\binom{M - R}{N - r}\binom{R}{r}}{\binom{M}{N}}$$

where $\binom{n}{m} = \dfrac{n!}{m!(n - m)!}$ and r is the number of defective items in the sample and is a sufficient statistic [see Section 8.4].

We shall restrict ourselves to quadratic loss functions. That is, we shall assume that, if the statistician chooses an estimate $a \, \varepsilon \, A$ and the true fraction defective is ω, the loss $L(\omega, a)$ is given by $\lambda(\omega)(a - \omega)^2$ where $\lambda(\omega) > 0$ for all ω.

Let $\xi = (\xi(0), \xi(1), \cdots, \xi(M))$ be an a priori probability distribution on Ω. If ξ is binomial, i.e., if

$$(6.4.25) \qquad \xi(R) = \binom{M}{R}\theta^R(1 - \theta)^{M-R}$$

for all $R = 0, 1, \cdots, M$ and $0 \le \theta \le 1$, then the machine producing the items from which the lots are formed is said to be in statistical control. Let $g(r \mid \theta)$ be the probability that r defective items will be found in a random sample selected from the lot when the machine is in statistical control. Then, since $M - R \ge N - r$, we have

$$(6.4.26) \quad g(r \mid \theta) = \sum_{R=r}^{M-N+r} \binom{M - R}{N - r}\binom{R}{r}\binom{M}{R}\theta^R(1 - \theta)^{M-R} \Big/ \binom{M}{N}$$

Setting $R^* = R - r$ and $M^* = M - N$ and simplifying, we get

$$(6.4.27) \quad g(r \mid \theta) = \sum_{R^*=0}^{M^*} \binom{M^*}{R^*}\theta^{R^*}(1 - \theta)^{M^*-R^*}\binom{N}{r}\theta^r(1 - \theta)^{N-r}$$

$$= \binom{N}{r}\theta^r(1 - \theta)^{N-r}$$

so that $g(r \mid \theta)$ is also binomial.

For any ξ and any estimate a, let $\tau_r(a)$ be the a posteriori risk [see Definition 3.6.5] for the quadratic risk function. Then

$$(6.4.28) \qquad \tau_r(a) = \frac{\sum\limits_{R=r}^{M-N+r} \lambda(R/M)\left(a - \dfrac{R}{M}\right)^2 q(r\mid R)\xi(R)}{\sum\limits_{R=r}^{M-N+r} q(r\mid R)\xi(R)}$$

which, when expanded, is a quadratic function of a and attains a minimum at

$$(6.4.29) \qquad a^* = \frac{\sum\limits_{R=r}^{M-N+r} \dfrac{R}{M}\lambda(R/M)q(r\mid R)\xi(R)}{\sum\limits_{R=r}^{M-N+r} \lambda(R/M)q(r\mid R)\xi(R)}$$

Thus the Bayes estimating procedure is to choose the function d with values $d(r)$ given by the right-hand side of equation (6.4.29).

As illustrations, consider the case where $\lambda(\omega) = 1$ for all ω and $\xi(R)$ is given by (6.4.25). Then a simple computation shows that

$$(6.4.30) \qquad d(r) = \left(1 - \frac{N}{M}\right)\theta + \frac{N}{M}\hat{\omega}$$

where $\hat{\omega} = r/N$ is the usual estimate of ω.

Example 6. Minimax Estimate of ω When the Loss Is Quadratic. Of considerable interest is the problem of finding a loss function $L(\omega, a)$ for which the minimax estimate d is the commonly employed estimate $\hat{\omega} = r/N$. We shall show that $\hat{\omega}$ is minimax for the quadratic loss function with $\lambda(\omega) = 1/\omega(1 - \omega)$ and that nature's least favorable distribution is given by $\xi(R) = 1/(M + 1)$ for all R.

We see from the assumed form of $L(\omega, a)$ that the only estimating procedure $d(r)$ that yields finite risk for all ω is one for which $d(0) = 0$ and $d(N) = 1$, unless, of course, the states $\omega = 0$ and $\omega = 1$ are considered impossible. We also note that $L(0, 0)$ and $L(1, 1)$ are undefined. For reasons that will become apparent shortly, we set

$$(6.4.31) \qquad L(0, 0) = L(1, 1) = \frac{M - N}{N(M - 1)}$$

If the statistician employs $\hat{\omega}$ as an estimate of ω, then his risk $\rho(\omega, \hat{\omega})$ for $\omega \neq 0$ or 1 is given by

$$(6.4.32) \quad \rho(\omega, \hat{\omega}) = \frac{\displaystyle\sum_{r=0}^{N} \left(\frac{r}{N} - \frac{R}{M}\right)^2 \binom{M-R}{N-r}\binom{R}{r}}{\frac{R}{M}\left(1 - \frac{R}{M}\right)\binom{M}{N}}$$

$$= \frac{\sigma^2_{\hat{\omega}}}{\omega(1-\omega)} = \frac{M-N}{N(M-1)}$$

Thus, in view of (6.4.31) the estimate $\hat{\omega}$ yields the constant risk $(M-N)/N(M-1)$ for all ω.

It remains to be shown that $\hat{\omega}$ is Bayes against the a priori distribution $\xi(R) = 1/(M+1)$ for all R. Now by (6.4.29) the Bayes estimate is given by

$$(6.4.33) \quad d(r) = \frac{\displaystyle\sum_{R=r}^{M-N+r} \frac{M}{M-R}\binom{M-R}{N-r}\binom{R}{r}}{\displaystyle\sum_{R=r}^{M-N+r} \frac{M^2}{R(M-R)}\binom{M-R}{N-r}\binom{R}{r}}$$

$$= \frac{1}{M} \frac{\displaystyle\sum_{R=r}^{M-N+r} \frac{(M-R-1)!R!}{(M-R-N+r)!(R-r)!}}{\displaystyle\sum_{R=r}^{M-N+r} \frac{(M-R-1)!(R-1)!}{(M-R-N+r)!(R-r)!}} = \frac{1}{M}\frac{a}{b}$$

We now use the fact that

$$\sum_{R=0}^{M} \int_0^1 \frac{\Gamma(\alpha+\beta)}{\Gamma(\alpha)\Gamma(\beta)}\theta^{\alpha-1}(1-\theta)^{\beta-1}\binom{M}{R}\theta^R(1-\theta)^{M-R}\,d\theta = 1$$

to derive the identity

$$\sum_{R=0}^{M}\binom{M}{R}\frac{\Gamma(\alpha+\beta)}{\Gamma(\alpha)\Gamma(\beta)}\frac{\Gamma(\alpha+R)\Gamma(\beta+M-R)}{\Gamma(\alpha+\beta+M)} = 1$$

or

$$\sum_{R=0}^{M}\frac{\Gamma(\alpha+R)\Gamma(\beta+M-R)}{R!(M-R)!} = \frac{\Gamma(\alpha)\Gamma(\beta)\Gamma(\alpha+\beta+M)}{M!\Gamma(\alpha+\beta)}$$

or

$$\sum_{R=0}^{M}\frac{(\alpha+R-1)!(\beta+M-R-1)!}{R!(M-R)!} = \frac{\Gamma(\alpha)\Gamma(\beta)\Gamma(\alpha+\beta+M)}{M!\Gamma(\alpha+\beta)}$$

Replacing R by $R - r$ and M by $M - N$, we obtain

$$(6.4.34) \quad \sum_{R=r}^{M-N+r} \frac{(\alpha + R - r - 1)!(\beta + M - N - R + r - 1)!}{(R - r)!(M - N - R + r)!}$$

$$= \frac{\Gamma(\alpha)\Gamma(\beta)\Gamma(\alpha + \beta + M - N)}{(M - N)!\Gamma(\alpha + \beta)}$$

Substituting $\alpha = r + 1$, $\beta = N - r$, in identity (6.4.34), we obtain

$$a = \frac{\Gamma(r + 1)\Gamma(N - r)\Gamma(M + 1)}{(M - N)!\Gamma(N + 1)}$$

Similarly, putting $\alpha = r$, $\beta = N - r$ in (6.4.34), we get

$$b = \frac{\Gamma(r)\Gamma(N - r)\Gamma(M)}{(M - N)!\Gamma(N)}$$

Applying the above expression for a and b to (6.4.33), we obtain

$$(6.4.35) \quad d(r) = \frac{1}{M}\frac{rM}{N} = \frac{r}{N}$$

Thus $\hat{\omega}$ is Bayes against the rectangular distribution and hence is a minimax estimate for the given quadratic risk function.

PROBLEMS

6.4.1. We are given two coins and are informed that one of them is biased, i.e., has a known probability $p > 1/2$ of falling "head," and the other is unbiased. The problem is to decide which of the two coins is biased on the basis of N tosses of each coin. Assuming a constant loss w due to a wrong decision, determine the minimax procedure for this problem.

6.4.2. Suppose we introduce in Problem 6.4.1 the possibility of deciding that the result of the experiment was inconclusive and assume that the loss due to this decision is v with $w > 2v$. Give a minimax procedure in this case.

6.4.3. Give two geometric interpretations of condition 6.4.22 in Example 4, Section 6.4. Generalize this condition to the case $A = (1, 2, 3, 4)$.

6.4.4. Show that in Example 6, Section 6.4, nature's least favorable distribution $\xi(R) = 1/(M + 1)$ is equivalent to the following. Nature first selected R with the binomial probability (6.4.25) and then selected θ with a rectangular distribution over the interval $(0, 1)$.

6.4.5. Suppose that in Example 6, Section 6.4, we take

$$L(0, 0) < \frac{M - N}{N(M - 1)}, \qquad L(1, 1) < \frac{M - N}{N(M - 1)}$$

Show that in this case $\hat{\omega}$ is still a minimax estimate of ω, but that nature has no least favorable a priori distribution.

6.4.6. Find the minimax estimate of ω in Example 6, Section 6.4, if $L(\omega, a) = (\omega - a)^2$. *Hint.* Show first that there exist constants α and β such that

$$E(\alpha\hat{\omega} + \beta - \omega)^2 \equiv \beta^2$$

Next show that the estimate $d = \alpha\hat{\omega} + \beta$ is Bayes against

$$\xi(R) = \int_0^1 \binom{M}{R} \theta^R (1 - \theta)^{M-R} \frac{\Gamma(a + b)}{\Gamma(a)\Gamma(b)} \theta^{a-1}(1 - \theta)^{b-1}\, d\theta$$

for an appropriate choice of a and b.

6.4.7. Let $G = (\Omega, D, \rho)$ be a game with $\Omega = (1, 2, \cdots, h)$ and a loss function L. Let \mathcal{B} be the class of Bayes procedures for G. Consider a class of procedures \mathcal{B}', each of which is Bayes against $\xi = (1/h, \cdots, 1/h)$ for one of the class of loss functions

$$\mathcal{L}(j, a) = \lambda_j L(j, a)$$

with $\lambda_j \geq 0$ for all j and $\sum_{j=1}^n \lambda_j = 1$. Show that $\mathcal{B} = \mathcal{B}'$.

6.4.8. Let $G_N = (\Omega_N, D_N, \rho_N)$ be a fixed sample-size game based on N observations. Let the cost of taking N observations be given by $c(N)$. Show how to obtain the optimal N and d_N for any a priori distribution ξ if the total risk is given by $c(N) + \rho_N(\xi, d_N)$, $d_N \in D_N$.

6.4.9. Let $G_u = (\Omega, D, \rho_u)$ be a fixed sample-size game in which $\Omega = (1, 2)$, $A = (1, 2)$, $L(1, 1) = L(2, 2) = 0$, $L(1, 2) = 1$, $L(2, 1) = u > 0$. Let S^* be the convex hull of the set S of attainable risk vectors in 2-space for the case $u = 1$. (a) How is the lower boundary of S^* related to the Neyman-Pearson theory of testing a simple hypothesis against a simple alternative? (b) Show that this lower boundary (excluding those points lying on the axes) can be generated by considering the minimax solutions of G_u for all values of u between 0 and ∞. (c) Sketch the lower boundary of S^* for the case $Z = (z_1, z_2, z_3)$,

$$p_1(z_1) = p_1(z_3) = 1/2, \quad p_1(z_2) = 0; \qquad p_2(z_2) = p_2(z_3) = 1/2, \quad p_2(z_1) = 0$$

CHAPTER 7

Fixed Sample-Size Games
with Finite A

7.1. Introduction

This chapter will be devoted to the study of a class of fixed sample-size statistical games in which the number of possible actions that the statistician can take is finite. (Games in which the number of possible actions is finite are commonly referred to as multidecision games.) More specifically, we shall consider a sample space $\mathcal{Z} = (Z, \Omega, p)$ and games $G = (\Omega, D, \rho)$ in which Ω is a parameter set determining a class of probability distributions \mathcal{P}_Ω on Z, the class of actions A is finite, i.e., $A = (1, 2, \cdots, k)$, the class D consists of decision functions d mapping Z into A, the risk function ρ is given by Definition 3.5.3, and the statistician performs a fixed sample-size experiment, resulting in a point $z \in Z$ on the basis of which he chooses an action employing a decision function $d \in D$.

The number of elements in Ω may be finite, denumerable, or non-denumerable. The special case where Ω is finite has already been treated in Chapter 6. Whether Ω is finite or not, as always, the proofs of theorems will be carried out under the assumption that for each of its elements p_ω is zero except on a countable set of points z_1, z_2, \cdots in Z. Also, if mixed strategies enter in a proof, it will be assumed that they are zero except on a countable number of elements in the respective spaces Ω and D. In many instances, the reader will have no difficulty in supplying the corresponding proofs in case Z is an n space and p_ω is a density, or nature's mixed strategy ξ is a density defined on an n space, or both are densities. This will usually involve simply replacing a summation sign by an integral sign.

In case of mixed strategies for the statistician, the very nature of the space D will preclude the considerations of anything but mixtures on a countable set of elements of D. However, it can be shown that for finite A this is the most general type of randomization that the statistician need consider.

171

7.2. On the Equivalence of Two Methods of Randomization

In Section 3.6 [see Definition 3.6.6] it was stated that the statistician has at his disposal two methods of randomization. He can either select an η from a class H of randomized strategies, i.e., mix a sequence d_1, d_2, \cdots of decision functions in the proportions λ_1, λ_2, \cdots with $\lambda_i \geq 0$ and $\Sigma\lambda_i = 1$, or he can choose an element $\varphi \, \varepsilon \, \Phi$ where φ is defined on $A \times Z$, $\varphi(a \mid z) \geq 0$ and $\sum_{a \, \varepsilon \, A} \varphi(a \mid z) = 1$, and, for every outcome z of the experiment, he takes action a with probability $\varphi(a \mid z)$. We shall now prove that these two methods of randomization are equivalent in case A is finite [see also Theorem 8.3.1].

Theorem 7.2.1. Let $G = (\Omega, D, \rho)$ be a fixed sample-size multi-decision game (i.e., a game in which A is finite), and let $\Gamma = (\Xi, H, \rho)$ be its mixed extension. Consider another game $\Gamma^* = (\Xi, \Phi, \rho)$ where each element φ of Φ has the property described above. Then Γ^* is equivalent to Γ in the sense that, for every $\eta \, \varepsilon \, H$, there exists an element $\varphi \, \varepsilon \, \Phi$, and, conversely, such that $\rho(\omega, \eta) = \rho(\omega, \varphi)$ for all $\omega \, \varepsilon \, \Omega$ and hence for all $\xi \, \varepsilon \, \Xi$.

Proof. Since by assumption $A = (1, \cdots, k)$ every element $d \, \varepsilon \, D$ can be considered as a partition of the sample space Z into k mutually exclusive sets S_1, \cdots, S_k with $\bigcup_{i=1}^{k} S_i = Z$, such that, if $z \, \varepsilon \, S_i$, action i is taken [see Section 3.5]. Hence, the value of the risk function ρ can be written as

$$(1) \quad \rho(\omega, d) = \sum_{i=1}^{k} L_i(\omega) \sum_{z \, \varepsilon \, S_i} p(z \mid \omega) = \sum_{i=1}^{k} \sum_{z} L_i(\omega)\psi(i \mid z)p(z \mid \omega)$$

where $\psi(i \mid z) = 1$ if $z \, \varepsilon \, S_i$ and $\psi(i \mid z) = 0$ otherwise and $L_i(\omega) = L(\omega, i)$ is the value of the loss function given by Definition 3.5.2. Consider a mixture of a denumerable number of elements of D, say d_1, d_2, \cdots. Then to each d_j there corresponds a function ψ_j on $A \times Z$ of the type considered. From mixing d_1, d_2, \cdots in the proportions λ_1, λ_2, \cdots; $\lambda_j \geq 0$ and $\Sigma\lambda_j = 1$; we get a procedure η with

$$(2) \quad \rho(\omega, \eta) = \sum_{j=1}^{\infty} \sum_{i=1}^{k} \sum_{z} L_i(\omega)\lambda_j\psi_j(i \mid z)p(z \mid \omega)$$

$$= \sum_{z} \sum_{i=1}^{k} L_i(\omega) \left[\sum_{j=1}^{\infty} \lambda_j\psi_j(i \mid z) \right] p(z \mid \omega)$$

where the interchange of summation is justified by the fact that the series is absolutely convergent.

Now, for a general φ the risk is given by

$$(3) \qquad \rho(\omega, \varphi) = \sum_z \sum_{i=1}^{k} L_i(\omega)\varphi(i \mid z)p(z \mid \omega)$$

Thus from (2) and (3) we see that any $\eta \, \varepsilon \, H$ determines a φ, namely

$$(4) \qquad \sum_{j=1}^{\infty} \lambda_j\psi_j(i \mid z) = \varphi(i \mid z)$$

which satisfies the condition of the theorem.

We must show now that given a φ we can find a probability sequence $\lambda_1, \lambda_2, \cdots$ and a sequence $\{\psi_j\}$ which satisfy (4) for each i and z. Choose

$$\lambda_n = \frac{1}{k}\left(\frac{k-1}{k}\right)^{n-1}$$

Fix z and define $\psi_n(i \mid z)$ and $\theta_n(i \mid z)$ inductively as follows:

$$\theta_1(i \mid z) = \varphi(i \mid z)$$

$$\theta^*_1(z) = \max\,[\theta_1(1 \mid z), \cdots, \theta_1(k \mid z)] = \theta_1(i_1 \mid z)$$

where i_1 is the smallest integer i $(i = 1, 2, \cdots, k)$ for which $\theta^*_1(z) = \theta_1(i \mid z)$.

$$\psi_1(i_1 \mid z) = 1, \qquad \psi_1(i \mid z) = 0 \quad \text{for} \quad i \neq i_1$$

Having defined $\psi_j(i \mid z)$ and $\theta_j(i \mid z)$ for $j < n$, let

$$(5) \qquad \theta_n(i \mid z) = \varphi(i \mid z) - \sum_{j=1}^{n-1} \lambda_j\psi_j(i \mid z)$$

$$(6) \qquad \theta^*_n(z) = \max\,[\theta_n(1 \mid z), \cdots, \theta_n(k \mid z)] = \theta_n(i_n \mid z)$$

where i_n is the smallest integer i $(i = 1, 2, \cdots, k)$ for which $\theta^*_n(z) = \theta_n(i \mid z)$.

$$(7) \qquad \psi_n(i_n \mid z) = 1, \qquad \psi_n(i \mid z) = 0 \quad \text{for} \quad i \neq i_n$$

We shall now show that

$$\sum_{n=1}^{\infty} \lambda_n\psi_n(i \mid z) = \varphi(i \mid z), \qquad i = 1, 2, \cdots, k$$

Since

$$\sum_{i=1}^{k} \sum_{n=1}^{\infty} \lambda_n\psi_n(i \mid z) = 1 = \sum_{i=1}^{k} \varphi(i \mid z)$$

it will suffice to prove that

$$\sum_n \lambda_n \psi_n(i \mid z) \leq \varphi(i \mid z), \qquad i = 1, 2, \cdots, k$$

However, to prove this inequality, it is enough to show that $\theta_n(i \mid z)$ is non-negative for all n, as can be seen from (5). We prove this by induction. We know that $\theta_1(i \mid z)$ is non-negative. We shall assume $\theta_j(i \mid z) \geq 0$ for $j \leq n$ and prove that $\theta_{n+1}(i \mid z) \geq 0$. Now

$$(8) \qquad \sum_{i=1}^{k} \sum_{j=1}^{n-1} \lambda_j \psi_j(i \mid z) = \sum_{j=1}^{n-1} \lambda_j = 1 - \left(\frac{k-1}{k}\right)^{n-1}$$

Also, summing (5) with respect to i yields

$$(9) \qquad \sum_{i=1}^{k} \theta_n(i \mid z) = \sum_{i=1}^{k} \varphi(i \mid z) - \sum_{i=1}^{k} \sum_{j=1}^{n-1} \lambda_j \psi_j(i \mid z)$$

$$= 1 - \sum_{i=1}^{k} \sum_{j=1}^{n-1} \lambda_j \psi_j(i \mid z)$$

Thus, from (8) and (9) we have

$$(10) \qquad \sum_{i=1}^{k} \theta_n(i \mid z) = \left(\frac{k-1}{k}\right)^{n-1}$$

By the induction hypothesis, $\theta_n(i \mid z) \geq 0$ for all i. Hence, in view of (10) we have

$$(11) \quad \theta^*_n(z) = \max [\theta_n(1 \mid z), \cdots, \theta_n(k \mid z)] \geq \frac{1}{k}\left(\frac{k-1}{k}\right)^{n-1} = \lambda_n$$

Now consider

$$(12) \qquad \theta_{n+1}(i \mid z) = \varphi(i \mid z) - \sum_{j=1}^{n} \lambda_j \psi_j(i \mid z)$$

$$= \varphi(i \mid z) - \sum_{j=1}^{n-1} \lambda_j \psi_j(i \mid z) - \lambda_n \psi_n(i \mid z)$$

$$= \theta_n(i \mid z) - \lambda_n \psi_n(i \mid z)$$

Case 1. $i \neq i_n$. Then, by (7), $\psi_n(i \mid z) = 0$, and, by (12), $\theta_{n+1}(i \mid z) = \theta_n(i \mid z)$, so that by the induction hypothesis $\theta_{n+1}(i \mid z) \geq 0$.

Case 2. $i = i_n$. Then, by (7), $\psi_n(i_n \mid z) = 1$, and hence, by (12), (6), and (11),

$$\theta_{n+1}(i \mid z) = \theta_n(i_n \mid z) - \lambda_n = \theta^*_n(z) - \lambda_n \geq 0$$

This completes the proof of the theorem.

Corollary 1. If for all ω, a risk $\rho(\omega, \eta)$ is attainable with an $\eta \in H$, it is also attainable by employing a mixture of a denumerable number of elements d_1, d_2, \cdots of D in the fixed proportions $\lambda_j = \dfrac{1}{k} \left(\dfrac{k-1}{k} \right)^{j-1}$ $(j = 1, 2, \cdots)$.

Proof. The proof of this corollary follows directly from Theorem 7.2.1.

<div align="center">PROBLEMS</div>

7.2.1. Let $Z = (0 \leq z \leq 1)$, $A = (1, 2)$ and $\varphi(1 \mid z) = z$, $\varphi(2 \mid z) = 1 - z$. Construct a sequence $\{\psi_j\}$ satisfying (4).

7.2.2. Show that there is no sequence of numbers $\lambda_1, \lambda_2, \cdots$, with $\lambda_n > 0, \Sigma\lambda_n = 1$, such that, for every sequence μ_1, μ_2, \cdots, with $\mu_n > 0, \Sigma\mu_n = 1$, the series $\Sigma\lambda_n$ can be partitioned into subseries $\Sigma'\lambda_n, \Sigma''\lambda_n, \cdots$ with $\Sigma^{(k)}\lambda_n = \mu_k$. How is this related to corollary 1 of Theorem 7.2.1?

7.3. Bayes Solutions in Fixed Sample-Size Games with Finite A

Let G be a fixed sample-size multidecision game, and let $\Gamma = (\Xi, H, \rho)$ be its mixed extension where ρ is defined on $\Xi \times H$. In view of Theorem 7.2.1 we can replace H by Φ so that $\Gamma = (\Xi, \Phi, \rho)$ where ρ is defined on $\Xi \times \Phi$. The problem of characterizing the class \mathfrak{B} of Bayes solutions for G is the problem of finding for each $\xi \in \Xi$, a $\varphi^* \in \Phi$ which minimizes $\rho(\xi, \varphi)$. We prove the following

Theorem 7.3.1. <u>For any $\xi \in \Xi$ let</u>

$$\tau_z(i) = \frac{\sum\limits_{\omega} L_i(\omega)p(z \mid \omega)\xi(\omega)}{\sum\limits_{\omega} p(z \mid \omega)\xi(\omega)}$$

<u>be the a posteriori risk [see Definition 3.6.4] if z is observed and action i is taken. Then a Bayes decision procedure φ^* is given by $\varphi^*(i \mid z)$ $= 1$ for an i for which $\tau_z(i)$ is the minimum of $\tau_z = \{\tau_z(1), \cdots, \tau_z(k)\}$ and $\varphi^*(i \mid z) = 0$ for all other i's.</u>

Proof. For any ξ and φ the value of the risk function ρ is given by

(1) $$\rho(\xi, \varphi) = \sum_{\omega} \sum_{z} \sum_{i=1}^{k} L_i(\omega)p(z \mid \omega)\varphi(i \mid z)\xi(\omega)$$

Since the series on the right is absolutely convergent, we can interchange the order of summation and obtain

(2) $$\rho(\xi, \varphi) = \sum_z \sum_\omega \sum_{i=1}^k L_i(\omega) p(z \mid \omega) \varphi(i \mid z) \xi(\omega)$$

$$= \sum_z \sum_i \tau_z(i) \varphi(i \mid z) \sum_\omega p(z \mid \omega) \xi(\omega)$$

But the expression on the right is clearly minimized if for every z we set $\varphi(i \mid z) = 1$ for an i for which

(3) $$\tau_z(i) = \min [\tau_z(1), \cdots, \tau_z(k)]$$

and $\varphi(i \mid z) = 0$ for all other i's. This proves the theorem.

Theorem 7.3.1 states that a Bayes solution is obtained by computing for each outcome of an experiment the value $\tau_z(i)$ for each i (note that only the numerator of the expression for $\tau_z(i)$ is relevant) and then selecting that action which corresponds to the smallest coordinate of τ_z. In case there is more than one minimum coordinate in the vector τ_z, it is immaterial which one of these is chosen.

As an illustration of a Bayes solution in a fixed sample-size multidecision game, consider the following: A manufacturer of cloth is faced with the problem of disposing of each bale as it is produced. The quality of a bale of cloth is measured by the average number of defects per yard of cloth in the bale, where a defect is defined as either a loose thread or a transparent spot.

For each bale, let ω stand for the average number of defects per yard of cloth. If ω were known to the manufacturer he would behave as follows: Whenever $0 \leq \omega < r$ he would sell the bale as "first quality" for \$500.00 (action 1). If $r \leq \omega < s$ he would sell the bale as "seconds" for \$300.00 (action 2). However, if $\omega \geq s$ he would sell the bale as "rejects" for \$100.00. The user of the cloth eventually knows the quality of each bale. He agrees to pay the manufacturer the sale price of a bale, provided its quality is as specified or better. However, if the quality of a bale is worse than specified, he pays the manufacturer the actual value of the bale but imposes a penalty equal to the amount he was overcharged.

The "payoff" matrix in terms of actual money income to the manufacturer is of the following form:

Quality of Bale	Action 1	Action 2	Action 3
$0 \leq \omega < r$	\$500.00	\$300.00	\$100.00
$r \leq \omega < s$	100.00	300.00	100.00
$\omega \geq s$	−300.00	−100.00	100.00

In terms of "loss" or "regret" [see Section 4.3] the payoff matrix is given by

Quality of Bale	Action 1	Action 2	Action 3
$0 \leq \omega < r$	$ 0.00	$200.00	$400.00
$r \leq \omega < s$	200.00	0.00	200.00
$\omega \geq s$	400.00	200.00	0.00

(It is to be remembered that the loss matrix is obtained from the income matrix by subtracting for each state of nature the actual income from a given action, from the maximum income that could have been obtained if that state were known.)

For every ω, the probability of getting x defects per yard, $x = 0, 1, 2, \cdots$ is assumed to be given by the Poisson distribution

$$p(x \mid \omega) = \frac{e^{-\omega}\omega^x}{x!}$$

From past experience, the manufacturer also knows that the a priori probability distribution of ω is given approximately by the density

$$\xi(\omega) = e^{-\omega}, \qquad (0 \leq \omega < \infty)$$

The manufacturer is willing to examine N yards of cloth in each bale for a decision. What is an optimum (i.e., Bayes) procedure for him to follow? For any outcome of the experiment $x = (x_1, \cdots, x_N)$ he has to compute $\tau_x(i)$ $i = 1, 2, 3$ and choose the action corresponding to the smallest coordinate of τ_x. Now for a Bayes solution it is immaterial whether the income or loss matrix is considered. Hence, employing the latter, we have

$$\tau_x(1) = \frac{200 \int_r^s e^{-(N+1)\omega}\omega^m \, d\omega + 400 \int_s^\infty e^{-(N+1)\omega}\omega^m \, d\omega}{\int_0^\infty e^{-(N+1)\omega}\omega^m \, d\omega}$$

$$\tau_x(2) = \frac{200 \int_0^r e^{-(N+1)\omega}\omega^m \, d\omega + 200 \int_s^\infty e^{-(N+1)\omega}\omega^m \, d\omega}{\int_0^\infty e^{-(N+1)\omega}\omega^m \, d\omega}$$

$$\tau_x(3) = \frac{400 \int_0^r e^{-(N+1)\omega}\omega^m \, d\omega + 200 \int_r^s e^{-(N+1)\omega}\omega^m \, d\omega}{\int_0^\infty e^{-(N+1)\omega}\omega^m \, d\omega}$$

where $m = \sum_{i=1}^{N} x_i$.

Comparing the coordinates of τ_x, we see that the manufacturer will take action 1 if

(1)
$$\int_r^\infty e^{-(N+1)\omega}\omega^m \, d\omega \le \int_0^r e^{-(N+1)\omega}\omega^m \, d\omega$$

and

(2)
$$\int_s^\infty e^{-(N+1)\omega}\omega^m \, d\omega \le \int_0^r e^{-(N+1)\omega}\omega^m \, d\omega$$

He will take action 2 if

(3)
$$\int_0^r e^{-(N+1)\omega}\omega^m \, d\omega \le \int_r^\infty e^{-(N+1)\omega}\omega^m \, d\omega$$

and

(4)
$$\int_s^\infty e^{-(N+1)\omega}\omega^m \, d\omega \le \int_0^s e^{-(N+1)\omega}\omega^m \, d\omega$$

He will take action 3 if

(5)
$$\int_0^r e^{-(N+1)\omega}\omega^m \, d\omega \le \int_s^\infty e^{-(N+1)\omega}\omega^m \, d\omega$$

and

(6)
$$\int_0^s e^{-(N+1)\omega}\omega^m \, d\omega \le \int_s^\infty e^{-(N+1)\omega}\omega^m \, d\omega$$

Let m_1 be a value of m (not necessarily integral) for which equality holds in (1). Then the inequality will hold for all $m < m_1$. For, let δ be any positive number; then

(7)
$$\int_r^\infty e^{-(N+1)\omega}\omega^{m_1}r^{-\delta} \, d\omega = \int_0^r e^{-(N+1)\omega}\omega^{m_1}r^{-\delta} \, d\omega$$

If we set $r = \omega$, the integral on the left-hand side of (7) will decrease while the integral on the right-hand side will increase. On the other hand, if $m \ge m_1$, the inequality will be reversed. It is clear that, for $m < m_1$, the inequality in (2) will surely hold. Similarly, let m_2 be a value for which equality holds in (6). Then, by a similar argument, we see that the inequality will hold for $m \ge m_2$ in both (5) and (6), and these inequalities will be reversed if $m < m_2$. It follows also that, for an m between m_1 and m_2, the inequalities in (3) and (4) will hold. Thus we can characterize the Bayes procedure for this problem as follows: Compute m_1 and m_2 in the manner indicated. Then, if $\sum_{i=1}^{N} x_i < m_1$,

take action 1; if $m_1 \leq \sum\limits_{i=1}^{N} x_i \leq m_2$, take action 2; and, if $\sum\limits_{i=1}^{N} x_i > m_2$, take action 3. The values of m_1 and m_2 may be computed with the help of tables of the incomplete gamma function.

The above is a special case of a general result [Theorem 7.4.3 and corollary 1] to be proved below.

PROBLEMS

7.3.1. With a given diet A the weight x of 8-month-old hogs is normally distributed with mean $\mu = 250$ lb. and a known variance σ^2. An alternative diet B is suggested which is expected either to increase the mean weight or leave the mean weight unchanged. In either case, diet B is not expected to affect the variance. With diet A the cost of feeding for the specified period is \$30.00 per hog; with diet B it is \$32.40 per hog. Hogs are worth \$16.00 per hundred pounds.

A farmer who ordinarily raises a crop of N hogs decides to experiment with the new diet. He selects a sample of n hogs on which to base a decision. Assuming that the farmer wishes to maximize his yearly expected profit, show that a class of Bayes strategies for this problem is as follows: Let k be a real constant and \bar{x} the arithmetic average weight of the n hogs. Then adopt diet B if $\bar{x} > k$, and reject diet B if $\bar{x} \leq k$.

7.3.2. A buyer measures the quality of lots submitted to him for inspection by the proportion p of defective items in each lot. If $p < p_0$, he wishes to accept a submitted lot. If $p > p_0$, he wishes to reject it. If he accepts a lot, his loss is measured by a function $L_1(p)$ which is positive for $p > p_0$ and zero for $p \leq p_0$. If he rejects the lot, his loss is measured by a function $L_2(p)$ which is positive for $p < p_0$ and zero for $p \geq p_0$. Assume that the buyer makes his decision on the basis of N observations and that the probability of getting r defective items in a sample of N is given by the binomial distribution $\binom{N}{r} p^r (1-p)^{N-r}$. Show that the class of Bayes solutions for this problem is of the form: Accept the lot if $r \leq a$; reject the lot if $r > a$, where a is an integer. *how is p distributed. $p = r/n$*

$\xi(p) = \binom{N}{r}\left(\frac{r}{N}\right)^r \left(\frac{N-r}{N}\right)^{N-r}$

7.4. Fixed Sample-Size Multidecision Games Where \mathcal{P}_Ω Is the Exponential Class

Many of the distributions studied in statistical literature belong to a class known as the exponential class. A probability distribution p_ω is said to be of the *exponential type* if

$$(7.4.1) \qquad p(x \mid \omega) = \beta(\omega) e^{\omega x} r(x) = \frac{e^{\omega x} r(x)}{\sum\limits_{x} e^{\omega x} r(x)}$$

where r is a non-negative function depending only on the real number x and ω ranges over an interval on the real line. Examples of distributions which are of the exponential type are the binomial and Poisson

for the discrete case, the normal with known variance, and chi square for the case of densities.

Theorem 7.4.1. Let x_1, x_2, \cdots, x_N be the values of N numerical random variables which are independently and identically distributed according to the exponential type. Then the probability distribution of the random variable t where $t(x) = \sum\limits_{i=1}^{N} x_i$ is also of the exponential type.

Proof. Let $x = (x_1, \cdots, x_N)$, and let

$$q(u \mid \omega) = P_\omega\{x : t(x) = u\}$$

Then

$$q(u \mid \omega) = \sum_{\{x : t(x) = u\}} [\beta(\omega)]^N e^{\omega t(x)} \prod_{i=1}^{N} r(x_i)$$

$$= [\beta(\omega)]^N e^{\omega u} \sum_{\{x : t(x) = u\}} \prod_{i=1}^{N} r(x_i)$$

$$= [\beta(\omega)]^N e^{\omega u} R(u) = \beta_0(\omega) e^{\omega u} R(u)$$

which completes the proof of the theorem.

Let $\mathfrak{X} = (X, \Omega, p)$ be a sample space where, for each $\omega \, \varepsilon \, \Omega$ and $x \, \varepsilon \, X$,

$$(7.4.2) \qquad p(x \mid \omega) = [\beta(\omega)]^N e^{\omega \sum\limits_{i=1}^{N} x_i} \prod_{i=1}^{N} r(x_i)$$

i.e., the coordinates of each $x \, \varepsilon \, X$ are the values of N numerical random variables which are independently distributed according to (7.4.1). Let $\mathfrak{J} = (T, \Omega, q)$ be another sample space in which T is the set of real numbers determined by the range of the random variable t with $t(x) = \sum\limits_{i=1}^{N} x_i$. By Theorem 7.4.1, \mathfrak{Q}_Ω consists of elements defined by

$$q(t \mid \omega) = \beta_0(\omega) e^{\omega t} R(t)$$

Theorem 7.4.2. Let $G = (\Omega, D, \rho)$ be any multidecision game in which the elements of \mathcal{O}_Ω are given by (7.4.2), and let Φ be a class of randomized strategies on $A \times X$. Let Ψ be the class of randomized strategies ψ on $A \times T$. Then for each $\varphi \, \varepsilon \, \Phi$ there exists a $\psi \, \varepsilon \, \Psi$ and conversely such that $\rho(\omega, \varphi) = \rho(\omega, \psi)$ for all $\omega \, \varepsilon \, \Omega$.

Proof. Let φ be given. For any $u \, \varepsilon \, T$ we define $\psi(i \mid u)$ as the conditional expectation of φ, given i and u; i.e.,

$$\psi(i \mid u) = \sum_{x \, \varepsilon \, S_u} \varphi(i \mid x) p(x \mid \omega) \big/ \sum_{x \, \varepsilon \, S_u} p(x \mid \omega)$$

where $S_u = \{x : t(x) = u\}$. Now since $[\beta(\omega)]^N e^{\omega \sum_i x_i} > 0$ we have for all i and u

$$\psi(i \mid u) = \sum_{x \, \varepsilon \, S_u} \varphi(i \mid x) \prod_{j=1}^{N} r(x_j) / R(u)$$

so that ψ is independent of ω for all $u \, \varepsilon \, T$. Also $\psi(i \mid u) \geq 0$ for all i and u and $\sum_{i=1}^{k} \psi(i \mid u) = 1$ for all u. Consequently, $\psi \, \varepsilon \, \Psi$. Now

$$\rho(\omega, \varphi) = \sum_{i=1}^{k} \sum_{x} L_i(\omega) \varphi(i \mid x) [\beta(\omega)]^N e^{\omega \Sigma x_j} \prod_{j=1}^{N} r(x_j)$$

$$= \sum_{i=1}^{k} L_i(\omega) \sum_{u \, \varepsilon \, T} \beta_0(\omega) e^{\omega u} \sum_{x \, \varepsilon \, S_u} \varphi(i \mid x) \prod_{j=1}^{N} r(x_j)$$

$$= \sum_{i=1}^{k} \sum_{u \, \varepsilon \, T} L_i(\omega) \beta_0(\omega) e^{\omega u} R(u) \psi(i \mid u)$$

$$= \sum_{i=1}^{k} \sum_{u \, \varepsilon \, T} L_i(\omega) \psi(i \mid u) q(u \mid \omega) = \rho(\omega, \psi)$$

which completes the proof of the first half of the theorem. The converse is left as an exercise. [See Problem 7.4.4.]

Theorem 7.4.2 is a special case of the more general Theorem 8.3.2 to be proved later.

In view of Theorem 7.4.2, every fixed sample-size multidecision game in which the observations are independent and distributed according to (7.4.1) can be treated as a game in which the sample space is $\mathfrak{X} = (X, \Omega, p)$ where X is a set of real numbers. Multidecision games of this type are known as games with a *numerical-valued single observation.*

Theorem 7.4.3. Let $G = (\Omega, D, \rho)$ be a multidecision game with a numerical-valued single observation in which the elements of φ_Ω are of the exponential type (7.4.1); ω ranges over an interval $\Omega = (a, b)$, the k elements of the action space A can be so labeled as to permit the subdivision of the interval Ω into k consecutive subintervals I_1, I_2, \cdots, I_k

(some of which may be empty and some consisting of a single point) with $\bigcup_{j=1}^{k} I_j = \Omega$ such that

1. For all $\omega \in I_i$, $L_i(\omega) = \min_j L_j(\omega)$.

2. If the integer j lies between s and i, $L_j(\omega) \leq L_s(\omega)$ for all $\omega \in I_i$. [See Fig. 11 for illustrations of conditions 1 and 2.]

Loss functions for monotone procedures

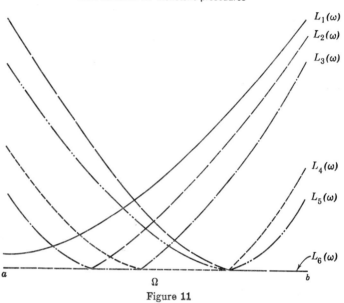

Figure 11

Then a complete class \mathcal{C} of decision procedures is a class of monotone procedures, i.e., procedures defined by a set of numbers $x_0 \leq x_1 \leq x_2 \leq \cdots \leq x_k$ (with $x_0 = -\infty$ and $x_k = +\infty$ permitted) such that action i is taken only if the outcome of an experiment is a point in the closed interval (x_{i-1}, x_i). Moreover, if the inequalities of condition 2 on the risk function are strict, then, given any decision procedure that is not monotone, we can find one that is monotone and that is uniformly better, i.e., that has smaller risk for all ω.

Proof. Before we prove this theorem we require the following

Lemma 7.4.1. Let $\theta \in \Omega$ and c be given, with $0 < c < 1$. Then among all those φ's which satisfy

(a) $\qquad\qquad 0 \leq \varphi(x) \leq 1 \quad \text{for all } x$

(b) $\qquad\qquad \sum_x \varphi(x)\beta(\theta)e^{\theta x}r(x) = c$

there is a unique $\hat\varphi$ that both maximizes $\sum_x \varphi(x)\beta(\omega)e^{\omega x}r(x)$ for all $\omega < \theta$ and minimizes the same sum for $\omega > \theta$. Furthermore, there exists an $x = x_c$ such that we may take $\hat\varphi(x) = 1$ for $x < x_c$ and $\hat\varphi(x) = 0$ for $x > x_c$.

Proof. We shall construct such a $\hat\varphi$ and then show that it satisfies these conditions.

Let x_c be the maximum of the numbers a such that $P_\theta(x < a) \le c$. Define $\hat\varphi(x) = 1$ if $x < x_c$, $\hat\varphi(x) = 0$ for $x > x_c$, and if $p(x_c \,|\, \theta) > 0$

$$(1) \qquad \hat\varphi(x_c) = \frac{c - P_\theta(x < x_c)}{p(x_c \,|\, \theta)}$$

It is easily seen that $\hat\varphi(x)$ satisfies conditions a and b. From condition b and the fact that $p(x_c \,|\, \theta) = 0$ implies $P_\theta(x < x_c) = c$, we have

$$(2) \qquad \sum_{x < x_c} [\hat\varphi(x) - \varphi(x)]\beta(\theta)e^{\theta x}r(x) = \sum_{x > x_c} [\varphi(x) - \hat\varphi(x)]\beta(\theta)e^{\theta x}r(x)$$

if $p(x_c \,|\, \theta) = 0$. If $p(x_c \,|\, \theta) \ne 0$ we include the x_c terms in either the left-hand side or the right-hand side of (2), depending on whether $\hat\varphi(x_c) - \varphi(x_c) \ge 0$ or $\hat\varphi(x_c) - \varphi(x_c) < 0$. With this convention we see that each term in the right- as well as left-hand sums of (2) is non-negative. We now multiply both sides of (2) by $[\beta(\omega)/\beta(\theta)]e^{(\omega-\theta)x_c}$ and get

$$(3) \qquad \sum_{x < x_c} [\hat\varphi(x) - \varphi(x)]\beta(\omega)e^{(\omega-\theta)x_c + \theta x}r(x)$$
$$= \sum_{x > x_c} [\varphi(x) - \hat\varphi(x)]\beta(\omega)e^{(\omega-\theta)x_c + \theta x}r(x)$$

Since, for $x_c > x$, $e^{(\omega-\theta)x_c + \theta x} \lessgtr e^{\omega x}$ according to whether $\omega \lessgtr \theta$, and for $x > x_c$ these inequalities are reversed, it follows that, if we substitute ωx for the exponent in (3), then, if $\omega < \theta$ the left-hand side of (3) is increased, while the right-hand side is decreased, but, if $\omega > \theta$, the reverse is true. This establishes the lemma.

We now return to the proof of Theorem 7.4.3. Since by defining $L^*_i(\omega) = L_i(\omega) - \min_j L_j(\omega)$ we do not alter either the class \mathcal{C} or the hypothesis of the theorem, we may assume, without any loss of generality, that $L_i(\omega) = 0$ for all $\omega \,\varepsilon\, I_i$. We may also assume that neither I_1 nor I_k are empty. For suppose I_1 were empty. Then $L_2(\omega) \le L_1(\omega)$ for $\omega \,\varepsilon\, I_2$ by assumption 1 and $L_2(\omega) \le L_1(\omega)$ for $\omega \,\varepsilon\, I_s$, $s > 2$ by assumption 2. Thus $L_2(\omega) \le L_1(\omega)$ for all ω, and we can delete action 1 from consideration. [See Fig. 11.] Similarly for I_k.

Let $S_i = \bigcup_{j \leq i} I_j$, and let ω_i ($i = 1, 2, \cdots, k - 1$) be the right end points of S_i. (Note that S_i is an interval since it is the union of adjacent intervals. Also, ω_i is always in the range of ω since I_1 and I_k are non-empty.)

Now let ψ be any decision procedure which is not of the type specified by the theorem, i.e., monotone. We shall show that we can find a monotone decision procedure which is better. We shall assume that $\psi(1 \mid x) \not\equiv 0$. (If $\psi(1 \mid x) \equiv 0$, the better procedure which we shall construct will simply never employ action 1.) Define

$$(4) \qquad \varphi(i \mid x) = \sum_{j=1}^{i} \psi(j \mid x), \qquad i = 1, \cdots, k, \qquad \varphi(0 \mid x) \equiv 0$$

Apply Lemma 7.4.1 to

$$(5) \qquad\qquad \sum_x \varphi(i \mid x)\beta(\theta)e^{\theta x}r(x) = c$$

with $\theta = \omega_i$, and obtain a $\hat{\phi}_i$ and a corresponding point x_i for $i = 1, 2, \cdots, k - 1$. Define $\hat{\phi}(0 \mid x) \equiv 0$, $\hat{\phi}(k \mid x) \equiv 1$. Observe that $\hat{\phi}(i \mid x)$ is monotone in i, for

$$(6) \quad \sum_x \hat{\phi}(i \mid x)\beta(\omega_i)e^{\omega_i x}r(x)$$

$$= \sum_x \varphi(i \mid x)\beta(\omega_i)e^{\omega_i x}r(x)$$

$$\leq \sum_x \varphi(i + 1 \mid x)\beta(\omega_i)e^{\omega_i x}r(x) \leq \sum_x \hat{\phi}(i + 1 \mid x)\beta(\omega_i)e^{\omega_i x}r(x)$$

The second inequality follows from Lemma 7.4.1 since $\omega_i \leq \omega_{i+1}$. Hence, from the form of the $\hat{\phi}$'s, $\hat{\phi}(i \mid x) \leq \hat{\phi}(i + 1 \mid x)$ for all x. Observe also that $\hat{\phi}(i \mid x)$ is either 0 or 1 for all x with the possible exception of the point x_i.

Consider a new decision procedure $\bar{\varphi}$ defined by

$$(7) \qquad\qquad \bar{\varphi}(i \mid x) = \hat{\phi}(i \mid x) - \hat{\phi}(i - 1 \mid x)$$

and let $\rho(\omega, \psi)$ be the risk with the given procedure. For any $\omega \, \varepsilon \, \Omega$

there is a j such that $\omega \,\varepsilon\, I_j$, so that we may write

(8) $$\rho(\omega, \psi) = \sum_{i=1}^{k} \sum_{x} L_i(\omega)\psi(i \mid x)\beta(\omega)e^{\omega x}r(x)$$

$$= \sum_{i=1}^{k} \sum_{x} L_i(\omega)[\widehat{\varphi}(i \mid x) - \widehat{\varphi}(i-1 \mid x)]\beta(\omega)e^{\omega x}r(x)$$

$$= \sum_{i=1}^{j-1} \sum_{x} L_i'(\omega)[\widehat{\varphi}(i \mid x) - \widehat{\varphi}(i-1 \mid x)]\beta(\omega)e^{\omega x}r(x)$$

$$+ \sum_{i=j+1}^{k} \sum_{x} L_i(\omega)[\widehat{\varphi}(i \mid x) - \widehat{\varphi}(i-1 \mid x)]\beta(\omega)e^{\omega x}r(x)$$

since $L_j(\omega) = 0$ for $\omega \,\varepsilon\, I_j$. Also by rearrangement of terms we get

(9) $$\rho(\omega, \psi) = \sum_{i=1}^{j-1} [L_i(\omega) - L_{i+1}(\omega)] \sum_{x} \varphi(i \mid x)\beta(\omega)e^{\omega x}r(x)$$

$$+ \sum_{i=j+1}^{k} [L_i(\omega) - L_{i-1}(\omega)] \left\{ 1 - \sum_{x} \varphi(i-1 \mid x)\beta(\omega)e^{\omega x}r(x) \right\}$$

The first term on the right-hand side of (9) is obtained from the corresponding term in (8) by collecting coefficients of $\varphi(i \mid x)$ for a fixed x. The second term of (9) is obtained from the corresponding term of (8) by writing $\varphi(i \mid x) = 1 - (1 - \varphi(i \mid x))$ and then collecting coefficients of $1 - \varphi(i \mid x)$ for a fixed x. Note also that $\varphi(0 \mid x) \equiv 0$ and $\varphi(1 \mid x) \equiv 1$.

Now, by hypothesis 2 of the theorem, the quantities in brackets in (9) are non-negative. Hence by Lemma 7.4.1 the first sum of (9) is minimized term by term by $\widehat{\varphi}(i \mid x)$ for each i since $i < j$ and hence $\omega_i < \omega$. The second sum is minimized term by term by $\widehat{\varphi}(i - 1 \mid x)$ since here $\omega < \omega_{i-1}$. Thus we have

(10) $$\rho(\omega, \psi) \geq \sum_{i=1}^{j-1} [L_i(\omega) - L_{i+1}(\omega)] \sum_{x} \widehat{\varphi}(i \mid x)\beta(\omega)e^{\omega x}r(x)$$

$$+ \sum_{i=j+1}^{k} [L_i(\omega) - L_{i-1}(\omega)] \left\{ 1 - \sum_{x} \widehat{\varphi}(i-1 \mid x)\beta(\omega)e^{\omega x}r(x) \right\}$$

Working back by the same process we get that the right-hand side of (10) is $\rho(\omega, \bar{\varphi})$ so that

(11) $$\rho(\omega, \psi) \geq \rho(\omega, \bar{\varphi})$$

This proves the theorem since clearly $\bar{\varphi}$ is a monotone-decision procedure of the required type.

Note that, if the inequalities of condition 2 of the hypotheses of the theorem are strict, then the inequality in (11) is also strict for all ω, as can be seen from (10) and Lemma 7.4.1.

Corollary 1. Let G be a game satisfying the hypotheses of Theorem 7.4.3, and let ξ be any a priori distribution of ω. Then, among all decision procedures which are Bayes against ξ, there exists one which is monotone. If the inequalities of condition 2 of the hypotheses of Theorem 7.4.3 are strict, where j can equal i but not s, then all Bayes solutions are monotone.

Proof. The proof follows directly from the definition of a Bayes solution.

Corollary 2. Let G be a two-decision game satisfying hypothesis 1 of Theorem 7.4.3. Furthermore, assume that θ is an interior point of $\Omega = (a, b)$ and that there exists no interval around θ in which either $L_1(\omega)$ or $L_2(\omega)$ is identically zero and that $L_1(\omega) = 0$ for $\omega \leq \theta$ and $L_2(\omega) = 0$ for $\omega \geq \theta$. Then for any procedure φ which is not monotone there exists one and only one monotone procedure which dominates it.

Proof. Let φ be any decision procedure which selects action 1 with probability $\varphi(x)$ and action 2 with probability $1 - \varphi(x)$, and for any $\omega \, \varepsilon \, \Omega$, let $\pi(\omega \mid \varphi)$ be the probability of taking action 1. Then

$$(1) \qquad \pi(\omega \mid \varphi) = \sum_x \varphi(x) p(x \mid \omega)$$

In terms of the function π the risk is given by

$$(2) \qquad \rho(\omega, \varphi) = L_1(\omega)\pi(\omega \mid \varphi) \qquad \text{for} \quad \omega \geq \theta$$

$$= L_2(\omega)(1 - \pi(\omega \mid \varphi)) \quad \text{for} \quad \omega \leq \theta$$

For a specified function φ a monotone dominating procedure $\hat{\varphi}$ is guaranteed by Lemma 7.4.1 without reference to Theorem 7.4.3 and is characterized by a number x_c and the rule that action 1 is to be taken if $x < x_c$, action 2 is to be taken if $x > x_c$, and if $p(x_c \mid \theta) > 0$ and $x = x_c$ action 1 is to be taken with probability $\hat{\varphi}(x_c)$ given by (1) Lemma 7.4.1, where $c = \pi(\theta \mid \varphi)$. Now let $\hat{\psi}$ be any monotone procedure, and let $\pi(\theta \mid \hat{\psi}) = c'$. We shall show that, unless $c' > c$ (and hence $\hat{\psi} = \hat{\varphi}$), $\hat{\psi}$ does not dominate φ. Assume first that $c' > c$. Then, since for a fixed-decision procedure π is a continuous function of ω, there exists an interval I containing θ such that, for all $\omega \, \varepsilon \, I$, $\pi(\omega \mid \hat{\psi}) > \pi(\omega \mid \varphi)$.

Also, by hypothesis there exists an $\omega = \omega_0$ in I such that $L_1(\omega_0) > 0$. Consequently, we have

(3) $\rho(\omega_0, \hat{\psi}) = L_1(\omega_0)\pi(\omega_0 \mid \psi) > L_1(\omega_0)\pi(\omega_0 \mid \varphi) = \rho(\omega_0, \varphi)$

and $\hat{\psi}$ does not dominate φ. A similar argument holds in case $c' < c$. This completes the proof of the corollary.

Corollary 3. Let G be a game satisfying hypothesis 1 of Theorem 7.4.3 with $A = (1, 2)$ and with neither $L_1(\omega)$ nor $L_2(\omega)$ identically zero. Then the monotone procedures form an admissible and hence a minimal complete class.

Proof. In view of Theorem 7.4.3, it is sufficient to show that no monotone procedure can dominate another monotone procedure. But this follows from the fact that, if we increase $\hat{\varphi}$, we increase $\pi(\omega \mid \hat{\varphi})$, where

(1) $\pi(\omega \mid \hat{\varphi}) = P_\omega(x < x_c) + \hat{\varphi}(x_c)p(x_c \mid \omega)$

and hence increase $\rho(\omega, \hat{\varphi})$ [see (2), corollary 2] for $\omega \geq \theta$; and, if we decrease $\hat{\varphi}$, we increase $1 - \pi(\omega \mid \hat{\varphi})$, and hence $\rho(\omega, \hat{\varphi})$ for $\omega \leq \theta$.

It can be shown that Theorem 7.4.3 applies to more general distributions than were considered here. For example, if the elements in $P\Omega$ are probability distributions or densities of the form

(i) $p(x \mid \omega) = f(x \mid \omega)g(x)$

where $f(x \mid \omega)$ satisfies the conditions that, if $x_1 > x_2$, $\omega_1 > \omega_2$, then

(ii) $f(x_1 \mid \omega_1)f(x_2 \mid \omega_2) - f(x_2 \mid \omega_1)f(x_1 \mid \omega_2) \geq 0$

and, if the range of ω is an interval, the class of monotone procedures is a complete class. Condition (ii) is clearly satisfied by the exponential class, since, in this case,

$$f(x_1 \mid \omega_1)f(x_2 \mid \omega_2) - f(x_2 \mid \omega_1)f(x_1 \mid \omega_2) = Ke^{x_1\omega_2 + x_2\omega_1}(e^{(x_1 - x_2)(\omega_1 - \omega_2)} - 1)$$

As an illustration of a monotone procedure where the distribution is not of the exponential type, consider the following problem: We are given a class of rectangular distributions defined over the range $(0, \omega)$. On the basis of N independent observations x_1, \cdots, x_N we wish to test the hypothesis that $\omega < \theta$ against the alternative hypothesis that $\omega > \theta$. The loss function $L_1(\omega) > 0$ for $\omega > \theta$ and zero elsewhere. The loss function $L_2(\omega) > 0$ for $\omega < \theta$ and zero elsewhere. It is desired to obtain a Bayes procedure against an a priori density $\xi(\omega)$. Let

$$\xi(\omega) = \alpha\lambda_1(\omega) + (1 - \alpha)\lambda_2(\omega)$$

where $\lambda_1(\omega)$ is a density defined over the interval $(0, \theta)$, $\lambda_2(\omega)$ is a den-

sity defined over the interval (θ, ∞) and $0 < \alpha < 1$. Let $x = (x_1, \cdots, x_N)$ and $t(x) = \max(x_1, \cdots, x_N)$. Then the density of x is given by

$$p(x \mid \omega) = 1/\omega^N \quad \text{for} \quad t < \omega$$
$$= 0 \qquad \text{for} \quad t > \omega$$

To obtain the density of t, we observe that the cumulative distribution function of t is given by

$$F(a \mid \omega) = P_\omega(t < a) = (a/\omega)^N$$

Differentiating the above expression with respect to a, we get $F'(a \mid \omega) = N(a^{N-1}/\omega^N)$. Hence

$$q(t \mid \omega) = (Nt^{N-1}/\omega^N) \quad \text{for} \quad t < \omega$$
$$= 0 \qquad \text{for} \quad t > \omega$$

The a posteriori risk if we decide that $\omega < \theta$ is given by [see Theorem 7.3.1]

$$\tau_t(1) = \frac{(1 - \alpha) \displaystyle\int_\theta^\infty L_1(\omega) q(t \mid \omega) \lambda_2(\omega)\, d\omega}{\displaystyle\int_0^\infty q(t \mid \omega) \xi(\omega)\, d\omega}$$

and the a posteriori risk if we decide that $\omega > \theta$ is given by

$$\tau_t(2) = \frac{\alpha \displaystyle\int_0^\theta L_2(\omega) q(t \mid \omega) \lambda_1(\omega)\, d\omega}{\displaystyle\int_0^\infty q(t \mid \omega) \xi(\omega)\, d\omega}$$

Hence the Bayes procedure is to accept the hypothesis that $\omega > \theta$ if

$$h(t) = \frac{\displaystyle\int_{\min[t,\,\theta]}^\theta Nt^{N-1} \frac{L_2(\omega)\lambda_1(\omega)}{\omega^N}\, d\omega}{\displaystyle\int_{\max[t,\,\theta]}^\infty Nt^{N-1} \frac{L_1(\omega)\lambda_2(\omega)}{\omega^N}\, d\omega}$$

$$= \frac{\displaystyle\int_{\min[t,\,\theta]}^\theta \frac{L_2(\omega)\lambda_1(\omega)}{\omega^N}\, d\omega}{\displaystyle\int_{\max[t,\,\theta]}^\infty \frac{L_1(\omega)\lambda_2(\omega)}{\omega^N}\, d\omega} < \frac{1 - \alpha}{\alpha}$$

and to accept the hypothesis $\omega < \theta$ if $h(t) \geq (1 - \alpha)/\alpha$.

We shall now show that $\{t\colon h(t) \geq (1 - \alpha)/\alpha\}$ is an interval $(0,\ t^*)$. To prove this, it will be sufficient to show that $h(t)$ is a decreasing function of t. But this follows since, if $t < \theta$, the denominator of the expression for $h(t)$ is constant and the numerator is of the form $\displaystyle\int_t^\theta g(\omega)\,d\omega$ where $g(\omega) \geq 0$ which is clearly a decreasing function of t. On the other hand, if $t > \theta$, the numerator is zero so that $h(t) = 0$ and we always accept the hypothesis $\omega > \theta$, as logically we should.

Fixed sample-size games in which the statistician has only one of two possible actions have been considered in Section 6.3 and will again be studied in Section 7.7. Although A contains only two elements, the space D of pure strategies for the statistician is usually infinite so that no general statement can be made about the number of pure strategies for either player that may be involved in a minimax solution to a game of this type. However, in the case of the exponential class the minimax solution is often in fact a dichotomy; i.e., nature's good strategy is to mix two points ω_1 and ω_2 in Ω and the statistician's good strategy is to employ a likelihood ratio test based on these two points, with possible randomization when the class \mathcal{P}_Ω is discrete. The results are incorporated in the next theorem. The proof of this theorem is intuitively simple but requires a somewhat lengthy argument in order to take care of the various types of behavior of the function p at the end points of the interval Ω [see Problem 7.4.2].

Theorem 7.4.4. Let G be a two-decision game with a single observation in which (I) the elements of \mathcal{P}_Ω are of the exponential type; i.e., for each $\omega\ \varepsilon\ \Omega$, p_ω is defined by

$$p(x \mid \omega) = \beta(\omega)e^{\omega x}r(x)$$

(II) Ω is an interval (possibly including $\pm\infty$) with left end point a and right end point b (III) if $a(b)$ does not belong to Ω then either

 (i) $a(b)$ is finite and $\displaystyle\lim_{\omega \to a(b)} \beta(\omega) = 0$, or

 (ii) $a(b)$ is infinite and there is no smallest (largest) value of x such that $r(x) > 0$.

(IV) The loss functions L_1 and L_2 are continuous and bounded and neither is identically zero. (V) There is a point θ interior to Ω such that $L_1(\omega) = 0$ for $\omega \leq \theta$ and $L_2(\omega) = 0$ for $\omega \geq \theta$.

Then there exists a good strategy for the statistician which is monotone and a corresponding good strategy for nature which is a mixture of only two points $\omega_1 > \theta$ and $\omega_2 < \theta$.

Proof. The proof of this theorem depends on the following auxiliary propositions:

A. Let $0 < c < 1$, and let $\varphi(x) \equiv c$. By Lemma 7.4.1 there is a dominating monotone procedure $\hat{\phi}_c$ for the given θ such that $\hat{\phi}_c(x) = 1$ for $x < x_c$, $\hat{\phi}_c(x) = 0$ for $x > x_c$, and, if $p(x_c \mid \theta) > 0$, $\hat{\phi}_c(x_c)$ is given by (1) of this lemma.

For any c, let $\pi(\omega \mid \hat{\phi}_c)$ be the probability that we take action 1 if we use the monotone procedure $\hat{\phi}_c$. That is

$$\pi(\omega \mid \hat{\phi}_c) = \beta(\omega) \sum_{x < x_c} e^{\omega x} r(x) + \hat{\phi}_c(x_c)\beta(\omega)e^{\omega x_c}r(x_c)$$

Then $\pi(\omega \mid \hat{\phi}_c)$ is for each c a monotone non-increasing function of ω. Moreover, since $\pi(\theta \mid \hat{\phi}_c) = c$, this result implies that

(1) $$\lim_{c \to 0} \pi(\omega \mid \hat{\phi}_c) = 0 \quad \text{uniformly in } \omega \text{ for } \quad \omega \geq \theta$$

(2) $$\lim_{c \to 1} \pi(\omega \mid \hat{\phi}_c) = 1 \quad \text{uniformly in } \omega \text{ for } \quad \omega \leq \theta$$

Proof of A. Let $\omega_1 < \omega_2$ be elements of Ω, and let

$$\gamma(\omega_1, \omega_2) = \pi(\omega_1 \mid \hat{\phi}_c)(1 - \pi(\omega_2 \mid \hat{\phi}_c)) - \pi(\omega_2 \mid \hat{\phi}_c)(1 - \pi(\omega_1 \mid \hat{\phi}_c))$$

Then, from the definition of $\pi(\omega \mid \hat{\phi}_c)$ and the fact that $\hat{\phi}_c(x) = 1$ for $x < x_c$, $\hat{\phi}_c(x) = 0$ for $x > x_c$, we have

$$\gamma(\omega_1, \omega_2) = K \sum_x \sum_y \hat{\phi}_c(x)(1 - \hat{\phi}_c(y))[e^{\omega_1 x + \omega_2 y} - e^{\omega_2 x + \omega_1 y}]r(x)r(y)$$

$$= K \sum_{x < y} \hat{\phi}_c(x)(1 - \hat{\phi}_c(y))e^{\omega_1 x + \omega_2 y}[e^{(\omega_2 - \omega_1)(y - x)} - 1]r(x)r(y)$$

$$\geq 0$$

where $K = \beta(\omega_1)\beta(\omega_2)$. Thus $\pi(\omega_1 \mid \hat{\phi}_c) \geq \pi(\omega_2 \mid \hat{\phi}_c)$.

B. Let c and $\hat{\phi}_c$ be defined as in A. Then

(3) $$\lim_{\omega \to a} \pi(\omega \mid \hat{\phi}_c) = \pi(a \mid \hat{\phi}_c) \quad \text{if} \quad a \, \varepsilon \, \Omega$$

$$= 1 \qquad\qquad \text{if} \quad a \notin \Omega$$

(4) $$\lim_{\omega \to b} \pi(\omega \mid \hat{\phi}_c) = \pi(b \mid \hat{\phi}_c) \quad \text{if} \quad b \, \varepsilon \, \Omega$$

$$= 0 \qquad\qquad \text{if} \quad b \notin \Omega$$

Proof of B. We shall prove (3); the proof of (4) is similar.

Suppose a is finite and $a \, \varepsilon \, \Omega$. Then (3) follows from the continuity of π as a function of ω for a fixed c. [See Problem 7.4.7.] If $a = -\infty$ and $a \, \varepsilon \, \Omega$, then there exists a smallest $x = x_0$ such that $r(x_0) > 0$. We may assume that $x_0 = 0$. Then it is clear that β is continuous at $-\infty$,

and consequently (3) holds. Suppose now $a \notin \Omega$. We may assume that $x_c > 0$. Then, taking any ω_0 interior to Ω, we have

$$1 - \pi(\omega \mid \hat{\phi}_c) = \beta(\omega)\left(\sum_{x > x_c} e^{\omega x} r(x) + [1 - \hat{\phi}_c(x_c)]e^{\omega x_c} r(x_c) \right)$$

$$\leq \beta(\omega)\left(\sum_{x > x_c} e^{\omega_0 x} r(x) + [1 - \hat{\phi}_c(x_c)]e^{\omega_0 x_c} r(x_c) \right)$$

for all $\omega < \omega_0$. Now, by conditions III(i), $\beta(\omega) \to 0$ as $\omega \to a$ if a is finite. If $a = -\infty$, then, by condition III(ii), we may assume there exists an $x = x_0$ which is negative and such that $r(x_0) > 0$. Hence $\sum_x e^{\omega x} r(x) \to \infty$ as $\omega \to -\infty$ so that in this case also $\lim_{\omega \to -\infty} \beta(\omega) = 0$. This completes the proof of B.

C. Let ρ be the risk function from the given procedure $\hat{\phi}_c$. That is

$$\rho(\omega, \hat{\phi}_c) = L_1(\omega)\pi(\omega \mid \hat{\phi}_c) = \rho_1(c, \omega) \qquad \text{for} \quad \omega \geq \theta$$

$$= L_2(\omega)(1 - \pi(\omega \mid \hat{\phi}_c)) = \rho_2(c, \omega) \quad \text{for} \quad \omega \leq \theta$$

Then

(5) $$\limsup_{c \to 0 \; \omega \geq \theta} \rho_1(c, \omega) = 0$$

(6) $$\limsup_{c \to 1 \; \omega \leq \theta} \rho_2(c, \omega) = 0$$

(7) $$\sup_{\omega \geq \theta} \rho_1(c, \omega) \text{ is monotone non-decreasing in } c$$

(8) $$\sup_{\omega \leq \theta} \rho_2(c, \omega) \text{ is monotone non-increasing in } c$$

Proof of C. The results (5) and (6) follow directly from (1) and (2). The results (7) and (8) hold because the function π is non-decreasing in c for each ω, and hence the supremum of ρ_i ($i = 1, 2$) has the desired property.

D. For each c with $0 < c < 1$, there is an $\omega_1 \, \varepsilon \, \Omega$ with $\omega_1 > \theta$ and an $\omega_2 \, \varepsilon \, \Omega$ with $\omega_2 < \theta$ such that

(9) $$\sup_{\omega \geq \theta} \rho_1(c, \omega) = \rho_1(c, \omega_1)$$

(10) $$\sup_{\omega \leq \theta} \rho_2(c, \omega) = \rho_2(c, \omega_2)$$

Proof of D. For a fixed c, π is a continuous function of ω. Hence by condition IV the risks ρ_i ($i = 1, 2$) are also continuous in ω. That is,

for a fixed c, ρ_1 is continuous in ω for $\omega \geq \theta$ and ρ_2 is continuous in ω for $\omega \leq \theta$. Also, if $b \notin \Omega$, then by (4)

$$\lim_{\omega \to b} \rho_1(c, \omega) = 0$$

Define

$$\rho'_1(c, \omega) = \rho_1(c, \omega) \quad \text{for} \quad \omega \geq \theta, \quad \omega \, \varepsilon \, \Omega$$

$$= 0 \qquad \text{for} \quad \omega = b, \quad b \notin \Omega$$

Then ρ'_1 is continuous on the closed interval (θ, b). It therefore has a maximum in this interval. Since

$$\sup_{\omega \geq \theta} \rho_1(c, \omega) > 0$$

the maximum cannot occur at θ, nor can it occur at b unless b is an element of Ω.

We similarly define $\rho'_2(c, \omega)$ and show that ρ'_2 has a maximum in the closed interval (a, θ) and this maximum occurs at an interior point in this interval if $a \notin \Omega$ but may occur at a if $a \, \varepsilon \, \Omega$.

E. There exists a c_1 and c_2 with $0 < c_1 < c_2 < 1$ such that

$$\max_{\omega \geq \theta} \rho_1(c, \omega) < \max_{\omega \leq \theta} \rho_2(c, \omega) \quad \text{for} \quad c < c_1$$

$$\max_{\omega \leq \theta} \rho_2(c, \omega) < \max_{\omega \geq \theta} \rho_1(c, \omega) \quad \text{for} \quad c > c_2$$

Proof of E. Define

$$\rho^*_1(c) = \max_{\omega \geq \theta} \rho_1(c, \omega), \qquad \rho^*_2(c) = \max_{\omega \leq \theta} \rho_2(c, \omega)$$

Then, by condition IV, $\rho^*_i(c) > 0$ for $i = 1, 2$, and by (5) and (8) we can find a c_1 such that for $c < c_1$

$$\max_{\omega \geq \theta} \rho_1(c, \omega) < \frac{\rho^*_2(c)}{2} < \rho^*_2(c) = \max_{\omega \leq \theta} \rho_2(c, \omega)$$

Similarly by (6) and (7) we can find a c_2 such that for $c > c_2$

$$\max_{\omega \leq \theta} \rho_2(c, \omega) < \frac{\rho^*_1(c)}{2} < \rho^*_1(c) = \max_{\omega \geq \theta} \rho_1(c, \omega)$$

F. There exists (i) a value σ with $c_1 < \sigma < c_2$ where c_1 and c_2 are defined in E, (ii) an ω_1 with $\omega_1 > \theta$, (iii) an ω_2 with $\omega_2 < \theta$, such that

$$\rho^*_1(\sigma) = \rho_1(\sigma, \omega_1) = \rho^*_2(\sigma) = \rho_2(\sigma, \omega_2) = v$$

Proof of F. Both $\rho^*_1(c)$ and $\rho^*_2(c)$ are continuous functions of c [see Problems 7.4.7 and 1.6.3]. Hence we let c vary in the closed interval (c_1, c_2) and apply D and E.

G. $\hat\phi_\sigma$ is a good strategy for the statistician, and nature's good strategy is to mix the points ω_1 and ω_2 given by F.

Proof of G. Suppose the statistician employs the strategy $\hat\phi_\sigma$. Then, for any a priori distribution ξ,

$$E[\rho(\omega, \hat\phi_\sigma)] = \sum_{\omega \le \theta} \rho_2(\sigma \mid \omega)\xi(\omega) + \sum_{\omega \ge \theta} \rho_1(\sigma \mid \omega)\xi(\omega)$$

$$\le \sum_{\omega \le \theta} \rho^*_2(\sigma)\xi(\omega) + \sum_{\omega \ge \theta} \rho^*_1(\sigma)\xi(\omega) = v$$

Thus the statistician, by employing $\hat\phi_\sigma$, can guarantee himself a risk not exceeding v. On the other hand, suppose nature mixes ω_1 and ω_2 in the proportions γ and $1 - \gamma$, respectively, where

$$\gamma = \frac{L_2(\omega_2)\beta(\omega_2)e^{(\omega_2 - \omega_1)x\sigma}}{L_1(\omega_1)\beta(\omega_1) + L_2(\omega_2)\beta(\omega_2)e^{(\omega_2 - \omega_1)x\sigma}}$$

then the best the statistician can do against this strategy is to employ procedure $\hat\phi_\sigma$, as can easily be verified.

Note that the boundedness condition on the $L_i(\omega)$ can be relaxed without impairing the truth of Theorem 7.4.4. It is clearly sufficient for example for the $L_i(\omega)$ to satisfy the condition

$$\lim_{\omega \to a} \rho_2(c, \omega) = \lim_{\omega \to b} \rho_1(c, \omega) = 0$$

for all c.

The reader is referred to Problem 7.4.8 for an illustrative example.

<div align="center">PROBLEMS</div>

7.4.1. Let $p(x \mid \omega)$ be given by (7.4.1), and let $\nu(\omega) = 1/\beta(\omega)$. Then

(a)
$$E_\omega(x) = \frac{d \log \nu}{d\omega}$$

(b)
$$\sigma^2(\omega) = E_\omega(x - E_\omega(x))^2 = \frac{d^2 \log \nu}{d\omega^2}$$

where the symbol log stands here for the logarithm to the base e.

7.4.2. Let \mathcal{P}_Ω be of the exponential type, and let $\Omega^* = \{\omega: \omega \text{ is finite and } \sum_x e^{\omega x} r(x)$ $< \infty; \omega = +\infty$ and there is a largest x such that $r(x) > 0; \omega = -\infty$ and there is a smallest x such that $r(x) > 0\}$. Then Ω^* is called the *natural range* of the class \mathcal{P}_Ω. Characterize the set Ω^* for the following classes \mathcal{P}_Ω: (a) binomial, (b) Poisson, (c) the

set X consists of all positive and negative integers including zero and

$$r(x) = e^{-|x|}$$

(d) The set X is as in (c) and

$$r(x) = e^{-|x|}/(1 + x^2)$$

(Note that the natural range for \mathcal{P}_Ω is an interval; see Lemma 11.5.1.)

7.4.3. Give an example of a discrete distribution p_θ of the exponential type such that (a) for some c, $0 < c < 1$, $p_\theta(x = x_c) = 0$ where x_c is given by Lemma 7.4.1, (b) for all c, $0 < c < 1$, $p_\theta(x = x_c) > 0$.

7.4.4. Prove the converse part in Theorem 7.4.2.

7.4.5. A sample of 10 observations is taken from a binomial distribution with probability ω of a "success." It is desired to test the following three alternative hypotheses:

$$\text{(1) } 0 \leq \omega \leq 0.4, \quad \text{(2) } 0.4 < \omega < 0.6, \quad \text{(3) } 0.6 \leq \omega \leq 1$$

The loss matrix is summarized in the following table.

States of Nature	Decisions		
	1	2	3
$0 \leq \omega \leq 0.4$	0	10	100
$0.4 < \omega < 0.6$	10	0	10
$0.6 \leq \omega \leq 1$	100	10	0

$L_1(\omega) = 0$

$L_2(\omega) = 0$

$L_3(\omega) = 0$

A decision procedure ψ of the following form has been suggested:

$$\psi(1 \mid m) = 0.6, \quad \psi(2 \mid m) = 0.3, \quad \psi(3 \mid m) = 0.1 \quad \text{for} \quad m = 0, 1, 2$$

$$\psi(1 \mid m) = 0.2, \quad \psi(2 \mid m) = 0.6, \quad \psi(3 \mid m) = 0.2 \quad \text{for} \quad m = 3, 4, 5, 6, 7$$

$$\psi(1 \mid m) = 0.1, \quad \psi(2 \mid m) = 0.3, \quad \psi(3 \mid m) = 0.6 \quad \text{for} \quad m = 8, 9, 10$$

where m is the number of successes in the sample.

Employing Theorem 7.4.3, compute the monotone procedure $\bar{\varphi}$ which dominates ψ, and compare the graphs of the risk function ρ for ψ and $\bar{\varphi}$.

7.4.6. Let G be a game satisfying the hypothesis of Theorem 7.4.3 with $A = (1, 2)$, and let d be a Bayes decision procedure against an a priori distribution ξ. Then, if $E_\xi[\rho(\omega, d)] \neq 0$, d is monotone.

7.4.7. Prove that the function π in Theorem 7.4.4 is jointly continuous in ω and c.

7.4.8. Consider Problem 7.3.1. Let Δ stand for the possible average increase in weight as a result of feeding the hogs diet B. The expected profit per hog if diet A is fed is $\$[0.16(250) - 30] = \10. If diet B is fed, the expected profit per hog is $\$[0.16(250 + \Delta) - 32.40] = \$(0.16\Delta - 7.60)$. It is equally profitable to feed diet A or B if $\$10 = \$(0.16\Delta - 7.60)$, i.e., if $\Delta = 15$ lb. Assume that, if the farmer feeds

diet A and $\Delta > 15$, his "loss" per hog is measured by $L_A(\Delta) = 0.16(\Delta - 15)$. If he feeds diet B and $0 \leq \Delta < 15$, his "loss" per hog is measured by $L_B(\Delta) = 0.16(15 - \Delta)$. Prove that if $\sigma \leq (15/t)\sqrt{n}$, where the constant t is approximately 0.75, then a minimax solution to this problem is as follows: Nature's good strategy is to select two values of $\mu_B : \mu_B = 265 - 0.75\sigma/\sqrt{n}$ and $\mu_B = 265 + 0.75\sigma/\sqrt{n}$ with equal probability. The farmer's good strategy is to adopt diet B if $\bar{x} > 265$ lb. and not adopt diet B if $x < 265$ lb. The value of the game is $0.0272N\sigma/\sqrt{n}$ (approx.).

7.5. Minimax Strategies in Fixed Sample-Size Multidecision Games

The main result of this section is the following:

Theorem 7.5.1. Every fixed sample-size multidecision game $G = (\Omega, D, \rho)$ in which Z is countable has a value and the statistician has a good strategy.

To prove this theorem, we shall need three lemmas which will be required in the proofs of later theorems also. Without loss of generality we shall assume that the elements of Z are the positive integers $1, 2, \cdots$.

Lemma 7.5.1. The space Ω contains a sequence $\{\omega_q\}$ such that, for every $\omega \, \varepsilon \, \Omega$, there is a subsequence $\{\omega_m\}$ of $\{\omega_q\}$ such that

$$\lim_{m \to \infty} \rho(\omega_m, \varphi) = \rho(\omega, \varphi)$$

for all $\varphi \, \varepsilon \, \Phi$.

Proof. For any ω and θ in Ω define a "distance" function δ by

$$(1) \qquad \delta(\omega, \theta) = \sum_{i=1}^{k} | L_i(\omega) - L_i(\theta) | + \sum_{i=1}^{\infty} \frac{1}{2^j} | p(j \,|\, \omega) - p(j \,|\, \theta) |$$

Consider sequences $r = (r_1, r_2, \cdots)$ of rational numbers which have only a finite number of non-zero terms. Define

$$(2) \qquad \delta(\omega, r) = \sum_{i=1}^{k} | L_i(\omega) - r_i | + \sum_{j=1}^{\infty} \frac{1}{2^j} | p(j \,|\, \omega) - r_{j+k} |$$

We first show that for any $\epsilon > 0$ and any $\omega \, \varepsilon \, \Omega$, there is an r such that $\delta(\omega, r) < \epsilon$. To do this, we select an integer M such that $1/2^M < \epsilon/3$. We also select a sequence r of rational numbers r_1, r_2, \cdots such that

$$(3) \qquad | L_i(\omega) - r_i | < \epsilon/3k, \qquad i = 1, 2, \cdots, k$$

and

$$(4) \qquad | p(j \,|\, \omega) - r_{j+k} | < \epsilon/3, \qquad j = 1, 2, \cdots, M$$

and set $r_j = 0$ for $j > M + k$. (This clearly can be done since there are

only a finite number of inequalities to be satisfied.) Then for such a sequence r

(5) $\delta(\omega, r) < \dfrac{\epsilon}{3} + \dfrac{\epsilon}{3} \sum\limits_{j=1}^{M} \dfrac{1}{2^j} + \sum\limits_{j=M+1}^{\infty} \dfrac{1}{2^j} p(j \mid \omega) < \dfrac{\epsilon}{3} + \dfrac{\epsilon}{3} + \dfrac{1}{2^M} < \epsilon$

Now for every r and n, let ω_{rn} be such that $\delta(\omega_{rn}, r) < 1/n$, if there is an element in Ω with this property. Clearly the set $\{\omega_{rn}\}$ is denumerable. Now we have seen that, for any $\omega \, \varepsilon \, \Omega$, $\epsilon > 0$ and $\epsilon \le 3$, there exists an r such that $\delta(\omega, r) < \epsilon/3$. Also we can find an n such that $\epsilon/3 \le 1/n \le 2\epsilon/3$. Then $\delta(\omega, r) < 1/n$, and hence there exists at least one ω_{rn} in the denumerable set such that $\delta(\omega_{rn}, r) < 1/n$. Moreover, it is easily verified from (1) and (2) that

(6) $\delta(\omega, \omega_{rn}) \le \delta(\omega, r) + \delta(\omega_{rn}, r)$

Therefore

(7) $\delta(\omega, \omega_{rn}) \le \epsilon/3 + 1/n \le \epsilon$

Thus we have exhibited a denumerable sequence $\{\omega_{rn}\}$ such that for any $\omega \, \varepsilon \, \Omega$ we can find a subsequence $\{\omega_{r_j n_j}\}$ with the property that $\lim\limits_{j \to \infty} \delta(\omega, \omega_{r_j n_j}) = 0$. We shall denote the sequence $\{\omega_{rn}\}$ by $\{\omega_q\}$ and any subsequence of it by $\{\omega_m\}$.

Now consider any $\omega \, \varepsilon \, \Omega$ and any $\varphi \, \varepsilon \, \Phi$, and let $\{\omega_m\}$ be a subsequence such that $\lim\limits_{m \to \infty} \delta(\omega, \omega_m) = 0$. Then

(8) $\big| \rho(\omega, \varphi) - \rho(\omega_m, \varphi) \big| \le A_m + B_m$

where

$A_m = \left| \sum\limits_{i=1}^{k} \sum\limits_{j=1}^{\infty} L_i(\omega)\varphi(i \mid j)p(j \mid \omega) - \sum\limits_{i=1}^{k} \sum\limits_{j=1}^{\infty} L_i(\omega)\varphi(i \mid j)p(j \mid \omega_m) \right|$

$B_m = \left| \sum\limits_{i=1}^{k} \sum\limits_{j=1}^{\infty} L_i(\omega)\varphi(i \mid j)p(j \mid \omega_m) - \sum\limits_{i=1}^{k} \sum\limits_{i=1}^{\infty} L_i(\omega_m)\varphi(i \mid j)p(j \mid \omega_m) \right|$

$\le \sum\limits_{j=1}^{\infty} p(j \mid \omega_m) \sum\limits_{i=1}^{k} \big| L_i(\omega) - L_i(\omega_m) \big| \varphi\Big(i \,\Big|\, j\Big) \le \sum\limits_{i=1}^{k} \big| L_i(\omega) - L_i(\omega_m) \big|$

since $0 \le \varphi(i \mid j) \le 1$ for all i and j and $\sum\limits_{j=1}^{\infty} p(j \mid \omega_m) = 1$

We observe from (1) that $\delta(\omega, \omega_m) \to 0$ if and only if $L_i(\omega_m) \to L_i(\omega)$ for every i and $p(j \mid \omega_m) \to p(j \mid \omega)$ for every j. Moreover, by assumption, $L_i(\omega)$ is a bounded function. Hence, by Theorem 3.11.5, $\lim\limits_{m \to \infty} A_m = 0$. Also, $\lim\limits_{m \to \infty} B_m = 0$. This proves the lemma.

Lemma 7.5.2. Any sequence $\{\varphi_n\}$ with $\varphi_n \, \varepsilon \, \Phi$ has a subsequence $\{\psi_n\}$ such that $\psi_n \to \psi \, \varepsilon \, \Phi$.

Proof. Since Z is countable and A is finite, $A \times Z$ is countable. Also, the sequence φ_n is uniformly bounded, so that the Cantor diagonal method yields a subsequence $\{\psi_n\}$ of $\{\varphi_n\}$ converging to a limit ψ. Since $\psi_n(i \mid j) \geq 0$ for all i, j and $\sum_i \psi_n(i \mid j) = 1$ for all j, ψ has the same properties, i.e., $\psi \, \varepsilon \, \Phi$.

Lemma 7.5.3. Let $\{\psi_q\}$ be a sequence in Φ such that

$$\lim_{q \to \infty} \psi_q(i \mid j) = \psi(i \mid j)$$

for each i and j. Then

$$\lim_{q \to \infty} \rho(\omega, \psi_q) = \rho(\omega, \psi)$$

for all $\omega \, \varepsilon \, \Omega$.

Proof. This lemma follows from Definition 3.6.7 and Theorem 3.11.5. We now return to the proof of Theorem 7.5.1.

Let $\{\omega_q\}$ be the countable sequence of elements in Ω considered in Lemma 7.5.1. Consider a game G_M in which nature is restricted to the pure strategies $\omega_1, \omega_2, \cdots, \omega_M$ of the sequence $\{\omega_q\}$. By corollary 1, Theorem 2.3.3, this game has a value v_M, and nature has a good strategy $\xi^*_M = (\xi^*_M(1), \cdots, \xi^*_M(M))$. Moreover, the statistician also has a good strategy φ^*_M, for, since G_M has a value, there exists a sequence $\{\varphi_q\}$ such that

$$\lim_{q \to \infty} \rho(\xi^*_M, \varphi_q) = v_M$$

But, by Lemmas 7.5.2 and 7.5.3, there exists a subsequence $\{\psi_n\}$ such that

$$\lim_{n \to \infty} \psi_n = \varphi^*_M, \quad \text{say}$$

and

$$\lim_{n \to \infty} \rho(\xi^*_M, \psi_n) = \rho(\xi^*_M, \varphi^*_M)$$

Hence we have for all $\varphi \, \varepsilon \, \Phi$

(1) $\rho(\omega_i, \varphi^*_M) \leq v_M \leq \rho(\xi^*_M, \varphi)$, $(i = 1, 2, \cdots, M)$

Now $v_M \leq \sup_{(\omega, a)} L(\omega, a) < +\infty$, and, denoting the set of a priori distributions over $(\omega_1, \cdots, \omega_M)$ by Ξ_M, $v_M = \sup_{\xi \, \varepsilon \, \Xi_M} \Lambda(\xi) \leq \sup_{\xi \, \varepsilon \, \Xi_{M+1}} \Lambda(\xi) =$

v_{M+1} since $\Xi_M \subset \Xi_{M+1}$. Hence we may write

$$(2) \qquad \lim_{M \to \infty} v_M = v^*$$

By Lemma 7.5.2, $\{\varphi^*_M\}$ contains a convergent subsequence $\{\varphi^*_{M_i}\}$ (without loss of generality we take $M_i < M_{i+1}$); let $\lim_{i \to \infty} \varphi^*_{M_i} = \varphi^*$.

Given $\omega_m \, \varepsilon \, \{\omega_q\}$, then by (a) we have, for $M_i > m$, $\rho(\omega_m, \varphi^*_{M_i}) \leq v_{M_i} \leq v^*$. From Lemma 7.5.3, $\lim_{i \to \infty} \rho(\omega_m, \varphi^*_{M_i}) = \rho(\omega_m, \varphi^*)$; hence $\rho(\omega_m, \varphi^*) \leq v^*$. For arbitrary $\omega \, \varepsilon \, \Omega$ there exists (Lemma 7.5.1) a subsequence $\{\omega_m\}$ of $\{\omega_q\}$ such that $\rho(\omega, \varphi^*) = \lim_{m \to \infty} \rho(\omega_m, \varphi^*)$. Therefore

$$(3) \qquad \rho(\omega, \varphi^*) \leq v^* \quad \text{for all} \quad \omega \, \varepsilon \, \Omega$$

From (3) it is clear that $v^*_G \leq v^*$ and that if G has the value v^* then φ^* is a good strategy for the statistician. But from (1) and (2) we see that G does have value v^* since for given $\epsilon > 0$ an M_ϵ can be found such that

$$\lambda^*_\Gamma = \sup_{\xi \, \varepsilon \, \Xi} \inf_{\varphi \, \varepsilon \, \Phi} \rho(\xi, \varphi) \geq \inf_{\varphi \, \varepsilon \, \Phi} \rho(\xi^*_{M_\epsilon}, \varphi) \geq v_{M_\epsilon} > v^* - \epsilon$$

Since ϵ is arbitrary, $\lambda^*_\Gamma \geq v^*$, and this together with $v^*_\Gamma \leq v^*$ implies that G has value v^*.

Theorem 7.5.1 as well as Lemmas 7.5.1 and 7.5.3 also hold for the case where the $p(x \mid \omega)$ are densities.

<div align="center">PROBLEM</div>

7.5.1. Let \mathcal{P}_{Ω_1} consist of a class of normal distributions with mean μ, $-\infty < \mu < \infty$ and a fixed variance $\sigma_1{}^2$. Let \mathcal{P}_{Ω_2} consist of a single normal distribution with fixed mean μ_2 and fixed variance $\sigma_2{}^2$ where $\sigma_1{}^2 < \sigma_2{}^2$. The loss from an error of the first kind is unity, and the loss from an error of the second kind is u. (See Section **7.7** for the definition of these terms.) It is desired to test the hypothesis Ω_1 against the alternative Ω_2 on the basis of N independent observations $x = (x_1, x_2, \cdots, x_N)$. Show that

(a) The good strategy for the statistician is to accept the hypothesis Ω_1 whenever $\sum_{i=1}^{N} (x_i - \bar{x})^2 \leq k$ and accept the alternative hypothesis Ω_2 whenever $\sum_{i=1}^{N} (x_i - \bar{x})^2 > k$ where k is a constant and $\bar{x} = 1/N \sum_{i=1}^{N} x_i$.

(b) Nature's good strategy is to select Ω_1 with a probability g and Ω_2 with a probability $1 - g$. In Ω_1 nature will select μ with density $\xi(\mu)$ where

$$\xi(\mu) = \sqrt{\frac{N}{2\pi(\sigma_2{}^2 - \sigma_1{}^2)}} \, e^{-N(\mu - \mu_2)^2/2(\sigma_2{}^2 - \sigma_1{}^2)}$$

Hint. Show that for any k there exists a value of g for which the proposed statistician's strategy is Bayes against that g and $\xi(\mu)$, and that there exists a value of g, and hence a value of k, which makes the maximum risk in Ω_1 and Ω_2 equal.

Note that, if nature employs the above $\xi(\mu)$, the distribution of \bar{x} will be the same for the hypothesis Ω_1 as it is for the alternative hypothesis. This makes \bar{x} useless for discriminating between Ω_1 and Ω_2.

7.6. The Completeness of the Classes \mathfrak{B}_0, \mathfrak{a}_0, and \mathfrak{a}

Theorem 7.6.1. In any fixed sample-size multidecision game $G = (\Omega, D, \rho)$ the class \mathfrak{B}_0 of extended Bayes strategies and the class \mathfrak{a}_0 of extended admissible strategies are complete.

Proof. The truth of this theorem will follow from Theorems 5.6.3 and 5.6.4 if we can establish that, for each φ in Φ, the game G_φ has a value and the statistician has in this game a good strategy, where

$$G_\varphi = (\Omega, D, \rho_\varphi)$$

$$\rho_\varphi(\omega, d) = \rho(\omega, d) - \rho(\omega, \varphi)$$

But the steps required to prove the latter result are identical with those employed in the proof of Theorem 7.5.1.

Theorem 7.6.2. In any fixed sample-size multidecision game $G = (\Omega, D, \rho)$ the class \mathfrak{a} of admissible strategies is complete.

Proof. In view of Theorem 5.7.1, we must establish that the game G satisfies the following two conditions:

1. There exists a sequence $\{\omega_q\}$ in Ω such that, for every $\omega \, \varepsilon \, \Omega$, there is a subsequence $\{\omega_m\}$ with the property that

$$\lim_{m \to \infty} \rho(\omega_m, \varphi) = \rho(\omega, \varphi)$$

for all φ in Φ.

2. For any sequence of mixed strategies $\varphi^{(1)}$, $\varphi^{(2)}$, \cdots in Φ such that

$$\rho(\omega, \varphi^{(q+1)}) \leq \rho(\omega, \varphi^{(q)})$$

for all $\omega \, \varepsilon \, \Omega$, there exists a φ^* such that

$$\rho(\omega, \varphi^*) \leq \rho(\omega, \varphi^{(q)})$$

for all q and ω.

That the game G satisfies condition 1 follows from Lemma 7.5.1. To prove that G satisfies condition 2, let $\{\varphi^{(q)}\}$ be a sequence such that

$$\rho(\omega, \varphi^{(q+1)}) \leq \rho(\omega, \varphi^{(q)})$$

Then by Lemmas 7.5.2 and 7.5.3, we can select a subsequence $\{\varphi^{(m)}\}$ from the sequence $\{\varphi^{(q)}\}$ such that

$$\lim_{m \to \infty} \varphi^{(m)} = \varphi^*$$

and such that

$$\lim_{m \to \infty} \rho(\omega, \varphi^{(m)}) = \rho(\omega, \varphi^*)$$

for all ω. Since by assumption $\{\rho(\omega, \varphi^{(q)})\}$ is a non-decreasing sequence of numbers, it must follow that

$$\rho(\omega, \varphi^*) \leq \rho(\omega, \varphi^{(q)})$$

for all q and ω. This completes the proof of the theorem.

7.7. Tests of Composite Hypotheses

Often in statistics a fixed sample-size two-decision problem is presented in the following manner: The space Ω of nature's pure strategies consists of two subspaces Ω_1 and Ω_2. The statistician wishes to make one decision if $\omega \varepsilon \Omega_1$ and another decision if $\omega \varepsilon \Omega_2$. The decision is to be made on the basis of a sample of N observations $x = (x_1, x_2, \cdots, x_N)$. The hypothesis that $\omega \varepsilon \Omega_1$ is often called the "null" hypothesis while the hypothesis that $\omega \varepsilon \Omega_2$ is called the "alternative" hypothesis. If Ω_1 consists of a single element, the null hypothesis is called "simple," and, if it consists of more than one element, it is called "composite." A similar definition is given to a "simple" alternative hypothesis and a "composite" alternative hypothesis. In this section we shall consider the case where at least one of the two hypotheses is composite.

If $\omega \varepsilon \Omega_1$ and the statistician decides on the alternative hypothesis, the error is known as "an error of the first kind." Conversely, if $\omega \varepsilon \Omega_2$, and the statistician accepts the null hypothesis, the error is known as "an error of the second kind."

Let φ be a randomized statistical-decision procedure such that, if x is observed, the null hypothesis is accepted with probability $\varphi(x)$ and the alternative hypothesis is accepted with probability $1 - \varphi(x)$. Furthermore, let $\bar{\alpha}$ and $\bar{\beta}$ be two functions defined by

$$(7.7.1) \qquad \bar{\alpha}(\omega \mid \varphi) = 1 - \sum_x \varphi(x) p(x \mid \omega), \qquad \omega \varepsilon \Omega_1$$

$$(7.7.2) \qquad \bar{\beta}(\omega \mid \varphi) = \sum_x \varphi(x) p(x \mid \omega), \qquad \omega \varepsilon \Omega_2$$

Then, for any $\omega \varepsilon \Omega_1$, $\bar{\alpha}(\omega \mid \varphi)$ is the probability of an error of the first kind, and, for $\omega \varepsilon \Omega_2$, $\bar{\beta}(\omega \mid \varphi)$ is the probability of an error of the second

kind, if the procedure φ is used. We also define

(7.7.3) $$\alpha(\varphi) = \sup_{\omega \, \varepsilon \, \Omega_1} \bar{\alpha}(\omega \mid \varphi)$$

(7.7.4) $$\beta(\varphi) = \sup_{\omega \, \varepsilon \, \Omega_2} \bar{\beta}(\omega \mid \varphi)$$

A problem of statistical interest is usually formulated as follows: Of all procedures φ satisfying the condition $\alpha(\varphi) = \alpha_0$ (i.e., $\bar{\alpha}(\omega \mid \varphi) \leq \alpha_0$ for all $\omega \, \varepsilon \, \Omega_1$) find that procedure φ^* which minimizes $\beta(\varphi)$. In this section we shall give a solution to this problem employing game-theoretic considerations.

Let Φ be the class of randomized strategies φ and let $\boldsymbol{\gamma}$ be a vector function with values $\boldsymbol{\gamma}(\varphi) = (\alpha(\varphi), \beta(\varphi))$ mapping Φ into a set S in 2-space. Unlike the case of a simple hypothesis against a simple alternative, it can be shown that the set S is not necessarily convex. However, consider the subset T of S defined by

(7.7.5) $T = \{\boldsymbol{\gamma}(\varphi) = (\alpha(\varphi), \beta(\varphi)): \varphi \, \varepsilon \, \Phi \; \text{and} \; \alpha(\varphi) + \beta(\varphi) \leq 1\}$

We shall show that T is a convex set in the positive quadrant and that the lower boundary of T belongs to T, at least for the case where X is denumerable. Let $\boldsymbol{\gamma}(\varphi^*)$ be a point on the lower boundary of T. Then clearly, if $\alpha(\varphi^*) = \alpha_0$,

$$\beta(\varphi^*) = \min_{\{\varphi:\, \alpha(\varphi) = \alpha_0\}} \beta(\varphi)$$

so that the points on this boundary are of primary interest in the solution of the statistical problem posed above.

To show that T is convex, we first observe that, for any two points $\boldsymbol{\gamma}(\varphi)$ and $\boldsymbol{\gamma}(\psi)$ and for $0 \leq t \leq 1$, we have

(7.7.6) $$t\boldsymbol{\gamma}(\varphi) + (1 - t)\boldsymbol{\gamma}(\psi) \geq \boldsymbol{\gamma}(t\varphi + (1 - t)\psi)$$

This result follows since for all ω

$$t\bar{\alpha}(\omega \mid \varphi) + (1 - t)\bar{\alpha}(\omega \mid \psi) = \bar{\alpha}(\omega \mid t\varphi + (1 - t)\psi)$$

so that taking the supremum with respect to $\omega \, \varepsilon \, \Omega_1$ on both sides of the above equation yields

(7.7.7) $$t\alpha(\varphi) + (1 - t)\alpha(\psi) \geq \alpha(t\varphi + (1 - t)\psi)$$

A similar argument holds for the function $\bar{\beta}$. Let q be the line segment joining the point $(0, 1)$ and $(1, 0)$, and let φ_a be a randomized strategy such that $\varphi_a(x) \equiv a$, $0 \leq a \leq 1$. Then by (7.7.1) and (7.7.2)

$$\bar{\alpha}(\omega \mid \varphi_a) = 1 - a \quad \text{for all} \quad \omega \, \varepsilon \, \Omega_1; \qquad \bar{\beta}(\omega \mid \varphi_a) = a \quad \text{for all} \quad \omega \, \varepsilon \, \Omega_2$$

so that $\boldsymbol{\gamma}(\varphi_a) = (1 - a, a)$ is a point on q. Conversely every point on

q can be obtained from a φ_a for some a. Also, for any $\boldsymbol{\gamma}(\varphi)$ ε T, the line segment joining $\boldsymbol{\gamma}(\varphi)$ and $\boldsymbol{\gamma}(\varphi_a)$ lies entirely in T since for this special case equality holds in (7.7.7) (with $\psi = \varphi_a$) for the functions α as well as β.

Now let $\boldsymbol{\gamma}_1$ ε T, $\boldsymbol{\gamma}_2$ ε T where $\boldsymbol{\gamma}_1 = \boldsymbol{\gamma}(\varphi)$, $\boldsymbol{\gamma}_2 = \boldsymbol{\gamma}(\psi)$. We shall show that $t\boldsymbol{\gamma}_1 + (1 - t)\boldsymbol{\gamma}_2$ ε T for all t with $0 \leq t \leq 1$. By (7.7.6) we have

$$t\boldsymbol{\gamma}_1 + (1 - t)\boldsymbol{\gamma}_2 \geq \boldsymbol{\gamma}(t\varphi + (1 - t)\psi) = \boldsymbol{\gamma}_3$$

If the equality sign holds in the above expression for all $\boldsymbol{\gamma}_1$, $\boldsymbol{\gamma}_2$, and t, then the convexity of T is established. Assume that the inequality

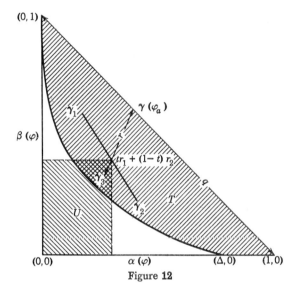

Figure 12

holds for some $\boldsymbol{\gamma}_1$, $\boldsymbol{\gamma}_2$, and t. Then $\boldsymbol{\gamma}_3$ is a point in the rectangle designated by U in Figure 12. We draw a line segment r from $\boldsymbol{\gamma}_3$ through the point $t\boldsymbol{\gamma}_1 + (1 - t)\boldsymbol{\gamma}_2$ intersecting q at a point, say, $\boldsymbol{\gamma}(\varphi_a)$. Then since, as we have seen, $r \subset T$, it follows that the point $t\boldsymbol{\gamma}_1 + (1 - t)\boldsymbol{\gamma}_2$ belongs to T. This completes the proof of the convexity of T.

The fact that the lower boundary of T belongs to T can be proved without great difficulty for a denumerable space X by means of Lemmas 7.5.1, 7.5.2, and 7.5.3 and will be left as an exercise for the reader [see Problem 7.7.3] since the result is also a consequence of a minimax method for obtaining the points on this boundary which we shall now present. Reference to Problem 6.4.9, especially parts b and c, will help to understand what follows.

Consider the game $\Gamma = (\Omega, \Phi, \rho)$ where Ω and φ are defined as above, the space X is denumerable, and the loss function L is defined by

$$L_1(\omega) = u \quad \text{for} \quad \omega \, \varepsilon \, \Omega_2$$

$$= 0 \quad \text{for} \quad \omega \, \varepsilon \, \Omega_1$$

$$L_2(\omega) = w \quad \text{for} \quad \omega \, \varepsilon \, \Omega_1$$

$$= 0 \quad \text{for} \quad \omega \, \varepsilon \, \Omega_2$$

with $u > 0$ and $w > 0$. Since the scale is arbitrary, we can, without loss of generality, assume that $w = 1$. The risk function $\rho(\omega, \varphi)$ is then given by

$$\rho(\omega, \varphi) = \bar{\alpha}(\omega \mid \varphi), \qquad \omega \, \varepsilon \, \Omega_1$$

$$\rho(\omega, \varphi) = u\bar{\beta}(\omega \mid \varphi), \qquad \omega \, \varepsilon \, \Omega_2$$

We thus have

(7.7.8)
$$\sup_{\omega \, \varepsilon \, \Omega_1} \rho(\omega, \varphi) = \alpha(\varphi)$$

$$\sup_{\omega \, \varepsilon \, \Omega_2} \rho(\omega, \varphi) = u\beta(\varphi)$$

Let

(7.7.9)
$$\Upsilon_u(\varphi) = \max \left[\alpha(\varphi), u\beta(\varphi) \right]$$

$$v^*{}_u = \inf_{\phi \, \varepsilon \, \Phi} \Upsilon_u(\varphi)$$

It follows from Theorem 7.5.1 that the game G has a value for all u and the statistician has a good strategy, say, $\varphi^*{}_u$. Hence, we have

$$v^*{}_u = \Upsilon_u(\varphi^*{}_u) = \max \left[\alpha(\varphi^*{}_u), u\beta(\varphi^*{}_u) \right]$$

Theorem 7.7.1.

$$\alpha(\varphi^*{}_u) = u\beta(\varphi^*{}_u) = v^*{}_u$$

Proof. Assume the contrary. Then either (a) $v^*{}_u = u\beta(\varphi^*{}_u)$ and $\alpha(\varphi^*{}_u) = v^*{}_u - \epsilon$, $\epsilon > 0$, or (b) $v^*{}_u = \alpha(\varphi^*)$ and $u\beta(\varphi^*{}_u) = v^*{}_u - \delta$, $\delta > 0$. We shall prove that case a is impossible. A similar argument shows that case b is impossible also.

Consider a strategy

(1) $\varphi_0 = (1 - \lambda)\varphi^*{}_u + \lambda I_2, \qquad 0 < \lambda < 1$

where I_2 is the strategy of always accepting the alternative hypothesis.

Then

(2) $\rho(\omega, \varphi_0) = (1 - \lambda)\rho(\omega, \varphi^*_u) + \lambda,$ $\omega \varepsilon \Omega_1$

$= (1 - \lambda)\rho(\omega, \varphi^*_u),$ $\omega \varepsilon \Omega_2$

Therefore

(3) $\alpha(\varphi_0) = (1 - \lambda)\alpha(\varphi^*_u) + \lambda$

$= (1 - \lambda)[v^*_u - \epsilon] + \lambda = v^*_u - \lambda[v^*_u - \epsilon - 1] - \epsilon$

and

(4) $u\beta(\varphi_0) = (1 - \lambda)u\beta(\varphi^*_u) = (1 - \lambda)v^*_u$

By a choice of λ sufficiently small we can make

(5) $\alpha(\varphi_0) < v^*_u,$ $u\beta(\varphi_0) < v^*_u$

so that φ^*_u cannot be minimax, which is contrary to the assumption.

Theorem 7.7.2. For any u, let φ^*_u be a minimax strategy. Then for any φ such that $\alpha(\varphi) \leq \alpha(\varphi^*_u)$ we have $\beta(\varphi) \geq \beta(\varphi^*_u)$.

Proof. Suppose there exists a φ such that

$$\alpha(\varphi) \leq \alpha(\varphi^*_u), \qquad \beta(\varphi) < \beta(\varphi^*_u)$$

Then

$$\max [\alpha(\varphi), u\beta(\varphi)] = \Upsilon_u(\varphi) \leq \Upsilon_u(\varphi^*_u)$$

Since φ^*_u is minimax it must follow that $\Upsilon_u(\varphi) = \Upsilon_u(\varphi^*_u)$. Thus φ is also a minimax strategy, and therefore by Theorem 7.7.1

$$\alpha(\varphi) = u\beta(\varphi) = \alpha(\varphi^*_u) = u\beta(\varphi^*_u)$$

which is a contradiction. Hence $\beta(\varphi) \geq \beta(\varphi^*_u)$.

Theorem 7.7.3. The minimax risk v^*_u is a monotone non-decreasing continuous function of u.

Proof. The monotonicity of v^*_u follows from the monotonicity of $\Upsilon_u(\varphi)$ for each φ. To prove the continuity of v^*_u, let $u' = u + \Delta u$ with $\Delta u > 0$. Then

$$v^*_{u'} = \inf_{\varphi} \max [\alpha(\varphi), u'\beta(\varphi)]$$

$$\leq \max [\alpha(\varphi^*_u), u'\beta(\varphi^*_u)]$$

$$= \max \left[v^*_u, \left(1 + \frac{\Delta u}{u}\right) v^*_u \right] = \left(1 + \frac{\Delta u}{u}\right) v^*_u$$

Thus $0 \leq v^*_{u+\Delta u} - v^*_u \leq \dfrac{\Delta u}{u} v^*_u$ which proves that v^*_u is continuous on the right. Taking $\Delta u < 0$ and interchanging the role of u and u' in the above argument shows that v^*_u is continuous on the left also.

Theorem 7.7.4.

(a) $$v^*_u \to 0 \qquad \text{as} \quad u \to 0$$

(b) $$v^*_u \to \Delta \leq 1 \quad \text{as} \quad u \to \infty$$

Proof. (a) Consider the strategy I_1 of always accepting the null hypothesis. Then

$$\rho(\omega, I_1) = 0, \qquad \omega \ \varepsilon \ \Omega_1$$

$$= u, \qquad \omega \ \varepsilon \ \Omega_2$$

Hence

$$v^*_u = \inf_{\varphi} \sup_{\omega} \rho(\omega, \varphi) \leq \sup_{\omega} \rho(\omega, I_1) = u$$

Thus since $0 \leq v^*_u \leq u$, it follows that $v^*_u \to 0$ as $u \to 0$. (b) Consider a strategy I_2 of always accepting the alternative hypothesis. Then

$$\rho(\omega, I_2) = 1, \qquad \omega \ \varepsilon \ \Omega_1$$

$$= 0, \qquad \omega \ \varepsilon \ \Omega_2$$

Again

$$v^*_u = \min_{\varphi} \sup_{\omega} \rho(\omega, \varphi) \leq \sup_{\omega} \rho(\omega, I_2) = 1$$

Therefore

$$\lim_{u \to \infty} v^*_u = \Delta \leq 1$$

Theorem 7.7.5. Let α_0 be given with $0 < \alpha_0 < \Delta$ where Δ is determined by Theorem 7.7.4. Then among all strategies φ such that $\alpha(\varphi) = \alpha_0$ there exists a strategy φ^* which minimizes $\beta(\varphi)$.

Proof. For any u, let φ^*_u be the corresponding minimax strategy. Then, by Theorem 7.7.1, $v^*_u = \alpha(\varphi^*_u)$, and, by Theorem 7.7.3, we can find a u such that $v^*(u) = \alpha_0$. The theorem now follows from Theorem 7.7.2.

Theorem 7.7.6. Let Φ_0 be a class of strategies such that $\alpha(\varphi) = \Delta_1 < \Delta$ for all $\varphi \ \varepsilon \ \Phi_0$. Then, $\inf_{\varphi \ \varepsilon \ \Phi_0} \beta(\varphi) > 0$. [See Figure 12.]

Proof. Assume that $\inf_{\varphi \ \varepsilon \ \Phi_0} \beta(\varphi) = 0$. Then for every $\epsilon > 0$ we can

find a $\varphi_\epsilon \in \Phi_0$ such that $\beta(\varphi_\epsilon) \leq \epsilon$. Take $\epsilon = \Delta_1/2u$. Then

$$v^*_u \leq \Upsilon_u(\varphi_\epsilon) = \max [\alpha(\varphi_\epsilon), u\beta(\varphi_\epsilon)] \leq \max [\Delta_1, \Delta_1/2] = \Delta_1$$

which is impossible since, by Theorem 7.7.4, $\lim_{u \to \infty} v^*_u = \Delta > \Delta_1$.

We remark that Theorem 7.7.6 no longer holds if we remove the condition $\Delta_1 < \Delta$. For in that case we simply choose u such that $1/u \leq \epsilon$. Then the minimax strategy φ^*_u satisfies $\alpha(\varphi^*_u) = v^*_u \leq \Delta$ and $\beta(\varphi^*_u) = (1/u)v^*_u \leq \Delta/u \leq 1/u \leq \epsilon$. In fact, we have the following

Theorem 7.7.7. There exists a decision procedure φ which is pure (i.e., $\varphi(x) = 1$ for all x on a set $S \subset X$ and $\varphi(x) = 0$ for all $x \in C(S)$) such that $\alpha(\varphi) = \Delta$, $\beta(\varphi) = 0$.

Proof. Let $u = 2^n$ and let φ^*_n be the corresponding minimax strategy. Then

$$\beta(\varphi^*_n) = \frac{1}{2^n} v^*_{2^n} \leq \frac{\Delta}{2^n} \leq \frac{1}{2^n}$$

Define
$$\psi_n(x) = \min [1, \sum_{j=n}^{\infty} \varphi^*_j(x)]$$

Then
$$\psi_n(x) \geq \varphi^*_n(x)$$

Moreover, $\psi_n(x)$ is monotonically decreasing as n increases. Now for $\omega \in \Omega_1$

$$\bar{\alpha}(\omega \mid \psi_n) = \sum_x [1 - \psi_n(x)p(x \mid \omega)] \leq \sum_x [1 - \varphi^*_n(x)p(x \mid \omega)]$$

$$\leq \bar{\alpha}(\omega \mid \varphi^*_n) \leq \Delta$$

for all n. Also for $\omega \in \Omega_2$

$$\bar{\beta}(\omega \mid \psi_n) = \sum_x \psi_n(x)p(x \mid \omega) \leq \sum_x \sum_{j=n}^{\infty} \varphi^*_j(x)p(x \mid \omega)$$

$$\leq \sum_{j=n}^{\infty} \sum_x \varphi^*_j(x)p(x \mid \omega) = \sum_{j=n}^{\infty} \bar{\beta}(\omega \mid \varphi^*_j) \leq \sum_{j=n}^{\infty} \frac{1}{2^j} = \frac{1}{2^{n-1}}$$

Since $\psi_n(x)$ is monotone decreasing in n, it approaches a limit, say $\psi^*(x)$ for every x as $n \to \infty$. Then

$$\lim_{n \to \infty} \bar{\alpha}(\omega \mid \psi_n) = \bar{\alpha}(\omega \mid \psi^*) \leq \Delta$$

for all $\omega \in \Omega_1$, and

$$\lim_{n \to \infty} \bar{\beta}(\omega \mid \psi_n) = \bar{\beta}(\omega \mid \psi^*) \leq \lim_{n \to \infty} \frac{1}{2^{n-1}} = 0$$

for all $\omega \, \varepsilon \, \Omega_2$. Thus $\beta(\psi^*) = 0$, and, in view of Theorem 7.7.6, $\alpha(\psi^*)$ $= \Delta$. We must now prove that we can find a φ which is pure. Let S be the set of all $x \, \varepsilon \, X$ such that $\psi^*(x) > 0$, and let $\varphi(x) = 1$ for all $x \, \varepsilon \, S$ and $\varphi(x) = 0$ otherwise. Then for $\omega \, \varepsilon \, \Omega_1$

$$\bar{\alpha}(\omega \mid \psi^*) = \sum_x [1 - \psi^*(x)]p(x \mid \omega)$$

$$= 1 - \sum_{x \, \varepsilon \, S} \psi^*(x)p(x \mid \omega) - \sum_{x \, \varepsilon \, C(S)} \psi^*(x)p(x \mid \omega)$$

$$= 1 - \sum_{x \, \varepsilon \, S} \psi^*(x)p(x \mid \omega) - 0 \geq 1 - \sum_{x \, \varepsilon \, S} p(x \mid \omega) = \bar{\alpha}(\omega \mid \varphi)$$

Similarly for $\omega \, \varepsilon \, \Omega_2$

$$\bar{\beta}(\omega \mid \psi^*) = \sum_x \psi^*(x)p(x \mid \omega) = 0$$

$$= \sum_{x \, \varepsilon \, S} \psi^*(x)p(x \mid \omega) + \sum_{x \, \varepsilon \, C(S)} \psi^*(x)p(x \mid \omega)$$

$$\geq \sum_{x \, \varepsilon \, S} p(x \mid \omega) = \bar{\beta}(\omega \mid \varphi) = 0$$

Consequently

$$\alpha(\varphi) = \sup_{\omega \, \varepsilon \, \Omega_1} \bar{\alpha}(\omega \mid \varphi) \leq \sup_{\omega \, \varepsilon \, \Omega_1} \bar{\alpha}(\omega \mid \psi^*) = \alpha(\psi^*) = \Delta$$

$$\beta(\varphi) = \sup_{\omega \, \varepsilon \, \Omega_2} \bar{\beta}(\omega \mid \varphi) = 0$$

which proves the theorem.

PROBLEMS

7.7.1. Write an explicit expression for v^*_u in Problem 7.5.1, compute a sufficient number of points on the lower boundary of T [see expression 7.7.5], and sketch the whole boundary of this set, for $\sigma_1^2 = 1$, $\sigma_2^2 = 2$, $N = 10$.

7.7.2. Employing Lemmas 7.5.1, 7.5.2, and 7.5.3, give a direct proof that the lower boundary of T belongs to T in case X is denumerable.

7.7.3. Under Ω_1 a coin falls "head" with probability either 0.3 or 0.7. Under Ω_2 it falls head with probability either 0.4 or 0.6. Characterize the test procedure based on N observations which for a given α minimizes β.

7.7.4. Let \mathcal{P}_Ω be the set of all distributions on the positive integers, let Ω_1 be any subset of Ω, and let $\Omega_2 = \Omega - \Omega_1$. Show that, for any sample size N and any φ, $\alpha(\varphi) + \beta(\varphi) \geq 1$.

Sufficient Statistics
and the Invariance Principle
in Statistical Games

8.1. Introduction

A statistical decision is usually made on the basis of the outcome of an experiment. The experiment will often contain information that is not necessarily relevant to the making of the decision. Thus, for example, in the rocket-firing experiment discussed in Section 3.8, the outcome reveals not only the number of defective rockets in the sample but also the order in which the defectives occurred. However, the order of occurrence of these defectives may, for example, be completely irrelevant to the decision whether to accept or reject the lot of propellent powder.

To discover what information is and what is not relevant in a given experiment is an important problem in statistical games. This problem may be more generally posed in the following manner: Suppose we are dealing with a statistical game $\Gamma = (\Omega, \Phi, \rho)$ where Φ is a class of randomized strategies defined on $A \times Z$. Does there exist a partition of Z with the property that every possible risk attainable with a complete knowledge of z is also attainable with only the information that z belongs to a set S of this partition? More technically, does there exist a partition S on Z and a class Ψ of randomized strategies such that each $\psi \in \Psi$ is defined on $A \times S$ and such that the class of probability distributions on an action space A induced by Ψ and Ω is the same as that induced by Φ and Ω? A partition of this type will be called a *partition which is as informative as Z*. Whether or not a partition S as informative as Z exists (other than the trivial partition $S = S_t$ where $t(z) = z$) must clearly depend on the structure of the sample space Z. If for some Z non-trivial such partitions exist, we shall be interested in finding the coarsest (minimal partition) among them, since clearly the original game can then be replaced by one in which the space of (ran-

domized) decision functions is only a subset, and sometimes a very small subset of the original space of decision functions. Partitions as informative as Z are given by the principle of sufficiency, or what is more commonly known as the principle of sufficient statistics.

A further reduction in the decision space can often be made, using the so-called invariance principle. Often, the invariance principle leads to simplifications even more striking than those obtained from the sufficiency principle, but the guarantees are somewhat weaker. We cannot assert that the invariance principle can be used without loss. However, weaker statements can be made such as that it can be used without enlarging the maximum risk. That is, the invariance principle states that under certain conditions there exists a subset Ψ of Φ with the property that for every $\varphi \, \varepsilon \, \Phi$ there is a $\psi \, \varepsilon \, \Psi$ such that

$$\sup_{\omega} \rho(\omega, \psi) \leq \sup_{\omega} \rho(\omega, \varphi)$$

Thus, if φ is minimax, so is ψ, and, if there is a minimax strategy, there is one in Ψ. Moreover, a minimax strategy in Ψ turns out often to be an admissible strategy.

Loosely speaking, the invariance principle asserts that, if a problem is invariant under a change of coordinates, the solution should also be invariant under this change of coordinates. For instance, if one wishes to estimate the mean height in a population on the basis of a random sample of N individuals with observed heights x_1, \cdots, x_N, the estimate will be a function t of x_1, \cdots, x_N. If the observed heights are measured in inches, and for some reason the estimate is wanted in centimeters, two plausible estimates in centimeters are $ct(x_1, \cdots, x_N)$, obtained simply by changing the estimate t to centimeters, and $t(cx_1, \cdots, cx_N)$, obtained by changing the observations to centimeters and using the original estimate t where $c = 2.54$, the number of centimeters in an inch. The invariance principle requires that the estimates should agree, i.e., that only those functions t should be considered as estimates which satisfy $ct(x_1, \cdots, x_N) = t(cx_1, \cdots, cx_N)$. Examples of estimates with this property are the arithmetic, geometric, and harmonic means of the x's; the median of the x's, etc. A further application of the principle of invariance, or the principle of sufficiency, for that matter, would lead us to consider only estimates that are symmetric functions of x's, thus rejecting estimates such as $(x_1 + x_N)/2$, or any weighted average with unequal weights.

This chapter will deal with the general problem of characterizing the sample spaces Z which admit non-trivial partitions that are statistically equivalent to Z. It will be shown that minimal such partitions

always exist, and a general method for constructing them will be given. This problem in a somewhat more general form will be again taken up in Chapter 12.

While the general formulation of the invariance principle, to say nothing of the proof, is beyond the scope of this book, a few special but important cases of this principle will be proved, and applications to sampling from a finite population will be given. We shall return briefly again to the problem of invariance in Chapter 11.

8.2. Partitions of Z Which Are Sufficient on \mathcal{Z}

In the next four sections we shall assume that the sample space $\mathcal{Z} = (Z, \Omega, p)$ is such that for each $z \in Z$ there exists at least one $\omega \in \Omega$ with $p(z \mid \omega) > 0$. When Z consists of a denumerable set of points, this simply requires that we restrict the sample spaces to points that can be considered as realizable through an actual experiment.

Definition 8.2.1. Let $\mathcal{Z} = (Z, \Omega, p)$ be a sample space. A partition \mathcal{S} of Z is said to be sufficient on \mathcal{Z} if for every bounded function f defined on Z and for every $S \in \mathcal{S}$, $E_\omega(f \mid S)$ [see Definition 3.6.1] is independent of ω for those $\omega \in \Omega$ for which $P_\omega(S) > 0$.

We remark that there always exists a sufficient partition on \mathcal{Z}, namely the partition formed by the individual points of Z. However, for many sample spaces, there exist less trivial sufficient partitions. Examples of such \mathcal{Z} will be given below.

Theorem 8.2.1. A necessary and sufficient condition that a partition \mathcal{S} on a sample space $\mathcal{Z} = (Z, \Omega, p)$ be sufficient is that there exist a factorization of the form

(i) $$p(z \mid \omega) = g_\omega(z)r(z) = g(z \mid \omega)r(z)$$

such that for each ω the partition \mathcal{S} is a subpartition [see Definition 3.11.5] of the partition of \mathcal{S}_{g_ω} determined by g_ω (i.e., $g_\omega(z)$ is constant on each $S \in \mathcal{S}$) and such that the function r depends only on z.

Proof. (a) Necessity: Let \mathcal{S} be a partition of Z which is sufficient on \mathcal{Z}, and let s be a function defined on Z with values in \mathcal{S} such that $s(z) = S$ if $z \in S$, where S is an element of \mathcal{S}. Now for any bounded function f on Z we have by definition

(1) $$E_\omega(f) = \sum_{S \in \mathcal{S}} E_\omega(f \mid S)P_\omega(S)$$

where the summation is taken over those elements $S \in \mathcal{S}$ for which $P_\omega(S)$

> 0. Let z be fixed and consider a function f defined by

$$f(y) = 1 \quad \text{if} \quad y = z$$

$$f(y) = 0 \quad \text{if} \quad y \neq z$$

Then, for this f, $E_\omega(f) = p(z \mid \omega)$, and by (1) we have for all ω for which $P_\omega(s(z)) > 0$

(2) $$p(z \mid \omega) = P_\omega(s(z))E_\omega(f \mid s(z))$$

Since \mathcal{S} is sufficient on \mathcal{Z}, $E_\omega(f \mid s(z))$ is independent of ω. Thus setting

(3) $$g(z \mid \omega) = P_\omega(s(z)), \qquad r(z) = E_\omega(f \mid s(z))$$

equation (2) becomes

(4) $$p(z \mid \omega) = g(z \mid \omega)r(z)$$

Moreover, it is clear from (3) that, for a fixed ω, \mathcal{S} is a subpartition of \mathcal{S}_{g_ω} [see, for example, Lemma 8.2.1 below], and that (4) holds trivially in case $P_\omega(s(z)) = 0$.

(b) Sufficiency: Assume that (i) holds and that for each ω the partition \mathcal{S} is a subpartition of \mathcal{S}_{g_ω}. To show that \mathcal{S} is sufficient on \mathcal{Z}, let f be a bounded function on Z, let θ be any element of Ω, and let $S \, \varepsilon \, \mathcal{S}$ be such that $P_\theta(S) > 0$. Now, by definition,

(5) $$E_\theta(f \mid S) = \frac{\sum\limits_{z \, \varepsilon \, S} f(z)g(z \mid \theta)r(z)}{\sum\limits_{z \, \varepsilon \, S} g(z \mid \theta)r(z)}$$

Since \mathcal{S} is a subpartition of \mathcal{S}_{g_θ}, it follows that $g(z \mid \theta)$ is a non-zero constant for all $z \, \varepsilon \, S$ so that

(6) $$E_\theta(f \mid S) = \frac{\sum\limits_{z \, \varepsilon \, S} f(z)r(z)}{\sum\limits_{z \, \varepsilon \, S} r(z)}$$

Thus \mathcal{S} is a sufficient partition on \mathcal{Z}. This completes the proof of the theorem.

Definition 8.2.2. Let $\mathcal{Z} = (Z, \Omega, p)$ be a sample space. A random variable t defined on Z is said to be sufficient on \mathcal{Z} if the partition \mathcal{S}_t of Z determined by t is sufficient on \mathcal{Z}.

Theorem 8.2.2. A necessary and sufficient condition that a random variable t be sufficient on \mathcal{Z} is that for each $\omega \, \varepsilon \, \Omega$ there exists a function

q_ω defined on the range of t and a function r defined on Z and independent of ω, such that

(i) $$p(z \mid \omega) = q_\omega(t(z))r(z) = q(t(z) \mid \omega)r(z)$$

Proof. In order to prove this theorem, we require the following lemma.

Lemma 8.2.1. Let u and v be two functions defined on Z, and let S_u and S_v be the corresponding partitions determined by them. Then a necessary and sufficient condition that S_u be a subpartition of S_v is that there exist a function w such that $v = w \circ u$; i.e.,

$$v(z) = w(u(z))$$

for all $z \, \varepsilon \, Z$.

Proof. (*a*) Sufficiency: Assume that a function w exists such that $v = w \circ u$. Let y be fixed, and let

(1) $$U_y = \{z : u(z) = y\}$$

Then by definition $U_y \, \varepsilon \, S_u$. Let $w(y) = v_0$, and let

(2) $$V_y = \{z : v(z) = v_0\}$$

Then, again by definition, $V_y \, \varepsilon \, S_v$. Now let z belong to U_y. Then for that z

$$v(z) = w(u(z)) = w(y) = v_0$$

and hence $z \, \varepsilon \, V_y$. Thus $U_y \subset V_y$ and consequently S_u is a subpartition of S_v.

(*b*) Necessity: Assume S_u is a subpartition of S_v, and for a fixed y define U_y as in (1). Then, for all $z \, \varepsilon \, U_y$, $v(z) = v_0$ where v_0 is some constant, since by assumption S_u is a subpartition of S_v. Define $w(y) = v(z)$ for all $z \, \varepsilon \, U_y$. Then $v = w \circ u$ which proves the lemma.

We now return to the proof of Theorem 8.2.2. Assume (i) holds, and let S_t be the partition determined by the random variable t, and for any ω let

$$g_\omega(z) = q_\omega(t(z))$$

Then, by Lemma 8.2.1, S_t is a subpartition of S_{g_ω}, and hence, by Theorem 8.2.1, S_t is a sufficient partition on Z, and therefore t is a sufficient statistic. This proves the necessity of condition (i). To prove the sufficiency of this condition, assume that S_t is a sufficient partition on Z. Then by Theorem 8.2.1

$$p(z \mid \omega) = g_\omega(z)r(z) = g(z \mid \omega)r(z)$$

and S_t is a subpartition of S_{g_ω}. Then by Lemma 8.2.1 there exists a function q_ω such that $g_\omega = q_\omega \circ t$; i.e.,

$$g(z \mid \omega) = q_\omega(t(z)) = q(t(z) \mid \omega)$$

which proves the theorem.

Theorem 8.2.3. <u>Every sufficient partition on \mathcal{Z} determines a sufficient statistic.</u>

Proof. Let $S = \{S_\alpha\}$ be a sufficient partition on \mathcal{Z}. Define, for example, $t(z) = \alpha$ for all $z \, \varepsilon \, S_\alpha$. Then, by definition, t is a sufficient statistic.

We note that to a given sufficient partition there can be made to correspond an arbitrary number of sufficient statistics so that the notion of a sufficient partition is a more fundamental notion than that of a sufficient statistic.

The following are two examples of sufficient partitions and sufficient statistics.

1. An experiment consists of N independent trials, each trial resulting either in an event E or an event \bar{E}. The probability that E occurs is ω, and the probability that \bar{E} occurs is $1 - \omega$. The sample space $\mathcal{Z} = (Z, \Omega, p)$ where Z contains 2^N points z, each of which is a sequence of N elements of the type E or \bar{E}, Ω is the closed interval $(0, 1)$. Consider the partition $S = (S_0, S_1, \cdots, S_N)$ where S_m consists of all points z containing exactly m events labeled E. It is easily verified that S_m contains $\binom{N}{m}$ points of Z, S is a sufficient partition on \mathcal{Z}, and m is a sufficient statistic defined on Z.

2. Let an experiment result in a point $x = (x_1, \cdots, x_N)$ where the x_i's are independent observations from a Poisson distribution having a mean value ω. Here the sample space $\mathcal{X} = (X, \Omega, p)$ where X consists of all points in N space with non-negative integral coordinates and p is defined by

$$p(x \mid \omega) = \frac{e^{-\omega N} \omega^{t(x)}}{\displaystyle\prod_{i=1}^{N} x_i!}, \qquad 0 \le \omega < \infty$$

where $t(x) = \displaystyle\sum_{i=1}^{N} x_i$. The function t is a sufficient statistic on \mathcal{X}, and the partition S_t determined by t is a sufficient partition on \mathcal{X}.

PROBLEMS

8.2.1. Let S be a partition of Z. A function f on Z is said to be S-measurable if $f(z)$ is constant on each $S \, \varepsilon \, S$. Prove that a function f is S-measurable if and only if S is a subpartition of S_f.

8.2.2. In view of the results of Problem 8.2.1, restate Theorem 8.2.1, in terms of an S-measurable function.

8.2.3. A coin with unknown probability ω of falling head is tossed repeatedly until exactly 10 heads have been obtained. Show that the number of tosses is a sufficient statistic on the appropriate sample space.

8.2.4. License numbers from a random sample of 100 automobiles registered in a certain state are observed. Show that the largest license number observed is sufficient for estimating ω, the total number of automobiles registered in the state.

8.2.5. A die with probabilities $\omega = (\omega_1, \cdots, \omega_6)$ of showing 1, \cdots, 6 is rolled N times. On what sample space is the number of observed 1's sufficient?

8.3. The Principle of Sufficiency

In this section we shall prove that, if $\mathcal{Z} = (Z, \Omega, p)$ is a sample space and S is a sufficient partition of Z, then S is as informative as Z. Before we prove this result and make the notion of "as informative" more precise, we shall first generalize Theorem 7.2.1 to statistical games in which the space A of actions is not restricted to be finite.

Let $\mathcal{Z} = (Z, \Omega, p)$ be a sample space, A an arbitrary space of actions, D a class of decision functions mapping Z into A, and H a class of randomized strategies; i.e., each element $\eta \varepsilon$ H is a mixture of a denumerable number of elements d_1, d_2, \cdots in D in proportions, say, $\lambda_1, \lambda_2, \cdots$, respectively. Furthermore, let Φ be a class of randomized strategies φ defined on $A \times Z$ [see Definition 3.6.6] such that, for a fixed z, $\varphi(a, z) = \varphi(a \mid z)$ is non-negative, is zero except for a countable number of elements a of A and $\sum_{a \varepsilon A} \varphi(a \mid z) = 1$ where it is understood that the summation is taken over a countable set.

Theorem 8.3.1. Let $G = (\Omega, D, \rho)$ be a fixed sample-size game, and let $\Gamma = (\Xi, H, \rho)$ be its mixed extension. Consider another game $\Gamma^* = (\Xi, \Phi, \rho)$ where each element $\varphi \varepsilon \Phi$ has the property described above. Then, (a) for each $\eta \varepsilon$ H there exists a $\varphi \varepsilon \Phi$ such that $\rho(\xi, \eta) = \rho(\xi, \varphi)$ for all $\xi \varepsilon \Xi$, and (b) for each $\varphi \varepsilon \Phi$ and each $\xi \varepsilon \Xi$ there exists a sequence $\eta_m, m = 1, 2, \cdots$ of randomized strategies in H such that

$$(1) \qquad \lim_{m \to \infty} \rho(\xi, \eta_m) = \rho(\xi, \varphi)$$

Proof. The proof of part a of this theorem is the same as that given in Theorem 7.2.1 since the finiteness of A did not enter into consideration. To prove part b, we let $Z' = \{z_1, z_2, \cdots\}$ be the denumerable subset of Z such that $\sum_{\omega} \xi(\omega) p(z \mid \omega) > 0$, and, for each i, let a_{ij} ($j = 1, 2, \cdots$) be the elements of A (which are assumed to be distinct for that i) such that

$$\sum_j \varphi(a_{ij} \mid z_i) = 1$$

Consider the totality of m-tuples of positive integers (j_1, j_2, \cdots, j_m) where for each fixed k $(k = 1, 2, \cdots, m)$ the range of j_k is finite or denumerable depending on whether the range of the subscript j in the element a_{kj} is finite or denumerable. We define

$$(2) \quad d_{j_1 j_2 \cdots j_m}(z_1) = a_{1j_1}, \quad d_{j_1 j_2 \cdots j_m}(z_2) = a_{2j_2}, \cdots, \quad d_{j_1 j_2 \cdots j_m}(z_m) = a_{mj_m}$$

and $d_{j_1 j_2 \cdots j_m}(z_i)$ is arbitrary for $i > m$. Now consider the randomized strategy η_m which selects $d_{j_1 j_2 \cdots j_m}$ with probability $\lambda_{j_1 j_2 \cdots j_m}$ where

$$\lambda_{j_1 j_2 \cdots j_m} = \varphi(a_{1j_1} \mid z_1)\varphi(a_{2j_2} \mid z_2) \cdots \varphi(a_{mj_m} \mid z_m)$$

By part a of this theorem there exists a φ in Φ, say φ_m, which is equivalent to η_m. Consider the element $z_1 \,\varepsilon\, Z$. The randomized strategy η_m will select the element a_{1n} when z_1 is observed if and only if the pure strategy $d_{j_1 j_2 \cdots j_m}$ is selected with $j_1 = n$. But the probability that this will occur is given by

$$\sum_{j_2, \cdots, j_m} \varphi(a_{1n} \mid z_1)\varphi(a_{2j_2} \mid z_2) \cdots \varphi(a_{mj_m} \mid z_m) = \varphi(a_{1n} \mid z_1)$$

for all n. A similar argument shows that for a given z_i $(i \le m)$ the strategy η_m will select the element a_{ij_i} with probability $\varphi(a_{ij_i} \mid z_i)$ for all j_i. It must follow therefore that

$$\varphi_m(a \mid z_i) = \varphi(a \mid z_i) \quad \text{for} \quad i = 1, 2, \cdots, m$$

The loss function L is bounded by assumption, so that there exists a K with $\mid L(\omega, a) \mid \,\le K$ for all $\omega \,\varepsilon\, \Omega$ and $a \,\varepsilon\, A$. Now

$$\mid \rho(\omega, \varphi_m) - \rho(\omega, \varphi) \mid \, = \Big| \sum_{i=1}^{\infty} \sum_{a \,\varepsilon\, A} L(\omega, a)p(z_i \mid \omega)[\varphi_m(a \mid z_i) - \varphi(a \mid z_i)] \Big|$$

$$\le \sum_{i=m+1}^{\infty} \sum_{a \,\varepsilon\, A} \mid L(\omega, a) \mid p(z_i \mid \omega) \mid \, \varphi_m(a \mid z_i) - \varphi(a \mid z_i) \mid$$

$$\le K \sum_{i=m+1}^{\infty} \sum_{a \,\varepsilon\, A} [\varphi_m(a \mid z_i) + \varphi(a \mid z_i)]p(z_i \mid \omega) \le 2K \sum_{i=m+1}^{\infty} p(z_i \mid \omega)$$

Let m be so large that $\sum\limits_{i=m+1}^{\infty} p(z_i \mid \omega) < \epsilon/2K$ where ϵ is an arbitrary positive quantity. Then

$$\mid \rho(\omega, \varphi_m) - \rho(\omega, \varphi) \mid \, < \epsilon$$

which in conjunction with the corollary to Theorem 3.11.5 proves the theorem.

We make the following remarks concerning the above theorem: (1) Unlike Theorem 7.2.1, this theorem does not establish complete equiv-

alence between H and Φ since it only guarantees that, given a $\varphi \, \varepsilon \, \Phi$, we can find an $\eta \, \varepsilon \, H$ which results in a Bayes risk which is within ϵ of the Bayes risk attainable with φ for any arbitrary $\epsilon > 0$. Complete equivalence can be established, however, if we admit more general types of randomized strategies in both H and Φ than can be considered in this book. (2) If Z is finite, say, $Z = (z_1, z_2, \cdots, z_M)$, then complete equivalence can be established from the following considerations: Let φ be given, and let a_{ij} $(i = 1, 2, \cdots, M; j = 1, 2, \cdots)$ be elements in A such that $\sum_j \varphi(a_{ij} \mid z_i) = 1$. As above, we define

$$d_{j_1 j_2 \cdots j_M}(z_i) = a_{i j_i}, \qquad i = 1, 2, \cdots, M$$

for all possible sets (j_1, j_2, \cdots, j_M) of positive integers. We then select a strategy $d_{j_1 j_2 \cdots j_M}$ with probability $\prod_{i=1}^{M} \varphi(a_{i j_i} \mid z_i)$.

We now turn to the proof of the main result of this section.

Let $\mathcal{Z} = (Z, \Omega, p)$ be a sample space, and let S be a partition of Z. Let Φ be the class of randomized strategies defined on $A \times Z$ where A is an arbitrary space of actions. For any $\omega \, \varepsilon \, \Omega$ and any $\varphi \, \varepsilon \, \Phi$ let $q_\varphi(a \mid \omega)$ be the probability that an action $a \, \varepsilon \, A$ will be taken. Then

$$(8.3.1) \qquad q_\varphi(a \mid \omega) = \sum_{z \, \varepsilon \, Z} \varphi(a \mid z) p(z \mid \omega)$$

Thus, for a fixed ω, q_φ is a probability distribution on A. Let \mathcal{R}_Φ be the class of functions q_φ defined on $A \times \Omega$ by (8.3.1) for all $\varphi \, \varepsilon \, \Phi$. We define a class Ψ of randomized strategies on $A \times S$ in the following manner: An element ψ belongs to Ψ if $\psi(a \mid S)$ is a non-negative real number which, for each $S \, \varepsilon \, S$, is zero except for a denumerable set in A, and $\sum_{a \, \varepsilon \, A} \psi(a \mid S) = 1$. The interpretation of the function ψ is as follows: If the outcome of the experiment is a point $z \, \varepsilon \, S$, we select $a \, \varepsilon \, A$ with probability $\psi(a \mid S)$. For any $\omega \, \varepsilon \, \Omega$ and any $\psi \, \varepsilon \, \Psi$, let $q^*_\psi(a \mid \omega)$ be the probability that an action $a \, \varepsilon \, A$ will be taken. Then

$$(8.3.2) \quad q^*_\psi(a \mid \omega) = \sum_{S \, \varepsilon \, S} \sum_{z \, \varepsilon \, S} \psi(a \mid S) p(z \mid \omega) = \sum_{S \, \varepsilon \, S} \psi(a \mid S) \sum_{z \, \varepsilon \, S} p(z \mid \omega)$$

$$= \sum_{S \, \varepsilon \, S} \psi(a \mid S) P_\omega(S)$$

Let \mathcal{R}^*_Ψ be the class of functions q^*_ψ defined on $A \times \Omega$ by (8.3.2) for all $\psi \, \varepsilon \, \Psi$.

Definition 8.3.1. Let $\mathcal{Z} = (Z, \Omega, p)$ be a sample space, let A be an arbitrary space of actions, let Φ be the class of randomized strategies defined on $A \times Z$, let S be a partition of Z, and let Ψ be the class of

randomized strategies on $A \times S$. Then the space Z and the partition S are said to be equally informative if $\mathcal{R}_\Phi = \mathcal{R}^*_\Psi$ where the elements of \mathcal{R}_Φ are defined by (8.3.1) and the elements of \mathcal{R}^*_Ψ are defined by (8.3.2).

We note that by (8.3.1) and (8.3.2) we have

$$\rho(\omega, \varphi) = \sum_{a \,\varepsilon\, A} \sum_{z \,\varepsilon\, Z} L(\omega, a)\varphi(a \mid z)p(z \mid \omega) = \sum_{a \,\varepsilon\, A} L(\omega, a)q_\varphi(a \mid \omega)$$

and

$$\rho(\omega, \psi) = \sum_{a \,\varepsilon\, A} \sum_{z \,\varepsilon\, S} \sum_{S \,\varepsilon\, S} L(\omega, a)\psi(a \mid z)p(z \mid \omega) = \sum_{a \,\varepsilon\, A} L(\omega, a)q^*_\psi(a \mid z)$$

Thus, if Z and S are equally informative, then every risk which is attainable by knowing the outcome of the experiment z is also attainable by only knowing which element S of S contains the outcome z.

Theorem 8.3.2. Let $Z = (Z, \Omega, p)$ be a sample space, and let S be a sufficient partition on Z. Then Z and S are equally informative.

Proof. Since by assumption S is sufficient on Z, then, by Theorem 8.2.1, every element of \mathcal{P}_Ω factors; i.e.,

$$(1) \qquad p(z \mid \omega) = g(z \mid \omega)r(z)$$

where, for a given $S \,\varepsilon\, S$, $g(z \mid \omega)$ is constant for all $z \,\varepsilon\, S$. Now let $\varphi \,\varepsilon\, \Phi$, and let $q_\varphi(a \mid \omega)$ be the probability that an $a \,\varepsilon\, A$ will be selected for any $\omega \,\varepsilon\, \Omega$. Then by equation 8.3.1

$$(2) \qquad q_\varphi(a \mid \omega) = \sum_{z \,\varepsilon\, Z} \varphi(a \mid z)g(z \mid \omega)r(z)$$

for all $\omega \,\varepsilon\, \Omega$. We now define a class Ψ of randomized strategies ψ on $A \times S$ as follows: For each $\varphi \,\varepsilon\, \Phi$ we let

$$(3) \qquad \psi(a \mid S) = \frac{\displaystyle\sum_{z \,\varepsilon\, S} \varphi(a \mid z)r(z)}{\displaystyle\sum_{z \,\varepsilon\, S} r(z)}$$

for all $S \,\varepsilon\, S$ and $a \,\varepsilon\, A$. (Note that the denominator in (3) is not zero by the assumption made on Z in the first paragraph of Section 8.2.) Clearly ψ is a non-negative function on $A \times S$, is zero except on a denumerable set of A, and for a fixed S

$$(4) \qquad \sum_{a \,\varepsilon\, A} \psi(a \mid S) = \frac{\displaystyle\sum_{z \,\varepsilon\, S} \sum_{a \,\varepsilon\, A} \varphi(a \mid z)r(z)}{\displaystyle\sum_{z \,\varepsilon\, S} r(z)} = 1$$

Now for any $\omega \, \varepsilon \, \Omega$ let $q^*_\psi(a \mid \omega)$ be the probability that action $a \, \varepsilon \, A$ will be selected if the strategy ψ is employed. Then by (8.3.2)

$$(5) \qquad q^*_\psi(a \mid \omega) = \sum_{S \, \varepsilon \, \mathcal{S}} \psi(a \mid z) \sum_{z \, \varepsilon \, S} g(z \mid \omega) r(z)$$

Now, on any S in \mathcal{S}, $g(z \mid \omega)$ is constant. Thus from (3) we obtain

$$(6) \qquad \psi(a \mid S) \sum_{z \, \varepsilon \, S} g(z \mid \omega) r(z) = \sum_{z \, \varepsilon \, S} \varphi(a \mid z) g(z \mid \omega) r(z)$$

and hence

$$(7) \quad q^*_\psi(a \mid \omega) = \sum_{S \, \varepsilon \, \mathcal{S}} \sum_{z \, \varepsilon \, S} \varphi(a \mid z) g(z \mid \omega) r(z) = \sum_{z \, \varepsilon \, Z} \varphi(a \mid z) g(z \mid \omega) r(z)$$

Comparing (2) and (7), we conclude that $\mathfrak{R}_\Phi \subset \mathfrak{R}^*_\Psi$. Conversely, let $\psi \, \varepsilon \, \Psi$. We define $\varphi(a \mid z) = \psi(a \mid S)$ for all $z \, \varepsilon \, S \, \varepsilon \, \mathcal{S}$. Then clearly $\mathfrak{R}^*_\Psi \subset \mathfrak{R}_\Phi$, and hence $\mathfrak{R}_\Phi = \mathfrak{R}^*_\Psi$.

We remark that, for those $S \, \varepsilon \, \mathcal{S}$ for which $P_\omega(S) > 0$, ψ defined by (3) is in fact the conditional expected value of φ, given that $z \, \varepsilon \, S$.

PROBLEMS

8.3.1. A coin with unknown probability ω of falling head is tossed five times. If at no time during the tosses does the number of tails exceed the number of heads, an observer will decide that $\omega > 1/2$; otherwise he will decide that $\omega \leq 1/2$. Construct an equivalent decision function based only on the number of heads obtained.

8.3.2. Give an example satisfying the hypothesis of Theorem 8.3.1, in which the classes H, Φ are not strictly equivalent.

8.3.3. Prove that, if Ω is finite, the convergence specified by (1) in Theorem 8.3.1 is uniform in ξ.

8.3.4. Prove the converse of Theorem 8.3.2. That is, show that, if $\mathcal{Z} = (Z, \Omega, p)$, \mathcal{S} is a partition on Z, and \mathcal{S} and Z are equally informative for any arbitrary A containing at least 2 elements, then \mathcal{S} is sufficient on \mathcal{Z}.

8.3.5. Prove that, if a partition \mathcal{S} on Z and Z are equally informative for an action space A containing 2 elements, then \mathcal{S} is sufficient on \mathcal{Z}.

8.4. Minimal Sufficient Partitions

Theorem 8.3.2 exhibits the importance of sufficient partitions (and therefore sufficient statistics) in statistical games and raises the question whether for a given sample space $\mathcal{Z} = (Z, \Omega, p)$ there exists a minimal partition which is sufficient. Formally, this concept is made precise in the following definition:

Definition 8.4.1. Let $\mathcal{Z} = (Z, \Omega, p)$ be a sample space. A partition \mathcal{S} of Z which is sufficient on \mathcal{Z} is minimal if any other sufficient partition of Z is a subpartition of \mathcal{S}. A sufficient statistic t on \mathcal{Z} is minimal if the partition \mathcal{S}_t is minimal.

We shall now prove that for every sample space in which Z is denumerable there always exists a minimal sufficient partition and therefore a minimal sufficient statistic. In order to prove this result, we need the following lemmas.

Lemma 8.4.1. Let \mathfrak{S} be any class of partitions on a space Y. Then there exists a partition \mathfrak{U} on Y such that (a) \mathfrak{U} is a subpartition of every \mathcal{S} in \mathfrak{S}, and (b) if \mathfrak{V} is any other subpartition of every \mathcal{S} in \mathfrak{S}, then \mathfrak{V} is a subpartition of \mathfrak{U} (i.e., \mathfrak{U} is the coarsest partition that is a subpartition of every $\mathcal{S}\,\varepsilon\,\mathfrak{S}$).

Proof. For any $y\,\varepsilon\,Y$ and any $\mathcal{S}\,\varepsilon\,\mathfrak{S}$, let \mathcal{S}_y be the set in \mathcal{S} which has y as an element, and let

$$(1) \qquad\qquad U_y = \bigcap_{\mathcal{S}\,\varepsilon\,\mathfrak{S}} \mathcal{S}_y$$

We first prove that the collection of sets U_y form a partition of Y. We observe that every $y\,\varepsilon\,Y$ belongs to U_y since y belongs to each \mathcal{S}_y. It remains to be shown that these sets are disjoint. Let $z\,\varepsilon\,U_y$. Then $z\,\varepsilon\,\mathcal{S}_y$ for every $\mathcal{S}\,\varepsilon\,\mathfrak{S}$. Hence $\mathcal{S}_z = \mathcal{S}_y$ for every $\mathcal{S}\,\varepsilon\,\mathfrak{S}$, and therefore $U_z = U_y$. Now suppose for some x and z in Y, $U_x \cap U_z$ is not empty, and assume $U_x \neq U_z$. Let y be a common element of U_x and U_z. Then $U_x = U_y$ and $U_z = U_y$, and therefore $U_x = U_z$ which is a contradiction. Also, by definition U_y is a subset of \mathcal{S}_y for every $\mathcal{S}\,\varepsilon\,\mathfrak{S}$ so that \mathfrak{U} is a subpartition of every $\mathcal{S}\,\varepsilon\,\mathfrak{S}$.

Assume now that \mathfrak{V} is a subpartition of every $\mathcal{S}\,\varepsilon\,\mathfrak{S}$. To show that \mathfrak{V} is a subpartition of \mathfrak{U}, let V be a non-empty set of \mathfrak{V}, and let $y\,\varepsilon\,V$. Now, by hypothesis, for every $\mathcal{S}\,\varepsilon\,\mathfrak{S}$ there is an $S\,\varepsilon\,\mathcal{S}$ such that $V \subset S$, therefore $y\,\varepsilon\,S$ since $y\,\varepsilon\,V$, and hence $S = \mathcal{S}_y$. Therefore $V \subset \mathcal{S}_y$ for every $\mathcal{S}\,\varepsilon\,\mathfrak{S}$. Consequently $V \subset U_y$ by (1) which completes the proof of the lemma.

Lemma 8.4.2. Let $\mathcal{Z} = (Z, \Omega, p)$ be a sample space in which Z is denumerable. There exists a sequence $\omega_1, \omega_2, \cdots$ in Ω such that for every $z\,\varepsilon\,Z$ there is an i such that $p(z \mid \omega_i) > 0$.

Proof. The proof of this lemma follows from the assumption we made about \mathcal{Z} in the beginning of Section 8.2.

Lemma 8.4.3. Let $\omega_1, \omega_2, \cdots$ be a sequence in Ω specified by Lemma 8.4.2, and define

$$(1) \qquad\qquad k_\omega(z) = \frac{p(z \mid \omega)}{\displaystyle\sum_{i=1}^{\infty} \frac{1}{2^i} p(z \mid \omega_i)}$$

Let S_{k_ω} be the partition of Z determined by the function k_ω, and let \mathfrak{S} be the class of partitions determined by k_ω for each $\omega \, \varepsilon \, \Omega$. Then a partition S of Z is sufficient on \mathcal{Z} if and only if it is a subpartition of every S_{k_ω} of \mathfrak{S}.

Proof. Suppose S is sufficient on \mathcal{Z}. Then by Theorems 8.2.2 and 8.2.3 there exists a random variable t such that $S_t = S$ and

$$p(z \mid \omega) = q(t(z) \mid \omega)r(z)$$

We then have

$$k_\omega(z) = \frac{q(t(z) \mid \omega)r(z)}{\displaystyle\sum_{i=1}^{\infty} \frac{1}{2^i} q(t(z) \mid \omega_i)r(z)}$$

By Lemma 8.4.2 the denominator in the above expression is positive so that $r(z) > 0$ for all z, and hence

$$k_\omega(z) = \frac{q(t(z) \mid \omega)}{\displaystyle\sum_i \frac{1}{2^i} q(t(z) \mid \omega_i)} = h_\omega(t(z))$$

Thus $k_\omega = h_\omega \circ t$, and, by Lemma 8.2.1, S is a subpartition of S_{k_ω}.

Conversely, assume S is a subpartition of S_{k_ω} for every $\omega \, \varepsilon \, \Omega$. We define

$$r(z) = \sum_i \frac{1}{2^i} p(z \mid \omega_i)$$

Then by (1)

$$p(z \mid \omega) = k_\omega(z)r(z)$$

Let t be a function such that $S_t = S$. Then by Lemma 8.2.1 there exists a function q_ω such that

$$k_\omega = q_\omega \circ t$$

and consequently

$$p(z \mid \omega) = q_\omega(t(z))r(z) = g(z \mid \omega)r(z)$$

and, by Theorem 8.2.1, S is sufficient on \mathcal{Z}. This completes the proof of the lemma.

We remark that in many statistical problems the sample space $\mathcal{Z} = (Z, \Omega, p)$ is such that there exists at least one element $\theta \, \varepsilon \, \Omega$ such that $p(z \mid \theta) > 0$ for all $z \, \varepsilon \, Z$. In such cases, all the ω_i that appear in the denominator of the definition of k_ω can be taken to be equal to θ so

that k_ω is then defined by a likelihood ratio, namely

$$k_\omega(z) = \frac{p(z \mid \omega)}{p(z \mid \theta)}$$

and Lemma 8.4.3 can then be stated in terms of this likelihood ratio.

Theorem 8.4.1. Let $\mathcal{Z} = (Z, \Omega, p)$ be an arbitrary sample space in which Z is denumerable. There always exists a minimal sufficient partition on \mathcal{Z} and hence a minimal sufficient statistic.

Proof. Let \mathfrak{S} be the class of partitions \mathcal{S}_{k_ω} on Z. By Lemma 8.4.1 there exists a partition \mathfrak{U} such that \mathfrak{U} is a subpartition of every \mathcal{S}_{k_ω} in \mathfrak{S}, and, by Lemma 8.4.3, \mathfrak{U} is sufficient on \mathcal{Z}. Also, by Lemma 8.4.1, if \mathfrak{V} is any other subpartition of every \mathcal{S}_{k_ω} (and hence by Lemma 8.4.3 is a sufficient partition), then \mathfrak{V} is a subpartition of \mathfrak{U}. That is, \mathfrak{U}, by Definition 8.4.1, is a minimal sufficient partition on \mathcal{Z} which proves the theorem.

It is to be pointed out that Lemma 8.4.1 gives a constructive method for obtaining the minimal partition from the class of partitions \mathfrak{S} determined by k_ω for each $\omega \varepsilon \Omega$.

As an illustration of minimal partitions and minimal sufficient statistics, consider the following two examples.

Example 1. Let $\mathfrak{X} = (X, \Omega, p)$ where X is a subset of N space and \mathcal{P}_Ω is a product of exponential distributions; i.e.,

$$p(x \mid \omega) = [\beta(\omega)]^N e^{\omega \sum_{i=1}^{N} x_i} \prod_{i=1}^{N} r(x_i)$$

where $x = (x_1, \cdots, x_N)$ and ω ranges over an interval (a, b) on the real line. Here any $\theta \varepsilon \Omega$ has the property that $p(x \mid \theta) > 0$ for all X; consequently, we can fix a θ and define k_ω by

$$k_\omega(x) = \frac{p(x \mid \omega)}{p(x \mid \theta)} = \left[\frac{\beta(\omega)}{\beta(\theta)}\right]^N e^{(\omega-\theta)\sum_{i=1}^{N} x_i}$$

It is clear that the class of partitions determined by k_ω is identical with the class of partitions determined by the function t where $t(x) = \sum_{i=1}^{N} x_i$. Thus trivially \mathcal{S}_t is a subpartition of every \mathcal{S}_{k_ω}, and \mathcal{S}_t is a minimal sufficient partition on \mathfrak{X}, and t is a minimal sufficient statistic.

Example 2. The probability of a coin falling head (H) is ϕ_1 with $(0 < \phi_1 < 1)$, if in the previous trial the outcome was tail (T); and the probability of its falling head is ϕ_2 with $(0 < \phi_2 < 1)$ if in the previous trial the outcome was head. A coin was tossed, and the outcome was tail. An experiment consists of tossing the coin 3 more times, each toss being an independent trial. We consider two sample spaces $\mathcal{Z}_1 = (Z, \Omega_1, p_1)$ and $\mathcal{Z}_2 = (Z, \Omega_2, p_2)$ where Z consists of 8 points representing the outcomes of the 3 tosses, $\Omega_1 = (0 < \phi_1 < 1) \times (0 < \phi_2 < 1)$ and $\Omega_2 = \{(\phi_1, \phi_2) \, \varepsilon \, \Omega_1 : \phi_1 = \phi_2 = \phi\}$. For any $\omega_1 \, \varepsilon \, \Omega_1$ and $\omega_2 \, \varepsilon \, \Omega_2$, the probability distribution on Z is summarized in the accompanying table. Let S_1 be the minimal sufficient partition on \mathcal{Z}_1 and S_2 be the

Z	$p_1(z \mid \omega_1)$	$p_2(z \mid \omega_2)$	S_1	S_2
HHH	$\phi_1\phi_2^2$	ϕ^3	(HHH)	(HHH)
HHT	$\phi_1\phi_2(1 - \phi_2)$	$\phi^2(1 - \phi)$	(HHT)	$\left(\begin{array}{c}HHT\\HTH\\THH\end{array}\right)$
HTH	$\phi_1^2(1 - \phi_2)$	$\phi^2(1 - \phi)$	(HTH)	
THH	$\phi_1\phi_2(1 - \phi_1)$	$\phi^2(1 - \phi)$	(THH)	
THT	$\phi_1(1 - \phi_1)(1 - \phi_2)$	$\phi(1 - \phi)^2$	$\left(\begin{array}{c}THT\\HTT\end{array}\right)$	$\left(\begin{array}{c}THT\\HTT\\TTH\end{array}\right)$
HTT	$\phi_1(1 - \phi_1)(1 - \phi_2)$	$\phi(1 - \phi)^2$		
TTH	$\phi_1(1 - \phi_1)^2$	$\phi(1 - \phi)^2$	(TTH)	
TTT	$(1 - \phi_1)^3$	$(1 - \phi)^3$	(TTT)	(TTT)

minimal sufficient partition on \mathcal{Z}_2. Then S_1 consists of 7 sets and S_2 of 4 sets as is indicated in the table. To show that these are minimal partitions we apply the results of Lemma 8.4.2 where we define

$$k_{\omega_j}(z) = \frac{p_i(z \mid \omega_j)}{p_i(z \mid \theta_j)}, \qquad (j = 1, 2; i = 1, 2)$$

where $\theta_1 = \theta_2$ is the point in Ω_1 with $\phi_1 = \phi_2 = 1/2$.

Example 2 is a good illustration of how the concept of sufficient partition and sufficient minimal partition on $\mathcal{Z} = (Z, \Omega, p)$ depends not only on Z but also on \mathcal{O}_Ω.

PROBLEMS

8.4.1. Determine the minimal sufficient partition for the class \mathcal{O}_Ω of discrete rectangular distributions $\omega = 1, 2, \cdots$, where $p_\omega(i) = 1/\omega$ for $i = 1, \cdots, \omega$, for a sample of size N.

8.4.2. Determine the minimal sufficient partition for the class \mathcal{O}_Ω of all discrete distributions on the set of positive integers for a sample of size N.

8.4.3. A necessary and sufficient condition that a partition of Z be sufficient on \mathcal{Z} is that for any set of the partition and any two distributions in the class \mathcal{O}_Ω the likelihood ratio is either constant or undefined.

8.5. Sufficient Statistics for Densities

It is beyond the scope of this book to give analogous definitions of the notions of sufficient partitions and sufficient statistics in case the sample space $\mathfrak{X} = (X, \Omega, p)$ is such that X is an N space and \mathcal{P}_Ω is a class of densities. Here we shall only remark that, if there exists a random variable t such that for each $\omega \, \varepsilon \, \Omega$ and each $x \, \varepsilon \, X$, $p(x \mid \omega) = q(t(x) \mid \omega)g(x)$ where the function g is independent of ω, then t is called a sufficient statistic on \mathfrak{X}. Most of the theorems proved in the previous sections are valid for densities—in particular it can be shown that any risk attainable by a randomized strategy defined on $A \times X$ can also be attained by a randomized strategy defined on $A \times T$ where T is the range of t.

The following are two examples of sufficient statistics for densities.

1. Let $x = (x_1, \cdots, x_N)$ be N independent observations from a rectangular distribution defined over the interval $(0, \omega)$, and let $t(x) = \max(x_1, \cdots, x_N)$. Then the density of x given ω is defined by

(i) $$p(x \mid \omega) = 1/\omega^N \quad \text{for} \quad t(x) \leq \omega$$

$$= 0 \qquad \text{for} \quad t(x) > \omega$$

Thus t is a sufficient statistic on $\mathfrak{X} = (X, \Omega, p)$ where p is defined by (i).

2. Let $x = (x_1, \cdots, x_N)$ be N independent observations from a normal distribution with mean μ and variance σ^2. Then the density $p(x \mid \omega)$, $\omega = (\mu, \sigma)$ is given by

(ii) $$p(x \mid \omega) = \left(\frac{1}{\sqrt{2\pi}\sigma}\right)^N e^{-\frac{N}{2}\left(\frac{\bar{x}-\mu}{\sigma}\right)^2} e^{-\frac{1}{2}\sum_1^N \left(\frac{x_i-\bar{x}}{\sigma}\right)^2}$$

where $\bar{x} = \dfrac{1}{N}\sum_{i=1}^N x_i$. Let t be defined by $t(x) = \left(\bar{x}, \sum_1^N (x_i - \bar{x})^2\right)$. Then t is a sufficient statistic on $\mathfrak{X} = (X, \Omega, p)$ where p is defined by (ii).

8.6. Principle of Invariance for Finite Groups

In this section we will develop the principle of invariance for the special case in which there is a finite group of transformations defined on $Z \times \Omega \times A$. To this end we first define formally the notion of a group of transformations.

Definition 8.6.1. Let E be a non-empty set. Then \mathcal{G} is a group of transformations on E if

1. Each element g of \mathcal{G} is a one-to-one function from E onto E.
2. For each g in \mathcal{G} and h in \mathcal{G}, the function $g \circ h$ is in \mathcal{G}.

3. For each g in \mathcal{G}, the function g^{-1} defined by

$$x = g^{-1}(y) \quad \text{if} \quad g(x) = y$$

is in \mathcal{G}.

It follows from the above definition that the identity transformation $I = g \circ g^{-1} = g^{-1} \circ g$ is in \mathcal{G}.

Definition 8.6.2. Let $\mathcal{Z} = (Z, \Omega, p)$ be a sample space, A an action space, L a loss function defined on $\Omega \times A$, let $G = (\Omega, D, \rho)$ be a game and \mathcal{G} a group of transformations defined on $Z \times \Omega \times A$. The group \mathcal{G} is said to be admissible with respect to the game G if for each $g \, \varepsilon \, \mathcal{G}$ there exist functions g_Z, g_Ω, g_A on Z, Ω, and A respectively such that, for every $z \, \varepsilon \, Z$, $\omega \, \varepsilon \, \Omega$, and $a \, \varepsilon \, A$,

(1) $$g(z, \omega, a) = (g_Z(z), g_\Omega(\omega), g_A(a))$$

(2) $$p(g_Z(z) \mid g_\Omega(\omega)) = p(z \mid \omega)$$

(3) $$L(g_\Omega(\omega), g_A(a)) = L(\omega, a)$$

(Note that, in case \mathcal{P}_Ω is a class of density functions defined on N space, condition 2 is to be replaced by

$$P(g_X(R) \mid g_\Omega(\omega)) = P(R \mid \omega)$$

where R is an arbitrary N-dimensional interval.)

The following is an illustration of an admissible group \mathcal{G}. Let $\mathcal{Z} = (Z, \Omega, p)$ be a sample space in which $z = (x_1, x_2, \cdots, x_N)$ is a point in N space and the coordinates of z are values of normally and independently distributed random variables with mean μ and standard deviation σ so that $\omega = (\mu, \sigma)$, $-\infty < \mu < \infty$, $0 < \sigma < \infty$ and

$$p(z \mid \omega) = \left(\frac{1}{\sqrt{2\pi}\,\sigma}\right)^N e^{-\frac{1}{2}\sum_{i=1}^{N}\left(\frac{x_i - \mu}{\sigma}\right)^2}$$

The problem is to estimate μ. The action space A is the entire real line $A = (-\infty < a < \infty)$. The loss function L is given by

$$L(\omega, a) = f\left(\frac{|\mu - a|}{\sigma}\right)$$

where f is an arbitrary function.

Let β, $\gamma \, \varepsilon \, A$, $\beta \neq 0$, $\epsilon = (1, 1, \cdots, 1)$, and let

$$g_Z{}^{\beta\gamma}(z) = \beta z + \gamma\epsilon, \qquad g_\Omega{}^{\beta\gamma}(\omega) = (\beta\mu + \gamma, |\beta|\sigma), \qquad g_A{}^{\beta\gamma}(\omega) = \beta a + \gamma$$

Consider the group \mathcal{G} with elements g defined by

$$g^{\beta\gamma}(z,\,\omega,\,a) = (g_Z{}^{\beta\gamma}(z),\, g_\Omega{}^{\beta\gamma}(\omega),\, g_A{}^{\beta\gamma}(a))$$

Then \mathcal{G} satisfies condition 1 for admissibility. It is easily verified that \mathcal{G} also satisfies conditions 2 and 3.

We observe that in many statistical problems $g_A = I$. Thus, for example, if in the above illustration, instead of estimating μ, we wish to decide whether $\mu/\sigma = \delta_1$ (action a_1) or $\mu/\sigma = \delta_2$ (action a_2) where the loss function L is defined by

$$L(\omega,\, a_i) = 0 \qquad \text{if} \quad \mu/\sigma = \delta_i \qquad (i = 1,\, 2)$$

$$L(\omega,\, a_1) = w_{21} \quad \text{if} \quad \mu/\sigma = \delta_2$$

$$L(\omega,\, a_2) = w_{12} \quad \text{if} \quad \mu/\sigma = \delta_1$$

then the group \mathcal{G} with elements

$$g^\beta = (g_Z{}^\beta,\, g_\Omega{}^\beta,\, I)$$

where $g_Z{}^\beta(z) = \beta z$, $g_\Omega{}^\beta = (\beta\mu,\, \beta\sigma)$ where $\beta > 0$ is an admissible group for this decision problem.

Definition 8.6.3. Let \mathcal{G} be an admissible group and Φ a class of randomized strategies. For $g \,\varepsilon\, \mathcal{G}$ and each $\varphi \,\varepsilon\, \Phi$ we define a function φ_g on $A \times Z$ as follows:

$$\varphi_g(a \mid z) = \varphi(g_A{}^{-1}(a) \mid g_Z{}^{-1}(z))$$

Definition 8.6.4. Let \mathcal{G} be an admissible group, $Z = (Z,\, \Omega,\, p)$ a sample space, and A a space of actions. A randomized strategy φ defined on $A \times Z$ is said to be invariant with respect to \mathcal{G} if, for all $g \,\varepsilon\, \mathcal{G}$, $z \,\varepsilon\, Z$, and $a \,\varepsilon\, A$,

$$\varphi(g_A(a) \mid g_Z(z)) = \varphi(a \mid z)$$

Theorem 8.6.1. If $\varphi \,\varepsilon\, \Phi$ is an invariant randomized strategy with respect to an admissible group \mathcal{G} then for all g,

$$\varphi_g = \varphi$$

Theorem 8.6.2. Let $\Gamma = (\Omega,\, \Phi,\, \rho)$ be a game and \mathcal{G} an admissible group. Then for each $\varphi \,\varepsilon\, \Phi$ and each $g \,\varepsilon\, \mathcal{G}$

$$\rho(\omega,\, \varphi) = \rho(g_\Omega(\omega),\, \varphi_g)$$

Proof. Since \mathcal{G} is admissible and each $g \,\varepsilon\, \mathcal{G}$ is a one-to-one function,

$$\begin{aligned}
\rho(\omega, \varphi) &= \sum_{z\,\varepsilon\,Z} \sum_{a\,\varepsilon\,A} L(\omega, a)\varphi(a \mid z)p(z \mid \omega) \\
&= \sum_{z\,\varepsilon\,Z} \sum_{a\,\varepsilon\,A} L(g_\Omega(\omega), g_A(a))\varphi_g(g_A(a)\mid g_Z(z))p(g_Z(z) \mid g_\Omega(\omega)) \\
&= \sum_{z'\,\varepsilon\,Z} \sum_{a'\,\varepsilon\,A} L(g_\Omega(\omega), a')\varphi_g(a' \mid z')p(z' \mid g_\Omega(\omega)) \\
&= \rho(g_\Omega(\omega), \varphi_g)
\end{aligned}$$

which proves the theorem.

Theorem 8.6.3. If φ is an invariant randomized strategy then for any $g \,\varepsilon\, \mathcal{G}$
$$\rho(g_\Omega(\omega), \varphi) = \rho(\omega, \varphi)$$

Proof. This theorem follows from Theorems 8.6.1 and 8.6.2.

Theorem 8.6.4. Let \mathcal{G} be a finite admissible group, and let Φ be the class of all randomized strategies. Then for every $\varphi \,\varepsilon\, \Phi$ there is a φ^* in Φ which is invariant and is such that

$$\sup_{\omega\,\varepsilon\,\Omega} \rho(\omega, \varphi^*) \le \sup_{\omega\,\varepsilon\,\Omega} \rho(\omega, \varphi)$$

Proof. Let M be the number of elements of \mathcal{G}. Define

(1) $$\varphi^* = \frac{1}{M} \sum_{h\,\varepsilon\,\mathcal{G}} \varphi_h$$

(a) φ^* is invariant. Take any arbitrary $g \,\varepsilon\, \mathcal{G}$. Then from Definition 8.6.3

$$\begin{aligned}
\varphi^*(a \mid z) &= \frac{1}{M} \sum_{h\,\varepsilon\,\mathcal{G}} \varphi_h(a \mid z) = \frac{1}{M} \sum_{h\,\varepsilon\,\mathcal{G}} \varphi(h_A^{-1}(a) \mid h_Z^{-1}(z)) \\
&= \frac{1}{M} \sum_{h\,\varepsilon\,\mathcal{G}} \varphi[(g \circ h)_A^{-1}(g_A(a)) \mid (g \circ h)_Z^{-1}(g_Z(z))] \\
&= \frac{1}{M} \sum_{h\,\varepsilon\,\mathcal{G}} \varphi_{g\circ h}(g_A(a), g_Z(z)) \\
&= \frac{1}{M} \sum_{k\,\varepsilon\,\mathcal{G}} \varphi_k(g_A(a), g_Z(z)) = \varphi^*(g_A(a) \mid g_Z(z))
\end{aligned}$$

$$(b) \qquad \sup_{\omega \,\varepsilon\, \Omega} \rho(\omega, \varphi^*) \lneq \frac{1}{M} \sum_{g \,\varepsilon\, \mathcal{G}} \sup_{\omega \,\varepsilon\, \Omega} \rho(\omega, \varphi_g)$$

$$= \frac{1}{M} \sum_{g \,\varepsilon\, \mathcal{G}} \sup_{\omega \,\varepsilon\, \Omega} \rho(g_\Omega(\omega), \varphi_g)$$

$$= \frac{1}{M} \sum_{g \,\varepsilon\, \mathcal{G}} \sup_{\omega \,\varepsilon\, \Omega} \rho(\omega, \varphi) = \sup_{\omega \,\varepsilon\, \Omega} \rho(\omega, \varphi)$$

which proves the theorem.

Corollary 1. If there exists a finite admissible group \mathcal{G} and if the game has a minimax procedure then it has a minimax invariant procedure.

Theorem 8.6.5. Let \mathcal{G} be a finite admissible group. Let φ^* be an invariant randomized strategy which is not admissible. Then there is an invariant strategy ψ^* which is better than φ^*; i.e., ψ^* is such that, for all $\omega \,\varepsilon\, \Omega$, $\rho(\omega, \psi^*) \leq \rho(\omega, \varphi^*)$, and, for some $\theta \,\varepsilon\, \Omega$, $\rho(\theta, \psi^*) < \rho(\theta, \varphi)$.

Proof. Since by assumption φ^* is not admissible, there exists a $\psi \,\varepsilon\, \Phi$ which is better. We construct a ψ^* as in (1) in the proof of the previous theorem. Then

$$(1) \qquad \rho(\omega, \psi^*) = \frac{1}{M} \sum_{g \,\varepsilon\, \mathcal{G}} \rho(\omega, \psi_g)$$

$$= \frac{1}{M} \sum_{g \,\varepsilon\, \mathcal{G}} \rho(g_\Omega{}^{-1}(\omega), \psi)$$

by Theorem 8.6.2. But ψ is better than φ^*, and hence

$$(2) \qquad \rho(\omega, \psi^*) \leq \frac{1}{M} \sum_{g \,\varepsilon\, \mathcal{G}} \rho(g_\Omega{}^{-1}(\omega), \varphi^*)$$

so that, by Theorem 8.6.3,

$$(3) \qquad \rho(\omega, \psi^*) \leq \frac{1}{M} \sum_{g \,\varepsilon\, \mathcal{G}} \rho(\omega, \varphi^*) = \rho(\omega, \varphi^*)$$

Now, for some $\theta \,\varepsilon\, \Omega$, $\rho(\theta, \psi) < \rho(\theta, \varphi^*)$ so that if we substitute θ for ω in (2) we get

(4)
$$\rho(\theta, \psi^*) = \frac{1}{M} \sum_{g \in \mathcal{G}} \rho(g_\Omega^{-1}(\theta), \psi)$$

$$= \frac{1}{M} [\rho(\theta, \psi) + \sum_{\substack{g \in \mathcal{G} \\ g \neq I}} \rho(g_\Omega^{-1}(\theta), \psi)]$$

$$< \frac{1}{M} [\rho(\theta, \varphi^*) + \sum_{\substack{g \in \mathcal{G} \\ g \neq I}} \rho(g_\Omega^{-1}(\theta), \varphi^*)]$$

$$= \frac{1}{M} \sum_{g \in \mathcal{G}} \rho(\theta, \varphi^*) = \rho(\theta, \varphi^*)$$

which completes the proof of the theorem.

Theorem 8.6.6. Let \mathcal{G} be a finite admissible group, and let Φ^* be the subclass of Φ of randomized strategies, each of which is invariant under \mathcal{G}. Then if $\varphi^* \varepsilon \Phi^*$ is admissible with respect to the elements of Φ^* then it is admissible.

Proof. Assume that φ^* is not admissible. Then by Theorem 8.6.5 there exists a $\psi^* \varepsilon \Phi^*$ which is better than φ^*. But this contradicts the assumption that φ^* is admissible in the class Φ^*.

Theorem 8.6.6 states that, in order to determine whether a strategy, invariant under a finite group, is admissible, we need only to test it against the class of invariant strategies.

Theorem 8.6.7. Let $G = (\Omega, D, \rho)$ be a game satisfying the conditions: (i) For any $a, b \varepsilon A$ with $a \neq b$ there exists an $\omega \varepsilon \Omega$ such that $L(\omega, a) \neq L(\omega, b)$. (ii) If $p(z \mid \omega) = p(z \mid \theta)$ for all $z \varepsilon Z$, then $\omega = \theta$. Let \mathcal{G} be a group which is admissible with respect to G. Then if g and h are elements of \mathcal{G} such that $g_Z = h_Z$ then $g = h$.

Proof. We first show that $g_Z = h_Z$ implies $g_\Omega = h_\Omega$. Since \mathcal{G} is admissible, we have

(1)
$$p(g_Z(z) \mid g_\Omega(\omega)) = p(z \mid \omega)$$

and hence

(2)
$$p(z \mid g_\Omega(\omega)) = p(g_Z^{-1}(z) \mid \omega)$$

Similarly, for any $h \varepsilon \mathcal{G}$,

(3)
$$p(z \mid h_\Omega(\omega)) = p(h_Z^{-1}(z) \mid \omega)$$

But $g_Z = h_Z$ and hence $g_Z^{-1} = h_Z^{-1}$, and, since the index ω is unique,

we have $g_\Omega = h_\Omega$. It remains to show that $g_A = h_A$. Now by (3) Definition 8.6.2,

$$(4) \qquad L(g_\Omega(\omega), g_A(a)) = L(\omega, a) = L(h_\Omega(\omega), h_A(a))$$

for all $a \, \varepsilon \, A$ and $\omega \, \varepsilon \, \Omega$. But $g_\Omega(\omega) = h_\Omega(\omega)$ for all ω, as we have first shown, so that (4) can be written as

$$(5) \qquad L(\omega, g_A(a)) = L(\omega, h_A(a))$$

for all $\omega \, \varepsilon \, \Omega$. Now suppose $g_A \neq h_A$; then by assumption there exists an $\omega \, \varepsilon \, \Omega$ such that $L(\omega, g_A(a)) \neq L(\omega, h_A(a))$ which contradicts (5). Hence $g_A = h_A$, and consequently $g = h$.

We remark that condition (i) of the theorem implies that the same label has been applied to all actions that result in the same loss for each state of nature, and condition (ii) simply states that distinct labels imply distinct distributions in \mathcal{P}_Ω. Thus, neither condition is restrictive.

Theorem 8.6.8. Let $G = (\Omega, D, \rho)$ be a game satisfying conditions (i) and (ii) of Theorem 8.6.7, and let \mathcal{G} be a group which is admissible with respect to G. Then if Z is finite so is \mathcal{G}.

Proof. Let $Z = (z_1, z_2, \cdots, z_M)$, and let $g \, \varepsilon \, \mathcal{G}$. Since \mathcal{G} is admissible,

$$g(z, \omega, a) = (g_Z(z), g_\Omega(\omega), g_A(a))$$

Also, g_Z is a one-to-one function on Z so that each g_Z simply permutes the subscripts of the elements of Z. Thus there are only a finite number of elements g in \mathcal{G} with distinct components g_Z. The theorem now follows from Theorem 8.6.7.

PROBLEMS

8.6.1. Show that in estimating the parameter ω (the probability of a success) of a binomial distribution from N observations x_1, \cdots, x_N with $L(\omega, a)$ an even convex function of $(\omega - a)$, there is a minimax estimate t such that

$$t(x_1, \cdots, x_N) = 1 - t(1 - x_1, \cdots, 1 - x_N)$$

8.6.2. Treat the problem of the n-faced die of Section 6.4 in terms of the invariance principle, and characterize the game G and the group \mathcal{G} involved.

8.7. Application of the Invariance Principle to Sampling from a Finite Population

The concept of a statistical game involving a finite population may be formulated in the following manner. We are given a sample space $\mathcal{Z} = (Z, \Omega', p')$, and either nature or a conscious player performs a fixed

sample-size experiment and obtains a value of a random variable which is a point $x = (x_1, x_2, \cdots, x_M)$ in a space X where each x_i is a real number or vector with real components. The statistician has to select one out of a class A of possible actions in complete or partial ignorance of x and ω'. He incurs a loss L which is a function of the action $a \varepsilon A$ selected and the point x, but usually not of the underlying $\omega' \varepsilon \Omega'$. Moreover, for a given a, $L(x, a)$ is assumed to be constant for all permutations of the coordinates of x. The statistician can obtain partial information on x by observing a fixed number of coordinates of x. The problem is, if the cost of observing x_i is independent of i, how should the statistician select the sample? We shall here show that the principle of invariance together with the principle of sufficiency leads to the well-known method of simple random sampling.

Formally we are dealing with the following entities.

1. A sample space $\mathfrak{X} = (X, \Omega, p)$ where each element $x \varepsilon X$ has M coordinates (x_1, x_2, \cdots, x_M) and each x_i is a real number or a vector. It is assumed that if $x \varepsilon X$ so does any arbitrary permutation of its coordinates. The space Ω is the same as X; i.e.,

$$p(x \mid \omega) = 1 \quad \text{if} \quad x = \omega, \qquad p(x \mid \omega) = 0 \quad \text{if} \quad x \neq \omega$$

2. An arbitrary space A of actions.

3. A set S of sampling plans consisting of all subsets $s = (j_1, j_2, \cdots, j_N)$ of the integers $(1, 2, \cdots, M)$ where $N < M$ and no two j_i's are equal. If $s \varepsilon S$ is selected, then the N coordinates (j_1, j_2, \cdots, j_N) of x are observed.

4. A decision function space $S \times D$ with elements (s, d) where d depends only on the coordinates specified by s and $d(x) \varepsilon A$ for all x.

5. A class of random procedures Φ where each $\varphi \varepsilon \Phi$ is defined on $S \times A \times X$, is non-negative, is zero except on a denumerable set in A, and is such that

(a) $$\sum_{s \varepsilon S} \sum_{a \varepsilon A} \varphi(s, a \mid x) = 1 \quad \text{for all } x$$

(b) $$\sum_{a \varepsilon A} \varphi(s, a \mid x) \quad \text{is independent of } x \text{ for all } s \varepsilon S$$

(c) For each $s \varepsilon S$, $\varphi(s, a \mid x)$ depends only on the coordinates of x named in s.

6. A group \mathcal{G} with elements g^T defined on $\bar{A} \times X$ where $\bar{A} = S \times A$, such that

$$g^T(x, \omega, \bar{a}) = (g_X{}^T(x), g_\Omega{}^T(\omega), g_{\bar{A}}{}^T(\bar{a}))$$

where T is a permutation of the integers 1, 2, \cdots, M, and, if $x = (x_1, \cdots, x_M)$,

$$g_X{}^T(x) = (X_{T1}, X_{T2}, \cdots, X_{TM})$$

and, if $\bar{a} = (s, a) = (j_1, j_2, \cdots, j_N, a)$,

$$g_{\bar{A}}{}^T(\bar{a}) = (T_{j1}, T_{j2}, \cdots, T_{jM}, a) = (g_S{}^T(s), a)$$

where, if k is an integer and T carries k into j, then by Tk is meant the integer j. Since there exists a one-to-one correspondence between X and Ω, the function $g_\Omega{}^T$ transforms the elements of Ω in the same manner as $g_X{}^T$ transforms the elements of X.

7. The loss function L is defined on $\Omega \times A$ and does not depend on s and is constant for all permutations of the coordinates of $\omega = x$. We shall write

$$L(\omega, a) = \mathcal{L}(\omega, \bar{a}) = \mathcal{L}(\omega, (s, a))$$

We observe that the group \mathcal{G} is admissible [see Definition 8.6.2] for by definition $g^T(x, \omega, \bar{a}) = (g_X{}^T(x), g_\Omega{}^T(\omega), g_{\bar{A}}{}^T(\bar{a}))$. Moreover, by the definition of \mathcal{L}

$$\mathcal{L}(\omega, \bar{a}) = \mathcal{L}(g_\Omega{}^T(\omega), g_{\bar{A}}{}^T(\bar{a}))$$

Also by definition $p(g_X{}^T(x) \mid g_\Omega{}^T(\omega)) = 1$ if $g_\Omega{}^T(\omega) = g_X{}^T(x)$ and the latter implies $\omega = x$ and hence $p(x \mid \omega) = 1$. A similar argument shows that if $p(g_X{}^T(x) \mid g_\Omega{}^T(\omega)) = 0$ then $p(x \mid \omega) = 0$. Consequently

$$p(g_X{}^T(x) \mid g_\Omega{}^T(\omega)) = p(x \mid \omega)$$

Also \mathcal{G} is finite. Hence by Theorem 8.6.4 for each $\varphi \varepsilon \Phi$ there exists an invariant procedure φ^* such that

$$\sup_{\omega \varepsilon \Omega} \rho(\omega, \varphi^*) \leq \sup_{\omega \varepsilon \Omega} \rho(\omega, \varphi)$$

Now by Definition 8.6.4

(a) $\varphi^*((s, a) \mid x) = \varphi^*(g_{\bar{A}}{}^T(s, a) \mid g_X{}^T(x)) = \varphi^*[(g_S{}^T(s), a) \mid g_X{}^T(x)]$

and hence

(b) $\displaystyle\sum_{a \varepsilon A} \varphi^*(s, a \mid x) = \sum_{a \varepsilon A} \varphi^*[(g_S{}^T(s), a) \mid g_X{}^T(x)]$

Now by definition of φ both sides of (b) are independent of x and represent the probability, say $\pi(s)$, that φ^* will result in a choice of s. Hence we have

(c) $\pi(s) = \pi(g_S{}^T(s))$

Summing both sides of (c) over all permutations T and remembering that $\sum_s \pi(s) = 1$, we get

$$M!\pi(s) = (M - N)!$$

or

$$\pi(s) = (M - N)!/M!$$

We note that invariance so far considers each subset of the integers in order. Although we could have defined the group \mathcal{G} so as to eliminate order, it is preferable to accomplish this by employing the principle of sufficiency since more is guaranteed by it. For this purpose we need only to show that the probability distribution of the observed sample factors.

Let $\mathfrak{U} = (U_N, \Omega, q)$ be a sample space in which each $u = (u_1, \cdots, u_N) \, \varepsilon \, U_N$ consists of N coordinates of some $x \, \varepsilon \, X$ and where each element $q_\omega \, \varepsilon \, \mathcal{Q}_\Omega$ is given by

$$(1) \quad q(u \mid \omega) = \sum_{j_1 \neq \cdots \neq j_N} P_\omega(\omega_{j_1} = u_1, \cdots, \omega_{j_N} = u_N) \frac{(M - N)!}{M!}$$

and is the probability that a sample will result in a point u such that $\omega_{j_1} = x_{j_1} = u_1, \cdots, \omega_{j_N} = x_{j_N} = u_N$. Note that $P_\omega(\omega_{j_1} = u_1, \cdots, \omega_{j_N} = u_N)$ is either 1 or 0.

We shall say that $u \, \varepsilon \, U_N$ is equivalent to $u' \, \varepsilon \, U_N$ if, for some permutation T of the integers 1 to N,

$$u'_1 = u_{T1}, \cdots, u'_N = u_{TN}$$

Consider a collection of sets \mathcal{S} in U_N with each set in \mathcal{S} consisting of all points equivalent to a given point. It is easy to show that \mathcal{S} is a partition.

In order to show that

$$q(u \mid \omega) = g(u \mid \omega)r(u)$$

it is sufficient to demonstrate that $q(u \mid \omega)$ is, for a given ω, constant over each set of the partition \mathcal{S} since we can then take $r(u) = 1$ for all u. Now assume that u and u' belong to the same set in \mathcal{S}. Then for some permutation T

$$(2) \quad q(u'_1, \cdots, u'_N \mid \omega)$$

$$= p(u_{T1}, \cdots, u_{TN} \mid \omega)$$

$$= \sum_{j_1 \neq \cdots \neq j_N} P_\omega(\omega_{j_1} = u_{T1}, \cdots, \omega_{j_N} = u_{TN}) \frac{(M - N)!}{M!}$$

$$= \sum_{j_1 \neq \cdots \neq j_N} P_\omega(\omega_{j_{T1}} = u_1, \cdots, \omega_{j_{TN}} = u_N) \frac{(M - N)!}{M!}$$

where $\tau = T^{-1}$. Since the summation extends over all values of $j_1 \neq \cdots \neq j_N$, equation 2 can also be written as

(3) $q(u'_1, \cdots, u'_N \mid \omega)$

$$= \sum_{j_{\tau 1} \neq \cdots \neq j_{\tau N}} P_\omega(\omega_{j_{\tau 1}} = u_1, \cdots, \omega_{j_{\tau N}} = u_N) \frac{(M - N)!}{M!}$$

$$= q(u_1, \cdots, u_N \mid \omega)$$

which establishes the result.

The above discussion shows that the invariance principle in conjunction with the sufficiency principle leads to a strategy which selects each set s of N distinct integers from 1 to M (without regard to order) with probability

(4) $$\pi(s) = 1 \bigg/ \binom{M}{N}$$

which is the strategy of simple random sampling.

8.8. A Special Case of the Invariance Principle with an Infinite Group

The illustration of the invariance principle involving an infinite group which we shall treat in this section is that of testing a composite hypothesis against a composite alternative, with special application to the Student t test, and it will be simpler to formulate the problem in terms of densities than in terms of discrete distributions. We consider a pair of densities $p_i(t, s)$, $i = 1, 2$, $-\infty < t < \infty$, $0 < s < \infty$, so that $p_i(t, s) \geq 0$, $\int p_i(t, s)\, dt\, ds = 1$, and suppose that a pair (t, s) is chosen according to p_1 or p_2, and that the statistician observes (t, u) where $u = cs$ and c is an unknown positive constant. The problem is to decide whether the true distribution is p_1 or p_2, and a decision procedure is a function φ with values $\varphi(i \mid t, u)$, where $\varphi(i \mid t, u)$ is the probability of deciding that p_i is the true distribution when (t, u) is observed. We measure the loss by the probabilities of errors, so that

$$\rho(i, c; \varphi) = \int \varphi(i \mid t, cs) p_i(t, s)\, dt\, ds$$

Now, if we change the units in which u is measured, say, $u = kv$, $k > 0$, the decision function φ, expressed in terms of t, v is $\psi_i(t, v) = \varphi_i(t, kv)$. But the problem in terms of t, v is precisely the same as that in terms of t, u, since $v = (c/k)s$ and (c/k) is, like c, an unknown positive constant. The invariance principle, applied to this case, requires that

$\psi(i \mid t, v) = \varphi(i \mid t, v)$; i.e., $\varphi(i \mid t, kv) = \varphi(i \mid t, v)$, so that, since k is arbitrary, the invariance principle requires that, for a fixed i, φ should be a function of t only.

A property of tests based on t only is given by

Theorem 8.8.1. For any φ and any $\epsilon > 0$ there is a φ^* based on t only such that

$$\alpha_i(\varphi^*) < \alpha_i(\varphi) + \epsilon, \qquad i = 1, 2$$

where

$$\alpha_i(\varphi) = \sup_c \rho(i, c; \varphi)$$

Proof. Write, for any $M > 1$,

$$f_M(i, \varphi) = \frac{\displaystyle\int_{1/M}^{M} \rho(i, c; \varphi)\, \frac{dc}{c}}{\displaystyle\int_{1/M}^{M} \frac{dc}{c}} = \int p_i(t, s) \left[\frac{1}{2 \log M} \int_{1/M}^{M} \varphi(i \mid t, cs)\, \frac{dc}{c} \right] dt\, ds$$

$$= \int p_i(t, s) \left[\frac{1}{2 \log M} \int_{s/M}^{sM} \varphi(i \mid t, c)\, \frac{dc}{c} \right]$$

so that, since $f_M(i, \varphi)$ is a weighted average of $\rho(i, c; \varphi)$, $f_M(i, \varphi) \leq \alpha_i(\varphi)$. We consider the decision function

$$\varphi_M(i \mid t) = \frac{1}{2 \log M} \int_{1/M}^{M} \varphi(i \mid t, c)\, \frac{dc}{c}$$

We have

$$\alpha_i(\varphi_M) = \int p_i(t, s) \left[\frac{1}{2 \log M} \int_{1/M}^{M} \varphi(i \mid t, c)\, \frac{dc}{c} \right] dt\, ds$$

so that

(1) $$\left| f_M(i, \varphi) - \alpha_i(\varphi_M) \right| \leq \int p_i(t, s) \left| g_i(M, t, s) \right| dt\, ds$$

where

$$g_i(M, t, s) = \frac{1}{2 \log M} \left[\int_{1/M}^{M} - \int_{s/M}^{sM} \varphi(i \mid t, c)\, \frac{dc}{c} \right]$$

Since $0 \leq \varphi(i \mid t, s) \leq 1$, $\left| g_i(M, t, s) \right| \leq 1$ and

$$\left| g_i(M, t, s) \right| \leq \frac{1}{2 \log M} \left\{ \left| \int_{sM}^{M} \frac{dc}{c} \right| + \left| \int_{s/M}^{1/M} \frac{dc}{c} \right| \right\} = \frac{\log |s|}{\log M}$$

so that

$$g_i(M, t, s) \to 0 \quad \text{as} \quad M \to \infty \quad \text{for all } t, s$$

Inequality 1 yields that

$$\left| f_M(i, \varphi) - \alpha_i(\varphi_M) \right| \to 0$$

as $M \to \infty$, so that, for sufficiently large M,

$$\alpha_i(\varphi_M) < f_M(i, \varphi) + \epsilon \le \alpha_i(\varphi) + \epsilon$$

Since each φ_M depends only on t, the proof is complete.

The reader will note that we have actually proved a little more than is asserted in the theorem: Not only was the maximum risk $\alpha_i(\varphi)$ not increased by restriction to invariant tests, but also a weighted average risk $f_M(i, \varphi)$ was approximable, for large M, by the (constant) risk of an invariant test. The particular weighted average used here, with density $1/c$, is the so-called invariant measure for the multiplicative group of positive real numbers, since it has the property

$$\int_a^b \frac{dc}{c} = \int_{ka}^{kb} \frac{dc}{c}$$

for all positive k, a, b.

As an application of Theorem 8.8.1, we consider the following problem: $x = (x_1, \cdots, x_N)$ is a sample of N independent observations from a normal distribution with parameters $\omega = (\mu, \sigma)$. Ω_i consists of all points such that

$$\int_0^\infty p(y \mid \omega) \, dy = p_i, \qquad i = 1, 2$$

where

$$p(y \mid \omega) = \frac{1}{\sigma \sqrt{2\pi}} e^{-\frac{1}{2}\left(\frac{x-\mu}{\sigma}\right)^2}$$

i.e., Ω_i consists of all ω for which the proportion of positive individuals is p_i, and we wish to test p_1 against p_2. If we have a_i so that

$$\int_{a_i}^\infty p(y, \omega_0) \, dy = p_i$$

where $\omega_0 = (0, 1)$, Ω_i consists of all $\omega = (\mu, \sigma)$ such that $\mu/\sigma = -a_i$, so that the problem may be regarded as testing $\mu/\sigma = -a_1$ against the alternative $\mu/\sigma = -a_2$. The sufficiency principle enables us to restrict attention to tests based on (\bar{x}, s), where $s = \sum_1^N (x_i - \bar{x})^2$, or equivalently, to tests based on (t, s), where $t = \bar{x}/s$. If we write s/σ for s, the joint density of (t, s) depends only on μ/σ; let $p_i(t, s)$, $-\infty < t < \infty$,

$s > 0$, be the joint density of (t, s) for $\omega \, \varepsilon \, \Omega_i$. If φ is any decision function, we have probabilities of errors

$$\rho(i, \sigma, \varphi) = \int \varphi(i \mid t, \sigma s) p_i(t, s) \, dt \, ds$$

Thus the problem is exactly that treated in Theorem 8.8.1, and we obtain that without increasing $\alpha_1(\varphi)$ or $\alpha_2(\varphi)$, we may restrict attention to tests based on $t = \bar{x}/s$. The famous t test emerges here as a test for μ/σ, rather than as a test for μ as it is often described.

CHAPTER 9

Sequential Games

9.1. Introduction

In Chapter 3 we have given a general description of the structure of truncated sequential games for the case where the sequence of possible subexperiments to be performed is prescribed in advance. In this chapter we shall be concerned with the characterization of the class of Bayes procedures for truncated sequential games of this type, and we shall extend these procedures to the non-truncated case for games with constant cost and independent and identically distributed observations. The main aim will be to develop the theory of sequential-decision procedures. Applications of this theory to several classes of problems will be given in the subsequent chapter. The reader will do well to refer back to this chapter after having become acquainted with the contents of Chapter 10.

In some statistical problems a sequential-sampling plan is given in advance. What remains to be determined is the decision procedure to be used once experimentation is terminated by this plan. For this and other technical reasons it is convenient, as was pointed out in Section 3.9, to separate the statistician's strategy into two components, the sequential-sampling plan and the terminal-decision procedure. For the sake of completeness, we shall summarize the contents of Definition 3.10.3.

The elements of a truncated sequential game are:

(i) A sample space $Z = (Z, \Omega, p')$.

(ii) Vector-valued random variables g_1, \cdots, g_N defined on Z.

Using (i) and (ii), we obtain the new sample space $\mathfrak{X} = (X, \Omega, p)$, where $X = X_1 \times \cdots \times X_N$ and X_i is the range of g_i, for $i = 1, \cdots, N$, and each p_ω in \mathcal{P}_Ω is obtained from a p'_ω in \mathcal{P}'_Ω according to Definition 3.4.2; i.e., p_ω is the joint probability distribution of g_1, \cdots, g_N given ω.

(iii) A space A of terminal actions. In general we place no restrictive assumptions on A; it may be any arbitrary set.

(iv) A set D of functions which map $J \times X$ into A, where J is the set $\{0, 1, \cdots, N\}$ and such that, if $x, y \in X$ and $x_i = y_i$, $i = 1, 2, \cdots$, j, then $d(j, x) = d(j, y)$ for all $d \in D$.

(v) A class \mathfrak{S} of partitions of X such that

(a) If $\mathcal{S} \in \mathfrak{S}$ then $\mathcal{S} = (S_0, S_1, \cdots, S_N)$.

(b) If $x, y \in X$ and $x_i = y_i$ for $i = 1, \cdots, j$, then $x \in S_j$ if and only if $y \in S_j$. That is, each S_j is a cylinder set over $K = \{r \in J : 0 < r \leq j\}$.

The product space $\mathfrak{S} \times D$ is the space of sequential-decision functions. A partition \mathcal{S} in \mathfrak{S} determines a sequential-sampling plan. The sets S_j of \mathcal{S} are sometimes referred to as "stopping regions." Since S_j is a cylinder set, it is always known in a sequence of experiments whether or not the observations belong to a stopping region, i.e., whether the experiment is to be continued or terminated.

In addition to the above notions, we also need a cost function and a loss function.

(vi) A non-negative bounded function c defined on $J \times X$ such that, if x and y are in X and $x_i = y_i$ for $i = 1, \cdots, j$, then

$$c(j, x) = c(j, y)$$

This last restriction on the cost function c amounts to saying that the sampling cost of experimentation depends only on the subexperiments actually performed. The function c may also be regarded as a set C of bounded cost functions c_j, $j = 0, 1, \cdots, N$, where $c_j(x)$ with $j \neq 0$ is the cost of observing x_1, \cdots, x_j, when x is the point in the sample space, and $c_0(x) = 0$.

(vii) A bounded non-negative function L defined on $\Omega \times A$. $L(\omega, a)$ represents the loss when p_ω is the true distribution of x and the statistician takes action a. Using (vi) and (vii), the risk to the statistician is given by the function ρ which is defined as follows [see Definition 3.10.2]:

$$\rho(\omega, \mathcal{S}, d) = \sum_{j=0}^{N} \sum_{x \in S_j} [c_j(x) + L(\omega, d(j, x))] p_\omega(x)$$

The triple $(\Omega, \mathfrak{S} \times D, \rho)$ is a *truncated sequential game*.

9.2. Bayes Procedures for Sequential Games

The main results of this section are: (1) For any arbitrary sampling plan \mathcal{S} and for any a priori probability distribution ξ on Ω, there always exists, at least to within any $\epsilon > 0$, an optimal terminal-decision procedure. (2) For any ξ, there always exists an optimal sampling plan which is briefly characterized as follows: At any stage of experimenta-

tion, if there exists a continuation that will reduce the risk below the present level, we perform an additional subexperiment. If, on the other hand, there exists no such continuation, we stop experimenting. The above two results are incorporated in Theorems 9.2.1 and 9.2.2 respectively.

Let Ξ be the class of a priori distributions over Ω, i.e., the class of mixed strategies for nature. Then, for any ξ in Ξ, the expected risk is

$$(9.2.1)\quad \rho(\xi, \mathsf{s}, d) = \sum_{j=0}^{N} \sum_{x \, \varepsilon \, S_j} \sum_{\omega} [c_j(x) + L(\omega, d(j, x))]\xi(\omega)p_\omega(x)$$

We introduce the following notation:

$$(9.2.2)\qquad\qquad P_\xi(x) = \sum_{\omega} \xi(\omega)p_\omega(x)$$

(9.2.3) $\mathfrak{B}_j =$ the collection of all sets B_j such that, for some $x \, \varepsilon \, X$, $y \, \varepsilon \, B_j$ if and only if $y_i = x_i$ for all $i \le j$. That is, B_j is a cylinder set over $K = \{r \, \varepsilon \, J : 0 < r \le j\}$. For any $x \, \varepsilon \, X$ we also define $F_j(x)$ as the set of all points having the same first j coordinates as x. Thus, for a fixed j, the sets $F_j(x)$ are equal for all $x \, \varepsilon \, B_j$.

For any bounded function h on $\Omega \times X$, let $E_{j\xi}(h)$ be the conditional expectation of h given x_1, x_2, \cdots, x_j, when ω has distribution ξ, and, for fixed ω, x has distribution p_ω. For any x, the value of $E_{j\xi}(h)$ at x is

$$(9.2.4)\qquad E_{j\xi}(h) = \frac{\displaystyle\sum_{y \, \varepsilon \, F_j(x)} \sum_{\omega} \xi(\omega)p_\omega(y)h(\omega, y)}{\displaystyle\sum_{y \, \varepsilon \, F_j(x)} P_\xi(y)}$$

Note that, if $j = 0$, $\mathfrak{B}_0 = \{X\}$, so that we can write $E_\xi(h)$ for $E_{0\xi}(h)$.

The function $E_{j\xi}(h) = v(x)$ is a function of x_1, x_2, \cdots, x_j only and has the following property: For any bounded function f on X which depends only on x_1, x_2, \cdots, x_j,

$$(9.2.5)\quad \sum_{\omega} \sum_{x} \xi(\omega)p_\omega(x)f(x)h(\omega, x) = \sum_{\omega} \sum_{x} \xi(\omega)p_\omega(x)f(x)v(x)$$

$$= \sum_{x} f(x)v(x)P_\xi(x)$$

The second equality is immediate, and the first is obtained by substituting for $v(x)$ its defining expression above, summing over the elements of the partition \mathfrak{B}_j, and using the fact that f is constant over a

given set $F_j(x)$. More specifically, we have

$$\sum_\omega \sum_x \xi(\omega)p_\omega(x)f(x)v(x)$$

$$= \sum_\omega \sum_x \xi(\omega)p_\omega(x)f(x) \left(\frac{\displaystyle\sum_{y\,\varepsilon\,F_j(x)} \sum_\theta \xi(\theta)p_\theta(y)h(\theta,\,y)}{\displaystyle\sum_{y\,\varepsilon\,F_j(x)} P_\xi(y)} \right)$$

$$= \sum_x P_\xi(x) \left(\frac{\displaystyle\sum_{y\,\varepsilon\,F_j(x)} \sum_\theta f(y)\xi(\theta)p_\theta(y)h(\theta,\,y)}{\displaystyle\sum_{y\,\varepsilon\,F_j(x)} P_\xi(y)} \right)$$

$$= \sum_{B_j\,\varepsilon\,\mathfrak{B}_j} \sum_{x\,\varepsilon\,B_j} P_\xi(x) \left(\frac{\displaystyle\sum_{y\,\varepsilon\,F_j(x)} \sum_\theta f(y)\xi(\theta)p_\theta(y)h(\theta,\,y)}{\displaystyle\sum_{y\,\varepsilon\,F_j(x)} P_\xi(y)} \right)$$

$$= \sum_{B_j\,\varepsilon\,\mathfrak{B}_j} \left(\sum_{x\,\varepsilon\,B_j} P_\xi(x) \right) \left(\frac{\displaystyle\sum_{y\,\varepsilon\,B_j} \sum_\theta f(y)\xi(\theta)p_\theta(y)h(\theta,\,y)}{\displaystyle\sum_{y\,\varepsilon\,B_j} P_\xi(y)} \right)$$

$$= \sum_{B_j\,\varepsilon\,\mathfrak{B}_j} \sum_{y\,\varepsilon\,B_j} \sum_\theta f(y)\xi(\theta)p_\theta(y)h(\theta,\,y)$$

$$= \sum_\omega \sum_x \xi(\omega)p_\omega(x)f(x)h(\omega,\,x)$$

In case h is a function of x only, i.e., $h(\omega,\,x) = g(x)$, we have from equation (9.2.5)

$$(9.2.6) \qquad \sum_x f(x)g(x)P_\xi(x) = \sum_x f(x)(E_{j\xi}[g(x)])P_\xi(x)$$

Let $f(x) = f_j(x)$ be the characteristic function of S_j, and let $h(\omega,\,x) = h_j(\omega,\,x) = c_j(x) + L(\omega,\,d(j,\,x))$; then (9.2.1) can be expressed as

$$(9.2.7) \qquad \rho(\xi,\,\mathcal{S},\,d) = \sum_{j=0}^{N} \sum_{x\,\varepsilon\,S_j} [c_j(x) + E_{j\xi}(L(\omega,\,d(j,\,x)))]P_\xi(x)$$

Since in most discussions ξ will be fixed, we shall sometimes fail to exhibit it. Thus, taking for h the function whose values are given by $h(\omega,\,x) = L(\omega,\,a)$ for a given a in A, we define

$$(9.2.8) \qquad\qquad \tau_j(x,\,a) = E_{j\xi}[L(\omega,\,a)]$$

$$(9.2.9) \qquad\qquad \tau^*_j(x) = \inf_{a\,\varepsilon\,A} \tau_j(x,\,a)$$

Theorem 9.2.1. For a fixed ξ, there is a sequence of terminal-decision functions d_n such that

$$(9.2.10) \qquad \lim_{n \to \infty} \rho(\xi, \, \text{S}, \, d_n) = \rho^*(\xi, \, \text{S}) = \inf_d \rho(\xi, \, \text{S}, \, d)$$

uniformly in S, where

$$(9.2.11) \qquad \rho^*(\xi, \, \text{S}) = \sum_{j=0}^{N} \sum_{x \, \varepsilon \, S_j} [c_j(x) + \tau^*_j(x)] P_\xi(x)$$

Proof. Fix j and x in (9.2.9). Then, for any n we can find a point $a(j, \, x)$ in A depending on j and x such that

$$(1) \qquad \tau_j(x, \, a(j, \, x)) \leq \tau^*_j(x) + \frac{1}{n}$$

Since for a fixed n we can define d_n by $d_n(j, \, x) = a(j, \, x)$, satisfying (1) for each j and x, then for this d_n

$$(2) \qquad \rho(\xi, \, \text{S}, \, d_n) \leq \rho^*(\xi, \, \text{S}) + \frac{1}{n}$$

for all S as can be seen by substituting (1) into (9.2.7). Thus

$$(3) \qquad \inf_d \rho(\xi, \, \text{S}, \, d) \leq \rho(\xi, \, \text{S}, \, d_n) \leq \rho^*(\xi, \, \text{S}) + \frac{1}{n}$$

On the other hand, it follows from (9.2.7) that for all d

$$(4) \qquad \rho(\xi, \, \text{S}, \, d) \geq \sum_{j=0}^{N} \sum_{x \, \varepsilon \, S_j} [c_j(x) + \tau^*_j(x)] P_\xi(x) = \rho^*(\xi, \, \text{S})$$

so that

$$(5) \qquad \inf_d \rho(\xi, \, \text{S}, \, d) \geq \rho^*(\xi, \, \text{S})$$

and, since (3) and (5) hold for all n and S, the theorem is proved.

Theorem 9.2.1 states that, for any arbitrary truncated sequential-sampling plan S and for a given ξ, there always exists (at least to within any $\epsilon > 0$) an optimal terminal-decision procedure. Moreover, the Bayes risk for a given ξ and arbitrary S may be taken to be $\rho^*(\xi, \, \text{S})$ (to be henceforth designated simply by $\rho(\xi, \, \text{S})$) since this value can be approximated to arbitrary accuracy by an appropriate choice of d_n.

It remains to show that, for a given ξ, there exists an optimal sequential-sampling plan S*. A constructive proof of this fact is given as follows:

Let ξ be fixed, and for any function $h(\omega, x)$ we write $E_j(h)$ for the expression in (9.2.4). We also write

(9.2.12) $$U_j(x) = c_j(x) + \tau^*_j(x)$$

We define

(9.2.13) $$\alpha_N(x) = U_N(x)$$

and, by induction backward,

(9.2.14) $$\alpha_j(x) = \min [U_j(x), E_j(\alpha_{j+1}(x))]$$

for $j < N$. More specifically,

(9.2.15)
$$\alpha_N(x) = U_N(x)$$
$$\alpha_{N-1}(x) = \min [U_{N-1}(x), E_{N-1}(\alpha_N(x))]$$
$$\alpha_{N-2}(x) = \min [U_{N-2}(x), E_{N-2}(\alpha_{N-1}(x))]$$

$$\cdot \qquad \cdot \qquad \cdot \qquad \cdot$$
$$\cdot \qquad \cdot \qquad \cdot \qquad \cdot$$
$$\cdot \qquad \cdot \qquad \cdot \qquad \cdot$$

$$\alpha_0 = \min [U_0, E(\alpha_1(x))]$$

where

(9.2.16) $$U_0 = \inf_{a \,\varepsilon\, A} E[L(\omega, a)] = \inf_{a \,\varepsilon\, A} \sum_\omega L(\omega, a)\xi(\omega)$$

Observe that if we had performed all N subexperiments and obtained $x = (x_1, \cdots, x_N)$ then $\alpha_N(x)$ would represent the best we can do with this x. Also, both $U_{N-1}(x)$ and $E_{N-1}(U_N(x))$ depend only on $x_1, x_2, \cdots, x_{N-1}$, and, moreover, $U_{N-1}(x)$ represents the best we can do with $N-1$ observations, and $E_{N-1}(U_N(x))$ represents the average of the best that we can do with an additional observation. Thus $\alpha_{N-1}(x)$ represents the smaller of two risks—the risk of stopping with $N-1$ observations and the average risk from an additional observation. Similarly, $\alpha_{N-2}(x)$ depends only on $x_1, x_2, \cdots, x_{N-2}$ and stands for the smaller of two risks—the risk of stopping with $N-2$ observations and the average risk of going on, provided that if we go on experimenting we do the best we can; i.e., we stop with one more observation if $\alpha_{N-1}(x) = U_{N-1}(x)$ and take a second observation if $\alpha_{N-1}(x) = E_{N-1}(U_N(x))$. The interpretation of $\alpha_{N-k}(x)$ for any k is now clear. Let

(9.2.17) $S^*_j = \{x: U_i(x) > \alpha_i(x)$ for $i < j, U_j(x) = \alpha_j(x)\}$

$$\mathbf{s}^* = (S^*_0, S^*_1, \cdots, S^*_N)$$

Then S^* forms a partition of the sample space X into disjoint sets. That the sets are disjoint follows from the fact that, for any $p < q$, $U_p(x) > \alpha_p(x)$ for all $x \, \varepsilon \, S^*_q$ while $U_p(x) = \alpha_p(x)$ for all $x \, \varepsilon \, S^*_p$. Moreover, every point of X belongs to some S_j. This follows since, for any x we have, by (9.2.13) and (9.2.14), $\alpha_j(x) \geq U_j(x)$ for all j, with equality holding for $j = N$. Let $r \leq N$ be the smallest non-negative integer for which the equality sign holds in this expression. Then $x \, \varepsilon \, S^*_r$. Also the sets S^*_j ($j \neq 0$) are clearly cylinder sets over $K = \{ r \, \varepsilon \, J : 0 < r \leq j \}$.

Thus S^* is a possible sequential-sampling procedure and is characterized as follows: At the jth stage of experimentation $j = 0, 1, \cdots$, we compare the present risk $U_j(x)$ with the average risk $\alpha_j(x)$ resulting from a continuation if at each future stage we did the best we could with the resulting observations. We stop sampling if $U_j(x) = \alpha_j(x)$ and take another observation if $U_j(x) > \alpha_j(x)$. We shall show that S^* is in fact a Bayes sequential-sampling plan.

Theorem 9.2.2. The sequential-sampling plan S^* defined by (9.2.17) is Bayes against ξ, that is,

$$(9.2.18) \qquad \rho(\xi, S^*) = \rho^*(\xi) = \min_{S} \rho(\xi, S)$$

and furthermore

$$(9.2.19) \qquad \rho^*(\xi) = \sum_{j=0}^{N} \sum_{x \, \varepsilon \, S^*_j} \alpha_j(x) P_\xi(x) = \alpha_0$$

Proof. Let $S = (S_0, S_1, \cdots, S_N)$ be any arbitrary truncated sequential-sampling plan, and let

$$(1) \qquad T_r = S_r \cup S_{r+1} \cup \cdots \cup S_N$$

Define

$$(2) \qquad g(r) = \sum_{j=0}^{r-1} \sum_{x \, \varepsilon \, S_j} \alpha_j(x) P_\xi(x) + \sum_{x \, \varepsilon \, T_r} \alpha_r(x) P_\xi(x)$$

$$= \sum_{j=0}^{r} \sum_{x \, \varepsilon \, S_j} \alpha_j(x) P_\xi(x) + \sum_{x \, \varepsilon \, T_{r+1}} \alpha_r(x) P_\xi(x)$$

so that

$$(3) \qquad g(N) = \sum_{j=0}^{N} \sum_{x \, \varepsilon \, S_j} \alpha_j(x) P_\xi(x), \qquad g(0) = \alpha_0$$

Now the set T_{r+1} is defined by $x \notin S_j$ for $j = 0, 1, \cdots, r$ so that T_{r+1} depends only on x_1, \cdots, x_r. Hence letting γ_{r+1} represent the charac-

teristic function of the set T_{r+1} and taking γ_{r+1} for f and α_{r+1} for g in (9.2.6), we obtain

$$(4) \qquad \sum_{x \,\varepsilon\, T_{r+1}} \alpha_{r+1}(x) P_\xi(x) = \sum_{x \,\varepsilon\, T_{r+1}} E_r[\alpha_{r+1}(x)] P_\xi(x)$$

Thus $g(r+1)$ can be written

$$(5) \qquad g(r+1) = \sum_{j=0}^{r} \sum_{x \,\varepsilon\, S_j} \alpha_j(x) P_\xi(x) + \sum_{x \,\varepsilon\, T_{r+1}} E_r[\alpha_{r+1}(x)] P_\xi(x)$$

However, by (9.2.14), $\alpha_r(x) \le E_r[\alpha_{r+1}(x)]$, so that

$$(6) \qquad g(r+1) \ge \sum_{j=0}^{r} \sum_{x \,\varepsilon\, S_j} \alpha_j(x) P_\xi(x) + \sum_{x \,\varepsilon\, T_{r+1}} \alpha_r(x) P_\xi(x) = g(r)$$

for $r = 0, 1, \cdots, N-1$. Thus $g(r)$ is an increasing function of r. Again by (9.2.11) and (9.2.12)

$$(7) \qquad \rho(\xi, \, \mathcal{S}) = \sum_{j=0}^{N} \sum_{x \,\varepsilon\, S_j} U_j(x) P_\xi(x)$$

and in view of (9.2.14) and (3)

$$(8) \qquad \rho(\xi, \, \mathcal{S}) \ge \sum_{j=0}^{N} \sum_{x \,\varepsilon\, S_j} \alpha_j(x) P_\xi(x) = g(N)$$

Hence, for all \mathcal{S} we have

$$(9) \qquad \rho(\xi, \, \mathcal{S}) \ge g(N) \ge g(0) = \alpha_0$$

However, if $\mathcal{S} = \mathcal{S}^*$, the inequality, preceding (6) becomes an equality for $x \,\varepsilon\, T_{r+1}$, since $U_r(x) > \alpha_r(x)$ by (9.2.17), and hence $\alpha_r(x) = E_r[\alpha_{r+1}(x)]$ by (9.2.14). Thus (6) becomes an equality for $r = 0, 1, \cdots, N-1$. Also inequality 8 becomes an equality since $U_j(x) = \alpha_j(x)$ for $x \,\varepsilon\, S_j$ by (9.2.17). This completes the proof of the theorem.

Theorem 9.2.3. The Bayes risk $\rho^*(\xi)$ for a truncated sequential procedure is a concave function of ξ; i.e., for any ξ_1 and ξ_2 and any α, $0 \le \alpha \le 1$,

$$\rho^*(\alpha \xi_1 + (1-\alpha)\xi_2) \ge \alpha \rho^*(\xi_1) + (1-\alpha)\rho^*(\xi_2)$$

Proof. Let $\xi = \alpha \xi_1 + (1-\alpha)\xi_2$. Then for any \mathcal{S} and d

$$(1) \qquad \rho(\xi, \, \mathcal{S}, \, d) = \alpha \rho(\xi_1, \, \mathcal{S}, \, d) + (1-\alpha)\rho(\xi_2, \, \mathcal{S}, \, d)$$

as can be seen from (9.2.1). But for all s and d

(2)

$$\rho(\xi, s, d) \geq \alpha \inf_{(s', d') \varepsilon \, \mathfrak{S} \times D} \rho(\xi_1, s', d') + (1 - \alpha) \inf_{(s', d') \varepsilon \, \mathfrak{S} \times D} \rho(\xi_2, s', d')$$

and hence

(3) $\rho^*(\xi) = \inf_{(s, d) \varepsilon \, \mathfrak{S} \times D} \rho(\xi, s, d) \geq \alpha \rho^*(\xi_1) + (1 - \alpha)\rho^*(\xi_2)$

PROBLEMS

9.2.1. Let y be a binomial random variable with $p_\omega(y = 1) \equiv \omega$, $p_\omega(y = 0) \equiv 1 - \omega$, $0 \leq \omega \leq 1$, and let $\xi(\omega) = 1$ for all ω; i.e., ξ is rectangular on the interval $(0, 1)$. Let s_N be the following sequential-sampling plan. Take independent observations on y in sequence, and stop as soon as $m > 1$ ones have been found, but in any case stop after N observations. Find the optimal estimate of ω if, for any estimate a, $0 \leq a \leq 1$, $L(\omega, a) = 200(\omega - a)^2$.

9.2.2. Consider the same situation as in Problem 9.2.1, but, instead of employing s_N, construct the optimal sequential procedure s^*_N for $N = 5$ if the cost per observation is 1 unit.

9.3. Bayes Sequential Procedures for Constant Cost and Identically and Independently Distributed Observations

We shall here consider the special case in which the random variables g_i $(i = 1, 2, \cdots, N)$ are independent [see Definition 3.11.4] with the same probability distribution f_ω and $c_j(x) = jc$ where c is a positive constant which, by a change in scale, can and will be taken as unity. We shall show that for this case the optimal sequential procedure s^*_N truncated at N observations can be described by means of a decreasing sequence of regions in the space Ξ of all distributions ξ on Ω and in terms of these regions extend these procedures to the non-truncated case as well. More specifically, we shall show that: (1) All the information contained in a sequence of r subexperiments is summarized in the a posteriori probability distribution to be designated by ξ_r, in the sense that we can compute ξ_{r+1}, knowing only ξ_r and x_{r+1}. Moreover, ξ_r is a point in Ξ. (2) There exists an infinite sequence Ξ_0, Ξ_1, Ξ_2, \cdots of subsets of Ξ such that $\Xi_0 = \Xi \supset \Xi_1 \supset \Xi_2 \supset \cdots$ with the property that, if, for a given ξ, s^*_m is the optimal sequential-sampling plan truncated at m observations where the observations are to be taken one at a time in sequence, then s^*_m requires taking no observations if and only if $\xi \varepsilon \Xi_m$. (3) For any ξ, the risk of the sequential plan s^*_N approaches a limit as $N \to \infty$, and the value of this limit is the

same as for the sequential plan S* defined by a stopping region Ξ^* where Ξ^* is the common part of Ξ_i ($i = 0, 1, 2, \cdots$).

In view of the above, S^*_N can be characterized in the following manner. Suppose we have performed j subexperiments and computed ξ_j. Then we are in the same situation as we were initially except that ξ has become ξ_j and the optimal continuation is now the sampling plan S^*_{N-j}. Hence we stop experimenting if and only if $\xi_j \, \varepsilon \, \Xi_{N-j}$. With the non-truncated sequential-sampling plan S*, we stop experimenting if and only if $\xi_j \, \varepsilon \, \Xi^*$.

The details of the above characterizations and extensions of Bayes sampling plans are incorporated in Theorems 9.3.1 and 9.3.3 below. Conditions under which the optimal sequential procedure is necessarily truncated, or is of fixed sample size, are also given in this section.

Let ξ be fixed, and let the symbol ξ_j stand for the a posteriori probability of ω, given the observations x_1, x_2, \cdots, x_j. (Note that the symbol exhibits only the number and not the values of the observed coordinates of a point x. This, however, will not cause any confusion.) Then

$$(9.3.1) \quad \xi_j(\omega) = \frac{\xi(\omega) \sum\limits_{y \, \varepsilon \, F_j(x)} p_\omega(y)}{\sum\limits_{\theta} \sum\limits_{y \, \varepsilon \, F_j(x)} \xi(\theta) p_\theta(y)}, \qquad y = (y_1, \cdots, y_N)$$

Now, since the x_i's are independent and have the same distribution, say $f_\omega(x_i)$, we have $p_\omega(x) = \prod\limits_{i=1}^{N} f_\omega(x_i)$. Let $x = (u, v)$ where $u = (x_1, \cdots, x_j)$ and $v = (x_{j+1}, \cdots, x_N)$, and let V be the set consisting of all points v. Then since $\sum\limits_{x \, \varepsilon \, V} \prod\limits_{i=j+1}^{N} f_\omega(x_i) = 1$, we have

$$(9.3.2) \quad \xi_j(\omega) = \frac{\xi(\omega) \prod\limits_{i=1}^{j} f_\omega(x_i)}{\sum\limits_{\theta} \prod\limits_{i=1}^{j} f_\theta(x_i) \xi(\theta)}$$

which is clearly independent of N.

By direct computation we also observe that

$$(9.3.3) \quad \xi_{j+1}(\omega) = \frac{\xi_j(\omega) f_\omega(x_{j+1})}{\sum\limits_{\theta} f_\theta(x_{j+1}) \xi_j(\theta)}$$

Thus the a posteriori probability distribution ξ_j becomes the a priori probability distribution for the next observation (or observations).

More generally, knowing only ξ_j and x_{j+1}, we can compute the a posteriori probability for ω, given all the x_i's from 1 to $j+1$. This, of course, no longer holds if the x_i's are not independent, since in that case additional information, viz., the conditional distribution of x_{j+1}, given x_1, \cdots, x_j, would be required for each ω. In addition, since the x_i's are identically distributed, the functional form of $\xi_{j+1}(\omega)$ in (9.3.3) is the same for all $j = 0, 1, \cdots$. The above can be summarized by saying that a given sequence of j observations results in a point $\xi = \xi_j$ in Ξ, and an additional observation transforms ξ into a different point in Ξ, the transformation being given by (9.3.3). We shall designate this transformation by T so that equation 9.3.3 becomes $\xi_{j+1} = T\xi_j$.

Let g be a real-valued and bounded function on Ξ (for example, $g(\xi) = \inf_{a} \sum_{\omega} L(\omega, a)\xi(\omega)$), and for any $\xi \in \Xi$ let

$$h(\xi) = E_0[g(T\xi)] = E[g(T\xi)]$$

where, by definition,

$$E[g(T\xi)] = \sum_{x_1} \sum_{\omega} g(T\xi)\xi(\omega)f_\omega(x_1)$$

Consider now the conditional expected value of ξ_{j+1}, given x_1, x_2, \cdots, x_j. This can be written as

$$(9.3.4) \qquad E_j[g(T\xi_j)] = \sum_{x_{j+1}} \sum_{\omega} g(T\xi_j)\xi_j(\omega)f_\omega(x_{j+1})$$

as can be seen from the definition of the symbol E_j and the fact that the x_i's are independent. Since the x_i's are also identically distributed, the above equation shows that, if we set $\xi' = \xi_j$, then

$$E_j[g(T\xi_j)] = E[g(T\xi')] = h(\xi')$$

These remarks are to be borne in mind in the subsequent discussions.

For any bounded function q defined on Ω, the conditional expected value of q, given x_1, x_2, \cdots, x_j, can be written in terms of ξ_j as

$$(9.3.5) \qquad E_j(q) = \sum_{\omega} \xi_j(\omega)q(\omega)$$

In particular, $\tau_j(x, a)$ [see 9.2.8] in this notation is given by

$$(9.3.6) \qquad \tau_j(x, a) = \sum_{\omega} \xi_j(\omega)L(\omega, a)$$

and hence

$$(9.3.7) \qquad \tau^*_j(x) = \inf_{a \,\varepsilon\, A} \tau_j(x, a) = \psi(\xi_j)$$

Note that the domain of ψ is the space Ξ, and the functional form of ψ is the same for all j. Hence, for the problem under consideration, the risk $\rho(\xi, \mathcal{S}_N)$ [see (9.2.11)] for any truncated sequential-sampling plan $\mathcal{S}_N = (S_0, S_1, \cdots, S_N)$ can be written as

$$(9.3.8) \qquad \rho(\xi, \mathcal{S}_N) = \sum_{j=0}^{N} \sum_{x \, \varepsilon \, S_j} [j + \psi(\xi_j)] P_\xi(x)$$

Theorem 9.3.1. (a) There is a monotonically non-increasing sequence of subsets of Ξ, $\Xi_0 = \Xi$, Ξ_1, Ξ_2, \cdots, such that, for any N and ξ, the best truncated sequential procedure $\mathcal{S}^*_N = (S^*_{0N}, S^*_{1N}, \cdots, S^*_{NN})$ is described by

$$(9.3.9) \qquad S^*_{jN} = \{x : \xi_r \notin \Xi_{N-r} \text{ for } r < j, \; \xi_j \, \varepsilon \, \Xi_{N-j}\}$$

(b) If $\rho^*_N(\xi)$ is the Bayes risk from \mathcal{S}^*_N, then $\rho^*_N(\xi)$ approaches a limit, say $\rho^*(\xi)$, as $N \to \infty$.

(c) If $\mathfrak{I}_m = (T_0, T_1, \cdots, T_{m-1}, V_m)$ is the procedure

$$(9.3.10) \qquad T_j = \{x : \xi_r \notin \Xi^* \text{ for } r < j, \; \xi_j \, \varepsilon \, \Xi^*\}$$

$$V_m = C(T_0 \cup T_1 \cup \cdots \cup T_{m-1}) = \{x : \xi_j \notin \Xi^* \text{ for } j < m\}$$

where Ξ^* is the common part of the sets Ξ_r $(r = 0, 1, \cdots)$ then $\rho^*(\xi, \mathfrak{I}_m) \to \rho^*(\xi)$ uniformly in ξ as $m \to \infty$.

(d) In (b), the approach of $\rho^*_N(\xi)$ to $\rho^*(\xi)$ is uniform in ξ.

Proof. (a) We define functions h_0, h_1, \cdots, on Ξ as follows:

$$(1) \qquad h_0(\xi) = \psi(\xi) = \inf_a \sum_\omega \xi(\omega) L(\omega, a)$$

(see (9.3.7)) and by induction on j, $j > 0$,

$$(2) \qquad h_j(\xi) = \min [\psi(\xi), 1 + E(h_{j-1}(T\xi))]$$

We shall later show that h_m is in fact the risk function of a sequential procedure truncated at m observations. We also define

$$(3) \qquad U_j = j + \psi(\xi_j)$$

$$(4) \qquad \alpha_{NN} = U_N$$

and by induction backward

$$(5) \qquad \alpha_{jN} = \min [U_j, E_j(\alpha_{j+1, \, N})]$$

for $j < N$. We note that

$$(6) \qquad \alpha_{NN} = N + \psi(\xi_N) = N + \psi(T\xi_{N-1}) = N + h_0(T\xi_{N-1})$$

$$\alpha_{N-1,\,N} = \min\,[N - 1 + \psi(\xi_{N-1}),\, N + E_{N-1}(h_0(T\xi_{N-1}))]$$

$$= N - 1 + \min\,[\psi(\xi_{N-1}),\, 1 + E_{N-1}(h_0(T\xi_{N-1}))]$$

$$= N - 1 + h_1(\xi_{N-1})$$

The last expression follows from (2) and the introductory remarks to this discussion.

By a similar argument we have

$$(7) \quad \alpha_{N-2,\,N} = \min\,[N - 2 + \psi(\xi_{N-2}),\, N - 1 + E_{N-2}(h_1(\xi_{N-1}))]$$

$$= N - 2 + \min\,[\psi(\xi_{N-2}),\, 1 + E_{N-2}(h_1(T\xi_{N-2}))]$$

$$= N - 2 + h_2(\xi_{N-2})$$

and so forth. In general, we have

$$(8) \quad \alpha_{N-j,\,N} = \min\,[N - j + \psi(\xi_{N-j}),$$

$$N - j + 1 + E_{N-j}(h_{j-1}(T\xi_{N-j}))] = N - j + h_j(\xi_{N-j})$$

By Theorem 9.2.2 the optimal sequential procedure is characterized by [see 9.2.17]

$$(9) \qquad S^*_{jN} = \{x: \alpha_{rN} < U_r \quad \text{for} \quad r < j,\ \alpha_{jN} = U_j\}$$

Hence, writing $r = N - (N - r)$ and employing (3) and (8), we have

$$(10) \quad S^*_{jN} = \{x: h_{N-r}(\xi_r) < \psi(\xi_r) \quad \text{for} \quad r < j,\ h_{N-j}(\xi_j) = \psi(\xi_j)\}$$

Now consider the sets Ξ_j in Ξ defined by

$$(11) \qquad\qquad \Xi_j = \{\xi: h_j(\xi) = \psi(\xi)\}$$

Then the following identity holds:

$$(12) \quad \{x: \xi_r \notin \Xi_{N-r} \quad \text{for} \quad r < j,\ \xi_j \,\varepsilon\, \Xi_{N-j}\}$$

$$= \{x: h_{N-r}(\xi_r) \neq \psi(\xi_r) \quad \text{for} \quad r < j,\ h_{N-j}(\xi_j) = \psi(\xi_j)\}$$

But, by (2), if $h_j(\xi) \neq \psi(\xi)$, then $h_j(\xi) < \psi(\xi)$ for all j, so that the \neq sign in the second expression in (12) can be replaced by the $<$ sign. This implies that the sequential procedure S^*_N defined by (10) can be expressed as

$$(13) \qquad S^*_{jN} = \{x: \xi_r \notin \Xi_{N-r} \quad \text{for} \quad r < j,\ \xi_j \,\varepsilon\, \Xi_{N-j}\}$$

which proves one part of (a).

To show that the sets Ξ_j are decreasing with j is equivalent to showing that $h_j(\xi)$ is a decreasing function of j for a fixed ξ. For suppose

the contrary, and let $\xi \varepsilon \Xi_{j+1}$ and $\xi \notin \Xi_j$. Then $h_{j+1}(\xi) = \psi(\xi)$ and $h_j(\xi) \neq \psi(\xi)$; i.e., $h_j(\xi) < \psi(\xi) = h_{j+1}(\xi)$ which contradicts the assumption that $h_j(\xi) \geq h_{j+1}(\xi)$. Now from (6)

$$(14) \qquad h_j(\xi) = \alpha_{N-j,\,N} + (j - N)$$

Replacing N by $N + 1$ and j by $j + 1$, we get

$$(15) \qquad h_{j+1}(\xi) = \alpha_{N-j,\,N+1} + (j - N)$$

so that

$$(16) \qquad h_j(\xi) - h_{j+1}(\xi) = \alpha_{N-j,\,N} - \alpha_{N-j,\,N+1}$$

It remains to show that the right side of (16) is non-negative. This is equivalent to showing that α_{kN} decreases as N increases. We have

$$(17) \qquad \alpha_{N,\,N+1} = \min\,[\alpha_{NN}, E_N(\alpha_{N+1,\,N+1})] \leq \alpha_{NN}$$

Applying an induction backward, we assume that $\alpha_{k,\,N+1} \leq \alpha_{kN}$ for $k > j$. Then

$$(18) \qquad \alpha_{j,\,N+1} = \min\,[U_j, E_j(\alpha_{j+1,\,N+1})]$$
$$\leq \min\,[U_j, E_j(\alpha_{j+1,\,N})] = \alpha_{jN}$$

which completes the proof of part a of Theorem 9.3.1.

Proof. (*b*) Since for a given ξ a possible sequential procedure truncated at $N + 1$ is to discard the $(N + 1)$st observation and employ the procedure s^*_N, it must follow that $\rho^*_{N+1}(\xi) \leq \rho^*_N(\xi)$. Thus $\rho^*_N(\xi)$ for a fixed ξ is a decreasing function of N and hence converges to a limit, say $\rho^*(\xi)$.

Proof. (*c*) To prove part c of Theorem 9.3.1 we need the following two lemmas.

Lemma 9.3.1. Let S^*_{jN} and T_j be defined as in (9.3.9) and (9.3.10) respectively. That is,

$$S^*_{jN} = \{x: \xi_r \notin \Xi_{N-r} \text{ for } r < j, \ \xi_j \varepsilon \Xi_{N-j}\}$$
$$T_j = \{x: \xi_r \notin \Xi^* \text{ for } r < j, \ \xi_j \varepsilon \Xi^*\}$$

Then

$$\lim_{N \to \infty} S^*_{jN} = T_j$$

Proof. We define

$$K_{jN} = \{x: \xi_j \varepsilon \Xi_{N-j}\}, \qquad K_j = \{x: \xi_j \varepsilon \Xi^*\}$$

Then

$$S^*_{jN} = K_{jN} - \bigcup_{r<j} K_{rN}$$

$$T_j = K_j - \bigcup_{r<j} K_r$$

Now the sets Ξ_q are monotonically non-increasing, and therefore

$$\lim_{N \to \infty} K_{jN} = K_j, \qquad \lim_{N \to \infty} \bigcup_{r<j} K_{rN} = \bigcup_{r<j} K_r$$

which proves the lemma.

Lemma 9.3.2. Let S_N be any sequential-sampling procedure resulting in a risk $\rho(\xi, S_N)$ for a given ξ, and let S_m with risk $\rho(\xi, S_m)$ be the truncation of S_N at $m \leq N$; i.e., S_m is the procedure that follows S_N up to $m - 1$ observations but always terminates at the mth observation. Then

(19) $$\rho(\xi, S_m) \leq \rho(\xi, S_N)\left[1 + \frac{M}{m}\right]$$

where

(20) $$M = \sup_{\omega, a} L(\omega, a)$$

Proof. From (9.2.11) we have, since $\tau^*_j(x)$ is non-negative for all j and x,

(21) $$\rho(\xi, S_N) = \sum_{j=0}^{N} \sum_{x \,\varepsilon\, S_j} (j + \tau^*_j(x))P_\xi(x)$$

$$\geq \sum_{j=0}^{m-1} \sum_{x \,\varepsilon\, S_j} (j + \tau^*_j(x))P_\xi(x) + m \sum_{x \,\varepsilon\, W_m} P_\xi(x)$$

where $W_m = C(S_0 \cup S_1 \cup \cdots \cup S_{m-1})$. Also

(22) $$\rho(\xi, S_m) = \sum_{j=0}^{m-1} \sum_{x \,\varepsilon\, S_j} (j + \tau^*_j(x))P_\xi(x) + \sum_{x \,\varepsilon\, W_m} (m + \tau^*_m(x)P_\xi(x)$$

$$\leq \rho(\xi, S_N) + M \sum_{x \,\varepsilon\, W_m} P_\xi(x)$$

But, by (21), $\sum_{x \,\varepsilon\, W_m} P_\xi(x) \leq \rho(\xi, S_N)/m$. Substituting this expression

into (22) yields (19). This completes the proof of Lemma 9.3.2.

Now, for a fixed ξ, let f_{jN} be the characteristic function of the set S^*_{jN} in (13) for $j < m$ and g_{mN} be the characteristic function of the

set $C(S_{0N} \cup S_{1N} \cup \cdots \cup S_{m-1, N})$. Also let \mathcal{S}_{mN} be the truncation of \mathcal{S}^*_N at $m < N$. Then, if $\rho^*_{mN}(\xi)$ is the risk of \mathcal{S}_{mN},

$$(23) \quad \rho^*_{mN}(\xi) = \sum_{j=0}^{m-1} \sum_x f_{jN}(x) U_j(x) P_\xi(x) + \sum_x g_{mN}(x) U_m(x) P_\xi(x)$$

Now, by Lemma 9.3.1, $f_{jN}(x) \to f^*_j(x)$ and $g_{mN}(x) \to g^*_m(x)$ as $N \to \infty$, where f^*_j is the characteristic function of the set T_j [see (9.3.10)] for $j < m$ and g^*_m is the characteristic function of the set V_m. Hence, by Theorem 3.11.5 and the fact that for a procedure truncated at m, $P_\xi(x)$ can be taken to be $\sum_\omega \xi(\omega) \prod_{i=1}^m f_\omega(x_i)$,

$$(24) \quad \lim_{N \to \infty} \rho^*_{mN}(\xi) = \sum_{j=0}^{m-1} \sum_x f^*_j(x) U_j(x) P_\xi(x) + \sum_x g^*_m(x) U_m(x) P_\xi(x)$$

$$= \rho(\xi, \mathfrak{I}_m)$$

Now $\rho^*_N(\xi) \le \rho^*_{mN}(\xi)$ for all N. Hence, applying Lemma 9.3.2, we get

$$(25) \qquad \rho^*_N(\xi) \le \rho^*_{mN}(\xi) \le \rho^*_N(\xi) \left(1 + \frac{M}{m}\right)$$

and, letting $N \to \infty$, we get

$$(26) \qquad \rho^*(\xi) \le \rho(\xi, \mathfrak{I}_m) \le \rho^*(\xi) \left(1 + \frac{M}{m}\right) \le \rho^*(\xi) + \frac{M^2}{m}$$

Consequently $\rho(\xi, \mathfrak{I}_m) \to \rho^*(\xi)$ as $m \to \infty$, and, moreover, the convergence is uniform in ξ.

Proof. (d) The truth of part (d) of Theorem 9.3.1 follows from the inequalities

$$(27) \qquad \rho^*(\xi) \le \rho^*_N(\xi) \le \rho(\xi, \mathfrak{I}_N) \le \rho^*(\xi) \left(1 + \frac{M}{N}\right)$$

Theorem 9.3.2. Let $\rho^*_N(\xi)$ for a given ξ be the Bayes risk from the optimal sequential procedure \mathcal{S}^*_N truncated at N. Then

$$(9.3.11) \qquad \rho^*_N(\xi) = \min \left[\psi(\xi), 1 + E(\rho^*_{N-1}(T\xi))\right]$$

Proof. From (9.2.19) together with (8) Theorem 9.3.1 with $j = N$, we have

$$(1) \qquad\qquad \rho^*_N(\xi) = \alpha_{0N} = h_N(\xi)$$

But by (2), Theorem 9.3.1,

(2) $h_N(\xi) = \min\,[\psi(\xi),\, 1 + E(h_{N-1}(T\xi))]$

Combining (1) and (2) yields the theorem.

Corollary. If, for a given ξ, $\rho^*(\xi)$ is the Bayes risk from the optimal non-truncated procedure, then

(9.3.12) $\rho^*(\xi) = \min\,[\psi(\xi),\, 1 + E(\rho^*(T\xi))]$

Proof. This corollary follows from Theorems 9.3.2 and 9.3.1.

For the type of decision problems under consideration, Theorem 9.3.1 describes the stopping regions S^*_{jN} of the optimal sequential procedure truncated at N observations in terms of sets of points $x \,\varepsilon\, X$ whose first j coordinates result in a posteriori probabilities which are points in a specified region Ξ_j of Ξ. This suggests an intrinsic characterization of S^*_N in terms of regions in Ξ without any direct reference to the space X. This is often advantageous, especially when Ξ is the fundamental probability simplex in h space; i.e., Ω consists only of h elements, and h is not large [see Chapter 10].

Suppose we are given an a priori probability ξ on Ω and wish to employ a sequential procedure truncated at N observations. Assume that the regions Ξ_j ($j = 0, 1, \cdots, N$) have been determined. (Note that the characterization of these regions on a given space Ξ depends only on the space A of possible actions, the loss function L, and the distribution function of a single coordinate.)

Now the set Ξ_N is such that, if the initial ξ is in Ξ_N, there will be no advantage in taking N or fewer observations before reaching a decision; in this case the risk is $\rho^*_N(\xi) = \psi(\xi)$. On the other hand, if the initial ξ is not in Ξ_N, we will incur a smaller risk, namely, $\rho^*_N(\xi) = 1 + E[\rho^*_{N-1}(T\xi)]$ by taking an observation and then following the optimal procedure S^*_{N-1}. Similarly the set Ξ_{N-1} is such that, if $\xi_1 = T\xi$ is in Ξ_{N-1}, we will gain nothing by expending any or all of our $N - 1$ remaining observations, whereas, if ξ_1 is not in Ξ_{N-1}, we will run a smaller risk by taking an observation and following S^*_{N-2}. It should be emphasized moreover that the taking of one observation has the effect of transforming the initial distribution ξ into a new distribution $\xi_1 = T\xi$, and that in terms of the new ξ_1 we are back to the original problem except that N has been reduced by 1. Keeping this point in mind, the extension of this argument is clear and justifies the description of the optimal sequential procedures given in the introduction to this section.

If a given problem does not specify an upper bound to the number of subexperiments one might perform, then the optimal sequential procedure for a fixed ξ is S^* defined by the limit of the sequential pro-

cedures \mathfrak{I}_m [see (9.3.10)] as $m \to \infty$. However, in certain cases \mathcal{S}^* is necessarily truncated and in fact may be of fixed sample size. The conditions under which this holds is given by the following theorem.

Theorem 9.3.3. If $\psi(\xi_j) \to 0$ uniformly in x, i.e., $\psi(\xi_j) \le \varphi(j)$ for all x and j, where $\varphi(j) \to 0$ as $j \to \infty$, then the optimal sequential procedure is truncated. If $\psi(\xi_j)$ is a function of j only, the optimal sequential procedure \mathcal{S}^* is a fixed sample-size procedure.

Proof. By (7), Theorem 9.3.1, we have that for all N

(1) $h_j(\xi_N) = \min [\psi(\xi_N), 1 + E_N(h_{j-1}(T\xi_N))]$

so that, for any j, $h_j(\xi_N) = \psi(\xi_N)$ whenever $\psi(\xi_N) < 1$. Since $\psi(\xi_N) < 1$ for sufficiently large N, say $N \ge N_0$, we have $h_j(\xi_{N_0}) = \psi(\xi_{N_0})$ for all j; i.e., $\xi N_0 \, \varepsilon \, \Xi_j$ for all j, and hence $\xi N_0 \, \varepsilon \, \Xi^*$. Thus the optimal procedure does not require more than N_0 observations.

Assume now that $\psi(\xi_j) = g(j)$; then, for any procedure \mathcal{S},

(2) $\rho(\xi, \mathcal{S}) = \sum_j \sum_{x \,\varepsilon\, S_j} [j + g(j)] P_\xi(x)$

$$= \sum_j P_\xi(S_j)[j + g(j)] \ge \min_j [j + g(j)] = j_0 + g(j_0)$$

Since the fixed sample-size procedure with j_0 observations has risk $j_0 + g(j_0)$, it is clearly optimal. Note that $g(j)$ will in general depend on ξ.

As an illustration, consider the problem of estimating the probability ω of a "success" from a binomial distribution $p_\omega(x)$ from a sequence of independent trials where for any estimate a the loss is $k(\omega - a)^2$, $k > 0$, and where ξ is rectangular over the interval $(0 \le \omega \le 1)$. The probability of r successes in a sequence of j trials is $\binom{j}{r} \omega^r (1 - \omega)^{j-r}$ so that the Bayes estimate $d(r)$ if sampling terminates with j trials is [see Section 11.2]

$$(9.3.13) \quad d(r) = E_j(\omega) = \frac{\displaystyle\int_0^1 \omega^{r+1}(1 - \omega)^{j-r} \, d\omega}{\displaystyle\int_0^1 \omega^r (1 - \omega)^{j-r} \, d\omega}$$

$$= \frac{\Gamma(r + 2)\Gamma(j - r + 1)\Gamma(j + 2)}{\Gamma(j + 3)\Gamma(r + 1)\Gamma(j - r + 1)} = \frac{r + 1}{j + 2}$$

The Bayes risk $\psi(\xi_j)$ is given by

$$(9.3.14) \qquad \psi(\xi_j) = \frac{k\int_0^1 (\omega - E_{j\xi}(\omega))^2 \omega^r (1-\omega)^{j-r}\, d\omega}{\int_0^1 \omega^r (1-\omega)^{j-r}\, d\omega}$$

$$= \frac{k\int_0^1 \omega^{r+2}(1-\omega)^{j-r}\, d\omega}{\int_0^1 \omega^r (1-\omega)^{j-r}\, d\omega} - k\left(\frac{r+1}{j+2}\right)^2$$

$$= \frac{k(r+2)(r+1)}{(j+3)(j+2)} - k\left(\frac{r+1}{j+2}\right)^2$$

$$= \frac{k(r+1)(j-r+1)}{(j+2)^2(j+3)} \le \frac{k(j+1)^2}{(j+2)^2(j+3)}$$

since $0 \le r \le j$. Thus $\psi(\xi_j) \to 0$ uniformly in r and the best sequential procedure is truncated.

On the other hand, if the loss is taken as $k(\omega - a)^2/\omega(1 - \omega)$, the Bayes estimate is

$$(9.3.15) \qquad d(r) = \frac{E_j(1/(1-\omega))}{E_j(1/\omega(1-\omega))} = \frac{r}{j}$$

as can be seen by direct computations, and $\psi(\xi_j) = k/j$ for all x. Thus the best sequential procedure for this estimation problem is a fixed sample-size procedure.

PROBLEMS

9.3.1. Prove that $E(\rho^*(T\xi))$ is a concave function of ξ. *Hint.* Show that it is a risk function of an optimal sequential procedure where the first observation is costless.

9.3.2. Let $\{G_N\}$ be a sequence of truncated sequential games of the type considered in Section 9.3, and let $\{G'_N\}$ be another sequence of games similar in all respects to G_N except that in each G'_N the loss due to the terminal decision is assumed to be zero whenever all N observations are taken; i.e., $\psi(\xi_N) = 0$ for all ξ and x. Prove

(1) The Bayes sequential procedures $\{S'^*_N\}$ in these modified games are characterized by regions $\Xi'_0 = \Xi$, and a sequence of *increasing* regions Ξ_1, Ξ_2, \cdots in Ξ such that, for a given ξ, S'^*_N will require taking no observations if and only if $\xi \in \Xi'_N$.

(2) $\Xi'_N \subset \Xi_N$ where Ξ_N is the corresponding stopping region in the original game G_N.

(3) If $r^*_N(\xi)$ is the Bayes risk for S'^*_N, then $r^*_N(\xi) \le r^*_{N+1}(\xi) \le \psi(\xi)$ for all N, and hence $r^*_N(\xi) \to r^*(\xi)$ say, as $N \to \infty$, where by definition $r^*_0(\xi) = 0$ for all ξ.

(4) $r^*_N(\xi) = \min [\psi(\xi),\ 1 + E(r^*_{N-1}(T\xi))]$.

(5) If $\rho^*_N(\xi)$ is the Bayes risk in G_N and $\rho^*(\xi) = \lim\limits_{N \to \infty} \rho^*_N(\xi)$, then $r^*_N(\xi) \le \rho^*_N(\xi)$ for all N and $r^*(\xi) = \rho^*(\xi)$.

(6) Let $\Xi'^* = \bigcup\limits_{j=1}^{\infty} \Xi_j$, and let $\mathfrak{I}'_m = (T'_0,\ \cdots,\ T'_{m-1},\ V'_m)$ be the sequential procedure defined by

$$T'_j = \{x : \xi_r \notin \Xi'^* \text{ for } r < j,\ \xi_j \in \Xi'^*\}$$

$$V'_m = C(T'_0 \cup T'_1 \cdots \cup T'_{m-1})$$

Furthermore, let $r^*(\xi, \mathfrak{I}'_m)$ be the risk from \mathfrak{I}'_m in the game G'_m. Then $r(\xi, \mathfrak{I}'_m) \to r^*(\xi)$ as $m \to \infty$. *Hint.* Corresponding to the functions α_{jN} and h_j of Section 9.3 define α'_{jN} and h'_j with $h'_0 = 0$ for the modified game, and prove by an induction backward that α'_{jN} is an *increasing* function of N and hence that h'_j is an *increasing* function of j. Also prove by induction that $h'_j(\xi) < h_j(\xi)$ for all j and ξ. The remaining steps are similar to those employed in the proof of Theorem 9.3.1.

We observe that, for any N, $\rho^*_N(\xi)$ is an upper bound for $\rho^*(\xi)$ and $r^*_N(\xi)$ is a lower bound. Also for any N we have $\Xi'_N \subset \Xi^* \subset \Xi_N$.

9.3.3. Given a decision procedure involving an action space A, a parameter space Ω, a loss function L on $\Omega \times A$, and two independent random variables f and g with respective distribution functions p_ω and q_ω for each $\omega \in \Omega$. Characterize the truncated Bayes sequential procedures in terms of regions in the space Ξ if at each stage the experimenter has the choice of (1) taking an action without further experimentation, (2) taking an observation on the random variable f at a cost of c_1 units, (3) taking an observation on the random variable g at the cost of c_2 units. The observations at all times are independent. *Hint.* For any $\xi \in \Xi$ let $T_f\xi$ be the a posteriori probability if a value on f is observed, and let $T_g\xi$ be the a posteriori probability if a value on g is observed. Define

(1) $$\psi(\xi) = \inf_a \sum_\omega L(\omega, a)\xi(\omega)$$

(2) $$h_0(\xi) = \psi(\xi)$$

and by induction on j

(3) $$h_j(\xi) = \min [\psi(\xi),\ c_1 + Eh_{j-1}(T_f\xi),\ c_2 + Eh_{j-1}(T_g\xi)]$$

Also for each j define

(4) $$\Xi_{0j} = \{\xi : h_j(\xi) = \psi(\xi)\}$$

(5) $$\Xi_{fj} = \{\xi : h_j(\xi) = c_1 + Eh_{j-1}(T_f\xi)\}$$

(6) $$\Xi_{gj} = \{\xi : h_j(\xi) = c_2 + Eh_{j-1}(T_g\xi)\}$$

Suppose that a sequential procedure truncated at N observations is contemplated. By an argument similar to that employed in Section 9.3 show that, after taking j observations, $(j = 0, 1, \cdots, N)$, the optimal procedure is as follows: Let ξ_j be the a posteriori probability distribution, given the j observations. If $\xi_j \in \Xi_{0,\,N-j}$, take the best possible action without further experimentation. If $\xi_j \in \Xi_{f,\,N-j}$, take an

observation on the random variable f; if $\xi_j \, \varepsilon \, \Xi_g, \, _{N-j}$, take an observation on the random variable g; in either case compute ξ_{j+1}, and follow the sequential procedure defined by the regions $\Xi_0, \, _{N-j-1}$, $\Xi_f, \, _{N-j-1}$, and $\Xi_g, \, _{N-j-1}$.

9.4. Bayes Sequential Procedures for Finite Ω

In this section we shall study sequential games of the type considered in Section 9.3, except that we shall restrict Ω to be finite, say, $\Omega = (1, 2, \cdots, h)$. In addition, we shall replace, as we may, the terminal action space A by a subset W of the h-dimensional Cartesian space, where the jth coordinate of a point $\mathbf{w} = (w_1, w_2, \cdots, w_h) \, \varepsilon \, W$ is $L(j, a)$, and assume that W is closed and bounded. In this equivalent game, a terminal-decision rule is a function d with values $d(j, x) = \mathbf{w}(j, x)$ mapping the space $J \times X$ into W where $J = (0, 1, \cdots)$.

Paralleling the definitions given in Section 9.2, we define

$$(9.4.1) \qquad \tau_j(x, \mathbf{w}) = \frac{\sum\limits_{i=1}^{h} w_i \prod\limits_{k=1}^{j} f_i(x_k)\xi(i)}{\sum\limits_{i=1}^{h} \prod\limits_{k=1}^{j} f_i(x_k)\xi(i)} = \sum\limits_{i=1}^{h} w_i\xi_j(i)$$

$$(9.4.2) \qquad \tau^*_j(x) = \inf_{\mathbf{w} \, \varepsilon \, W} \tau_j(x, \mathbf{w}) = \psi(\xi_j)$$

where $\boldsymbol{\xi} = (\xi(1), \cdots, \xi(h)) \, \varepsilon \, \Xi$ represents the a priori probability distribution over Ω and $f_i(x_k)$ is the probability (or density) of x_k when nature is in state i.

Since W is closed and $\tau_j(x, \mathbf{w})$ is linear and hence continuous in the w_i, there exists a terminal-decision procedure d^* with $d^*(j, x) = \mathbf{w}^*(j, x)$ such that $\tau_j(x) = \tau_j(x, \mathbf{w}^*)$. Hence, in view of Theorem 9.2.1, we have

Theorem 9.4.1. For a fixed $\boldsymbol{\xi}$, there exists a terminal-decision function d^* such that

$$(9.4.3) \qquad \rho^*(\boldsymbol{\xi}, \, \mathbb{S}, \, d^*) = \min_d \rho^*(\boldsymbol{\xi}, \, \mathbb{S}, \, d)$$

uniformly in \mathbb{S} where $\boldsymbol{\xi} = (\xi(1), \cdots, \xi(h))$.

Theorem 9.4.2. Let \mathbb{S}^*_N be the Bayes sequential procedure truncated at N, and let \mathbb{S}^* be the Bayes non-truncated procedure. Furthermore, let $\rho^*_N(\boldsymbol{\xi}) = \rho(\boldsymbol{\xi}, \mathbb{S}^*_N, d^*)$ and $\rho^*(\boldsymbol{\xi}) = \rho(\boldsymbol{\xi}, \mathbb{S}^*, d^*)$ be the corresponding risk functions. Then $\rho^*_N(\boldsymbol{\xi})$ and $\rho^*(\boldsymbol{\xi})$ are continuous and concave functions of $\boldsymbol{\xi}$ where $\boldsymbol{\xi} = (\xi(1), \cdots, \xi(h))$.

Proof. Since W is bounded,

$$(1) \qquad \psi(\xi) = \min_{w \, \varepsilon \, W} \sum_{i=1}^{h} w_i \xi(i)$$

is a continuous function of ξ by Theorem 2.2.7. Also, by Theorem 9.3.2

$$(2) \qquad \rho^*_N(\xi) = \min \, [\psi(\xi), \, 1 + E(\rho^*_{N-1}(T\xi))]$$

for all N, so that, for $N = 0$, $\rho^*_0(\xi) = \psi(\xi)$ is a continuous function of ξ. We shall prove this theorem by an induction on N. Assume that $\rho^*_k(\xi)$ is a continuous function of ξ for all $k = 0, 1, \cdots, N - 1$. Then $\rho^*_{N-1}(T\xi)$ is a continuous function of $T\xi$, where

$$(3) \qquad T\xi = \xi_{x_1} = (\xi_{x_1}(1), \, \cdots, \, \xi_{x_1}(h))$$

and

$$(4) \qquad \xi_{x_1}(i) = \frac{f_i(x_1)\xi(i)}{\displaystyle\sum_{j=1}^{h} f_j(x_1)\xi(j)}$$

Now for a fixed x_1, ξ_{x_1} is a continuous function of $\xi = (\xi(1), \cdots, \xi(h))$, so that, for a fixed x_1, $\rho^*_{N-1}(T\xi) = g(\xi, x_1)$ is a continuous function of ξ, since the composition of a continuous function with a continuous function is continuous. It remains to show that $E[g(\xi, x_1)]$, and hence $\min \, [\psi(\xi), \, 1 + E(g(\xi, x_1))]$ is a continuous function of ξ. Now $g(\xi, x_1)$ is uniformly bounded by some number, say K, so that

$$(5) \qquad E(\rho^*_{N-1}(T\xi)) = \sum_{i=1}^{h} \sum_{x_1} f_i(x_1)g(\xi, x_1)\xi(i)$$

$$\leq \sum_{i=1}^{h} \sum_{x_1} K f_i(x_1)\xi(i) = K$$

Thus the series (5) converges uniformly in ξ since it is term by term less than the convergent series $\sum_{i=1}^{h} \sum_{x_i} K f_i(x_1)\xi(i)$, and hence $E(\rho^*_{N-1}(T\xi))$ is continuous.

Now, if Q is a continuous function of u and v, and if k and h are continuous functions of ξ, then $Q(k(\xi), h(\xi))$ is a continuous function of ξ. In particular, $Q(u, v) = \min \, (u, v)$ is a continuous function of u and v, so that, if we set $u = \psi(\xi)$ and $v = 1 + E(\rho^*_{N-1}(T\xi))$, we conclude that $\rho^*_N(\xi)$ is a continuous function of ξ. This completes the induction. The continuity of $\rho^*(\xi)$ follows from Theorem 9.3.1(*d*) which states that $\rho^*_N(\xi) \rightarrow \rho^*(\xi)$ uniformly in ξ.

That $\rho^*_N(\xi)$ is a concave function of ξ has been proved in Theorem 9.2.3. The concavity of $\rho^*(\xi)$ is an immediate consequence of Theorem 2.2.7.

Corollary 1. If Ω is finite, the functions $h_j(\xi)$ defined by equation 8 of Theorem 9.3.1 are continuous and concave functions of ξ for all j.

Proof. The truth of this corollary follows from Theorem 9.4.2 and (1) Theorem 9.3.2.

Let Ω be finite, and for each $\mathbf{w} \; \varepsilon \; W$ let $T(\mathbf{w})$ be a set in Ξ defined by

$$(9.4.4) \qquad T(\mathbf{w}) = \{\xi : \psi(\xi) = \sum_{i=1}^{h} \xi(i) w_i\}$$

That is, $T(\mathbf{w})$ consists of all ξ's for which an optimal terminal decision is \mathbf{w}. Furthermore, let

$$(9.4.5) \qquad \Delta_m(\mathbf{w}) = \Xi_m \cap T(\mathbf{w})$$

where Ξ_m is defined in (11), Theorem 9.3.1. Then $\Delta_m(\mathbf{w})$ is a set in Ξ such that, if $\xi \; \varepsilon \; \Delta_m(\mathbf{w})$, the best procedure truncated at m observations is to decide \mathbf{w} without experimentation [see Theorem 9.3.3].

Theorem 9.4.3. The sets $\Delta_m(\mathbf{w})$ defined in (9.4.5) are closed and convex. If \mathbf{w}_1, $\mathbf{w}_2 \; \varepsilon \; W$ with $\mathbf{w}_1 \neq \mathbf{w}_2$, then $\Delta_m(\mathbf{w}_1)$ and $\Delta_m(\mathbf{w}_2)$ have no interior points in common.

Proof. Both $T(\mathbf{w})$ and Ξ_m are defined by equations involving continuous functions [see Corollary 1, Theorem 9.4.2], and consequently they are closed sets, and, since the intersection of closed sets is closed, it follows that $\Delta_m(\mathbf{w})$ is closed.

Now let λ_1 and λ_2 belong to $\Delta_m(\mathbf{w})$, and let

$$\xi = \alpha\lambda_1 + (1 - \alpha)\lambda_2, \qquad 0 \le \alpha \le 1$$

To show that $\xi \; \varepsilon \; \Delta_m(\mathbf{w})$ also. From (9.3.11) and (1), Theorem 9.4.2, we have

$$(1) \qquad \rho^*_m(\xi) \le \psi(\xi) \le \sum_{i=1}^{h} \xi(i) w_i = \alpha \sum_{i=1}^{h} \lambda_1(i) w_i + (1 - \alpha) \sum_{i=1}^{h} \lambda_2(i) w_i$$

But, since $\lambda_1, \lambda_2 \; \varepsilon \; \Delta_m(\mathbf{w})$, then by (9.4.4) and (11), Theorem 9.3.1,

$$(2) \qquad \sum_{i=1}^{h} \xi(i) w_i = \alpha\psi(\lambda_1) + (1 - \alpha)\psi(\lambda_2)$$

$$= \alpha\rho^*_m(\lambda_1) + (1 - \alpha)\rho^*_m(\lambda_2)$$

Also, by Theorem 9.4.2, $\rho^*_m(\boldsymbol{\xi})$ is a concave function of $\boldsymbol{\xi}$. That is

(3) $$\rho^*_m(\boldsymbol{\xi}) \geq \alpha\rho^*_m(\lambda_1) + (1 - \alpha)\rho^*_m(\lambda_2)$$

We therefore have

(4) $$\alpha\rho^*_m(\lambda_1) + (1 - \alpha)\rho^*_m(\lambda_2) \leq \rho^*_m(\boldsymbol{\xi}) \leq \psi(\boldsymbol{\xi}) \leq \sum_{i=1}^{n} \xi(i)w_i$$

$$= \alpha\rho^*_m(\lambda_1) + (1 - \alpha)\rho^*_m(\lambda_2)$$

Thus $\psi(\boldsymbol{\xi}) = \sum_{i=1}^{n} \xi(i)w_i$ and $\boldsymbol{\xi} \, \varepsilon \, T(w)$. Also, from (4), $\rho^*_m(\boldsymbol{\xi}) = \psi(\boldsymbol{\xi})$, and hence, by (11), Theorem 9.3.1, $\boldsymbol{\xi} \, \varepsilon \, \Xi_m$, which completes the proof of the convexity of $\Delta_m(w)$. The proof of the last part of the theorem follows the same argument as that employed in the proof of Theorem 6.3.1.

Theorem 9.4.4. Let $T(w)$ be defined by (9.4.4), and let $\Delta(w) = \Xi^* \cap T(w)$ where Ξ^* is the intersection of Ξ_m for all m. Then $\Delta(w)$ is closed and convex, and for any w_1, $w_2 \, \varepsilon \, W$, the sets $\Delta(w_1)$ and $\Delta(w_2)$ have no interior points in common unless $w_1 = w_2$.

Proof. The truth of this theorem follows from Theorem 9.4.3 by noting that the intersection of closed convex sets is a closed convex set. [See Problem 2.2.1.]

PROBLEM

9.4.1. Determine the regions $\Delta_m(w_i)$ for $m = 0, 1, 2, 3$ in Example 1 of Section 10.7.

Bayes and Minimax Sequential Procedures When Both Ω and A Are Finite

10.1. Introduction

The general characterization of Bayes sequential procedures, for the case where $\Omega = (1, 2, \cdots, h)$, $A = (1, 2, \cdots, k)$, where the observations are independent with the same distribution, and where the cost per observation is constant, follows directly from the results of the previous chapter and can be briefly summarized as follows:

Let Ξ be the space of a priori probability distributions on Ω. Then Ξ can be represented as an $(h - 1)$-dimensional simplex with points $\boldsymbol{\xi} = (\xi(1), \xi(2), \cdots, \xi(h))$, $\xi(i) \geq 0$ for all i and $\sum_{j=1}^{h} \xi(j) = 1$. Let W be an $h \times k$ matrix with elements $w_{ij} = L(i, j)$ where $L(i, j)$ is the loss if nature is in state i and the statistician decides j. We shall designate the columns of W by column vectors $\mathbf{w}_1, \mathbf{w}_2, \cdots, \mathbf{w}_k$ so that a decision j is equivalent to the selection of the column \mathbf{w}_j from W. For any sequence of observations x_1, x_2, \cdots, x_r, let $\boldsymbol{\xi}_r = (\xi_r(1), \cdots, \xi_r(h))$ be the a posteriori probability distribution on Ω where

$$(10.1.1) \quad \xi_r(s) = \frac{\xi(s) \prod_{j=1}^{r} f_s(x_j)}{\sum_{i=1}^{h} \xi(i) \prod_{j=1}^{r} f_i(x_j)}, \quad (s = 1, 2, \cdots, h, \quad r = 0, 1, \cdots)$$

and where $f_s(x_j)$ is the probability distribution of x_j $(j = 1, 2, \cdots)$, given that nature is in state s.

First consider the class of Bayes sequential procedures \mathcal{S}^*_N truncated at N observations. Then according to Theorem 9.4.3 there ex-

ist $k(N + 1)$ closed and convex regions $\Delta_m(\mathbf{w}_j)$ $(m = 0, 1, \cdots, N;$ $j = 1, \cdots, k)$ in Ξ which completely characterize this class in the following sense: Initially we are given a $\boldsymbol{\xi}$. If $\boldsymbol{\xi} \; \varepsilon \; \Delta_N(\mathbf{w}_j)$ for some j, we make decision j without any observations. If $\boldsymbol{\xi} \notin \Delta_N(\mathbf{w}_j)$ for any j, we take one observation and compute the a posteriori probability distribution $\boldsymbol{\xi}_1$. We then look at the regions $\Delta_{N-1}(\mathbf{w}_j)$. If $\boldsymbol{\xi}_1 \; \varepsilon \; \Delta_{N-1}(\mathbf{w}_j)$ for some j, we stop taking observations and make decision j. If $\boldsymbol{\xi}_1 \notin \Delta_{N-1}(\mathbf{w}_j)$ for any j, we take a second observation, and so forth. In general, if we have not stopped with the first $r - 1$ observations, we take an additional observation and compute $\boldsymbol{\xi}_r$. If $\boldsymbol{\xi}_r \; \varepsilon \; \Delta_{N-r}(\mathbf{w}_j)$ for some j, we terminate sampling and make decision j. If $\boldsymbol{\xi}_r \notin \Delta_{N-r}(\mathbf{w}_j)$ for any j, we take an additional observation. The quantity $\boldsymbol{\xi}_N$ will belong to $\Delta_0(\mathbf{w}_j) = \Xi_0 \cap T(\mathbf{w}_j)$ for some j since every $\boldsymbol{\xi}$ belongs to some $T(\mathbf{w}_j)$ and $\Xi_0 = \Xi$, so that a decision will be reached at the Nth observation if none was reached before.

The class of non-truncated Bayes procedures \mathcal{S}^* has a somewhat simpler structure since it is completely specified by only k convex regions $\Delta(\mathbf{w}_1), \cdots, \Delta(\mathbf{w}_k)$ in Ξ [see Theorem 9.4.4]. As in the previous case, we take observations in sequence and at the rth stage $(r = 0, 1, 2, \cdots)$ we compute $\boldsymbol{\xi}_r$. If there exists a j such that $\boldsymbol{\xi}_r \; \varepsilon \; \Delta(\mathbf{w}_j)$, we terminate sampling and make decision j. If, on the other hand, $\boldsymbol{\xi}_r \notin \bigcup_{j=1}^{k} \Delta(\mathbf{w}_j)$, we take an additional observation. That sampling in the non-truncated case will terminate with probability one follows from the finiteness of the Bayes risk $\rho^*(\xi)$ [see, for example, proof of (b) in Theorem 9.3.1].

We see then that the problem of characterizing the class of Bayes sequential procedures under consideration is equivalent to the problem of delineating in the space Ξ the convex regions $\Delta_m(\mathbf{w}_j)$ for the truncated case and $\Delta(\mathbf{w}_j)$ for the non-truncated case. We shall indicate here a step-by-step method, beginning with $m = 0$, for determining the boundaries of the regions $\Delta_m(\mathbf{w}_j)$, which will converge to the boundaries of $\Delta(\mathbf{w}_j)$, for the case $h = k = 2$, i.e., dichotomies. This method, as will be seen, can be generalized to any h and k, but a detailed description which would take care of the various pathological cases that might arise seems hardly worth the effort in view of the computational difficulties involved even in the special case to be considered. No direct method has as yet been developed for determining the boundaries of $\Delta(\mathbf{w}_j)$ in the general case. However, for $h = k = 2$ such a method exists, at least from a theoretical point of view, and will be discussed in some detail.

10.2. Method for Determining the Boundaries of the Stopping Regions for Truncated Sequential Dichotomies

Let $\Omega = (1, 2)$, $A = (1, 2)$, $W = \begin{pmatrix} 0 & w_{12} \\ w_{21} & 0 \end{pmatrix}$. That is, we are faced with two alternative hypotheses H_1 and H_2 where under H_1 the probability distribution of an observation x_s is $f_1(x_s)$ $(s = 1, 2, \cdots)$ and under H_2 it is $f_2(x_s)$. If H_i is true and we decide H_j the loss is w_{ij} for $i \neq j$ and zero otherwise. Let $\boldsymbol{\xi} = (\zeta, 1 - \zeta)$ where ζ is the a priori probability for H_1, and hence $1 - \zeta$ is the a priori probability for H_2. Then, writing any function of $\boldsymbol{\xi}$ as a function of ζ, we have

$$(10.2.1) \qquad \rho^*_0(\zeta) = \psi(\zeta) = \min \left[\zeta w_{12}, (1 - \zeta) w_{21} \right]$$

and hence, setting $\gamma_0 = \delta_0 = w_{21}/(w_{21} + w_{12})$, we have

$$(10.2.2) \quad \mathrm{T}(\mathbf{w}_1) = [\delta_0 \leq \zeta \leq 1], \qquad \mathrm{T}(\mathbf{w}_2) = [0 \leq \zeta \leq \gamma_0]$$

Now let $\rho^*_m(\zeta)$ be the risk function from the optimal sequential procedure truncated at m observations. Then by Theorem 9.3.2

$$(10.2.3) \qquad \rho^*_m(\zeta) = \min \{\psi(\zeta), 1 + E[\rho^*_{m-1}(T\zeta)]\}$$

Consider the sets $\Delta_m(\mathbf{w}_1)$ and $\Delta_m(\mathbf{w}_2)$. Since they are closed and convex, they must be closed intervals. But clearly $\zeta = 0$ is an element of $\Delta_m(\mathbf{w}_2)$ and $\zeta = 1$ is an element of $\Delta_m(\mathbf{w}_1)$. Thus there must exist two values of ζ, say $\zeta = \gamma_m$ and $\zeta = \delta_m$ with $\gamma_m \leq \delta_m$ such that

$$(10.2.4) \quad \Delta_m(\mathbf{w}_1) = [\delta_m \leq \zeta \leq 1], \qquad \Delta_m(\mathbf{w}_2) = [0 \leq \zeta \leq \gamma_m]$$

Thus it remains to determine γ_m and δ_m for $m = 0, 1, 2, \cdots$. To this end we prove the following theorem.

Theorem 10.2.1. A necessary and sufficient condition that $\zeta = \zeta_1$ be a boundary point of the set $\Delta_m(\mathbf{w}_j)$, $j = 1$ or 2 is that

$$(10.2.5) \qquad \psi(\zeta_1) = 1 + E[\rho^*_{m-1}(T\zeta_1)]$$

Proof. That the condition is necessary follows from the continuity of the risk function $\rho^*_m(\zeta)$ [see Theorem 9.4.2] which implies that for a boundary point the risk of making an optimal decision without observations must equal the risk of taking one observation and employing the optimal sequential procedure from then on. To prove the sufficiency of the condition, we observe that $E[\rho^*_{m-1}(T\zeta)]$ is a risk function of a Bayes sequential procedure truncated at m observations when the first observation is costless [see Problem 9.4.1] so that it is a continuous

and concave function of ζ. Moreover, this function vanishes at $\zeta = 0$ and $\zeta = 1$.

Now suppose first that $\psi(\zeta_1) = \zeta_1 w_{21}$, and consider any $\zeta_2 < \zeta_1$ for which it definitely pays to make decision \mathbf{w}_2 without experimentation; i.e.,

$$(1) \qquad \zeta_2 w_{21} < 1 + E[\rho^*_{m-1}(T\zeta_2)]$$

Then if we multiply (10.2.5) by α and (1) by $1 - \alpha$ where $0 < \alpha < 1$ and set $\zeta = \alpha\zeta_1 + (1 - \alpha)\zeta_2$ we get

$$(2) \qquad \zeta w_{21} < 1 + \alpha E[\rho^*_{m-1}(T\zeta_1)] + (1 - \alpha)E[\rho^*_{m-1}(T\zeta_2)]$$
$$\leq 1 + E[\rho^*_{m-1}(T\zeta)]$$

Thus, for all $\zeta < \zeta_1$,

$$\zeta w_{21} < 1 + E[\rho^*_{m-1}(T\zeta)]$$

and, since equality holds for $\zeta = \zeta_1$, it must follow that, for a ζ in a small neighborhood beyond ζ_1,

$$\zeta w_{21} > 1 + E[\rho^*_{m-1}(T\zeta)]$$

A similar argument can be applied to the case $\psi(\zeta_1) = (1 - \zeta_1)w_{12}$. Thus either $\psi(\zeta) \leq 1 + E[\rho^*_{m-1}(T\zeta)]$ for all ζ, i.e., there exists no ζ for which it pays to take observations, or the curve $y = \psi(\zeta)$ will intersect the curve $y = 1 + E[\rho^*_{m-1}(T\zeta)]$ at exactly two values of ζ which are the boundary points of the stopping regions $\Delta_m(\mathbf{w}_1)$ and $\Delta_m(\mathbf{w}_2)$. [See Figure 13.]

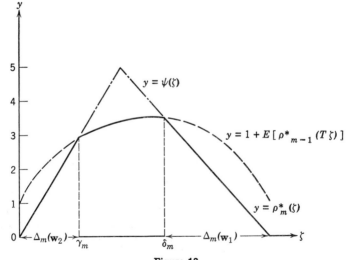

Figure 13

We see then that the problem of determining γ_m and δ_m, as well as $\rho^*_m(\zeta)$, reduces itself to the problem of obtaining the functional form of $E[\rho^*_{m-1}(T\zeta)]$. The latter is in turn solvable if we know the functional form of $\rho^*_{m-1}(\zeta)$ and are able to compute the expectation of $\rho^*_{m-1}(T\zeta)$ for each ζ.

Assume that the function $\rho^*_{m-1}(\zeta)$ is known, and let y be the generic symbol for the observations x_i. Then the expectation of $\rho^*_{m-1}(T\zeta)$ is given by

$$(10.2.6) \quad E[\rho^*_{m-1}(T\zeta)] = \zeta \sum_y \rho^*_{m-1}\left(\frac{\zeta f_1(y)}{\zeta f_1(y) + (1 - \zeta)f_2(y)}\right)f_1(y)$$

$$+ (1 - \zeta) \sum_y \rho^*_{m-1}\left(\frac{\zeta f_1(y)}{\zeta f_1(y) + (1 - \zeta)f_2(y)}\right)f_2(y)$$

which is an explicit function of ζ. Now, for $m = 1$, $\rho^*_0(\zeta)$ given by (10.2.1) is a very simple function of ζ so that $E[\rho^*_0(T\zeta)]$ can be obtained from (10.2.6) in a straightforward manner. Knowing $E[\rho^*_0(T\zeta)]$, we can compute $\rho^*_1(\zeta)$ from (10.2.3) and hence $E[\rho^*_1(T\zeta)]$ from (10.2.6) and therefore $\rho^*_2(\zeta)$ from (10.2.3) and so forth.

It is to be observed that, while the averaging process involved in (10.2.6) is laborious from a computational point of view, the fact that the determination of the stopping regions and the Bayes risk involves nothing more complicated than taking expectations is of theoretical interest. Also this method can be considered as an iterative procedure for obtaining the Bayes risk and stopping regions of the non-truncated sequential procedure. It yields at each stage an upper bound for $\rho^*(\zeta)$ and upper bounds for the regions $\Delta(\mathbf{w}_1)$ and $\Delta(\mathbf{w}_2)$. A similar iterative procedure implied in Problem 9.4.2 yields lower bounds for these quantities. More specifically, we employ the equation [see Problem 9.4.2]

$$(10.2.7) \qquad r^*_m(\zeta) = \min[\psi(\zeta), 1 + E[r^*_{m-1}(T\zeta)]]$$

where $E[r^*_{m-1}(T\zeta)]$ is given by (10.2.6) with ρ^* replaced by r^* and where

$$(10.2.8) \qquad r^*_1(\zeta) = \min[\psi(\zeta), 1]$$

to obtain increasing lower bounds for $\rho^*(\zeta)$; and the equation

$$(10.2.9) \qquad \psi(\zeta) = 1 + E(r^*_{m-1}(T\zeta))$$

to obtain increasing lower bounds for $\Delta(\mathbf{w}_1)$ and $\Delta(\mathbf{w}_2)$.

PROBLEMS

10.2.1. Let y be a binomial random variable taking on the values 0 and 1, and let $f_1(1) = \frac{1}{3}, f_2(1) = \frac{2}{3}$. Let $W = \begin{pmatrix} 0 & 15 \\ 15 & 0 \end{pmatrix}$. Determine the regions $\Delta_m(\mathbf{w}_1)$ and $\Delta_m(\mathbf{w}_2)$, and compute $\rho^*_m(\zeta)$ for $m = 0, 1, 2$.

10.2.2. Consider the same problem as 10.2.1 with $W = \begin{pmatrix} 0 & 15 & 6 \\ 15 & 0 & 6 \end{pmatrix}$. Determine the regions $\Delta_m(\mathbf{w}_j)$, $j = 1, 2, 3$, and compute $\rho^*_m(\zeta)$ for $m = 0, 1$. Note that we have here an entire interval in which $h_1(\zeta) = \psi(\zeta) = 1 + Eh_0(T\zeta)$.

10.2.3. Compute $r^*_m(\zeta)$ for Problem 10.2.1 for $m = 0, 1, 2$, and obtain γ'_m and δ'_m and hence $\Delta'_m(\mathbf{w}_1) = [\delta'_m \leq \zeta \leq 1]$, $\Delta'_m(\mathbf{w}_2) = [0 \leq \zeta \leq \gamma'_m]$ from equation 10.2.9. Plot $r^*_2(\zeta)$ and $\rho^*_2(\zeta)$ on the same graph, and indicate on the abscissa the four regions $\Delta_2(\mathbf{w}_1)$, $\Delta'_2(\mathbf{w}_1)$, $\Delta_2(\mathbf{w}_2)$, $\Delta'_2(\mathbf{w}_2)$.

10.2.4. Let h and k be general, and let ξ_0 be a point in Ξ satisfying the equation

$$\psi(\bar{\xi}) = 1 + E[\rho^*_{m-1}(T\xi)]$$

Furthermore, let V be the face of the simplex Ξ of lowest dimensionality such that $\xi_0 \varepsilon V$. Then either ξ_0 is a boundary point of $\Delta_m(\mathbf{w}_j)$ for some j or every point in $\Delta_m(\mathbf{w}_j) \bigcap V$ satisfies the above equation.

10.2.5. What general conditions must a 3×3 loss matrix W satisfy in order for the stopping regions $\Delta_m(\mathbf{w}_j)$ $j = 1, 2, 3$ to have the general shape indicated in Figure 14?

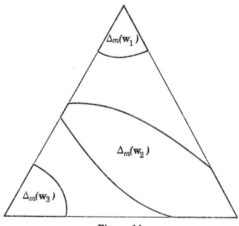

Figure 14

10.3. Method for Determining the Boundaries of the Stopping Regions for Non-Truncated Sequential Dichotomies

The Bayes non-truncated sequential procedures S^* for the dichotomy defined in the beginning of Section 10.2 are characterized by the two intervals

(10.3.1) $\Delta(w_1) = (\delta \le \zeta \le 1)$, $\Delta(w_2) = (0 \le \zeta \le \gamma)$

with $\gamma \le \delta$. Assume for the moment that γ and δ are determined. Let $j = 0, 1, 2, \cdots$ represent the number of observations taken in sequence. At each stage we compute ζ_j where

$$(10.3.2) \quad \zeta_j = \frac{\zeta \prod_{i=1}^{j} f_1(x_i)}{\zeta \prod_{i=1}^{j} f_1(x_i) + (1 - \zeta) \prod_{i=1}^{j} f_2(x_i)}, \qquad \zeta_0 = \zeta$$

We continue taking observations as long as $\gamma < \zeta_j < \delta$. We stop as soon as, for some $j = n$, either $\zeta_n \ge \delta$ or $\zeta_n \le \gamma$. In the former case, we accept H_1; in the latter case, we accept H_2.

It is easy to see that the above-described procedure (if S* requires taking at least one observation) is identical with the following likelihood ratio procedure (called the sequential probability ratio test). Let

$$(10.3.3) \qquad \lambda_j = \prod_{i=1}^{j} f_2(x_i) \Big/ \prod_{i=1}^{j} f_1(x_i)$$

$$(10.3.4) \qquad A_\zeta = \frac{\zeta(1 - \gamma)}{(1 - \zeta)\gamma}, \qquad B_\zeta = \frac{\zeta(1 - \delta)}{(1 - \zeta)\delta}$$

Observations are taken in sequence, and sampling continues as long as $B_\zeta < \lambda_j < A_\zeta$. Sampling terminates as soon as, for some sample size n, either $\lambda_n \le B_\zeta$ or $\lambda_n \ge A_\zeta$. In the former case H_1 is accepted. In the latter case H_2 is accepted.

We define

$$(10.3.5) \qquad z_i = \log \frac{f_2(x_i)}{f_1(x_i)}$$

$$(10.3.6) \qquad a_\zeta = \log A_\zeta, \qquad -b_\zeta = \log B_\zeta$$

(Note that a_ζ and b_ζ are non-negative for all ζ in the interval (γ, δ).) In terms of these quantities the sequential procedure S* can be defined as follows: Continue sampling as long as $-b_\zeta < \sum_{i=1}^{j} z_i < a_\zeta$. Terminate sampling and accept the appropriate hypothesis as soon as, for some n, $\sum_{=1}^{n} z_i \ge a_\zeta$ or $\sum_{i=1}^{n} z_i \le -b_\zeta$.

We now turn to the problem of determining γ and δ. It follows from the continuity and concavity of the Bayes risk $\rho^*(\zeta)$ that γ and δ satisfy the two equations:

$$(10.3.7) \qquad \gamma w_{12} = 1 + E[\rho^*(T\gamma)]$$

$$(10.3.8) \qquad \delta w_{21} = 1 + E[\rho^*(T\delta)]$$

That is, at both of these points, the risk of making the appropriate decision without taking observations is equal to the expected risk from taking one observation and then going on with S^*. It remains therefore to obtain an expression for $E[\rho^*(T\zeta)]$ for $\zeta = \gamma$ and $\zeta = \delta$.

Consider first the case $\zeta = \gamma$. If we set $\zeta = \gamma$ in (10.3.2) we get

$$(10.3.9) \quad a_\gamma = \log A_\gamma = 0, \qquad -b_\sim = \log B_\gamma = \log \frac{\gamma(1-\delta)}{(1-\gamma)\delta}$$

It is clear that for this case the first observation, to be designated by y, will either terminate the sampling or result in a new sequential-probability ratio test with boundaries $a'_\gamma = -z$ and $b'_\gamma = -(b_\gamma + z)$ where $z = \log \dfrac{f_2(y)}{f_1(y)}$ and $-b_\gamma < z < 0$.

For any sequential-probability ratio test defined by boundaries $-b$ and a with $a \geq 0$, $b \geq 0$, let

$$(10.3.10) \quad \pi_\omega(-b, a) = P\left(\sum_{j=1}^n z_j \leq -b \mid H_\omega\right), \qquad \omega = 1, 2$$

Then $\pi_\omega(-b, a)$ is the probability that we accept H_1 when H_ω is true. We also have $1 - \pi_\omega(-b, a) = P\left(\sum_{j=1}^n z_j \geq a \mid H_\omega\right)$ [see, for example, Theorem 10.4.1 below]. Further, let $E_\omega[n \mid -b, a]$ stand for the expected number of observations required to reach a decision when H_ω is true, and let

$$(10.3.11) \quad \rho_1(-b, a) = E_1[n \mid -b, a] + w_{12}(1 - \pi_1(-b, a))$$

$$(10.3.12) \quad \rho_2(-b, a) = E_2[n \mid -b, a] + w_{21}\pi_2(-b, a)$$

Then $\rho_\omega(-b, a)$ is the risk from the sequential-probability ratio test when H_ω is true. In terms of the above quantities we can express $E[\rho^*(T\gamma)]$ as

$$(10.3.13) \quad E[\rho^*(T\gamma)] = \gamma[w_{12}P(z \geq 0 \mid H_1)$$

$$+ \sum_{-b_\gamma < z < 0} \rho_1(-(b_\gamma + z), -z)g_1(z)]$$

$$+ (1 - \gamma)[w_{21}P(z \leq -b_\gamma \mid H_2) + \sum_{-b_\gamma < z < 0} \rho_2(-(b + z), -z)g_2(z)]$$

where $g_\omega(z) = P\left\{y: \log \dfrac{f_2(y)}{f_1(y)} = z \mid H_\omega\right\}$, $\qquad \omega = 1, 2$

Similarly, if we set $\zeta = \delta$ in (10.3.4) we get

$$(10.3.14) \quad a_\delta = \log A_\delta = \log \frac{\delta(1 - \gamma)}{(1 - \delta)\gamma} = b_\gamma, \qquad b_\delta = \log B_\delta = 0$$

Hence the first observation will either terminate the sampling or result in a new sequential-probability ratio test with boundaries $a'_\delta = b_\gamma - z$, $-b'_\delta = -z$. We therefore have

$$(10.3.15) \quad E[\rho^*(T\delta)]$$

$$= \delta[w_{12}P(z \geq b_\gamma \mid H_1) + \sum_{0 < z < b_\gamma} \rho_1(-z, b_\gamma - z)g_1(z)]$$

$$+ (1 - \delta)[w_{21}P(z \leq 0 \mid H_2) + \sum_{0 < z < b_\gamma} \rho_2(-z, b_\gamma - z)g_2(z)]$$

We note that $E[\rho^*(T\gamma)]$ and $E[\rho^*(T\delta)]$ are both functions of γ and δ so that (10.3.7) and (10.3.8) are two equations involving two unknowns which, at least theoretically, can be solved. The major difficulty, from a computational point of view, is obtaining explicit expressions for the two risks $\rho_1(-b, a)$ and $\rho_2(-b, a)$ as functions of a and b. This, in general, involves the solution of fairly complicated "random walk with absorbing barrier" problems which is beyond the scope of this book. However, approximate expressions for ρ_1 and ρ_2 can be obtained [see also Problem 10.5.5], and the underlying theory will be given below. We shall also consider a few simple situations where this theory gives exact solutions to ρ_1 and ρ_2. It is of interest to point out that the expressions enclosed in brackets in equations 10.3.13 and 10.3.15 depend only on $b_\gamma = \log \dfrac{(1 - \gamma)\delta}{\gamma(1 - \delta)}$ and that equations 10.3.7 and 10.3.8 are linear in w_{12} and w_{21}. Hence, assuming that we computed the quantities in the brackets for a fixed b_γ we can solve for $w_{ij} = u_{ij}(\gamma, \delta)$ with $ij = 12$, 21, and by varying γ and δ so as to keep b_γ fixed obtain a whole se-

quence of sequential procedures which are optimal for the loss matrix

$$\begin{pmatrix} 0 & u_{12}(\gamma,\ \delta) \\ u_{21}(\gamma,\ \delta) & 0 \end{pmatrix}.$$

PROBLEMS

10.3.1. Let $\Omega = (1,\ 2)$; $A = (1,\ 2,\ 3)$; $W = \begin{pmatrix} 0 & w_{12} & w_{13} \\ w_{21} & 0 & w_{23} \end{pmatrix}$. Prove that a neces-

sary and sufficient condition that $\Delta(w_3)$ be non-empty is that the line $y = \zeta w_{12} + (1 - \zeta)w_{23}$ intersect the curve $y = \rho^*(\zeta)$ where $\rho^*(\zeta)$ is the Bayes risk of the dichotomy $\Omega = (1,\ 2)$, $A = (1,\ 2)$, $W = \begin{pmatrix} 0 & w_{12} \\ w_{21} & 0 \end{pmatrix}$.

10.3.2. Assuming that $\Delta(w_3)$ in the above problem is not empty, characterize the regions of $\Delta(w_1)$, $\Delta(w_2)$, and $\Delta(w_3)$, and derive equations for determining their boundaries.

10.4. Some Theory in Sequential Analysis

In the previous section we showed that the class of Bayes non-truncated sequential procedures for a dichotomy requiring at least one observation is equivalent to the class of likelihood ratio tests which in turn is equivalent to the following procedures. We are given a numerical random variable z which on the hypothesis H_ω ($\omega = 1, 2$) has probability distribution $g_\omega(z)$. Then, corresponding to any a priori probability ζ for H_1, and any loss matrix $W = \begin{pmatrix} 0 & w_{12} \\ w_{21} & 0 \end{pmatrix}$ there exist two non-negative constants a and b. Observations z_i, ($i = 1, 2, \cdots$), are taken in sequence, and at each stage j we compute $Z_j = \sum_{i=1}^{j} z_i$. We continue sampling as long as $-b < Z_j < a$. We terminate sampling at the nth stage if n is the smallest value of j such that $Z_n \geq a$ or $Z_n \leq -b$. In the former case we accept H_2, and in the latter case we accept H_1.

Let a and b be fixed, and let us consider the general situation where the probability distribution of z is $g_\omega(z)$ with arbitrary ω. We note that n (the sample size at which we terminate sampling) and Z_n (the value of $\sum_{i=1}^{n} z_i$ when sampling is terminated) are both random variables whose joint probability distribution depends on ω. We shall investigate some of the properties of this distribution.

Theorem 10.4.1. If, for a given ω, $P_\omega(z = 0) \neq 1$, then there exists a ν with $0 < \nu < 1$ and a $c > 0$ such that

$$(10.4.1) \qquad P_\omega(n > N) < c\nu^N \quad \text{for} \quad N \geq N_0$$

Proof. Since $z \not\equiv 0$, then either $P_\omega(z > 0) > 0$ or $P_\omega(z < 0) > 0$. Assume first that $P_\omega(z > 0) > 0$. Then, since $P_\omega(z > 0) = \lim_{d \to 0} P_\omega(z > d)$, there exists a positive number d, say d_0, for which $P_\omega(z > d_0) = p_0 > 0$. Choose an N_0 such that $N_0 d_0 > a + b$, and define

$$(1) \qquad \begin{aligned} y_1 &= z_1 &&+ \cdots + z_{N_0} \\ y_2 &= z_{N_0+1} &&+ \cdots + z_{2N_0} \\ &\quad\vdots \\ y_k &= z_{(k-1)N_0+1} + \cdots + z_{kN_0}, &&\quad k = 1, 2, \cdots \end{aligned}$$

The random variables y_1, \cdots, y_k are independent with identical probability distributions. Moreover,

$$(2) \qquad P_\omega(y_1 > a + b) \geq P_\omega(z_1 > d_0, \cdots, z_{N_0} > d_0) = p_0^{N_0} = p^*$$

Thus each y_i has a probability of at least p^* of exceeding $a + b$.

Let E be the event that at least one y_i ($i = 1, 2, \cdots, k$) exceeds $a + b$. Then

$$(3) \qquad P_\omega(n \leq kN_0) \geq P_\omega(E)$$

For assume $y_r > a + b$ for some $r \leq k$. Then if the sequential test did not terminate before or at $(r - 1)N_0$ observations, we have $-b < \sum_{i=1}^{r-1} y_i < a$, so that $\sum_{i=1}^{r} y_i > -b + y_r > a$, and hence it must terminate with r observations. Now, from (2)

$$(4) \qquad P_\omega(y_1 \leq a + b, \cdots, y_k \leq a + b) \leq (1 - p^*)^k$$

and hence $P_\omega(E) \geq 1 - (1 - p^*)^k$. Setting $N = N_0 k + h$ ($0 \leq h \leq N_0 - 1$), $\nu = (1 - p^*)^{1/N_0}$, and employing (3), we obtain

$$(5) \qquad 1 - \left(\frac{1}{1 - p^*}\right)^h \nu^N \leq P_\omega(n \leq kN_0) \leq P_\omega(n \leq N) \leq 1$$

Finally, letting $c = (1/1 - p^*)^{N_0-1}$, we get

$$(6) \qquad P_\omega(n > N) < c\nu^N \quad \text{for} \quad N \geq N_0$$

The argument for the case $P_\omega(z < 0) > 0$ is similar.

Theorem 10.4.2. Let $E_\omega(n \mid -b, a)$ be the expected number of observations required for sampling to terminate, $E_\omega[Z_n \mid -b, a]$ and $E_\omega[Z^2_n \mid -b, a]$, the expected value of Z_n and Z^2_n, respectively, $E_\omega(z)$

and $\sigma_\omega{}^2$, the expected value and variance of z, all under the condition that the distribution of z is $g_\omega(z)$. Then always

(10.4.2)
$$E_\omega[Z_n \mid -b, a] = E_\omega[n \mid -b, a] E_\omega(z)$$

and, if $E_\omega(z) = 0$,

(10.4.3)
$$E_\omega[Z^2{}_n \mid -b, a] = E_\omega[n \mid -b, a]\sigma_\omega{}^2$$

Proof. Let \mathcal{S}_N, $N \geq N_0$, be a truncation of the sequential procedure under consideration; i.e., \mathcal{S}_N follows the sequential procedure for N observations and then terminates. Taking expectations of $\sum_{i=1}^{N} z_i$ with respect to the joint event n and Z_n arising from the procedure \mathcal{S}_N, we have

(1) $NE_\omega(z) = E_\omega\left(\sum_{i=1}^{N} z_i\right) = \sum_{j=1}^{N} P_\omega(n = j)E_\omega\left[\sum_{i=1}^{N} z_i \mid n = j\right]$

$$+ P_\omega(n > N)E_\omega\left[\sum_{i=1}^{N} z_i \mid n > N\right]$$

where the event $(n > N)$ means that the non-truncated procedure did not terminate at N. Now, for $n = j$,

(2) $E_\omega\left[\sum_{i=1}^{N} z_i \mid n = j\right] = E_\omega\left(\sum_{i=1}^{j} z_i \mid n = j\right)$

$$+ E_\omega(z)\{E_\omega[(N - j) \mid n = j]\}$$

Substituting (2) into (1), we get

(3) $0 = \sum_{j=1}^{N} P_\omega(n = j)E_\omega\left[\sum_{i=1}^{j} z_i \mid n = j\right] - E_\omega(z)\sum_{j=1}^{N} jP_\omega(n = j)$

$$+ P_\omega(n > N)E_\omega\left[\sum_{i=1}^{N} z_i \mid n > N\right] + E_\omega(z)N \sum_{j=N+1}^{\infty} P_\omega(n = j)$$

We observe that, for $n > N$, $-b < \sum_{i=1}^{N} z_i < a$, so that by Theorem 10.4.1

$$\lim_{N \to \infty} P_\omega(n > N)E_\omega\left(\sum_{i=1}^{N} z_i \mid n > N\right) = 0$$

and

$$\lim_{N \to \infty} N \sum_{j=N+1}^{\infty} P_\omega(n = j) = 0$$

This proves the first part of the theorem. The second part is proved in

a similar fashion by taking the expectation of $\left(\sum\limits_{i=1}^{N} z_i\right)^2$ with respect to the joint events n and Z_n.

Theorem 10.4.3. Let $\varphi_\omega(t) = E_\omega(e^{tz})$ be the moment-generating function of z, and let it be assumed to exist for all real t. Then a necessary and sufficient condition that there exists a $t = t_\omega$ with $t_\omega \neq 0$ such that $\varphi_\omega(t_\omega) = 1$ is that $E_\omega(z) \neq 0$ and that z take on both positive and negative values with positive probability.

Proof. To prove the sufficiency, we observe that $\varphi''_\omega(t) = E_\omega(z^2 e^{tz})$ > 0 unless $z \not\equiv 0$. [Since $\varphi_\omega(t)$ exists for all t, it is differentiable any number of times as is shown by Lemma 11.5.1.] Thus $\varphi(t)$ is a convex function of z. Now by assumption there exists a value $z' > 0$ such that $P_\omega(z > z') = u > 0$. Hence for $t > 0$

$$(1) \qquad \sum_z e^{tz} g_\omega(z) \geq \sum_{z > z'} e^{tz} g_\omega(z) \geq u e^{tz'}$$

and consequently $\varphi_\omega(t) \to \infty$ as $t \to \infty$. A similar argument shows that $\varphi_\omega(t) \to \infty$ as $t \to -\infty$. Thus $\varphi_\omega(t)$ assumes a minimum value at a unique point say, t^* for which $\varphi'_\omega(t^*) = 0$. Now $\varphi'_\omega(0) = E_\omega(z)$, so that $t^* \neq 0$ unless $E_\omega(z) = 0$. Since $\varphi_\omega(0) = 1$ and $\varphi_\omega(t^*) < \varphi_\omega(0)$ whenever $E_\omega(z) \neq 0$, it must follow that there exists a $t = t_\omega \neq 0$ such that $\varphi_\omega(t) = 1$. To prove that the condition is necessary, suppose $P_\omega(z \geq 0) = 1$, and let $P_\omega(z = 0) = \alpha < 1$. Then $P_\omega(z > 0) = 1 - \alpha$. We shall show that $\varphi_\omega(t) \to \alpha$ as $t \to -\infty$. Let $t < 0$. For any ϵ, $0 < \epsilon < 1 - \alpha$, we can find a positive number c such that $P_\omega(0 < z \leq c)$ $\leq \epsilon$. Then

$$(2) \qquad \alpha \leq \varphi_\omega(t) = E_\omega(e^{tz}) \leq [\alpha + \epsilon] + [1 - \alpha - \epsilon]e^{ct}$$

and hence

$$(3) \qquad \alpha \leq \lim_{t \to -\infty} \varphi_\omega(t) \leq \alpha + \epsilon$$

Since ϵ is arbitrary, $\lim\limits_{t \to -\infty} \varphi_\omega(t) = \alpha$. We see then that $\varphi'(t) > 0$ for all t, and hence $\varphi(t) = 1$ has no solutions other than $t = 0$. A similar argument shows that, if $P_\omega(z \leq 0) = 1$ and $P_\omega(z = 0) < 1$, then $\varphi'(t)$ < 0 for all t. This completes the proof of the theorem.

Corollary 1. The value of t_ω in the above theorem is opposite in sign to $E_\omega(z)$.

Proof. For all real y, $e^y \geq 1 + y$ so that $\varphi_\omega(t) = E_\omega(e^{tz}) \geq 1 + tE_\omega(z)$, and, since $\varphi_\omega(t_\omega) = 1$, $t_\omega E_\omega(z) \leq 0$.

Theorem 10.4.4. (The fundamental identity for real values of t.) For a given ω and for all real t such that $\varphi_\omega(t) > \nu$ (where ν is defined in Theorem 10.4.1)

$$(10.4.4) \qquad E_\omega[e^{tZ_n}(\varphi_\omega(t))^{-n}] = 1$$

and, if $P_\omega(z > 0) > 0$ and $P_\omega(z < 0) > 0$, then (10.4.4) holds for all real t.

Proof. Let the sequential procedure \mathcal{S}_N be defined as in Theorem 10.4.2. Then since

$$(1) \qquad E_\omega\left[e^{t\sum\limits_{i=1}^{N} z_i}\right] = \{E_\omega(e^{tz_1})\} \cdots \{E_\omega(e^{tz_N})\} = [\varphi_\omega(t)]^N$$

we can write

$$(2) \quad 1 = E_\omega\left[e^{t\sum\limits_{i=1}^{N} z_i}(\varphi_\omega(t))^{-N}\right]$$

$$= \sum_{j=1}^{N} P_\omega(n = j)E_\omega\left[e^{t\sum\limits_{i=1}^{N} z_i}(\varphi_\omega(t))^{-N} \,\middle|\, n = j\right]$$

$$+ P_\omega(n > N)E_\omega\left[e^{t\sum\limits_{i=1}^{N} z_i}(\varphi_\omega(t))^{-N} \,\middle|\, n > N\right]$$

But, for $n = j$, $\sum\limits_{i=1}^{j} z_i$ is independent of $\sum\limits_{i=j+1}^{N} z_i$, and therefore

$$(3) \qquad E_\omega\left[e^{t\sum\limits_{i=1}^{N} z_i}(\varphi_\omega(t))^{-N} \,\middle|\, n = j\right] = E_\omega[e^{tZ_j}(\varphi_\omega(t))^{-j} \,|\, n = j]$$

Equation 1 thus becomes

$$(4) \quad 1 = \sum_{j=1}^{N} P_\omega(n = j)E_\omega[e^{tZ_j}(\varphi_\omega(t))^{-j} \,|\, n = j]$$

$$+ \frac{P_\omega(n > N)}{[\varphi_\omega(t)]^N} E_\omega\left[e^{t\sum\limits_{i=1}^{N} z_i} \,\middle|\, n > N\right]$$

Since, for $n > N$, $-b < \sum\limits_{i=1}^{N} z_i < a$, then, by (4) and Theorem 10.4.1, for N sufficiently large,

$$(5) \quad 0 \le 1 - \sum_{j=1}^{N} P_\omega(n = j)E_\omega[e^{tZ_j}(\varphi_\omega(z))^{-j} \,|\, n = j] \le \left[\frac{\nu}{\varphi_\omega(t)}\right]^N K(t)$$

where $K(t)$ is positive and for fixed ω depends only on t. Letting $N \to \infty$, we see that, for all real t such that $\varphi_\omega(t) > \nu$, equation 10.4.4 holds.

Suppose now that z takes on both positive and negative values so that $\varphi_\omega(t)$ has a minimum which is assumed at, say, $t = t^*$. Then it follows from (4) that for all real t

$$(6) \qquad P_\omega(n > N) < \frac{[\varphi_\omega(t)]^N}{K(t)}, \qquad P_\omega(n > N) < \frac{[\varphi_\omega(t^*)]^N}{K(t^*)}$$

and hence

$$(7) \quad 0 \leq 1 - \sum_{j=1}^{N} P_\omega(n = j) E_\omega[e^{tZ_j}(\varphi_\omega(z))^{-j} \mid n = j] \leq \left[\frac{\varphi_\omega(t^*)}{\varphi_\omega(t)}\right]^N \frac{K(t)}{K(t^*)}$$

Thus, if we let $N \to \infty$, we see that in this case equation 10.4.4 holds for all t with the possible exception of $t = t^*$. Even in this case, the fundamental identity holds, but the proof will be omitted.

We observe that for all ω for which $E_\omega(z) \neq 0$ equation 6 gives an upper bound for $P_\omega(n > N)$ in terms of the minimum of $\varphi_\omega(t)$.

PROBLEMS

10.4.1. Prove that the moment-generating function of n exists for all real t such that $e^t < 1/\nu$. *Hint.* Write

$$E_\omega(e^{tn}) = \sum_{j=1}^{\infty} P_\omega(n = j) e^{tj} \leq \sum_{j=1}^{N} P_\omega(n = j) e^{tj} + \sum_{j=N+1}^{\infty} P_\omega(n \geq j) e^{tj}$$

and employ Theorem 10.4.1.

10.4.2. Prove that, if $\varphi_\omega(t)$ exists for all real t, the fundamental identity can be differentiated any number of times with respect to t. Then, using this fact, give an alternative proof of Theorem 10.4.2. *Hint.* Show that the kth derivative of the remainder in equation 4, Theorem 10.4.4, converges to zero for all k as $N \to \infty$.

10.4.3. Show that the fundamental identity holds for all t in the complex plane for which $\mid \varphi_\omega(t) \mid > \nu$ where $\mid \varphi_\omega(t) \mid$ stands for the modulus of $\varphi_\omega(t)$.

10.4.4. Using the results of Problem 10.4.3 show that $E_\omega(e^{tZ_n}) = 1$ for all t in the complex plane for which $\varphi_\omega(t) = 1$.

10.5. Approximation for $P_\omega(Z_n \leq -b)$ and for $E_\omega(n)$

Let z have probability distribution $g_\omega(z)$, and let $P_\omega(z > 0) > 0$ and $P_\omega(z < 0) > 0$. We define

$$(10.5.1) \quad \pi_\omega(-b, a) = P_\omega(Z_n \leq -b); \qquad 1 - \pi_\omega(-b, a) = P_\omega(Z_n \geq a)$$

Furthermore, let $E_\omega(n \mid -b, a)$ stand for the expected number of observations required by the sequential procedure under consideration.

Assume that $E_\omega(z) \neq 0$ and that $\varphi_\omega(t)$ exists for all real t. Then, by Theorem 10.4.3, there exists a $t = t_\omega \neq 0$ such that $\varphi_\omega(t_\omega) = 1$. Substituting t_ω for t in the fundamental identity (10.4.4) we get

$$E_\omega(e^{t_\omega Z_n}) = 1 \tag{10.5.2}$$

We shall neglect the excess of Z_n over the boundaries $-b$ and a and assume that Z_n takes on only the two values $-b$ and a. Then, keeping in mind this approximation, we can write (10.5.2) as

$$\pi_\omega(-b, a)e^{-bt_\omega} + [1 - \pi_\omega(-b, a)]e^{at_\omega} = 1 \tag{10.5.3}$$

Multiplying (10.5.3) by e^{bt_ω} and solving for $\pi_\omega(-b, a)$, we get

$$\pi_\omega(-b, a) = \frac{e^{(a+b)t_\omega} - e^{bt_\omega}}{e^{(a+b)t_\omega} - 1} \tag{10.5.4}$$

Employing the same approximation, we also get

$$E_\omega(Z_n \mid -b, a) = -b\pi_\omega(-b, a) + a[1 - \pi_\omega(-b, a)] \tag{10.5.5}$$

and consequently from (10.4.2)

$$E_\omega(n \mid -b, a) = \frac{a - (a + b)\pi_\omega(-b, a)}{E_\omega(z)} \tag{10.5.6}$$

If $E_\omega(z) = 0$, then $t_\omega = 0$, so that (10.5.4) becomes indeterminate. However, if we apply L'Hospital's rule and differentiate the numerator and denominator of (10.5.4) with respect to t_ω and set $t_\omega = 0$, we get

$$\pi_\omega(-b, a) = \frac{a}{a + b}, \qquad (E_\omega(z) = 0) \tag{10.5.7}$$

Also from (10.4.3), the above approximations and (10.5.7)

$$E_\omega(n \mid -b, a) = \frac{ab}{\sigma_\omega^2}, \qquad (E_\omega(z) = 0) \tag{10.5.8}$$

As an illustration of the application of the above formulas, let z be a binomial random variable which takes on the value u with probability ω and $-u$ with probability $1 - \omega$. Then $\varphi_\omega(t) = \omega e^{ut} + (1 - \omega)e^{-ut}$, $E_\omega(z) = u(2\omega - 1)$ and $\sigma_\omega^2 = 4u^2\omega(1 - \omega)$. Setting $\varphi_\omega(t) = 1$ and solving for $e^{t\omega}$, we easily obtain $e^{t\omega} = \left(\dfrac{1 - \omega}{\omega}\right)^{1/u}$. Substituting these expressions in the approximate formulas, we get for $\omega \neq 1/2$

$$(10.5.9) \qquad \pi_\omega(-b, a) = \frac{\left(\dfrac{1-\omega}{\omega}\right)^{(a+b)/u} - \left(\dfrac{1-\omega}{\omega}\right)^{b/u}}{\left(\dfrac{1-\omega}{\omega}\right)^{(a+b)/u} - 1}$$

$$(10.5.10) \qquad E_\omega(n \mid -b, a) = \frac{a - (a + b)\pi_\omega(-b, a)}{u(2\omega - 1)}$$

and, for $\omega = 1/2$, $E_\omega(n \mid -b, a) = \dfrac{ab}{4u^2\omega(1 - \omega)}$.

Note that, if $u = 1$ and a and b are integers, there will be no excess over the boundaries, so that formulas 10.5.9 and 10.5.10 are exact. These formulas, in fact, represent a solution to the "Gambler's Ruin" problem which has been frequently treated in the literature. Two special classes of statistical problems where $u = 1$ and a and b are integers will be considered in the next section.

PROBLEMS

10.5.1. Employing the approximations, obtain expressions for $\pi_\omega(-b, a)$ and $E_\omega(n \mid -b, a)$ in case

(a) $g_\omega(z)$ is normal with unit variance and mean ω.

(b) $z = x - u$ where u is a positive constant and x has a Poisson distribution with mean ω.

10.5.2. In Problem 10.5.1, plot $\pi_\omega(-b, a)$ and $E_\omega(n \mid -b, a)$ as functions of ω for $a = 5$, $b = 10$.

10.5.3. Let y be a numerical-valued random variable with probability distribution $f_\omega(y)$ under the hypothesis H_ω ($\omega = 1, 2$), and let $z = \log \dfrac{f_2(y)}{f_1(y)}$. Consider a sequential-probability ratio test with boundaries $A \geq 1$, $B \leq 1$, and let $a = \log A$, $-b = \log B$. Let $\alpha = 1 - \pi_1(-b, a)$ be the error of accepting H_2 when H_1 is true, and $\beta = \pi_2(-b, a)$ be the error of accepting H_1 when H_2 is true. Employing the given approximations, show that

$$A = \frac{1 - \beta}{\alpha}, \qquad B = \frac{\beta}{1 - \alpha}.$$

Hint. Let $g_\omega(z)$ ($\omega = 1, 2$) be the distribution of z under H_ω. Show that $t_\omega = 1$ for $\omega = 1$ and $t_\omega = -1$ for $\omega = 2$. Hence solve for A and B in terms of α and β from equation 10.5.3.

10.5.4. Let x be a numerical random variable with probability distribution $f(x) = \beta(\omega)e^{\omega x}r(x)$. Show that any sequential-probability ratio test for testing the hypothesis H_1 that $\omega = \omega_1$ against the alternative H_2 that $\omega = \omega_2$ is reducible to a sequential test of the type: Accept H_1 if $\sum_{i=1}^{n} z_i \leq -b$; accept H_2 if $\sum_{i=1}^{n} z_i \geq a$; continue sampling otherwise, where $z_i = x_i - u$ and u is a constant.

10.5.5. Express the risk function ρ^* for a non-truncated sequential dichotomy in terms of the approximate values of $E_\omega(n \mid -b, a)$ and $\pi_\omega(-b, a)$ given in (10.5.4) and (10.5.6) respectively, and obtain approximate expressions for γ and δ by minimizing this function with respect to these quantities.

10.6. The Determination of the Stopping Regions for a Special Class of Dichotomies

We shall consider in this section two cases of dichotomies in which the boundaries γ and δ [see Section 10.3] can be obtained with relative ease without any approximations.

Case 1. Binomial Dichotomies with Hypotheses Symmetric about 1/2. Let y be a binomial random variable which takes on the values 1 and 0 with respective probabilities p_1 and $q_1 = 1 - p_1$ under the hypothesis H_1, p_2 and $q_2 = 1 - p_2$ under the hypothesis H_2. We assume that $p_1 < p_2$ and that $p_1 + p_2 = 1$; i.e., p_1 and p_2 are symmetric about 1/2. Let ζ be the a priori probability for H_1, and let the loss matrix be given by $\begin{pmatrix} 0 & w_{12} \\ w_{21} & 0 \end{pmatrix}$. The problem is to determine γ and δ which define the class of Bayes procedures for testing H_1 against H_2.

Let y_1, y_2, \cdots be a sequence of observations on y, and let $m_j = \sum_{i=1}^{j} y_i$. Then the likelihood ratio [see (10.3.3)] is given by

$$(10.6.1) \qquad \lambda_j = \frac{p_2{}^{m_j} q_2{}^{j-m_j}}{p_1{}^{m_j} q_1{}^{j-m_j}} = \left(\frac{p_2}{p_1}\right)^{2m_j} \left(\frac{p_1}{p_2}\right)^{j}$$

so that [see (10.3.5)]

$$(10.6.2) \qquad \sum_{i=1}^{j} z_i = 2m_j \log \frac{p_2}{p_1} - j \log \frac{p_1}{p_2}$$

Hence, defining a_ζ and $-b_\zeta$ as in (10.3.6), we see that the class of Bayes procedures can be characterized as follows: Continue sampling as long as

$$(10.6.3) \qquad \frac{-b_\zeta}{2 \log (p_2/p_1)} + \frac{j}{2} < m_j < \frac{a_\zeta}{2 \log (p_2/p_1)} + \frac{j}{2}$$

and terminate sampling and accept the appropriate hypothesis as soon as, for some $j = n$, one of the two inequalities in (10.6.3) does not hold.

We define $x_i = 1$ if $y_i = 1$, $x_i = -1$ if $y_i = 0$. Then (10.6.3) can easily be shown to be equivalent to

$$(10.6.4) \qquad \frac{-b_\zeta}{\log (p_2/p_1)} < \sum_{i=1}^{j} x_i < \frac{a_\zeta}{\log (p_2/p_1)}$$

Moreover, since when we terminate sampling, the quantity $\sum\limits_{i=1}^{N} x_i$ is an integer, we might as well take the boundaries in (10.6.4) as integers. Thus, if γ and δ are known, the Bayes procedure for a given ζ is defined as follows: We set

$$(10.6.5) \quad a^*_\zeta = \left[\frac{\log \dfrac{(1-\gamma)\zeta}{(1-\zeta)\gamma}}{\log (p_2/p_1)} \right]', \qquad -b^*_\zeta = \left[\frac{\log \dfrac{(1-\delta)\zeta}{(1-\zeta)\delta}}{\log (p_2/p_1)} \right]'$$

where the symbol $[k]'$ stands for the smallest integer greater than or equal to k. We continue sampling as long as $-b^*_\zeta < \sum\limits_{i=1}^{n} x_i < a^*_\zeta$.

We terminate sampling as soon as for some sample size n either $\sum\limits_{i=1}^{n} x_i = a^*_\zeta$ or $\sum\limits_{i=1}^{n} x_i = -b^*_\zeta$. In the former case we accept H_2; in the latter case we accept H_1.

Let $\pi_\omega(-b^*_\zeta, a^*_\zeta) = P_\omega \left(\sum\limits_{i=1}^{n} x_i = -b^*_\zeta \right)$, and let $E_\omega(n \mid -b^*_\zeta, a^*_\zeta)$ be the expected number of observations required to reach a decision when H_ω ($\omega = 1, 2$) is true. Then without any approximations [see remark at end of Section 10.5]

$$(10.6.6) \qquad \pi_1(-b^*_\zeta, a^*_\zeta) = \frac{(p_2/p_1)^{a^*_\zeta + b^*_\zeta} - (p_2/p_1)^{b^*_\zeta}}{(p_2/p_1)^{a^*_\zeta + b^*_\zeta} - 1}$$

$$(10.6.7) \qquad \pi_2(-b^*_\zeta, a^*_\zeta) = \frac{(p_1/p_2)^{a^*_\zeta + b^*_\zeta} - (p_1/p_2)^{b^*_\zeta}}{(p_1/p_2)^{a^*_\zeta + b^*_\zeta} - 1}$$

$$(10.6.8) \quad E_1[n \mid -b^*_\zeta, a^*_\zeta] = \frac{a^*_\zeta - (a^*_\zeta + b^*_\zeta)\pi_1(-b^*_\zeta, a^*_\zeta)}{p_1 - p_2}$$

$$(10.6.9) \quad E_2[n \mid -b^*_\zeta, a^*_\zeta] = \frac{a^*_\zeta - (a^*_\zeta + b^*_\zeta)\pi_2(-b^*_\zeta, a^*_\zeta)}{p_2 - p_1}$$

Now let $\zeta = \gamma$. Then the Bayes procedure is defined by the boundaries [see (10.6.5)] $a^* = 0$, $-b^*_\gamma$. Hence, employing equation 10.3.13

and excluding the trivial case $b^*_\gamma = 1$, we get

(10.6.10) $E[\rho^*(T\gamma)] = (1 - \gamma)p_2[E_2(n \,|-(b^* - 1), 1)$

$+ w_{21}\pi_2(-(b^*_\gamma - 1), 1)] + \gamma\{w_{12}(1 - p_1) + p_1[E_1(n \,|-(b^*_\gamma - 1), 1)$

$+ w_{12}\{1 - \pi_1(-(b^*_\gamma - 1), 1)\}]\}$

Similarly, if we set $\zeta = \delta$ in (10.6.5), we get

(10.6.11) $E[\rho^*(T\delta)] = \delta p_2[E_1(n \,|-1, b^*_\gamma - 1)$

$+ w_{12}(1 - \pi_1(-1, b^*_\gamma - 1))] + (1 - \delta)\{w_{21}(1 - p_1)$

$+ p_1[E_2(n \,|-1, b^*_\gamma - 1) + w_{21}\pi_2(-1, b^*_\gamma - 1)]\}$

Setting

(10.6.12) $w_{12}\gamma = 1 + E[\rho^*(T\gamma)]$, $(1 - \delta)w_{21} = 1 + E[\rho^*(T\delta)]$

we obtain two equations in two unknowns which may be solved in the

The Bayes Risk as a Function of the a priori Distribution for a Dichotomy with
$H_1: p_1 = \frac{1}{3}$, $H_2: p_2 = \frac{2}{3}$, $c = 1$, $w_{12} = w_{21} = 38.25$

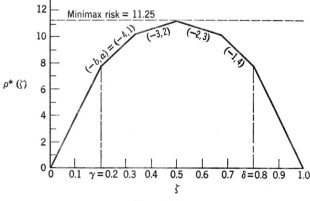

Figure 15

Minimax strategy for the statistician: A sequential probability ratio test with bound-
aries $(-3, 3)$ or $(-2, 2)$, or any mixture of the two, or a 50:50 mixture of two se-
quential probability ratio tests with boundaries $(-3, 2)$ and $(-2, 3)$, respectively.
Nature's least favorable distribution:

$$\xi = (\zeta, 1 - \zeta) = (0.5, 0.5)$$

following manner: Guess an integer b^*_γ. Then the equations in (10.6.12)
are linear in γ and δ. Solve for γ and δ, and substitute these values in
the formula

(10.6.13)
$$b = \left[\frac{\log \dfrac{\delta(1-\gamma)}{\gamma(1-\delta)}}{\log (p_2/p_1)} \right]'$$

If the resulting quantity has a value equal to the guessed b^*_γ, the computed γ and δ are correct. If not, repeat the process.

The risk from the optimum sequential procedure under consideration

The Bayes Risk as a Function of the a priori Distribution for a Dichotomy with $H_1: p_1 = \frac{1}{3}, H_2: p_2 = \frac{2}{3}, c = 1, w_{12} = 50, w_{21} = 100$

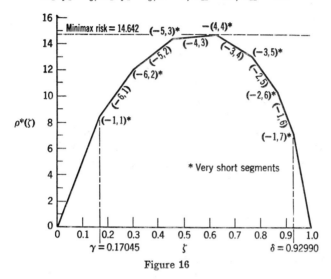

Figure 16

Minimax strategy for the statistician: A mixture of two sequential probability ratio tests, one with boundaries $(-4, 3)$, the other with boundaries $(-4, 4)$, in the proportions 0.58682 and 0.41318, respectively. Nature's least favorable distribution:

$$\xi = (\zeta, 1 - \zeta) = (0.62175, 0.37825)$$

can be computed as a function of ζ as soon as γ and δ are known and is given by

(10.6.14) $\rho^*(\zeta) = \zeta E_1(n \,|-b^*_\zeta, a^*_\zeta) + (1 - \zeta)E_2(n \,|-b^*_\zeta, a^*_\zeta)$

$+ \zeta w_{12}[1 - \pi_1(-b^*_\zeta, a^*_\zeta)] + (1 - \zeta)w_{21}\pi_2(-b^*_\zeta, a^*_\zeta)$

where for a fixed ζ, a^*_ζ and b^*_ζ are given by (10.6.5). Since a^*_ζ and b^*_ζ are integers, the curve obtained by plotting $\rho^*(\zeta)$ against ζ will consist of connected line segments. This is illustrated in Figures 15 and 16.

Case 2. Double Dichotomies. We are given two binomial populations Π_1 and Π_2 defined by two parameters p_1 and p_2 where $p_\omega =$

$P_\omega \, (y = 1)$, $q_\omega = 1 - p_\omega = P_\omega \, (y = 0)$ for $\omega = 1, 2$ and $p_1 < p_2$. Let H_1 stand for the hypothesis that p_1 is associated with Π_1 and p_2 is associated with Π_2, and let H_2 stand for the hypothesis that p_2 is associated with Π_1 and p_1 is associated with Π_2. Let w_{12} be the loss in accepting H_2 when H_1 is true and w_{21} be the loss in accepting H_1 when H_2 is true. Let ζ be the a priori probability that H_1 is true. The problem is to determine γ and δ which characterize the Bayes procedures for testing these hypotheses.

We shall assume that the sequence of observations will be taken in pairs, one from Π_1 and one from Π_2, and we shall designate this sequence by (y_{11}, y_{21}), (y_{12}, y_{22}), \cdots where y_{ij} $(i = 1, 2; j = 1, 2, \cdots)$ takes on the value 0 or 1. If the above assumption is made, the steps required to compute γ and δ parallel those of case 1, provided we define $x_i = y_{2i} - y_{1i}$ and substitute in each formula, beginning with (10.6.5), $p_1 q_2$ for p_1 and $p_2 q_1$ for p_2. The verification of this fact is left to the reader [see Problem 10.6.1]. Note that, for each i, the random variable $x_i = y_{2i} - y_{1i}$ takes on the values -1, 0, 1, with respective probabilities $q_2 p_1$, $p_1 p_2 + q_1 q_2$, $p_2 q_1$ under H_1; and $q_1 p_2$, $p_1 p_2 + q_1 q_2$, $p_1 q_2$ under H_2. Thus $x_i = 0$ has the same probability of occurring under either hypothesis and consequently yields no useful information for discriminating between them.

10.7. Examples of Trichotomies, i.e., $\Omega = (1, 2, 3)$, $A = (1, 2, 3)$

Example 1. Assume that the random variables y_1, y_2, \cdots are independently distributed and all have the same distribution. Each y_n takes on the values 1, 2, 3 with probabilities specified by one of the following alternative hypotheses:

States of Nature	Event		
	1	2	3
H_1	0	1/2	1/2
H_2	1/2	0	1/2
H_3	1/2	1/2	0

Let w_{ij} be the loss if H_j is accepted when H_i is true; the values are given by the following table.

States of Nature	Decisions		
	H_1	H_2	H_3
H_1	0	4	6
H_2	6	0	6
H_3	4	6	0

Note that both of these matrices are invariant under a cyclic permutation of the hypotheses and events.

Let $\xi(i)$ be the a priori probability of H_i. As we have seen, a point $\boldsymbol{\xi} = (\xi(1),\ \xi(2),\ \xi(3)) \,\varepsilon\, \Xi$ with $\xi(1) + \xi(2) + \xi(3) = 1$, may be represented by a point in an equilateral triangle with unit altitudes [see Section 6.3], the distance from the point to the three sides being the values $\xi(1)$, $\xi(2)$, and $\xi(3)$. Let P_i be the point where $\xi(i) = 1$ $(i = 1, 2, 3)$.

Let $\rho(\boldsymbol{\xi},\ \mathcal{S})$ be the average risk under a non-truncated sequential procedure \mathcal{S} when the a priori distribution is $\boldsymbol{\xi}$. Let \mathcal{S}^*_0 be the optimal sequential procedure where no observations are taken and let $T(\mathbf{w}_i)$ be the region in Ξ where H_i is accepted under \mathcal{S}^*_0. Let $\boldsymbol{\xi}\cdot\mathbf{w}_j = \sum_{i=1}^{3} w_{ji}\xi(i)$ be the risk in accepting H_j without experimentation when the a priori distribution is $\boldsymbol{\xi}$. Then $T(\mathbf{w}_1)$ is defined by $\psi(\boldsymbol{\xi}) = \min \boldsymbol{\xi}\cdot\mathbf{w}_j = \boldsymbol{\xi}\cdot\mathbf{w}_1$, i.e., by the inequalities

(10.7.1) $\boldsymbol{\xi}\cdot\mathbf{w}_1 \leq \boldsymbol{\xi}\cdot\mathbf{w}_2, \qquad \boldsymbol{\xi}\cdot\mathbf{w}_1 \leq \boldsymbol{\xi}\cdot\mathbf{w}_3$

or

(10.7.2) $6\xi(2) + 4\xi(3) \leq 4\xi(1) + 6\xi(3)$

$$6\xi(2) + 4\xi(3) \leq 6\xi(1) + 4\xi(2)$$

That is

(10.7.3) $\xi(1) \geq \max\left(\tfrac{3}{2}\xi(2) - \tfrac{1}{2}\xi(3),\ \tfrac{1}{3}\xi(2) + \tfrac{2}{3}\xi(3)\right)$

At P_1, $\xi(2) = \xi(3) = 0, \xi(1) = 1$, so that $P_1\,\varepsilon\,T(\mathbf{w}_1)$. When $\xi(3) = 0$, (10.7.3) becomes $\xi(1) \geq \tfrac{3}{2}\xi(2)$, while $\xi(1) + \xi(2) = 1$, so that $\xi(1) \geq \tfrac{3}{5}$; when $\xi(2) = 0$, $\xi(1) \geq \tfrac{2}{3}\xi(3)$, $\xi(1) + \xi(3) = 1$, so that $\xi(1) \geq \tfrac{2}{5}$. Also, the two lower bounding lines for $\xi(1)$ are equal when $\tfrac{3}{2}\xi(2) - \tfrac{1}{2}\xi(3) = \tfrac{1}{3}\xi(2) + \tfrac{2}{3}\xi(3) = \xi(1)$, or $\xi(1) = \xi(2) = \xi(3) = \tfrac{1}{3}$. Thus $T(\mathbf{w}_1)$ contains

all points above the boundary defined by the polygon with vertices $(\frac{3}{5}, \frac{2}{5}, 0)$, $(\frac{1}{3}, \frac{1}{3}, \frac{1}{3})$, and $(\frac{2}{5}, 0, \frac{3}{5})$. $T(w_2)$ and $T(w_3)$ can be obtained by successive cyclic permutation of the coordinates. [See Figure 17.]

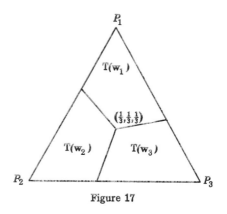

Figure 17

Let $S^*(\xi)$ be the optimal non-truncated sequential procedure for a given a priori distribution ξ, and let $\xi_j(i)$ be the a posteriori probability of H_i given that $y_1 = j$ where

$$(10.7.4) \qquad \xi_j(i) = \frac{\xi(i)p_{ij}}{\sum\limits_{k=1}^{3} p_{kj}\xi(k)}$$

and where p_{ij} is the probability that $y_1 = j$ under H_i (note that here the subscript j in $\xi_j(i)$ designates the value of the first observation and not the number of coordinates observed). Let $S^*_1(\xi)$ be the sequential procedure defined as taking one observation and then using the procedure $S^*(\xi_j)$ based on $\xi_j = (\xi_j(1), \xi_j(2), \xi_j(3))$ when $y_1 = j$. $S^*_1(\xi)$ is the best sequential procedure involving taking at least one observation. In the present case, $p_{jj} = 0$, so that $\xi_j(j) = 0$ by (10.7.4); therefore $S^*(\xi_j)$ is the optimal sequential test for a dichotomy.

Let $\Delta(w_i)$ be the region in Ξ for which H_i is accepted without any observations under $S^*(\xi)$. As has been shown, the regions $\Delta(w_i)$ are all that is needed to determine all the tests $S^*(\xi)$. They are convex, and their boundaries are characterized by the relations

$$(10.7.5) \qquad \psi(\xi) = 1 + E[\rho^*(T\xi)] = \rho^*(\xi, S^*_1(\xi))$$

so that

$$(10.7.6) \qquad \Delta(w_i) \subset T(w_i)$$

It is first necessary to find the optimal tests for each of the dichoto-
mies formed by taking pairs from the trichotomy H_1, H_2, H_3. Consider
the dichotomy H_1, H_2. Then $\xi(1) + \xi(2) = 1$. Suppose $\xi(1)$ is such
that it pays to take at least one observation. From (10.7.4), since
$p_{i3} = 1/2$ $(i = 1, 2)$,

$$(10.7.7) \qquad \xi_3(i) = \frac{\xi(i)}{\xi(1) + \xi(2)} = \xi(i)$$

Hence, if $y_1 = 3$, the a posteriori probabilities are unchanged, and, as
shown previously, the optimal test calls for taking another observa-
tion. On the other hand, $p_{11} = 0$, so that $\xi_1(2) = 1$. Therefore, if
$y_1 = 1$, the process should be terminated and H_2 accepted. Similarly,
if $y_1 = 2$, the process should be terminated and H_1 accepted. It fol-
lows that, if $\xi(1)$ is such that the best sequential procedure calls for
taking at least one observation, then the best procedure is to sample
indefinitely until $y_n = 1$ or 2; in the former case, accept H_2; in the
latter, H_1. The probability of accepting the wrong hypothesis is zero
under either hypothesis; the risk is then the expected number of obser-
vations, which is 2 under either hypothesis.

The boundaries γ_{12} and δ_{12} of the interval of $\xi(1)$'s in which it pays
to go on are then determined by the equation,

$$(10.7.8) \qquad w_{12}\gamma_{12} = 2 \quad \text{or} \quad \gamma_{12} = 1/2$$

$$w_{21}(1 - \delta_{12}) = 2 \quad \text{or} \quad \delta_{12} = 2/3$$

Returning to the specification of $S^*_1(\boldsymbol{\xi})$, we note that, if $y_1 = 3$,

$$\xi_3(i) = \frac{\xi(1)p_{i3}}{\displaystyle\sum_{k=1}^{3} \xi(k)p_{k3}}$$

As $p_{33} = 0$, $p_{i3} = 1/2$ for $i = 1, 2$,

$$\xi_2(i) = \frac{\xi(i)}{\xi(1) + \xi(2)}, \qquad (i = 1, 2)$$

Therefore $S^*_1(\boldsymbol{\xi})$ can be described as follows: If $y_1 = 3$, H_3 is rejected
entirely; if $\xi(1)/(\xi(1) + \xi(2)) \leq 1/2$, stop and accept H_2; if $\xi(1)/(\xi(1)$
$+ \xi(2)) \geq 2/3$, stop and accept H_1; if $1/2 < \xi(1)/(\xi(1) + \xi(2)) < 2/3$,
continue sampling until $y_n = 1$ or 2, at which point stop and accept
H_2 or H_1, respectively. The three conditions on $\xi(1)/(\xi(1) + \xi(2))$ can
be written in the simpler form,

$$(10.7.9) \quad \xi(1) \leq \xi(2), \qquad \xi(1) \geq 2\xi(2), \qquad \xi(2) < \xi(1) < 2\xi(2)$$

respectively. The cases where $y_1 = 1$ or 2 can be obtained from the preceding case by cyclic permutation of the numbers 1, 2, 3.

Let $\rho^*_j(\boldsymbol{\xi})$ be the conditional expected risk associated with $S^*_1(\boldsymbol{\xi})$ when the a priori probability distribution is $\boldsymbol{\xi}$, given that $y_1 = j$; and let p_i be the a priori probability that $y_1 = j$. Then

$$(10.7.10) \qquad \rho^*(\boldsymbol{\xi}, S^*_1(\boldsymbol{\xi})) = \sum_{j=1}^{3} p_j \rho^*_j(\boldsymbol{\xi})$$

$$(10.7.11) \qquad pj = \sum_{i=1}^{3} p_{ij}\xi(i)$$

$$(10.7.12) \quad \rho^*_3(\boldsymbol{\xi}) = 1 + \frac{4\xi(1)}{\xi(1) + \xi(2)} \quad \text{if} \quad \xi(1) \leq \xi(2)$$

$$= 3 \quad \text{if} \quad \xi(2) \leq \xi(1) \leq 2\xi(2)$$

$$= 1 + \frac{6\xi(2)}{\xi(1) + \xi(2)} \quad \text{if} \quad \xi(1) \geq 2\xi(2)$$

$\rho^*_1(\boldsymbol{\xi})$ and $\rho^*_2(\boldsymbol{\xi})$ can be obtained from (10.7.12) by cyclic permutation of the subscripts.

The region $\Delta(w_1)$ can now be determined by relations 10.7.5 and 10.7.10 to 10.7.12. First note that, when $\xi(3) = 0$, the problem reduces to the dichotomy between H_1 and H_2 already discussed, so that the interval from $\xi(1) = 1$ to $\xi(1) = 2/3$ on the line $\xi(3) = 0$ belongs to $\Delta(w_1)$. Hence the point $(2/3, 1/3, 0)$ lies on the boundary of $\Delta(w_1)$. This point satisfies the conditions,

$$(10.7.13) \quad \xi(2) \leq \xi(1) \leq 2\xi(2), \qquad \xi(2) \geq 2\xi(3), \qquad \xi(3) \leq \xi(1)$$

Consider the intersection, if any, of the boundary of $\Delta(w_1)$ with the region Δ_1 defined by (10.7.13). Using (10.7.10–11) and (10.7.5),

$$\frac{\xi(1) + \xi(2)}{2} \rho^*_3(\boldsymbol{\xi}) + \frac{\xi(2) + \xi(3)}{2} \rho^*_1(\boldsymbol{\xi}) + \frac{\xi(1) + \xi(3)}{2} \rho^*_2(\boldsymbol{\xi}) = \boldsymbol{\xi} \cdot w$$

From above, (10.7.12) and (10.7.2), we obtain

$$3\frac{\xi(1) + \xi(2)}{2} + \frac{\xi(2) + \xi(3)}{2}\left(1 + \frac{6\xi(3)}{\xi(2) + \xi(3)}\right)$$

$$+ \frac{\xi(1) + \xi(3)}{2}\left(1 + \frac{4\xi(3)}{\xi(1) + \xi(3)}\right) = 6\xi(2) + 4\xi(3)$$

or

(10.7.14) $\xi(2) = 1/3$

The intersection of (10.7.14) with the line $\xi(2) = 2\xi(3)$ occurs at the point $(1/2, 1/3, 1/6)$, which satisfies the conditions (10.7.13) and so lies on the boundary of the region Δ_1. As Δ_1 is convex, it follows that the boundary of $\Delta(w_1)$ actually does intersect Δ_1 and there coincides

Boundaries of Regions Determining the Optimum Test for a Trichotomy:

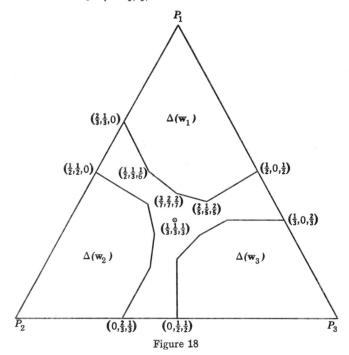

$$y = 1, 2, 3$$
$$H_1: \quad p = 0, \tfrac{1}{2}, \tfrac{1}{2}$$
$$H_2: \quad p = \tfrac{1}{2}, 0, \tfrac{1}{2} \qquad W = \begin{pmatrix} 0 & 4 & 6 \\ 6 & 0 & 4 \\ 4 & 6 & 0 \end{pmatrix}$$
$$H_3: \quad p = \tfrac{1}{2}, \tfrac{1}{2}, 0$$

Figure 18

Nature's strategy least favorable to the statistician: $\xi = (\tfrac{1}{3}, \tfrac{1}{3}, \tfrac{1}{3})$

with the line segment joining $(2/3, 1/3, 0)$ and $(1/2, 1/3, 1/6)$. The latter point satisfies also the conditions

(10.7.15) $\xi(2) \leq \xi(1) \leq 2\xi(2), \qquad \xi(3) \leq \xi(2) \leq 2\xi(3), \qquad \xi(3) \leq \xi(1)$

Let Δ_2 be the region defined by (10.7.15). Then we can find as before

the intersection of the boundary of $\Delta(\mathbf{w}_1)$ with Δ_2; the boundary hits the line $\xi(2) = \xi(3)$ at the point $(3/7, 2/7, 2/7)$, which point lies in Δ_2. Hence the boundary of $\Delta(\mathbf{w}_1)$ actually does intersect Δ_2 and there coincides with the segment joining $(1/2, 1/3, 1/6)$ to $(3/7, 2/7, 2/7)$. If we continue this method, it can be shown that $\Delta(\mathbf{w}_1)$ is bounded by the polygon with vertices $(2/3, 1/3, 0)$, $(1/2, 1/3, 1/6)$, $(3/7, 2/7, 2/7)$, $(2/5, 1/5, 2/5)$, $(1/2, 0, 1/2)$, and $(1, 0, 0)$. It is easily verified that $\Delta(\mathbf{w}_1)$ actually is a subset of $T(\mathbf{w}_1)$ as demanded by (10.7.6). The vertices of the polygons bounding $\Delta(\mathbf{w}_2)$ and $\Delta(\mathbf{w}_3)$ can be obtained by cyclic permutation of the coordinates. [See Figure 18.]

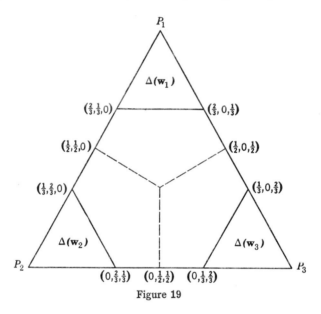

Figure 19

Example 2. The boundaries of the regions $\Delta(\mathbf{w}_i)$ might also be straight lines, as shown by the following example: Let x_1, x_2, \cdots be independently distributed with the same distribution, and x_n takes on the values 1, 2, or 3. Let H_i be the hypothesis that $x_n = i$ with probability 1 ($i = 1, 2, 3$), and let $w_{ij} = 3$ for $i \neq j$, $w_{ii} = 0$. Assume the cost of each observation is 1. Then the best test involving at least one observation is clearly to take exactly one observation and accept H_i if $x_1 = i$. The expected loss due to incorrect decision is 0, so that the risk of this test is 1. Hence the boundary of $\Delta(\mathbf{w}_1)$ is characterized by the relation, $w_{21}\xi(2) + w_{31}\xi(3) = 3(\xi(2) + \xi(3)) = 1$, or $\xi(1) = 2/3$. Similarly, $\Delta(\mathbf{w}_2)$, $\Delta(\mathbf{w}_3)$ are defined by the inequalities $\xi(2) \geq 2/3$, $\xi(3) \geq 2/3$, respectively.

If no observations are taken, the region $T(w_1)$ in which H_1 is accepted is characterized by $w_{21}\xi(2) + w_{31}\xi(3) \leq \min (w_{12}\xi(1) + w_{32}\xi(3), w_{13}\xi(1) + w_{23}\xi(2))$ or $1 - \xi(1) \leq \min (\xi(1) + \xi(3), \xi(1) + \xi(2)), 2\xi(1) \geq \max (1 - \xi(2), 1 - \xi(3))$.

The boundary is the polygonal line with vertices $(1/2, 1/2, 0)$, $(1/3, 1/3, 1/3)$, and $(1/2, 0, 1/2)$. The boundaries of $T(w_2)$ and $T(w_3)$ are found similarly. The regions $\Delta(w_1)$, $\Delta(w_2)$, $\Delta(w_3)$ clearly lie inside $T(w_1)$, $T(w_2)$, $T(w_3)$, respectively. [See Figure 19.]

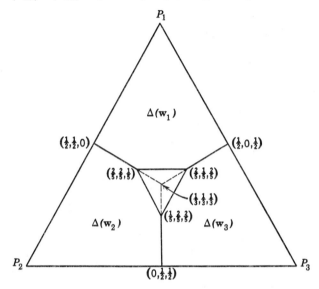

Figure 20

Example 3. In both previous examples, inner boundaries of the regions $\Delta(w_i)$ were found by equating the risk of accepting H_i if no observations are taken with the risk under the best procedure calling for taking at least one observation. The regions so found were in both cases subsets of $T(w_i)$. However, this relation need not hold in general, as shown by the following example.

Let all conditions be the same as in Example 2 except that $w_{ij} = 5/3$ for $i \neq j$. Then the risk of accepting H_1 without observations is equal to the risk of the best test, taking at least one observation when $\xi(1) = 2/5$. But the region $\xi(1) \geq 2/5$ is not a subset of $T(w_1)$ (which is the same here as in Example 2). $\Delta(w_1)$ is the intersection of $T(w_1)$ and the region $\xi(1) \geq 2/5$. $\Delta(w_1)$ is bound from below by the polygonal line with vertices $(1/2, 1/2, 0)$, $(2/5, 2/5, 1/5)$, $(2/5, 1/5, 2/5)$, and $(1/2, 0, 1/2)$. [See Figure 20.]

<div align="center">PROBLEM</div>

10.7.1. Obtain the stopping regions for the sequential trichotomy given in Figure 18 with $W = \begin{pmatrix} 0 & 6 & 6 \\ 6 & 0 & 6 \\ 6 & 6 & 0 \end{pmatrix}$.

10.8. Minimax Strategies in Sequential Games with Finite Ω and A

We have shown that when both Ω and A are finite there exists a sequential-sampling plan and a terminal-decision procedure which minimizes the average risk for every ξ. This means that, for every mixed strategy of nature, the statistician has a pure strategy which is optimal against it. Thus, if nature's mixed strategy were known, the statistician's problem would be solved, except for the problem of characterizing the optimal sequential procedure S^*. But often nature's mixed strategy is unknown. In this case, the minimax strategy might be employed; that is, the statistician might select that decision procedure which minimizes the maximum risk. Since the Bayes risk $\rho^*(\xi)$ is a concave and continuous function of ξ defined over a closed and convex set Ξ in a finite dimensional Cartesian space, it will attain a maximum at some point $\xi = \xi^* \varepsilon \Xi$. Hence ξ^* will be nature's least favorable distribution. If the Bayes sequential procedure against ξ^* requires at least one observation and if $f_\omega(x_i)$ is a density for each ω, then this Bayes procedure, which is a pure strategy for the statistician, will in fact be a minimax strategy. This, however, no longer holds if $f_\omega(x_i)$ is a discrete probability distribution, and in this case the statistician may have to resort to mixed strategies.

As an illustration consider the dichotomy discussed in Section 10.6. Suppose we have obtained γ and δ and found that $\rho^*(\zeta)$ given in (10.6.14) has a maximum at $\zeta = \zeta^*$ and ζ^* does not belong to a stopping region. Then in order that the sequential test S^* (defined by the boundaries $-b^*_{\zeta*}$ and $a^*_{\zeta*}$) be independent of ζ, which is required here for a minimax solution, we must have

$$(10.8.1) \quad E_1[n \mid -b^*_{\zeta*}, a^*_{\zeta*}] + w_{12}[1 - \pi_1(-b^*_{\zeta*}, a^*_{\zeta*})]$$

$$= E_2(n \mid -b^*_{\zeta*}, a^*_{\zeta*}) + w_{21}\pi_2(-b^*_{\zeta*}, a^*_{\zeta*})$$

But, since $a^*_{\zeta*}$ and $b^*_{\zeta*}$ are necessarily integers, this equation will usually not be satisfied. This implies that nature's strategy ζ^* must have the property that when we set $\zeta = \zeta^*$ in (10.6.5) (removing the braces) either $a^*_{\zeta*}$ is exactly an integer, or $b^*_{\zeta*}$ is exactly an integer, or both are

integers. Suppose for example that $a^*_{\zeta*}$ is an integer but not $b^*_{\zeta*}$. This means that when $\sum_{i=1}^{n} x_i = a^*_{\zeta*}$ we have two courses of action to follow. We can either stop and accept H_2 or go on experimenting with the best sequential procedure defined by boundaries $a = a^*_{\zeta*} + 1$, $-b = -b^*_{\zeta*}$. But these two procedures will not always have the same risk for $\zeta \neq \zeta^*$. Thus, in order to make the risk independent of ζ we shall have to employ a mixed strategy. That is, we shall have to employ one procedure some specified fraction α of the time and the other procedure, $1 - \alpha$ of the time, where $0 < \alpha < 1$. The above is illustrated in Figures 15 and 16.

Another remark which might be of interest is that the minimax sequential procedure even in relatively simple situations need not be unique as is illustrated in the problem dealt with in Figure 15. As another illustration, consider the trichotomy discussed in Section 10.7. Here the minimax procedure is to stop with one observation and accept H_3 if $y_1 = 1$, H_2 if $y_1 = 2$, and H_1 if $y_1 = 3$. This can be seen from the following considerations.

By (10.7.12) the maximum conditional risk, given that $y_1 = 1$, is 3, and it occurs when $\xi(3) \leq \xi(2) \leq 2\xi(3)$. Similarly, the maximum conditional expected risk, given that $y_1 = 2$ and 3, respectively, are both equal to 3, and they occur when $\xi(1) \leq 2\xi(2)$, $\xi(2) \leq \xi(1) \leq 2\xi(2)$, respectively. Any $\boldsymbol{\xi}$ satisfying these three conditions will be a least favorable a priori distribution, and, clearly, the only set of values is $\xi(1) = \xi(2) = \xi(3) = 1/3$. If $y_1 = 1$, the corresponding a posteriori distribution is $(0, 1/2, 1/2)$. This is the boundary of $\Delta(\mathbf{w}_3)$. In general, then, the minimax procedure is to take one observation, stop, and accept H_3 if $y_1 = 1$, H_1 if $y_1 = 2$, and H_2 if $y_1 = 3$. The risk associated with this test is 3, of which the cost of observation is 1, and the expected loss due to incorrect decision is 2, independent of the true a priori distribution.

The above minimax test, however, is not unique, the lack of uniqueness corresponding exactly to the inclusion or exclusion of the boundaries of $\Delta(\mathbf{w}_1)$, $\Delta(\mathbf{w}_2)$, and $\Delta(\mathbf{w}_3)$ in those sets. If we exclude the boundaries, then, when $y_1 = 1$, we continue. So long as $y_j = 1$, the a posteriori probabilities remain at $(0, 1/2, 1/2)$: when $y_j = 2(3)$, the a posteriori probability of $H_3(H_2)$ becomes unity. Therefore, a second minimax procedure is to stop the first time $y_n \neq y_{n-1}$ and then accept that hypothesis whose subscript equals neither y_n nor y_{n-1}. The maximum risk is again 3; all of this is represented by the expected number of observations which is the same for all a priori distributions.

10.9. Another Optimal Property of the Sequential-Probability Ratio Test

In Section 10.3 we have shown that the sequential-probability ratio test is optimal in the sense that for a given a priori distribution $\boldsymbol{\xi} = (\zeta, 1 - \zeta)$ it minimizes the average risk. We shall now prove that for a fixed probability of making erroneous decisions, this test minimizes the average number of observations when H_1 is true as well as when H_2 is true.

Theorem 10.9.1. Let a sequential-probability ratio test S^* be defined by the boundaries $A \geq 1$ and $B \leq 1$, and let α be the probability of accepting H_2 when H_1 is true, β the probability of accepting H_1 when H_2 is true, when S^* is employed: Let S be any other test procedure that results in probabilities $\alpha' \leq \alpha$, $\beta' \leq \beta$ of making erroneous decisions. Then

$$(10.9.1) \qquad E[n \mid S^*; H_1] \leq E(n \mid S; H_1)$$

and

$$(10.9.2) \qquad E(n \mid S^*; H_2) \leq E(n \mid S; H_2)$$

where the symbols in (10.9.1) and (10.9.2) represent the expected number of observations required under the specified decision procedure and hypothesis.

Proof. Choose any $\boldsymbol{\xi} = (\zeta, 1 - \zeta)$ such that $0 < \zeta < 1$, and solve for γ and δ from (10.3.4) in terms of A and B. Then since the quantity b_γ entering in (10.3.13) and (10.3.15) is equal to $\log (A/B)$ [see (10.3.4)] we can solve for $w_{12} = u_{12}(\gamma, \delta)$ and $w_{21} = u_{21}(\gamma, \delta)$.

The three quantities $u_{12}(\gamma, \delta)$, $u_{21}(\gamma, \delta)$, and $\boldsymbol{\xi}$ have the property that, if the a priori distribution is $\boldsymbol{\xi}$ and if the risk of accepting H_2 when H_1 is true is $u_{12}(\gamma, \delta)$ and the risk of accepting H_1 when H_2 is true is $u_{21}(\gamma, \delta)$, then S^* has minimum average risk. The average risk under S^* is given by

$$(1) \quad \rho(\boldsymbol{\xi}, S^*) = \zeta E(n \mid S^*; H_1) + (1 - \zeta)E(n \mid S^*; H_2)$$
$$+ \zeta u_{12}(\gamma, \delta)\alpha + (1 - \zeta)u_{21}(\gamma, \delta)\beta$$

Similarly, the average risk under S for the same triple, $\boldsymbol{\xi}$, $u_{12}(\gamma, \delta)$, $u_{21}(\gamma, \delta)$ is

$$(2) \quad \rho(\boldsymbol{\xi}, S) = \zeta E(n \mid S; H_1) + (1 - \zeta)E(n \mid S; H_2)$$
$$+ \zeta u_{12}(\gamma, \delta)\alpha' + (1 - \zeta)u_{21}(\gamma, \delta)\beta'$$

Now since $\rho(\boldsymbol{\xi}, \mathrm{S}^*) \leq \rho(\boldsymbol{\xi}, \mathrm{S})$ we must have

(3) $\zeta E(n \mid \mathrm{S}^*; H_1) + (1 - \zeta)E(n \mid \mathrm{S}^*; H_2) \leq E(n \mid \mathrm{S}; H_1)$
$$+ (1 - \zeta)E(n \mid \mathrm{S}; H_2)$$

But inequality 3 must hold for all values of ζ, $0 < \zeta < 1$. Hence, from continuity considerations we must have

(4) $E(n \mid \mathrm{S}^*; H_1) \leq E(n \mid \mathrm{S}; H_1)$ and $E(n \mid \mathrm{S}^*; H_2) \leq E(n \mid \mathrm{S}; H_2)$

This proves the theorem.

CHAPTER 11

Estimation

11.1. Introduction

A statistical-estimation problem with a fixed sample-size experiment has the following structure: We are given a sample space $\mathcal{Z} = (Z, \Omega, p)$ and a numerical-valued function θ defined on Ω whose value the statistician wishes to estimate on the basis of the outcome of an experiment $z \, \varepsilon \, Z$. (For the sake of simplicity we restrict ourselves to the consideration of numerical-valued functions θ. Many of the results of this chapter carry over easily to the case where θ is vector-valued.) A non-randomized decision function for the statistician, usually called an estimate, is a numerical function t defined on Z, specifying for each z the number $a \, \varepsilon \, A$ which will be chosen to estimate $\theta(\omega)$ when that z is observed. The space of actions A is here the real line. The loss function L defined on $\Omega \times A$ is non-negative and for many estimation problems is usually bounded only from below. Thus the only functions t that can be considered as possible estimates for θ are those for which the risk function ρ with

$$\rho(\omega, t) = \sum_{z \, \varepsilon \, Z} L(\omega, t(z)) p(z \mid \omega)$$

is finite. Another restriction which is usually placed on L and which is often not unreasonable is that, for any $\omega \, \varepsilon \, \Omega$, $L(\omega, a)$ is assumed to be convex in a and further that, as $a \to \pm\infty$, $L(\omega, a) \to +\infty$ for all ω. This assumption has two interesting consequences. One is that the statistician never needs to consider randomized estimates. The other is that any estimate u which is not a function of a sufficient statistic t is inadmissible, and that $v = E_\omega(u \mid t)$ (which is independent of ω [see Definition 8.2.1 and Definition 8.2.2]) constitutes an improvement. These facts are incorporated in the following two theorems.

Theorem 11.1.1. In any estimation problem where $L(\omega, a)$ is for a fixed ω convex in a and $\to +\infty$ as $a \to \pm\infty$, the class of pure estimates is complete: In fact, if η is any randomized estimate, mixing pure esti-

mates t_1, t_2, \cdots, with probabilities λ_1, λ_2, \cdots, the pure estimate

$$t^*(z) = \sum_j \lambda_j t_j(z)$$

is superior, i.e.,

$$\rho(\omega, t^*) \le \rho^*(\omega, \eta)$$

for all ω.

Proof.

$$\rho^*(\omega, \eta) = \sum_j \sum_\omega \lambda_j L(\omega, t_j(z)) p(z \mid \omega)$$

$$= \sum_\omega p(z \mid \omega) \left[\sum_j \lambda_j L(\omega, t_j(z)) \right]$$

Now, by Theorem 2.2.8, $t^*(z)$ exists since by assumption the series $\sum_j \lambda_j L(\omega, t_j(z))$ converges for all z for which $p(z \mid \omega) > 0$, and

$$\sum_j \lambda_j L(\omega, t_j(z)) \ge L(\omega, t^*(z))$$

These two facts prove the theorem.

Theorem 11.1.2. Consider an estimation problem where $L(\omega, a)$ is for fixed ω convex in a. Then for any statistic t which is sufficient on $\mathcal{Z} = (Z, \Omega, p)$ and any estimate u of the function θ, the estimate $v = E_\omega(u \mid t)$ which is a function of t only, has the property that

(i) $$\rho(\omega, v) \le \rho(\omega, u)$$

for all ω. If $L(\omega, a)$ is for a given ω strictly convex in a, actual inequality holds in (i) for that ω unless u is a function of t, i.e., unless v and u coincide.

Proof. To prove this theorem we first restate Theorem 2.2.8 as a lemma involving conditional expectations.

Lemma 11.1.1. For any real-valued random variable y, any convex function h, and any random variable t,

$$E[h(y) \mid t] \ge h[E(y \mid t)]$$

for all t. If h is strictly convex, actual inequality holds unless y is constant for the given u.

We now return to the proof of the theorem. For fixed ω

(1) $$\rho(\omega, u) = E_\omega[L(\omega, u)], \qquad \rho(\omega, v) = E_\omega[L(\omega, v)]$$

Application of Lemma 11.1.1 with $y = u$ and

$$(2) \qquad\qquad h(u) = L(\omega, u)$$

yields

$$(3) \qquad\qquad E[L(\omega, u) \mid t] \geq L(\omega, v(t))$$

for all t. Multiplying both sides of (3) by $p(t \mid \omega)$ and summing with respect to t yields

$$(4) \qquad\qquad \rho(\omega, u) \geq \rho(\omega, v)$$

If $L(\omega, a)$ is strictly convex in a, we have actual inequality in (3) unless $u \equiv v$ for the given t, so that we have inequality in (4) unless $u \equiv v$ for all t.

The remainder of this chapter will deal with several classes of problems in estimation where some general results are available. It is a fact that thus far only the framework of the general theory of estimation has been established. Specific applications to many general classes of problems await further research. This is particularly true in the case of sequential-estimation procedures.

In the sequential games considered in Chapters 9 and 10, a decision procedure specifies a sampling plan S and a terminal-decision function d. For general sequential-estimation problems, little is known about the structure of Bayes and minimax sampling plans, though in certain cases the hypotheses of Theorem 9.3.3 can be verified (as in the illustration following that theorem) so that the Bayes S will be truncated or of fixed sample size. The Bayes terminal-decision functions d, on the other hand, present no additional difficulties in the sequential case, since Theorem 9.2.1 reduces the choice of d to the solution of fixed sample-size problems: *for any ξ, the Bayes estimate $d = a(j, x)$ is for each j the Bayes estimate $t_j(x)$ against ξ in the fixed sample-size estimation problem in which x_1, \cdots, x_j are observed.* Thus, for estimation problems with a prescribed S, which are of some interest, the Bayes solutions are easily described. These remarks are illustrated in several of the problems in this chapter.

PROBLEMS

11.1.1. If $z = (x_1, \cdots, x_N)$, where x_1, \cdots, x_N are independent with $p_\omega\{x_i = j\} = 1/\omega, j = 1, \cdots, \omega, \omega = 1, 2, \cdots$, and $L(\omega, a) = (a - \omega)^2$, show that

$$t = 2\,\frac{x_1 + \cdots + x_N}{N} - 1$$

is not an admissible estimate for ω.

11.1.2. If t is admissible in a given estimation problem, it remains admissible if $L(\omega, a)$ is replaced by $L_1(\omega, a) = \lambda(\omega)L(\omega, a)$, $\lambda(\omega) > 0$.

11.2. Bayes Estimates for Special Loss Functions

We are given a sample space $\mathcal{Z} = (Z, \Omega, p)$ a numerical-valued function θ on Ω, and a priori distribution ξ on Ω, and a space of actions A which is the real line. The problem is to find a Bayes estimate of θ on the basis of the outcome of an experiment $z \; \varepsilon \; Z$, i.e., to find a real-valued function t on Z which minimizes the average risk where for each $\omega \; \varepsilon \; \Omega$ and each $a \; \varepsilon \; A$ the loss is given by $L(\omega, a)$.

The solution to the above problem is as follows: Let

$$(11.2.1) \qquad P_\xi(z) = \sum_{\omega \, \varepsilon \, \Omega} p(z \mid \omega)\xi(\omega)$$

and let $\tau_z(t)$ be the a posteriori risk, given that the estimating procedure t is used and z is observed. (Note that we do not exhibit the dependence of the function τ_z on ξ.) Then it follows from Definition 3.6.5 that, if $\rho(\xi, t)$ is the risk from t,

$$(11.2.2) \qquad \rho(\xi, t) = \sum_z \tau_z(t(z))P_\xi(z)$$

Although in this case the function L is not necessarily bounded, the arguments of Theorems 6.2.2 and 9.2.1 still apply to show that, for a given z and ξ, the Bayes estimate is obtained by choosing that value t such that

$$(11.2.3) \qquad \tau_z(t) = \inf_{a \, \varepsilon \, A} \tau_z(a)$$

If $\tau_z(a)$ has, for a given z, a minimum in A, then a Bayes estimate will actually exist. This situation arises very frequently in many statistical problems. It may happen that the right-hand side of (11.2.3) is infinite for some z for which $P_\xi(z) > 0$, in which case no estimating procedure of finite risk exists. In most cases of interest, however, the Bayes risk is finite.

The above remarks together with the pertinent theorems proved in Chapter 6 concerning the class \mathcal{B} of Bayes solutions furnish a fairly complete description of Bayes estimates when considered from a general point of view. However, specific properties and characterizations of such estimates are generally difficult to obtain except for relatively simple types of loss functions. In this section we shall consider 3 types of such loss functions which are of theoretical and practical interest. We shall also consider a prediction problem which can be cast into the framework of a Bayes estimation problem.

1. Bayes Estimates for Quadratic Loss Functions. Let

$$(11.2.4) \qquad L(\omega, a) = \lambda(\omega)[\theta(\omega) - a]^2, \qquad \lambda(\omega) > 0$$

For any function γ on Ω and any $\xi \, \varepsilon \, \Xi$ we shall denote by $E_\xi[\gamma \mid z]$ the conditional expected value of γ, given z. Thus fixing a and setting $\gamma = L$, in (11.2.4), we get

$$(11.2.5) \qquad \tau_z(a) = E_\xi[\lambda(\theta - a)^2 \mid z]$$

Theorem 11.2.1. For each z, $\tau_z(a) < \infty$ either for no a, for exactly one a, or for every $a \, \varepsilon \, A$. The second case implies that $E_\xi[\lambda \mid z] = \infty$ and the third that $E_\xi[\lambda \mid z] < \infty$.

Proof. We first show that, if $\tau_z(a)$ is finite for two distinct points, say, a_1, a_2 with $a_1 < a_2$ in A, then it is finite for all $a \, \varepsilon \, A$.

The function $\lambda(\theta - a)^2$ is convex in a so that, for all a in the closed interval (a_1, a_2) and all ω,

$$(1) \quad \lambda(\omega)[\theta(\omega) - a]^2 \leq \frac{a_2 - a}{a_2 - a_1} \lambda(\omega)[\theta(\omega) - a_1]^2$$
$$+ \frac{a - a_1}{a_2 - a_1} \lambda(\omega)[\theta(\omega) - a_2]^2$$

and hence, for all $a \, \varepsilon \, (a_1, a_2)$, $\tau_z(a) < \infty$ since

$$(2) \qquad \tau_z(a) \leq \frac{a_2 - a}{a_2 - a_1} \tau_z(a_1) + \frac{a - a_1}{a_2 - a_1} \tau_z(a_2)$$

Now let $b \, \varepsilon \, (a_1, a_2)$, and let c be any arbitrary point in A with $c \neq b$. Then from the identity

$$(3) \qquad (b - \theta)^2 = (b - c + c - \theta)^2$$
$$= (b - c)^2 + 2(b - c)(c - \theta) + (c - \theta)^2$$

we readily obtain

$$(4) \qquad (b - c)^2 + 2(b - c)(c - \theta) \leq (b - \theta)^2$$

and consequently we conclude that

$$(5) \qquad E_\xi[\{\lambda(b - c)^2 + 2\lambda(b - c)(c - \theta)\} \mid z] < \infty$$

Setting $c = 0$, we get

$$(6) \qquad E_\xi[\{b\lambda - 2\theta\lambda\} \mid z] < \infty$$

Since b is any arbitrary point in (a_1, a_2) it follows that $E_\xi[\lambda \mid z] < \infty$ and therefore $E_\xi[\theta\lambda \mid z] < \infty$. The finiteness of $E_\xi[\lambda\theta^2 \mid z]$ now follows from the finiteness of $\tau_z(a_1)$. Thus $\tau_z(a)$ is finite for all $a \, \varepsilon \, A$.

We next show that if $\tau_z(a_1) < \infty$ and $E_\xi[\lambda \mid z] < \infty$ then $\tau_z(a) < \infty$ for all $a \, \varepsilon \, A$.

Since $\lambda(\omega) > 0$, Schwarz' inequality yields

$$(7) \quad \left| E_\xi[\lambda(\theta - a_1) \mid z] \right| \leq E_\xi[\lambda \mid \theta - a_1 \mid \mid z] = E_\xi[\sqrt{\lambda}(\sqrt{\lambda} \mid \theta - a_1 \mid) \mid z]$$

$$\leq [E_\xi(\lambda \mid z)]^{1/2}[E_\xi(\lambda \mid \theta - a_1 \mid^2 \mid z)]^{1/2}$$

$$= [E_\xi(\lambda \mid z)]^{1/2}[\tau_z(a)]^{1/2} < \infty$$

But, since

$$(8) \quad E_\xi[\lambda\theta \mid z] = E_\xi[a_1\lambda + \lambda(\theta - a_1) \mid z]$$

we have by (7) and the assumption of the finiteness of $E_\xi[\lambda \mid z]$ that $E_\xi[\lambda\theta \mid z] < \infty$. The finiteness of $E_\xi[\lambda\theta^2 \mid z]$ follows from the finiteness of $\tau_z(a_1)$. Thus $\tau_z(a) < \infty$ for all $a \, \varepsilon \, A$.

Finally, if $\tau_z(a) < \infty$ for all $a \, \varepsilon \, A$ then $E_\xi[\lambda \mid z] < \infty$. This follows since in that case (6) holds for all $b \, \varepsilon \, A$.

From Theorem 11.2.1 we see that if $\tau_z(a)$ exists for two values of $a \, \varepsilon \, A$, or, equivalently, if $\tau_z(a)$ exists for one value of a and $E_\xi[\lambda \mid z] < \infty$, then $\tau_z(a)$ exists for all a, and, moreover,

$$(9) \quad E_\xi[\lambda\theta^i \mid z] < \infty, \qquad i = 0, 1, 2$$

Hence $\tau_z(a)$ can be written as

$$(10) \quad \tau_z(a) = a^2 E_\xi[\lambda \mid z] - 2aE_\xi[\lambda\theta \mid z] + E_\xi[\lambda\theta^2 \mid z]$$

which for a given z is a quadratic function in a and therefore has a minimum at $a^* = t(z)$ where

$$(11) \qquad t(z) = \frac{E_\xi[\lambda\theta \mid z]}{E_\xi[\lambda \mid z]}$$

We thus have the following.

Theorem 11.2.2. In any estimation problem where the loss is defined by (11.2.4), if the a priori distribution ξ admits any estimate of finite expected risk then it admits a Bayes estimate, and essentially only one, defined thus:

$$t^*(z) = b \qquad \text{if} \quad \tau_z(b) < \infty \quad \text{only for} \quad b \, \varepsilon \, A$$

$$= \frac{E_\xi[\lambda\theta \mid z]}{E_\xi[\lambda \mid z]}, \quad \text{if} \quad \tau_z(a) < \infty \quad \text{for all} \qquad a \, \varepsilon \, A$$

Theorem 11.2.3. Let the loss function be given by (11.2.4). Then, if for a given a priori distribution ξ which admits an estimate of finite risk the expectation of the function λ exists, then the Bayes estimate t^* is biased (i.e., the expectation of t^* is not identically equal to θ) or the Bayes risk is zero.

Proof. Let $E_\xi(\lambda)$ be the expected value of λ with respect to an a priori distribution ξ. Then the existence of $E_\xi(\lambda)$ implies the existence of $E_\xi(\lambda \mid z)$ for all z for which $P_\xi(z) > 0$ as can be seen from the equation

$$(1) \qquad E_\xi(\lambda) = \sum_z E_\xi(\lambda \mid z) P_\xi(z)$$

We define

$$(2) \qquad \xi_\lambda(\omega) = \frac{\lambda(\omega)\xi(\omega)}{E_\xi(\lambda)}$$

Then the Bayes estimate with respect to the loss function (11.2.4) and ξ is the same as the Bayes estimate with respect to the loss function L^* defined by

$$(3) \qquad L^*(\omega, a) = [\theta(\omega) - a]^2$$

and the a priori distribution ξ_λ. Since ξ and hence ξ_λ admits an estimate of finite risk, then the Bayes estimate with respect to ξ_λ exists and is given by

$$(4) \qquad t^*(z) = E_{\xi_\lambda}(\theta \mid z) = E_{\xi_\lambda}(\theta \mid t^*)$$

by Problem 3.11.6. Now suppose t^* is unbiased; i.e.,

$$(5) \qquad E(t^* \mid \omega) = \theta(\omega)$$

for all ω. Then

$$(6) \qquad E(\theta t^*) = E[t^* E(\theta \mid z)] = E(t^2) = E[\theta E(t^* \mid \omega)] = E(\theta^2)$$

from which it follows that

$$(7) \qquad \rho(\xi, t^*) = \sum_\omega \sum_\xi [\theta(\omega) - t^*(z)]^2 p(z \mid \omega) \xi(\omega) = 0$$

The assumption of the existence of the second moments of θ and t^* which is implied in the above proof can be removed.

If $E_\xi(\lambda)$ does not exist, then Theorem 11.2.3 no longer holds, as can be seen from the following example:

It is desired to obtain a Bayes estimate of a binomial probability ω of a success, on the basis of N independent trials when the a priori distribution ξ is rectangular over the interval $(0, 1)$ and the loss function L is given by

$$L(\omega, a) = \frac{(\omega - a)^2}{\omega(1 - \omega)}, \qquad 0 \le a \le 1$$

Here

$$\lambda(\omega) = \frac{1}{\omega(1 - \omega)} = \frac{1}{\omega} + \frac{1}{1 - \omega}$$

so that $\int_0^1 \lambda(\omega)\, d\omega = \infty$. On the other hand, if m represents the number of successes in the N trials, then, by Theorem 11.2.2, the Bayes estimate $t^*(m)$ if $m \neq 0$ or 1 is given by

$$t^*(m) = \frac{\displaystyle\int_0^1 \frac{\omega^{m+1}(1-\omega)^{N-m}}{\omega(1-\omega)}\, d\omega}{\displaystyle\int_0^1 \frac{\omega^m(1-\omega)^{N-m}}{\omega(1-\omega)}\, d\omega}$$

this results in a β function

$$= \frac{\Gamma(m+1)\Gamma(N-m)}{\Gamma(N+1)} \times \frac{\Gamma(N)}{\Gamma(m)\Gamma(N-m)} = \frac{m}{N}$$

which is unbiased. For this example, it is also easily verified that $E_\xi\left[\dfrac{(\omega-a)^2}{\omega(1-\omega)}\,\middle|\, m\right]$ exists for only one value of a, viz. $a = 0$, when $m = 0$, and only one value of a, viz. $a = 1$, when $m = N$, so that $t^*(0) = 0$ and $t^*(N) = 1$.

2. Bayes Estimates Where the Loss Depends on the Absolute Error, i.e.,

$$(11.2.6) \qquad L(\omega, a) = \lambda(\omega)\big|\,\theta(\omega) - a\,\big|, \qquad \lambda(\omega) > 0$$

As in the case of the quadratic risk function, let $\tau_z(a)$ be the conditional expected value of the above loss function with respect to a fixed a priori distribution ξ when z is observed. Then

$$(11.2.7) \qquad \tau_z(a) = E_\xi[\lambda(\omega)\big|\,\theta(\omega) - a\,\big|\,|\,z]$$

As in Theorem 11.2.2, we have,

Theorem 11.2.4. For each z, $\tau_z(a) < \infty$ either for no a, for exactly one a, or for every $a \,\varepsilon\, A$. The second case implies $E_\xi(\lambda \,|\, z) = \infty$, and the third case implies $E_\xi(\lambda \,|\, z) < \infty$.

We first show that, if $\tau_z(a) < \infty$ for a_1 and a_2 with $a_1 < a_2$, then $E_\xi(\lambda \,|\, z) < \infty$. This follows since

$$(1) \qquad \lambda(\omega)(a_2 - a_1) \leq \lambda(\omega)(\big|\,a_2 - \theta(\omega)\,\big| + \big|\,\theta(\omega) - a_1\,\big|)$$

and hence

$$(2) \qquad (a_2 - a_1)E_\xi[\lambda \,|\, z] \leq \tau_z(a_2) + \tau_z(a_1) < \infty$$

Now consider any $b \,\varepsilon\, A$, and let $a = a_1 - b$. Then

$$(3) \qquad \lambda(\omega)\big|\,\theta(\omega) - a\,\big| \leq \lambda(\omega)\big|\,\theta(\omega) - a_1\,\big| + \lambda(\omega)\big|\,b\,\big|$$

and hence, since by (2), $E_\xi(\lambda \mid z) < \infty$, we have

(4) $\tau_z(a) \leq \tau_z(a_1) + |b| E_\xi(\lambda \mid z) < \infty$

and, since b is arbitrary, we see that $\tau_z(a) < \infty$ for all $a \, \varepsilon \, A$ which proves the theorem.

We see from the above that, if for a given z, $\tau_z(a)$ is finite for two points of A, or, what is equivalent, if $\tau_z(a)$ is finite for any one value of a and $E_\xi(\lambda \mid z) < \infty$, then $\tau_z(a) < \infty$ for all $a \, \varepsilon \, A$. This fact will permit us to give a complete characterization of the Bayes solutions for the loss function under consideration. However, before we do this, we require a preliminary definition and theorem.

Definition 11.2.1. Let $p(x)$ be the distribution of a real-valued random variable, let A be the real line, let

$$m_1 = \inf_{a \, \varepsilon \, A} \, [P(x \leq a) \geq 1/2]$$

$$m_2 = \sup_{a \, \varepsilon \, A} \, [P(x \geq a) \geq 1/2]$$

and let I be the closed interval (m_1, m_2). Then any $m \, \varepsilon \, I$ is called a median of the distribution $p(x)$.

Lemma 11.2.1. Let m be a median of $p(x)$, and let

$$g(a) = E|x - a| = \sum_x |x - a| p(x)$$

exist for at least one $a \, \varepsilon \, A$ (and hence for all a). Then $g(a)$ is minimized by $a = m$.

Proof. Let $c \, \varepsilon \, A$ and $c \notin I$. We shall show that

(1) $\psi(c) = E[|x - c| - |x - m|] > 0$

Assume for the sake of argument that $c > m$. Then

(2) $\psi(c) = \sum_{x \leq m} (c - m)p(x) + \sum_{x > c} (m - c)p(x)$

$$+ \sum_{m < x \leq c} (c + m - 2x)p(x)$$

Now the third term of (2) is clearly positive and moreover,

(3) $\sum_{x \leq m} (c - m)p(x) > \frac{1}{2}(c - m), \qquad \left| \sum_{x > c} (m - c)p(x) \right| < \frac{1}{2}(c - m)$

and hence $\psi(c) > 0$ which proves the lemma.

Now by definition, the quantity $\tau_z(a)$ in (11.2.7) is given by

$$(11.2.8) \qquad \tau_z(a) = \sum_{\omega \, \varepsilon \, \Omega} \lambda(\omega) \big| \theta(\omega) - a \big| \xi_z(\omega)$$

where

$$\xi_z(\omega) = \frac{p(z \mid \omega)\xi(\omega)}{\sum\limits_{\omega' \, \varepsilon \, \Omega} p(z \mid \omega')\xi(\omega')}$$

We now define

$$(11.2.9) \qquad r_\xi(\theta_0 \mid z) = \sum_{\{\omega : \, \theta(\omega) = \theta_0\}} \frac{\lambda(\omega)\xi_z(\omega)}{E_\xi(\lambda \mid z)}$$

and

$$(11.2.10) \qquad \tau^*_z(a) = \sum_\theta \big| \theta - a \big| r_\xi(\theta \mid z)$$

It is clear that any a which minimizes $\tau^*_z(a)$ in (11.2.10) will also minimize $\tau_z(a)$ in (11.2.8). This in conjunction with Theorem 11.2.4 and Lemma 11.2.1 gives a complete characterization of Bayes solutions for the loss function 11.2.6 and is incorporated in the following.

Theorem 11.2.5. In any estimation problem where the loss is defined by (11.2.6), if the a priori distribution ξ admits any estimate of finite expected risk then it admits a Bayes estimate defined thus:

$$t^*(z) = b \quad \text{if} \quad \tau^*_z(b) < \infty \quad \text{only for} \quad b \, \varepsilon \, A$$

$$= \text{median of the distribution } r_\xi(\theta \mid z)$$

if $\tau^*_z(a) < \infty$ for all $a \, \varepsilon \, A$, where τ^*_z is defined in (11.2.10) and $r_\xi(\theta \mid z)$ is defined in (11.2.9).

As an illustration, consider again the problem of estimating a binomial probability ω of a success on the basis of N independent trials when ξ is rectangular over the interval $(0, 1)$ and

$$L(\omega, a) = \frac{\big| \omega - a \big|}{\omega(1 - \omega)}$$

Let m be the number of successes. Then, if $m = 0$, the Bayes estimate of ω is zero; if $m = N$, the Bayes estimate is unity; and, if $m \neq 0$ or N, the Bayes estimate of ω is the median of the distribution density

$$r_\xi(\omega \mid m) = \frac{\Gamma(N)}{\Gamma(m)\Gamma(N - m)} \omega^{m-1}(1 - \omega)^{N-m-1}$$

3. Bayes Estimates of Bounded Absolute and Relative Errors. Consider the following two loss functions:

$$(11.2.11) \qquad L(\omega, a) = 0 \quad \text{if} \quad |\theta(\omega) - a| \leq k$$
$$= 1 \quad \text{if} \quad |\theta(\omega) - a| > k$$

where $k > 0$.

$$(11.2.12) \qquad L(\omega, a) = 0 \quad \text{if} \quad |\theta(\omega) - a| \leq \alpha a$$
$$= 1 \quad \text{if} \quad |\theta(\omega) - a| > \alpha a$$

where $0 < \alpha < 1$.

The loss function 11.2.11 is of particular interest in case z is a vector in N space and $\theta(\omega)$ is a location (i.e., translation) parameter in a distribution. The loss function 11.2.12 is of interest in case $\theta(\omega)$ is a positive scale parameter in a distribution of a positive random variable. In this case a is also assumed to be positive. The latter loss function can also be written as

$$(11.2.13) \qquad L(\omega, a) = 0 \quad \text{if} \quad (1 - \alpha) \leq \theta(\omega)/a \leq 1 + \alpha$$
$$= 1 \quad \text{otherwise}$$

In particular, if we take logarithms of the quantities involved, this loss function (employing the same symbols $\theta(\omega)$ and a) can be expressed as

$$(11.2.14) \qquad L(\omega, a) = 0 \quad \text{if} \quad -c \leq \theta(\omega) - a \leq d$$
$$= 1 \quad \text{otherwise}$$

where c and d are positive numbers. It can be seen that (11.2.11) is a special case of (11.2.14).

To obtain a Bayes estimate for the loss functions under consideration and for an a priori distribution ξ, we set

$$r_\xi(\theta_0 \mid z) = \sum_{\{\omega:\, \theta(\omega) = \theta_0\}} \xi_z(\omega)$$

where $\xi_z(\omega)$ is the a posteriori probability of ω, given z. Now, for each $a \, \varepsilon \, A$, we define an interval

$$I_a = \{\theta: a - c \leq \theta \leq a + d\}$$

We also define the function R_ξ by

$$(11.2.15) \qquad R_\xi(I_a \mid z) = \sum_{\theta \, \varepsilon \, I_a} r_\xi(\theta \mid z)$$

It is clear then that the Bayes estimate for this problem is obtained by finding that $a \, \varepsilon \, A$ which maximizes $R_\xi(I_a \mid z)$ for each z.

The interval I_a which maximizes (11.2.15) is called a *modal interval*. In particular, if $c = d = 0$ the modal interval reduces to a point which is the mode of the distribution $r_\xi(\theta \mid z)$. In case the a priori distribution of θ is rectangular, the mode of the resulting conditional distribution is known as the *maximum likelihood estimate* of θ. If $r_\xi(\theta \mid z)$ is a density, every estimate for the case $c = d = 0$ is Bayes since the probability of zero error with any estimate is zero.

Let $t^*(z)$ be the value of a which maximizes (11.2.15), and let $\beta^*(z) = R_\xi(I_{t^*} \mid z)$. Then, for the location parameter case, $\beta^*(z)$ is the conditional probability that the estimate of θ does not differ by more than k units from the true value, and, for the case of a scale parameter, it is the conditional probability that the estimate does not differ by more than a fraction α from the true value. The quantity

$$\beta = \sum_z \beta^*(z) P_\xi(z)$$

will be called the *confidence coefficient of these estimates*. The estimates t^* will be termed *estimates of bounded absolute error* in the case of translation parameters and *estimates of bounded relative error* in the case of scale parameters. Minimax estimates of the above type both for location and scale parameters will be considered in Sections 11.3 and 11.4 respectively.

4. Prediction Problems Which Can Be Cast into the Framework of Bayes Estimation. Let y, x_1, \cdots, x_k be $k + 1$ random variables having a joint distribution $q(y, x_1, \cdots, x_k)$ which is assumed to be known. A decision problem, which takes the form of a prediction, is usually formulated as follows: The statistician observes only x_1, \cdots, x_k and on the basis of this information desires to predict the value of y. There may be many reasons for deciding to predict rather than observe y. In some cases y can be observed only after a time lag. Thus, for example, if y represents the performance of a complex mechanism, its value can be known only after the mechanism has been assembled. Or again, if y represents the possible average grades in college of an applicant, then y can be observed only after a lag of four years. Another possible reason for not wishing to observe y directly might be the destructiveness of the experiment which yields the value of y. This, for example, is the case where y represents the tensile strength of a given metallic object or the presence or absence of an internal tumor in a human body.

A predictor of y is a function t which maps each vector $x = (x_1, x_2, \cdots, x_k)$ into a decision space A. Since y need not be either a numerical- or vector-valued random variable, the space A can be fairly complex.

We shall here consider only the case where y is numerical valued so that A is the real line. We shall also assume that, if the true outcome is y and $a \, \varepsilon \, A$ is a prediction, then $L(y, a)$ measures the loss due to the departure of y from a and that $L(y, a) \geq 0$ for all y and a.

Since $q(y, x_1, \cdots, x_k)$ is assumed to be known, we can compute the conditional distribution of $x = (x_1, \cdots, x_k)$, given y, to be designated by $p(x \mid y)$, as well as the marginal distribution of y to be designated by $\xi(y)$. We observe that the variable y is in the nature of a parameter in the distribution $p(x \mid y)$ and that $\xi(y)$ is in the nature of an a priori distribution of y. Thus the problem of obtaining an optimal predictor of y is identical with that of obtaining a Bayes estimate of y for the given a priori distribution ξ and the given loss function L. More specifically, the best predictor of y for a given $x = (x_1, \cdots, x_k)$ is that real number t such that

$$\sum_y L(y, t) r(y \mid x) = \inf_{a \, \varepsilon \, A} \Sigma L(y, a) r(y \mid x)$$

where $r(y \mid x)$ is the conditional distribution of y for that x. (In case $r(y \mid x)$ is a density, then the summation sign in the above equation is replaced by an integral sign.)

As an illustration, consider the case where the joint distribution of y, x_1, \cdots, x_k are multivariate normal. Then $r(y \mid x)$ is normal with constant variance for all x and a mean value which is a linear function of x_1, \cdots, x_k known as the *regression plane* of y on x_1, \cdots, x_k. Since, for each x in this case, the density $r(y \mid x)$ is symmetric around its mean, the value of the regression is the optimal predictor for any of the following 3 loss functions:

(1) $L(y, a) = k(y - a)^2$

(2) $L(y, a) = k| y - a |$

(3) $L(y, a) = 0 \qquad$ if $\; | y - a | \leq k$

$\qquad\qquad\qquad = 1 \qquad$ if $\; | y - a | > k$

where k is a positive constant. Also, since the variance of $r(y \mid x)$ is independent of x, the conditional risk for each of the 3 loss functions is constant for all x and is therefore equal to the average risk. Thus for the loss function (1) the average risk is $k\sigma^2$, for (2) it is $\sqrt{\dfrac{2}{\pi}}\, k\sigma$, and for (3) it is $1 - \beta$ where

$$\beta = \frac{1}{\sqrt{2\pi}} \int_{-k/\sigma}^{k/\sigma} e^{-(\frac{1}{2}) z^2} \, dz$$

and where σ^2 is the conditional variance of y, given x.

PROBLEMS

11.2.1. If $L(\omega, a)$ is for each ω strictly convex in a and $\to +\infty$ as $a \to \pm\infty$, the Bayes estimate for any ξ is unique and hence admissible.

11.2.2. Determine the Bayes estimate t of the probability ω of a success in a binomial distribution with a sample of size N when $L(\omega, a) = (\omega - a)^2$ and ω has a rectangular a priori distribution over $(0, 1)$.

11.2.3. Show that the estimate t of Problem 11.2.2 has a smaller mean square error than the estimate $\bar{x} = \dfrac{1}{N} \sum_{i=1}^{N} x_i$ (where $x_i = 1$ if the outcome is a success and $x_i = 0$ otherwise) for all ω such that $\left| \frac{1}{2} - \omega \right| \leq \sqrt{2}/4$, and all N.

11.2.4. Show that the Bayes estimate t for the probability ω of a success in a binomial distribution with a sample of size N and $L(\omega, a) = 0$ if $\left| \omega - a \right| \leq \delta$, $L(\omega, a) = 1$ if $\left| \omega - a \right| > \delta$, where δ is a given positive number, and ω has a uniform distribution, has the property that $\left| t(x) - \bar{x} \right| \leq \delta$ and that the modal interval always includes the sample mean, where \bar{x} is defined in Problem 11.2.3.

11.2.5. If $p(t)$ is a continuous unimodal density, the modal interval $(a, a + h)$ satisfies $p(a) = p(a + h)$.

11.2.6. (a) In estimating ω, the probability of a success in a binomial distribution, from a sample of size N with $L(\omega, a) = (\omega - a)^2$, the Bayes estimate for $\xi(\omega) = K\omega^u(1 - \omega)^v$, $u > -1$, $v > -1$ has the form $\alpha\bar{x} + \beta = t_{u,v}$ where \bar{x} is defined in Problem 11.2.3.

(b) Find u', v' such that $\rho(\omega, t_{u',v'})$ is a constant ρ' independent of ω, so that $t_{u',v'} = \alpha'\bar{x} + \beta'$ is the minimax estimate of ω.

(c) In estimating the mean of an unknown distribution over $(0, 1)$ from a sample of size N, show that $\rho(\omega, t_{u',v'}) \leq \rho'$, so that $t_{u',v'}$ is minimax for this problem.

11.2.7. Let x assume values 1, ω, each with probability $1/2$. Show that, for any loss function $L(\omega, a)$ and any ξ, the Bayes sequential-estimation procedure with constant cost per observation is (i) no observations with ω estimated by that number $a = a^*$ which minimizes $E_\xi L(\omega, a)$, or else (ii) continue taking observations until a value of x different from 1 occurs, and estimate ω as this value of x.

11.2.8. Let t_N for any arbitrary N be the unique Bayes estimate of ω for a loss function $L(\omega, a)$, a given a priori distribution ξ, when x_1, \cdots, x_N are observed. Prove that $t(x) = t_N(x)$ is admissible for any prescribed sequential plan S when S terminates with N observations.

11.2.9. In estimating ω in a binomial distribution, let S be the sampling plan of taking observations until m successes occur. Show that $t = (m - 1)/(n - 1)$, where n is the number of observations required, is the unique Bayes solution when $\xi(\omega)$ is rectangular and $L(\omega, a) = (\omega - a)^2/\omega^2(1 - \omega)$, and conclude that t is admissible when $L(\omega, a) = (\omega - a)^2$. Prove that t is an unbiased estimate of ω; i.e., $E_\omega(t) \equiv \omega$.

11.3. The Translation-Parameter Problem

An interesting special case of the general estimation problem is that in which the distribution is known except for an additive constant ω, and in which the loss depends only on our error in estimating ω. Thus there is given a distribution q over an N-dimensional Cartesian space S_N, and with each real number ω is associated the distribution p defined by

$$p(x \mid \omega) = q(x - \omega\epsilon)$$

where $\epsilon = (1, 1, \cdots, 1)$. A point $y \in S_N$ is chosen with probability $q(y)$, an unknown constant ω is added to each coordinate of y, and the result x is observed by the statistician, who is required to estimate ω. A pure strategy for the statistician is a numerical function t defined on S_N. For any choice of t, the risk function ρ is given by

$$(11.3.1) \qquad \rho(\omega, t) = \sum_y q(y) L(t(y + \omega) - \omega)$$

where $L(s)$ is a non-negative function, specifying the statistician's loss when his error of estimate is s, $-\infty < s < \infty$.

We now reformulate the problem slightly. Let $y = (y_1, \cdots, y_N) \in S_N$, and let

$$z_i(y) = y_i - y_1, \qquad i = 2, \cdots, N, \qquad r(y) = y_1$$

Then for each y, $z = (z_2, \cdots, z_N)$ is a point in S_{N-1} and r is a point in S_1. The distribution p determines a distribution g of the vectors z in S_{N-1} and, for each z, a distribution h_z of the numbers r in S_1. Thus, for each $y = (r, z_2 + r, \cdots, z_N + r)$, we have

$$q(y) = g(z) h_z(r)$$

In terms of the new variables z and r the translation problem can be formulated as follows: A pair (z, r) is chosen according to the distribution $g(z) h_z(r)$ on the space $S_{N-1} \times S_1$, and the pair (z, x_1) with $x_1 = r + \omega$ is observed by the statistician who is required to estimate ω. Thus an estimate in this formulation is a function t on $S_{N-1} \times S_1$ and the risk function is given by

$$(11.3.2) \qquad \rho(\omega, t) = \sum_{z, r} g(z) h_z(r) L(t(z, r + \omega) - \omega)$$

Notice that, if we are given z and x_1 we can either estimate ω directly or estimate r and subtract it from x_1 to obtain an estimate of ω. Thus, if $t(z, x_1)$ is an estimate of ω, the function

$$(11.3.3) \qquad u(z, x_1) = x_1 - t(z, x_1)$$

is an estimate of r and conversely, if $u(z, x_1)$ is an estimate of r, $t(z, x) = x_1 - u(z, x_1)$ is an estimate of ω. In terms of the function u, the risk ρ can be written as

$$(11.3.4) \qquad \rho(\omega, u) = \sum_z \sum_r g(z) h_z(r) L[r - u(z, r + \omega)]$$

We shall thus consider the problem of estimating r, having observed z and $x_1 = r + \omega$, where the risk of an error is given by (11.3.4).

Now, since ω is merely an unknown real number, the observation x_1 will ordinarily be of little value in estimating r, and the invariance principle discussed in Chapter 8 leads us to expect that we can ignore x_1, i.e., restrict attention to the class I of invariant estimates u based on z only, without increasing the maximum risk.

Note that, if u is a function of z only, the estimate

$$t(z, x) = t(x_1, x_2, \cdots, x_N) = x_1 - u(z)$$

has the property that, for any real number s,

$$t(x_1 + s, \cdots, x_N + s) = s + t(x_1, x_2, \cdots, x_N)$$

An estimate satisfying the above is said to possess the *translation* property.

From (11.3.4) we observe that, if u is an invariant estimate, the risk $\rho(\omega, u)$ is independent of ω. Moreover, if we set

$$(11.3.5) \qquad F_z(v) = \sum_r h_z(r) L(r - v)$$

we get

$$(11.3.6) \qquad \rho(\omega, u) = \sum_z g(z) F_z(u(z)) = \rho(u)$$

We now define

$$(11.3.7) \qquad F(z) = \inf_v F_z(v)$$

so that

$$(11.3.8) \qquad \rho^* = \sum_z g(z) F(z) \leq \rho(u)$$

for all $u \varepsilon I$, and choosing $u^*(z)$ so that $F_z(u^*(z)) < F(z) + \epsilon$ for all z makes

$$(11.3.9) \qquad \rho(u^*) < \rho^* + \epsilon$$

Moreover, no $u \varepsilon I$ has a risk less than ρ^*, and we see how to choose $u \varepsilon I$ so as to approximate ρ^* as closely as required. Thus, if we restrict ourselves to invariant estimates, we can find the optimum of such estimates by evaluating the infimum of (11.3.5) with respect to v, which, of course, is a function of z. This result also follows directly from the discussion of Section 11.2 as can be seen from an examination of the risk function given in (11.3.6). Thus we have transformed the translation-parameter problem into the framework of a Bayes estimation problem by restricting ourselves to invariant estimates for the quantity r. More specifically, we have reformulated the problem so that the random variable r becomes a location parameter, in the distribu-

tion of z_2, \cdots, z_n, which we are required to estimate. But its a priori distribution is known, since it is precisely the distribution of x_1 for $\omega = 0$. The above remark makes it possible to characterize the optimal estimates of this type for the various loss functions considered in the previous section. Thus, for example, if

$$L(r - v) = k(r - v)^2, \qquad k > 0$$

then the optimal invariant estimate u^* of the number r is given by

$$u^*(z) = \sum_r rh_z(r) = E(r \mid z) = E(x_1 \mid x_2 - x_1, \cdots, x_N - x_1)$$

and consequently the corresponding estimate of ω is given by

$$t^*(z, x_1) = x_1 - u(z) = x_1 - E(x_1 \mid x_2 - x_1, \cdots, x_N - x_1)$$

Referring again to the invariance principle, we would suspect that the estimate u^* not only is optimal among all invariant estimates, but that, for all estimates u,

(11.3.10) $$\rho_0(u) = \sup_\omega \rho(\omega, u) \geq \rho^*$$

(Note that the definition of $\rho_0(u)$ for all u in (11.3.10) is consistent with that in (11.3.5) for $u \, \varepsilon \, I$.) The main result of this section is that under certain mild restrictions on the loss function L, the inequality 11.3.10 holds.

Theorem 11.3.1. If for every $\epsilon > 0$ and every $z \, \varepsilon \, Z$ there is a set R such that

(11.3.11) $$\sum_{r \, \varepsilon \, R} h_z(r)L(r - v) > F(z) - \epsilon$$

for all v, then (11.3.10) holds.

We remark that the hypothesis of this theorem will be satisfied if either

(1) $L(s)$ is bounded for $-\infty < s < \infty$

or

(2) $L(s) \to +\infty$ as $s \to \pm\infty$ and L is continuous

Proof of (1). If L is bounded, the series 11.3.5 converges uniformly in v, and there is a finite set R such that

$$\sum_{r \, \varepsilon \, R} h_z(r)L(r - v) > F_z(v) - \epsilon$$

for all v. Since $F(z) \leq F_z(v)$ for all v, it follows that (11.3.11) holds.

Proof of (2). We show that, if $b_1(v)$, $b_2(v)$, \cdots is an increasing sequence of non-negative continuous functions with $b_N(v) \to +\infty$ as $v \to \pm\infty$ for all N, and, if $b(v) = \lim b_N(v)$ and $b = \inf_v b(v)$ is finite, then, for every $\epsilon > 0$, there is an N with $bN(v) \geq b - \epsilon$ for all v. The proof of (2) then follows since we can take

$$b_N(v) = \sum_{i=1}^{N} h_z(r_i)L(r_i - v)$$

where r_1, r_2, \cdots is an enumeration of the r's for which $h_z(r) > 0$.

Since by hypothesis $b_1(v) \to \infty$ as $v \to \pm\infty$, we can choose an interval (A, B), such that $b_1(v) \geq b + 1$ for v outside (A, B). Let v_N be the value of v that minimizes $b_N(v)$ and, say,

$$\min_v b_N(v) = b^*{}_N = b_N(v_N)$$

Then $A \leq v_N \leq B$ for all N, and we may suppose, choosing a subsequence of $b^*{}_N$ if necessary, that $v_N \to v^*$. Also $b^*{}_N \leq b$ for all N, say, $b^*{}_N \to b^*$. Then

$$b_N(v_n) \leq b_n(v_n) \leq b^*$$

for $N < n$, so that $b_N(v^*) \leq b^*$ for all N, and $b(v^*) \leq b^*$. Thus $b(v^*) = b^* = b$, and $b^*{}_N \to b$; i.e., there is an N for which

$$\min_v b_N(v) = b^*{}_N \geq b - \epsilon$$

We proceed to the proof of Theorem 11.3.1. Let r_1, r_2, \cdots be an enumeration of the possible r values, i.e., those values of r for which $g(z)h_z(r) > 0$ for some z. With each sequence $\alpha = (n_1, n_2, \cdots)$ of integers n_i with $n_i = 0$ for sufficiently large i, we associate the number $v(\alpha) = \sum_i n_i r_i$. Then from (11.3.2),

(1) $$\rho[v(\alpha), u] = \sum_{z, r_i} g(z)h_z(r_i)L[r_i - u[z, v(\alpha + \delta_i)]]$$

where δ_i has $n_i = 1$, $n_j = 0$ for $j \neq i$.

Let A_{MN} consist of all sequences α with $|\alpha_i| \leq M$, for all i, $\alpha_i = 0$ for $i \geq N$. Then

(2) $$\sum_{\alpha \,\varepsilon\, A_{MN}} \rho[v(\alpha), u] = \sum_z g(z) \left[\sum_\beta \sum_{i \,\varepsilon\, J(M, N, \beta)} h_z(r_i)L[r_i - u(\beta)] \right]$$

where $J(M, N, \beta)$ consists of all i for which $\beta - \delta_i \,\varepsilon\, A_{MN}$.

Since $\beta - \delta_i \, \varepsilon \, A_{MN}$ for $\beta \, \varepsilon \, A_{M-1, N}$, $i \leq N$, we have

$$(3) \qquad \sum_{\alpha \, \varepsilon \, A_{MN}} \rho[v(\alpha), u] \geq \sum_z g(z) \sum_{\beta \, \varepsilon \, A_{M-1, N}} H_N(z, u(\beta))$$

where

$$(4) \qquad H_N(z, t) = \sum_{i=1}^{N} h_z(r_i) L[r_i - t]$$

For any $\epsilon > 0$, choose z_1, \cdots, z_k so that

$$(5) \qquad \sum_1^k g(z_i) F(z_i) > \rho^* - \epsilon$$

and choose N, as can be done by hypothesis, so that

$$(6) \qquad H_N(z_i, t) > F(z_i) - \epsilon$$

for all $i = 1, \cdots, k$ and all t. Then from (3) and (6) we obtain

$$(7) \qquad \sum_{\alpha \, \varepsilon \, A_{MN}} \rho[v(\alpha), u] \geq \left\{ \sum_{i=1}^{k} g(z_i)[F(z_i) - \epsilon] \right\} a(M - 1, N)$$

$$\geq (\rho^* - 2\epsilon) a(M - 1, N)$$

where $a(M, N) = (2M + 1)^N$ is the number of points in A_{MN}. Now

$$\sum_{\alpha \, \varepsilon \, A_{MN}} \rho[v(\alpha), u] \leq a(M, N)\rho^*(u)$$

which together with (7) yields

$$\rho_0(u) \geq \frac{a(M - 1, N)}{a(M, N)} [\rho^* - 2\epsilon]$$

Letting $M \to \infty$ yields $\rho_0(u) \geq \rho^* - 2\epsilon$ which, since ϵ is arbitrary, completes the proof.

We remark that *randomized estimates play no essential role in the translation-parameter problem*. The explanation here is not convexity, as in Theorem 11.3.1, but the fact that the invariant estimates have constant risk. For, if t_1, t_2, \cdots are pure estimates with constant risk ρ_1, ρ_2, \cdots, the mixed estimate η using t_1, t_2, \cdots with probabilities λ_1, λ_2, \cdots has constant risk $\rho = \Sigma \lambda_n \rho_n$. Necessarily $\rho_n \leq \rho$ for some n, so that there is a pure estimate whose constant risk is less than or equal to that of η; i.e., we have

Theorem 11.3.2. In any translation-parameter estimation problem, the class of pure invariant estimates is a complete class, among the class of all invariant estimates.

An example in which (11.3.10) fails is the following. $N = 1$;

$$q(K) = \frac{1}{K(K+1)}, \qquad K = 1, 2, \cdots, \qquad f(s) = \max{(s, 0)}$$

An invariant estimate is a constant u, and

$$\rho(u) = \sum_{K>u} \frac{K-u}{K(K+1)} = +\infty \quad \text{for all} \quad u \, \varepsilon \, I$$

so that $\rho^* = +\infty$. The non-invariant estimate $u(s) = M|\,s\,|$, where $M > 1$, has risk

$$\rho(\omega, u) = \sum_{K > M|\,K+\omega\,|} \frac{K - M|\,K+\omega\,|}{K(K+1)}$$

For $\omega > -(M-1)/M$, $K > M|\,K+\omega\,|$ is impossible, and $\rho(\omega, u) = 0$. For $\omega \leq -(M-1)/M$, $K > M|\,K+\omega\,|$ implies $K > M|\,K+\omega\,|$ and $K > -M(K+\omega)$. Thus letting $c = \frac{M}{M+1}|\,\omega\,|, d = \frac{M}{M-1}|\,\omega\,|$, we have $c < K < d$. Consequently

$$\rho(\omega, u) < \sum_{c < K < d} \frac{1}{K+1} < \int_c^{d+1} \frac{dx}{x}$$

$$= \log\left[\frac{M+1}{M-1} + \frac{M+1}{M|\,\omega\,|}\right] \leq \log\left[2\frac{M+1}{M-1}\right]$$

From this it follows that

$$\sup_{\omega} \rho(\omega, u) \leq \log\left[2\frac{M+1}{M-1}\right]$$

so that (11.3.10) fails.

The most interesting statistical problems involving translation or scale parameters concern probability distributions which are not discrete. For this reason, the illustrative examples to be given in this and the following section will deal with densities. Theorem 11.3.1 holds for densities and more general distributions in case the loss function is bounded or quadratic. The proof of this can be found in an appropriate reference at the end of the book.

Let x_1, x_2, \cdots, x_N be N independent observations with each x_i having distribution $f(x_i - \omega)$ where $-\infty < x_i < \infty$ and $-\infty < \omega < \infty$ and f is a density. It is desired to obtain the minimax estimate of ω possess-

ing the translation property when the loss function L is given by

$$L(\omega, a) = k(\omega - a)^2, \qquad k > 0$$

Let t^* be the desired estimate. We shall show that t^* is given by

$$(11.3.12) \qquad t^*(x_1, \cdots, x_N) = \frac{\displaystyle\int_{-\infty}^{\infty} \theta \prod_{i=1}^{N} f(x_i - \theta) \, d\theta}{\displaystyle\int_{-\infty}^{\infty} \prod_{i=1}^{N} f(x_i - \theta) \, d\theta}$$

whenever an invariant estimate of ω of finite quadratic risk exists. To see this we set $z_j = x_j - x_1, j = 2, \cdots, N$ and let $\theta = x_1 - r$. Then

$$t^*(x_1, \cdots, x_N) = x_1 - \frac{\displaystyle\int_{-\infty}^{\infty} r f(r) \prod_{i=2}^{N} f(z_i + r) \, dr}{\displaystyle\int_{-\infty}^{\infty} f(r) \prod_{i=2}^{N} f(z_i + r) \, dr}$$

$$= x_1 - E(x_1 \,|\, x_2 - x_1, \cdots, x_N - x_1)$$

since it is easily seen that

$$(11.3.13) \qquad h_z(r) = \frac{f(r) \displaystyle\prod_{i=2}^{N} f(z_i + r)}{\displaystyle\int_{-\infty}^{\infty} f(u) \prod_{i=2}^{N} f(z_i + u) \, du}$$

Let again x_1, x_2, \cdots, x_N be N independent observations with density $f(x_i - \omega)$ for each x_i, and for any estimate a of ω let the loss be given by

$$L(\omega, a) = 0 \quad \text{if} \quad |\omega - a| \le k$$

$$= 1 \quad \text{otherwise}$$

It is desired to obtain a minimax estimate of ω possessing the translation property. To accomplish this, we find the modal interval of length $2k$ in the distribution 11.3.13 and take the midpoint of this interval, say, $u^*(z_2, \cdots, z_N)$ as an estimate of r. Then the minimax estimate of ω is given by

$$t^*(z_2, \cdots, z_N) = x_1 - u^*(z_2, \cdots, z_N)$$

Let β be the probability that t^* will be within k units of ω. Then

$$(11.3.14) \quad \beta = \int_{-\infty}^{\infty} \cdots \int_{-\infty}^{\infty} \left(\int_{u^*-k}^{u^*+k} h_z(r) \right) g(z_2, \cdots, z_N) \, dz_2, \cdots, dz_N$$

where $h_z(r)$ is given by (11.3.13) and

$$g(z_2, \cdots, z_N) = \int_{-\infty}^{\infty} f(u) \prod_{i=2}^{N} f(z_i + u) \, du$$

Since the risk of using t^* is constant, we see that t^* is an estimate of ω of bounded absolute error with confidence coefficient β which is independent of ω. These results are quite general, and we thus have

Theorem 11.3.3. If ω is a translation parameter and it is the only unknown parameter in the distribution, then there always exists a minimax estimate of it which is of bounded absolute error with a confidence coefficient β which is independent of ω.

We remark that the value of the confidence coefficient β will depend on the sample size and can ordinarily be made to assume any desired value by adjusting the sample size. We also remark that when, $N = 1$, $r = x_1$ and $h_z(r) = f(x_1)$. This is of particular interest in case the class of distributions under consideration admits a sufficient statistic which can be treated as a single observation. To illustrate, if the loss function is quadratic and $N = 1$, the minimax estimate is given by

(11.3.15) $t^*(x_1) = x_1 - E(x_1) = x_1 - \text{constant}$

PROBLEMS

11.3.1. If $x = (x_1, \cdots, x_n)$ is a sample of size n from a translation-parameter distribution and $u(x)$ is any random variable with the translation property $u(x + \epsilon h) = u(x) + h$ for all x, h, then $u - E_0(u \mid x_2 - x_1, \cdots, x_k - x_1) = x_1 - E_0(x_1 \mid x_2 - x_1, \cdots, x_k - x_1)$ where E_0 denotes expectation with respect to the distribution of x where $\omega = 0$.

11.3.2. Consider the following translation-parameter problem: $q(1) = q(-1) = 1/2$, $L(\omega, a) = \min [|\omega - a|, 1]$, $N = 1$. (a) Show that there are two invariant minimax estimates for ω: $t_1(x) = x + 1$, $t_{-1}(x) = x - 1$. (b) Show that $t(x) = x + 1$ if $x \leq 0$, $t(x) = x - 1$ if $x > 0$ is better than either t_1 or t_{-1}, so that no invariant estimate is admissible.

11.3.3. Obtain the minimax invariant estimate of θ based on N independent observations from a rectangular distribution defined over the interval $(\theta, \theta + 1)$ for the loss functions

(1) $L(\theta, a) = (\theta - a)^2$

(2) $L(\theta, a) = |\theta - a|$

(3) $L(\theta, a) = 0$ \qquad if $|\theta - a| \leq k$

\qquad\qquad\qquad\quad $= 1$ \qquad if $|\theta - a| > k$

where $k > 0$.

11.3.4. In Problem 11.3.3 and loss function (3), consider the following sequential procedure: Take observations in sequence, and at the nth observation $n = 1, 2, \cdots$ compute

$$\beta_n = \int_{u^*-k}^{u^*+k} h_z(r)\, dr$$

Stop sampling as soon as, for some n, $\beta_n \geq \gamma$ where $0 < \gamma < 1$.

(a) Characterize this sequential procedure.

(b) Compute $E(n)$.

(c) Let N be the nearest integer to $E(n)$, and compute β from equation 11.3.14 for N observations. How does β compare to γ?

11.4. The Scale-Parameter Problem

In some statistical problems we may be dealing with a positive random variable whose distribution is known except for a multiplicative positive constant θ, and the loss in estimating θ depends only on the relative error. That is, for any estimate $b > 0$, the loss function L is given by

$$(11.4.1) \qquad\qquad L(\theta, b) = L(\theta/b)$$

As in the translation-parameter case, we may assume that we are given a distribution q over an N-dimensional Cartesian space S_N, and, with each real positive number θ, there is associated a distribution p_θ defined by

$$(11.4.2) \qquad p(v \mid \theta) = p(v/\theta) = p(v_1/\theta, \cdots, v_N/\theta)$$

A point $w \, \varepsilon \, S_N$ is chosen with probability $q(w)$, each coordinate of w is multiplied by a positive constant θ, and the resulting vector v is observed by the statistician, who is required to estimate θ.

The above scale-parameter problem is easily reducible to the translation-parameter problem, as can be seen from the following considerations: We set

$$x_i = \log v_i, \quad y_i = \log w_i, \quad \omega = \log \theta, \quad a = \log b$$

Then

$$(11.4.3) \qquad L(\theta/b) = L(e^{\omega - a}) = L^*(\omega - a)$$

$$p(v \mid \theta) = p(e^{x_1 - \omega}, \cdots, e^{x_N - \omega}) = p_0(x - \epsilon\omega)$$

We see then that all the results derived in Section 11.3, when properly translated, are also applicable to the problem under consideration. In particular, if L in (11.4.3) satisfies the conditions of Theorem 11.3.1,

then we can state that a minimax estimate of θ exists and is obtained as follows: Let

$$r = w_1, \qquad z_j = w_j/w_1, \qquad j = 2, \cdots, N$$

and let $h_z(r)$ be the conditional distribution of r given $z = (z_2, \cdots, z_N)$ and given that $\theta = 1$. Also let

$$F_z(b) = \sum_r h_z(r) L\left(\frac{r}{b}\right)$$

For the sake of simplicity, we shall assume that there exists a b^* such that

$$F_z(b^*) = \inf_b F_z(b)$$

Then, for any z_2, \cdots, z_N,

$$b^*(z_2, \cdots, z_N) = b^*(v_2/v_1, \cdots, v_N/v_1)$$

is a Bayes estimate of $r = w_1$ and

(11.4.4) $$t^*(v_1, \cdots, v_N) = v_1/b^*$$

is a minimax estimate of θ. Observe that the estimate t^* satisfies the condition

(11.4.5) $$t^*(cv_1, \cdots, cv_N) = ct^*(v_1, \cdots, v_N)$$

where c is any constant. Estimates of this type are said to possess the *multiplicative* property.

Of particular interest is the loss function

(11.4.6) $\quad L(\theta/b) = 1 \quad$ if $\ \left| \theta - b \right| \leq \alpha b, \quad$ or equivalently

$$\text{if} \ \ 1 - \alpha \leq \theta/b \leq 1 + \alpha$$

$$= 0 \quad \text{otherwise}$$

and the random variables v_i, $0 \leq v_i \leq \infty$ have a distribution density $f(v_i/\theta)$. Here the minimax estimate is obtained as follows: As above, let $h_z(r)$ be the conditional distribution of r, given z, and given that $\theta = 1$. Then

(11.4.7) $$h_z(r) = \frac{f(r) \prod\limits_{i=2}^{N} f(rz_i)}{\displaystyle\int_{-\infty}^{\infty} f(u) \prod\limits_{i=2}^{N} f(uz_i)\, du}$$

Also, let

(11.4.8) $$Q(b) = \int_{b(1-\alpha)}^{b(1+\alpha)} h_z(r)\, dr$$

Then the Bayes estimate of r is that $b = b^*$ which maximizes $Q(b)$, and the minimax estimate of θ is given by

$$(11.4.9) \qquad t^*(v_1, \cdots, v_N) = v_1/b^*$$

Let β represent the confidence coefficient of the estimate t^*, i.e., the probability that the relative error in the estimate will not exceed α. Then

$$(11.4.10) \quad \beta = \int_{-\infty}^{\infty} \cdots \int_{-\infty}^{\infty} Q(b^*) \left[\int_{-\infty}^{\infty} f(u) \prod_{i=2}^{N} f(uz_i)\, du \right] dz_2, \cdots, dz_N$$

Since the risk of using t^* in (11.4.9) is constant, we can state the following theorem.

Theorem 11.4.1. If θ is a scale parameter and it is the only unknown parameter in the distribution of the type considered, then there always exists a minimax estimate of it which is of bounded relative error with a confidence coefficient β which is independent of θ.

As an illustration, consider the following problem. A chemist desires to estimate the average concentration of inert particles per unit volume in a liquid. He desires his estimate to be no more than a specified fraction α away from the true concentration and wishes to be right with a specified probability β. He assumes that the particles are well mixed in the liquid so that the distribution of the number of particles in any volume of the liquid can be considered to be Poisson. He spreads a known amount of this liquid on a plate which he will examine with a microscope. Let λ be the expected number of particles in a unit area of the plate. The problem then becomes one of estimating λ.

In any specified area A on the plate, the distribution of the number of particles m is given by

$$(11.4.11) \qquad p(m \mid \lambda) = \frac{e^{-\lambda A}(\lambda A)^m}{m!}$$

We observe that the quantity λ is in the nature of a scale parameter, but it is not a scale parameter in the distribution (11.4.11). This seems to indicate that there exists another random variable for which λ is a scale parameter. We shall now show that, if the chemist were to focus the microscope on the plate and then continuously increase the aperture and stop as soon as the observed area contains exactly m particles, then the size of this area is the required random variable. To see this, let z designate the size of such an area. Then the event $z \geq x$ is equiv-

alent to the event "The area of size x has fewer than m particles." Thus

$$P(z > x) = \sum_{j=0}^{m-1} \frac{e^{-\lambda x}(\lambda x)^j}{j!}$$

Let $F_\lambda(z)$ be the c.d.f. of the random variable z, and let $g(z \mid \lambda)$ be the density of z. Then

$$F_\lambda(x) = 1 - \sum_{j=0}^{m-1} \frac{e^{-\lambda x}(\lambda x)^j}{j!}$$

and

$$\frac{dF_\lambda(x)}{dx} = \lambda e^{-\lambda x} + \sum_{j=1}^{m-1} \frac{(\lambda e^{-\lambda x}(\lambda x)^j - \lambda e^{-\lambda x}(\lambda x)^{j-1})}{j!}$$

$$= \frac{\lambda e^{-\lambda x}(\lambda x)^{m-1}}{(m-1)!} = g(x \mid \lambda)$$

Thus λ is a scale parameter in the distribution of x, and, if $\lambda = 1$, x has a chi-square distribution with $2m$ degrees of freedom.

Now suppose the chemist observes n non-overlapping areas of size x_1, \cdots, x_n, each having the property of being the minimum area that includes m particles. Then since $2\lambda \sum_{i=1}^{n} x_i$ has a χ^2 distribution with $2mn$ degrees of freedom, the distribution of $w = \sum_{i=1}^{n} x_i$ is

$$(11.4.12) \qquad f(w \mid \lambda) = \frac{\lambda e^{-\lambda w}(\lambda w)^{mn-1}}{(mn-1)!}$$

Thus we can consider our problem as that of estimating λ on the basis of a single observation w whose distribution is (11.4.12). The minimax estimate of λ is here given by

$$t^*(w) = b^*/w$$

where b^* is the value of b which maximizes

$$(11.4.13) \qquad Q(b) = \frac{1}{(mn-1)!} \int_{b(1-\alpha)}^{b(1+\alpha)} e^{-y} y^{mn-1} \, dy$$

Note that b^* depends on mn only. Thus the value of mn can be so chosen as to make the confidence coefficient $\beta = Q(b^*)$ as large as desired.

PROBLEMS

11.4.1. Show that, for small α and large β, $N = mn = (1/\alpha^2)z^2_{(1+\beta)/2}$ where $z_{(1+\beta)/2}$ is the normal deviate which is exceeded with probability $(1 + \beta)/2$. *Hint.* Employ the fact that if χ^2 is based on a large number of degrees of freedom s, then

$$z = (\sqrt{2\chi^2} - \sqrt{2s - 1})$$

is approximately normally distributed with zero mean and unit standard deviation.

11.4.2. Find the Bayes estimate of bounded relative error for λ in the particle-counting problem when λ has a priori distribution $e^{-\lambda}$, $\lambda \geq 0$.

11.4.3. Obtain the minimax invariant estimate of θ based on N independent observations from a rectangular distribution defined over the interval $(0, \theta)$ for the loss function

$$L(\theta, b) = 0 \quad \text{if} \quad |\theta - b| \leq \alpha b$$
$$= 1 \quad \text{if} \quad |\theta - b| > \alpha b \qquad 0 < \alpha < 1$$

11.4.4. In Problem 11.4.3, characterize the following sequential procedure: Take observations in sequence, and at the nth observation $n = 1, 2, \cdots$ compute

$$\beta_n = \int_{b^*(1-\alpha)}^{b^*(1+\alpha)} h_z(r) \, dr$$

where $h_z(r)$ is given by (11.4.7). Stop sampling as soon as, for some n, $\beta_n \geq \gamma$, where $0 < \gamma < 1$.

11.5. Admissible Minimax Estimates for the Exponential Class

Let x_1, \cdots, x_N be N independent observations with each x_i having the distribution

$$(11.5.1) \qquad\qquad p(x_i \mid \omega) = \beta(\omega)e^{\omega x_i}r(x_i)$$

where the x_i's are real numbers and ω ranges over an interval on the real line. The class of distributions 11.5.1 called the exponential class was studied in Section 6.7, and it was proved there that the distribution of the random variable $t(x) = (x_1 + \cdots + x_N)/N$ is also of the exponential type. Let

$$\nu(\omega) = \frac{1}{\beta(\omega)} = \sum_x e^{\omega x}r(x)$$

Then by direct differentiation [see Problem 7.4.1] it follows that

$$(11.5.2) \qquad\qquad \theta(\omega) = E_\omega(x) = \frac{d \log \nu(\omega)}{d\omega}$$

$$(11.5.3) \qquad\quad \sigma^2(\omega) = E_\omega(x - E_\omega(x))^2 = \frac{d^2\nu(\omega)}{d\omega^2} = \frac{d\theta(\omega)}{d\omega}$$

The problem we shall consider is that of estimating $\theta(\omega)$ when the loss function is

$$(11.5.4) \qquad L(\omega, a) = \frac{k(\theta(\omega) - a)^2}{\sigma^2(\omega)}, \qquad k > 0$$

In Chapter 8 we have seen that the function t is a sufficient statistic for this class of distributions. Moreover, by (11.5.2), $E_\omega(t) = \theta(\omega)$, and the variance of t is σ^2_ω/N. Thus, if t were used to estimate $\theta(\omega)$ with the loss function 11.5.4, the risk ρ would be given by

$$(11.5.5) \qquad \rho(\omega, t) = k/N$$

for all ω. This suggests that t might be a minimax estimate of θ. We shall show that, if the range of ω is the entire real line, t is not only a minimax estimate but also admissible. More correctly, we shall show that under this condition t is admissible, and from (11.5.5) it will then follow that t is minimax.

Theorem 11.5.1. If the range of ω is the entire real line, then $t(x) = \frac{1}{N}\sum_{i=1}^{N} x_i$ is an admissible, and hence minimax estimate of $\theta(\omega)$ for the loss function 11.5.4.

Proof. Before we prove this theorem, we need the following lemma.

Lemma 11.5.1. If $\lambda_n > 0$, x_n are sequences of numbers, the set of τ values for which

$$\varphi(\tau) = \sum_{1}^{\infty} \lambda_n e^{\tau x_n}$$

is finite is an interval, i.e., if $\varphi(a)$ and $\varphi(b)$ are finite, so is $\varphi(t)$ for $a < t < b$. Moreover, $\varphi^{(k)}$, the kth derivative of φ, is finite and is given by

$$\sum_{n=1}^{\infty} \lambda_n x^k_n e^{\tau x_n}.$$

Proof. Suppose $\varphi(a)$ and $\varphi(b)$ are finite. We first show that, for any $k \geq 0$, the series $\sum_{1}^{\infty} \lambda_n x^k_n e^{\tau x_n}$ is absolutely and uniformly convergent in any interval $a_1 \leq t \leq b_1$ with $a < a_1 < b_1 < b$. Consider the function f defined by

$$f(x) = \frac{|x|^k e^{b_1 x}}{e^{bx}}$$

It is clear that f is continuous for all x and $f(x) \to 0$ as $x \to +\infty$.

Since $f(0) = 0$, it follows that f is bounded above for $x \geq 0$. Say

$$\left| x \right|^k e^{b_1 x} \leq M_1 e^{bx}, \qquad x \geq 0$$

Similarly, we have

$$\left| x \right|^k e^{a_1 x} < M_2 e^{ax}, \qquad x < 0$$

Thus, for $a_1 \leq \tau \leq b_1$,

$$\lambda_n \left| x_n \right|^k e^{\tau x_n} \leq M_1 \lambda_n e^{b x_n} + M_2 \lambda_n e^{a x_n} = u_n(x)$$

Since by hypothesis the series $\Sigma u_n(x)$ converges, the series $\Sigma \lambda_n x_n^k e^{\tau x_n}$ converges absolutely and uniformly in τ in the interval $a_1 \leq \tau \leq b_1$. Using the theorem that a series can be differentiated term by term over any interval in which the resulting series is uniformly convergent completes the proof of the lemma.

We now return to the proof of the theorem. Assume that t is not admissible. Then there exists an estimate u better than t. In view of Theorem 11.1.2, we might as well assume that u is a function of t. Let

$$(1) \qquad \psi(\omega) = E_\omega(u) = \beta_0(\omega) \sum_t u(t) e^{t\omega} R(t)$$

and set $\mu(\omega) = 1/\beta_0(\omega)$. Then

$$(2) \qquad \psi'(\omega) = \beta_0(\omega) \left(\sum_t u(t) \left[t - \frac{\mu'(\omega)}{\mu(\omega)} \right] e^{t\omega} R(t) \right)$$

$$= \beta_0(\omega) \sum_t u(t)[u - \theta(\omega)] e^{t\omega} R(t)$$

$$= E_\omega[u(t - \theta)]$$

when the differentiation of the series is justified by Lemma 11.5.1.

Now, by Schwarz' inequality applied to equation 2,

$$(3) \qquad [\psi'(\omega)]^2 = \{E_\omega[u(t - \theta)]\}^2 \leq \sigma_t^2(\omega)\sigma_u^2(\omega)$$

Now let

$$(4) \qquad \psi(\omega) = b(\omega) + \theta(\omega), \qquad \psi'(\omega) = b'(\omega) + \sigma_t^2(\omega)$$

We also have

$$(5) \qquad \sigma_u^2(\omega) = E_\omega[(u - \theta(\omega))^2] - b^2(\omega)$$

Substituting (4) and (5) into (3), we get

$$(6) \qquad \sigma_u^2(\omega) b^2(\omega) + [b'(\omega) + \sigma_t^2(\omega)]^2 \leq \sigma_t^2(\omega) E_\omega(u - \theta)^2$$

Now by hypothesis

(7) $$E_\omega[(u - \theta)^2] \leq \sigma_t^2(\omega)$$

Therefore

(8) $$\sigma_t^2(\omega)b^2(\omega) + [b'(\omega) + \sigma_t^2(\omega)]^2 \leq \sigma_t^4(\omega)$$

It follows from (8) that $b'(\omega)$ is never positive, so that $b(\omega)$ is non-decreasing in ω. Now dropping the term $[b'(\omega)]^2$ from the left-hand side of (8) and simplifying, we get

(9) $$b^2(\omega) + 2b'(\omega) \leq 0 \quad \text{or} \quad \frac{d}{d\omega}\left[\frac{1}{b(\omega)}\right] \geq \frac{1}{2}$$

where $b(\omega) \neq 0$.

Since $b'(\omega) \leq 0$, it is true that either $b(\omega) = 0$ for all sufficiently large ω, or, above some value ω_0, $b(\omega) \neq 0$. In either event $1/b(\omega) \geq \frac{1}{2}\omega - \frac{1}{2}[\omega_0 - 1/b(\omega_0)]$. Therefore, in either event, $b(\omega) \to 0$ as $\omega \to \infty$, and, by the same argument $b(\omega) \to 0$ as $\omega \to -\infty$. Now, if $b'(\omega) \leq 0$ and $b(\omega) \to 0$ as $\omega \to \pm\infty$, $b(\omega) = 0$ for all ω. This in turn implies that

(10) $$\sigma_t^2(\omega) \leq E_\omega[(u - \theta)^2]$$

as can be seen from equation 6. Consequently, no better estimate can exist.

PROBLEMS

11.5.1. Show that, in the distribution 11.4.12 with $1/\lambda = \theta$, the estimate $t = w/mn$ of θ is not admissible for the loss function $(t - \theta)^2$ and hence that Theorem 11.5.1 no longer holds if ω does not range over the entire real line. *Hint.* Show that if $t^* = w/(mn + 1)$ then $E(t^* - \theta)^2 < E(t - \theta)^2$ for all θ.

11.5.2. Prove Theorem 11.5.1 directly for the case $a \leq x_i \leq b$ with a and b finite by showing that nature's least favorable distribution for θ is rectangular over the interval (a, b) and that t is the unique minimax strategy for the statistician. Also show that the estimate t satisfies the conditions of Theorem 9.2.1 and consequently is of fixed sample size.

CHAPTER 12

Comparison of Experiments

12.1. Introduction

A fixed sample-size game with finite Ω is an S game specified by a sample space $\mathcal{Z} = (Z, \Omega, p)$, $\Omega = (\omega_1, \cdots, \omega_n)$, a closed bounded convex subset W of n space, and a loss function described as follows: When the state of nature is ω_i, the statistician observes z selected according to ω_i, after which he chooses $w = (w_1, \cdots, w_n) \, \varepsilon \, W$, incurring loss w_i. (See Section 6.1. Henceforth we shall identify the set W with the action space A.) If, instead of observing z, the statistician observes merely the value of a random variable f defined on Z, he will generally have less information about ω than had z itself been observed. However, if f is sufficient on \mathcal{Z}, we saw in Chapter 8 that f is as informative as Z (more precisely, the partition of Z determined by f is as informative as Z) in the sense that any risk function attainable with Z is also attainable with f.

Any random variable defined on Z will be called an *experiment* associated with the sample space \mathcal{Z}, and in this chapter we shall be concerned with the problem of comparing two experiments f and g defined on the same sample space: If the statistician may observe values of either f or g but not both, and if f and g are equally costly, which should he observe? Generally, the answer to this question depends on the set A of actions associated with the problem, and even when A is specified some Bayes solutions may involve observing values of f while others may involve observing values of g. We shall study those pairs of experiments f, g for which f is preferable to g in the strong sense that for any A the class of decision functions specifying that values of f be observed is a complete class.

As an example of the kind of problem with which we are concerned, consider a large population in which each individual has or has not each of two characteristics H, S and in which the proportions h, s of individuals with characteristics H, S are known. What is not known is the proportion ω of individuals having both characteristics; however, we suppose it known that either $\omega = hs$, so that the characteristics are in-

dependent, or $\omega = \delta \neq hs$, a specified alternative proportion. One experiment which the statistician might perform is the observation of 1000 individuals with characteristic H, another is the observation of 1000 individuals with characteristic S, and a third is the observation of 1000 individuals from the general population. Denote by x_H, x_S, x_{CH}, x_{CS}, x, observations of 1000 individuals from H, S, CH, CS, and the general population respectively, where CH, CS denote the characteristics non-H, non-S. It turns out that there is one of these experiments which is preferable to all the others, no matter what set A is associated with the problem. This best experiment is obtained simply by comparing the proportions h, s, $1 - h$, $1 - s$ of individuals with characteristics H, S, CH, CS and selecting 1000 individuals with that characteristic which is rarest in the general population.

This example may be formally described as follows, restricting ourselves to observations x_H, x_S, x_{CH}, x_{CS}. The set Z of the sample space $\mathcal{Z} = (Z, \Omega, p)$ is the set of all sequences of 1's and 0's

$$u_1, \cdots, u_{1000}; \quad v_1, \cdots, v_{1000}; \quad w_1, \cdots, w_{1000}; \quad y_1, \cdots, y_{1000}$$

where the u_i correspond to a sequence of 1000 individuals with characteristic H and $u_i = 1$ or 0 as individual i does or does not possess characteristic S; the v_i correspond to a sequence of 1000 individuals with characteristic S and $v_i = 1$ or 0 as the ith individual of this sequence does or does not possess characteristic H; the w_i correspond to a sequence of 1000 individuals with characteristic CH and $w_i = 1$ or 0 as the ith individual of this sequence does or does not possess characteristic S; the y_i correspond to a sequence of 1000 individuals with characteristic CS and $y_i = 1$ or 0 as the ith individual of this sequence does or does not possess characteristic H. There are thus 2^{4000} points in Z. Ω consists of two elements ω_1 and ω_2, which may be described as follows:

$$\omega_1: \quad p_{\omega_1}(u_i = 1) = s, \quad p_{\omega_1}(v_i = 1) = h$$

$$p_{\omega_1}(w_i = 1) = s, \quad p_{\omega_1}(y_i = 1) = h$$

$$\omega_2: \quad p_{\omega_2}(u_i = 1) = \delta/h, \quad p_{\omega_2}(v_i = 1) = \delta/s$$

$$p_{\omega_2}(w_i = 1) = \frac{s - \delta}{1 - h}, \quad p_{\omega_2}(y_i = 1) = \frac{h - \delta}{1 - s}$$

The random variable f_H, defined on Z, takes as values the sequences $\{u_i\}$, $i = 1, \cdots, 1000$; correspondingly the random variables f_S, f_{CH}, f_{CS}, take as values the sequences $\{v_i\}$, $\{w_i\}$, $\{y_i\}$ respectively.

For simplicity, we shall restrict attention to experiments with a finite number of possible outcomes. If the random variable f which consti-

tutes the experiment assumes the N distinct values x_1, \cdots, x_N, and if $\Omega = (\omega_1, \cdots, \omega_n)$, then the experiment f is described by the $n \times N$ matrix $P = \| p_{ij} \|$, where

$$P_{ij} = P\omega_i(\{z : f(z) = x_j\})$$

We have $p_{ij} \geq 0$ and $\sum_j p_{ij} = 1$ for each i, so that P is what is called a *Markov matrix*. Thus every experiment in which both Ω and the number of possible outcomes are finite corresponds to a Markov matrix, and every Markov matrix can be interpreted as an experiment. The experiment f_H of the preceding paragraph, for instance, is represented by the 2×1001 Markov matrix with

$$p_{1j} = \binom{1000}{j} s^j (1 - s)^{1000-j}$$

$$p_{2j} = \binom{1000}{j} \left(\frac{\delta}{h}\right)^j \left(1 - \frac{\delta}{h}\right)^{1000-j}$$

We remark that an experiment can be formally characterized in several ways other than as a random variable or a Markov matrix. It may also be regarded as a partition of the sample space—we have in previous chapters seen what a close relation there is between random variables and partitions; from this standpoint the comparison of experiments is a comparison of partitions of the sample space.

12.2. Some Equivalent Conditions

A fixed sample-size decision problem with finite $\Omega = (\omega_1, \cdots, \omega_n)$ is specified by a pair (P, A) where P is an experiment, i.e., an $n \times N$ Markov matrix, A is a closed bounded convex subset of n space: a terminal action is a point $a = (a_1, \cdots, a_n)$ in A, and the loss from action a when the state of nature is ω_i is a_i. A decision function is specified by an $N \times n$ matrix $d = \| d_{ji} \|$, whose jth row is a point in A, specifying the action to be taken when sample point j is observed, and every $N \times n$ matrix D, each row of which is a point in A, is a possible decision function. When the state of nature is ω_i, the risk is $\sum_{j=1}^{N} p_{ij} d_{ji}$, the ith diagonal element of the matrix PD, so that the worth of D is specified by the risk vector $b(P, D)$ whose n coordinates are the diagonal elements of PD. The set of possible risk vectors in the problem (P, A) is the set $B(P, A)$ of all points $b(P, D)$ as D varies over all possible decision functions for the problem.

These notions are illustrated in the following simple example. Let $n = N = 2$. Let

$$P = \begin{array}{c|cc} & x_1 & x_2 \\ \hline \omega_1 & \frac{1}{3} & \frac{2}{3} \\ & & \\ \omega_2 & \frac{3}{5} & \frac{2}{5} \end{array} \qquad A = \{(x, y) : x^2 + y^2 \leq 1\}$$

$$D = \begin{array}{c|cc} & \omega_1 & \omega_2 \\ \hline x_1 & x & y \\ & & \\ x_2 & u & v \end{array} \quad \text{with} \quad \begin{array}{c} x^2 + y^2 \leq 1 \\ \\ u^2 + v^2 \leq 1 \end{array}$$

Then

$$PD = \begin{pmatrix} \frac{1}{3}x + \frac{2}{3}u & \frac{1}{3}y + \frac{2}{3}v \\ \frac{3}{5}x + \frac{2}{5}u & \frac{3}{5}y + \frac{2}{5}v \end{pmatrix}$$

and consequently

$$B(P, A) = \{(\alpha, \beta) : \alpha = \tfrac{1}{3}x + \tfrac{2}{3}u, \quad \beta = \tfrac{3}{5}y + \tfrac{2}{5}v,$$
$$x^2 + y^2 \leq 1, \quad u^2 + v^2 \leq 1\}$$

Since we may take $x = u$ and $y = v$, it is easily seen that $B(P, A) \supset A$. The relation between the two sets is shown in Figure 21.

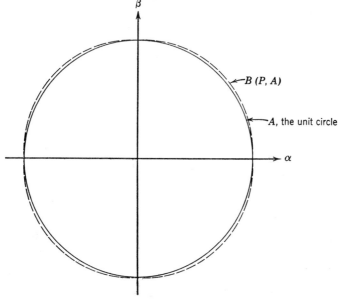

Figure 21

Theorem 12.2.1. In any decision problem (P, A), the set $B(P, A)$ is a closed bounded convex set containing A.

Proof. Closure, boundedness, and convexity of B follow immediately from Theorem 6.2.1. For any $a \, \varepsilon \, A$, choosing D with all rows equal to a yields $b(P, D) = a$, so that $B(P, D) \supset A$.

Definition 12.2.1. Let P, Q be any experiments with the same n. We say that P is more informative than Q, written $P \supset Q$, if for every closed bounded convex set A of n space

$$B(P, A) \supset B(Q, A)$$

Thus $P \supset Q$ means that, for any specification of the set of terminal actions and their losses, any loss vector attainable with Q is also attainable with P. For a given n, the least informative experiment is one with identical rows, so that the distribution of x is independent of ω; the most informative experiment is the $n \times n$ identity matrix, where observing x identifies ω; and other experiments are intermediate. Generally speaking, two experiments will not be comparable; i.e., neither will be more informative than the other.

Theorem 12.2.2. Let P, Q be $n \times N_1$, $n \times N_2$ Markov matrices, i.e., any two experiments with the same n. Each of the following conditions is equivalent to $P \supset Q$.

(1) For every $N_2 \times n$ matrix C there is an $N_1 \times N_2$ Markov matrix M such that every diagonal element of PMC equals the corresponding diagonal element of QC.

(2) There is an $N_1 \times N_2$ Markov matrix M with $PM = Q$.

(3) For every $N_2 \times n$ matrix C there is an $N_1 \times N_2$ Markov matrix M with

$$\text{Trace of } PMC \leq \text{trace of } QC$$

(The trace of a matrix is the sum of its diagonal elements.)

(4) Writing

$$\alpha_j = \sum_i p_{ij}, \qquad\qquad \beta_j = \sum_i q_{ij}$$

$$e_j = \left(\frac{p_{1j}}{\alpha_j}, \cdots, \frac{p_{nj}}{\alpha_j} \right), \qquad f_j = \left(\frac{q_{1j}}{\beta_j}, \cdots, \frac{q_{nj}}{\beta_j} \right)$$

for any continuous convex function φ defined for all $y = (y_1, \cdots, y_n)$ with $y_i \geq 0$, $\sum_1^n y_i = 1$ we have

$$\sum_1^{N_1} \alpha_j \varphi(e_j) \geq \sum_1^{N_2} \beta_j \varphi(f_j)$$

(5) With α_j, β_j, e_j, f_j as in (4), there is an $N_2 \times N_1$ Markov matrix T with

(a) $$\sum_{k=1}^{N_1} t_{jk} e_k = f_j \quad \text{for} \quad j = 1, \cdots, N_2$$

(b) $$\sum_{j=1}^{N_2} \beta_j t_{jk} = \alpha_k \quad \text{for} \quad k = 1, \cdots, N_1$$

Proof. $P \supset Q \Rightarrow$ (1). (The symbol \Rightarrow stands for "implies.") Let C be any $N_2 \times n$ matrix, and let A be the convex hull determined by the rows of C. Then C is a possible decision function in (Q, A). Any decision function in (P, A) is an $N_1 \times n$ matrix D, each row of which is a convex linear combination of the rows of C, and so there is an $N_1 \times N_2$ Markov matrix M with $D = MC$. Choosing D with $b(P, D) = b(Q, A)$ yields an M satisfying (1).

(1) $\Rightarrow P \supset Q$. Let A be any closed bounded convex set in n space, and let C be any decision function in (Q, A); i.e., C is an $N_2 \times n$ matrix, each row of which is a point of A. From (1), there is an $N_1 \times N_2$ Markov matrix M with $b(P, MC) = b(Q, C)$. Since A is convex, $MC = D$ is a decision function in (P, A), so that $b(Q, C) \varepsilon B(P, A)$ and $B(Q, A) \subset B(P, A)$.

The implications (2) \Rightarrow (1) \Rightarrow (3) are clear. (3) \Rightarrow (2): Consider the game in which I chooses any $N_2 \times n$ matrix C with $0 \le c_{ji} \le 1$ for all j, i; II chooses any $N_1 \times N_2$ Markov matrix M, with payoff $\Pi(C, M)$ = trace of $[(PM - Q)C]$. Since the sets of strategies are closed bounded convex subsets of $N_2 n$ and $N_1 N_2$ space respectively and the payoff Π is bilinear, by corollary 2 of Theorem 2.5.1 the game has a value v_0, and the players have good strategies C_0, M_0; i.e., $\Pi(C_0, M) \ge v_0 \ge \Pi(C, M_0)$ for all C, M. From (3) there is an M_1 with $\Pi(C_0, M_1) \le 0$, so that $v_0 \le 0$. Thus $\Pi(C, M_0) \le 0$ for all C; i.e., the trace of UC is ≤ 0 for all C with $0 \le c_{ji} \le 1$, where $U = PM_0 - Q$. Then $u_{ij} \le 0$ for all i, j, for the choice $c_{j_0 i_0} = 1$, $c_{ji} = 0$ otherwise, makes the trace of UC equal $u_{i_0 j_0}$. Since PM_0 and Q are both $n \times N_2$ Markov matrices, $\sum_j u_{ij} = 0$ for every i, so that $u_{ij} = 0$ for all i, j, and $PM_0 = Q$.

(4) \Rightarrow (3): Let C be any $N_2 \times n$ matrix, and let $\varphi(y) = -\min_j$ $\sum_{i=1}^{n} c_{ji} y_i$. For any $N_2 \times N_2$ Markov matrix V,

$$\text{Trace of } QVC = \sum_{i=1, j=1, k=1}^{n, N_2, N_2} q_{ij} v_{jk} c_{ki} = \sum_{j=1}^{N_2} \beta_j \sum_{k=1}^{N_2} v_{jk} \left(\sum_{i=1}^{n} c_{ki} \left(\frac{q_{ij}}{\beta_j} \right) \right)$$

$$\ge -\sum_{j=1}^{N_2} \beta_j \sum_{k=1}^{N_2} v_{jk} \varphi(f_j) = -\sum_{1}^{N_2} \beta_j \varphi(f_j)$$

with equality if V is chosen so that $v_{jk} = 1$ for the smallest k with

$$\sum_{i=1}^{n} c_{ki}\left(\frac{q_{ij}}{\beta_j}\right) = -\varphi(f_j)$$

We have shown that

$$\min_{V} [\text{trace of } QVC] = -\sum_{j=1}^{N_2} \beta_j \varphi(f_j)$$

A similar argument shows that

$$\min_{M} [\text{trace of } PMC] = -\sum_{j=1}^{N_1} \alpha_j \varphi(e_j)$$

where M varies over all $N_1 \times N_2$ Markov matrices. Consequently (4) implies the existence of an $N_1 \times N_2$ Markov matrix M with trace of $PMC \leq$ trace of QVC for all V. In particular, choosing for V the $N_2 \times N_2$ identity matrix yields (3).

(2) \Rightarrow (5): Define

$$t_{jk} = \frac{\alpha_k m_{kj}}{\sum\limits_{k=1}^{N_1} \alpha_k m_{kj}} = \frac{\alpha_k m_{kj}}{\beta_j}$$

Clearly T is an $N_2 \times N_1$ Markov matrix. The ith coordinate of $\sum\limits_{k=1}^{N_1} t_{jk} e_k$ is

$$\sum_{k=1}^{N_1} \left(\frac{\alpha_k m_{kj}}{\beta_j}\right)\left(\frac{p_{ik}}{\alpha_k}\right) = \frac{1}{\beta_j}\sum_{k=1}^{N_1} p_{ij} m_{kj} = \frac{q_{ij}}{\beta_j}$$

$$= i\text{th coordinate of } f_j, \text{ proving } (a)$$

Also $\sum\limits_{j=1}^{N_2} \beta_j t_{jk} = \sum\limits_{j=1}^{N_2} \alpha_k m_{kj} = \alpha_k$, proving (b)

(5) \Rightarrow (4): We have

$$\sum_{1}^{N_1} \alpha_k \varphi(e_k) = \sum_{k=1}^{N_1}\sum_{j=1}^{N_2} \beta_j t_{jk} \varphi(e_k)$$

$$\geq \sum_{j=1}^{N_2} \beta_j \varphi\left(\sum_{k=1}^{N_1} t_{jk} e_k\right) = \sum_{j=1}^{N_2} \beta_j \varphi(f_j)$$

We remark that (2) asserts that, if we observe the result of experiment P and, when the result is $x = j$, select $y = k$ with probability m_{jk}, $k = 1, \cdots, N_2$, the resulting y is equivalent to experiment Q;

thus (2) asserts that Q can be duplicated from P with the aid of a table of random numbers. Equivalence of (2) with $P \supset Q$ implies that P is more informative than Q if and only if Q can be duplicated from P.

Condition (3) also has a simple interpretation, for the trace of QC is n times the expected loss from decision function C and experiment Q where all alternatives ω_i are equiprobable and the trace of PMC has a similar interpretation. Thus $P \supset Q$ if and only if for any A the Bayes risk when all alternatives are equiprobable in (P, A) is less than or equal to the corresponding Bayes risk in (Q, A).

A sixth equivalent condition is that for every A, in the decision problem in which the statistician may without cost observe either P or Q but not both, followed by the choice of $a \, \varepsilon \, A$, the class of decision functions that involves observing P is a complete class; i.e.,

(6) For every A, the set T of admissible points of S, the convex set determined by the union of $B(P, A)$ and $B(Q, A)$ is a subset of $B(P, A)$.

For $P \supset Q$ implies $S = B(P, A)$, so that (6) follows, and (6) implies (3), in view of the interpretation of (3) given above.

12.3. Combinations of Experiments

If P and Q are $n \times N_1$ and $n \times N_2$ experiments, both of which may be performed, the combined experiment (P, Q) corresponds to an $n \times N_1N_2$ matrix R with $r_{ijk} = \text{Prob} \{x = j, y = k \mid \omega = \omega_i\}$ where x, y denote the result of P and Q. If P and Q are independent, i.e., if x and y are independent under each ω_i, we have $r_{ijk} = p_{ij}q_{ik}$.

Consider any $m \times n$ matrix A, and any $r \times s$ matrix B. We define the $rm \times sn$ "partitioned" matrix $(a_{ij}B)$ to be

$$\begin{bmatrix} a_{11}B & \cdots & a_{1n}B \\ \vdots & & \vdots \\ a_{m1}B & \cdots & a_{mn}B \end{bmatrix}$$

where the ijth element $a_{ij}B$ is itself an $r \times s$ matrix. (We remark that the matrix multiplication rule of rows by columns holds for partitioned matrices.)

If P and Q are independent experiments, the matrix associated with the combined experiment (P, Q) may be written as a partitioned matrix $(q_{ij}P_i)$ where P_i is a matrix consisting of the ith row of P. This representation of a combined experiment will facilitate the proofs of the next two theorems.

Theorem 12.3.1. If P, S are $n \times N_1$, $n \times N_2$ experiments and R is an $n \times N_3$ experiment which is independent of both, then $P \supset S$ implies

$$(P, R) \supset (S, R)$$

Proof. If $P \supset S$, there is an $N_1 \times N_2$ Markov matrix M with $PM = S$. Let $M^* = (\delta_{ij}M)$, $\delta_{ij} = 1$ if $1 \le i = j \le N_3$, $\delta_{ij} = 0$ otherwise. M^* is a $N_1 N_3 \times N_2 N_3$ Markov matrix. Then

$$(P, R)M^* = (r_{ij}P_i)(\delta_{ij}M) = (r_{ij}P_iM) = (r_{ij}S_i) = (S, R)$$

Therefore, by condition 2, Theorem 12.2.2,

$$(P, R) \supset (S, R)$$

Theorem 12.3.2. If $P^{(1)} \supset S^{(1)}$ and $P^{(2)} \supset S^{(2)}$, $P^{(1)}$ and $P^{(2)}$ are independent and $S^{(1)}$ and $S^{(2)}$ are independent, then

$$(P^{(1)}, P^{(2)}) \supset (S^{(1)}, S^{(2)})$$

Proof. If $P^{(1)} \supset S^{(1)}$ and $P^{(2)} \supset S^{(2)}$, then there are Markov matrices $M^{(1)}$ and $M^{(2)}$ such that $P^{(1)}M^{(1)} = S^{(1)}$ and $P^{(2)}M^{(2)} = S^{(2)}$. Let $M = (m_{ij}{}^{(2)}M^{(1)})$, then M is a Markov matrix and

$$(P^{(1)}, P^{(2)})M = (p_{ij}{}^{(2)}P_i{}^{(1)})(m_{ij}{}^{(2)}M^{(1)}) = (P_i{}^{(1)}M^{(1)} \sum_k p_{ik}{}^{(2)}m_{kj}{}^{(2)})$$

$$= (s_{ij}{}^{(2)}S_i{}^{(1)}) = (S^{(1)}, S^{(2)})$$

where $m_{ij}{}^{(k)}$, $p_{ij}{}^{(k)}$, and $s_{ij}{}^{(k)}$ are the general elements of $M^{(k)}$, $P^{(k)}$, and $S^{(k)}$, respectively, for $k = 1, 2$. Therefore, by condition (2), Theorem 12.2.2, $(P^{(1)}, P^{(2)}) \supset (S^{(1)}, S^{(2)})$.

The extension of Theorem 12.3.2 to N independent experiments is clear. In particular, we obtain that, if $P \supset S$, N independent observations from P are more informative than N independent observations from S.

12.4. Dichotomies

For two given experiments P, Q, neither the definition of \supset nor any of the six equivalent conditions of Theorem 12.2.2 yields a systematic method for deciding whether $P \supset Q$. For the case of dichotomies, i.e., $n = 2$, there is a seventh equivalent condition which is useful in deciding whether $P \supset Q$. It is given by

Theorem 12.4.1. For any experiment P with $n = 2$, write $F_P(t) = \sum_{p_{1j} \le \alpha_j t} \alpha_j$, $C_P(t) = \int_0^t F_P(u)\, du$. Then $C_P(t)$ is an increasing convex function of t on $0 \le t \le 1$ with $C_P(1) = 1$. $P \supset Q$ if and only if $C_P(t) \ge C_Q(t)$ for all t, $0 \le t \le 1$.

Proof. Define

$$f(t, u) = (t - u) \quad \text{for} \quad 0 \leq u \leq t \leq 1$$
$$= 0 \qquad \text{for} \quad t \leq u \leq 1$$

For each t, $f(t, u)$ is convex in u so that $\varphi(t, y) = f(t, y_1)$ is a convex function of $y = (y_1, y_2)$ defined over $y_i \geq 0$, $y_1 + y_2 = 1$. We have

$$\sum_1^{N_1} \alpha_j \varphi(t, e_j) = \sum_{p_{1j} \leq \alpha_j t} \alpha_j \left(t - \frac{p_{1j}}{\alpha_j} \right)$$

$$= t F_P(t) - \sum_{p_{1j} \leq \alpha_j t} p_{1j}$$

Also, integrating by parts

$$C_P(t) = u F_P(u) \Big|_0^t - \int_0^t u \, dF_P(u) = t F_P(t) - \sum_{p_{1j} \leq \alpha_j t} \alpha_j \left(\frac{p_{1j}}{\alpha_j} \right)$$

$$= \sum_1^{N_1} \alpha_j \varphi(t, e_j)$$

Thus $C_P(t) \geq C_Q(t)$ for all t if and only if

(i) $$\Sigma \alpha_j \varphi(e_j) \geq \Sigma \beta_j \varphi(f_j)$$

for all convex $\varphi(y) = f(t, y)$ for some t. Moreover, for linear $\varphi(y) = Ay_1 + B$

$$\Sigma \alpha_j \varphi(e_j) = A \sum_j p_{1j} + B \Sigma \alpha_j = A + 2B = \Sigma \beta_j \varphi(f_j)$$

Then $C_P(t) \geq C_Q(t)$ for all t is equivalent to (i) for all functions $\varphi(y) = \Sigma h_k f(t_k, y) + l(y)$ where $h_k \geq 0$ and l is linear. Since every continuous convex function can be uniformly approximated by φ of this form, $C_P(t) \geq C_Q(t)$ for all t is equivalent to condition (4) of Theorem 12.2.2. Finally $C_P(1) = \sum_j \alpha_j - \sum_j p_{1j} = 1$.

For dichotomies, $P \supset Q$ has a simple description in terms of errors of the first and second kind, as follows: If we consider the problem of testing ω_1 against ω_2, a test, i.e., decision function, is a function φ, $0 \leq \varphi(x) \leq 1$ for all x, specifying the probability with which we accept ω_2 when x is observed. For any φ, write

$$\alpha_P(\varphi) = \Sigma p_{1j} \varphi_j$$

$$\beta_P(\varphi) = \Sigma p_{2j} (1 - \varphi_j)$$

The set S_P of possible pairs $\alpha_P(\varphi)$, $\beta_P(\varphi)$ is clearly a closed bounded convex subset of the plane; let $\beta_P(\alpha) = \min_{\alpha_P(\varphi) = \alpha} \beta_P(\varphi)$, $0 \leq \alpha \leq 1$. Then

$\beta_P(\alpha)$ is a convex decreasing function of α associated with the dichotomy P, specifying the minimum attainable β for a given α.

Theorem 12.4.2. $P \supset Q$ if and only if $\beta_P(\alpha) \leq \beta_Q(\alpha)$ for all α.

Proof. Clearly $\beta_P(\alpha) \leq \beta_Q(\alpha)$ for all α if and only if $f_P(k) = \min_{\varphi} \alpha_P(\varphi)$ $+ k\beta_P(\varphi) \leq f_Q(k) = \min_{\varphi} \alpha_Q(\varphi) + k\beta_Q(\varphi)$ for all $k \geq 0$. Now $\overset{\varphi}{\alpha_P(\varphi)} +$ $k\beta_P(\varphi) = k + \Sigma\varphi_j(p_{1j} - kp_{2j})$ is minimized for $\varphi_j = 1$ when $p_{1j} < kp_{2j}$, $\varphi_j = 0$ when $p_{1j} \geq kp_{2j}$, so that, in the notation of (4) of Theorem 12.2.2,

$$f_P(k) = \sum_{kp_{2j} \geq p_{1j}} \alpha_j \left(\frac{p_{1j}}{\alpha_j}\right) + \sum_{kp_{2j} < p_{1j}} \alpha_j \left(\frac{kp_{2j}}{\alpha_j}\right) = \Sigma\alpha_j\psi_k(e_j)$$

where

$$\psi_k(y_1, y_2) = \min(y_1, ky_2)$$

Similarly $f_Q(k) = \Sigma\beta_j\psi_k(f_j)$, so that $\beta_P(\alpha) \leq \beta_Q(\alpha)$ for all α if and only if

(i) $\Sigma\alpha_j\psi_k(e_j) \leq \Sigma\beta_j\psi_k(f_j)$ for all $k \geq 0$

As in the proof of Theorem 12.4.1, every continuous concave ψ can be uniformly approximated by functions $\Sigma h_j\psi_{k_j} + l$, where $h_j \geq 0$ and l is linear, so that (i) is equivalent to

$$\Sigma\alpha_j\psi(e_j) \leq \Sigma\beta_j\psi(f_j)$$

for all concave ψ, which is equivalent to (4) of Theorem 12.2.2.

12.5. Binomial Dichotomies

For a sample of size 1, a binomial dichotomy has a matrix of the form

$$P = \left\| \begin{array}{cc} p_1 & q_1 \\ p_2 & q_2 \end{array} \right\|$$

where $q_i = 1 - p_i$, and is characterized by the pair (p_1, p_2). We now construct the function $C_P(t)$ for this experiment. Writing

$$A(p_1, p_2) = \min\left(\frac{p_1}{p_1 + p_2}, \frac{q_1}{q_1 + q_2}\right)$$

$$B(p_1, p_2) = \max\left(\frac{p_1}{p_1 + p_2}, \frac{q_1}{q_1 + q_2}\right)$$

we have

$$F_P(t) = 0 \qquad\qquad \text{for} \quad 0 \le t < A$$
$$ = 2 \qquad\qquad \text{for} \quad B \le t \le 1$$
$$ = p_1 + p_2 \quad \text{or} \quad q_1 + q_2 \quad \text{for} \quad A \le t < B$$

It is clear then that

$$C_P(t) = 0 \quad \text{for} \quad t < A$$

To obtain $C_P(t)$ for $t \ge B$, we first observe that, if for $A \le t \le B$,

$$F_P(t) = p_1 + p_2 \quad (\text{or} \quad q_1 + q_2)$$

then

$$F_P(t) = p_1/A \qquad (\text{or} \quad q_1/A)$$

Suppose for definiteness that $F_P(t) = p_1/A$, then $B = q_1/(q_1 + q_2)$. From this we easily conclude that for $A \le t < B$

$$F_P(t) = \frac{2B - 1}{B - A}$$

Thus, for $t \ge B$

$$C_P(t) = \int_B^t 2\,du + \int_A^B \frac{2B - 1}{B - A}\,du = 2t - 1$$

and for $A \le t < B$

$$C_P(t) = \left(\frac{2B - 1}{B - A}\right)(t - A)$$

By Theorem 12.4.1, for binomial experiments P and R, $P \supset R$ if and only if $A(P) \le A(R)$ and $B(P) \ge B(R)$. [See Figure 22.] More spe-

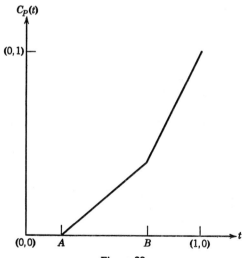

Figure 22

cifically, writing, for any dichotomy R,

$$A(R) = \min_{j} \left(\frac{r_{1j}}{r_{1j} + r_{2j}} \right), \qquad B(R) = \max_{j} \left(\frac{r_{1j}}{r_{1j} + r_{2j}} \right)$$

we have

$$C_R(t) = 0 \qquad \text{for} \quad t \le A(R)$$

$$= 2t - 1 \quad \text{for} \quad t \ge B(R)$$

Thus, if P is any binomial dichotomy of sample size 1 with $A(P) \le A(R)$ and $B(P) \ge B(R)$, since $C_P(t) = C_R(t)$ for $t \le A(P)$ and $t \ge B(P)$ and C_P is linear over $(A(P), B(P))$ while C_R is convex over this interval, $C_P(t) \ge C_R(t)$ for all t, so that $P \supset R$. We now apply these facts to the problem mentioned in the introduction.

For samples of size 1, the experiments H, S, CH, CS are binomial dichotomies characterized by the pairs $\left(s, \frac{\delta}{h} \right)$, $\left(h, \frac{\delta}{s} \right)$, $\left(s, \frac{s - \delta}{1 - h} \right)$, $\left(h, \frac{h - \delta}{1 - s} \right)$ respectively. Suppose for definiteness that $\delta > hs$. Computing A, B for each of H, S, CH, CS yields

	H	S	CH	CS
A	$\dfrac{hs}{hs + \delta}$	$\dfrac{hs}{hs + \delta}$	$\dfrac{(1 - s)(1 - h)}{(1 - s)(1 - h) + 1 - h - s + \delta}$	$\dfrac{(1 - s)(1 - h)}{(1 - s)(1 - h) + 1 - h - s + \delta}$
B	$\dfrac{h(1 - s)}{h(1 - s) + h - \delta}$	$\dfrac{s(1 - h)}{s(1 - h) + s - \delta}$	$\dfrac{s(1 - h)}{s(1 - h) + s - \delta}$	$\dfrac{h(1 - s)}{h(1 - s) + h - \delta}$

Since $A(H) = A(S)$, we have $H \supset S$ if and only if $B(H) \ge B(S)$; i.e.,
$$\frac{h(1 - s)}{h(1 - s) + h - \delta} \ge \frac{s(1 - h)}{s(1 - h) + s - \delta} \; ; \text{ i.e., } (\delta - hs)(s - h) \ge 0; \text{ i.e.,}$$
$h \le s$. Comparing H with CH, CS yields $H \supset CH$ if and only if $h \le s$ and $h \le 1 - s$, and $H \supset CS$ if and only if $h \le 1 - s$. Thus H is the most informative of the four experiments if and only if h is the smallest of the four numbers, h, s, $1 - h$, $1 - s$. The computations for $\delta < hs$ yield the same conclusion. If h is the smallest of the four numbers, it is easily verified that $S \supset CH$, $CS \supset CH$, while S and CS are not comparable. The extension of Theorem 12.3.1 to samples of size n guarantees that, if h is the smallest of the four numbers h, s, $1 - h$, $1 - s$, a sample of n H's is more informative than any other sample of n individuals, selected from H, S, CH, and CS in specified amounts. Finally, selection at random from the general population can be considered as a mixture of experiments H, CH with probabilities h, $1 - h$, so that $H \supset CH$ implies that H is more informative than random sampling from the general population.

References

The numbers in brackets refer to the corresponding numbers in the bibliography which follows.

Chapter 1. [22], [26], [27], [34], [39], [58], [83], [84], [85], [95], [96], [97], [98], [120], [128], [129], [130], [141], [142], [144], [146], [147], [149], [177].

Chapter 2. [8], [12], [22], [23], [24], [25], [26], [30], [31], [35], [37], [39], [40], [41], [42], [46], [49], [53], [54], [55], [56], [57], [59], [64], [72], [73], [74], [75], [76], [77], [79], [82], [86], [87], [94], [96], [98], [101], [104], [106], [108], [124], [126], [127], [128], [131], [132], [134], [136], [143], [144], [147], [148], [149], [157], [158], [175], [176], [177].

Chapter 3. [38], [48], [102], [128], [151], [152], [156], [159], [166], [167].

Chapter 4. [6], [7], [28], [29], [32], [47], [50], [52], [65], [70], [99], [100], [103], [105], [107], [121], [125], [128], [139], [140], [149], [168].

Chapter 5. [21], [79], [87], [88], [93], [128], [155], [166], [167], [171], [178].

Chapter 6. [8], [33], [36], [128], [166], [167], [171].

Chapter 7. [3], [4], [16], [21], [28], [43], [44], [81], [89], [90], [91], [102], [112], [113], [114], [117], [128], [152], [166], [167], [173].

Chapter 8. [10], [18], [45], [51], [63], [67], [81], [89], [90], [91], [93], [102], [111], [115], [116], [117], [122], [123], [128].

Chapter 9. [9], [62], [156], [160], [161], [162], [163], [164], [165], [166], [167], [169], [170], [172].

Chapter 10. [1], [2], [5], [9], [15], [19], [20], [38], [48], [60], [61], [68], [71], [78], [92], [113], [118], [119], [135], [137], [138], [145], [153], [154], [156], [160], [161], [162], [163], [164], [165], [169], [170], [172], [174], [179].

Chapter 11. [11], [14], [18], [32], [38], [63], [66], [69], [80], [91], [92], [102], [109], [110], [115], [116], [122], [123], [128], [150], [152], [166], [167], [179], [180].

Chapter 12. [13], [17], [45], [128], [133].

[1] Albert, G. E., "A note on the fundamental identity of sequential analysis," *Ann. Math. Stat.*, *18*, 593–596 (1947).

[2] Albert, G. E., correction to "A note on the fundamental identity of sequential analysis," *Ann. Math. Stat.*, *19*, 426–427 (1948).

[3] Allen, S. G., Jr., "A class of minimax tests for one-sided composite hypotheses," *Ann. Math. Stat.*, *24*, 295–298 (1953).

[4] Anderson, T. W., "Classification by multivariate analysis," *Psychometrika*, *16*, 31–50 (1951).

[5] Armitage, P., "Sequential analysis with more than two alternative hypotheses, and its relation to discriminant function analysis," *J. Roy. Stat. Soc.*, Ser. B, *12*, 137–144 (1950).

[6] Arrow, K. J., "Alternative approaches to the theory of choice in risk-taking situations," *Econometrica*, *19*, 404–437 (1951).

337

[7] Arrow, K. J., *Social choice and individual values*, Cowles Commission Monograph 12, John Wiley & Sons, New York, 1951.

[8] Arrow, K. J., Barankin, E. W., and Blackwell, D., "Admissible points of convex sets," Contributions to the theory of games, *Ann. Math. Stud.*, *28*, 87–91 (1953).

[9] Arrow, K. J., Blackwell, D., and Girshick, M. A., "Bayes and minimax solutions of sequential decision problems," *Econometrica*, *17* (1949).

[10] Bahadur, R. R., and Goodman, L. A., "Impartial decision rules and sufficient statistics," *Ann. Math. Stat.*, *23*, 553–562 (1952).

[11] Barankin, E. W., "Conditional expectation and convex functions," *Proc. Second Berkeley Symp. on Math. Stat. and Probability*, 167–169 (1950), University of California Press, Berkeley and Los Angeles, 1951.

[12] Bellman, Richard, and Blackwell, David, "Some two-person games involving bluffing," *Proc. Nat. Acad. Sci. Wash.*, *35*, 600–605 (1949).

[13] Blackwell, David, "Comparison of experiments," *Proc. Second Berkeley Symp. on Math. Stat. and Probability*, 93–102 (1950), University of California Press, Berkeley and Los Angeles, 1951.

[14] Blackwell, David, "Conditional expectation and unbiased sequential estimation," *Ann. Math. Stat.*, *18*, 105–110 (1947).

[15] Blackwell, David, "On an equation of Wald," *Ann. Math. Stat.*, *17*, 84–87 (1946).

[16] Blackwell, David, "On randomization in statistical games with k terminal actions," Contributions to the theory of games, *Ann. Math. Stud.*, *28*, 183–187 (1953).

[17] Blackwell, David, "Equivalent comparisons of experiments," *Ann. Math. Stat.*, *24*, 265–272 (1953).

[18] Blackwell, David, "On the translation parameter problem for discrete variables," *Ann. Math. Stat.*, *22*, 393–399 (1951).

[19] Blackwell, David, and Girshick, M. A., "On functions of sequences of independent chance vectors with applications to the problem of the 'random walk' in k dimensions," *Ann. Math. Stat.*, *17*, 310–317 (1946).

[20] Blackwell, David, and Girshick, M. A., "A lower bound for the variance of some unbiased sequential estimates," *Ann. Math. Stat.*, *18*, 277–280 (1947).

[21] Blyth, Colin R., "On minimax statistical decision procedures and their admissibility," *Ann. Math. Stat.*, *22*, 22–42 (1951).

[22] Bohnenblust, H., Dresher, M., Girshick, M. A., Harris, T. E., Helmer, D., McKinsey, J. C. C., Shapley, L. S., and Snow, R. N., "Mathematical theory of zero-sum two-person games with a finite number or a continuum of strategies," Rand Corp., Santa Monica, Calif., 1948.

[23] Bohnenblust, H., and Karlin, S., "On a theorem of Ville," Contributions to the theory of games, *Ann. Math. Stud.*, *24*, 155–160 (1950).

[24] Bohnenblust, H., Karlin, S., and Shapley, L. S., "Games with continuous convex pay-off," Contributions to the theory of games, *Ann. Math. Stud.*, *24*, 181–192 (1950).

[25] Bohnenblust, H., Karlin, S., and Shapley, L. S., "Solutions of discrete two-person games," Contributions to the theory of games, *Ann. Math. Stud.*, *24*, 51–72 (1950).

[26] Borel, E., "La théorie du jeu et les équations intégrales à noyau symétrique," *C. R. Acad. Sci. Paris*, *173*, 1304–1308 (1921). Translated by L. J. Savage in *Econometrica*, *21*, 97–100 (1953).

[27] Bott, Raoul, "Symmetric solutions to majority games," Contributions to the theory of games, *Ann. Math. Stud.*, *28*, 319–324 (1953).

[28] Brookner, Ralph J., "Choice of one among several statistical hypotheses," *Ann. Math. Stat.*, *16*, 221–242 (1945).

[29] Bross, Irwin D. J., *Design for decision*, Macmillan Co., New York, 1953.

[30] Brown, George W., "Notes on the solution of linear systems in solving inequalities," *Proc. Second Symp. on Large-Scale Digital Calculating Machinery*, 137–140 (1949), Harvard University Press, Cambridge, Mass., 1951.

[31] Brown, George W., and von Neumann, J., "Solutions of games by differential equations," Contributions to the theory of games, *Ann. Math. Stud.*, *24*, 73–79 (1950).

[32] Carnap, R., *The continuum of inductive methods*, Chicago, 1951.

[33] Chernoff, H., and Scheffè, H., "A generalization of the Neyman-Pearson fundamental lemma," *Ann. Math. Stat.*, *23*, 213–225 (1952).

[34] Dalkey, Norman, "Equivalence of information patterns and essentially determinate games," Contributions to the theory of games, *Ann. Math. Stud.*, *28*, 217–244 (1953).

[35] Dantzig, George B., "A proof of the equivalence of the programming problem and the game problem," pp. 330–335 in Koopman's *Activity analysis of production and allocation*, Cowles Commission Monograph 13, John Wiley & Sons, New York; Chapman & Hall, London, 1951.

[36] Dantzig, George B., and Wald, A., "On the fundamental lemma of Neyman and Pearson," *Ann. Math. Stat.*, *22*, 87–93 (1951).

[37] Dines, L. L., "On a theorem of von Neumann," *Proc. Nat. Acad. Sci. Wash.*, *33*, 329–331 (1947).

[38] Doob, J. L., *Stochastic processes*, John Wiley & Sons, New York, 1953.

[39] Dresher, Melvin, "Games of strategy," *Math. Mag.*, *25*, 93–99 (1951).

[40] Dresher, Melvin, "Methods of solution in game theory," *Econometrica*, *18*, 179–181 (1950).

[41] Dresher, M., and Karlin, S., "Solutions of convex games as fixed-points," Contributions to the theory of games, *Ann. Math. Stud.*, *28*, 75–86 (1953).

[42] Dresher, M., Karlin, S., and Shapley, L. S., "Polynomial games," Contributions to the theory of games, *Ann. Math. Stud.*, *24*, 161–180 (1950).

[43] Dvoretzky, A., Wald, A., and Wolfowitz, J., "Elimination of randomization in certain problems of statistics and of the theory of games," *Proc. Nat. Acad. Sci. Wash.*, *36*, 256–260 (1950).

[44] Dvoretzky, A., Wald, A., and Wolfowitz, J., "Elimination of randomization in certain statistical decision problems and zero-sum two-person games," *Ann. Math. Stat.*, *22*, 1–21 (1951).

[45] Elfving, G., "Sufficiency and completeness in decision function theory," *Ann. Acad. Sci. Fennicae*, 135, (1952).

[46] Fan, Ky, "Fixed point and minimax theorems in locally convex topological linear spaces," *Proc. Nat. Acad. Sci. Wash.*, *38*, 121–126 (1952).

[47] Feller, W., "Note on the law of large numbers and fair games," *Ann. Math. Stat.*, *16*, 301–304 (1945).

[48] Feller, W., *An introduction to probability theory and its applications*, John Wiley & Sons, New York, 1950.

[49] Fisher, R. A., "Randomization and an old enigma of card play," *Math. Gaz.*, *18*, 294–297 (1934).

[50] Frank, P., and Kiefer, J., "Almost subminimax and biased minimax procedures," *Ann. Math. Stat.*, *22*, 465–468 (1951).

[51] Fraser, D. A. S., "Sufficient statistics and selection depending on the parameter," *Ann. Math. Stat.*, *23*, 417–425 (1952).

[52] Friedman, M., and Savage, L. J., "The utility analysis of choices involving risk," *J. Polit. Econ.*, *56*, 279–304 (1948).

[53] Gale, David, Kuhn, Harold W., and Tucker, Albert W., "Linear programming and the theory of games," pp. 317–329 in Koopman's *Activity analysis of production and allocation*, Cowles Commission Monograph 13, John Wiley & Sons, New York; Chapman & Hall, London, 1951.

[54] Gale, David, Kuhn, Harold W., and Tucker, Albert W., "Reductions of game matrices," Contributions to the theory of games, *Ann. Math. Stud.*, *24*, 89–96 (1950).

[55] Gale, David, Kuhn, Harold W., and Tucker, Albert W., "On symmetric games," Contributions to the theory of games, *Ann. Math. Stud.*, *24*, 81–87 (1950).

[56] Gale, D., and Sherman, S., "Solutions of finite two-person games," Contributions to the theory of games, *Ann. Math. Stud.*, *24*, 37–49 (1950).

[57] Gale, D., and Stewart, F. M., "Infinite games with perfect information," Contributions to the theory of games, *Ann. Math. Stud.*, *28*, 245–266 (1953).

[58] Gillies, D. B., "Discriminatory and bargaining solutions to a class of symmetric *n*-person games," Contributions to the theory of games, *Ann. Math. Stud.*, *28*, 325–342 (1953).

[59] Gillies, D. B., Mayberry, J. P., and von Neumann, J., "Two variants of poker," Contributions to the theory of games, *Ann. Math. Stud.*, *28*, 13–50 (1953).

[60] Girshick, M. A., "Contributions to the theory of sequential analysis, I," *Ann. Math. Stat.*, *17*, 123–143 (1946).

[61] Girshick, M. A., "Contributions to the theory of sequential analysis, II, III," *Ann. Math. Stat.*, *17*, 212–298 (1946).

[62] Girshick, M. A., and Rubin, H., "A Bayes approach to a quality control model," *Ann. Math. Stat.*, *23*, 114–125 (1952).

[63] Girshick, M. A., and Savage, L. J., "Bayes and minimax estimates for quadratic loss functions," *Proc. Second Berkeley Symp. on Math. Stat. and Probability*, 53–73 (1950), University of California Press, Berkeley and Los Angeles, 1951.

[64] Glicksberg, I., and Gross, O., "Notes on games over the square," Contributions to the theory of games, *Ann. Math. Stud.*, *28*, 173–184 (1953).

[65] Good, I. J., *Probability and the weighing of evidence*, Hafner, 1950.

[66] Goodman, Leo, "A simple method for improving some unbiased estimates," *Ann. Math. Stat.*, *24*, 114–117 (1953).

[67] Halmos, P. R., and Savage, L. J., "Applications of the Radon-Nikodym theorem to the theory of sufficient statistics," *Ann. Math. Stat.*, *20*, 225–241 (1949).

[68] Harris, T. E., "Note on differentiation under the expectation sign in the fundamental identity of sequential analysis," *Ann. Math. Stat.*, *18*, 294–295 (1947).

[69] Hodges, J. L., Jr., and Lehmann, E. L., "Some problems in minimax point estimation," *Ann. Math. Stat.*, *21*, 182–197 (1950).

[70] Hodges, J. L., Jr., and Lehmann, E. L., "The use of previous experience in reaching statistical decisions," *Ann. Math. Stat.*, *23*, 396–407 (1952).

[71] Jones, Howard L., "Formulas for the group sequential sampling of attributes," *Ann. Math. Stat.*, *23*, 72–87 (1952).

[72] Kaplansky, I., "A contribution to von Neumann's theory of games," *Ann. Math.*, (2), *46*, 474–479 (1945).

[73] Karlin, S., "Continuous games," *Proc. Nat. Acad. Sci. Wash.*, *37*, 220–223 (1951).

[74] Karlin, S., "Operator treatment of minimax principle," Contributions to the theory of games, *Ann. Math. Stud.*, *24*, 134–154 (1950).

[75] Karlin, S., "Reduction of certain classes of games to integral equation," Contributions to the theory of games, *Ann. Math. Stud.*, *28*, 125–158 (1953).

[76] Karlin, S., "On a class of games," Contributions to the theory of games, *Ann. Math. Stud.*, *28*, 159–172 (1953).

[77] Karlin, S., and Shapley, L. S., "Some applications of a theorem on convex functions," *Ann. Math.* (2), *52*, 148–153 (1950).

[78] Kemperman, J. H. B., "The general one-dimensional random walk with absorbing barriers with applications to sequential analysis," Excelsiors Foto-Offset, 's Gravenhage, 1950.

[79] Kiefer, J., "On Wald's complete class theorems," *Ann. Math. Stat.*, *24*, 70–75 (1953).

[80] Kiefer, J., "Sequential minimax estimation for the rectangular distribution with unknown range," *Ann. Math. Stat.*, *23*, 586–593 (1952).

[81] Koopman, B. O., "On distributions admitting a sufficient statistic," *Trans. Amer. Math. Soc.*, *39*, 399–409 (1936).

[82] Koopmans, T. (editor), *Activity analysis of production and allocation*, Cowles Commission Monograph 13; John Wiley & Sons, New York, 1951.

[83] Krentel, W. D., McKinsey, J. C. C., and Quine, W. V., "A simplification of games in extensive form," *Duke Math. J.*, *18*, 885–900 (1951).

[84] Kuhn, H. W., "Extensive games," *Proc. Nat. Acad. Sci. Wash.*, *36*, 570–576 (1950).

[85] Kuhn, H. W., "Extensive games and the problem of information," Contributions to the theory of games, *Ann. Math. Stud.*, *28*, 193–216 (1953).

[86] Kuhn, H. W., "A simplified two-person poker," Contributions to the theory of games, *Ann. Math. Stud.*, *24*, 97–103 (1950).

[87] Lehmann, E. L., "On the existence of least favorable distributions," *Ann. Math. Stat.*, *23*, 408–416 (1952).

[88] Lehmann, E. L., "On families of admissible tests," *Ann. Math. Stat.*, *18*, 97–104 (1947).

[89] Lehmann, E. L., "Some principles of the theory of testing hypotheses," *Ann. Math. Stat.*, *21*, 1–26 (1950).

[90] Lehmann, E. L., "Theory of testing hypotheses" (mimeographed notes recorded by Colin Blyth), University of California, Berkeley, 1949.

[91] Lehmann, E. L., and Scheffe, H., "Completeness, similar regions, and unbiased estimation," *Sankhya*, *10*, 305–339 (1950).

[92] Lehmann, E. L., and Stein, Charles, "Completeness in the sequential case," *Ann. Math. Stat.*, *21*, 376–385 (1950).

[93] Lehmann, E. L., and Stein, Charles, "The admissibility of certain invariant statistical tests involving a translation parameter," *Ann. Math. Stat.*, *24*, 473–479 (1953).

[94] Loomis, L. H., "On a theorem of von Neumann," *Proc. Nat. Acad. Sci. Wash.*, *32*, 213–215 (1946).

[95] McDonald, J., *Strategy in poker, business and war*, W. W. Norton & Co., New York, 1950.

[96] McKinsey, J. C. C., *Introduction to the theory of games*, Rand Corp., Santa Monica, Calif., 1952.

[97] McKinsey, J. C. C., "Isomorphism of games and strategic equivalence," Contributions to the theory of games, *Ann. Math. Stud.*, *24*, 117–130 (1950).

[98] McKinsey, J. C. C., "Some notions and problems in game theory," *Bull. Amer. Math. Soc.*, 591ff (1952).

[99] Marschak, J., "Rational behavior, uncertain prospects, and measurable utility," *Econometrica*, *18*, 111–141 (1950).

[100] Mays, W. J., "The valuation of risks," *Amer. Math. Monthly*, *52*, 138–148 (1945).

[101] Milnor, John, "Sums of positional games," Contributions to the theory of games, *Ann. Math. Stud.*, *28*, 291–302 (1953).

[102] Mood, A. M., *Introduction to the theory of statistics*, McGraw-Hill Book Co., New York, 1950.

[103] Mosteller, Frederick, and Nogee, Philip, "An experimental measurement of utility," *J. Polit. Econ.*, *59*, 371–404 (1951).

[104] Motzkin, T. S., Raiffa, H., Thompson, G. L., and Thrall, R. M., "The double description method," Contributions to the theory of games, *Ann. Math. Stud.*, *28*, 51–74 (1953).

[105] Nash, J. F., "The bargaining problem," *Econometrica*, *18*, 155–162 (1950).

[106] Nash, J. F., "Equilibrium points in n-person games," *Proc. Nat. Acad. Sci. Wash.*, *36*, 48–49 (1950).

[107] Nash, J. F., "Non-cooperative games," *Ann. Math.* (2), *54*, 286–295 (1951).

[108] Nash, J. F., and Shapley, L. S., "A simple three-person poker game," Contributions to the theory of games, *Ann. Math. Stud.*, *24*, 105–116 (1950).

[109] Neyman, J., "L'estimation statistique traité comme un problème classique de probabilité," *Actualités sci. ind.*, *739* (1938).

[110] Neyman, J., "Outline of a theory of statistical estimation based on the classical theory of probability," *Phil. Trans. Roy. Soc.*, A *236* (1937).

[111] Neyman, J., "Su un teorema concernente le considette statistiche sufficienti," *Giornale Ist. Ital. Attuari*, *6*, 320–334 (1934).

[112] Neyman, J., and Pearson, E. S., "Contributions to the theory of testing statistical hypotheses," *Stat. Research Mem.*, parts I and II (1936 and 1938).

[113] Neyman, J., and Pearson, E. S., "The testing of statistical hypotheses in relation to probability a priori," *Proc. Camb. Phil. Soc.*, *29* (1933).

[114] Paulson, E., "An optimum solution to the k-sample slippage problem for the normal distribution," *Ann. Math. Stat.*, *23*, 610–616 (1952).

[115] Peterson, Raymond P., "Uniformly best constant risk and minimax point estimates," *J. Research Nat. Bur. Standards*, *48*, 49–53 (1952).

[116] Pitman, E. J. G., "The estimation of location and scale parameters of a continuous population of any given form," *Biometrika*, *30* (1939).

[117] Pitman, E. J. G., "Tests of hypotheses concerning location and scale parameters," *Biometrika*, *31*, 200–215 (1939).

[118] Polya, George, "Exact formulas in the sequential analysis of attributes," *Univ. California Publ. Math.* (N.S.), *1*, 229–239 (1948).

[119] Polya, George, "Sur une généralisation d'un problème élémentaire classique, importante dans l'inspection des produits industriels," *C. R. Acad. Sci. Paris*, *222*, 1422–1424 (1946).

[120] Raiffa, Howard, "Arbitration schemes for generalized two-person games," Contributions to the theory of games, *Ann. Math. Stud.*, *28*, 361–389 (1953).

[121] Ramsey, Frank P., *The foundations of mathematics and other logical essays*, Humanities Press, New York, 1950.

[122] Rao, C. R., "Information and accuracy attainable in the estimation of statistical parameters," *Bull. Calcutta Math. Soc.*, *37*, 81–91 (1945).

[123] Rao, C. R., "Sufficient statistics and minimum variance estimates," *Proc. Camb. Phil. Soc.*, *45*, 213–218 (1949).

[124] Reich, Edgar, "The game of 'gossip' analyzed by the theory of information," *Bull. Math. Biophys.*, *13*, 313–318 (1951).

[125] Robbins, Herbert, "Asymptotically subminimax solutions of compound statistical decision problems," *Proc. Second Berkeley Symp. on Math. Stat. and Probability*, 131–148 (1950), University of California Press, Berkeley and Los Angeles, 1951.

[126] Robinson, Julia, "An iterative method of solving a game," *Ann. Math.* (2), *54*, 296–301 (1951).

[127] Robinson, Julia, "A note on exact sequential analysis," *Univ. California Publ. Math.* (N.S.), *1*, 241–246 (1948).

[128] Savage, Leonard J., *The foundations of statistics*, John Wiley & Sons, New York, 1954.

[129] Shapley, L. S., "A value for *n*-person games," Contributions to the theory of games, *Ann. Math. Stud.*, *28*, 307–318 (1953).

[130] Shapley, L. S., "Quota solutions of *n*-person games," Contributions to the theory of games, *Ann. Math. Stud.*, *28*, 343–360 (1953).

[131] Shapley, L. S., and Snow, R. N., "Basic solutions of discrete games," Contributions to the theory of games, *Ann. Math. Stud.*, *24*, 27–35 (1950).

[132] Sherman, Seymour, "Games and sub-games," *Proc. Amer. Math. Soc.*, *2*, 186–187 (1951).

[133] Sherman, Seymour, "On a theorem of Hardy, Littlewood, Pólya, and Blackwell," *Proc. Nat. Acad. Sci. Wash.*, *37*, 826–831 (1951); errata: *38*, 382 (1952).

[134] Shiffman, Max, "Games of timing," Contributions to the theory of games, *Ann. Math. Stud.*, *28*, 97–124 (1953).

[135] Sobel, M., "An essentially complete class of decision functions for certain standard sequential problems," *Ann. Math. Stat.*, *24*, 319–337 (1953).

[136] Spacek, A., "Note on minimax solutions of statistical decision problems," *Colloquium Math.*, *2*, 275–281 (1951).

[137] Stein, Charles, "A note on cumulative sums," *Ann. Math. Stat.*, *17*, 498–499 (1946).

[138] Stein, Charles, "A two-sample test for a linear hypothesis whose power is independent of the variance," *Ann. Math. Stat.*, *16*, 243–258 (1945).

[139] Steinhaus, H., "Sur la division pragmatique," *Econometrica*, *17* (supplement), 315–319 (1949).

[140] Steinhaus, H., "Quality control by sampling (a plea for Bayes' rule)," *Colloquium Math.*, *2*, 98–108 (1951).

[141] Thompson, G. L., "Bridge and signaling," Contributions to the theory of games, *Ann. Math. Stud.*, *28*, 279–290 (1953).

[142] Thompson, G. L., "Signaling strategies in *n*-person games," Contributions to the theory of games, *Ann. Math. Stud.*, *28*, 267–278 (1953).

[143] Tukey, J. W., "A problem in strategy," *Econometrica*, *17*, 73 (1949).

[144] Ville, J., "Note sur la théorie générale des jeux où intervient l'habilité des joueurs," in *Applications aux jeux de hasard*, by Emile Borel and Jean Ville, tome IV, fascicule II of the *Traité du calcul des probabilités et de ses applications*, by Emile Borel (1938).

[145] Ville, J., and Schutzenberger, Marcel Paul, "Les problèmes de diagnostic sequentiel," *C. R. Acad. Sci. Paris, 232*, 206–207 (1951).

[146] von Mises, R., "On the probabilities in a set of games and the foundation of probability theory," *Revista Cienc. Lima, 47*, 435–456 (1945).

[147] von Neumann, J., "Zur Theorie der Gesellschaftspiele," *Math. Annalen, 100*, 295–320 (1928).

[148] von Neumann, J., "A certain zero-sum two-person game equivalent to the optimal assignment problem," Contributions to the theory of games, *Ann. Math. Stud., 28*, 5–12 (1953).

[149] von Neumann, J., and Morgenstern, Oskar, *Theory of games and economic behavior*, 2nd ed., Princeton University Press, New Jersey, 1947.

[150] Wald, A., "Asymptotic minimax solutions of sequential point estimation problems," *Proc. Second Berkeley Symp. on Math. Stat. and Probability*, 1–11 (1950), University of California Press, Berkeley and Los Angeles, 1951.

[151] Wald, A., "Basic ideas of a general theory of statistical decision rules," *Proc. Int. Cong. Math., 1*, 231–243 (1950); *Amer. Math. Soc.*, Providence, R. I. (1952).

[152] Wald, A., "Contributions to the theory of statistical estimation and testing hypotheses," *Ann. Math. Stat., 10*, 299–326 (1939).

[153] Wald, A., "On cumulative sums of random variables," *Ann. Math. Stat., 15*, 283–296 (1944).

[154] Wald, A., "Differentiation under the expectation sign in the fundamental identity of sequential analysis," *Ann. Math. Stat., 17*, 493–497 (1946).

[155] Wald, A., "An essentially complete class of admissible decision functions," *Ann. Math. Stat., 18*, 549–555 (1947).

[156] Wald, A., "Foundations of a general theory of sequential decision functions," *Econometrica, 15*, 279–313 (1947).

[157] Wald, A., "Generalization of a theorem by von Neumann concerning zero-sum two-person games," *Ann. Math. (2), 46*, 281–286 (1945).

[158] Wald, A., "Note on zero-sum two-person games," *Ann. Math. (2), 52*, 739–742 (1950).

[159] Wald, A., "On the principles of statistical inference," *Notre Dame Math. Lectures, 1*, University of Notre Dame, Indiana (1942).

[160] Wald, A., *Sequential analysis*, John Wiley & Sons, New York; Chapman & Hall, London, 1947.

[161] Wald, A., "Sequential analysis," 25th session International Statistical Institute, Sept. 1947, Washington, D. C., *Int. Stat. Inst. Proc., III*, 67–73; discussion, 74–80.

[162] Wald, A., "Sequential method of sampling for deciding between two courses of action," *J. Amer. Stat. Assoc., 40*, 277–306 (1945).

[163] Wald, A., "Sequential tests of statistical hypotheses," *Ann. Math. Stat., 16*, 117–186 (1945).

[164] Wald, A., "Some generalizations of the theory of cumulative sums of random variables," *Ann. Math. Stat., 16*, 287–293 (1945).

[165] Wald, A., "Some improvements in setting limits for the expected number of observations required by a sequential probability ratio test," *Ann. Math. Stat., 17*, 466–474 (1946).

[166] Wald, A., "Statistical decision functions," *Ann. Math. Stat., 20*, 165–205 (1949).

[167] Wald, A., *Statistical decision functions*, John Wiley & Sons, New York; Chapman & Hall, London, 1950.

[168] Wald, A., "Statistical decision functions which minimize the maximum risk," *Ann. Math.* (2), *46*, 265–280 (1945).

[169] Wald, A., and Wolfowitz, J., "Bayes solutions of sequential decision problems," *Proc. Nat. Acad. Sci. Wash., 35*, 99–102 (1949).

[170] Wald, A., and Wolfowitz, J., "Bayes solutions of sequential decision problems," *Ann. Math. Stat., 21*, 82–99 (1950).

[171] Wald, A., and Wolfowitz, J., "Characterization of the minimal complete class of decision functions when the number of distributions and decisions is finite," *Proc. Second Berkeley Symp. on Math. Stat. and Probability*, 149–157 (1950), University of California Press, Berkeley and Los Angeles, 1951.

[172] Wald, A., and Wolfowitz, J., "Optimum character of the sequential probability ratio test," *Ann. Math. Stat., 19*, 326–339 (1948).

[173] Wald, A., and Wolfowitz, J., "Two methods of randomization in statistics and the theory of games," *Ann. Math.* (2), *53*, 581–586 (1951).

[174] Weiss, Lionel, "Testing one simple hypothesis against another," *Ann. Math. Stat., 24*, 273–281 (1953).

[175] Weyl, H., "Elementary proof of a minimax theorem due to von Neumann," Contributions to the theory of games, *Ann. Math. Stud., 24*, 19–25 (1950).

[176] Weyl, H., "The elementary theory of convex polyhedra," Contributions to the theory of games, *Ann. Math. Stud., 24*, 3–18 (1950).

[177] Williams, J. D., *The compleat strategist*, McGraw-Hill Book Co., New York, 1954.

[178] Wolfowitz, J., "On ε-complete classes of decision functions," *Ann. Math. Stat., 22*, 461–465 (1951).

[179] Wolfowitz, J., "The efficiency of sequential estimates and Wald's equation for sequential processes," *Ann. Math. Stat., 18*, 215–230 (1947).

[180] Wolfowitz, J., "Minimax estimates of the mean of a normal distribution with known variance," *Ann. Math. Stat., 21*, 218–230 (1950).

References to Unpublished Papers

1. Blackwell, D., Girshick, M. A., and Rubin, H., "Optimal invariant decision procedures," Unpublished. (Chapters 8 and 11.)

2. Girshick, M. A., Rubin, H., and Sitgreaves, R., "Estimates of bounded relative error in particle counting," Unpublished. (Chapter 11.)

3. Paulson, Edward, "Optimum selection procedures," Abstract, *Ann. Math. Stat., 23* (1952). (Chapter 11.)

4. Rubin, Herman, "A complete class of decision procedures for distributions with monotone likelihood ratio," Abstract, *Ann. Math. Stat., 22* (1951). (Chapter 7.)

5. Rubin, H., and Wesler, Oscar, "Convexity properties of the α,β-set under composite hypotheses," Abstract, *Ann. Math. Stat., 25* (1954). (Chapter 7.)

6. Rubin, H., and Wesler, Oscar, "A note on convexity in n-space," Unpublished. (Chapter 2.)

Index

Conditional risk function, definition, 87
see also A posteriori risk
Confidence coefficient, 305
for scale parameter, 318
for translation parameter, 314
Convergence theorems, for Bayes procedures, 248
for expectations, 100, 101
Convex functions, definition, 38
expectation of, 41, 101, 295
properties, 39–42, 295
sequences of, 42
Convex hull, 36, 38, 42, 48
definition, 32
Convex loss function, consequence for estimation, 294
Convex mixture, 48
Convex payoff function, 51–54
Convex sets, 30–38, 42, 50
Cost function, definition, 95
Critical region, 82
Cumulative distribution function, 88
Cylinder set, definition, 92
property of stopping regions, 93, 238

Decision function, as a partition, 81
as sequence of vectors, 145
definition, 81
randomized, *see* Randomized strategies
terminal, 93, 94–96, 238, 241
truncated sequential, 91, 94
see also Strategies
Decision problem, general formulation, 103
Decision space, 78, 81
Densities, 88, 146, 171, 233, 313
Density function, as extended mixed strategy, 55, 56, 58
definition, 56
Derived games G_η, class of strategies in, ε-good, 135
minimax, 135
definition, 133
value, 134
lower, 133, 134
upper, 133, 134
Diameter of a set, 31
Discriminant analysis, 157, 158

Distributions, with monotone likelihood ratio, 187
see also Probability distributions

ε-admissible strategies, completeness of class, 139
definition, 136
ε-Bayes strategies, completeness conditions, 140
definition, 135
ε-good strategies, definition, 46, 47
Equivalent games, definition, 11
examples, 11, 12, 124, 125
invariance under, 12, 16, 17, 28
Equivalent methods of randomization, 172, 214, 216
Equivalent strategies, definition, 133
Error, absolute, 301–305, 315
first and second kind, 200
relative, 305, 318–320
Essentially complete class, 137, 140, 141, 146
definition, 137
Estimate of Poisson parameter, 82
of bounded relative error, 318–320
Estimates, admissible, 296, 320–323
based on sufficient statistics, 294–296
Bayes, 296–305
biased, 299
multiplicative property of, 317
non-randomized, 294, 312
of bounded error, absolute, 304, 305, 315
relative, 304, 305, 318
of fixed sample size, 323
of proportion defective in finite lot, 144, 165, 167, 169, 170
of scale parameter, 316–320
of translation parameter, 307–315
translation property of, 309
Estimation problem, structure of, 294
Event, concept of, 76
probability of, 77
Events, independence of, 96
Expectation, conditional, 84, 85, 101, 239, 295
convergence theorems, 100, 101
definition, 80
for exponential class, 193